THE CLASSIC SLAVE NARRATIVES

Edited and

with an Updated Introduction by

Henry Louis Gates, Jr.

SIGNET CLASSICS

SIGNET CLASSICS
Published by New American Library, a division of
Penguin Group (USA) Inc., 375 Hudson Street,
New York, New York 10014, USA
Penguin Group (Canada), 90 Eglinton Avenue East, Suite 700, Toronto,
Ontario M4P 2Y3, Canada (a division of Pearson Penguin Canada Inc.)
Penguin Books Ltd., 80 Strand, London WC2R 0RL, England
Penguin Ireland, 25 St. Stephen's Green, Dublin 2,
Ireland (a division of Penguin Books Ltd.)
Penguin Group (Australia), 250 Camberwell Road, Camberwell, Victoria 3124,
Australia (a division of Pearson Australia Group Pty. Ltd.)
Penguin Books India Pvt. Ltd., 11 Community Centre, Panchsheel Park,
New Delhi - 110 017, India
Penguin Group (NZ), 67 Apollo Drive, Rosedale, Auckland 0632,
New Zealand (a division of Pearson New Zealand Ltd.)
Penguin Books (South Africa) (Pty.) Ltd., 24 Sturdee Avenue,
Rosebank, Johannesburg 2196, South Africa

Penguin Books Ltd., Registered Offices:
80 Strand, London WC2R 0RL, England

Published by Signet Classics, an imprint of New American Library, a division of
Penguin Group (USA) Inc. Previously published in a Mentor edition.

First Signet Classics Printing, January 2002
20   19   18   17   16   15   14   13

Introduction and selection copyright © Henry Louis Gates, Jr., 1987, 2012
All rights reserved

℃ REGISTERED TRADEMARK—MARCA REGISTRADA

Printed in the United States of America

THE CLASSIC SLAVE NARRATIVES
Edited by Henry Louis Gates, Jr.

The Interesting Narrative of the Life of Olaudah Equiano, a bestseller when first published in 1789, is the prototype for the nineteenth-century slave narrative. The movement of Equiano's story from African freedom through European enslavement to Anglican freedom, combined with his truly astonishing adventures, created the first large audience for any black writer in England or America.

The History of Mary Prince, A West Indian Slave is a brief, poignant tale of suffering and degradation, emblematic of narrators "not telling of themselves alone," but seeking to tell the world of the plight of an entire race.

Narrative of the Life of Frederick Douglass is perhaps the best known of all the slave narratives. Its elegant simplicity and gripping readability make it a moving testimony to the facts of human bondage. His is one of the quintessential instances of chiasmus in all of literature: "You have seen how a man became a slave," writes Frederick Douglass. "You will see how a slave became a man."

Incidents in the Life of a Slave Girl is the incredible story of Harriet Jacobs, writing as Linda Brent. From her sexual harassment by a cruel master to a harrowing escape to freedom, this work is an outstanding example of a woman's extraordinary courage.

Henry Louis Gates, Jr., is the director of the W. E. B. Du Bois Institute for African and African American Research and holder of the distinguished title of Alphonse Fletcher University Professor at Harvard University. He is the author of several award-winning works of literary criticism as well as *Colored People: A Memoir, The Future of the Race* (co-authored with Cornel West), *Thirteen Ways of Looking at a Black Man,* and *Life Upon These Shores: Looking at African American History, 1513–2008.*

For Paul Edward Gates

CONTENTS

INTRODUCTION

A REMARKABLE AND enduringly visible legacy of Africans' enslavement in the New World is the slave narrative, the genre of literature created by formerly enslaved black people at once to testify against their captors and to bear witness to the urge of every black slave to be free and literate and accorded all the "rights of man." The slave narrative is a unique creation in the long history of human bondage, designed by a small but exceptionally gifted group of men and women who escaped and who went on to write books about the severe conditions of their bondage within the brutally inhumane social and economic system euphemistically—and inadequately—dubbed "the peculiar institution." These people of African descent *wrote*: once enslaved in the United States or the West Indies, and once secure and free in London or in the North, and with the generous encouragement and assistance of antislavery advocates, they wrote their own stories about life in slavery and about the meaning of freedom.

The Enlightenment discourse on rights and reason gave rise to the slave's discourse on race and reason, and abolitionists in London and in the centers of antislavery sentiment in the United States, such as Boston, Philadelphia, and New York, fueled the development of this genre, in intimate collaboration with these extraordinarily intelligent former slaves, black men and women who were as eager to testify to their intellectual capacities as they were to testify against the evils of slavery to hasten its end. In fact, it is fair to say that the writing and publishing of the slave narratives, especially between 1772 and 1808 (particularly in London), and then again between 1831 and 1865, under the lead initially of William Lloyd Garrison and then of Frederick Douglass, became the basis of the first interracial intellectual movements in the history of England and the United States. As Richard S. Newman observes, "African American writers and readers also forged alliances with white abolitionists. It is no accident, for instance, that much of the extant black protest literature from the eighteenth century flowed from Anglo-American abolitionist capitals: London, New York, and Philadelphia. Wherever African peoples came into contact with abolitionist groups, black-authored antislavery literature appeared."[1] And this was especially the case after William Lloyd Garrison founded the *Liberator* newspaper as America's principal organ of abolitionist advocacy in 1831.

As several scholars have shown, there is an inextricable link in the African American tradition between literacy and freedom. And this linkage composes the structuring principle of the slave narratives. As the novelist Ishmael Reed put the matter in his fictional slave narrative, *Flight to Canada* (1976), the slave who was the first to learn to read and write was the first to run away. While not literally true, the mastery of literacy signified a measure of metaphysical freedom in the realm of the slave, willfully kept illiterate by the masters and their laws, laws that were enacted to perpetuate the myth that persons of African descent were either not actually human beings or were human beings fundamentally different or inferior to other kinds of human beings, destined by nature to be enslaved, in perpetuity.

In literacy lay a peculiar kind of freedom—or burden—for the black person who was enslaved. We do not know exactly how many slaves escaped to freedom across the Ohio River and the Mason-Dixon Line, but some historians estimate that as many as forty or fifty thousand did. (By 1860, 3.9 million black people were in bondage in the slave states, while another 488,000 were free.) Of that number, William L. Andrews has discovered that 102 wrote book-length slave narratives between 1760 and the end of the Civil War. Following the abolition of slavery in 1865 and well into the twentieth century, Andrews concludes that another 102 former slaves also published books about their enslavement. In a sense, this cadre of former slaves formed the nucleus of the black intellectual tradition, the group that W. E. B. Du Bois would define as "the talented tenth," a figure that, not by accident, I believe, parallels the percentage of black people who were free and most probably literate in 1860. Statistically, these authors were very special people. Despite their small number, however, no group of slaves anywhere, at any other period in history, has left such a large repository of testimony about the horror of becoming the legal property of another human being.

The black slave narrators sought to indict both those who enslaved them and the metaphysical system drawn upon to justify their enslavement. They did so using the most enduring weapon at their disposal, the printing press. Sometimes serving an apprenticeship in rhetoric and oratory on the antislavery lecture circuit, these individuals would publish accounts of their lives and times in the house of bondage, narratives that were polished, formal extensions of the speeches that they delivered. Sometimes these were dictated, as in the case of Mary Prince, but more often than not they were "written by themselves," a crucial argument in the discourse of race and reason. These slave narratives came to resemble one another, both in their content and in their formal shape. So similar was their structure that it sometimes seems to the modern reader that the slave authors were drawing upon shared patterns, and then imposing these patterns upon different pieces of cloth. There can be little doubt that when the ex-slave author decided to write his or her story, he or she did so only after reading, and rereading, the telling stories of other former slaves who preceded them as authors.

In the process of imitation, revision, and repetition, the black slave's narrative came to be a communal utterance, a collective tale, rather than merely an individual's autobiography. Each slave author, in writing about his or her personal life experiences, simultaneously wrote on behalf of the millions of silent slaves still held captive throughout the Caribbean, Latin America, and the American South. Each author, then, knew that *all* black slaves would be judged—on their character, integrity, intelligence, manners, and morals, and their claims to warrant emancipation, citizenship, and equality—on this published evidence provided by one of their number. The slave authors therefore had to satisfy the dual expectations of shaping the random events of their lives into a meaningful and compelling pattern—just as all autobiographers do—while also making the narrative of their odyssey from slavery to freedom an emblem of every black person's potential for higher education and the right to be free. This was no easy task. Nevertheless, the ex-slave author met this challenge squarely, creating the largest body of literature ever created by former slaves and giving birth thereby to the African American literary tradition.

In 1969, the poet and novelist Arna Bontemps put the matter well in a statement about black literary ancestry that has influenced African American literary history ever since:

> From the narrative came the spirit and vitality and the angle of vision responsible for the most effective prose writing by black American writers from William Wells Brown to Charles W. Chesnutt, from W. E. B. Du Bois to Richard Wright, Ralph Ellison and James Baldwin.[2]

The first century of the African American literary tradition was created when its authors and their black readers were all slaves, former slaves, or descendants of former slaves. In fact, the first nonfiction work by an African American was Britton Hammon's slave narrative published in Boston in 1760. Have there ever been more curious origins of a literary tradition, especially when we recall that the slave narrative arose as a response to, and refutation of, claims that blacks lacked reason, therefore could not write, and therefore were somehow less than human?

Since the status of the slave narrative as history and literature seems self-evident to us now, how could the narratives have been "lost" to us for such a long period in American literary history and slave historiography? How indeed, especially when the apparent "silence" of the black person was drawn upon by a host of commentators as "evidence" of either the unrelentingly brutal environment of slavery or else of an inherent mental deficiency within the slave? After all, slave narratives were extraordinarily popular texts. Here is just a sampling of how well they sold: According to Charles H. Nichols, "At least six editions of Charles Ball's *Slavery in the United States* were issued between 1836 and 1859. By 1856, *Narrative of the Adventures and Escape of Moses Roper, from American Slavery*, first published in 1837, had reached ten editions and had been translated into Celtic. Josiah Henson's narrative had sold six thousand copies in 1852, having been published in England as well as in America. By 1858 advance orders for the 'Stowe edition' of Henson's book totaled 5,000 copies. In the 1878 edition it is claimed that 100,000 copies of the earlier book had been sold. Henson's life story was translated into Dutch and into French. Within two years after its publication in 1853 *The Narrative of Solomon Northup* had sold 27,000 copies. *The Narrative of William Wells Brown* sold 8,000 copies by 1849, and Douglass's narrative had, by the same year, gone through seven editions."[3]

Arna Bontemps, moreover, says that by 1879 Josiah Henson's slave narrative had sold 100,000 copies. "Indeed, good sales had become the rule for slave narratives. *The Narrative of Solomon Northup* sold 27,000 copies in 1853 and 1854. *Narrative of the Life of William Wells Brown, a Fugitive Slave, Written by Himself* went through four editions in its first year. According to a piece in the *Christian Examiner* of July 1849, the *Frederick Douglass Narrative* had achieved seven editions since its publication in 1845."[4]

The antislavery press and lecture circuit fostered the discourse of the slave. John A. Collins, general agent of the Massachusetts Anti-Slavery Society, wrote to William Lloyd Garrison in 1842, "The public have itching ears to hear a colored man speak, and particularly a *slave*. Multitudes will flock to hear one of his class."[5] And multitudes would read their books. The lecture circuit afforded the former slave— such as Frederick Douglass and William Wells Brown—the opportunity to grow in her or his command of English. But it also helped to ensure the veracity of the slave's tale, a very important factor after the popular 1838 narrative of James Williams had to be withdrawn from circulation because charges that it fictionalized his experiences could not be disproven. Comparing spoken and written versions of these tales (as we can do with Douglass, for example) provides an ideal opportunity for scholars to study the complex relation between oral and written forms of narrative, and especially the trope of orality itself that remains central in much of contemporary black fiction. A former slave's mastery of words could have profound implications for that individual's fame and fortune, and for the larger thrust of the antislavery movement more broadly.

We can gain some idea of the role that the words of ex-slaves were able to play in the fight against slavery by considering the following comments. Lucius C. Matlack wrote in 1849:

> Naturally and necessarily, the enemy of literature, [American slavery] has [be]come the prolific theme of much that is profound in argument, sublime in poetry, and thrilling in narrative. From the soil of slavery itself have sprang forth some of the most brilliant productions, whose logical levers will ultimately upheave and overthrow the system.... Startling incidents authenticated, far excelling fiction in their touching pathos, from the pen of self-emancipated slaves do now exhibit slavery in such revolting aspects, as to secure the execrations of all good men and become a monument more enduring than marble, in testimony strong as sacred writ against it.[6]

In 1855, in a review of Frederick Douglass's second slave narrative, *Putnam's Monthly* said:

> Our English literature has recorded many an example of genius struggling against adversity,—of the poor Ferguson, for instance, making himself an astronomer, of Burns becoming a poet, of Hugh Miller finding his geology in a stone quarry, and a thousand similar cases—yet none of these are so impressive as the case of a solitary slave, in a remote district, surrounded by none but enemies, conceiving the project of his escape, teaching himself to read and write to facilitate it, accomplishing it at last, and subsequently raising himself to a leadership in a great movement on behalf of his brethren.[7]

The direct relation between reading and writing, on one hand, and legal freedom on the other, was patently evident to both the slave narrators and to their reviewers.

There are measures other than sales figures that attest to the popularity of the form. A reviewer of Henry Bibb's narrative wrote in 1849: "This fugitive slave literature is destined to be a powerful lever. We have the most profound conviction of its potency. We see in it the easy and infallible means of abolitionizing the free States. Argument provides argument, reason is met by sophistry. But narratives of slaves go right to the heart of men."[8]

The narratives of ex-slaves, as Arna Bontemps pointed out, became the very foundation upon which so very many subsequent canonical African American fictional and nonfictional narrative forms were based. This is as true of Booker T. Washington's *Up from Slavery* and *The Autobiography of Malcolm X* as it is of Zora Neale Hurston's *Their Eyes Were Watching God*, Richard Wright's *Black Boy*, Ralph Ellison's *Invisible Man*, Alice Walker's *The Color Purple*, Toni Morrison's *Beloved*, and Colson Whitehead's *The Intuitionist*. And the legion of contemporary fictional, or "neoslave narratives," illustrates this formal literary history quite explicitly. Alone among all literary traditions, the canon of African American literature rests on the framework built, by fits and starts, by these first-person narratives of persons who were once legally defined as property—as things.

Collected in this volume are four classic narratives written or narrated by former slaves: Olaudah Equiano, Mary Prince, Frederick Douglass, and Harriet Jacobs. Chronologically, these authors' texts span nearly three-quarters of a century (1789 to 1861); the authors, two men and two women, include one African, one West Indian, and two African Americans, thereby helping us to understand a broad range of the black experience in slavery between the Enlightenment period following the American Revolution and the start of the Civil War.

The most famous of them all is Frederick Douglass's 1845 *Narrative*. Classic and elegant in its simplicity and its gripping readability, Douglass's compelling lucidity belies his narrative's literary complexity, a complexity that masks or disguises itself precisely because Douglass was a master rhetorician, expert in both spoken *and* written English. Douglass tells such a good tale that his text opens itself to all classes of readers, from those who love a good adventure story to those who wish to have rendered for them in startling detail the facts of human bondage—what it meant to discover that one was a slave and what one proceeded to do about it, while someone else simultaneously was doing all manner of horrendous things to keep that slave from imagining himself or herself otherwise. Douglass's rhetorical power convinces us that he is "the" black slave, that he embodies the structures and thoughts and feelings of all black slaves, that he is the resplendent, articulate part that stands for the whole, for the collective slave community. His superb command of several rhetorical figures—metaphor, irony, synecdoche, apostrophe, and especially chiasmus—enables him to chart with fine precision in only a few pages not only "how a man was made a slave," but also "how a slave was made a man." And that chiasmus most succinctly summarizes the political intention of the genre of the slave narratives.

Douglass's narrative demonstrates not only how the deprivation of the hallmarks of identity can affect the slave but also how the slaveowner's world negates and even perverts its own values. Deprivation of a birth date, a name, a family structure, and of legal rights makes of the deprived a brute, a subhuman, says Douglass, until he comes to a consciousness of these relations: through that consciousness, he comes to see that it is the human depriver who is inhumane, the actual barbarian within the plantation system. With painstaking verisimilitude, Douglass reproduces a system of signs that we have come to call plantation culture, an ordering of the world based on a profoundly relational type of thinking. In this world, a strict barrier of difference forms the basis of a class rather than, as in other classification schemes, an ordering based on resemblances or the identity of two or more elements. Douglass's narrative strategy seems to be this: he brings together two terms in special relationships suggested by some quality that they share; then, by opposing two seemingly unrelated elements, such as the sheep, cattle, or horses on the plantation and the specimen of life known as a slave, Douglass's language is made to signify the presence and absence of some quality—in this case, humanity itself. Douglass uses this device to explicate the slave's understanding of himself and of his relation to the world. Not only does his *Narrative* depict two diametrically opposed notions of genesis, origins, and meaning, but its structure actually turns on an opposition between nature and culture as well.

What great slave narrative informed Douglass's? Although it is obvious that Douglass read widely, and avidly devoured those narratives published by other ex-slaves between 1831 and 1845, was he revising another classic slave narrative, one whose form and themes he could appropriate and "rewrite" in that profound art of grounding that creates a literary tradition? I am not the only scholar who believes that Douglass was, and that the 1789 slave narrative of Olaudah Equiano was his "silent second text."

Equiano's *Life* has remained a favorite of readers since its late-eighteenth-century publication in London. Eight British editions and one American edition were published in Equiano's lifetime, and by 1837 there had been an additional eight editions, including Dutch and German translations in 1790 and 1791. Equiano's tale is of innocence betrayed, of wisdom earned, as he passes from one phase of enslavement to the next on the high seas. His is an adventure story, one that charts a human being's passage from an idyllic Igbo childhood to slavery in the New World.

Equiano's narrative is so richly structured that it became the prototype of the nineteenth-century slave narrative. From his subtitle "Written by Himself" and a signed engraving of the black author holding an open text (the Bible) in his lap, to more subtle rhetorical strategies such as the overlapping of the slave's arduous journey to freedom and his simultaneous journey from orality to literacy, Equiano's strategies of self-preservation most certainly influenced the shape of black narrative before 1865, especially those of Douglass and Harriet Jacobs.

Equiano told an exceptionally good story, and even gives a believable account of cultural life among the Igbo peoples of what is now eastern Nigeria. The movement of his plot, then, is from African freedom, through European enslavement, to Anglican freedom. Both his remarkable command of narrative devices and his detailed accounts of his stirring adventures combined to create a readership broader than that enjoyed by any black writer before 1789. When we recall that his adventures include service in the Seven Years' War with General Wolfe in Canada and Admiral Boscawen in the Mediterranean, voyages to the Arctic with the 1772–73 Phipps expedition, six months among Miskito Indians in Central America, and "a grand tour of the Mediterranean as personal servant to an English gentleman," it is clear that this ex-slave was one of the best-traveled people in the world when he decided to write the story of his life.

Like Ottobah Cugoano, Equiano's close friend in London, Equiano was extraordinarily well read, and, like Cugoano, he borrowed freely from other texts, including Constantine Phipps's *A Journal of a Voyage Towards the North Pole* (London, 1771) and Thomas Clarkson's *Essay on the Slavery and Commerce of the Human Species* (London, 1785). He also paraphrased frequently, sometimes inventing "direct" quotations from Milton, Pope, and Thomas Day. Nevertheless, Equiano was an impressively self-conscious writer and developed highly influential rhetorical strategies, especially his use of two distinct voices: the simple wonder with which the young Equiano approaches the New World of his captors, and a more eloquent voice to describe the author's narrative present. The frequent reversal of plot, too, serves to highlight the sense of becoming, of a development of a self that not only has a past and a present but multiple languages, all of which serve to enliven the narrative present. Rarely would a slave narrator match Equiano's mastery of self-representation. Equiano's self-confident writing led one *Monthly Review* critic to ask whether "some English writer" had participated in the writing of his narrative. Equiano's text seems to anticipate such a response by making repeated references to his various lessons in literacy.

Central to Equiano's text is his use of what I call the "Trope of the Talking Book," revising it from Cugoano's use of it just two years before, in his third chapter, in which he describes his voyages from Barbados to Virginia and on to England—a portentous voyage, on which he begins to learn the English language. Exploring a shipboard cabin, a wide-eyed Equiano confronts the sublime artifacts of Western Culture:

> The first object that engaged my attention was a watch which hung on the chimney, and was going. I was quite surprised at the noise it made, and was afraid it would

tell the gentleman anything I might do amiss: and when I immediately after observed a picture hanging in the room, which appeared constantly to look at me, I was still more affrighted, having never seen such things as these before. At one time, I thought it was something relative to magic; and not seeing it move, I thought it might be some ways the whites had to keep their great men when they died, and offer them libations as we used to do to our friendly spirits. . . .

I was astonished at the wisdom of the white people in all the things I saw.   (pages 62, 67)

From these wonderments, Equiano proceeds to describe another marvelous sight:

I had often seen my master . . . employed in reading; and I had great curiosity to talk to the books, as I thought [he] did; and so to learn how all things had a beginning; for that purpose I have often taken up a book, and have talked to it, and then put my ears to it, when alone, in hopes it would answer me; and I have been very much concerned when I found it remained silent.   (page 67)

A watch, a portrait, a book that speaks—these are signs through which Equiano represents the difference in subjectivity. The portrait seems to be watching him as he moves through the room; the watch, he fears, can see, hear, and speak. The watch is his master's surrogate overseer, standing in for the master as an authority figure, even while he sleeps. The Talking Book talks only to "my master." By presenting these objects in this manner, Equiano dramatizes the sensitive child's naïveté and curiosity, as well as his ability to interpret the culture of the Europeans from a distinctly African point of reference. But he also, implicitly, contrasts this earlier self with the self that narrates his text. His ability to show his readers his own naïveté, rather than merely to tell us about it or to claim it, and to make this earlier self the focus of his readers' sympathy and amusement, are extraordinarily effective rhetorical strategies that serve to heighten our identification with the openly honest subject.

There is another purpose to this bestowal of subjectivity on the master's things. The young Equiano, as a slave, is a thing: the master's object, to be used and enjoyed, purchased, sold, or discarded, just like a watch, a portrait, or a book. By law, the slave has no more and no fewer rights than the other objects that the master endows with his subjectivity. When Equiano, the object, attempts to speak to the book, there follows only the deafening silence that obtains between two lifeless objects. When the master's book looks to see whose face is behind the voice that Equiano speaks, it can only see an absence, the invisibility that dwells in an unattended looking glass. Only through the act of writing can Equiano announce and preserve his newfound status as a subject. It is he who is the master of his text, a text that speaks volumes of experience and subjectivity. Equiano the author has changed, from African to Anglo-African, from slave to potential freedman, from an absence to a presence, from an object to a subject. Like Cugoano, Equiano could not simply make the trope a part of a linear narrative. So he subordinates it to a list of latent readings of the "true" nature of Western culture, and simultaneously allows it to function as an allegory of his own act of fashioning an Anglo-African self through language.

Scholars have recently been engaged in a debate about Equiano's birthplace. The pioneering Equiano scholar Paul Edwards long ago noted that a baptismal record lists Equiano's birthplace as South Carolina. Drawing upon Edwards's discovery, plus naval records that he believes also list South Carolina as Equiano's birthplace, Vincent Carretta, in *Equiano, the African: Biography of a Self-Made Man* (2005), questions Equiano's claim that eastern Nigeria, or Igboland, is his home. Carretta defends his position thus: "Some commentators assert that the records must be erroneous, while others conjecture that Equiano fabricated a North American birth and then suppressed that information in his autobiography. The truth about where Equiano was born may never be known. But certainly Equiano's claim to an African nativity rendered his description of the Middle Passage the eyewitness account that both proponents and opponents of the Trans-Atlantic slave trade were calling for." Carretta concludes: "From the available evidence, one could argue that the author of 'The Interesting Narrative' invented an African identity rather than reclaimed one. If so, his literary achievement has often been underestimated."*

On the other hand, the historian Paul Lovejoy makes a persuasive case for the authenticity of Equiano's claim, especially given the fact that many documents—such as federal census data, for instance—contain all sorts of errors, introduced by an official or even by the person being interviewed, for one reason or another. Lovejoy argues passionately, "The preponderant evidence derived from culture and context confirms his African birth, in my opinion, and the documents that claim otherwise have to be interpreted accordingly. What appears to establish his place of birth as South Carolina disappears when the chronology of his narrative is more carefully deciphered, suggesting that Vassa [Equiano was known as Gustavus Vassa, but used his African name in the title of his book] was likely two or three years older than he thought, not younger as Carretta has concluded. When all factors are considered, especially in consequence of what he reveals about eighteenth-century culture and society in Igboland, the most reasonable conclusion in assessing whether or not Vassa was born in Africa or America is to believe what Vassa claimed, that he was born in a place called 'Essaka.' Hence his account of his homeland and the terror of the 'Middle Passage' should be considered as being derived from his memory."[9]

Lovejoy makes an even stronger case for Equiano's African origins because he tells us that he was circumcised. As Lovejoy persuasively argues, "At that time in Britain, circumcision was considered barbaric. It was not even practiced in hospitals for medical reasons until one century later. He could not and would not have been circumcised in South Carolina. There was no ritual context, and masters would not have tolerated the practice in any event. We know he was circumcised because on the way to the coast, he passed through a land where people did not circumcise, and his reference makes these people sound barbaric. This is an unconscious demonstration of his authenticity; he mentions and discusses circumcision at least five times in a

---

*Vincent Carretta to Henry Louis Gates, Jr., August 25, 2011.

book aimed at a public to garner support. He does not say the practice is barbaric; far from it. Why did he mention it so much if the memory of the ritual and the context was not important to him? He would not have gotten this sensitivity from someone else, or by reading about it. The rituals involved in circumcision, as with the significance of *ichi* scarification, were essential in Vassa's memory of his homeland and his identity as an African."*

Given my own extensive research experience with the legion of discrepancies in names and ages in public records concerning African Americans—such as the federal census, for instance, and estate records—I have to say that I am inclined to agree with Lovejoy. There is absolutely no way to know how or why a South Carolina provenance appears on these documents that Carretta has found. And forcing Equiano (and scholars inclined to take him at his word) in effect to disprove a negative claim fostered in circumstances impossible to ascertain seems unfair to the subject. I am also forced to wonder at implicit support of his claims tendered by the absence of protest from Equiano's close African friends and intimates in London, such as Ottobah Cugoano. It is difficult to imagine their total silence about such a discrepancy, if their friend's claims to an African birth were untrue. But no doubt this debate among scholars will continue.

Mary Prince, born a slave at Brackish-Pond in Bermuda, enjoys the distinction of being the first woman to publish a slave narrative. This short narrative of twenty-three pages appeared in two editions in London in 1831. Although it is noteworthy for being the first woman's slave narrative, it is even more noteworthy because it altered fundamentally the very genre of the slave narrative.

Though Prince's story begins in the classic "I was born" mode common to all slave narratives, she quickly alerts her readers to the fact that hers is a tale that has not been told before, the very tale of the female slave who heretofore had been spoken for but who had not yet spoken *for herself.* Whereas both Equiano and Douglass were concerned with

*Paul Lovejoy to Henry Louis Gates, Jr., August 25, 2011.

depicting the cruelties of slavery by providing a few vivid scenes of sadism and sexual abuse practiced by white masters and mistresses against black women, Prince's account makes her readers acutely aware that the sexual brutalization of the black woman slave—along with the enforced severance of a mother's natural relation to her children and the lover of her choice—defined more than any other aspect of slavery the daily price of her bondage. Whereas black women are objects of narration in the tales written by black men, Prince's slim yet compelling story celebrates their self-transformation into subjects, subjects as defined by those who have gained a voice.

Prince is a convincing narrator, one who combines a fine sense of metaphor with the compulsion to testify against and indict her oppressors: "slavery hardens white people's hearts towards the blacks; and many of them were not slow to make their remarks upon us aloud, without regard to our grief—though their light words fell like cayenne on the fresh wounds of our hearts." Prince also reveals that sadism was as commonly practiced by white women as by white men; her own mistress "caused me to know the exact difference between the smart of the rope, the cart-whip, and the cow-skin, when applied to my naked body by her own cruel hand. . . . To strip me naked—to hang me up by the wrists and lay my flesh open with the cow-skin, was an ordinary punishment for even a slight offense" (pages 235, 239). Her master beat her in the same way, but also forced her "to wash him in a tub of water after he had stripped himself quite naked." This, she confesses, was "worse to me than all the licks" (page 249). Slavery brutalized men and women, master and mistress, the enslaved and the free.

Prince's narrative is also central to the development of the slave narrative because she repeatedly comments upon the differences between popular white myths or impressions about the feelings of slaves and the actual feelings of the slaves themselves: "Oh the Buckra [white] people who keep slaves think that black people are like cattle, without natural affection. But my heart tells me it is far otherwise" (page 243). Near the conclusion of her narrative, Prince makes an even bolder claim: "All slaves want to be free—to be free is very sweet. . . . I have been a slave myself—and I know what slaves feel—I can tell by myself what other slaves feel, and by what they have told me. The man that says slaves be quite happy in slavery—that they don't want to be free—that man is either ignorant or a lying person" (page 263). As William Andrews concludes about the historical significance of Prince's assertion:

> In this remark a black female slave declares herself to be a more reliable authority on slavery than any white man and fully capable of speaking for all her fellow slaves, both male and female, against any white man. The implication of this declaration should not be underestimated, since it provides the first claim in the Afro-American autobiographical tradition for the black woman as singularly authorized to represent all black people, regardless of gender, in Western discourse about "what slaves feel" about the morality of slavery.[10]

If Prince's narrative "broke the silence" of the black woman slave, Harriet Jacobs's *Incidents in the Life of a Slave Girl* brought this category of slave narratives to its summit. As William Andrews says, Jacobs's *Incidents* is "the major black woman's autobiography of the mid-nineteenth century."[11] *Incidents* is also one of the major autobiographies of the African American tradition.

Although Jacobs's narrative was a remarkably well-written and riveting testament to a black female slave's will to survive, it has only recently been authenticated as "written by herself," as her subtitle claims. Published under the pseudonym of "Linda Brent," "edited" by the well-known antislavery writer Lydia Maria Child, and constructed around an astonishing plot (in which the heroine remains concealed from her master for seven years in a garret in her grandmother's home), Jacobs's narrative was long thought to be either a novel assuming the shape of a slave narrative—as was Mattie Griffiths's *Autobiography of a Female Slave* (1857) or Richard Hildreth's *The Slave; or, Memoirs of Archie Moore* (1836)—or else a ghostwritten autobiography that strained credibility. The classic statement of the fraudulence of Jacobs's work is that written by John W. Blassingame in *The Slave Community* (1972):

In spite of Lydia Maria Child's insistence that she had only revised the manuscript of Harriet Jacobs "mainly for purposes of condensation and orderly arrangement," the work is not credible. In the first place, *Incidents in the Life of a Slave Girl* (1861) is too orderly; too many of the major characters meet providentially after years of separation. Then, too, the story is too melodramatic; miscegenation and cruelty, outraged virtue, unrequited love, and planter licentiousness appear on practically every page. The virtuous Harriet sympathizes with her wretched mistress who has to look on all of the mulattoes fathered by her husband, she refuses to bow to the lascivious demands of her master, bears two children for another white man, and then runs away and hides in a garret in her grandmother's cabin for seven years until she is able to escape to New York. In the meantime, her white lover has acknowledged his paternity of her children, purchased their freedom, and been elected to Congress. In the end, all live happily ever after.[12]

Despite the fact that an 1861 reviewer writing in *The Anti-Slavery Advocate* claims an extended acquaintance with the author and vouches with great confidence for the authenticity of her tale, it was not until 1981 that a scholar, Jean Fagan Yellin, demonstrated conclusively that Jacobs indeed wrote the narrative of her bondage and freedom. Among other things, Yellin discovered the actual historical identities of each of the major characters in the narrative to whom Jacobs gave pseudonyms. She also found examples of other writings by Jacobs, demonstrating that she had the capacity to write such a sophisticated autobiography. And she traced the details of Jacobs's life, and her dealings with abolitionists, after she made her successful escape to the North, and after her children joined her there. Few instances of scholarly sleuthing have been more important to African American Studies than has Yellin's.

Jacobs's narrative is a bold and gripping fusion of two major literary forms: she borrowed from the popular sentimental novel on one hand, and the slave narrative genre on the other. Jacobs's tale gains its importance in that she charts, in great and painful detail, the sexual exploitation that daily haunted her life—and the lives of every other black female slave. In the character of the unrelentingly evil Dr. Flint, and in the hard choices that his vulgar pursuit forces Jacobs to make, Jacobs graphically renders the sexual aspect of economic exploitation in a manner unimaginable before. Whereas the black male slave narrators' accounts of sexual brutality remain suggestive, if gruesome, Jacobs—enlarging upon the precedent created by Mary Prince—charts vivid detail by vivid detail precisely how the shape of her life and the choices she makes are defined by her reduction to a sexual object, an object to be raped, bred, or abused.

To escape the repulsive advances of Dr. Flint, she becomes the lover of a white man called Sands, to whom she bears two children, whom Sands promises to free. Banished by an outraged Flint to another plantation and taunted by the threat of the permanent loss of the possibility of freedom for her children, Jacobs escapes, hiding in a garret in her grandmother's home (three feet high, nine feet long, and seven feet wide) for seven years. Jacobs even writes letters in her garret, then has these mailed to Flint from Boston and New York, cleverly deceiving him. Sands does purchase and free his children, called Ellen and Ben in the narrative. He sends Ellen to work for a cousin of his in New York, and later, after Jacobs's escape, she writes her grandmother to send Ben to Boston, where they are finally reunited.

Jacobs revises the received structure of the genre as practiced by its two great exemplars, Equiano and Douglass, by framing her entire story with descriptions of the inherent strength, dignity, and nobility of her family, and especially that of her maternal grandmother, in whom she "had a great treasure," as she informs her readers in her very first paragraph. In so doing, she engages in one of the earliest examples of literary female bonding in the black tradition. And she also appeals directly to a female readership, including whites, by selecting as one of her epigraphs Isaiah 32:9: "Rise up, ye women that are at ease! Hear my voice, ye careless daughters!" This act, what feminists today would call "gendering," represents a major break from the male tradition she inherited.

In the final paragraph of the narrative, Jacobs reflects

upon the pains of her enslavement, finding comfort only in one set of memories:

> It has been painful to me, in many ways, to recall the dreary years I passed in bondage. I would gladly forget them if I could. Yet the retrospection is not altogether without solace; for with those gloomy recollections come tender memories of my good old grandmother, like light, fleecy clouds floating over a dark and troubled sea.
>
> (page 61)

In this way, Jacobs stresses not only the central importance of her grandmother in her own life, but also the crucial centrality of female bonding in the life of the slave woman. This declaration, along with the fact that Jacobs here has remodeled the forms of the black slave narrative and the white female sentimental novel to create a new literary form—a narrative at once black and female—underscores the major importance of *Incidents in the Life of a Slave Girl* to the African American tradition.

In these four narratives, then, written or related by one African, one West Indian, and two African Americans, the bondage of black human beings assumes a voice and a face that testify—as all classics do—against human bondage and on behalf of the will to be free, black, and human. For these authors, inevitably, the will to power was the will to write.

—HENRY LOUIS GATES, JR.
Oak Bluffs, MA
August 29, 2011

ENDNOTES

1. Richard S. Newman, "Liberation Technology: Black Printed Protest in the Age of Franklin." *Early American Studies: An Interdisciplinary Journal* 8.1 (Winter 2010), 191.
2. Arna Bontemps, ed., *Great Slave Narratives* (Boston: Beacon Press, 1969), x.
3. Charles S. Nichols, *Many Thousands Gone: The Ex-*

Slaves' Account of their Bondage and Freedom (Leiden: E. J. Brill, 1963), xiv–xv.

4. Bontemps, p. xviii.

5. Quoted in Robert L. Hall, "Massachusetts Abolitionists Document the Slave Experience," in Donald M. Jacobs, ed., *Courage and Conscience: Black and White Abolitionists in Boston* (Bloomington: Indiana University Press, 1993), 83.

6. Quoted in Henry Bibb, *Narrative of the Life Adventures of Henry Bibb, An American Slave, Written by Himself*, introduction by Lucius C. Matlack (New York: published by the author, 1849), i.

7. "American Literature and Reprints," *Putnam's Monthly* (Nov 1855), 547.

8. From *The Chronotype*, quoted in Bibb, *Narrative*, 207.

9. Paul E. Lovejoy, "Autobiography and Memory: Gustavus Vassa, alias Olaudah Equiano, the African." *Slavery and Abolition* 27.3 (2006), 47.

10. William L. Andrews and Henry Louis Gates, Jr., eds., *The Civitas Anthology of African American Slave Narratives* (Washington, D.C.: Civitas/Counterpoint, 1999), 9.

11. William L. Andrews, *To Tell a Free Story: The First Century of Afro-American Autobiography, 1760–1865* (Urbana: University of Illinois Press, 1986), 239.

12. John W. Blassingame, *The Slave Community: Plantation Life in the Antebellum South* (New York: Oxford University Press, 1972), 234.

ACKNOWLEDGMENTS

I would like to thank William L. Andrews, Houston A. Baker, Jr., Hazel V. Carby, James Olney, Robert Harris, Mary Helen Washington, and Jean Fagan Yellin for their recommendations about which slave narratives should be considered "classic" and why. I would also like to thank LuAnn Walther for suggesting that I edit this volume and Tracy Bernstein for suggesting that I publish this second edition of *The Classic Slave Narratives*, and also to thank them both for their superb editorial skills and for their patience. I would also like to thank Cynthia Bond, Marial Iglesias Utset, Nicholas Nardini, Samuel Otter, Abby Wolf, and Donald Yacovone for their research assistance, and Nina Tar, Phyllis Mollock, Amy Gosdanian, and Janice Stenger for typing the versions of this manuscript so expertly. Finally, I would like to thank Tina Bennett and Paul Lucas for their counsel and guidance.

THE
INTERESTING NARRATIVE
OF
THE LIFE
OF
OLAUDAH EQUIANO,
OR
GUSTAVUS VASSA,
THE AFRICAN.

WRITTEN BY HIMSELF.

Behold, God is my salvation; I will trust, and not be afraid, for the Lord Jehovah is my strength and my song; be also is become my salvation.

And in that day shall ye say, Praise the Lord, call upon his name, declare his doings among the people. Isa. xii. 2. 4.

NINTH EDITION ENLARGED.

LONDON:
PRINTED FOR, AND SOLD BY THE AUTHOR.

1794.

PRICE FIVE SHILLINGS,
Formerly sold for 7s.

[*Entered at Stationers' Hall.*]

To the Reader

An invidious falsehood having appeared in the Oracle of the 25th, and the Star of the 27th of April 1792, with a view to hurt my character, and to discredit and prevent the sale of my Narrative, asserting, that I was born in the Danish island of Santa Cruz, in the West Indies, it is necessary that, in this edition, I should take notice thereof, and it is only needful of me to appeal to those numerous and respectable persons of character who knew me when I first arrived in England, and could speak no language but that of Africa.

Under this appeal, I now offer this edition of my Narrative to the candid reader, and to the friends of humanity, hoping it may still be the means, in its measure, of showing the enormous cruelties practiced on my sable brethren, and strengthening the generous emulation now prevailing in this country, to put a speedy end to a traffic both cruel and unjust.

Edinburgh, June 1792.

Letter,
of
Alexander Tillock to John Montieth, Esq.
Glasgow.

DEAR SIR,

YOUR note of the 30th ult. I would have answered in course; but wished first to inform you what paper we had taken the article from which respected GUSTAVUS VASSA. By this day's post, have sent you a copy of the Oracle of Wednesday the 25th—in the last column of the 3rd page, you will find the article from which we inserted the one in the Star of the 27th ult.—If it be erroneous, you will see it had not its origin with us. As to G.V. I know nothing about him.

After examining the paragraph in the Oracle which immediately follows the one in question, I am inclined to believe that the one respecting G.V. may have been fabricated by some of the advocates for continuing the Slave Trade, for the purpose of weakening the force of the evidence brought against that trade; for, I believe, if they could, they would stifle the evidence altogether.

Having sent you the Oracle, we have sent all that we can say about the business. I am,

DEAR SIR,

Your most humble Servant,

ALEX. TILLOCH.

Star Office, 5th May, 1792.

LETTER

FROM THE REV. DR. J. BAKER, OF MAY FAIR
CHAPEL, LONDON, TO MR. GUSTAVUS
VASSA, AT DAVID DALE'S ESQ.
GLASGOW.

DEAR SIR,

I went after Mr. [Buchanan] Millan (the printer of the Oracle), but he was not at home. I understood that an apology would be made to you, and I desired it might be a proper one, such as would give fair satisfaction, and take off any disadvantageous impressions which the paragraph alluded to may have made. Whether the matter will bear an action or not, I do not know, and have not inquired whether you can punish by law; because I think it is not worth while to go to the expence of a law-suit, especially if a proper apology is made; for, can any man that reads your Narrative believe that you are not a native of Africa? I see therefore no good reason for not printing a fifth edition, on account of a scandalous paragraph in a newspaper.

I remain,

DEAR SIR,

Your sincere Friend,

J. BAKER.

Grosvenor-street, May 14, 1792.

TO THE LORDS SPIRITUAL AND TEMPORAL, AND THE
COMMONS OF THE PARLIAMENT OF GREAT BRITAIN.

My Lords and Gentlemen,

PERMIT me with the greatest deference and respect, to
lay at your feet the following genuine Narrative; the chief
design of which is to excite in your august assemblies a
sense of compassion for the miseries which the Slave Trade
has entailed on my unfortunate countrymen. By the horrors
of that trade I was first torn away from all the tender connexions that were dear to my heart; but these, through the
mysterious ways of Providence, I ought to regard as infinitely more than compensated by the introduction I have
thence obtained to the knowledge of the Christian religion,
and of a nation which, by its liberal sentiments, its humanity,
the glorious freedom of its government, and its proficiency
in arts and sciences, has exalted the dignity of human nature.

I am sensible I ought to entreat your pardon for addressing to you a work so wholly devoid of literary merit; but, as
the production of an unlettered African, who is actuated by
the hope of becoming an instrument towards the relief of
his suffering countrymen. I trust that *such a man,* pleading
in *such a cause,* will be acquitted of boldness and presumption.

May the god of Heaven inspire your hearts with peculiar
benevolence on that important day when the question of
Abolition is to be discussed, when thousands, in consequence of your determination, are to look for Happiness or
Misery!

I am,

My LORDS and GENTLEMEN,

Your most obedient,

And devoted humble servant,

OLAUDAH EQUIANO,

OR

GUSTAVUS VASSA.

March 1789.

To the CHAIRMEN of the COMMITTEE for the ABOLITION of the SLAVE TRADE.

Magdalen College, Cambridge, May 26 1790.

GENTLEMEN,

I TAKE the liberty, as being joined with you in the same laudable endeavours to support the cause of humanity in the Abolition of the Slave Trade, to recommend to your protection the bearer of this note GUSTAVUS VASSA, an African; and to beg the favour of your assistance to him in the sale of his book.

I am, with great respect,
GENTLEMEN,
Your most obedient servant,
P. PECKARD.

Manchester, July 23, 1790.

THOMAS WALKER has great pleasure in recommending the sale of the NARRATIVE of GUSTAVUS VASSA to the friends of justice and humanity, he being well entitled to their protection and support, from the united testimonies of the Rev. T. Clarkson, of London; Dr. Peckard, of Cambridge; and Sampson and Charles Lloyd, Esqrs. of Birmingham.

Sheffield, August 20 1790.

In consequence of the recommendation of Dr. Peckard, of Cambridge; Messrs. Lloyd, of Birmingham; the Rev. T. Clarkson, of London; Thomas Walker, Thomas Cooper, and Isaac Moss, Esqrs. of Manchester, we beg leave also to recommend the sale of the NARRATIVE of GUSTAVUS VASSA to the friends of humanity in the town and neighbourhood of Sheffield.

Dr. Brown,	Rev. Ja. Wilkinson,
Wm. Shore, Esq,	Rev. Edw. Goodwin,
Samuel Marshall,	John Barlow.

Nottingham, January 17, 1791.

IN consequence of the respectable recommendation of several gentlemen of the first character, who have born testimony to the good sense, intellectual improvements, and integrity of GUSTAVUS VASSA, lately of that injured and oppressed class of men, the injured Africans; and further convinced of the justice of his recommendations, from our own personal interviews with him, we take the liberty also to recommend the said GUSTAVUS VASSA to the protection and assistance of the friends of humanity.

Rev. G. Walker,
John Morris,
Joseph Rigsby, Rector, St. Peter's,
Samuel Smith,
John Wright,

F. Wakefield,
T. Bolton,

Thomas Hawksley,
S. White, M.D.
J. Hancock.

LETTER
TO MR. O'BRIEN, CARRICKFERGUS,
(*PER FAVOUR OF* MR. GUSTAVUS VASSA.)

Belfast, December 25, 1791.

DEAR SIR,

The bearer of this, Mr. GUSTAVUS VASSA, an enlightened African, of good sense, agreeable manners, and of an excellent character, and who comes well recommended to this place, and noticed by the first people here, goes to-morrow for your town, for the purpose of vending some books, written by himself, which is a Narrative of his own Life and Sufferings, with some account of his native country and its inhabitants. He was torn from his relatives and country (by the more savage white men of England) at an early period in life; and during his residence in England, at which time I have seen him, during my agency for the American prisoners, with Sir William Dolben, Mr. Granville Sharp, Mr. Wilkes, and many other distinguished characters; he supported an irreproachable character, and was a principal instrument in bringing about the motion for the repeal of the Slave-Act. I beg leave to introduce him to your notice and civility; and if you can spare the time, your introduction of him personally to your neighbours may be of essential benefit to him.

I am,

SIR,

Your obedient servant,

THOS. DIGGES.

LETTER
TO ROWLAND WEBSTER, ESQ. STOCKTON.
(*PER FAVOUR OF* MR. GUSTAVUS VASSA.)

DEAR SIR,

I TAKE the liberty to introduce to your knowledge Mr. GUSTAVUS VASSA, an African of distinguished merit. He has recommendations to Stockton, and I am happy in adding to the number. To the principal supporters of the Bill for the Abolition of the Slave Trade he is well known; and he has, himself, been very instrumental in promoting a plan so truly conducive to the interests of religion and humanity. Mr. VASSA has published a Narrative which clearly delineates the iniquity of that unnatural and destructive commerce; and I am able to assert, from my own experience, that he has not exaggerated in a single particular. This work has been mentioned in very favourable terms by the Reviewers, and fully demonstrates that genius and worth are not limited to country or complexion. He has with him some copies for sale, and if you can conveniently assist him in the disposal thereof, you will greatly oblige,

DEAR SIR,

Your friend and servant,

WILLIAM EDDIS.

Durham, October 25, 1792.

Hull, November 12, 1792.

THE bearer hereof, Mr. GUSTAVUS VASSA, an African, is recommended to us by the Rev. Dr. Peckard, Dean of Peterborough, and by many other very respectable characters, as an intelligent and upright man; and as we have no doubt but the accounts we have received are grounded on the best authority, we recommend him to the assistance of the friends of humanity in this town, in promoting subscriptions to an interesting Narrative of his Life.

John Sykes, Mayor,   R.A. Harrison, Esq.

Thomas Clarke, Vicar,   Jos. R. Pease, Esq.

William Hornby, Esq. of Gainsborough.

LETTER
TO WILLIAM HUGHES, ESQ. *DEVIZES.*

DEAR SIR,

WHETHER you will consider my introducing to your acquaintance the bearer of this letter, OLAUDAH EQUIANO, the enlightened African, (or GUSTAVUS VASSA) as a liberty or favour, I shall not anticipate.

He came recommended to me by men of distinguished talents and exemplary virtue, as an honest and benevolent man; and his conversation and manners as well as his book do more than justice to the recommendation.

The active part he took in bringing about the motion for a repeal of the Slave Act, has given him much celebrity as a public man; and, in all the varied scenes of chequered life, through which he has passed, his private character and conduct have been irreproachable.

His *business* in your part of the world is to promote the sale of his book, and [it] is a part of *my business*, as a friend to the cause of humanity, to do all the little service that is in my poor power to a man who is engaged in so noble a cause as the freedom and salvation of his enslaved and unenlightened countrymen.

The simplicity that runs through his Narrative is singularly beautiful, and that beauty is heightened by the idea that it is *true*; this is all I shall say about this book, save only that I am sure those who buy it will not regret that they have laid out the price of it in the purchase.

Your notice, civility, and personal introduction of this fair minded black man, to your friends in Devizes, will be gratifying to your own feelings, and laying a considerable weight of obligation on,

DEAR SIR,

Your most obedient and obliged servant,

WILLIAM LANGWORTHY.

Bath, October 10, 1793.

MONTHLY REVIEW FOR JUNE 1789. PAGE 551.

WE entertain no doubt of the authenticity of this very intelligent African's story; though it is not improbable that some English writer has assisted him in the compilement, or, at least, the correction of his book; for it is sufficiently well-written. The Narrative wears an honest face; and we have conceived a good opinion of the man, from the artless manner in which he has detailed the variety of adventures and vicissitudes which have fallen to his lot. His publication appears very seasonable, at a time when negro-slavery is the subject of public investigation; and it seems calculated to increase the odium that has been excited against the West-India planters, on account of the cruelties that some are said to have exercised on their slaves, many instances of which are here detailed.

The sable author of this volume appears to be a very sensible man; and he is, surely, not the less worthy of credit from being a convert to Christianity. He is a Methodist, and has filled many pages towards the end of his work, with accounts of his dreams, visions, and divine influences; but all this, supposing him to have been under any delusive influence, only serves to convince us that he is guided by principle, and that he is not one of those poor converts, who, having undergone the ceremony of baptism, have remained content with that portion only of the christian religion; instances of which are said to be almost innumerable in America and the West Indies.

GUSTAVUS VASSA appears to possess a very different character; and, therefore, we heartily wish success to his publication, which we are glad to see has been encouraged by a very respectable subscription.

THE GENERAL MAGAZINE AND IMPARTIAL
REVIEW FOR JULY 1789, CHARACTERIZES THIS
WORK IN THE FOLLOWING TERMS:

"This is 'a round unvarnished tale' of the chequered adventures of an African, who early in life, was torn from his native country, by those savage dealers in a traffic disgraceful to humanity, and which has fixed a stain on the legislature of Britain. The Narrative appears to be written with much truth and simplicity. The Author's account of the manners of the natives of his own province (Eboe) is interesting and pleasing; and the reader, unless, perchance he is either a West-India planter, or Liverpool merchant, will find his humanity often severely wounded by the shameless barbarity practised towards the author's hapless countrymen in all our colonies: if he feels, as he ought, the oppressed and the oppressors will equally excite his pity and indignation. That so unjust, so iniquitous a commerce may be abolished, is our ardent wish; and we heartily join in our author's prayer, 'That the God of Heaven may inspire the hearts of our Representatives in Parliament, with peculiar benevolence on that important day when so interesting a question is to be discussed; when thousands, in consequence of their determination, are to look for happiness or misery!' "

N.B. These letters, and the Reviewers' remarks would not have appeared in the Narrative, were it not on the account of the false assertions of my enemies to prevent its circulation.

THE kind reception which this work has met with from many hundred persons, of all denominations, demand the Author's most sincere thanks to his numerous friends; and he most respectfully solicits the favour and encouragement of the candid and unprejudiced friends of the Africans.

LIST
OF
ENGLISH SUBSCRIBERS.

His Royal Highness the Prince of Wales.
His Royal Highness the Duke of York.
His Royal Highness the Duke of Cumberland.

A

The Earl of Ailesbury
Admiral Affleck
Mr. William Abingdon
James Adair, Esq.
Rev. Mr. Charles Adams
John Ady
Rev. Mr. Aldridge
Mr. Law Atkinson, of
    Huddersfield
Rev. Mr. Atkinson of Leeds
Mr. Audley
———Atkinson, Esq.
Rev. Mr. Astley, of Chesterfield

B

The Duke of Bedford
The Duchess of Buccleugh
The Lord Bishop of Bangor
Lord Belgrade
Rev. Dr. Baker
Mrs. Baker
Matthew Baillie, M.D.

Mrs. Baillie
Miss Baillie
Miss J. Baillie
Wm. Bliss, of Birmingham
David Barclay, Esq.
Mrs. Baynes
Mr. Thomas Bellamy
Admiral Geo. Balfour
Mr. J. Benjafield
Mr. Bensley
Rev. Mr. Bentley
Mr. Thomas Bently
Sir John Berney, Bart.
Alexander Blair, Esq.
Sir Brooke Boothby, of
    Ashborne
Mrs. E. Boverie
Alderman Boydell
Mr. Beanson, of Doncaster
F.J. Brown, Esq. M.P.
Dr. Brown, of Sheffield
Rev. Mr. Burgess, of Durham
Edward Burch, Esq. R.A.
———Buxton, Esq. of Leicester

C

Rt. Hon. Lord Cathcart
Lord Bishop of Chester
Hon. H.S. Conway
Lady Almiria Carpenter
Captain John Clarkson of the
    Royal Navy
Rev. Tho. Clarkson
Rev. Mr. Carlow of Mansfield
Mrs. Chambers of Derby
Tho. Clark of Northampton
Thomas Cooper, Esq. of
    Manchester
Richard Cosway, Esq.
William B. Crafton, of
    Tewksbury
Alderman Curtis, M.P.

D

The Earl of Dartmouth
The Earl of Derby
Thomas Digges, Esq. of
    America
Sir William Dolben, Bart.
John English Dolben, Esq.
Mrs. Dolben
Rev. C.E. De Coetlogon
John Delemain, Esq.
Dr. William Dickson
Mr. Charles Dilly
Andrew Drummond, Esq.
Rev. Mr. William Dunn
Rev. Mr. James Dyer, Devizes

E

The Earl of Essex
The Countess of Essex
Sir Gilbert Elliot, Bart.
Wm. Eddis, Esq. of Durham
Lady Ann Erskine

G. Noel Edwards, Esq. M.P.
Rev. Mr. John Eyre

F

Mary Ann Fothergill of York
Rev. Mr. Foster
Richard Fishwick, Esq. of
    Newcastle

G

The Earl of Gainsborough
The Earl of Grosvenor
Rt. Hon. Visc. Gallway
Rt. Hon. Viscountess Gallway
Mrs. Garrick
W.P. Gilliess, Esq.
John Grove, Esq.
Sir Philip Gibbes, Bart.
Wm. Green, Esq. of Newcastle
Dr. Grieve, of ditto
Mrs. Guerin
Rev. Mr. Gwinnup

H

The Earl of Hopetoun
Rt. Hon. Lord Hawke
Rt. Hon. Countess of
    Harrington
Rt. Hon. Dowager Countess of
    Huntingdon
Dr. Hey, Leeds
Charles Hamilton, Esq.
Thomas Hammersley, Esq.
Capt. Hare, of Lincoln
Hugh Josiah Hansard, Esq.
Mr. Moses Hart
Sir Richard Hill, Bart.
Rev. Mr. Rowland Hill
Captain John Hill, Royal Navy

Edmund Hill, Esq.
Rev. Mr. Edward Hoare
Rev. Mr. John Holmes
William Hornsby, Esq. of
  Gainsborough
Rev. Mr. Houseman, of
  Leicester
Mr. Martin Hopkins
Mr. Philip Hurlock, sen.

I
Rev. Mr. James
Mr. Jefferys, Royal Navy
Rev. Dr. Jowett
Thomas Irving, Esq.
Edward Ind, Esq.
George Johnson, Esq. of Byker,
  100 copies

K
Rt. Hon. Lord Kinnaird
James Karr, Esq.
Rev. Dr. Kippis
Mr. Robert Kent, Soham
Rev. Mr. Kingsbury,
  Southampton

L
The Ld. Bishop of London
Bennet Langton, Esq.
Sir Egerton Leigh, of
  Northampton
Charles Loyd, Esq.
Edw. Lovedon, Lovedon, Esq.
  M.P.
Mr. William Loyd
Charles and Sampson Loyd,
  Esqs. of Birmingham

Mr. John Low, jun. of
  Manchester
William Langworth, Esq.

M
The Duke of Marlborough
The Duke of Montague
Sir Herbert Mackworth, Bart.
Rt. Hon. Lord Mulgrave
Sir Charles Middleton, Bt.
Lady Middleton
Morris Morgan, Esq.
Mr. Musgrove
James Martin, Esq. M.P.
Mr. Martin, of Hayesgrove,
  Kent
Paul Le Mesurier, Esq. M.P.
Miss Hannah More
Mr. Thomas Musgrove
Lindly Murry, of York

N
The Duke of Northumberland
Capt. Norman, Navy
Pim Nevins, of Leeds
Mr. Deputy Nichols
John Nelthorpe, Esq. of Lincoln
Rev. Robert Boucher Nichols,
  Dean of Middleham

O
Rev. Mr. J. Owen
Edward Ogle, Esq.

P
Rt. Hon. W. Pickett, Esq. Lord
  Mayor of London
Rev. Dr. Peckard, of Cambridge
The Hon. George Pitt, M.P.
Joseph Peas, of Darlington

J. Penn, Esq. of Philadelphia
David Priestman of Malton
Stanley Pumphrey, of Worcester
George Peters, Esq.
John Plowes, Esq. Mayor of
    Leeds
Rev. Mr. Edward Packer, of
    Durham

Q
The Duke of Queensberry
Robert Quarme, Esq.

R
Rt. Hon. Lord Rawdon
Rt. Hon. Lord Rivers
Geo. Rose, Esq. M.P.
Dan. Roberts of Painswick
Rev. Mr. Robinson, of
    Dewsbery
Rev. James Ramsay
Lieut. Gen. Rainsford
Admiral Roddam
Isaac Richardson, of Newcastle
Thomas Richardson, of
    Sunderland

S
The Duke of St. Alban's
The Duchess of St. Alban's
The Lord Bishop of St. David's
The Earl of Stanhope
The Earl of Scarborough
William, the son of Ignatius
    Sancho
Granville Sharp, Esq.
Mrs. M. Shaw
William Shore, Esq. of Sheffield
Sir Sidney Smith of the Royal
    Navy

General Smith
John Smith, Esq.
Colonel Simcoe
Rev. Mr. Southgate
Tho. Steel. Esq. M.P.
Rev. Mr. Sloper, Devizes

T
Hen. Thornton, Esq. M.P.
Alex. Thomson, M.D.
Rev. Mr. John Till
Dr. Thackery
Rev. Mr. Rob. Thornton
Clement Todway, Esq.
William Tuke, of York
Dr. Trotter, of Newcastle
Rev. Mr. Townshend, of
    Cockermouth
Rev. Mr. C. La Trobe
Thomas Talford, Esq.
    Shrewsbury

W
Hon. Earl of Warwick
The Bishop of Worcester
Hon. William Windham, Esq.
    M.P.
Mr. C.B. Wadstrom
Thomas Walker, Esq. of
    Manchester
Dr. White, Nottingham
Jonathan Walker, Esq. of
    Rotherham
Samuel Walker, Esq. of
    Rotherham
Joshua Walker, Esq. ditto
Joseph Walker, Esq. ditto
Rev. Mr. George Walker, of
    Nottingham
Josiah Wedgwood, Esq.

Rev. Mr. John Wesley
Samuel Whitbread, Esq. M.P.
Rev. Mr. Tho. Wigzell
Rev. James Wilkinson, of
    Sheffield
Rev. Mr. Wills
Rev. Mr. Ward
Rev. Elhanan Winchester

Rev. Mr. Wraith, of
    Wolverhampton

Y
Mr. Yeo, of Portsmouth
Mr. Samuel Yockney

LIST
OF
SUBSCRIBERS AT HULL.

A
Mr. Robert Atkinson
Dr. Alderson
Mr. George Adams
Captain Antoine
Mr. Anthony Atkinson
Mr. Thomas Althorp

B
Mr. Charles Broadley
Mr. John Bayes
Mr. Richard Brigham
Mr. Harrison Briggs
The Rev. Mr. Barker
Mr. Isaac Burnett
Miss Bolton
Mr. Peter John Bulmer
Miss Bine
Captain Thomas Brown
Mr. Jonas Brown
Mr. Peter Buttery
Mrs. and Miss Burn
Mr. John Briggs
Dr. Baynes
William Johnson Bell
Mr. George Wm. Brown
Dr. Bertram

Mr. William Barnes
Mr. John Burstale
Mr. William Baker
Mr. Eldred Brown
Mr. John Boyd
Mr. John Brookes
Mr. William Brown
Miss Ann Bateman

C
Rev. Mr. Tho. Clark
Mr. J.N. Cross
Mr. Johnson Cotton
Mr. Henry Coates
Mr. Richard Capes
Mr. Joseph Chapman
Miss Rachael Ann Cook
Mr. Thomas Cutsworth
Mr. Edward Chapman
Mr. William Coslass
Mr. J.S. Crosley
Mr. Joseph Cockerill
Mess. Cook and Walmsley

D
The Rev. Mr. Thomas Dykes
Major Ditmas

Mr. James Delemain
Mr. Dodsworth
Ralph Darling, Esq.
Mr. Joseph Denton
Mr. John Delvitte
Mr. Joseph Dickinson
Mr. Robert Dear

E
Mr. Joseph Eglin
Mr. Gardiner Egginton
Mr. Joseph Egginton
Mr. Thomas Escrett

F
Mr. John Fox
Mr. George Fletcher
Mr. Edmund Foster
Mr. George Fowler
Mr. Thomas Fishwick
Mr. Thomas Fletcher
Mr. John Fearnley
Mr. Thomas Frost
Mr. Henry Feasherston
Captain James Frank

G
The Rev. Edmund Garwood
Mr. John Gilder
Mr. William Green

H
R.A. Harrison, Esq.
Miss Harrison
Mr. Francis Hall
Mr. John Hutchinson
Mr. John Hall
Mr. Richard Hirst
Mr. Joseph Howard, jun.
Mr. Thomas Hall

Mr. Richard Howard
Mr. Wm. Huntingdon
Miss Howard, 5 copies
Mr. John Harrap
Mr. Bachus Huntingdon
Mr. Samuel Hall
Mr. J.P. Hendry
Mr. John Hardy

J
Mr. Anthony Jones
Mr. John Jackson
Mr. Thomas Jackson
Mr. Joseph Jewett
John Jarret, Esq.
Mr. Robert Jackson
Mr. Wm. Johnson
Mr. Robert Jennings

K
Mr. Samuel King
Mr. William Kirby
Mr. George Knowsley
Mr. Robert Kinder

L
Mr. William Levett
The Rev. Mr. George Lambert
Mr. Thomas Lee
Mr. John Lawson
Mr. John B. Lambert

M
John Melling, Esq.
Mr. Samuel Martin
The Rev. Mr. Joseph Milner
Mr. Michael Metcalfe
Mr. Richard Matson
Mr. Bailey Marley
Mr. Godfrey Martin

N
Mr. John Newmarch
Mr. Norris

O
Mr. Benjamin Outram
Mr. Thomas Outram
Mr. Joseph Outram
Robert Osbourne, Esq.
Wm. Osbourne, Esq.
Mr. John Orton

P
Mr. Wm. Proud
Miss Ann Pead
Joseph R. Pearse, Esq.
Mr. William Parker
Mr. John Parker
Isaac Pleasance, Esq.
Mr. Peter Peasegood
Mr. Josiah Prickett
Mr. Robert C. Pease
Mr. John Pickerd
Mr. Benjamin Pullan
Mr. John Popplewell
Charles Pool, Esq.
Mr. Thomas Parkinson

R
Mr. Joseph Rennard
Miss Ann Ramsey
Mr. Joseph Randall
Mr. Richard Rennard
Mr. Thomas Robinson
Mr. Robinson
Rev. Mr. A. Robinson
Mr. Wm. Reest
Mr. Edward Riddle
Mr. Wm. Richmon
Mr. George Roberts

Mr. Josiah Rhodes
Mr. William Ramsden
Mr. Edward Roisbeck
Mr. John Robinson

S
John Sykes, Esq. Mayor
Mr. Richard Stainton
Mr. Charles Smith
Mr. Thomas Scratchard
Mr. Thoms Sanderson
Mrs. Smith
Mr. Samuel Steekney
Mr. John Simpson
Mr. Wm. Shackles
James Stoven, Esq.
Mr. Wm. Steeple
Mr. Wm. Sedgwick
Mr. John Spouncer
Mr. John Spence
Mr. Wm. Stickney
Mr. Thomas Sargent

T
Mr. Thomas Thompson
Mr. Richard Taylor
Mr. William Thorp
Mr. John Thompson
Mr. John Travis
Mr. John Todd
Doctor Tucker
Mr. Richard Terry
Mr. Edward Terry
Mr. Simon Teale
Mr. Charles Trevor
Miss H. Travis
Mr. Thomas Turner
Mr. Tho. A. Terrington
Mr. Wm. Terrington
Mr. Christ. Thorley

Mr. Edward Thompson
Mr. Stephen Thorpe

W
Mr. Thomas Wasney
Mr. William Wasney
Mr. Benjamin Wright
Will. Williamson, Esq.
Mr. William Wasney
Mr. John Wilson
Mr. Isaac Womersley

Mr. George Wallis
Mr. Edward West
Mr. William Waring
Mr. John Wilson
Mr. Jonathan Walker
Mr. John Wray
Mr. J. Watson

V
Mr. John Voare

LIST
OF
SUBSCRIBERS AT BRISTOL.

A
Edward Ash
Sam. Atkins, 3 copies

B
Dan. Bailey
Mr. A. Barber
Mr. John Innes Baker
Joseph Baker
Thomas Bonville
John Bradley
Rev. Mr. Samuel Bradburn, 2
    copies
Mr. Robert Bruce
John Burt
Mr. Geo. Bush
Mr. Tho. Baynton
Mr. Dan. Baynton

C
Robert Charlton
Fred. Cockworthy

E
George Eaton

F
Anthony Fletcher
Dr. Fox, 5 copies
Charles Fox, 2 ditto
Arnee Frank
Robert Fry
Cornelius Fry
Joseph Storrs Fry

G
Mess. Granger and Cropper
Mr. Joseph Green
John Godwin, 2 copies

H
Love Hammond
Henry Hale
Edward Harwood
James Harford
Richard S. Harford
Mr. Job Harril
Mr. Robert Hazel
Rev. Mr. Hey
Joseph Hughes

I
Mr. William James
William Impey
Rev. Mr. Robt. Jacomb, 2 copies

L
Robert Lawson
Alice Ludlow
Mr. Wm. Peter Lunall
John Lury, 6 copies
John Lury, jun.

M
Mr. Tho. Morgan
Mr. Joseph Maurice, 2 copies
Jacob Merchant
Mrs. Moore, of Minehead, 2
   copies
Mr. Wm. Moore, ditto
Cath. Morgan

N
George Napper
John Newman

P
Mr. Wm. Painter, 2 cop.

Henry Parson
D.P. Pearce
William Pink

R
Rev. Mr. Richardson, Bradford

S
William Stansell
W.T. Simpson
William Smith

T
Miss M. Thatcher
John Thomas, 2 copies
John Tuckett, ditto
P.D. Tuckett, ditto

W
John Waring, 3 copies
Edward Welmat
John Wills
Matthew Wright, 3 cop.

LIST
OF
SUBSCRIBERS AT NORWICH.

A
Mr. Wm. Atthill
Miss Amelia Alderson
James Alderson, M.D.
Mrs. Aggs
Mr. E. Amond, Wyndham
Mr. Atkins
Rev. L. Adkin
J. Addey, Esq.

Mr. Hugh Alcock
Joseph Ainges, Yarmouth

B
John Buckle, Esq. Mayor
J.G. Baseley, Esq.
Mr. William Barnard
Mr. Wm. Barnard, jun.
Mrs. Barnard

Sam. Barnard, Esq.
Mr. Thomas Barnard
Mr. John Barnard
Mr. S.C. Barnard
Mr. John Corsbie Barnard
Master Joseph Barnard
Augustus Brevor, Esq.
Mr. John Bidwell
Miles Branthwaite, Esq.
Mr. Samuel Bond
Mr. Blunderfield
Mr. Edward Barrow, Esq.
Mr. Edward Booth
Mr. John Beckwith
Mr. Robert Bowen
Mr. Isaac Barnes, Bungay
Mr. Browne, Coltishall
Mr. William Burt
Wm. Buck, Esq. Bury
Miss Buck, Bury
Rev. C.R. Bond
Mr. James Back
Edward Bridgeman, Esq.
    Botesdale
Mr. Henry Brown, Diss
Mr. Tho. Bidwell, ditto
Mr. B. Boardman
Mr. Henry Baker
Mr. John Bouzell

C
Mr. Cubitt, Ludham
Mr. John Coleman
Mr. Bernard Church
Mr. Crouse
Miss E.B. Crouse
Miss Coe
Mr. Cully, Taverham
Mr. Crickmore, Seething
Mr. Cozens
Mr. Crane

Mr. Sam. Cole, sen.
Mr. Coke
Mr. H. Catton, Elmham
Mr. Christian
Mr. John Cully
Mr. Wright Coldham
Mr. Joseph Clarke
Mr. T. Cattermoul, jun.
Miss Crisp, Ipswich

D
B.G. Dillingham, Esq.
Mrs. Dillingham
Mr. E. De Hague
Mr. Danser
Rev. Tho. Drake, Shelton
Mr. Benjamin Dowson
Mr. Daveney
Mr. Ditchell, Cromer
Mr. Dairy
Mr. Dalrymple
Mr. Tho. Dyson, Diss

E
Wm. Enfield, LL.D.
Mr. Joseph English
Miss Eliza Errington, of
    Yarmouth
Miss Everett, Wyndham
Mr. J. Ebbets, Hellesdon

F
Rev. Sam. Forster, D.D.
Miss Frost
Travel Fuller, Yarmouth
Miss Firth
Mr. Firth
Mr. D. Fromanteel
Wm. Foster, jun. Esq.
Mr. Freshfield, sen.
Miss Fellows

G

J. Grigby, Esq. Drinkstone,
  Suffolk
Mrs. Gainsborough
Bartlett Gurney, Esq.
Miss Gurney
Miss H. Gurney
Mrs. Gray
Mrs. Goddard
Mr. Thomas Goff
Mr. H. Gurney
Mr. John Graves
Mr. Gardiner
Mr. F. Gostling, jun.

H

James Hudson, Esq.
Miss Hart
Rev. Peter Hansel
John Harvey, Esq.
William Herring, Esq.
Robert Herring, Esq.
Mr. Samuel Harmer
Mr. Hawkins
Mr. James Hayward
Miss Headley
Rev. P. Houghton
Mr. John Herring
J. Harvey, Esq.
Miss Ann Harvey, Catton
Miss Hagon
Mr. William Hankes
Miss Hammond
Mr. James Herring

I

J. Ives, Esq.
Mr. J.L. Johnson
Miss Jackson
Miss Jarrold

K

Henry Kett, Esq.

L

Mr. Leyson Lewis
Mr. J. Langley, Long Melford
Miss Lay
Mr. John Lovick
Mr. J. Landy
Rev. Mr. Lindley
Mr. Robert Larke

M

Mr. Edward Marsh
Mr. Muskett
Mr. James Moore
Mr. J. March
Mr. Matchett, printer
Rev. Mr. Millard
Mr. David Martineau
Miss Mildred, Diss
Mr. R. Mindham of Wells
Mr. Thomas Martineau
Miss Maling, Bury

N

Rev. Samuel Newton
Mr. William Newson

O

Mr. Olier
Mr. Edward Ollett
Mr. John Oxley
Miss Olier

P

Mr. Pitchford, jun.
Mr. Plowman, Bungay
Mr. J. Paul, Mettingham
Mr. Prentice, Bungay

Miss Plumtree
Joseph Parker, Esq. of
    Mettingham
Mr. E. Peckover
Mr. Thomas Paul
Mr. Robert Pearson
Robert Partridge, Esq.
Mr. Robert Paul, Starston
Mrs. Pullyn, Beccles
Mr. Parkinson, Hellesdon

R
Mr. John Reymes
Rev. Mr. Ray, Sudbury
Mr. Wm. Rye
Rev. H. Robinson, Diss
H. Raven, Esq. Bramerton
Mr. James Rump

S
Miss E. Smith
Miss F. Smith
Mr. Edward Sparshall
Rev. J.G. Smith
Mr. Stevenson
Miss Stevenson
Mr. Simpson
N. Styleman, Esq.
Mr. J. Simpson
Robert Suffield, Esq.
Mr. Jacob Shalders
Mr. John Scott, jun.
Mr. Charles Starkey

T
Mr. John Taylor
Mr. J.S. Taylor
Mr. Thomas Theobald
Mr. Taylor, Ipswich
Mr. John Toll, sen.
Mr. Taylor, jun.
Mr. John Tuthill, jun.
Mr. M. Taylor, Diss
Mr. Charles Tuthill
Rev. Dr. Temple, near [Beccles]

U
Mr. Unthank

W
Mr. R. Woodhouse
Mr. George Watson
Rev. John Walker
Mr. S. Wilkin
Mr. John Wright, Buxton
Mr. William Wilkins
Mr. John Webb
Mr. Robert Ward
Rev. S. Westby, Diss
Mr. B. Wiseman, ditto
Rev. Mr. Willins

Y
Mess. Yarington and Bacon
Mr. Wm. Youngman

Subscribers at Lynn.

Mr. Thomas Ayre
Mr. James Ayre
Mr. Samuel Baker
Mr. Birkboek
Mr. William Currie

Mr. William Cooper
Mr. James Coulton
Mr. Wm. Dunn, Docking
Mr. G. Edwards, 4 cop.
Rev. Mr. E. Edwards

Mr. John Egleton
Mr. John Benson Friend
Mr. Gamble
Mr. T. Gales, 2 copies
Mr. Harry Goodwin
Mr. Michael Gage
Mr. Samuel Hadley
Rev. Mr. W. Hardyman
Mr. J. Hedley, 4 copies
Mr. Michael Jackson

John Marshall, M.D.
Mr. Samuel Newham
Mr. Richard Newman
Mr. George Peeke
J. Packwood, M. D.
Mr. Henry Reggester
Rev. W. Richards, M.A. 2 copies
Mr. W.C. Tooke
Mr. R. Whincop

AT WISBEACH.

Mr. John Cockett
Mrs. Clarkson
Mrs. John Clarkson
Mr. J. Clark, Gosberton

Mr. William Fallows
Mr. William Friend
Elizabeth Heightholme
Mr. J. Peckover, 2 cop.

LIST
OF
SUBSCRIBERS IN IRELAND.
DUBLIN.

His Grace the Archbishop of Dublin

A
Richard Abel, of Cork
William Adamson
William Armstrong
John Allen, Esq.

B
Right Hon. the Earl of
   Belvedere
Mr. Mark Blair
Oliver Bond, Esq.

C
Right Rev. the Lord Bishop of
   Cork
James Christy, of Lurgan

Rev. Mr. Adam Clarke

D
Capt. Drough, of Mote
Robert Dudley of Clonmel
Mr. Frederick Darley
James Dale, Esq.

E
Rev. Dr. Ellison, of Kilkenny

F
Fisher and Hervey of Limerick
Mr. Samuel Forbes
Mr. Samuel Fayle
Capt. William Fitch

G
Dr. William Gray

H
The Right Hon. Henry Howson,
    Lord Mayor
Thomas Hancocks, of Lisborn
Sir Henry Hays of Cork
Joseph Henry, Esq.
John Hill, Esq.
Henry Hornton, of Carlow

I
Dr. Irving, of Lisborn

K
Alex. Kirkpatrick, Esq.
Fran. Kirkpatrick, Esq.
Wm. Kirkpatrick, Esq.
Mr. Wm. Kidd, of Mulingar
Rev. Walter B. Kirwan

L
His Grace the Duke of Leinster
Mr. Michael Lewis
—— Le Strange, Esq.
Lady Louth, of Drogheda

M
The Rt. Hon. the Earl of
    Miltown
Lady Miltown
The Rt. Rev. Lord Bishop of
    Meath
Lady Moira
Colin M'Kay, Esq. Belfast
Rev. Mr. W. Mann
S. M'Guire, Esq.
Rev. Dean Morgan

N
Samuel Neal, of Corke
Sam Neilson, Esq. Belfast

O
Rt. Hon. Earl of Ormond
Right Hon. John O'Neal

P
Wm. Penrose, Esq. Waterford
Mr. Thomas Prentice of
    Armaugh
Dr. Patten, of Tandragee
Richard Purcell, Esq. of Cork

R
Sir Samuel Rowland, Cork
Rev. Thomas Rutherford

S
Dr. F. Skelton, Drogheda
Mr. W. Sproule, Athlone
Mr. Joseph Sandwich
William Smyth, Esq.
James Stewart, Esq.
Mr. William Sleater

T
Right Hon. David La Touche,
    Esq., jun.
Lady Celia La Touche
Rev. Dr. Trail of Lisborn
Jas. Napper Tandy, Esq.

W
Robert Waller, Esq.
Joseph Williams
Joseph C. Walker, Esq.
John Walker

LIST
OF
SUBSCRIBERS IN SCOTLAND.
EDINBURGH.

A
Hon. Lord Ankerville
Professor Anderson, of Glasgow
Mr. J. Anderson, Leith
Dr. J. Anderson, Leith

B
Rev. Mr. Buchanan
Mr. James Bonar
Mr. Elphinston Balfour
Bailie Brown, Esq. Paisley
Rev. Mr. Balfour Glasgow
Messrs. Bogle & Scott, do.
Rev. Mr. Bogg, of Paisley

C
Mr. John Campbell, W.S.
Mr. Cathcart, Advocate
William Creech, Esq.
Misses Chancellors
Mr. J. Cochrane, Paisley
Rev. Mr. Colquhoun, Leith
James Christie, Esq.

D
David Dale, Esq. Glasgow
Mr. Donaldson
Mr. Wm. Dallas, W.S.
Mr. Wm. Dalziell, W.S.
Mr. Dickson

E
Hon. Hen. Erskine, D.F.
Col. Francis Erskine
Rev. Dr. Erskine

F
Sir William Forbes

G
Lord Adam Gordon
Capt. Gallia, of Greenock
Rev. Mr. Greenfield
Mr. Robert Graham of Glasgow
Wm. Gillespie, Esq. of do.
Rev. Dr. Gilles, of ditto

H
Rev. Mr. Hall
Rev. Dr. Andrew Hunter
Sir James Hall
Rev. Mr. Headrick

I
Dr. Jaffray, of Glasgow
Mrs. Irving

K
Rev. Mr. John Kemp
William Ker, Esq.

L
Mr. Laing, Advocate
J. Love, Esq. of Paisley

M
The Hon. Ld. Monboddo
R. Scott-Moncrief, Esq. of
　　Glasgow
Mr. Wm. Mayne, do.
John Monteith, Esq. do.
Rev. Mr. Moyse
Mr. Andrew M'Kenzie
Mr. Christ. Moubray

Mr. Kenneth M'Kenzie
Mr. Colin M'Donald
Rev. Mr. Moodie
Rev. Sir H. Moncrieff-Welwood,
   Bart. D.D.

N
Mr. Alexander Nairne, of
   Paisley
Mr. Adam Neal, of Glasgow

O
Mr. Oswald, Advocate
Mr. W. Orhart, Glasgow

P
Mr. Richard Prentice
Mr. Robert Plenderleath
John Pattison, Esq. of Glasgow

R
Rev. Mr. Thos. Randall
Mr. Rolland, Advocate
Mr. Ross, ditto
Mr. Rae, ditto
Mr. David Ramsay
George Ramsay, Esq.

S
Hon. Lord Swinton
Mr. Swinton

Mr. Robertson Scott, Advocate
David Stewart, Esq.
Francis Scott, Esq.
Mr. C. Stewart, W.S.
Dr. Charles Stewart
Sir John Sinclair, M.P.
Professor Dugald Stewart
Dr. Somerville, Edinburgh
Mr. John Swanston, of Glasgow
Mr. G. Stewart, W.S.

T
Mr. Crawford Tait, W.S.
Mr. John Tawse, ditto
Mr. Todd
Jn. Trotter, Esq. of Glasgow
Wm. Turnbull, printer

W
Mr. Wauchop, Advocate
Mr. Williamson, ditto
Mr. J. Watson, Writer
Mr. Kirkpatrick Williamson
Mr. Wardlow, Glasgow

Y
Mr. Charles Young
Mr. Robert Young
Alexander Young, Esq.
Dr. Yuile

CONTENTS

THE
LIFE
OF
GUSTAVUS VASSA

CHAPTER I.

The Author's account of his country, and their manners and customs—Administration of justice—Embrenché—Marriage ceremony, and public entertainments—Mode of living—Dress—Manufactures—Buildings—Commerce—Agriculture—War and Religion—Superstition of the natives—Funeral ceremonies of the priests or magicians—Curious mode of discovering poison—Some hints concerning the origin of the Author's countrymen, with the opinions of different writers on that subject.

I BELIEVE it is difficult for those who publish their own memoirs to escape the imputation of vanity; nor is this the only disadvantage under which they labour; it is also their misfortune, that whatever is uncommon is rarely, if ever, believed; and what is obvious we are apt to turn from with disgust, and to charge the writer with impertinence. People generally think those memoirs only worthy to be read or remembered which abound in great or striking events; those, in short, which in a high degree excite either admiration or pity: all others they consign to contempt and oblivion. It is, therefore, I confess, not a little hazardous, in a private and obscure individual, and a stranger too, thus to solicit the indulgent attention of the public; especially when I own I offer here the history of neither a saint, a hero, nor a tyrant. I believe there are a few events in my life which have not happened to many; it is true the incidents of it are numerous; and, did I consider myself an European, I might say my sufferings were great; but, when I compare my lot with that of most of my countrymen, I regard myself as a *particular favourite of Heaven,* and acknowledge the mercies of Providence in every occurrence of my life. If, then, the following narrative does not appear sufficiently interesting to engage general attention, let my motive be some excuse for its publication. I am not so foolishly vain as to expect from it either immortality or literary reputation. If it affords any satisfaction to my numerous friends, at whose request it has been written, or in the smallest degree promotes the interest of humanity, the ends for which it was undertaken will be fully attained, and every wish of my heart gratified. Let it therefore be remembered that, in wishing to avoid censure, I do not aspire to praise.

That part of Africa, known by the name of Guinea, to which the trade for slaves is carried on, extends along the coast above 3400 miles, from Senegal to Angola, and includes a variety of kingdoms. Of these the most considerable is the kingdom of Benin, both as to extent and wealth, the richness and cultivation of the soil, the power of its king, and the number and warlike disposition of the inhabitants. It is situated nearly under the line and extends along the coast about 170 miles, but runs back into the interior part of Africa to a distance hitherto I believe unexplored by any traveller; and seems only terminated at length by the empire of Abyssinia, near 1500 miles from its beginning. This kingdom is divided into many provinces or districts: in one of the most remote and fertile of which [, called Eboe,] I was born, in the year 1745, in a charming fruitful vale, named Essaka. The distance of this province from the capital of Benin and the sea coast must be very considerable; for I had never heard of white men or Europeans, nor of the sea; and our subjection to the king of Benin was little more than nominal; for every transaction of the government, as far as my slender observation extended, was conducted by the chiefs or elders of the place. The manners and government of a people who have little commerce with other countries are generally very simple; and the history of what passes in one family or village may serve as a specimen of the whole nation. My father was one of those elders or chiefs I have spoken of, and was styled Embrenché; a term, as I remember, importing the highest distinction, and signifying in our language a mark of grandeur. This mark is conferred on the person entitled to it, by cutting the skin across at the top of the forehead, and drawing it down to the eyebrows; and, while it is in this situation, applying a warm hand, and rubbing it until it shrinks up into a thick *weal* across the lower part of the forehead. Most of the judges and senators were thus marked; my father had long borne it: I had seen it conferred on one of my brothers, and I was also *destined* to receive it by my parents. Those Embrenché, or chief men, decided disputes and punished crimes; for which purpose they always assembled together. The proceedings were generally short; and in most cases the law of retaliation prevailed. I remember a man was brought before my father, and the other judges, for kidnapping a boy; and, although he was the son of a chief or senator, he was condemned to make recompense by a man or woman slave. Adultery, however, was sometimes punished with slavery or death; a punishment which I believe is inflicted on it throughout most of the nations of Africa: so sacred among them is the honour of the marriage bed, and so jealous are they of the fidelity of their wives. Of this I recollect an instance.—A woman was convicted before the judges of adultery, and delivered over, as the custom was, to her husband to be punished. Accordingly he determined to put her to death: but it being found, just before her execution, that she had an infant at her breast; and no woman being prevailed on to perform the part of a nurse, she was spared on account of the child. The men, however, do not preserve the same constancy to their wives, which they expect from them; for they indulge in a plurality, though seldom in more than two. Their mode of marriage is thus:—both parties are usually betrothed when young by their parents (though I have known the males to betroth themselves). On this occasion a feast is prepared, and the bride and bridegroom stand up in the midst of all their friends, who are assembled for the purpose, while he declares she is thenceforth to be looked upon as his wife, and that no other person is to pay any addresses to her. This is also immediately proclaimed in the vicinity, on which the bride retires from the assembly. Some time after, she is brought home to her husband, and then another feast is made, to which the relations of both parties are invited: her parents then deliver her to the bridegroom, accompanied with a number of blessings, and at the same time they tie round her waist a cotton string of the thickness of a goose-quill, which none but married women are permitted to wear: she is now considered as completely his wife; and at this time the dowry is given to the new married pair, which generally consists of portions of land, slaves, and cattle, household goods, and implements of husbandry. These are offered by the friends of both parties; besides which the parents of the bridegroom present gifts to those of the bride, whose property she is looked upon before marriage; but after it she is esteemed the sole property of her husband. The ceremony being now ended, the festival begins, which is celebrated with bonfires, and loud acclamations of joy, accompanied with music and dancing.

We are almost a nation of dancers, musicians, and poets. Thus every great event, such as a triumphant return from battle, or other cause of public rejoicing, is celebrated in public dances, which are accompanied with songs and music suited to the occasion. The assembly is separated into four divisions, which dance either apart or in succession, and each with a character peculiar to itself. The first division contains the married men, who in their dances frequently exhibit feats of arms, and the representation of a battle. To these succeed the married women, who dance in the second division. The young men occupy the third; and the maidens the fourth. Each represents some interesting scene of real life, such as a great achievement, domestic employment, a pathetic story, or some rural sport; and as the subject is generally founded on some recent event, it is therefore ever new. This gives our dances a spirit and variety which I have scarcely seen elsewhere. We have many musical instruments, particularly drums of different kinds, a piece of music which resembles a guitar, and another much like a stickado. These last are chiefly used by betrothed virgins, who play on them on all grand festivals.

As our manners are simple, our luxuries are few. The dress of both sexes is nearly the same. It generally consists of a long piece of calico, or muslin, wrapped loosely round the body, somewhat in the form of a Highland plaid. This is usually dyed blue, which is our favourite colour. It is extracted from a berry, and is brighter and richer than any I have seen in Europe. Besides this, our women of distinction wear golden ornaments, which they dispose with some profusion on their arms and legs. When our women are not employed with the men in tillage, their usual occupation is spinning and weaving cotton, which they afterwards dye, and make into garments. They also manufacture earthen vessels, of which we have many kinds. Among the rest tobacco pipes, made after the same fashion, and used in the same manner, as those in Turkey.

Our manner of living is entirely plain; for as yet the natives are unacquainted with those refinements in cookery which debauch the taste: bullocks, goats, and poultry supply the greatest part of their food. These constitute likewise the principal wealth of the country, and the chief articles of its commerce. The flesh is usually stewed in a pan. To make it savory, we sometimes use also pepper, and other spices, and we have salt made of wood ashes. Our vegetables are mostly plantains, eadas, yams, beans, and Indian corn. The head of the family usually eats alone; his wives and slaves have also their separate tables. Before we taste food, we always wash our hands: indeed our cleanliness on all occasions is extreme; but on this it is an indispensable ceremony. After washing, libation is made, by pouring out a small portion of the drink on the floor, and tossing a small quantity of the food in a certain place, for the spirits of departed relations, which the natives suppose to preside over their conduct, and guard them from evil. They are totally unacquainted with strong or spiritous liquours; and their principal beverage is palm wine. This is got from a tree of that name, by tapping it at the top, and fastening a large gourd to it; and sometimes one tree will yield three or four gallons in a night. When just drawn it is of a most delicious sweetness; but in a few days it acquires a tartish and more spirituous flavour: though I never saw any one intoxicated by it. The same tree also produces nuts and oil. Our principal luxury is in perfumes; one sort of these is an odoriferous wood of delicious fragrance: the other a kind of earth; a small portion of which thrown into the fire diffuses a most powerful odour. We beat this wood into powder, and mix it with palm-oil; with which both men and women perfume themselves.

In our buildings we study convenience rather than ornament. Each master of a family has a large square piece of ground, surrounded with a moat or fence, or enclosed with a wall made of red earth tempered, which, when dry, is as hard as brick. Within this are his houses to accommodate his family and slaves; which, if numerous, frequently present the appearance of a village. In the middle stands the principal building, appropriated to the sole use of the master, and consisting of two apartments; in one of which he sits in the day with his family, the other is left apart for the reception of his friends. He has besides these a distinct apartment in which he sleeps, together with his male children. On each side are the apartments of his wives, who have also their separate day and night houses. The habitations of the slaves and their families are distributed throughout the rest of the enclosure. These houses never exceed one story in height; they are always built of wood, or stakes driven into the ground, crossed with wattles, and neatly plastered within, and without. The roof is thatched with reeds. Our dayhouses are left open at the sides; but those in which we sleep are always covered, and plastered in the inside, with a composition mixed with cow-dung, to keep off the different insects which annoy us during the night. The walls and floors also of these are generally covered with mats. Our beds consist of a platform, raised three or four feet from the ground, on which are laid skins, and different parts of a spungy tree called plaintain. Our covering is calico or muslin, the same as our dress. The usual seats are a few logs of wood; but we have benches, which are generally perfumed, to accommodate strangers; these compose the greater part of our household furniture. Houses so constructed and furnished require but little skill to erect them. Every man is a sufficient architect for the purpose. The whole neighbourhood afford their unanimous assistance in building them, and, in return, receive and expect no other recompense than a feast.

As we live in a country where nature is prodigal of her favours, our wants are few and easily supplied; of course we have few manufactures. They consist for the most part of calicoes, earthen ware, ornaments, and instruments of war and husbandry. But these make no part of our commerce, the principal articles of which, as I have observed, are provisions. In such a state money is of little use; however we have some small pieces of coin, if I may call them such. They are made something like an anchor; but I do not remember either their value or denomination. We have also markets, at which I have been frequently with my mother. These are sometimes visited by stout, mahogany-coloured men from the south west of us: we call them *Oye-Eboe*, which term signifies red men living at a distance. They generally bring us fire-arms, gun-powder, hats, beads, and dried fish. The last we esteemed a great rarity, as our waters were only brooks and springs. These articles they barter with us for odoriferous woods and earth, and our salt of wood-ashes. They always carry slaves through our land; but the strictest account is exacted of their manner of procuring them before they are suffered to pass. Sometimes indeed we sold slaves to them, but they were only prisoners of war, or such among us as had been convicted of kidnapping, or adultery, and some other crimes which we esteemed heinous. This practice of kidnapping induces me to think, that, notwithstanding all our strictness, their principal business among us was to trepan our people. I remember too they carried great sacks along with them, which, not long after, I had an opportunity of fatally seeing applied to that infamous purpose.

Our land is uncommonly rich and fruitful, and produces all kinds of vegetables in great abundance. We have plenty of Indian corn, and vast quantities of cotton and tobacco. Our pine apples grow without culture; they are about the size of the largest sugarloaf, and finely flavoured. We have also spices of different kinds, particularly pepper; and a variety of delicious fruits which I have never seen in Europe; together with gums of various kinds, and honey in abundance. All our industry is exerted to improve those blessings of nature. Agriculture is our chief employment; and every one, even the children and women, are engaged in it. Thus we are all habituated to labour from our earliest years. Every one contributes something to the common stock; and as we are unacquainted with idleness, we have no beggars. The benefits of such a mode of living are obvious. The West-India planters prefer the slaves of Benin or Eboe to those of any other part of Guinea, for their hardiness, intelligence, integrity, and zeal. Those benefits are felt by us in the general healthiness of the people, and in their vigour and activity; I might have added too in their comeliness. Deformity is indeed unknown amongst us, I mean that of shape. Numbers of the natives of Eboe now in London might be brought in support of this assertion; for, in regard to complexion, ideas of beauty are wholly relative. I remember while in Africa to have seen three negro children, who were tawny, and another quite white, who were universally regarded by myself and the natives in general, as far as related to their complexions, as deformed. Our women too were, in my eyes at least, uncommonly graceful, alert, and modest to a degree of bashfulness; nor do I remember to have ever heard of an instance of incontinence amongst them before marriage. They are also remarkably cheerful. Indeed cheerfulness and affability are two of the leading characteristics of our nation.

Our tillage is exercised in a large plain or common, some hours walk from our dwellings, and all the neighbours resort thither in a body. They use no beasts of husbandry; and their only instruments are hoes, axes, shovels, and beaks, or pointed iron to dig with. Sometimes we are visited by locusts, which come in large clouds, so as to darken the air, and destroy our harvest. This however happens rarely, but when it does, a famine is produced by it. I remember an instance or two wherein this happened. This common is oftimes the theatre of war; and therefore when our people go out to till their land, they not only go in a body, but generally take their arms with them, for fear of a surprise; and when they apprehend an invasion they guard

the avenues to their dwellings, by driving sticks into the
ground, which are so sharp at one end as to pierce the foot,
and are generally dipt in poison. From what I can recollect
of these battles, they appear to have been irruptions of one
little state or district on the other, to obtain prisoners or
booty. Perhaps they were incited to this by those traders
who brought the European goods I mentioned amongst us.
Such mode of obtaining slaves in Africa is common; and I
believe more are procured this way, and by kidnapping,
than any other. When a trader wants slaves, he applies to a
chief for them, and tempts him with his wares. It is not extraordinary, if on this occasion he yields to the temptation
with as little firmness, and accepts the price of his fellow
creature's liberty with as little reluctance, as the enlightened merchant. Accordingly, he falls on his neighbours, and
a desperate battle ensues. If he prevails, and takes prisoners, he gratifies his avarice by selling them; but, if his party
be vanquished, and he falls into the hands of the enemy, he
is put to death: for, as he has been known to foment their
quarrels, it is thought dangerous to let him survive, and no
ransom can save him, though all other prisoners may be
redeemed. We have fire-arms, bows and arrows, broad two-
edged swords and javelins; we have shields also, which
cover a man from head to foot. All are taught the use of the
weapons. Even our women are warriors, and march boldly
out to fight along with the men. Our whole district is a kind
of militia: on a certain signal given, such as the firing of a
gun at night, they all rise in arms and rush upon their
enemy. It is perhaps something remarkable, that when our
people march to the field, a red flag or banner is borne
before them. I was once a witness to a battle in our common. We had been all at work in it one day as usual when
our people were suddenly attacked. I climbed a tree at
some distance, from which I beheld the fight. There were
many women as well as men on both sides; among others
my mother was there and armed with a broad sword. After
fighting for a considerable time with great fury, and many
had been killed, our people obtained the victory, and took
their enemy's Chief prisoner. He was carried off in great
triumph, and, though he offered a large ransom for his life,
he was put to death. A virgin of note among our enemies

had been slain in the battle, and her arm was exposed in our market-place, where our trophies were always exhibited. The spoils were divided according to the merit of the warriors. Those prisoners which were not sold or redeemed we kept as slaves: but how different was their condition from that of the slaves in the West-Indies! With us they do no more work than other members of the community, even their master. Their food, cloathing, and lodging were nearly the same as theirs, except that they were not permitted to eat with those who were free born and there was scarce any other difference between them, than a superior degree of importance which the head of a family possesses in our state, and that authority which, as such, he exercises over every part of his household. Some of these slaves have even slaves under them, as their own property, and for their own use.

As to religion, the natives believe that there is one Creator of all things, and that he lives in the sun, and is girded round with a belt, that he may never eat or drink; but, according to some, he smokes a pipe, which is our own favourite luxury. They believe he governs events, especially our deaths or captivity; but, as for the doctrine of eternity, I do not remember to have ever heard of it: some however believe in the transmigration of souls in a certain degree. Those spirits, which are not transmigrated, such as our dear friends or relations, they believe always attend them, and guard them from the bad spirits of their foes. For this reason, they always, before eating, as I have observed, put some small portion of the meat, and pour some of their drink, on the ground for them; and they often make oblations of the blood of beasts or fowls at their graves. I was very fond of my mother, and almost constantly with her. When she went to make these oblations at her mother's tomb, which was a kind of small solitary thatched house, I sometimes attended her. There she made her libations, and spent most of the night in cries and lamentations. I have been often extremely terrified on these occasions. The loneliness of the place, the darkness of the night, and the ceremony of libation, naturally awful and gloomy, were heightened by my mother's lamentations; and these, concurring with the doleful cries of birds, by which these places were frequented, gave an inexpressible terror to the scene.

We compute the year from the day on which the sun crosses the line, and, on its setting that evening, there is a general shout throughout the land; at least I can speak from my own knowledge throughout our vicinity. The people at the same time make a great noise with rattles, not unlike the basket rattles used by children here, though much larger, and hold up their hands to heaven for a blessing. It is then the greatest offerings are made; and those children whom our wise men foretell will be fortunate are then presented to different people. I remember many used to come to see me, and I was carried about to others for that purpose. They have many offerings, particularly at full moons; generally two at harvest, before the fruits are taken out of the ground: and, when any young animals are killed, sometimes they offer up part of them as a sacrifice. These offerings, when made by one of the heads of a family, serve for the whole. I remember we often had them at my father's and my uncle's, and their families have been present. Some of our offerings are eaten with bitter herbs. We had a saying among us to any one of a cross temper, "That if they were to be eaten, they should be eaten with bitter herbs."

We practised circumcision like the Jews, and made offerings and feasts on that occasion in the same manner as they did. Like them also, our children were named from some event, some circumstance, or fancied foreboding at the time of their birth. I was named *Olaudah,* which, in our language, signifies vicissitude, or fortunate also; one favoured, and having a loud voice and well spoken. I remember we never polluted the name of the object of our adoration; on the contrary, it was always mentioned with the greatest reverence; and we were totally unacquainted with swearing, and all those terms of abuse and reproach which find the way so readily and copiously into the languages of more civilized people. The only expressions of that kind I remember were "May you rot, or may you swell, or may a beast take you."

I have before remarked, that the natives of this part of Africa are extremely cleanly. This necessary habit of decency was with us a part of religion, and therefore we had many purifications and washings; indeed almost as many,

and used on the same occasions, if my recollection does not
fail me, as the Jews. Those that touched the dead at any time
were obliged to wash and purify themselves before they
could enter a dwelling-house. Every woman too, at certain
times, was forbidden to come into a dwelling-house, or
touch any person, or any thing we ate. I was so fond of my
mother I could not keep from her, or avoid touching her at
some of those periods, in consequence of which I was
obliged to be kept out with her, in a little house made for
that purpose, till offering was made, and then we were purified.

   Though we had no places of public worship, we had
priests and magicians, or wise men. I do not remember
whether they had different offices, or whether they were
united in the same persons but they were held in great reverence by the people. They calculated our time, and foretold events, as their name imported, for we called them
Ah-affoe-way-cah, which signifies calculators, or yearly
men, our year being called Ah-affoe. They wore their
beards; and, when they died, they were succeeded by their
sons. Most of their implements and things of value were
interred along with them. Pipes and tobacco were also put
into the grave with the corpse, which was always perfumed
and ornamented; and animals were offered in sacrifice to
them. None accompanied their funerals but those of the
same profession or tribe. These buried them after sunset,
and always returned from the grave by a different way from
that which they went.

   These magicians were also our doctors or physicians.
They practised bleeding by cupping, and were very successful in healing wounds and expelling poisons. They had likewise
some extraordinary method of discovering jealousy, theft,
and poisoning; the success of which no doubt they derived
from their unbounded influence over the credulity and superstition of the people. I do not remember what those
methods were, except that as to poisoning. I recollect an
instance or two, which I hope it will not be deemed impertinent here to insert, as it may serve as a kind of specimen
of the rest, and is still used by the negroes in the West Indies. A young woman had been poisoned, but it was not
known by whom; the doctors ordered the corpse to be

taken up by some persons, and carried to the grave. As soon as the bearers had raised it on their shoulders, they seemed seized with some sudden impulse, and ran to and fro', unable to stop themselves. At last, after having passed through a number of thorns and prickly bushes unhurt, the corpse fell from them close to a house, and defaced it in the fall: and the owner being taken up, he immediately confessed the poisoning.

The natives are extremely cautious about poison. When they buy any eatable the seller kisses it all round before the buyer, to shew him it is not poisoned; and the same is done when any meat or drink is presented, particularly to a stranger. We have serpents of different kinds, some of which are esteemed ominous when they appear in our houses, and these we never molest. I remember two of those ominous snakes, each of which was as thick as the calf of a man's leg, and in colour resembling a dolphin in the water, crept at different times into my mother's night-house, where I always lay with her, and coiled themselves into folds, and each time they crowed like a cock. I was desired by some of our wise men to touch these, that I might be interested in the good omens, which I did, for they were quite harmless, and would tamely suffer themselves to be handled; and then they were put into a large open earthen pan, and set on one side of the highway. Some of our snakes, however, were poisonous: one of them crossed the road one day when I was standing on it, and passed between my feet, without offering to touch me, to the great surprise of many who saw it; and these incidents were accounted by the wise men, and likewise by my mother and the rest of the people, as remarkable omens in my favour.

Such is the imperfect sketch my memory has furnished me with of the manners and customs of a people among whom I first drew my breath. And here I cannot forbear suggesting what has long struck me very forcibly, namely, the strong analogy which even by this sketch, imperfect as it is, appears to prevail in the manners and customs of my countrymen, and those of the Jews, before they reached the Land of Promise, and particularly the patriarchs, while they were yet in that pastoral state which is described in Genesis—an analogy, which alone would induce me to think that the one people had sprung from the other. Indeed this is the opinion of Dr. Gill, who, in his commentary on Genesis, very ably deduces the pedigree of the Africans from Afer and Afra, the descendants of Abraham by Keturah his wife and concubine, (for both these titles are applied to her). It is also conformable to the sentiments of Dr. John Clarke, formerly Dean of Sarum, in his Truth of the Christian Religion: both these authors concur in ascribing to us this original. The reasonings of these gentlemen are still further confirmed by the Scripture Chronology of the Rev. Arthur Bedford; and if any further corroboration were required, this resemblance in so many respects is a strong evidence in support of the opinion. Like the Israelites in their primitive state, our government was conducted by our chiefs, our judges, our wise men, and elders; and the head of a family with us enjoyed a similar authority over his household with that which is ascribed to Abraham and the other patriarchs. The law of retaliation obtained almost universally with us as with them: and even their religion appeared to have shed upon us a ray of its glory, though broken and spent in its passage, or eclipsed by the cloud with which time, tradition, and ignorance might have enveloped it: for we had our circumcision (a rule I believe peculiar to that people): we had also our sacrifices and burnt-offerings, our washings and purifications, on the same occasions as they had.

As to the difference of colour between the Eboan Africans and the modern Jews, I shall not presume to account for it. It is a subject which has engaged the pens of men of both genius and learning, and is far above my strength. The most able and Reverend Mr. T. Clarkson, however, in his much-admired Essay on the Slavery and Commerce of the Human Species, has ascertained the cause, in a manner that at once solves every objection on that account, and, on my mind at least, has produced the fullest conviction. I shall therefore refer to that performance for the theory, contenting myself with extracting a fact as related by Dr. Mitchel. "The Spaniards, who have inhabited America, under the torrid zone, for any time, are become as dark coloured as our native Indians of Virginia, *of which I myself have been a witness.* There is also another instance of a Portuguese settlement at Mitomba, a river in Sierra Leona, where the inhabitants are bred from a mixture of the first Portuguese discoverers with the natives, and are now become, in their complexion, and in the woolly quality of their hair, *perfect negroes,* retaining however a smattering of the Portuguese language."

These instances, and a great many more which might be adduced, while they shew how the complexions of the same persons vary in different climates, it is hoped may tend also to remove the prejudice that some conceive against the natives of Africa on account of their colour. Surely the minds of the Spaniards did not change with their complexions! Are there not causes enough to which the apparent inferiority of an African may be ascribed, without limiting the goodness of God, and supposing he forbore to stamp understanding on certainly his own image, because "carved in ebony"? Might it not naturally be ascribed to their situation? When they come among Europeans, they are ignorant of their language, religion, manners, and customs. Are any pains taken to teach them these? Are they treated as men? Does not slavery itself depress the mind, and extinguish all its fire, and every noble sentiment? But, above all, what advantages do not a refined people possess over those who are rude and uncultivated? Let the polished and haughty European recollect that *his* ancestors were once, like the Africans, uncivilized, and even barbarous. Did Nature make *them* inferior to their sons? and should *they too* have been made slaves? Every rational mind answers, No. Let such reflections as these melt the pride of their superiority into sympathy for the wants and miseries of their sable brethren, and compel them to acknowledge, that understanding is not confined to feature or colour. If, when they look round the world, they feel exultation, let it be tempered with benevolence to others, and gratitude to God, "who hath made of one blood all nations of men for to dwell on all the face of the earth; and whose wisdom is not our wisdom, neither are our ways his ways."

CHAP. II.

The Author's birth and parentage—His being kidnapped with his sister—Their separation—Surprise at meeting again— Are finally separated—Account of the different places and incidents the Author met with till his arrival on the coast— The effect the sight of a slave-ship had on him—He sails for the West-Indies—Horrors of a slave-ship—Arrives at Barbadoes, where the cargo is sold and dispersed.

I HOPE the reader will not think I have trespassed on his patience in introducing myself to him with some account of the manners and customs of my country. They had been implanted in me with great care, and made an impression on my mind, which time could not erase, and which all the adversity and variety of fortune I have since experienced served only to rivet and record: for, whether the love of one's country be real or imaginary, or a lesson of reason, or an instinct of nature, I still look back with pleasure on the first scenes of my life, though that pleasure has been for the most part mingled with sorrow.

I have already acquainted the reader with the time and place of my birth. My father, besides many slaves, had a numerous family, of which seven lived to grow up, including myself and a sister, who was the only daughter. As I was the youngest of the sons, I became, of course, the greatest favourite with my mother, and was always with her; and she used to take particular pains to form my mind. I was trained up from my earliest years in the arts of agriculture and war: my daily exercise was shooting and throwing javelins; and my mother adorned me with emblems, after the manner of our greatest warriors. In this way I grew up till I was turned the age of eleven, when an end was put to my happiness in the following manner:—Generally, when the grown people in the neighbourhood were gone far in the fields to labour, the children assembled together in some of the neighbours' premises to play; and commonly some of us used to get up a tree to look out for any assailant, or kidnapper, that might come upon us; for they sometimes took those opportunities of our parents' absence, to attack and carry off as many as they could seize. One day, as I was watching at the top of a tree in our yard, I saw one of those people come into the yard of our next neighbour but one, to kidnap, there being many stout young people in it. Immediately, on this, I gave the alarm of the rogue, and he was surrounded by the stoutest of them, who entangled him with cords, so that he could not escape till some of the grown people came and secured him. But, alas! ere long it was my fate to be thus attacked, and to be carried off, when none of the grown people were nigh. One day, when all our people were gone out to their works as usual, and only I and my dear sister were left to mind the house, two men and a woman got over our walls, and in a moment seized us both; and, without giving us time to cry out, or make resistance, they stopped our mouths, tied our hands, and ran off with us into the nearest wood: and continued to carry us as far as they could, till night came on, when we reached a small house, where the robbers halted for refreshment, and spent the night. We were then unbound, but were unable to take any food; and, being quite overpowered by fatigue and grief, our only relief was some sleep, which allayed our misfortune for a short time. The next morning we left the house, and continued travelling all the day. For a long time we had kept the woods, but at last we came into a road which I believed I knew. I had now some hopes of being delivered; for we had advanced but a little way before I discovered some people at a distance, on which I began to cry out for their assistance; but my cries had no other effect than to make them tie me faster, and stop my mouth, and then they put me into a large sack. They also stopped my sister's mouth, and tied her hands; and in this manner we proceeded till we were out of the sight of these people.—When we went to rest the following night they offered us some victuals; but we refused them; and the only comfort we had was in being in one another's arms all that night, and bathing each other with our tears. But, alas! we were soon deprived of even the smallest comfort of weeping together. The next day proved a day of greater sorrow than I had yet experienced; for my sister and I were then separated, while we lay clasped in each other's arms. It was in vain that we besought them not to part us: she was torn from me, and immediately carried away, while I was left in a state of distraction not to be described. I cried and grieved continually; and for several days I did not eat any thing but what they forced into my mouth. At length, after many days travelling, during which I had often changed masters, I got into the hands of a chieftain, in a very pleasant country. This man had two wives and some children, and they all used me extremely well, and did all they could to comfort me; particularly the first wife, who was something like my mother. Although I was a great many days journey from my father's house, yet these people spoke exactly the same language with us. This first master of mine, as I may call him, was a smith, and my principal employment was working his bellows, which were the same kind as I had seen in my vicinity. They were in some respects not unlike the stoves here in gentlemen's kitchens; and were covered over with leather; and in the middle of that leather a stick was fixed, and a person stood up, and worked it, in the same manner as is done to pump water out of a cask with a hand-pump. I believe it was gold he worked, for it was of a lovely bright yellow colour, and was worn by the women on their wrists and ancles. I was there I suppose about a month, and they at last used to trust me some little distance from the house. This liberty I used in embracing every opportunity to inquire the way to my own home: and I also sometimes, for the same purpose, went with the maidens, in the cool of the evenings, to bring pitchers of water from the springs for the use of the house. I had also remarked where the sun rose in the morning, and set in the evening, as I had travelled along; and I had observed that my father's house was towards the rising of the sun. I therefore determined to seize the first opportunity of making my escape, and to shape my course for that quarter; for I was quite oppressed and weighed down by grief after my mother and friends; and my love of liberty, ever great, was strengthened by the mortifying circumstance of not daring to eat with the free-born children, although I was mostly their companion.—While I was projecting my escape one day, an unlucky event happened, which quite disconcerted my plan, and put an end to my hopes. I used to be sometimes employed in assisting an elderly woman slave to cook and take care of the poultry; and one morning, while I was feeding some chickens, I happened to toss a small pebble at one of them, which hit it on the middle, and directly killed it. The old slave, having soon after missed the chicken, inquired after it; and on my relating the accident (for I told her the truth, because my mother would never suffer me to tell a lie) she flew into a violent passion, threatened that I should suffer for it; and, my master being out, she immediately went and told her mistress what I had done. This alarmed me very much, and I expected an instant correction, which to me was uncommonly dreadful; for I had seldom been beaten at home. I therefore resolved to fly; and accordingly I ran into a thicket that was hard by, and hid myself in the bushes. Soon afterwards my mistress and the slave returned, and, not seeing me, they searched all the house, but, not finding me, and I not making answer when they called to me, they thought I had run away, and the whole neighbourhood was raised in the pursuit of me. In that part of the country (as well as ours) the houses and villages were skirted with woods, or shrubberies, and the bushes were so thick, that a man could readily conceal himself in them, so as to elude the strictest search. The neighbours continued the whole day looking for me, and several times many of them came within a few yards of the place where I lay hid. I expected every moment, when I heard a rustling among the trees, to be found out, and punished by my master; but they never discovered me, though they were often so near that I even heard their conjectures as they were looking about for me; and I now learned from them, that any attempt to return home would be hopeless. Most of them supposed I had fled towards home; but the distance was so great, and the way so intricate, that they thought I could never reach it, and that I should be lost in the woods. When I heard this I was seized with a violent panic, and abandoned myself to despair. Night too began to approach, and aggravated all my fears. I had before entertained hopes of getting home, and I had determined when it should be dark to make the attempt; but I was now convinced it was fruitless, and I began to consider that, if possibly I could escape all other animals, I could not those of the human kind; and that, not knowing the way, I must perish in the woods.—Thus was I like the hunted deer:

> Ev'ry leaf and ev'ry whisp'ring breath
> Convey'd a foe, and ev'ry foe a death.

I heard frequent rustlings among the leaves; and, being pretty sure they were snakes, I expected every instant to be stung by them.—This increased my anguish, and the horror of my situation became now quite insupportable. I at length quitted the thicket, very faint and hungry, for I had not eaten or drank any thing all the day, and crept to my master's kitchen, from whence I set out at first, and which was an open shed, and laid myself down in the ashes, with an anxious wish for death to relieve me from all my pains. I was scarcely awake in the morning when the old woman slave, who was the first up, came to light the fire, and saw me in the fire-place. She was very much surprised to see me, and could scarcely believe her own eyes. She now promised to intercede for me, and went for her master, who soon after came, and, having slightly reprimanded me, ordered me to be taken care of, and not ill-treated.

Soon after this my master's only daughter and child by his first wife sickened and died, which affected him so much that for some time he was almost frantic, and really would have killed himself had he not been watched and prevented. However, in a small time afterwards he recovered, and I was again sold. I was now carried to the left of the sun's rising, through many dreary wastes and dismal woods, amidst the hideous roarings of wild beasts.—The people I was sold to used to carry me very often, when I was tired, either on their shoulders or on their backs. I saw many convenient well-built sheds along the roads, at proper distances, to accommodate the merchants and travellers, who lay in those buildings along with their wives, who often accompany them; and they always go well armed.

From the time I left my own nation I always found somebody that understood me till I came to the sea coast. The languages of different nations did not totally differ, nor were they so copious as those of the Europeans, particularly the English. They were therefore easily learned; and, while I was journeying thus through Africa, I acquired two or three different tongues. In this manner I had been travelling for a considerable time, when one evening, to my great surprise, whom should I see brought to the house where I was but my dear sister. As soon as she saw me she gave a loud shriek, and ran into my arms.—I was quite overpowered; neither of us could speak, but, for a considerable time, clung to each other in mutual embraces, unable to do any thing but weep. Our meeting affected all who saw us; and indeed I must acknowledge, in honour of those sable destroyers of human rights, that I never met with any ill treatment, or saw any offered to their slaves, except tying them, when necessary, to keep them from running away. When these people knew we were brother and sister they indulged us to be together; and the man, to whom I supposed we belonged, lay with us, he in the middle, while she and I held one another by the hands across his breast all night; and thus for a while we forgot our misfortunes in the joy of being together: but even this small comfort was soon to have an end; for scarcely had the fatal morning appeared, when she was again torn from me for ever! I was now more miserable, if possible, than before. The small relief which her presence gave me from pain was gone, and the wretchedness of my situation was redoubled by my anxiety after her fate, and my apprehensions lest her sufferings should be greater than mine, when I could not be with her to alleviate them. Yes, thou dear partner of all my childish sports! thou sharer of my joys and sorrows! happy should I have ever esteemed myself to encounter every misery for you, and to procure your freedom by the sacrifice of my own. Though you were early forced from my arms, your image has been always rivetted in my heart, from which neither *time nor fortune* have been able to remove it: so that, while the thoughts of your sufferings have damped my prosperity, they have mingled with adversity, and increased its bitterness.—To that heaven which protects the weak from the strong, I commit the care of your innocence and virtues, if they have not already received their full reward; and if your youth and delicacy have not long since fallen victims to the violence of the African trader, the pestilential stench of a Guinea ship, the seasoning in the European colonies, or the lash and lust of a brutal and unrelenting overseer.

I did not long remain after my sister. I was again sold, and carried through a number of places, till, after travelling a considerable time, I came to a town called Tinmah, in the most beautiful country I had yet seen in Africa. It was extremely rich, and there were many rivulets which flowed through it; and supplied a large pond in the center of the town, where the people washed. Here I first saw and tasted cocoa nuts, which I thought superior to any nuts I had ever tasted before; and the trees, which were loaded, were also interspersed amongst the houses, which had commodious shades adjoining, and were in the same manner as ours, the insides being neatly plastered and whitewashed. Here I also saw and tasted for the first time sugar-cane. Their money consisted of little white shells, the size of the finger nail: they are known in this country by the name of *core*. I was sold here for one hundred and seventy-two of them by a merchant who lived and brought me there. I had been about two or three days at his house, when a wealthy widow, a neighbour of his, came there one evening, and brought with her an only son, a young gentleman about my own age and size. Here they saw me; and, having taken a fancy to me, I was bought of the merchant, and went home with them. Her house and premises were situated close to one of those rivulets I have mentioned, and were the finest I ever saw in Africa: they were very extensive, and she had a number of slaves to attend her. The next day I was washed and perfumed, and when meal-time came, I was led into the presence of my mistress, and ate and drank before her with her son. This filled me with astonishment: and I could scarce help expressing my surprise that the young gentleman should suffer me, who was bound, to eat with him who was free; and not only so, but that he would not at any time either eat or drink till I had taken first, because I was the eldest, which was agreeable to our custom. Indeed every thing here, and all their treatment of me, made me forget that I was a slave. The language of these people resembled ours so nearly, that we understood each other perfectly. They had also the very same customs as we. There were likewise slaves daily to attend us, while my young master and I, with other boys, sported with our darts and bows and arrows, as I had been used to do at home. In this resemblance to my former happy state I passed about two months, and I now began to think I was to be adopted into the family, and was beginning to be reconciled to my situation, and to forget by degrees my misfortunes, when all at once the delusion vanished; for, without the least previous knowledge, one morning early, while my dear master and companion was still asleep, I was awakened out of my reverie to fresh sorrow, and hurried away even among the uncircumcised.

Thus, at the very moment I dreamed of the greatest happiness, I found myself most miserable: and it seemed as if fortune wished to give me this taste of joy only to render the reverse more poignant. The change I now experienced was as painful as it was sudden and unexpected. It was a change indeed from a state of bliss to a scene which is inexpressible by me, as it discovered to me an element I had never before beheld, and till then had no idea of, and wherein such instances of hardship and cruelty continually occurred as I can never reflect on but with horror.

All the nations and people I had hitherto passed through resembled our own in their manners, customs and language: but I came at length to a country, the inhabitants of which differed from us in all those particulars. I was very much struck with this difference, especially when I came among a people who did not circumcise, and eat without washing their hands. They cooked also in iron pots, and had European cutlasses and cross bows, which were unknown to us, and fought with their fists among themselves. Their women were not so modest as ours, for they eat, and drank, and slept with their men. But, above all, I was amazed to see no sacrifices or offerings among them. In some of those places the people ornamented themselves with scars, and likewise filed their teeth very sharp. They wanted sometimes to ornament me in the same manner, but I would not suffer them; hoping that I might some time be among a people who did not thus disfigure themselves, as I thought they did. At last, I came to the banks of a large river, which was covered with canoes, in which the people appeared to live with their household utensils and provisions of all kinds. I was beyond measure astonished at this, as I had never before seen any water larger than a pond or a rivulet; and my surprise was mingled with no small fear when I was put into one of these canoes, and we began to paddle and move along the river. We continued going on thus till night; and when we came to land, and made fires on the banks, each family by themselves, some dragged their canoes on shore, others staid and cooked in theirs, and laid in them all night. Those on the land had mats, of which they made tents, some in the shape of little houses: In these we slept; and after the morning meal we embarked again, and proceeded as before. I was often very much astonished to see some of the women, as well as the men, jump into the water, dive to the bottom, come up again, and swim about. Thus I continued to travel, sometimes by land, sometimes by water, through different countries, and various nations, till, at the end of six or seven months after I had been kidnapped, I arrived at the sea coast. It would be tedious and uninteresting to relate all the incidents which befel me during this journey, and which I have not yet forgotten; of the various hands I passed through, and the manners and customs of all the different people among whom I lived: I shall therefore only observe, that, in all the places where I was, the soil was exceedingly rich; the pomkins, eadas, plantains, yams, &c. &c. were in great abundance, and of incredible size. There were also vast quantities of different gums, though not used for any purpose; and every where a great deal of tobacco. The cotton even grew quite wild; and there was plenty of red wood. I saw no mechanics whatever in all the way, except such as I have mentioned. The chief employment in all these countries was agriculture, and both the males and females, as with us, were brought up to it, and trained in the arts of war.

The first object which saluted my eyes when I arrived on the coast was the sea, and a slave-ship, which was then riding at anchor, and waiting for its cargo. These filled me with astonishment, which was soon converted into terror, which I am yet at a loss to describe, nor the then feelings of my mind. When I was carried on board I was immediately handled, and tossed up, to see if I were sound, by some of the crew; and I was now persuaded that I had gotten into a world of bad spirits, and that they were going to kill me. Their complexions too differing so much from ours, their long hair, and the language they spoke, which was very different from any I had ever heard, united to confirm me in this belief. Indeed, such were the horrors of my views and fears at the moment, that, if ten thousand worlds had been my own, I would have freely parted with them all to have exchanged my condition with that of the meanest slave in my own country. When I looked round the ship too, and saw a large furnace of copper boiling, and a multitude of black people of every description chained together, every one of their countenances expressing dejection and sorrow, I no longer doubted of my fate, and, quite overpowered with horror and anguish, I fell motionless on the deck and fainted. When I recovered a little, I found some black people about me, who I believed were some of those who brought me on board, and had been receiving their pay; they talked to me in order to cheer me, but all in vain. I asked them if we were not to be eaten by those white men with horrible looks, red faces, and long hair? They told me I was not; and one of the crew brought me a small portion of spirituous liquor in a wine glass; but, being afraid of him, I would not take it out of his hand. One of the blacks therefore took it from him and gave it to me, and I took a little down my palate, which, instead of reviving me, as they thought it would, threw me into the greatest consternation at the strange feeling it produced, having never tasted any such liquor before. Soon after this, the blacks who brought me on board went off, and left me abandoned to despair. I now saw myself deprived of all chance of returning to my native country, or even the least glimpse of hope of gaining the shore, which I now considered as friendly: and I even wished for my former slavery in preference to my present situation, which was filled with horrors of every kind, still heightened by my ignorance of what I was to undergo. I was not long suffered to indulge my grief; I was soon put down under the decks, and there I received such a salutation in my nostrils as I had never experienced in my life; so that with the loathsomeness of the stench, and crying together, I became so sick and low that I was not able to eat, nor had I the least desire to taste any thing. I now wished for the last friend, Death, to relieve me; but soon, to my grief, two of the white men offered me eatables; and, on my refusing to eat, one of them held me fast by the hands, and laid me across, I think, the windlass, and tied my feet, while the other flogged me severely. I had never experienced any thing of this kind before; and although, not being used to the water, I naturally feared that element the first time I saw it; yet, nevertheless, could I have got over the nettings, I would have jumped over the side, but I could not; and, besides, the crew used to watch us very closely who were not chained down to the decks, lest we should leap into the water; and I have seen some of these poor African prisoners most severely cut for attempting to do so, and hourly whipped for not eating. This indeed was often the case with myself. In a little time after, amongst the poor chained men, I found some of my own nation, which in a small degree gave ease to my mind. I inquired of these what was to be done with us? they gave me to understand we were to be carried to these white people's country to work for them. I then was a little revived, and thought, if it were no worse than working, my situation was not so desperate: but still I feared I should be put to death, the white people looked and acted, as I thought, in so savage a manner; for I had never seen among any people such instances of brutal cruelty; and this not only shewn towards us blacks, but also to some of the whites themselves. One white man in particular I saw, when we were permitted to be on deck, flogged so unmercifully with a large rope near the foremast, that he died in consequence of it; and they tossed him over the side as they would have done a brute. This made me fear these people the more; and I expected nothing less than to be treated in the same manner. I could not help expressing my fears and apprehensions to some of my countrymen: I asked them if these people had no country, but lived in this hollow place the ship? they told me they did not, but came from a distant one. "Then," said I, "how comes it in all our country we never heard of them?" They told me, because they lived so very far off. I then asked where were their women? had they any like themselves! I was told they had: "And why," said I, "do we not see them?" they answered, because they were left behind. I asked how the vessel could go? they told me they could not tell; but that there were cloths put upon the masts by the help of the ropes I saw, and then the vessel went on; and the white men had some spell or magic they put in the water when they liked in order to stop the vessel. I was exceedingly amazed at this account, and really thought they were spirits. I therefore wished much to be from amongst them, for I expected they would sacrifice me: but my wishes were vain; for we were so quartered that it was impossible for any of us to make our escape. While we staid on the coast I was mostly on deck; and one day, to my great astonishment, I saw one of these vessels coming in with the sails up. As soon as the whites saw it, they gave a great shout, at which we were amazed; and the more so as the vessel appeared larger by approaching nearer. At last she came to an anchor in my sight, and when the anchor was let go, I and my countrymen who saw it were lost in astonishment to observe the vessel stop; and were now convinced it was done by magic. Soon after this the other ship got her boats out, and they came on board of us, and the people of both ships seemed very glad to see each other. Several of the strangers also shook hands with us black people, and made motions with their hands, signifying, I suppose, we were to go to their country; but we did not understand them. At last, when the ship we were in had got in all her cargo, they made ready with many fearful noises, and we were all put under deck, so that we could not see how they managed the vessel. But this disappointment was the least of my sorrow. The stench of the hold while we were on the coast was so intolerably loathsome, that it was dangerous to remain there for any time, and some of us had been permitted to stay on the deck for the fresh air; but now that the whole ship's cargo were confined together, it became absolutely pestilential. The closeness of the place, and the heat of the climate, added to the number in the ship, which was so crowded that each had scarcely room to turn himself, almost suffocated us. This produced copious perspirations, so that the air soon became unfit for respiration, from a variety of loathsome smells, and brought on a sickness among the slaves, of which many died, thus falling victims to the improvident avarice, as I may call it, of their purchasers.

This wretched situation was again aggravated by the galling of the chains, now become insupportable; and the filth of the necessary tubs, into which the children often fell, and were almost suffocated. The shrieks of the women, and the groans of the dying, rendered the whole a scene of horror almost inconceiveable. Happily perhaps for myself I was soon reduced so low here that it was thought necessary to keep me almost always on deck; and from my extreme youth I was not put in fetters. In this situation I expected every hour to share the fate of my companions, some of whom were almost daily brought upon deck at the point of death, which I began to hope would soon put an end to my miseries. Often did I think many of the inhabitants of the deep much more happy than myself; I envied them the freedom they enjoyed, and as often wished I could change my condition for theirs. Every circumstance I met with served only to render my state more painful, and heighten my apprehensions, and my opinion of the cruelty of the whites. One day they had taken a number of fishes; and when they had killed and satisfied themselves with as many as they thought fit, to our astonishment who were on the deck, rather than give any of them to us to eat, as we expected, they tossed the remaining fish into the sea again, although we begged and prayed for some as well as we could, but in vain; and some of my countrymen, being pressed by hunger, took an opportunity, when they thought no one saw them, of trying to get a little privately; but they were discovered, and the attempt procured them some very severe floggings.

One day, when we had a smooth sea, and moderate wind, two of my wearied countrymen, who were chained together (I was near them at the time), preferring death to such a life of misery, somehow made through the nettings, and jumped into the sea: immediately another quite dejected fellow, who, on account of his illness, was suffered to be out of irons, also followed their example; and I believe many more would very soon have done the same, if they had not been prevented by the ship's crew, who were instantly alarmed. Those of us that were the most active were, in a moment, put down under the deck; and there was such a noise and confusion amongst the people of the ship as I never heard before, to stop her, and get the boat out to go after the slaves. However, two of the wretches were drowned, but they got the other, and afterwards flogged him unmercifully, for thus attempting to prefer death to slavery. In this manner we continued to undergo more hardships than I can now relate; hardships which are inseparable from this accursed trade.—Many a time we were near suffocation, from the want of fresh air, which we were often without for whole days together. This, and the stench of the necessary tubs, carried off many. During our passage I first saw flying fishes, which surprised me very much: they used frequently to fly across the ship, and many of them fell on the deck. I also now first saw the use of the quadrant. I had often with astonishment seen the mariners make observations with it, and I could not think what it meant. They at last took notice of my surprise; and one of them, willing to increase it, as well as to gratify my curiosity, made me one day look through it. The clouds appeared to me to be land, which disappeared as they passed along. This heightened my wonder: and I was now more persuaded than ever that I was in another world, and that every thing about me was magic. At last we came in sight of the island of Barbadoes, at which the whites on board gave a great shout, and made many signs of joy to us. We did not know what to think of this; but as the vessel drew nearer we plainly saw the harbour, and other ships of different kinds and sizes: and we soon anchored amongst them off Bridge Town. Many merchants and planters now came on board, though it was in the evening. They put us in separate parcels, and examined us attentively. They also made us jump, and pointed to the land, signifying we were to go there. We thought by this we should be eaten by these ugly men, as they appeared to us; and, when soon after we were all put down under the deck again, there was much dread and trembling among us, and nothing but bitter cries to be heard all the night from these apprehensions, insomuch that at last the white people got some old slaves from the land to pacify us. They told us we were not to be eaten, but to work, and were soon to go on land, where we should see many of our country people. This report eased us much; and sure enough, soon after we were landed, there came to us Africans of all languages. We were conducted immediately to the merchant's yard, where we were all pent up together like so many sheep in a fold, without regard to sex or age. As every object was new to me, every thing I saw filled me with surprise. What struck me first was, that the houses were built with bricks, in stories, and in every other respect different from those in I have seen in Africa: but I was still more astonished on seeing people on horseback. I did not know what this could mean; and indeed I thought these people were full of nothing but magical arts. While I was in this astonishment, one of my fellow prisoners spoke to a countryman of his about the horses, who said they were the same kind they had in their country. I understood them, though they were from a distant part of Africa, and I thought it odd I had not seen any horses there; but afterwards, when I came to converse with different Africans, I found they had many horses amongst them, and much larger than those I then saw. We were not many days in the merchant's custody before we were sold after their usual manner, which is this:—On a signal given, (as the beat of a drum), the buyers rush at once into the yard where the slaves are confined, and make choice of that parcel they like best. The noise and clamour with which this is attended, and the eagerness visible in the countenances of the buyers, serve not a little to increase the apprehensions of the terrified Africans, who may well be supposed to consider them as the ministers of that destruction to which they think themselves devoted. In this manner, without scruple, are relations and friends separated, most of them never to see each other again. I remember in the vessel in which I was brought over, in the men's apartment, there were several brothers, who, in the sale, were sold in different lots; and it was very moving on this occasion to see and hear their cries at parting. O, ye nominal Christians! might not an African ask you, learned you this from your God? who says unto you, Do unto all men as you would men should do unto you? Is it not enough that we are torn from our country and friends to toil for your luxury and lust of gain? Must every tender feeling be likewise sacrificed to your avarice? Are the dearest friends and relations, now rendered more dear by their separation from their kindred, still to be parted from each other, and thus prevented from cheering the gloom

of slavery with the small comfort of being together and mingling their sufferings and sorrows? Why are parents to lose
their children, brothers their sisters, or husbands their
wives? Surely this is a new refinement in cruelty, which,
while it has no advantage to atone for it, thus aggravates
distress, and adds fresh horrors even to the wretchedness of
slavery.

CHAP. III.

*The Author is carried to Virginia—His distress—Surprise at see-
ing a picture and a watch—Is bought by Captain Pascal, and
sets out for England—His terror during the voyage—Arrives
in England—His wonder at a fall of snow—Is sent to Guernsey, and in some time goes on board a ship of war with his
master—Some account of the expedition against Louis-
bourg, under the command of Admiral Boscawen, in 1758.*

I NOW totally lost the small remains of comfort I had
enjoyed in conversing with my countrymen; the women too,
who used to wash and take care of me, were all gone different ways, and I never saw one of them afterwards.

I stayed in this island for a few days; I believe it could
not be above a fortnight; when I and some few more slaves,
that were not saleable among the rest, from very much fretting, were shipped off in a sloop for North America. On the
passage we were better treated than when we were coming
from Africa, and we had plenty of rice and fat pork. We
were landed up a river a good way from the sea, about Virginia county, where we saw few or none of our native Africans, and not one soul who could talk to me. I was a few
weeks weeding grass, and gathering stones in a plantation;

and at last all my companions were distributed different ways, and only myself was left. I was now exceedingly miserable, and thought myself worse off than any of the rest of my companions; for they could talk to each other, but I had no person to speak to that I could understand. In this state I was constantly grieving and pining, and wishing for death, rather than any thing else. While I was in this plantation, the gentleman, to whom I supposed the estate belonged, being unwell, I was one day sent for to his dwelling house to fan him: when I came into the room where he was, I was very much affrighted at some things I saw, and the more so as I had seen a black woman slave as I came through the house, who was cooking the dinner, and the poor creature was cruelly loaded with various kinds of iron machines; she had one particularly on her head, which locked her mouth so fast that she could scarcely speak; and could not eat nor drink. I was much astonished and shocked at this contrivance, which I afterwards learned was called the iron muzzle. Soon after I had a fan put into my hand, to fan the gentleman while he slept; and so I did indeed with great fear. While he was fast asleep I indulged myself a great deal in looking about the room, which to me appeared very fine and curious. The first object that engaged my attention was a watch which hung on the chimney, and was going. I was quite surprised at the noise it made, and was afraid it would tell the gentleman any thing I might do amiss: and when I immediately after observed a picture hanging in the room, which appeared constantly to look at me, I was still more affrighted, having never seen such things as these before. At one time I thought it was something relative to magic; and not seeing it move, I thought it might be some way the whites had to keep their great men when they died, and offer them libations as we used to do our friendly spirits. In this state of anxiety I remained till my master awoke, when I was dismissed out of the room, to my no small satisfaction and relief, for I thought that these people were all made of wonders. In this place I was called Jacob; but on board the African snow I was called Michael. I had been some time in this miserable, forlorn, and much dejected state, without having any one to talk to, which made my life a burden, when the kind and unknown hand of the Creator (who in very deed leads the blind in a way they know not) now began to appear, to my comfort; for one day the captain of a merchant ship, called the Industrious Bee, came on some business to my master's house. This gentleman, whose name was Michael Henry Pascal, was a lieutenant in the royal navy, but now commanded this trading ship, which was somewhere in the confines of the county many miles off. While he was at my master's house it happened that he saw me, and liked me so well that he made a purchase of me. I think I have often heard him say he gave thirty or forty pounds sterling for me; but I do not now remember which. However, he meant me for a present to some of his friends in England; and I was sent accordingly from the house of my then master (one Mr. Campbell) to the place where the ship lay; I was conducted on horseback by an elderly black man (a mode of travelling which appeared very odd to me). When I arrived I was carried on board a fine large ship, loaded with tobacco, &c. and just ready to sail for England. I now thought my condition much mended; I had sails to lie on, and plenty of good victuals to eat; and every body on board used me very kindly, quite contrary to what I had seen of any white people before; I therefore began to think that they were not all of the same disposition. A few days after I was on board we sailed for England. I was still at a loss to conjecture my destiny. By this time, however, I could smatter a little imperfect English; and I wanted to know as well as I could where we were going. Some of the people of the ship used to tell me they were going to carry me back to my own country, and this made me very happy. I was quite rejoiced at the idea of going back; and thought if I should get home what wonders I should have to tell. But I was reserved for another fate, and was soon undeceived when we came within sight of the English coast. While I was on board this ship, my captain and master named me *Gustavus Vasa*. I at that time began to understand him a little, and refused to be called so, and told him as well as I could that I would be called Jacob; but he said I should not, and still called me Gustavus; and when I refused to answer to my new name, which at first I did, it gained me many a cuff; so at length I submitted, and by which I have been known ever since. The ship had a very long passage; and on that account we had very short allowance of provisions. Towards the last we had only one pound and a half of bread per week, and about the same quantity of meat, and one quart of water a day. We spoke with only one vessel the whole time we were at sea, and but once we caught a few fishes. In our extremities the captain and people told me in jest they would kill and eat me, but I thought them in earnest, and was depressed beyond measure, expecting every moment to be my last. While I was in this situation one evening they caught, with a good deal of trouble, a large shark, and got it on board. This gladdened my poor heart exceedingly, as I thought it would serve the people to eat instead of their eating me; but very soon, to my astonishment, they cut off a small part of the tail, and tossed the rest over the side. This renewed my consternation; and I did not know what to think of these white people; I very much feared they would kill and eat me. There was on board the ship a young lad who had never been at sea before, about four or five years older than myself: his name was Richard Baker. He was a native of America, had received an excellent education, and was of a most amiable temper. Soon after I went on board he shewed me a great deal of partiality and attention, and in return I grew extremely fond of him. We at length became inseparable; and for the space of two years, he was of very great use to me, and was my constant companion and instructor. Although this dear youth had many slaves of his own, yet he and I have gone through many sufferings together on shipboard; and we have many nights lain in each other's bosoms when we were in great distress. Thus such a friendship was cemented between us as we cherished till his death, which, to my very great sorrow, happened in the year 1759, when he was up the Archipelago, on board his majesty's ship the Preston: an event which I have never ceased to regret, as I lost at once a kind interpreter, an agreeable companion, and a faithful friend; who, at the age of fifteen, discovered a mind superior to prejudice; and who was not ashamed to notice, to associate with, and to be the friend and instructor of one who was ignorant, a stranger, of a different complexion, and a slave! My master had lodged in his mother's house in America: he respected him very much, and made him always eat with him in the cabin. He used often to tell him jocularly that he would kill and eat me. Sometimes he would say to me—the black people were not good to eat, and would ask me if we did not eat people in my country. I said, No: then he said he would kill Dick (as he always called him) first, and afterwards me. Though this hearing relieved my mind a little as to myself, I was alarmed for Dick, and whenever he was called I used to be very much afraid he was to be killed; and I would peep and watch to see if they were going to kill him: nor was I free from this consternation till we made the land. One night we lost a man overboard; and the cries and noise were so great and confused, in stopping the ship, that I, who did not know what was the matter, began, as usual, to be very much afraid, and to think they were going to make an offering with me, and perform some magic; which I still believed they dealt in. As the waves were very high, I thought the Ruler of the seas was angry, and I expected to be offered up to appease him. This filled my mind with agony, and I could not any more that night close my eyes again to rest. However, when day-light appeared, I was a little eased in my mind; but still every time I was called I used to think it was to be killed. Some time after this we saw some very large fish, which I afterwards found were called grampusses. They looked to me extremely terrible, and made their appearance just at dusk, and were so near as to blow the water on the ship's deck. I believed them to be the rulers of the sea; and, as the white people did not make any offerings at any time, I thought they were angry with them; and, at last, what confirmed my belief was, the wind just then died away, and a calm ensued, and in consequence of it the ship stopped going. I supposed that the fish had performed this, and I hid myself in the fore-part of the ship, through fear of being offered up to appease them, every minute peeping and quaking; but my good friend Dick came shortly towards me, and I took an opportunity to ask him, as well as I could, what these fish were? not being able to talk much English, I could but just make him understand my question; and not at all, when I asked him if any offerings were to be made to them? However, he told me these fish would swallow any body; which sufficiently alarmed me. Here he was called away by the captain, who was leaning over the quarter-deck railing and looking at the fish; and most of the people were busied in getting a barrel of pitch to light, for them to play with. The captain now called me to him, having learned some of my apprehensions from Dick; and having diverted himself and others for some time with my fears, which appeared ludicrous enough in my crying and trembling, he dismissed me. The barrel of pitch was now lighted and put over the side into the water: by this time it was just dark, and the fish went after it; and, to my great joy, I saw them no more.

However, all my alarms began to subside when we got sight of land; and at last the ship arrived at Falmouth, after a passage of thirteen weeks. Every heart on board seemed gladdened on our reaching the shore, and none more than mine. The captain immediately went on shore, and sent on board some fresh provisions, which we wanted very much: we made good use of them, and our famine was soon turned into feasting, almost without ending. It was about the beginning of the spring 1757 when I arrived in England, and I was near twelve years of age at that time. I was very much struck with the buildings and the pavement of the streets in Falmouth; and, indeed, any object I saw filled me with new surprise. One morning, when I got upon deck, I saw it covered all over with the snow that fell over-night: as I had never seen any thing of the kind before, I thought it was salt; so I immediately ran down to the mate, and desired him, as well as I could, to come and see how somebody in the night had thrown salt all over the deck. He, knowing what it was, desired me to bring some of it down to him: accordingly I took up a handful of it, which I found very cold indeed; and when I brought it to him he desired me to taste it. I did so, and I was surprised beyond measure. I then asked him what it was? he told me it was snow: but I could not in any wise understand him. He asked me if we had no such thing in my country? and I told him, No. I then asked him the use of it, and who made it; he told me a great man in the heavens, called God: but here again I was to all intents and purposes at a loss to understand him; and the more so, when a little after I saw the air filled with it, in a heavy shower, which fell down on the same day. After this I went to church; and having never been at such a place before, I was again amazed at seeing and hearing the service. I asked all I could about it; and they gave me to understand it was worshipping God, who made us and all things. I was still at a great loss, and soon got into an endless field of inquiries, as well as I was able to speak and ask about things. However, my little friend Dick used to be my best interpreter; for I could make free with him, and he always instructed me with pleasure: and from what I could understand by him of this God, and in seeing these white people did not sell one another, as we did, I was much pleased; and in this I thought they were much happier than we Africans. I was astonished at the wisdom of the white people in all things I saw; but was amazed at their not sacrificing, or making any offerings, and eating with unwashed hands, and touching the dead. I likewise could not help remarking the particular slenderness of their women, which I did not at first like; and I thought they were not so modest and shamefaced as the African women.

I had often seen my master and Dick employed in reading; and I had a great curiosity to talk to the books, as I thought they did; and so to learn how all things had a beginning: for that purpose I have often taken up a book, and have talked to it, and then put my ears to it, when alone, in hopes it would answer me; and I have been very much concerned when I found it remained silent.

My master lodged at the house of a gentleman in Falmouth, who had a fine little daughter about six or seven years of age, and she grew prodigiously fond of me; insomuch that we used to eat together, and had servants to wait on us. I was so much caressed by this family that it often reminded me of the treatment I had received from my little noble African master. After I had been here a few days, I was sent on board of the ship; but the child cried so much after me that nothing could pacify her till I was sent for again. It is ludicrous enough, that I began to fear I should be betrothed to this young lady; and when my master asked me if I would stay there with her behind him, as he was going away with the ship, which had taken in the tobacco again? I cried immediately, and said I would not leave him. At last, by stealth, one night I was sent on board the ship again; and in a little time we sailed for Guernsey, where she was in part owned by a merchant, one Nicholas Doberry. As I was now amongst a people who had not their faces scarred, like some of the African nations where I had been, I was very glad I did not let them ornament me in that manner when I was with them. When we arrived at Guernsey, my master placed me to board and lodge with one of his mates, who had a wife and family there; and some months afterwards he went to England, and left me in the care of this mate, together with my friend Dick. This mate had a little daughter aged about five or six years, with whom I used to be much delighted. I had often observed, that when her mother washed her face it looked very rosy; but when she washed mine it did not look so; I therefore tried oftentimes myself if I could not by washing make my face of the same colour as my little play-mate (Mary), but it was all in vain; and I now began to be mortified at the difference in our complexions. This woman behaved to me with great kindness and attention; and taught me every thing in the same manner as she did her own child, and indeed in every respect treated me as such. I remained here till the summer of the year 1757, when my master, being appointed first lieutenant of his Majesty's ship the Roebuck, sent for Dick and me, and his old mate: on this we all left Guernsey, and set out for England in a sloop bound for London. As we were coming up towards the Nore, where the Roebuck lay, a man of war's boat came along-side to press our people; on which each man ran to hide himself. I was very much frightened at this, though I did not know what it meant, or what to think or do. However, I went and hid myself also under a hencoop. Immediately the press-gang came on board with their swords drawn, and searched all about, pulled the people out by force, and put them into the boat. At last I was found out also; the man that found me held me up by the heels while they all made their sport of me, I roaring and crying out all the time most lustily; but at last the mate, who was my conductor, seeing this, came to my assistance, and did all he could to pacify me; but all to very little purpose, till I had seen the boat go off. Soon afterwards we came to the Nore, where the Roebuck lay; and, to our great joy, my master came on board to us, and brought us to the ship. I was amazed indeed to see the quantity of men and the guns.

However my surprise began to diminish, as my knowledge increased; and I ceased to feel those apprehensions and alarms which had taken such strong possession of me when I first came among the Europeans, and for some time after. I began now to pass to an opposite extreme; I was so far from being afraid of any thing new which I saw, that, after I had been some time in this ship, I even began to long for an engagement. My griefs too, which in young minds are not perpetual, were now wearing away; and I soon enjoyed myself pretty well, and felt tolerably easy in my present situation. There was a number of boys on board, which still made it more agreeable; for we were always together, and a great part of our time was spent in play. I remained in this ship a considerable time, during which we made several cruises, and visited a variety of places: among others we were twice in Holland, and brought over several persons of distinction from it, whose names I do not now remember. On the passage, one day, for the diversion of those gentlemen, all the boys were called on the quarter-deck, and were paired proportionably, and then made to fight; after which the gentlemen gave the combatants from five to nine shillings each. This was the first time I ever fought with a white boy; and I never knew what it was to have a bloody nose before. This made me fight most desperately; I suppose considerably more than an hour; and at last, both of us being weary, we were parted. I had a great deal of this kind of sport afterwards, in which the captain and the ship's company used very much to encourage me. Sometime afterwards the ship went to Leith, in Scotland, from thence to the Orkneys, where I was surprised in seeing scarcely any night; and from thence we sailed with a great fleet, full of soldiers, for England. All this time we had never come to an engagement, though we were frequently cruising off the coast of France; during which we chased many vessels, and took in all seventeen prizes. I had been learning many of the manoeuvres of the ship during our cruise; and I was several times made to fire the guns.

One evening, off Havre de Grace, just as it was growing dark, we were standing off shore, and met with a fine large French-built frigate. We got all things immediately ready for fighting; and I now expected I should be gratified in seeing an engagement, which I had so long wished for in vain. But the very moment the word of command was given to fire, we heard those on board the other ship cry "Haul down the jib"; and in that instant she hoisted English colours. There was instantly with us an amazing cry of—"Avast!" or "stop firing!" and I think one or two guns had been let off, but happily they did no mischief. We had hailed them several times; but they not hearing, we received no answer, which was the cause of our firing. The boat was then sent on board of her, and she proved to be the Ambuscade man of war, to my no small disappointment. We returned to Portsmouth, without having been in any action, just at the trial of Admiral Byng (whom I saw several times during it); and my master, having left the ship, and gone to London for promotion, Dick and I were put on board the Savage sloop of war, and we went in her to assist in bringing off the St. George man of war, that had run ashore somewhere on the coast. After staying a few weeks on board the Savage, Dick and I were sent on shore at Deal, where we remained some short time, till my master sent for us to London, the place I had long desired exceedingly to see. We therefore both with great pleasure got into a waggon, and came to London, where we were received by a Mr. Guerin, a relation of my master. This gentleman had two sisters, very amiable ladies, who took much notice and great care of me. Though I had desired so much to see London, when I arrived in it I was unfortunately unable to gratify my curiosity; for I had at this time the chilblains to such a degree that I could not stand for several months, and I was obliged to be sent to St. George's Hospital. There I grew so ill, that the doctors wanted to cut my left leg off at different times, apprehending a mortification; but I always said I would rather die than suffer it; and happily (I thank God) I recovered without the operation. After being there several weeks, and just as I had recovered, the small-pox broke out on me, so that I was again confined; and I thought myself now particularly unfortunate. However, I soon recovered again: and by this time my master having been promoted to be first lieutenant of the Preston man of war of fifty guns, then new at Deptford, Dick and I were sent on board her, and soon we went to Holland to bring over the late Duke of Cumberland to

England. While I was in this ship an incident happened, which though trifling, I beg leave to relate, as I could not help taking particular notice of it, and considering it then as a judgment of God. One morning a young man was looking up to the fore-top, and in a wicked tone, common on ship-board, d——d his eyes about something. Just at the moment some small particles of dirt fell into his left eye, and by the evening it was very much inflamed. The next day it grew worse; and within six or seven days he lost it. From this ship my master was appointed a lieutenant on board the Royal George. When he was going he wished me to stay on board the Preston, to learn the French horn; but the ship being ordered for Turkey, I could not think of leaving my master, to whom I was very warmly attached; and I told him, if he left me behind it would break my heart. This prevailed on him to take me with him; but he left Dick on board the Preston, whom I embraced at parting for the last time. The Royal George was the largest ship I had ever seen; so that when I came on board of her I was surprised at the number of people, men, women, and children, of every denomina-tion; and the largeness of the guns, many of them also of brass, which I had never seen before. Here were also shops or stalls of every kind of goods, and people crying their dif-ferent commodities about the ship as in a town. To me it appeared a little world, into which I was again cast without a friend, for I had no longer my dear companion Dick. We did not stay long here. My master was not many weeks on board before he got an appointment to be sixth lieutenant of the Namur, which was then at Spithead, fitting up for Vice-Admiral Boscawen, who was going with a large fleet on an expedition against Louisbourgh. The crew of the Royal George were turned over to her, and the flag of that gallant Admiral was hoisted on board, the blue at the main-top gallant-mast head. There was a very great fleet of men of war of every description assembled together for this ex-pedition, and I was in hopes soon to have an opportunity of being gratified with a sea-fight. All things being now in readiness, this mighty fleet (for there was also Admiral Cor-nish's fleet in company, destined for the East Indies) at last weighed anchor, and sailed. The two fleets continued in company for several days, and then parted; Admiral Cornish, in the Lenox, having first saluted our Admiral in the Namur, which he returned. We then steered for America; but, by contrary winds, we were driven to Teneriffe, where I was struck with its noted peak. Its prodigious height, and its form, resembling a sugar loaf, filled me with wonder. We remained in sight of this island some days, and then proceeded for America, which we soon made, and got into a very commodious harbour called St. George, in Halifax, where we had fish in great plenty, and all other fresh provisions. We were here joined by different men of war and transport ships with soldiers; after which, our fleet being increased to a prodigious number of ships of all kinds, we sailed for Cape Breton in Nova Scotia. We had the good and gallant General Wolfe on board our ship, whose affability made him highly esteemed and beloved by all the men. He often honoured me, as well as other boys, with marks of his notice; and saved me once a flogging for fighting with a young gentleman. We arrived at Cape Breton in the summer of 1758: and here the soldiers were to be landed, in order to make an attack upon Louisbourgh. My master had some part in superintending the landing; and here I was in a small measure gratified in seeing an encounter between our men and the enemy. The French were posted on the shore to receive us, and disputed our landing for a long time: but at last they were driven from their trenches, and a complete landing was effected. Our troops pursued them as far as the town of Louisbourgh. In this action many were killed on both sides. One thing remarkable I saw this day;—A lieutenant of the Princess Amelia, who, as well as my master, superintended the landing, was giving the word of command, and while his mouth was open a musket ball went through it, and passed out at his cheek. I had that day in my hand the scalp of an Indian king, who was killed in the engagement: the scalp had been taken off by an Highlander. I saw this king's ornaments too, which were very curious, and made of feathers.

Our land forces laid siege to the town of Louisbourgh, while the French men of war were blocked up in the harbour by the fleet, the batteries at the same time playing upon them from the land. This they did with such effect, that one day I saw some of the ships set on fire by the shells from the batteries, and I believe two or three of them were quite burnt. At another time, about fifty boats belonging to the English men of war, commanded by Captain George Balfour of the Aetna fireship, and Mr. Laforey, another junior captain, attacked and boarded the only two remaining French men of war in the harbour. They also set fire to a seventy-gun ship, but they brought off a sixty-four, called the Bienfaisant. During my stay here I had often an opportunity of being near Captain Balfour, who was pleased to notice me, and liked me so much that he often asked my master to let him have me, but he would not part with me; and no consideration would have induced me to leave him. At last Louisbourgh was taken, and the English men of war came into the harbour before it, to my very great joy; for I had now more liberty of indulging myself, and I went often on shore. When the ships were in the harbour, we had the most beautiful procession on the water I ever saw. All the admirals and captains of the men of war, full dressed, and in their barges, well ornamented with pendants, came alongside of the Namur. The Vice-admiral then went on shore in his barge, followed by the other officers in order of seniority, to take possession, as I suppose, of the town and fort. Some time after this the French governor and his lady, and other persons of note, came on board our ship to dine. On this occasion our ships were dressed with colours of all kinds, from the topgallant-mast head to the deck; and this, with the firing of guns, formed a most grand and magnificent spectacle.

As soon as every thing here was settled, Admiral Boscawen sailed with part of the fleet for England, leaving some ships behind with Rear Admirals Sir Charles Hardy and Durell. It was now winter; and one evening, during our passage home, about dusk, when we were in the channel, or near soundings, and were beginning to look for land, we descried seven sail of large men of war, which stood off shore. Several people on board of our ship said, as the two fleets were (in forty minutes from the first sight) within hail of each other, that they were English men of war; and some of our people even began to name some of the ships. By this time both fleets began to mingle, and our admiral ordered his flag to be hoisted. At that instant, the other fleet, which were French, hoisted their ensigns, and gave us a broadside as they passed by. Nothing could create greater surprise and confusion among us than this. The wind was high, the sea rough, and we had our lower and middle deck guns housed in, so that not a single gun on board was ready to be fired at any of the French ships. However, the Royal William and the Somerset, being our sternmost ships, became a little prepared, and each gave the French ships a broadside as they passed by. I afterwards heard this was a French squadron, commanded by Mons. Conflans; and certainly had the Frenchman known our condition, and had a mind to fight us, they might have done us great mischief. But we were not long before we were prepared for an engagement. Immediately many things were tossed overboard; the ships were made ready for fighting as soon as possible; and about ten at night we had bent a new main sail, the old one being split. Being now in readiness for fighting, we wore ship, and stood after the French fleet, who were one or two ships in number more than we. However, we gave them chase, and continued pursuing them all night; and at day-light we saw six of them, all large ships of the line, and an English East-Indiaman, a prize they had taken. We chased them all day till between three and four o'clock in the evening, when we came up with, and passed within a musquet shot of one seventy-four gun ship and the Indiaman also, who now hoisted her colours, but immediately hauled them down again. On this we made a signal for the other ships to take possession of her; and, supposing the man of war would likewise strike, we cheered, but she did not; though if we had fired into her, from being so near, we must have taken her. To my utter surprise the Somerset, who was the next ship a-stern of the Namur, made way likewise; and, thinking they were sure of this French ship, they cheered in the same manner, but still continued to follow us. The French Commodore was about a gun-shot a-head of all, running from us with all speed; and about four o'clock he carried his fore-top-mast overboard. This caused another loud cheer with us; and a little after the top-mast came close by us; but, to our great surprise, instead of coming up with her, we found she went as fast as ever, if not faster. The sea grew now much smoother; and the wind lulling, the seventy-four gun ship we had passed came again by us in the very same direction, and so near, that we heard her people talk as she went by; yet not a shot was fired on either side; and about five or six o'clock, just as it grew dark, she joined her Commodore. We chased all night; but the next day they were out of sight, so that we saw no more of them; and we only had the old Indiaman (called Carnarvon I think) for our trouble. After this, we stood in for the channel, and soon made the land; and, about the close of the year 1758–9, we got safe to St. Helen's. Here the Namur ran a-ground; and also another large ship a-stern of us; but, by starting our water, and tossing many things overboard to lighten her, we got the ships off without any damage. We stayed for a short time at Spithead, and then went into Portsmouth harbour to refit; from whence the Admiral went to London; and my master and I soon followed, with a press-gang, as we wanted some hands to complete our complement.

CHAP. IV.

The Author is baptized—Narrowly escapes drowning—Goes on an expedition to the Mediterranean—Incidents he met with there—Is witness to an engagement between some English and French ships—A particular account of the celebrated engagement between Admiral Boscawen and Mons. Le Clue, off Cape Logas, in August 1759—Dreadful explosion of a French ship—The Author sails for England—His master appointed to the command of a fire-ship—Meets a negro boy, from whom he experiences much benevolence—Prepares for an expedition against Belle-Isle—A remarkable story of a disaster which befel his ship—Arrives at Belle-Isle—Operations of the landing and siege—The Author's danger and distress, with his manner of extricating himself—Surrender of Belle-Isle—Transactions afterwards on the

coast of France—Remarkable instance of kidnapping—The
Author returns to England—Hears a talk of peace, and ex-
pects his freedom—His ship sails for Deptford to be paid off,
and when he arrives there he is suddenly seized by his master,
and carried forcibly on board a West India ship, and sold.

It was now between three and four years since I first
came to England, a great part of which I had spent at sea; so
that I became inured to that service, and began to consider
myself as happily situated; for my master treated me always
extremely well; and my attachment and gratitude to him
were very great. From the various scenes I had beheld on
shipboard, I soon grew a stranger to terror of every kind, and
was, in that respect at least, almost an Englishman. I have
often reflected with surprise that I never felt half the alarm
at any of the numerous dangers I have been in, that I was
filled with at the first sight of the Europeans, and at every
act of theirs, even the most trifling, when I first came among
them, and for some time afterwards. That fear, however,
which was the effect of my ignorance, wore away as I began
to know them. I could now speak English tolerably well, and
I perfectly understood every thing that was said. I now not
only felt myself quite easy with these new countrymen, but
relished their society and manners. I no longer looked upon
them as spirits, but as men superior to us; and therefore I
had the stronger desire to resemble them; to imbibe their
spirit, and imitate their manners; I therefore embraced
every occasion of improvement; and every new thing that I
observed I treasured up in my memory. I had long wished
to be able to read and write; and for this purpose I took
every opportunity to gain instruction, but had made as yet
very little progress. However, when I went to London with
my master, I had soon an opportunity of improving myself,
which I gladly embraced. Shortly after my arrival, he sent
me to wait upon the Miss Guerins, who had treated me with
much kindness when I was there before; and they sent me
to school.

While I was attending these ladies, their servants told
me I could not go to heaven, unless I was baptized. This

made me very uneasy; for I had now some faint idea of a future state: accordingly I communicated my anxiety to the eldest Miss Guerin, with whom I was become a favourite, and pressed her to have me baptized; when, to my great joy, she told me I should. She had formerly asked my master to let me be baptized, but he had refused; however, she now insisted on it; and he, being under some obligation to her brother, complied with her request; so I was baptized at St. Margaret's church, Westminster, in February 1759, by my present name. The clergyman, at the same time, gave me a book, called a guide to the Indians, written by the Bishop of Sodor and Man. On this occasion, Miss Guerin and her brother did me the honour to stand as godfather and godmother, and afterwards gave me a treat. I used to attend these ladies about the town, in which service I was extremely happy; as I had thus very many opportunities of seeing London, which I desired of all things. I was sometimes, however, with my master at his rendezvous-house, which was at the foot of Westminster bridge. Here I used to enjoy myself in playing about the bridge stairs, and often in the watermen's wherries with other boys. On one of these occasions there was another boy with me in a wherry, and we went out into the current of the river; while there, two more stout boys came to us in another wherry, and, abusing us for taking the boat, desired me to get into the other wherry-boat. Accordingly I went to get out of the wherry I was in; but just as I had got one of my feet into the other boat, the boys shoved it off, so that I fell into the Thames and, not being able to swim, I should unavoidably have been drowned, but for the assistance of some watermen, who providentially came to my relief.

The Namur being again got ready for sea, my master, with his gang, was ordered on board; and, to my no small grief, I was obliged to leave my school-master, whom I liked very much, and always attended while I stayed in London, to repair on board with my master. Nor did I leave my kind patronesses, the Miss Guerins, without uneasiness and regret. They often used to teach me to read, and took great pains to instruct me in the principles of religion, and the knowledge of God. I therefore parted from those amiable ladies with reluctance; after receiving from them many friendly cautions how to conduct myself, and some valuable presents.

When I came to Spithead, I found we were destined for the Mediterranean, with a large fleet, which was now ready to put to sea. We only waited for the arrival of the admiral, who soon came on board; and about the beginning of the spring 1759, having weighed anchor and got under way, sailed for the Mediterranean; and in eleven days from the Land's End, we got to Gibraltar. While we were here I used to be often on shore, and got various fruits in great plenty, and very cheap.

I had frequently told several people, in my excursions on shore, the story of my being kidnapped with my sister, and of our being separated, as I have related before; and I had as often expressed my anxiety for her fate, and my sorrow at having never met her again. One day, when I was on shore, and mentioning these circumstances to some persons, one of them told me he knew where my sister was, and if I would accompany him, he would bring me to her. Improbable as this story was, I believed it immediately, and agreed to go with him, while my heart leaped for joy; and, indeed, he conducted me to a black young woman, who was so like my sister that, at first sight, I really thought it was she; but I was quickly undeceived; and, on talking to her, I found her to be of another nation.

While we lay here the Preston came in from the Levant. As soon as she arrived, my master told me I should now see my old companion Dick, who was gone in her when she sailed for Turkey. I was much rejoiced at this information, and expected every minute to embrace him; and when the captain came on board of our ship, which he did immediately after, I ran to enquire about my friend; but, with inexpressible sorrow, I learned from the boat's crew that the dear youth was dead! and that they had brought his chest, and all his other things to my master: these he afterwards gave to me, and I regarded them as a memorial of my friend, whom I loved and grieved for as a brother.

While we were at Gibraltar I saw a soldier hanging by

the heels at one of the moles. I thought this a strange sight, as I had seen a man hanged in London by his neck. At another time I saw the master of a frigate towed to shore on a grating, by several of the men of war's boats, and discharged the fleet, which I understood was a mark of disgrace for cowardice. On board the same ship a sailor was also hung up at the main-yard-arm.

After lying at Gibraltar for some time, we sailed up the Mediterranean, a considerable way above the gulf of Lyons: where we were one night overtaken by a terrible gale of wind, much greater than any I had ever yet experienced. The sea ran so high that, though all the guns were well housed, there was great reason to fear their getting loose, the ship rolled so much; and if they had, it must have proved our destruction. After we had cruised here for a short time, we came to Barcelona, a Spanish sea-port, remarkable for its silk manufactories. Here the ships were all to be watered; and my master, who spoke different languages, and used often to interpret for the admiral, superintended the watering of ours. For that purpose he and the officers of the other ships, who were on the same service, had tents pitched in the bay; and the Spanish soldiers were stationed along the shore, I suppose to see that no depredations were committed by our men.

I used constantly to attend my master, and I was charmed with this place. All the time of our stay it was like a fair with the natives, who brought us fruits of all kinds, and sold them to us much cheaper than I had got them in England. They used also to bring wine down to us in hog and sheep skins, which diverted me very much. The Spanish officers here treated our officers with great politeness and attention; and some of them, in particular, used to come often to my master's tent to visit him; where they did sometimes divert themselves by mounting me on the horses or mules, so that I could not fall, and setting them off at full gallop; my imperfect skill in horsemanship all the while affording them no small entertainment. After the ships were watered, we returned to our old station of cruizing off Toulon, for the purpose of intercepting a fleet of French men of war that lay there. One Sunday, in our cruize, we came off a place where there were two small French frigates lying in shore; and our admiral, thinking to take or destroy them, sent two ships in after them—the Culloden and the Conqueror. They soon came up to the Frenchmen, and I saw a smart fight here, both by sea and land: for the frigates were covered by batteries, and they played upon our ships most furiously, which they as furiously returned, and for a long time a constant firing was kept up, on all sides, at an amazing rate. At last one frigate sunk; but the people escaped, though not without much difficulty: and a little after some of the people left the other frigate also, which was a mere wreck. However, our ships did not venture to bring her away, they were so much annoyed from the batteries, which raked them both in going and coming; their top-masts were shot away, and they were otherwise so much shattered, that the admiral was obliged to send in many boats to tow them back to the fleet. I afterwards sailed with a man who fought in one of the French batteries during the engagement, and he told me our ships had done considerable mischief that day on shore, and in the batteries.

After this we sailed for Gibraltar, and arrived there about August 1759. Here we remained with all our sails unbent, while the fleet was watering and doing other necessary things. While we were in this situation, one day the admiral, with most of the principal officers, and many people of all stations, being on shore, about seven o'clock in the evening we were alarmed by signals from the frigates stationed for that purpose; and in an instant there was a general cry that the French fleet was out, and just passing through the streights. The admiral immediately came on board with some other officers; and it is impossible to describe the noise, hurry, and confusion, throughout the whole fleet, in bending their sails, and slipping their cables; many people and ship's boats were left on shore in the bustle. We had two captains on board of our ship, who came away in the hurry and left their ships to follow. We shewed lights from the gun-wales to the main-top-mast-head; and all our lieutenants were employed amongst the fleet to tell the ships not to wait for their captains, but to put the sails to the yards, slip their cables and follow us; and in this confusion of making ready for fighting, we set out for sea in the dark

after the French fleet. Here I could have exclaimed with
Ajax,

> Oh Jove! O father! if it be thy will
> That we must perish, we thy will obey,
> But let us perish by the light of day.

They had got the start of us so far that we were not able to
come up with them during the night; but at day-light we saw
seven sail of ships of the line some miles a-head. We immediately chased them till about four o'clock in the evening,
when our ships came up with them; and though we were
about fifteen large ships, our gallant admiral only fought
them with his own division, which consisted of seven; so that
we were just ship for ship. We passed by the whole of the
enemy's fleet in order to come at their commander, Mons.
La Clue, who was in the Ocean, an eighty-four gun ship: as
we passed they all fired on us; and at one time three of them
fired together, continuing to do so for some time. Notwithstanding which our admiral would not suffer a gun to be
fired at any of them, to my astonishment; but made us lie on
our bellies on the deck till we came quite close to the Ocean,
who was a-head of them all; when we had orders to pour the
whole three tiers into her at once.

The engagement now commenced with great fury on
both sides: the Ocean immediately returned our fire, and we
continued engaged with each other for some time; during
which I was frequently stunned with the thundering of the
great guns, whose dreadful contents hurried many of my
companions into awful eternity. At last the French line was
entirely broken, and we obtained the victory, which was immediately proclaimed with loud huzzas and acclamations.
We took three prizes, La Modeste, of sixty-four guns, and
Le Temeraire and Centaur, of seventy-four guns each. The
rest of the French ships took to flight with all the sail they
could crowd. Our ship being very much damaged, and quite
disabled from pursuing the enemy, the admiral immediately
quitted her, and went in the broken, and only boat we had
left, on board the Newark, with which, and some other
ships, he went after the French. The Ocean, and another
large French ship, called the Redoutable, endeavouring to

escape, ran ashore at Cape Logas, on the coast of Portugal; and the French admiral and some of the crew got ashore; but we, finding it impossible to get the ships off, set fire to them both. About midnight I saw the Ocean blow up, with a most dreadful explosion. I never beheld a more awful scene. About the space of a minute, the midnight seemed turned into day by the blaze, which was attended with a noise louder and more terrible than thunder, that seemed to rend every element around us.

My station during the engagement was on the middle deck, where I was quartered with another boy, to bring powder to the aftermost gun; and here I was a witness of the dreadful fate of many of my companions, who, in the twinkling of an eye, were dashed in pieces, and launched into eternity. Happily I escaped unhurt, though the shot and splinters flew thick about me during the whole fight. Towards the latter part of it my master was wounded, and I saw him carried down to the surgeon; but, though I was much alarmed for him, and wished to assist him, I dared not leave my post. At this station my gun-mate (a partner in bringing powder for the same gun) and I ran a very great risk for more than half an hour of blowing up the ship. For, when we had taken the cartridges out of the boxes, the bottoms of many of them proving rotten, the powder ran all about the deck, near the match-tub: we scarcely had water enough at the last to throw on it. We were also, from our employment, very much exposed to the enemy's shots; for we had to go through nearly the whole length of the ship to bring the powder. I expected therefore every minute to be my last; especially when I saw our men fall so thick about me; but, wishing to guard as much against the dangers as possible, at first I thought it would be safest not to go for the powder till the Frenchmen had fired their broadside; and then, while they were charging, I could go and come with my powder: but immediately afterwards I thought this caution was fruitless; and, cheering myself with the reflection that there was a time allotted for me to die as well as to be born, I instantly cast off all fear or thought whatever of death, and went through the whole of my duty with alacrity; pleasing myself with the hope, if I survived the battle, of relating it and the dangers I had es-

caped to the Miss Guerins, and others, when I should return to London.

Our ship suffered very much in this engagement; for, besides the number of our killed and wounded, she was almost torn to pieces, and our rigging so much shattered, that
our mizen-mast, main-yard, &c. hung over the side of the
ship; so that we were obliged to get many carpenters and
others, from some of the ships of the fleet, to assist in setting
us in some tolerable order; and, notwithstanding which, it
took us some time before we were completely refitted; after
which we left Admiral Broderick to command, and we, with
the prizes, steered for England. On the passage, and as soon
as my master was something recovered of his wounds, the
Admiral appointed him captain of the Aetna fire-ship, on
which he and I left the Namur, and went on board of her at
sea. I liked this small ship very much. I now became the
captain's steward, in which situation I was very happy, for I
was extremely well treated by all on board, and I had leisure to improve myself in reading and writing. The latter I
had learned a little before I left the Namur, as there was a
school on board. When we arrived at Spithead, the Aetna
went into Portsmouth harbour to refit, which being done,
we returned to Spithead, and joined a large fleet that was
thought to be intended against the Havannah. But about
that time the king died; whether that prevented the expedition I know not; but it caused our ship to be stationed at
Cowes, in the Isle of Wight, till the beginning of the year
sixty-one. Here I spent my time very pleasantly; I was much
on shore all about this delightful island, and found the inhabitants very civil.

While I was here, I met with a trifling incident which surprised me agreeably. I was one day in a field belonging to a
gentleman who had a black boy about my own size; this boy
having observed me from his master's house, was transported at the sight of one of his own countrymen, and ran
to meet me with the utmost haste. I not knowing what he
was about, turned a little out of his way at first, but to no
purpose; he soon came close to me, and caught hold of me
in his arms as if I had been his brother, though we had never
seen each other before. After we had talked together for
some time, he took me to his master's house, where I was

treated very kindly. This benevolent boy and I were very happy in frequently seeing each other, till about the month of March 1761, when our ship had orders to fit out again for another expedition. When we got ready, we joined a very large fleet at Spithead, commanded by Commodore Keppel, destined against Belle-Isle; and having a number of transport ships in company, with troops on board, to make a descent on the place, we sailed once more in quest of fame. I longed to engage in new adventures, and to see fresh wonders.

I had a mind on which every thing uncommon made its full impression, and every event which I considered as marvellous. Every extraordinary escape, or signal deliverance, either of myself or others, I looked upon to be effected by the interposition of Providence. We had not been above ten days at sea before an incident of this kind happened; which, whatever credit it may obtain from the reader, made no small impression upon my mind.

We had on board a gunner, whose name was John Mondle, a man of very indifferent morals. This man's cabin was between the decks, exactly over where I lay, a-breast of the quarter-deck ladder. One night, the 5th of April, being terrified with a dream, he awoke in so great a fright that he could not rest in his bed any longer, nor even remain in his cabin; and he went upon deck about four o'clock in the morning extremely agitated. He immediately told those upon the deck of the agonies of his mind, and the dream which occasioned it; in which he said he had seen many things very awful, and had been warned by St. Peter to repent, who told him his time was short. This he said had greatly alarmed him, and he was determined to alter his life. People generally mock the fears of others when they are themselves in safety; and some of his shipmates who heard him only laughed at him. However, he made a vow that he never would drink strong liquors again; and he immediately got a light, and gave away his sea-stores of liquor. After which, his agitation still continuing, he began to read the scriptures, hoping to find some relief; and soon afterwards he laid himself down again on his bed, and endeavoured to compose himself to sleep, but to no purpose; his mind still continuing in a state of agony. By this time it was exactly half after seven in the morning; I was then under the half deck at the great cabin door; and all at once I heard the people in the waist cry out most fearfully— "The Lord have mercy upon us! We are all lost! The Lord have mercy upon us!"—Mr. Mondle hearing the cries, immediately ran out of his cabin; and we were instantly struck by the Lynne, a forty-gun ship, Captain Clerk, which nearly ran us down. This ship had just put about, and was by the wind, but had not got full head-way, or we must all have perished; for the wind was brisk. However, before Mr. Mondle had got four steps from his cabin door, she struck our ship, with her cutwater, right in the middle of his bed and cabin, and ran it up to the combings of the quarter deck hatchway, and above three feet below water, and in a minute there was not a bit of wood to be seen where Mr. Mondle's cabin stood; and he was so near being killed, that some of the splinters tore his face. As Mr. Mondle must inevitably have perished from this accident, had he not been alarmed in the very extraordinary way I have related, I could not help regarding this as an awful interposition of Providence for his preservation. The two ships for some time swinged alongside of each other; for ours being a fire-ship, our grappling-irons caught the Lynne every way, and the yards and rigging went at an astonishing rate. Our ship was in such a shocking condition that we all thought she would instantly go down, and every one ran for their lives, and got as well as they could on board the Lynne; but our lieutenant being the aggressor, he never quitted the ship. However, when we found she did not sink, immediately, the captain came on board again and encouraged our people to return and try to save her. Many of them came back, but some would not venture. Some of the ships in the fleet, seeing our situation, immediately sent their boats to our assistance; but it took us the whole day to save the ship with all their help. And by using every possible means, particularly frapping her together with many hawsers, and putting a great quantity of tallow below water where she was damaged, she was kept together; but it was well we did not meet with any gales of wind, or we must have gone to pieces; for we were in such a crazy condition that we had ships to attend us till we arrived at Belle-Isle, the place of our destination; and then we had all things taken out of the ship, and she was properly repaired. This escape of Mr. Mondle, which he, as well as myself, always considered as a singular act of Providence, I believe had a great influence on his life and conduct ever afterwards.

Now that I am on this subject, I beg leave to relate another instance or two which strongly raised my belief of the particular interposition of Heaven, and which might not otherwise have found a place here, from their insignificance. I belonged for a few days, in the year 1758, to the Jason, of fifty-four guns, at Plymouth; and one night, when I was on board, a woman, with a child at her breast, fell from the upper deck down into the hold, near the keel. Every one thought that the mother and child must be both dashed to pieces; but, to our great surprise, neither of them was hurt. I myself one day fell headlong from the upper deck of the Aetna down the after-hold, when the ballast was out; and all who saw me fall called out I was killed; but I received not the least injury. And in the same ship a man fell from the mast-head on the deck without being hurt. In these, and in many more instances, I thought I could very plainly trace the hand of God, without whose permission a sparrow cannot fall. I began to raise my fear from man to him alone, and to call daily on his holy name with fear and reverence: and I trust he heard my supplications, and graciously condescended to answer me according to his holy word, and to implant the seeds of piety in me, even one of the meanest of his creatures.

When we had refitted our ship, and all things were in readiness for attacking the place, the troops on board the transports were ordered to disembark; and my master, as a junior captain, had a share in the command of the landing. This was on the 12th of April. The French were drawn up on the shore, and had made every disposition to oppose the landing of our men, only a small part of them this day being able to effect it; most of them, after fighting with great bravery, were cut off, and General Crawford, with a number of others, were taken prisoners. In this day's engagement we had also our lieutenant killed.

On the 21st of April we renewed our efforts to land the men, while all the men of war were stationed along the

shore to cover it, and fired at the French batteries and
breastworks, from early in the morning till about four
o'clock in the evening, when our soldiers effected a safe
landing. They immediately attacked the French; and, after a
sharp encounter, forced them from the batteries. Before the
enemy retreated, they blew up several of them, lest they
should fall into our hands. Our men then proceeded to besiege the citadel, and my master was ordered on shore to
superintend the landing of all the materials necessary for
carrying on the siege; in this service I mostly attended him.
While I was there I went about to different parts of the island; and one day, particularly, my curiosity almost cost me
my life. I wanted very much to see the mode of charging the
mortars, and letting off the shells, and for that purpose I
went to an English battery that was but a very few yards
from the walls of the citadel. There indeed I had an opportunity of completely gratifying myself in seeing the whole
operation, and that not without running a very great risk,
both from the English shells that burst while I was there,
but likewise from those of the French. One of the largest of
their shells bursted within nine or ten yards of me: there
was a single rock close by, about the size of a butt; and I got
instant shelter under it in time to avoid the fury of the shell.
Where it burst the earth was torn in such a manner that two
or three butts might easily have gone into the hole it made,
and it threw great quantities of stones and dirt to a considerable distance. Three shot were also fired at me, and another boy who was along with me, one of them in particular
seemed

Wing'd with red lightning and impetuous rage;

for, with a most dreadful sound, it hissed close by me, and
struck a rock at a little distance, which it shattered to pieces.
When I saw what perilous circumstances I was in, I attempted to return the nearest way I could find, and thereby
I got between the English and the French centinels. An
English serjeant, who commanded the outposts, seeing me,
and surprised how I came there (which was by stealth along
the sea-shore), reprimanded me very severely for it, and
instantly took the centinel off his post into custody, for his

negligence in suffering me to pass the lines. While I was in this situation I observed at a little distance a French horse belonging to some islanders, which I thought I would now mount, for the greater expedition of getting off. Accordingly, I took some cord which I had about me, and making a kind of bridle of it, I put it round the horse's head, and the tame beast very quietly suffered me to tie him thus and mount him. As soon as I was on the horse's back I began to kick and beat him, and try every means to make him go quick, but all to very little purpose: I could not drive him out of a slow pace. While I was creeping along, still within reach of the enemy's shot, I met with a servant well mounted on an English horse. I immediately stopped; and, crying, told him my case; and begged of him to help me, and this he effectually did; for, having a fine large whip, he began to lash my horse with it so severely, that he set off full speed with me towards the sea, while I was quite unable to hold or manage him. In this manner I went along till I came to a craggy precipice. I now could not stop my horse; and my mind was filled with apprehensions of my deplorable fate, should he go down the precipice, which he appeared fully disposed to do: I therefore thought I had better throw myself off him at once, which I did immediately with a great deal of dexterity, and fortunately escaped unhurt. As soon as I found myself at liberty, I made the best of my way for the ship, determined I would not be so fool-hardy again in a hurry.

We continued to besiege the citadel till June, when it surrendered. During the siege I have counted above sixty shells and carcases in the air at once. When this place was taken I went through the citadel, and in the bomb-proofs under it, which were cut in the solid rock; and I thought it a surprising place, both for strength and building: notwithstanding which our shots and shells had made amazing devastation, and ruinous heaps all around it.

After the taking of this island, our ships, with some others commanded by Commodore Stanhope, in the Swiftsure, went to Basse-road, where we blocked up a French fleet. Our ships were there from June till February following; and in that time I saw a great many scenes of war, and stratagems on both sides, to destroy each other's fleet. Sometimes we would attack the French with some ships of the line; at other times with boats; and frequently we made prizes. Once or twice the French attacked us, by throwing shells with their bomb-vessels; and one day, as a French vessel was throwing shells at our ships, she broke from 1er springs behind the Isle of Rhe: the tide being complicated, she came within a gun-shot of the Nassau; but the Nassau could not bring a gun to bear upon her, and thereby the Frenchman got off. We were twice attacked by their fire-floats, which they chained together, and then let them float down with the tide; but each time we sent boats with grapplings, and towed them safe out of the fleet.

We had different commanders while we were at this place, Commodores Stanhope, Dennis, Lord Howe, &c. From thence, before the Spanish war began, our ship and the Wasp sloop were sent to St. Sebastian, in Spain, by Commodore Stanhope; and Commodore Dennis afterwards sent our ship as a cartel to Bayonne in France; after which we went in February 1762, to Belle-Isle, and there stayed till the summer, then we left it, and returned to Portsmouth.

After our ship was fitted out again for service, in September she went to Guernsey, where I was very glad to see my old hostess, who was now a widow, and my former little charming companion her daughter. I spent some time here very happily with them, till October, when we had orders to repair to Portsmouth. We parted from each other with a great deal of affection, and I promised to return soon, and see them again, not knowing what all-powerful fate had determined for me. Our ship having arrived at Portsmouth, we went into the harbour, and remained there till the end of November, when we heard great talk about peace; and, to our very great joy, in the beginning of December we had orders to go up to London with our ship, to be paid off. We received this news with loud huzzas, and every other demonstration of gladness; and nothing but mirth was to be seen through every part of the ship. I too was not without my share of the general joy on this occasion. I thought now of nothing but being freed, and working for myself, and thereby getting money to enable me to get a good education; for I always had a great desire to be able at least to

read and write; and while I was on shipboard I had endeavoured to improve myself in both. While I was in the Aetna
particularly, the captain's clerk taught me to write, and gave
me a smattering of arithmetic as far as the rule of three.
There was also one Daniel Queen, about forty years of age,
a man very well educated, who messed with me on board
this ship, and he likewise dressed and attended the captain.
Fortunately this man soon became very much attached to
me, and took very great pains to instruct me in many things.
He taught me to shave and dress hair a little, and also to
read in the Bible, explaining many passages to me, which I
did not comprehend. I was wonderfully surprised to see the
laws and rules of my country written almost exactly here; a
circumstance which I believe tended to impress our manners and customs more deeply on my memory. I used to tell
him of this resemblance; and many a time we had sat up the
whole night together at this employment. In short he was
like a father to me; and some even used to call me after his
name; they also styled me the black Christian. Indeed I almost loved him with the affection of a son. Many things I
have denied myself that he might have them; and when I
used to play at marbles, or any other game, and won a few
halfpence, or got any little money, which I did sometimes,
for shaving any one, I used to buy him a little sugar or tobacco, as far as my stock of money would go. He used to say,
that he and I never should part; and that when our ship was
paid off, as I was as free as himself or any other man on
board, he would instruct me in his business, by which I
might gain a good livelihood. This gave me new life and
spirits, and my heart burned within me, while I thought the
time long till I obtained my freedom: for though my master
had not promised it to me, yet besides the assurances I had
received that he had no right to detain me, he always
treated me with the greatest kindness, and reposed in me an
unbounded confidence; he even paid attention to my morals; and would never suffer me to deceive him, or tell lies, of
which he used to tell me the consequences; and that if I did
so, God would not love me; so that from all this tenderness,
I had never once supposed, in all my dreams of freedom,
that he would think of detaining me any longer than I
wished.

In pursuance of our orders we sailed from Portsmouth for the Thames, and arrived at Deptford the 10th of December; where we cast anchor just as it was high water. The ship was up about half an hour, when my master ordered the barge to be manned; and all in an instant, without having before given me the least reason to suspect any thing of the matter, he forced me into the barge, saying, I was going to leave him, but he would take care I should not. I was so struck with the unexpectedness of this proceeding, that for some time I could not make a reply, only I made an offer to go for my books and chest of clothes, but he swore I should not move out of his sight; and if I did he would cut my throat, at the same time taking his hanger. I began, however, to collect myself: and, plucking up courage, I told him I was free, and he could not by law serve me so. But this only enraged him the more; and he continued to swear, and said he would soon let me know whether he would or not, and at that instant sprung himself into the barge from the ship, to the astonishment and sorrow of all on board. The tide, rather unluckily for me, had just turned downward, so that we quickly fell down the river along with it, till we came among some outward-bound West-Indiamen; for he was resolved to put me on board the first vessel he could get to receive me. The boat's crew, who pulled against their will, became quite faint at different times, and would have gone ashore; but he would not let them. Some of them strove then to cheer me, and told me he could not sell me, and that they would stand by me, which revived me a little, and encouraged my hopes; for as they pulled along he asked some vessels to receive me, and they would not. But, just as we had got a little below Gravesend, we came alongside of a ship which was going away the next tide for the West Indies; her name was the Charming Sally, Capt. James Doran; and my master went on board and agreed with him for me; and in a little time I was sent for into the cabin. When I came there, Captain Doran asked me if I knew him. I answered that I did not; "Then," said he, "you are now my slave." I told him my master could not sell me to him, nor to any one else. "Why," said he, "did not your master buy you?" I confessed he did. But I have served him, said I, many years, and he has taken all my wages and prize-money, for I only got one sixpence during the war; besides this I have been baptized; and by the laws of the land no man has a right to sell me: and I added, that I had heard a lawyer, and others at different times, tell my master so. They both then said that those people who told me so were not my friends: but I replied—It was very extraordinary that other people did not know the law as well as they. Upon this Captain Doran said I talked too much English; and if I did not behave myself well, and be quiet, he had a method on board to make me. I was too well convinced of his power over me to doubt what he said: and my former sufferings in the slave-ship presenting themselves to my mind, the recollection of them made me shudder. However, before I retired, I told them that as I could not get any right among men here, I hoped I should hereafter in Heaven; and I immediately left the cabin, filled with resentment and sorrow. The only coat I had with me my master took away with him, and said, "If your prize-money had been 10,000£ I had a right to it all, and would have taken it." I had about nine guineas, which during my long sea-faring life, I had scraped together from trifling perquisites and little ventures; and I hid it that instant, lest my master should take that from me likewise, still hoping that by some means or other I should make my escape to the shore, and indeed some of my old shipmates told me not to despair, for they would get me back again; and that, as soon as they could get their pay, they would immediately come to Portsmouth to me, where this ship was going: but, alas! all my hopes were baffled, and the hour of my deliverance was yet far off. My master, having soon concluded his bargain with the captain, came out of the cabin, and he and his people got into the boat, and put off; I followed them with aching eyes as long as I could, and when they were out of sight I threw myself on the deck, with a heart ready to burst with sorrow and anguish.

CHAP. V.

The Author's reflections on his situation—Is deceived by a promise of being delivered—His despair at sailing for the West-Indies—Arrives at Montserrat, where he is sold to Mr. King—Various interesting instances of oppression, cruelty, and extortion, which the Author saw practised upon the slaves in the West-Indies during his captivity, from the year 1763 to 1766—Address to the planters.

THUS, at the moment I expected all my toils to end, was I plunged, as I supposed, in a new slavery: in comparison of which all my service hitherto had been perfect freedom; and whose horrors, always present to my mind, now rushed on it with tenfold aggravation. I wept very bitterly for some time: and began to think that I must have done something to displease the Lord, that he thus punished me so severely. This filled me with painful reflections on my past conduct; I recollected that on the morning of our arrival at Deptford I had rashly sworn that as soon as we reached London I would spend the day in rambling and sport. My conscience smote me for this unguarded expression: I felt that the Lord was able to disappoint me in all things, and immediately considered my present situation as a judgment of Heaven on account of my presumption in swearing: I therefore, with contrition of heart, acknowledged my transgression to God, and poured out my soul before him with unfeigned repentance, and with earnest supplications I besought him not to abandon me in my distress, nor cast me from his mercy for ever. In a little time my grief, spent with its own violence, began to subside; and after the first confusion of my thoughts was over, I reflected with more calmness on my present condition: I considered that trials and disappointments are sometimes for our good, and I thought God might perhaps have permitted this in order to teach me wisdom and resignation; for he had hitherto shadowed me with the wings of his mercy, and by his invisible but powerful hand brought me the way I knew not. These reflections gave me a little comfort, and I rose at last from the deck with dejection and sorrow in my countenance, yet mixed with some faint hope that the *Lord would appear* for my deliverance.

Soon afterwards, as my new master was going ashore, he called me to him, and told me to behave myself well, and do the business of the ship the same as any of the rest of the boys, and that I should fare the better for it; but I made him no answer. I was then asked if I could swim, and I said, No. However I was made to go under the deck, and was well watched. The next tide the ship got under way, and soon after arrived at the Mother Bank, Portsmouth; where she waited a few days for some of the West India convoy. While I was here I tried every means I could devise among the people of the ship to get me a boat from the shore, as there was none suffered to come along side of the ship; and their own, whenever it was used, was hoisted in again immediately. A sailor on board took a guinea from me on pretence of getting me a boat; and promised me, time after time, that it was hourly to come off. When he had the watch upon deck I watched also; and looked long enough, but all in vain; I could never see either the boat or my guinea again. And what I thought was still the worst of all, the fellow gave information, as I afterwards found, all the while to the mates of my intention to go off, if I could in any way do it; but, rogue-like, he never told them he had got a guinea from me to procure my escape. However, after we had sailed, and his trick was made known to the ship's crew, I had some satisfaction in seeing him detested and despised by them all for his behaviour to me. I was still in hopes that my old shipmates would not forget their promise to come for me to Portsmouth; and they did at last, but not till the day before we sailed, some of them did come there, and sent me off some oranges, and other tokens of their regard. They also sent me off word they would come off to me themselves the next day or the day after; and a lady also, who lived in Gosport, wrote to me that she would come and take me out of the ship at the same time. This lady had been once very intimate with my former master; I used to sell and take care of a great deal of property for her in different ships; and in return she always shewed great friendship for me; and used to tell my master that she would take me away to live with her: but unfortunately for me, a disagreement soon afterwards took place between them; and she was succeeded in my master's good graces by another lady, who appeared sole mistress of the Aetna, and mostly lodged on board. I was not so great a favourite with this lady as with the former; she had conceived a pique against me on some occasion when she was on board, and she did not fail to instigate my master to treat me in the manner he did.

However the next morning, the 30th of December, the wind being brisk and easterly, the Aeolus frigate, which was to escort the convoy, made a signal for sailing. All the ships then got up their anchors; and, before any of my friends had an opportunity to come off to my relief, to my inexpressible anguish, our ship had got under way. What tumultuous emotions agitated my soul when the convoy got under sail, and I, a prisoner on board, now without hope! I kept my swimming eyes upon the land in a state of unutterable grief; not knowing what to do, and despairing how to help myself. While my mind was in this situation, the fleet sailed on, and in one day's time I lost sight of the wished-for land. In the first expressions of my grief I reproached my fate, and wished I had never been born. I was ready to curse the tide that bore us, the gale that wafted my prison, and even the ship that conducted us; and I called on death to relieve me from the horrors I felt and dreaded, that I might be in that place

> Where slaves are free, and men oppress no more,
> Fool that I was, inur'd so long to pain,
> To trust to hope, or dream of joy again.
>
> * * * * * * * * * *
>
> Now dragg'd once more beyond the western main,
> To groan beneath some dastard planter's chain;
> Where my poor countrymen in bondage wait
> The long enfranchisement of a ling'ring fate:
> Hard ling'ring fate! while, ere the dawn of day,
> Rous'd by the lash, they go their cheerless way;
> And as their souls with shame and anguish burn,
> Salute with groans unwelcome morn's return,
> And, chiding ev'ry hour the slow-pac'd sun,

> Pursue their toils till all his race is run.
> No eye to mark their suff'rings with a tear;
> No friend to comfort, and no hope to cheer:
> Then, like the dull unpity'd brutes, repair
> To stalls as wretched, and as coarse a fare;
> Thank heaven one day of mis'ry was o'er,
> Then sink to sleep, and wish to wake no more.

The turbulence of my emotions, however, naturally gave way to calmer thoughts, and I soon perceived what fate had decreed no mortal on earth could prevent. The convoy sailed on without any accident, with a pleasant gale and smooth sea, for six weeks, till February, when one morning the Aeolus ran down a brig, one of the convoy, and she instantly went down and was ingulfed in the dark recesses of the ocean. The convoy was immediately thrown into great confusion till it was day-light; and the Aeolus was illuminated with lights to prevent any farther mischief. On the 13th of February 1763, from the mast-head, we descried our destined island Montserrat; and soon after I beheld those

> Regions of sorrow, doleful shades, where peace
> And rest can rarely dwell. Hope never comes
> That comes to all, but torture without end
> Still urges.

At the sight of this land of bondage, a fresh horror ran through all my frame, and chilled me to the heart. My former slavery now rose in dreadful review to my mind, and displayed nothing but misery, stripes, and chains; and, in the first paroxysm of my grief, I called upon God's thunder, and his avenging power, to direct the stroke of death to me, rather than permit me to become a slave, and to be sold from lord to lord.

In this state of my mind our ship came to an anchor, and soon after discharged her cargo. I now knew what it was to work hard; I was made to help to unload and load the ship. And, to comfort me in my distress in that time, two of the sailors robbed me of all my money, and ran away from the ship. I had been so long used to an European climate that at first I felt the scorching West-India sun very painful, while the dashing surf would toss the boat and the people in it frequently above high-water mark. Sometimes our limbs were broken with this, or even attended with instant death, and I was day by day mangled and torn.

About the middle of May, when the ship was got ready to sail for England, I all the time believing that Fate's blackest clouds were gathering over my head, and expecting their bursting would mix me with the dead, Captain Doran sent for me ashore one morning, and I was told by the messenger that my fate was then determined. With trembling steps and fluttering heart I came to the captain, and found with him one Mr. Robert King, a Quaker and the first merchant in the place. The captain then told me my former master had sent me there to be sold; but that he had desired him to get me the best master he could, as he told him I was a very deserving boy, which Captain Doran said he found to be true, and if he were to stay in the West Indies he would be glad to keep me himself; but he could not venture to take me to London, for he was very sure that when I came there I would leave him. I at that instant burst out a crying, and begged much of him to take me to England with him, but all to no purpose. He told me he had got me the very best master in the whole island, with whom I should be as happy as if I were in England, and for that reason he chose to let him have me, though he could sell me to his own brother-in-law for a great deal more money than what he got from this gentleman. Mr. King, my new master, then made a reply, and said the reason he had bought me was on account of my good character; and, as he had not the least doubt of my good behaviour, I should be very well off with him. He also told me he did not live in the West Indies, but at Philadelphia, where he was going soon; and, as I understood something of the rules of arithmetic, when we got there he would put me to school, and fit me for a clerk. This conversation relieved my mind a little, and I left those gentlemen considerably more at ease in myself than when I came to them; and I was very thankful to Captain Doran, and even to my old master, for the character they had given me; a character which I afterwards found of infinite service to me. I went on board again, and took my leave of all my shipmates; and the next day the ship sailed. When she weighed

anchor I went to the waterside and looked at her with a
very wishful and aching heart, and followed her with my
eyes until she was totally out of sight. I was so bowed down
with grief that I could not hold up my head for many
months; and if my new master had not been kind to me, I
believe I should have died under it at last. And indeed I
soon found that he fully deserved the good character which
Captain Doran had given me of him; for he possessed a
most amiable disposition and temper, and was very charitable and humane. If any of his slaves behaved amiss, he did
not beat or use them ill, but parted with them. This made
them afraid of disobliging him; and as he treated his slaves
better than any other man on the island, so he was better
and more faithfully served by them in return. By this kind
treatment I did at last endeavour to compose myself; and
with fortitude, though moneyless, determined to face whatever fate had decreed for me. Mr. King soon asked me what
I could do; and at the same time said he did not mean to
treat me as a common slave. I told him I knew something of
seamanship, and could shave and dress hair pretty well; and
I could refine wines, which I had learned on shipboard,
where I had often done it; and that I could write, and understood arithmetic tolerably well as far as the Rule of Three.
He then asked me if I knew any thing of gauging; and, on
my answering that I did not, he said one of his clerks should
teach me to gauge.

Mr. King dealt in all manner of merchandize, and kept
from one to six clerks. He loaded many vessels in a year;
particularly to Philadelphia, where he was born, and was
connected with a great mercantile house in that city. He had
besides many vessels and droggers of different sizes, which
used to go about the island and other places to collect rum,
sugar, and other goods. I understood pulling and managing
those boats very well; and this hard work, which was the first
that he set me to, in the sugar seasons, used to be my constant employment. I have rowed the boat, and slaved at the
oars, from one hour to sixteen in the twenty-four; during
which I had fifteen pence sterling per day to live on, though
sometimes only ten pence. However, this was considerably
more than was allowed to other slaves that used to work
often with me, and belonged to other gentlemen on the is-

land: these poor souls had never more than nine-pence a day, and seldom more than six-pence, from their masters or owners, though they earned them three or four pisterines a day: for it is a common practice in the West Indies, for men to purchase slaves, though they have not plantations themselves, in order to let them out to planters and merchants, at so much a-piece by the day, and they give what allowance they choose out of this produce of their daily work to their slaves for subsistence; this allowance is often very scanty. My master often gave the owners of those slaves two and a half of these pieces per day, and found the poor fellows in victuals himself, because he thought their owners did not feed them well enough according to the work they did. The slaves used to like this very well, and as they knew my master to be a man of feeling, they were always glad to work for him in preference to any other gentleman; some of whom, after they had been paid for these poor people's labours, would not give them their allowance out of it. Many times have I seen these unfortunate wretches beaten for asking for their pay; and often severely flogged by their owners if they did not bring them their daily or weekly money exactly to the time; though the poor creatures were obliged to wait on the gentlemen they had worked for, sometimes more than half the day, before they could get their pay; and this generally on Sundays, when they wanted the time for themselves. In particular, I knew a countryman of mine, who once did not bring the weekly money directly that it was earned; and though he brought it the same day to his master, yet he was staked to the ground for his pretended negligence, and was just going to receive a hundred lashes, but for a gentleman who begged him off fifty. This poor man was very industrious, and by his frugality had saved so much money, by working on shipboard, that he had got a white man to buy him a boat, unknown to his master. Some time after he had this little estate, the governor wanted a boat to bring his sugar from different parts of the island; and, knowing this to be a negro-man's boat, he seized upon it for himself, and would not pay the owner a farthing. The man on this went to his master, and complained to him of this act of the governor; but the only satisfaction he received was to be damned very heartily by his master, who asked him how dared any of his negroes to have a boat. If the justly-merited ruin of the governor's fortune could be any gratification to the poor man he had thus robbed, he was not without consolation. Extortion and rapine are poor providers; and some time after this, the governor died in the King's Bench, in England, as I was told, in great poverty. The last war favoured this poor negro-man, and he found some means to escape from his Christian master; he came to England, where I saw him afterwards several times. Such treatment as this often drives these miserable wretches to despair, and they run away from their masters at the hazard of their lives. Many of them in this place, unable to get their pay when they have earned it, and fearing to be flogged as usual, if they return home without it, run away where they can for shelter, and a reward is often offered to bring them in dead or alive. My master used sometimes in these cases, to agree with their owners, and to settle with them himself; and thereby he saved many of them a flogging.

Once, for a few days, I was let out to fit a vessel, and I had no victuals allowed me by either party; at last I told my master of this treatment, and he took me away from him. In many of the estates, on the different islands where I used to be sent for rum or sugar, they would not deliver it to me, or to any other negro; he was therefore obliged to send a white man along with me to those places; and then he used to pay him from six to ten pisterines a day. From being thus employed, during the time I served Mr. King, in going about the different estates on the island, I had all the opportunity I could wish for, to see the dreadful usage of the poor men; usage that reconciled me to my situation, and made me bless God for the hands into which I had fallen.

I had the good fortune to please my master in every department in which he employed me; and there was scarcely any part of his business, or household affairs, in which I was not occasionally engaged. I often supplied the place of a clerk, in receiving and delivering cargoes to the ships, in tending stores, and delivering goods; and, besides this, I used to shave and dress my master when convenient, and take care of his horse; and when it was necessary, which was very often, I worked likewise on board of different vessels of his. By these means I became very useful to my master, and saved him, as he used to acknowledge, above a hundred pounds a year. Nor did he scruple to say I was of more advantage to him than any of his clerks; though their usual wages in the West Indies are from sixty to a hundred pounds current a year.

I have sometimes heard it asserted, that a negro cannot earn his master the first cost; but nothing can be further from the truth. I suppose nine tenths of the mechanics throughout the West Indies are negro slaves; and I well know the coopers among them earn two dollars a day; the carpenters the same, and oftentimes more; also the masons, smiths, and fishermen, &c. and I have known many slaves whose masters would not take a thousand pounds current for them. But surely this assertion refutes itself; for, if it be true, why do the planters and merchants pay such a price for slaves? And, above all, why do those, who make this assertion, exclaim the most loudly against the abolition of the slave trade? So much are we blinded, and to such inconsistent arguments are they driven by mistaken interest! I grant, indeed, that slaves are sometimes, by half-feeding, half-cloathing, overworking, and stripes, reduced so low, that they are turned out as unfit for service, and left to perish in the woods, or expire on a dunghill.

My master was several times offered by different gentlemen one hundred guineas for me; but he always told them he would not sell me, to my great joy: and I used to double my diligence and care for fear of getting into the hands of those men who did not allow a valuable slave the common support of life. Many of them used to find fault with my master for feeding his slaves so well as he did; although I often went hungry, and an Englishman might think my fare very indifferent; but he used to tell them he always would do it, because the slaves thereby looked better and did more work.

While I was thus employed by my master, I was often a witness to cruelties of every kind, which were exercised on my unhappy fellow slaves. I used frequently to have different cargoes of new negroes in my care for sale; and it was almost a constant practice with our clerks, and other whites, to commit violent depredations on the chastity of the female slaves; and these I was, though with reluctance, obliged to submit to at all times, being unable to help them. When we have had some of these slaves on board my master's vessels to carry them to other islands, or to America, I have known our mates to commit these acts most shamefully, to the disgrace, not of Christians only, but of men. I have even known them gratify their brutal passion with females not ten years old; and these abominations some of them practised to such scandalous excess, that one of our captains discharged the mate and others on that account. And yet in Montserrat I have seen a negro-man staked to the ground, and cut most shockingly, and then his ears cut off bit by bit, because he had been connected with a white woman who was a common prostitute: as if it were no crime in the whites to rob an innocent African girl of her virtue; but most heinous in a black man only to gratify a passion of nature, where the temptation was offered by one of a different colour, though the most abandoned woman of her species.

One Mr. Drummond told me that he had sold 41,000 negroes, and that he once cut off a negro-man's leg for running away.—I asked him, if the man had died in the operation? How he, as a Christian, could answer for the horrid act before God? And he told me, answering was a thing of another world; but what he thought and did were policy. I told him that the Christian doctrine taught us to do unto others as we would that others should do unto us. He then said that his scheme had the desired effect—it cured that man and some others of running away.

Another negro man was half hanged, and then burnt, for attempting to poison a cruel overseer. Thus by repeated cruelties are the wretched first urged to despair, and then murdered, because they still retain so much of human nature about them as to wish to put an end to their misery, and retaliate on their tyrants! These overseers are indeed for the most part persons of the worst character of any denomination of men in the West Indies. Unfortunately, many humane gentlemen, by not residing on their estates, are obliged to leave the management of them in the hands of these human butchers, who cut and mangle the slaves in a shocking manner on the most trifling occasions, and altogether treat them in every respect like brutes. They pay no regard to the situation of pregnant women, nor the least attention to the lodging of the field-negroes. Their huts, which ought to be well covered, and the place dry where they take their little repose, are often open sheds, built in damp places; so that, when the poor creatures return tired from the toils of the field, they contract many disorders, from being exposed to the damp air in this uncomfortable state, while they are heated, and their pores are open. This neglect certainly conspires with many others to cause a decrease in the births as well as in the lives of the grown negroes. I can quote many instances of gentlemen who reside on their estates in the West Indies, and then the scene is quite changed; the negroes are treated with lenity and proper care, by which their lives are prolonged, and their masters are profited. To the honour of humanity, I knew several gentlemen who managed their estates in this manner; and they found that benevolence was their true interest. And, among many I could mention in several of the islands, I knew one in Montserrat whose slaves looked remarkably well, and never needed any fresh supplies of negroes; and there are many other estates, especially in Barbadoes, which, from such judicious treatment, need no fresh stock of negroes at any time. I have the honour of knowing a most worthy and humane gentleman, who is a native of Barbadoes, and has estates there. This gentleman has written a treatise on the usage of his own slaves. He allows them two hours for refreshment at mid day; and many other indulgencies and comforts, particularly in their lying; and, besides this, he raises more provisions on his estate than they can destroy; so that by these attentions he saves the lives of his negroes, and keeps them healthy, and as happy as the condition of slavery can admit. I myself, as shall appear in the sequel, managed an estate, where, by those attentions, the negroes were uncommonly cheerful and healthy, and did more work by half than by the common mode of treatment they usually do. "For want, therefore, of such care and attention to the poor negroes, and otherwise oppressed as they are, it is no wonder that the decrease should require 20,000 new negroes annually to fill up the vacant places of the dead.

"Even in Barbadoes, notwithstanding those humane exceptions which I have mentioned, and others I am acquainted with, which justly make it quoted as a place where slaves meet with the best treatment, and need fewest recruits of any in the West Indies, yet this island requires 1000 negroes annually to keep up the original stock, which is only 80,000. So that the whole term of a negro's life may be said to be there but sixteen years! and yet the climate here is in every respect the same as that from which they are taken, except in being more wholesome." Do the British colonies decrease in this manner? And yet what a prodigious difference is there between an English and West India climate.

While I was in Montserrat, I knew a negro man, named Emanuel Sankey, who endeavoured to escape from his miserable bondage, by concealing himself on board of a London ship: but fate did not favour the poor oppressed man; for being discovered when the vessel was under sail, he was delivered up again to his master. This *Christian master* immediately pinned the wretch down to the ground at each wrist and ankle, and then took some sticks of sealing-wax, and lighted them, and dropped it all over his back. There was another master who was noted for cruelty, and I believe he had not a slave but what had been cut, and had pieces fairly taken out of the flesh: and after they had been punished thus, he used to make them get into a long wooden box or case he had for that purpose, in which he shut them up during pleasure. It was just about the height and breadth of a man; and the poor wretches had no room when in the case to move.

It was very common in several of the islands, particularly in St. Kitt's, for the slaves to be branded with the initial letters of their master's name, and a load of heavy iron hooks hung about their necks. Indeed, on the most trifling occasions they were loaded with chains, and often other instruments of torture were added. The iron muzzle, thumb-screws, &c. are so well known, as not to need a description, and were sometimes applied for the slightest faults. I have seen a negro beaten till some of his bones were broken, for only letting a pot boil over. It is not uncommon, after a flogging, to make slaves go on their knees, and thank their owners, and pray, or rather say, God bless them. I have often asked many of the men slaves (who used to go several miles to their wives, and late in the night, after having been wearied with a hard day's labour) why they went so far for wives, and why they did not take them of their own master's negro women, and particularly those who lived together as household slaves? Their answers have ever been—"Because when the master or mistress choose to punish the women, they make the husbands flog their own wives, and that they could not bear to do." Is it surprising that usage like this should drive the poor creatures to despair, and make them seek a refuge in death from those evils which render their lives intolerable—while,

> With shudd'ring horror pale, and eyes aghast,
> They view their lamentable lot, and find
> No rest!

This they frequently do. A negro man on board a vessel of my master's, while I belonged to her, having been put in irons for some trifling misdemeanor, and kept in that state for some days, being weary of life, took an opportunity of jumping overboard into the sea; however, he was picked up without being drowned. Another, whose life was also a burden to him, resolved to starve himself to death, and refused to eat any victuals: this procured him a severe flogging; and he also, on the first occasion which offered, jumped overboard at Charles Town, but was saved.

Nor is there any greater regard shewn to the little property than there is to the persons and lives of the negroes. I have already related an instance or two of particular oppression out of many which I have witnessed; but the following is frequent in all the islands. The wretched field slaves, after toiling all the day for an unfeeling owner, who gives them but little victuals, steal sometimes a few moments from rest or refreshment to gather some small portion of grass, according as their time will admit. This they commonly tie up in a parcel; either a bit's worth (six-pence) or half a bit's worth; and bring it to town, or to the market, to sell. Nothing is more common than for the white people on this occasion to take the grass from them without paying for it; and not only so, but too often also to my knowledge, our clerks, and many others, at the same time, have committed acts of violence on the poor, wretched, and helpless females, whom I have seen for hours stand crying to no purpose, and get no redress or pay of any kind. Is not this one common and crying sin, enough to bring down God's judgment on the islands? He tells us, the oppressor and the oppressed are both in his hands; and if these are not the poor, the brokenhearted, the blind, the captive, the bruised, which our Saviour speaks of, who are they? One of these depredators once, in St. Eustatia, came on board of our vessel, and bought some fowls and pigs of me; and a whole day after his departure with the things, he returned again and wanted his money back: I refused to give it, and, not seeing my captain on board, he began the common pranks with me; and swore he would even break open my chest and take my money. I therefore expected, as my captain was absent, that he would be as good as his word; and he was just proceeding to strike me, when fortunately a British seaman on board, whose heart had not been debauched by a West India climate, interposed and prevented him. But had the cruel man struck me, I certainly should have defended myself at the hazard of my life; for what is life to a man thus oppressed? He went away, however, swearing; and threatened that whenever he caught me on shore he would shoot me, and pay for me afterwards.

The small account in which the life of a negro is held in the West Indies is so universally known, that it might seem impertinent to quote the following extract, if some people had not been hardy enough of late to assert that negroes are on the same footing in that respect as Europeans. By the 329th Act, page 125, of the Assembly of Barbadoes, it is enacted, "That if any negro, or other slave, under punishment by his master, or his order, for running away, or any other crime or misdemeanor towards his said master, unfortunately shall suffer in life or member, no person whatsoever shall be liable to a fine; but if any man shall out of *wantonness, or only of bloody-mindedness, or cruel intention, wilfully kill a negro, or other slave, of his own, he shall pay into the public treasury fifteen pounds sterling.*" And it is the same in most, if not all, of the West India islands. Is not this one of the many acts of the islands which call loudly for redress? And do not the assembly which enacted it, deserve the appellation of savages and brutes rather than of Christians and men? It is an act at once unmerciful, unjust, and unwise; which for cruelty would disgrace an assembly of those who are called barbarians; and for its injustice and *insanity* would shock the morality and common sense of a Samaide or a Hottentot.

Shocking as this and many other acts of the bloody West India code at first view appear, how is the iniquity of it heightened when we consider to whom it may be extended. Mr. James Tobin, a zealous labourer in the vineyard of slavery, gives an account of a French planter, of his acquaintance, in the island of Martinico, who shewed him many Mulattoes working in the fields like beasts of burden; and he told Mr. Tobin, these were all the produce of his own loins! And I myself have known similar instances. Pray, reader, are these sons and daughters of the French planter less his children by being begotten on black women! And what must be the virtue of those legislators, and the feelings of those fathers, who estimate the lives of their sons, however begotten, at no more than fifteen pounds, though they should be murdered, as the act says, *out of wantonness and bloody-mindedness*? But is not the slave trade entirely at war with the heart of man? And surely that which is begun, by breaking down the barriers of virtue, involves in its continuance destruction to every principle, and buries all sentiments in ruin!

I have often seen slaves, particularly those who were meagre, in different islands, put into scales and weighed, and then sold from three-pence to six-pence, or nine-pence a pound. My master, however, whose humanity was shocked at this mode, used to sell such by the lump. And at or after a sale, even those negroes born in the islands, it is not uncommon to see taken from their wives, wives taken from their husbands, and children from their parents, and sent off to other islands, and wherever else their merciless lords choose; and probably never more during life see each other! Oftentimes my heart has bled at these partings; when the

friends of the departed have been at the water-side, and
with sighs and tears have kept their eyes fixed on the vessel
till it went out of sight.

A poor Creole negro I knew well, who, after having
often been thus transported from island to island, at last
resided in Montserrat. This man used to tell me many mel-
ancholy tales of himself. Generally, after he had done working for his master, he used to employ his few leisure
moments to go a fishing. When he had caught any fish, his
master would frequently take them from him without paying him; and at other times some other white people would
serve him in the same manner. One day he said to me, very
movingly, "Sometimes when a white man take away my fish,
I go to my master, and he get me my right; and when my
master, by strength, take away my fishes, what me must do?
I can't go to any body to be righted"; then, said the poor
man, looking up above, "I must look up to God Mighty in
the top for right." This artless tale moved me much, and I
could not help feeling the just cause Moses had in redress-
ing his brother against the Egyptian. I exhorted the man to
look up still to the God on the top, since there was no redress below. Though I little thought then that I myself
should more than once experience such imposition, and
need the same exhortation hereafter, in my own transactions in the islands; and that even this poor man and I
should some time after suffer together in the same manner,
as shall be related hereafter.

Nor was such usage as this confined to particular places
or individuals; for, in all the different islands in which I
have been (and I have visited no less than fifteen) the treatment of the slaves was nearly the same; so nearly indeed,
that the history of an island, or even a plantation, with a
few such exceptions as I have mentioned, might serve for a
history of the whole. Such a tendency has the slave-trade to
debauch men's minds, and harden them to every feeling of
humanity! For I will not suppose that the dealers in slaves
are born worse than other men—No! it is the fatality of this
mistaken avarice, that it corrupts the milk of human kindness, and turns it into gall. And, had the pursuits of those
men been different, they might have been as generous, as
tender-hearted, and just, as they are unfeeling, rapacious,

and cruel. Surely this traffic cannot be good, which spreads like a pestilence, and taints what it touches! Which violates that first natural right of mankind, equality and independency, and gives one man a dominion over his fellows which God could never intend! For it raises the owner to a state as far above man as it depresses the slave below it; and, with all the presumption of human pride, sets a distinction between them, immeasurable in extent, and endless in duration! Yet how mistaken is the avarice even of the planters. Are slaves more useful by being thus humbled to the condition of brutes, than they would be if suffered to enjoy the privileges of men? The freedom which diffuses health and prosperity throughout Britain answers you—No. When you make men slaves, you deprive them of half their virtue, you set them, in your own conduct, an example of fraud, rapine, and cruelty, and compel them to live with you in a state of war; and yet you complain that they are not honest or faithful! You stupify them with stripes, and think it necessary to keep them in a state of ignorance; and yet you assert that they are incapable of learning; that their minds are such a barren soil or moor, that culture would be lost on them; and that they came from a climate, where nature (though prodigal of her bounties in a degree unknown to yourselves) has left man alone scant and unfinished, and incapable of enjoying the treasures she has poured out for him! An assertion at once impious and absurd. Why do you use those instruments of torture? Are they fit to be applied by one rational being to another? And are ye not struck with shame and mortification, to see the partakers of your nature reduced so low? But, above all, are there no dangers attending this mode of treatment? Are you not hourly in dread of an insurrection? Nor would it be surprising; for when

> . . . No peace is given
> To us enslav'd, but custody severe;
> And stripes and arbitrary punishment
> Inflicted—What peace can we return?
> But to our power, hostility and hate;
> Untam'd reluctance, and revenge, tho' slow,
> Yet ever plotting how the conqueror least

> May reap his conquest, and may least rejoice
> In doing what we most in suff'ring feel.

But, by changing your conduct, and treating your slaves as men, every cause of fear would be banished. They would be faithful, honest, intelligent and vigorous; and peace, prosperity, and happiness would attend you.

CHAP. VI.

Some account of Brimstone-hill in Montserrat—The Author surprised by two earthquakes—Favourable change in the Author's situation—He commences merchant with three-pence—His various success in dealing in the different islands, and America, and the impositions he meets with in his transactions with white people—A curious imposition on human nature—Danger of the surfs in the West Indies—Remarkable instance of kidnapping a free mulatto—The Author is nearly murdered by Dr. Perkins, in Savannah.

In the preceding chapter I have set before the reader a few of those many instances of oppression, extortion and cruelty, to which I have been a witness in the West Indies; but, were I to enumerate them all, the catalogue would be tedious and disgusting. The punishments of the slaves, on every trifling occasion, are so frequent, and so well known, together with the different instruments with which they are tortured, that it cannot any longer afford novelty to recite them; and they are too shocking to yield delight either to the writer or the reader. I shall therefore hereafter only mention such as incidentally befel myself in the course of my adventures.

In the variety of departments in which I was employed

by my master, I had an opportunity of seeing many curious scenes in different islands; but, above all, I was struck with a celebrated curiosity called Brimstone-hill, which is a high and steep mountain, some few miles from the town of Plymouth, in Montserrat. I had often heard of some wonders that were to be seen on this hill, and I went once with some white and black people to visit it. When we arrived at the top, I saw under different cliffs great flakes of brimstone, occasioned by the steams of various little ponds, which were then boiling naturally in the earth. Some of these ponds were as white as milk, some quite blue, and many others of different colours. I had taken some potatoes with me, and I put them into different ponds, and in a few minutes they were well boiled. I tasted some of them, but they were very sulphurous; and the silver shoe-buckles, and all the other things we had among us of that metal, were, in a little time, turned as black as lead.

Whilst I was in the island, one night I felt a strange sensation, viz. I was told that the house where I lived was haunted by spirits. And once, at midnight, as I was sleeping on a large chest, I felt the whole building shake in an uncommon and astonishing manner; so much so, that it shook me off the chest where I then lay; I was exceedingly frightened, and thought it was the visitation of the spirits. It threw me into such a tremor as is not to be described. I instantly covered my head all over as I lay, and did not know what to think or do; and in this consternation, a gentleman, who lay in the next room just by me came out, and I was glad to hear him, and made a sham cough, and he asked me, if I felt the earthquake. I told him I was shook off the chest where I lay, but did not know what occasioned it; and he told me it was an earthquake, and shook him out of his bed. At hearing this I became easy in my mind.

At another time a circumstance of this kind happened, when I was on board of a vessel in Montserrat-road, at midnight, as we were asleep, and it shook the vessel in the most unaccountable manner imaginable, and to me it seemed as when a vessel or a boat runs on gravel, as near as I can describe it. Many things on board were moved out of their places, but happily no damage was done.

About the end of the year 1763, kind Providence seemed

to be rather more favourable to me. One of my master's vessels, a Bermudas sloop, about sixty tons burthen, was commanded by one Captain Thomas Farmer, an Englishman, a very alert and active man, who gained my master a great deal of money by his good management in carrying passengers from one island to another; but very often his sailors used to get drunk, and run away with the vessel's boat, which hindered him in his business very much. This man had taken a liking to me; and had many different times begged of my master to let me go a trip with him as a sailor: but he would tell him he could not spare me, though the vessel sometimes could not go for want of hands, for sailors were generally very scarce in the island. However, at last, from necessity, or force, my master was prevailed on, though very reluctantly, to let me go with this captain; but he gave him great charge to take care that I did not run away; for, if I did, he would make him pay for me. This being the case, the captain had for some time a sharp eye upon me whenever the vessel anchored: and as soon as she returned I was sent for on shore again. Thus was I slaving, as it were for life, sometimes at one thing, and sometimes at another; so that the captain and I were nearly the most useful men in my master's employment. I also became so useful to the captain on ship board, that many times, when he used to ask for me to go with him, though it should be but twenty-four hours, to some of the islands near us, my master would answer he could not spare me; at which the captain would swear, and would not go the trip, and tell my master that I was better to him on board than any three white men he had; for they used to behave ill in many respects, particularly in getting drunk, and then they frequently got the boat stove, so as to hinder the vessel from coming back so soon as she might have done. This my master knew very well; and, at last, by the captain's constant entreaties, after I had been several times with him, one day, to my great joy, told me the captain would not let him rest, and asked whether I would go aboard as a sailor, or stay on shore and mind the stores, for he could not bear any longer to be plagued in this manner. I was very happy at this proposal, for I immediately thought I might in time stand a chance by being on board to get a little money, or possibly make my escape if I should be used ill: I also expected to get better food, and in greater abundance; for I had oftentimes felt much hunger, though my master treated his slaves, as I have observed, uncommonly well; I therefore, without hesitation, answered him, that I would go and be a sailor if he pleased. Accordingly I was ordered on board directly. Nevertheless, between the vessel and the shore, when she was in port, I had little or no rest, as my master always wished to have me along with him. Indeed he was a very pleasant gentleman, and but for my expectations on shipboard I should not have thought of leaving him. But the captain liked me also very much, and I was entirely his right-hand man. I did all I could to deserve his favour, and in return I received better treatment from him than any other I believe ever met with in the West-Indies in my situation.

After I had been sailing for some time with this captain, I at length endeavoured to try my luck and commence merchant. I had but a very small capital to begin with; for one single half bit, which is equal to three pence in England, made up my whole stock. However I trusted to the Lord to be with me; and at one of our trips to *St. Eustatia*, a Dutch island, I bought a glass tumbler with my half bit, and when I came to Montserrat I sold it for a bit, or sixpence. Luckily we made several successive trips to St. Eustatia (which was a general mart for the West Indies, about twenty leagues from Montserrat), and in our next, finding my tumbler so profitable, with this one bit I bought two tumblers more; and when I came back I sold them for two bits, equal to a shilling sterling. When we went again, I bought with these two bits four more of these glasses, which I sold for four bits on our return to Montserrat; and in our next voyage to St. Eustatia, I bought two glasses with one bit, and with the other three I bought a jug of Geneva, nearly about three pints in measure. When we came to Montserrat I sold the gin for eight bits, and the tumblers for two, so that my capital now amounted in all to a dollar, well husbanded and acquired in the space of a month or six weeks, when I blessed the Lord that I was so rich. As we sailed to different islands, I laid this money out in various things occasionally, and it used to turn out to very good account, especially when we went to Guadaloupe, Grenada, and the rest of the French islands. Thus was I going all about the islands upwards of four years, and ever trading as I went, during which I experienced many instances of ill usage, and have seen many injuries done to other negroes in our dealings with whites; and, amidst our recreations, when we have been dancing and merry-making, they, without cause, have molested and insulted us. Indeed I was more than once obliged to look up to God on high, as I had advised the poor fisherman some time before. And I had not been long trading for myself in the manner I have related above, when I experienced the like trial in company with him as follows: This man being used to the water, was upon an emergency put on board of us by his master to work as another hand, on a voyage to Santa Cruz; and at our sailing he had brought his little all for a venture, which consisted of six bits worth of limes and oranges in a bag; I had also my whole stock; which was about twelve bits' worth of the same kind of goods, separate in two bags; for we had heard these fruits sold well in that island. When we came there, in some little convenient time, he and I went ashore with our fruits to sell them; but we had scarcely landed, when we were met by two white men, who presently took our three bags from us. We could not at first guess what they meant to do, and for some time we thought they were jesting with us; but they too soon let us know otherwise; for they took our ventures immediately to a house hard by adjoining the fort, while we followed all the way begging of them to give us our fruits, but in vain. They not only refused to return them, but swore at us, and threatened if we did not immediately depart, they would flog us well. We told them these three bags were all we were worth in the world; and that we brought them with us to sell when we came from Montserrat, and shewed them the vessel. But this was rather against us, as they now saw we were strangers as well as slaves. They still therefore swore, and desired us to be gone; and even took sticks to beat us; while we, seeing they meant what they said, went off in the greatest confusion and despair. Thus, in the very minute of gaining more by three times than I ever did by any venture in my life before, was I deprived of every farthing I was worth. An insupportable misfortune! but how to help ourselves we

knew not. In our consternation we went to the commanding
officer of the fort, and told him how we had been served by
some of his people; but we obtained not the least redress: he
answered our complaints only by a volley of imprecations
against us, and immediately took a horse-whip, in order to
chastise us, so that we were obliged to turn out much faster
than we came in. I now, in the agony of distress and indignation, wished that the ire of God, in his forked lightning,
might transfix these cruel oppressors among the dead. Still,
however, we persevered; went back again to the house, and
begged and besought them again and again for our fruits,
till at last some other people that were in the house asked
if we would be contented if they kept one bag, and gave us
the other two. We, seeing no remedy whatever, consented
to this; and they, observing one bag to have both kinds of
fruit in it, which belonged to my companion, kept that; and
the other two, which were mine, they gave us back. As soon
as I got them, I ran as fast as I could and got the first negro
man I could to help me off; my companion, however, stayed
a little longer to plead; he told them the bag they had was
his, and likewise all that he was worth in the world; but this
was of no avail, and he was obliged to return without it. The
poor old man, wringing his hands, cried bitterly for his loss;
and, indeed, he then did look up to God on high, which so
moved me with pity for him, that I gave him nearly one
third of my fruits. We then proceeded to the market to sell
them; and Providence was more favourable to us than we
could have expected, for we sold our fruits uncommonly
well; I got for mine about thirty-seven bits. Such a surprising reverse of fortune in so short a space of time seemed
like a dream to me, and proved no small encouragement for
me to trust the Lord in any situation. My captain afterwards
frequently used to take my part, and get me my right when
I have been plundered or used ill by these tender Christian
depredators; among whom I have shuddered to observe the
unceasing blasphemous execrations which are wantonly
thrown out by persons of all ages and conditions; not only
without occasion, but even as if they were indulgencies and
pleasures.

At one of our trips to St. Kitt's, I had eleven bits of my

own; and my friendly captain lent me five bits more, with which I bought a Bible. I was very glad to get this book, which I scarcely could meet with any where. I think there was none sold in Montserrat; and, much to my grief, from being forced out of the Aetna in the manner I have related, my Bible, and the Guide to the Indians, the two books I loved above all others, were left behind.

While I was in this place, St. Kitt's, a very curious imposition on human nature took place:—A white man wanted to marry in the church a free black woman that had land and slaves at Montserrat: but the clergyman told him it was against the law of the place to marry a white and a black in the church. The man then asked to be married on the water, to which the parson consented, and the two lovers went in one boat, and the parson and clerk in another, and thus the ceremony was performed. After this the loving pair came on board our vessel, and my captain treated them extremely well, and brought them safe to Montserrat.

The reader cannot but judge of the irksomeness of this situation to a mind like mine, in being daily exposed to new hardships and impositions, after having seen many better days, and been, as it were, in a state of freedom and plenty; added to which, every part of the world in which I had hitherto been seemed to me a paradise in comparison of the West-Indies. My mind was therefore hourly replete with inventions and thoughts of being freed, and, if possible, by honest and honourable means; for I always remembered the old adage, and I trust that it has ever been my ruling principle, "that Honesty is the best policy"; and likewise that other golden precept—"To do unto all men as I would they should do unto me." However, as I was from early years a predestinarian, I thought whatever fate had determined must ever come to pass; and therefore, if ever it were my lot to be freed, nothing could prevent me, although I should at present see no means or hope to obtain my freedom; on the other hand, if it were my fate not to be freed, I never should be so, and all my endeavours for that purpose would be fruitless. In the midst of these thoughts I therefore looked up with prayers anxiously to God for my liberty; and at the same time used every honest means, and did all that was possible on my part to obtain it. In process of time I became master of a few pounds, and in a fair way of making more, which my friendly captain knew very well: this occasioned him sometimes to take liberties with me; but whenever he treated me waspishly, I used plainly to tell him my mind, and that I would die before I would be imposed upon as other negroes were, and that to me life had lost its relish when liberty was gone. This I said, although I foresaw my then well-being or future hopes of freedom (humanly speaking) depended on this man. However, as he could not bear the thoughts of my not sailing with him, he always became mild on my threats: I therefore continued with him; and, from my great attention to his orders and his business, I gained him credit, and, through his kindness to me, I at last procured my liberty. While I thus went on, filled with the thoughts of freedom, and resisting oppression as well as I was able, my life hung daily in suspense, particularly in the surfs I have formerly mentioned, as I could not swim. These are extremely violent throughout the West-Indies, and I was ever exposed to their howling rage and devouring fury in all the islands. I have seen them strike and toss a boat right up on end, and maim several on board. Once in the island of Grenada, when I and about eight others were pulling a large boat with two puncheons of water in it, a surf struck us, and drove the boat and all in it about half a stone's throw among some trees, and above the high-water mark. We were obliged to get all the assistance we could from the nearest estate to mend the boat, and launch it into the water again. At Montserrat one night, in pressing hard to get off the shore on board, the punt was overset with us four times; the first time I was very near being drowned; however, the jacket I had on kept me above water a little space of time, while I called on a man near me who was a good swimmer, and told him I could not swim; he then made haste to me, and, just as I was sinking, he caught hold of me and brought me to sounding, and then he went and brought the punt also. As soon as we turned the water out of her, lest we should be used ill for being absent, we attempted again three times more, and as often the horrid surfs served us as at first; but at last, the fifth time we attempted, we gained our point, at the imminent hazard of our lives. One day also, at Old Road, in Montserrat, our captain and three men besides myself, were going in a large canoe in quest of rum and sugar, when a single surf tossed the canoe an amazing distance from the water, and some of us near a stone's throw from each other; most of us were very much bruised; so that I and many more often said, and really thought, that there was not such another place under the heavens as this. I longed, therefore, much to leave it, and daily wished to see my master's promise performed of going to Philadelphia.

While we lay in this place, a very cruel thing happened on board of our sloop, which filled me with horror; though I found afterwards such practices were frequent. There was a very clever and decent free young mulatto-man who sailed a long time with us; he had a free woman for his wife, by whom he had a child; and she was then living on shore, and all very happy. Our captain and mate, and other people on board, and several elsewhere, even the natives of Bermudas, then with us, all knew this young man from a child that he was always free, and no one had ever claimed him as their property: however, as might too often overcomes right in these parts, it happened that a Bermudas captain, whose vessel lay there for a few days in the road, came on board of us, and seeing the mulatto-man, whose name was Joseph Clipson, he told him he was not free, and that he had orders from his master to bring him to Bermudas. The poor man could not believe the captain to be in earnest; but he was very soon undeceived, his men laying violent hands on him; and although he shewed a certificate of his being born free in St. Kitt's, and most people on board knew that he served his time to boat building and always passed for a free man, yet he was forcibly taken out of our vessel. He then asked to be carried ashore, before the secretary or magistrates, and these infernal invaders of human rights promised him he should; but, instead of that, they carried him on board of the other vessel; and the next day, without giving the poor man any hearing on shore, or suffering him even to see his wife or child, he was carried away, and probably doomed never more in this world to see them again. Nor was this the only instance of this kind of barbarity I was a witness to. I have since often seen in Jamaica, and other islands, free men, whom I have known in America, thus villainously trepanned and held in bondage. I have heard of two similar practices even in Philadelphia: and were it not for the benevolence of the Quakers in that city, many of the sable race, who now breathe the air of liberty, would, I believe, be groaning under some planter's chains. These things opened my mind to a new scene of horror, to which I had been before a stranger. Hitherto I had thought only slavery dreadful; but the state of a free negro appeared to me now equally so at least, and in some respects even worse, for they live in constant alarm for their liberty, which is but nominal, for they are universally insulted and plundered without the possibility of redress; for such is the equity of the West Indian laws, that no free negro's evidence will be admitted in their courts of justice. In this situation, is it surprising that slaves, when mildly treated, should prefer even the misery of slavery to such a mockery of freedom? I was now completely disgusted with the West Indies, and thought I never should be entirely free till I had left them.

> With thoughts like these my anxious boding mind
> Recall'd those pleasing scenes I left behind;
> Scenes where fair Liberty, in bright array
> Makes darkness bright, and e'en illumines day;
> Where no complexion, wealth, or station can
> Protect the wretch who makes a slave of man.

I determined to make every exertion to obtain my freedom, and to return to Old England. For this purpose, I thought a knowledge of navigation might be of use to me; for, though I did not intend to run away unless I should be ill used, yet, in such a case, if I understood navigation, I might attempt my escape in our sloop, which was one of the swiftest sailing vessels in the West Indies, and I could be at no loss for hands to join me: and, if I should make this attempt, I had intended to have gone for England; but this, as I said, was only to be in the event of my meeting with any ill usage. I therefore employed the mate of our vessel to teach me navigation, for which I agreed to give him twenty-four dollars, and actually paid him part of the money down; though, when the captain, some time after, came to know that the mate was to have such a sum for teaching me, he rebuked him, and said it was a shame for him to take any money from me. However, my progress in this useful art was much retarded by the constancy of our work. Had I wished to run away, I did not want opportunities, which frequently presented themselves; and particularly at one time, soon after this. When we were at the island of Guadaloupe there was a large fleet of merchantmen bound for Old France; and, seamen then being very scarce, they gave from fifteen to twenty pounds a man for the run. Our mate, and all the white sailors, left our vessel on this account, and went on board of the French ships. They would have had me also gone with them, for they regarded me, and swore to protect me, if I would go; and, as the fleet was to sail the next day, I really believe I could have got safe to Europe at that time. However, as my master was kind, I would not attempt to leave him; still remembering the old maxim, that "honesty is the best policy," I suffered them to go without me. Indeed my captain was much afraid of my leaving him and the vessel at that time, as I had so fair an opportunity: but I thank God, this fidelity of mine turned out much to my advantage hereafter, when I did not in the least think of it; and made me so much in favour with the captain, that he used now and then to teach me some parts of navigation himself. But some of our passengers, and others, seeing this, found much fault with him for it, saying, it was a very dangerous thing to let a negro know navigation; thus I was hindered again in my pursuits. About the latter end of the year 1764, my master bought a larger sloop, called the Prudence, about seventy or eighty tons, of which my captain had the command. I went with him into this vessel, and we took a load of new slaves for Georgia and Charles Town. My master now left me entirely to the captain, though he still wished me to be with him; but I, who always much wished to lose sight of the West Indies, was not a little rejoiced at the thoughts of seeing any other country. Therefore, relying on the goodness of my captain, I got ready all the little venture I could; and, when the vessel was ready, we sailed to my great joy. When we got to our destined places, Georgia and Charles Town, I expected I should have an opportunity of selling my little property to advantage; but here, particularly in Charles Town, I met with buyers, white men, who imposed on me as in other places. Notwithstanding, I was resolved to have fortitude: thinking no lot or trial too hard when kind Heaven is the rewarder.

We soon got loaded again, and returned to Montserrat; and there, among the rest of the islands, I sold my goods well; and in this manner I continued trading during the year 1764; meeting with various scenes of imposition, as usual. After this, my master fitted out his vessel for Philadelphia, in the year 1765; and during the time of loading her, and getting ready for the voyage, I worked with double alacrity, from the hope of getting money enough by these voyages to buy my freedom, if it should please God; and also to see the city of Philadelphia, which I had heard a great deal about for some years past; besides which, I had always longed to prove my master's promise the first day I came to him. In the midst of these elevated ideas, and while I was about getting my little merchandise in readiness, one Sunday my master sent for me to his house. When I came there I found him and the captain together; and, on my going in, I was struck with astonishment at his telling me he heard that I meant to run away from him when I got to Philadelphia: "And therefore," said he "I must sell you again: you cost me a great deal of money, no less than forty pounds sterling; and it will not do to lose so much. You are a valuable fellow," continued he, "and I can get any day for you one hundred guineas, from many gentlemen in this island." And then he told me of Captain Doran's brother-in-law, a severe master, who ever wanted to buy me to make him his overseer. My captain also said, he could get much more than a hundred guineas for me in Carolina. This I knew to be a fact: for the gentleman that wanted to buy me, came off several times on board of us, and spoke to me to live with him, and said he would use me well. When I asked what work he would put me to, he said, as I was a sailor, he would make me a captain of one of his rice vessels. But I refused; and fearing, at the same time, by a sudden turn I saw in the captain's temper, he might mean to sell me, I told the gentleman I would not live with him on any condition, and that I certainly would run away with his vessel: but he said he did not fear that, as he would catch me again: and then he told me how cruelly he would serve me if I should do so. My captain, however, gave him to understand that I knew something of navigation: so he thought better of it; and, to my great joy, he went away. I now told my master, I did not say I would run away in Philadelphia, neither did I mean it, as he did not use me ill, nor yet the captain: for if they did, I certainly would have made some attempts before now; but as I thought that if it were God's will I ever should be freed it would be so; and, on the contrary, if it was not his will it would not happen; so I hoped, if ever I were freed, whilst I was used well, it should be by honest means; but as I could not help myself, he must do as he please! I could only hope and trust in the God of heaven; and at that instant my mind was big with inventions, and full of schemes to escape. I then appealed to the captain, whether ever he saw any sign of my making the least attempt to run away; and asked him if I did not always come on board according to the time for which he gave me liberty; and, more particularly, when all our men left us at Guadaloupe, and went on board the French fleet, and advised me to go with them, whether I might not, and that he could not have got me again. To my no small surprise, and very great joy, the captain confirmed every syllable I said, and even more; for he said he had tried different times to see if I would make any attempt of this kind, both at St. Eustatia and in America, and he never found that I made the smallest; but, on the contrary, I always came on board according to his orders; and he did really believe, if ever I meant to run away, that, as I could never have had a better opportunity, I would have done it the night the mate and all the people left our vessel at Guadaloupe. The captain then informed my master, who had been thus imposed on by our mate (though I did not know who was my enemy), the reason the mate had for imposing this lie upon him; which was, because I had acquainted the captain with the provisions the mate had given away, or taken out of the vessel. This speech of the captain was like life to the dead to me, and instantly my soul glorified God; and still more so on hearing my master immediately say that I was a sensible fellow, and he never did intend to use me as a common slave; and that, but for the entreaties of the captain, and his character of me, he would not have let me go from the stores about as I had done; that also, in so doing, he thought by carrying one little thing or other to different places to sell I might make money. That he also intended to encourage me in this, by crediting me with half a puncheon of rum and half a hogshead of sugar at a time; so that, from being careful, I might have money enough, in some time, to purchase my freedom: and, when that was the case, I might depend upon it he would let me have it for forty pounds sterling money, which was only the same price he gave for me. This soon gladdened my poor heart beyond measure; though indeed it was no more than the idea I had formed in my mind of my master long before; and I immediately made him this reply: "Sir, I always had that very thought of you, indeed I had, and that made me so diligent in serving you." He then gave me a large piece of silver coin, such as I had never seen or had before, and told me to get ready for the voyage, and he would credit me with a tierce of sugar and another of rum; he also said that he had two amiable sisters in Philadelphia, from whom I might get some necessary things. Upon this my noble captain desired me to go aboard; and, knowing the African mettle, he charged me not to say any thing of this matter to any body; and he promised that the lying mate should not go with him any more. This was a change indeed; in the same hour to feel the most exquisite pain, and in the turn of a moment, the fullest joy. It caused in me such sensations as I was only able to express in my looks; my heart was so overpowered with gratitude that I could have kissed both of their feet. When I left the room, I immediately went, or rather flew, to the vessel, which being loaded, my master, as good as his word, trusted me with a tierce of rum and another of sugar, when we sailed, and arrived safe at the elegant town of Philadelphia. I soon sold my goods here pretty well; and in this charming town I found every thing plentiful and cheap.

While I was in this place a very extraordinary occurrence befel me. I had been told one evening of a *wise* woman, a

Mrs. Davis, who revealed secrets, foretold events, &c. I put little faith in this story at first, as I could not conceive that any mortal could foresee the future disposals of Providence, nor did I believe in any other revelation than that of the holy Scriptures; however, I was greatly astonished at seeing this woman in a dream that night, though a person I never before beheld in my life; this made such an impression on me, that I could not get the idea the next day out of my mind, and I then became as anxious to see her as I was before indifferent; accordingly, in the evening, after we left off working, I enquired where she lived, and being directed to her, to my inexpressible surprise, beheld the very woman in the very same dress she appeared to me to wear in the vision. She immediately told me I had dreamed of her the preceding night; related to me many things that had happened with a correctness that astonished me; and finally told me I should not be long a slave. This was the more agreeable news, as I believed it the more readily from her having so faithfully related the past incidents of my life. She said I should be twice in very great danger of my life within eighteen months, which, if I escaped, I should afterwards go on well; so, giving me her blessing, we parted. After staying here some time till our vessel was loaded and I had bought in my little traffic, we sailed from this agreeable spot for Montserrat, once more to encounter the raging surfs.

We arrived safe at Montserrat, where we discharged our cargo, and I sold my things well. Soon after that we took slaves on board for St. Eustatia, and from thence to Georgia. I had always exerted myself, and did double work, in order to make our voyage as short as possible; and from thus overworking myself while we were at Georgia I caught a fever and ague. I was very ill for eleven days, and near dying; eternity was now exceedingly impressed on my mind, and I feared very much that awful event. I prayed the Lord therefore to spare me; and I made a promise in my mind to God, that I would be good if ever I should recover. At length, from having an eminent doctor to attend me, I was restored again to health: and soon after we got the vessel loaded, and set off for Montserrat. During the passage, as I was perfectly restored, and had much business of the vessel to mind, all my endeavours to keep up my integrity, and perform my promise to God, began to fail; and in spite of all I could do, as we drew nearer and nearer to the islands, my resolutions more and more declined, as if the very air of that country or climate seemed fatal to piety. When we were safe arrived at Montserrat, and I had got ashore, I forgot my former resolutions.—Alas! how prone is the heart to leave that God it wishes to love! And how strongly do the things of this world strike the senses and captivate the soul!— After our vessel was discharged, we soon got her ready, and took in, as usual, some of the poor oppressed natives of Africa, and other negroes; we then set off again for Georgia and Charlestown. We arrived at Georgia, and, having landed part of our cargo, proceeded to Charlestown with the remainder. While we were there I saw the town illuminated; the guns were fired, and bonfires and other demonstrations of joy shewn, on account of the repeal of the stamp-act. Here I disposed of some goods on my own account; the white men buying them with smooth promises and fair words, giving me, however, but very indifferent payment. There was one gentleman particularly who bought a puncheon of rum of me, which gave me a great deal of trouble; and although I used the interest of my friendly captain, I could not obtain any thing for it; for, being a negro man, I could not oblige him to pay me. This vexed me much, not knowing how to act; and I lost some time in seeking after this Christian; and though, when the sabbath came (which the negroes usually make their holiday) I was inclined to go to public worship, but, instead of that, I was obliged to hire some black men to help me to pull a boat across the water to go in quest of this gentleman. When I found him, after much entreaty, both from myself and my worthy captain, he at last paid me in dollars, some of them, however, were copper, and of consequence of no value; but he took advantage of my being a negro man, and obliged me to put up with those or none, although I objected to them. Immediately after, as I was trying to pass them in the market amongst other white men, I was abused for offering to pass bad coin; and though I shewed them the man I had got them from, I was within one minute of being tied up and flogged without either judge or jury; however, by the help of a good pair of heels, I ran off and so escaped the bastinadoes I should have received. I got on board as fast as I could, but still continued in fear of them until we sailed, which, I thank God, we did, not long after; and I have never been amongst them since.

We soon came to Georgia, where we were to complete our lading: and here worse fate than ever attended me: for one Sunday night, as I was with some negroes, in their master's yard, in the town of Savannah, it happened that their master, one Doctor Perkins, who was a very severe and cruel man, came in drunk; and not liking to see any strange negroes in his yard, he, and a ruffian of a white man he had in his service, beset me in an instant, and both of them struck me with the first weapons they could get hold of. I cried out as long as I could for help and mercy; but though I gave a good account of myself, and he knew my captain, who lodged hard by him, it was to no purpose. They beat and mangled me in a shameful manner, leaving me nearly dead. I lost so much blood from the wounds I received, that I lay quite motionless, and was so benumbed that I could not feel any thing for many hours. Early in the morning they took me away to the jail. As I did not return to the ship all night, my captain not knowing where I was, and being uneasy that I did not then make my appearance, he made inquiry after me; and, having found where I was, immediately came to me. As soon as the good man saw me so cut and mangled, he could not forbear weeping; he soon got me out of jail to his lodgings, and immediately sent for the best doctors in the place, who at first declared it as their opinion that I could not recover. My captain, on this, went to all the lawyers in the town for their advice, but they told him they could do nothing for me as I was a negro. He then went to Dr. Perkins, the hero who had vanquished me, and menaced him, swearing he would be revenged of him, and challenged him to fight. But cowardice is ever the companion of cruelty—and the Doctor refused. However, by the skilfulness of one Doctor Brady of that place, I began at last to amend; but, although I was so sore and bad, with the wounds I had all over me, that I could not rest in any posture, yet I was in more pain on account

of the captain's uneasiness about me than I otherwise
should have been. The worthy man nursed and watched
me all the hours of the night and I was, through his attention, and that of the doctor, able to get out of bed in about
sixteen or eighteen days. All this time I was very much
wanted on board, as I used frequently to go up and down
the river for rafts, and other parts of our cargo, and stow
them, when the mate was sick or absent. In about four
weeks I was able to go on duty; and in a fortnight after,
having got in all our lading, our vessel set sail for Montserrat; and in less than three weeks we arrived there safe, towards the end of the year. This ended my adventures in
1765; for I did not leave Montserrat again till the beginning of the following year.

CHAP. VII.

*The Author's disgust at the West Indies—Forms schemes to ob-
tain his freedom—Ludicrous disappointment he and his
Captain meet with in Georgia—At last, by several successful
voyages, he acquires a sum of money sufficient to purchase
it—Applies to his master, who accepts it, and grants his manumission, to his great joy—He afterwards enters as a freeman
on board one of Mr. King's ships, and sails for Georgia—
Impositions on free negroes as usual—His venture of
turkies—Sails for Montserrat, and, on his passage, his friend,
the Captain, falls ill and dies.*

Every day now brought me nearer my freedom, and I
was impatient till we proceeded again to sea, that I might
have an opportunity of getting a sum large enough to purchase it. I was not long ungratified; for in the beginning of
the year 1766, my master bought another sloop, named the
Nancy, the largest I had ever seen. She was partly laden, and

was to proceed to Philadelphia. Our captain had his choice of three, and I was well pleased he chose this, which was the largest, for, from his having a large vessel, I had more room, and could carry a larger quantity of goods with me. Accordingly, when we had delivered our old vessel, the Prudence, and completed the lading of the Nancy, having made near three hundred per cent. by four barrels of pork I brought from Charlestown, I laid in as large a cargo as I could, trusting to God's Providence to prosper my undertaking. With these views I sailed for Philadelphia. On our passage, when we drew near the land, I was for the first time surprised at the sight of some whales, having never seen any such large sea monsters before; and, as we sailed by the land, one morning I saw a puppy whale close by the vessel; it was about the length of a wherry boat, and it followed us all the day until we got within the Capes. We arrived safe and in good time at Philadelphia, and I sold my goods there chiefly to the Quakers. They always appeared to be a very honest discreet sort of people, and never attempted to impose on me; I therefore liked them, and ever after chose to deal with them in preference to any others.

One Sunday morning, while I was here, as I was going to church, I chanced to pass a meeting house. The doors being open, and the house full of people, it excited my curiosity to go in. When I entered the house, to my great surprise, I saw a very tall woman standing in the midst of them, speaking in an audible voice something which I could not understand. Having never seen any thing of this kind before, I stood and stared about me for some time, wondering at this odd scene. As soon as it was over, I took an opportunity to make enquiry about the place and people, when I was informed they were called Quakers. I particularly asked what that woman I saw in the midst of them had said, but none of them were pleased to satisfy me; so I quitted them, and soon after, as I was returning, I came to a church crowded with people; the church-yard was full likewise, and a number of people were even mounted on ladders, looking in at the windows. I thought this a strange sight, as I had never seen churches, either in England or the West Indies, crowded in this manner before. I therefore made bold to ask some people the meaning of all this, and they told me the Rev. George Whitfield was preaching. I had often heard of this gentleman, and had wished to see and hear him; but I had never before had an opportunity. I now therefore resolved to gratify myself with the sight, and pressed in amidst the multitude. When I got into the church I saw this pious man exhorting the people with the greatest fervour and earnestness, and sweating as much as ever I did while in slavery on Montserrat beach. I was very much struck and impressed with this; I thought it strange I had never seen divines exert themselves in this manner before, and was no longer at a loss to account for the thin congregations they preached to.

When we had discharged our cargo here, and were loaded again, we left this fruitful land once more, and set sail for Montserrat. My traffic had hitherto succeeded so well with me, that I thought, by selling my goods when we arrived at Montserrat, I should have enough to purchase my freedom. But as soon as our vessel arrived there, my master came on board, and gave orders for us to go to St. Eustatia, and discharge our cargo there, and from thence to proceed to Georgia. I was much disappointed at this; but thinking, as usual, it was of no use to murmur at the decrees of fate, I submitted without repining, and we went to St. Eustatia. After we had discharged our cargo there, we took in a live cargo (as we call a cargo of slaves). Here I sold my goods tolerably well; but not being able to lay out all my money in this small island to as much advantage as in many other places, I laid out only part, and the remainder I brought away with me neat. We sailed from hence for Georgia, and I was glad when we got there, though I had not much reason to like the place from my last adventure in Savannah; but I longed to get back to Montserrat and procure my freedom, which I expected to be able to purchase when I returned. As soon as we had arrived here I waited on my careful doctor, Mr. Brady, to whom I made the most grateful acknowledgments in my power for his former kindness and attention during my illness.

While we were here, an odd circumstance happened to the captain and me, which disappointed us both a good deal. A silversmith, whom we had brought to this place some voyages before, agreed with the captain to return to the West Indies, and promised at the same time to give the captain a great deal of money, having pretended to take a liking to him, and being as we thought very rich. But while we stayed to load our vessel this man was taken ill in a house where he worked, and in a week's time became very bad. The worse he grew, the more he used to speak of giving the captain what he had promised him, so that he expected something considerable from the death of this man, who had no wife or child, and he attended him day and night. I used also to go with the captain, at his own desire, to attend him; especially when we saw there was no appearance of his recovery; and in order to recompence me for my trouble, the captain promised me ten pounds, when he should get the man's property. I thought this would be of great service to me, although I had nearly money enough to purchase my freedom, if I should get safe this voyage to Montserrat. In this expectation I laid out above eight pounds of my money for a suit of superfine cloathes to dance in at my freedom, which I hoped was then at hand. We still continued to attend this man, and were with him even on the last day he lived, till very late at night, when we went on board. After we were got to bed, about one or two o'clock in the morning, the captain was sent for, and informed the man was dead. On this he came to my bed, and, waking me, informed me of it, and desired me to get up and procure a light, and immediately go with him. I told him I was very sleepy, and wished he would take somebody else with him; or else, as the man was dead, and could want no farther attendance, to let all things remain as they were till the next morning. "No, no," said he, "we will have the money to-night, I cannot wait till to-morrow; so let us go." Accordingly I got up and struck a light, and away we both went and saw the man as dead as we could wish. The captain said he would give him a grand burial, in gratitude for the promised treasure; and desired that all the things belonging to the deceased might be brought forth. Among others, there was a nest of trunks of which he had kept the keys whilst the man was ill, and when they were produced we opened them with no small eagerness and expectation; and as there were a great number within one another, with much impatience we took them one out of the other. At last, when we came to the smallest, and had opened it, we saw it was full of papers, which we supposed to be notes; at the sight of which our hearts leapt for joy; and that instant the captain, clapping his hands, cried out, "Thank God, here it is." But when we took up the trunk, and began to examine the supposed treasure and long-looked-for bounty (alas! alas! how uncertain and deceitful are all human affairs!) what had we found? While we thought we were embracing a substance, we grasped an empty nothing!! The whole amount that was in the nest of trunks was only one dollar and a half; and all that the man possessed would not pay for his coffin. Our sudden and exquisite joy was now succeeded by as sudden and exquisite pain; and my captain and I exhibited, for some time, most ridiculous figures—pictures of chagrin and disappointment! We went away greatly mortified, and left the deceased to do as well as he could for himself, as we had taken so good care of him when alive for nothing. We set sail once more for Montserrat, and arrived there safe, but much out of humour with our friend the silversmith. When we had unladen the vessel, and I had sold my venture, finding myself master of about forty-seven pounds—I consulted my true friend, the captain, how I should proceed in offering my master the money for my freedom. He told me to come on a certain morning, when he and my master would be at breakfast together. Accordingly, on that morning, I went, and met the captain there, as he had appointed. When I went in I made my obeisance to my master, and with my money in my hand, and many fears in my heart, I prayed him to be as good as his offer to me, when he was pleased to promise me my freedom as soon as I could purchase it. This speech seemed to confound him; he began to recoil; and my heart that instant sunk within me. "What!" said he, "give you your freedom? Why, where did you get the money; Have you got forty pounds sterling?" "Yes, sir," I answered. "How did you get it," replied he; I told him, "Very honestly." The captain then said he knew I got the money very honestly, and with much industry, and that I was particularly careful. On which my master replied, I got money much faster than he did; and said he would not have made me the promise he did if he had thought I should have got money so soon. "Come, come," said my worthy captain, clapping my master on the back, "Come, Robert, (which was his name), I think you must let him have his freedom;—you have laid your money out very well; you have received good interest for it all this time, and here is now the principal at last. I know Gustavus has earned you more than an hundred a-year, and he will still save you money, as he will not leave you: Come, Robert, take the money." My master then said, he would not be worse than his promise; and, taking the money, told me to go to the Secretary at the Register Office, and get my manumission drawn up. These words of my master were like a voice from heaven to me; in an instant all my trepidation was turned into unutterable bliss; and I most reverently bowed myself with gratitude, unable to express my feelings, but by the overflowing of my eyes, and a heart replete with thanks to God; while my true and worthy friend the captain congratulated us both with a peculiar degree of heartfelt pleasure. As soon as the first transports of my joy were over, and I had expressed my thanks to these my worthy friends in the best manner I was able, I rose with a heart full of affection and reverence, and left the room in order to obey my master's joyful mandate of going to the Register Office. As I was leaving the house, I called to mind the words of the Psalmist, in the 126th Psalm, and like him, "I glorified God in my heart, in whom I trusted." These words had been impressed on my mind from the very day I was forced from Deptford to the present hour, and I now saw them, as I thought, fulfilled and verified. My imagination was all rapture as I flew to the Register Office: and, in this respect, like the apostle Peter, (whose deliverance from prison was so sudden and extraordinary, that he thought he was in a vision), I could scarcely believe I was awake. Heavens! who could do justice to my feelings at this moment? Not conquering heroes themselves, in the midst of a triumph—Not the tender mother who has just regained her long-lost infant, and presses it to her heart—Not the weary hungry mariner, at the sight of the desired friendly port—Not the lover, when he once more embraces his beloved mistress, after she had been ravished from his arms!—All within my breast was tumult, wildness, and delirium! My feet scarcely touched the ground, for they were winged with joy, and, like Elijah, as he rose to Heaven, they "were with lightning sped as I went on." Every one I met I told of my happiness, and blazed about the virtue of my amiable master and captain.

When I got to the office and acquainted the Register with my errand, he congratulated me on the occasion, and told me he would draw up my manumission for half price, which was a guinea. I thanked him for his kindness; and having received it, and paid him, I hastened to my master to get him to sign it, that I might fully be released. Accordingly he signed the manumission that day; so that, before night, I who had been a slave in the morning, trembling at the will of another, now became my own master, and compleatly free. I thought this was the happiest day I had ever experienced; and my joy was still heightened by the blessings and prayers of the sable race, particularly the aged, to whom my heart had ever been attached with reverence.

As the form of my manumission has something peculiar in it, and expresses the absolute power and dominion one man claims over his fellow, I shall beg leave to present it before my readers at full length:

Montserrat.—To all men unto whom these presents shall come: I Robert King, of the parish of St. Anthony, in the said island, merchant, send greeting: Know ye, that I the aforesaid Robert King, for, and in consideration of the sum of seventy pounds current money of the said island, to me in hand paid, and to the intent that a negro man slave, named Gustavus Vasa, shall and may become free, have manumitted, emancipated, enfranchised, and set free, and by these presents do manumit, emancipate, enfranchise, and set free, the aforesaid negro man-slave, named Gustavus Vasa, for ever; hereby giving, granting, and releasing unto him, the said Gustavus Vasa, all right, title, dominion, sovereignty, and property, which, as lord and master over the aforesaid Gustavus Vasa, I have had, or which I now have, or by any means whatsoever I may or can hereafter possibly have over him the aforesaid Negro, for ever. In witness whereof, I the abovesaid Robert King, have unto these presents set my hand and seal, this tenth day of July, in the year of our Lord one thousand seven hundred and sixty-six.

ROBERT KING

Signed, sealed, and delivered in the presence of Terry Legay.

Montserrat,
    Registered the within manumission, at full length, this eleventh day of July, 1766, in liber D. TERRY LEGAY, Register.

In short, the fair as well as black people immediately styled me by a new appellation, to me the most desirable in the world, which was freeman, and at the dances I gave, my Georgia super-fine blue cloathes made no indifferent appearance, as I thought. Some of the sable females, who formerly stood aloof, now began to relax, and appear less coy, but my heart was still fixed on London, where I hoped to be ere long. So that my worthy captain, and his owner my late master, finding that the bent of my mind was towards London, said to me, "We hope you won't leave us, but that you will still be with the vessels." Here gratitude bowed me down; and none but the generous mind can judge of my feelings, struggling between inclination and duty. However, notwithstanding my wish to be in London, I obediently answered my benefactors that I would go in the vessel, and not leave them; and from that day I was entered on board as an able-bodied sailor, at thirty-six shillings per month, besides what perquisites I could make. My intention was to make a voyage or two, entirely to please these my honoured patrons; but I determined that the year following, if it pleased God, I would see Old England once more, and surprise my old master, Capt. Pascal, who was hourly in my mind; for I still loved him, notwithstanding his usage of me, and I pleased myself with thinking of what he would say when he saw what the Lord had done for me in so short a time, instead of being, as he might perhaps suppose, under the cruel yoke of some planter. With these kind of reveries I often used to entertain myself, and shorten the time till my return: and now, being as in my original free African state, I embarked on board the Nancy, after having got all things ready for our voyage. In this state of serenity we sailed for St. Eustatia; and having smooth seas and pleasant weather, we soon arrived there: after taking our cargo on board, we proceeded to Savannah in Georgia, in August 1766. While we were there, as usual, I used to go for the cargo up the rivers in boats: and when on this business, I have been frequently beset by Alligators, which were very numerous on that coast and river. I have shot many of them when they have been near getting into our boats; which we have with great difficulty sometimes prevented, and have been very much frightened at them. I have seen young ones sold alive in Georgia for six-pence.

During our stay at this place, one evening a slave belonging to Mr. Read, a merchant of Savannah, came near to our vessel, and began to use me very ill. I entreated him, with all the patience I was master of, to desist, as I knew there was little or no law for a free negro here; but the fellow, instead of taking my advice, persevered in his insults, and even struck me. At this I lost all temper, and fell on him and beat him soundly. The next morning his master came to our vessel as we lay alongside the wharf, and desired me to come ashore that he might have me flogged all round the town, for beating his negro slave. I told him he had insulted me, and had given the provocation by first striking me. I had told my captain also the whole affair that morning, and desired him to go along with me to Mr. Read, to prevent bad consequences; but he said that it did not signify, and if Mr. Read said any thing he would make matters up, and desired me to go to work, which I accordingly did. The captain being on board when Mr. Read came and applied to him to deliver me up, he said he knew nothing of the matter, I was a free man. I was astonished and frightened at this, and thought I had better keep where I was, than go ashore and be flogged round the town, without judge or jury. I therefore refused to stir; and Mr. Read went away, swearing he would bring all the constables in the town, for he would have me out of the vessel. When he was gone, I thought his threat might prove too true to my sorrow; and I was confirmed in this belief, as well by the many instances I had seen of the treatment of free negroes, as from a fact that had happened within my own knowledge here a short time before.

There was a free black man, a carpenter, that I knew, who for asking a gentleman that he had worked for, for the money he had earned, was put into gaol; and afterwards this oppressed man was sent from Georgia, with false accusations, of an intention to set the gentleman's house on fire, and run away with his slaves. I was therefore much embarrassed, and very apprehensive of a flogging at least. I dreaded, of all things, the thoughts of being stripped, as I never in my life had the marks of any violence of that kind. At that instant a rage seized my soul, and for a while I determined to resist the first man that should attempt to lay violent hands on me, or basely use me without a trial; for I would sooner die like a free man, than suffer myself to be scourged by the hands of ruffians, and my blood drawn like a slave. The captain and others, more cautious, advised me to make haste and conceal myself; for they said Mr. Read was a very spiteful man, and he would soon come on board with constables, and take me. At first I refused this council, being determined to stand my ground; but at length, by the prevailing entreaties of the Captain and Mr. Dixon, with whom we lodged, I went to Mr. Dixon's house, which was a little out of the town, at a place called *Yea-ma-chra*. I was but just gone when Mr. Read, with the constables, came for me, and searched the vessel; but not finding me there he swore he would have me dead or alive. I was secreted about five days; however, the good character which my Captain always gave me, as well as some other gentlemen, who also knew me, procured me some friends. At last some of them told my Captain that he did not use me well, in suffering me thus to be imposed upon, and said they would see me redressed, and get me on board some other vessel. My captain, on this, immediately went to Mr. Read, and told him, that ever since I eloped from the vessel, his work had been neglected, and he could not go on with her loading, himself and mate not being well; and, as I had managed things on board for them, my absence must have retarded his voyage, and consequently hurt the owner; he therefore begged of him to forgive me, as he said he never heard any complaint of me before, during the several years I had been with him. After repeated entreaties, Mr. Read said I might go to hell, and that he would not meddle with me; on which my Captain came immediately to me at his lodging, and telling me how pleasantly matters had gone on, desired me to go on board.

Some of my other friends then asked him if he had got the constable's warrant from them? the Captain said, No. On this I was desired by them to stay in the house; and they said they would get me on board of some other vessel before the evening. When the Captain heard this, he became almost distracted. He went immediately for the warrants, and, after using every exertion in his power, he at last got them from my hunters; but I had all the expences to pay.

After I had thanked all my friends for their kindness, I went on board again to my work, of which I had always plenty. We were in haste to complete our lading, and were to carry twenty head of cattle with us to the West Indies, where they are a very profitable article. In order to encourage me in working, and to make up for the time I had lost, my Captain promised me the privilege of carrying two bullocks of my own with me; and this made me work with redoubled ardour. As soon as I had got the vessel loaded, in doing which I was obliged to perform the duty of the mate as well as my own work, and when the bullocks were near coming on board, I asked the captain leave to bring my two, according to his promise; but, to my great surprise, he told me there was no room for them. I then asked him to permit me to take one; but he said he could not. I was a good deal mortified at this usage, and told him I had no notion that he intended thus to impose on me: nor could I think well of any man that was so much worse than his word. On this we had some disagreement, and I gave him to understand that I intended to leave the vessel. At this he appeared to be very much dejected; and our mate, who had been very sickly, and whose duty had long devolved upon me, advised him to persuade me to stay: in consequence of which he spoke very kindly to me, making many fair promises, telling me that as the mate was so sickly, he could not do without me; and that as the safety of the vessel and cargo depended greatly upon me, he therefore hoped that I would not be offended at what had passed between us, and swore he would make up all matters when we arrived in the West Indies, so I consented to slave on as before. Soon after this, as the bullocks were coming on board, one of them ran at the captain, and butted him so furiously in the breast, that he never recovered of the blow. In order to make me some amends for this treatment about the bullocks, the captain now pressed me very much to take some turkies, and other fowls, with me, and gave me liberty to take as many as I could find room for; but I told him he knew very well I had never carried any turkies before, as I always thought they were such tender birds that they were not fit to cross the seas. However, he continued to press me to buy them for once: and, what seemed very surprising to me, the more I was against it, the more he urged my taking them, insomuch that he ensured me from all losses that might happen by them, and I was prevailed on to take them; but I thought this very strange, as he had never acted so with me before. This, and not being able to dispose of my paper money in any other way, induced me at length to take four dozen. The turkies, however, I was so dissatisfied about, that I determined to make no more voyages to this quarter, nor with this captain; and was very apprehensive that my free voyage would be the very worst I had ever made.

We set sail for Montserrat. The Captain and mate had been both complaining of sickness when we sailed, and as we proceeded on our voyage they grew worse. This was about November, and we had not been long at sea before we began to meet with strong northerly gales and rough seas; and in about seven or eight days all the bullocks were near being drowned, and four or five of them died. Our vessel, which had not been tight at first, was much less so now: and, though we were but nine in the whole, including five sailors and myself, yet we were obliged to attend to the pump, every half or three quarters of an hour. The captain and mate came on deck as often as they were able, which was now but seldom; for they declined so fast, that they were not well enough to make observations above four or five times the whole passage. The whole care of the vessel rested therefore upon me; and I was obliged to direct her by mere dint of reason, not being able to work a traverse. The Captain was now very sorry he had not taught me navigation, and protested, if ever he should get well again, he would not fail to do so: but in about seventeen days his illness increased so much, that he was obliged to keep his bed, continuing sensible, however, till the last, constantly having the owner's interest at heart; for this just and benevolent man ever appeared much concerned about the welfare of what he was intrusted with. When this dear friend found the symptoms of death approaching, he called me by my name; and, when I came to him, he asked (with almost his last breath) if he had ever done me any harm? "God forbid I should think so," I replied, "I should then be the most ungrateful of wretches to the best of benefactors." While I was thus expressing my affection and sorrow by his bed-side, he expired without saying another word, and the day following we committed his body to the deep. Every man on board loved him, and regretted his death; but I was exceedingly affected at it, and found that I did not know, till he was gone, the strength of my regard for him. Indeed I had every reason in the world to be attached to him; for, besides that he was in general mild, affable, generous, faithful, benevolent, and just, he was to me a friend and father; and had it pleased Providence that he had died but five months before, I verily believe I should not have obtained my freedom when I did; and it is not improbable that I might not have been able to get it at any rate afterwards.

The captain being dead, the mate came on the deck, and made such observations as he was able, but to no purpose. In the course of a few days more, the few bullocks that remained were found dead; but the turkies I had, though on the deck, and exposed to so much wet and bad weather, did well, and I afterwards gained near three hundred per cent. on the sale of them; so that in the event it proved a happy circumstance for me that I had not bought the bullocks I intended, for they must have perished with the rest; I could not help looking upon this, otherwise trifling circumstance, as a particular providence of God, and was thankful accordingly. The care of the vessel took up all my time, and engaged my attention entirely. As we were now out of the variable winds, I thought I should not be much puzzled to hit the islands. I was persuaded I steered right for Antigua, which I wished to reach, as the nearest to us; and in the course of nine or ten days we made that island, to our great joy; and the day after we came safe to Montserrat.

Many were surprised when they heard of my conducting the sloop into the port, and I now obtained a new appellation, and was called captain. This elated me not a little, and it was quite flattering to my vanity to be thus styled by as high a title as any sable freeman in this place possessed. When the death of the captain became known, he was much regretted by all who knew him; for he was a man universally respected. At the same time the sable captain lost no fame; for the success I had met with increased the affection of my friends in no small measure; and I was offered, by a gentleman of the place, the command of his sloop to go amongst the islands, but I refused.

CHAP. VIII.

The Author, to oblige Mr. King, once more embarks for Georgia in the Nancy—A new captain is appointed—They sail, and steer a new course—Three remarkable dreams—The vessel is wrecked on Bahama Banks, but the crew are preserved, principally by means of the Author—He sets out from an

island, with the captain, in a small boat, in quest of a ship—
Their distress—Meet with a wrecker—Sail for Providence—
Are overtaken again by a terrible storm, and are all near
perishing—Arrive at New Providence—The Author, after
some time, sails from thence to Georgia—Meets with another
storm, and is obliged to put back and refit—Arrives at
Georgia—Meets new impositions—Two white men attempt to
kidnap him—Officiates as a parson at a funeral ceremony—
Bids adieu to Georgia, and sails for Martinico.

As I had now, by the death of my captain, lost my great benefactor and friend, I had little inducement to remain longer in the West Indies, except my gratitude to Mr. King, which I thought I had pretty well discharged in bringing back his vessel safe, and delivering his cargo to his satisfaction. I began to think of leaving this part of the world, of which I had been long tired, and of returning to England, where my heart had always been; but Mr. King still pressed me very much to stay with his vessel; and he had done so much for me, that I found myself unable to refuse his requests, and consented to go another voyage to Georgia, as the mate from his ill state of health, was quite useless in the vessel. Accordingly, a new captain was appointed, whose name was William Phillips, an old acquaintance of mine; and, having refitted our vessel, and taken several slaves on board, we set sail for St. Eustatia, where we staid but a few days; and on the 30th of January, 1767, we steered for Georgia. Our new captain boasted strangely of his skill in navigating and conducting a vessel; and, in consequence of this, he steered a new course, several points more to the westward than we ever did before; this appeared to me very extraordinary.

On the 4th of February, which was soon after we had got into our new course, I dreamt the ship was wrecked amidst the surfs and rocks, and that I was the means of saving every one on board; and on the night following I dreamed the very same dream. These dreams, however, made no impression on my mind; and the next evening, it being my watch below, I was pumping the vessel a little after eight o'clock, just before I went off the deck, as is the custom, and being weary with the duty of the day, and tired at the pump (for we made a good deal of water), I began to express my impatience, and I uttered with an oath, "Damn the vessel's bottom out." But my conscience instantly smote me for the expression. When I left the deck I went to bed, and had scarcely fallen asleep when I dreamed the same dream again about the ship that I had dreamt the two preceding nights. At twelve o'clock the watch was changed; and, as I had always the charge of the captain's watch, I then went upon deck. At half after one in the morning, the man at the helm saw something under the lee-beam that the sea washed against, and he immediately called to me that there was a grampus, and desired me to look at it. Accordingly I stood up and observed it for some time; but when I saw the sea wash up against it again and again, I said it was not a fish but a rock. Being soon certain of this, I went down to the captain, and, with some confusion, told him the danger we were in, and desired him to come upon deck immediately. He said it was very well, and I went up again. As soon as I was upon deck, the wind, which had been pretty high, having abated a little, the vessel began to be carried sideways towards the rock, by means of the current. Still the captain did not appear. I therefore went to him again and told him the vessel was then near a large rock, and desired he would come up with all speed. He said he would, and I returned on the deck. When I was upon the deck again I saw we were not above a pistol shot from the rock, and I heard the noise of the breakers all around us. I was exceedingly alarmed at this; and the captain not having yet come on the deck, I lost all patience; and, growing quite enraged, I ran down to him again, and asked him, why he did not come up, and what he could mean by all this? "The breakers," said I, "are around us, and the vessel is almost on the rock." With that he came on the deck with me, and we tried to put the vessel about, and get her out of the current, but all to no purpose, the wind being very small. We then called all hands up immediately; and after a little we got up one end of a cable, and fastened it to the anchor. By this time the surf foamed round us, and made a dreadful noise on the breakers, and the very moment we let the anchor go, the vessel struck against the rocks. One swell now succeeded another, as it were one wave calling on its fellow. The roaring of the billows increased, and, with one single heave of the swells, the sloop was pierced and transfixed among the rocks! In a moment a scene of horror presented itself to my mind, such as I never had conceived or experienced before. All my sins stared me in the face; and especially I thought that God had hurled his direful vengeance on my guilty head for cursing the vessel on which my life depended. My spirits at this forsook me, and I expected every moment to go to the bottom: I determined if I should still be saved, that I would never swear again. And in the midst of my distress, while the dreadful surfs were dashing with unremitting fury among the rocks, I remembered the Lord, though fearful that I was undeserving of forgiveness, and I thought that as he had often delivered he might yet deliver; and, calling to mind the many mercies he had shewn me in times past, they gave me some small hope that he might still help me. I then began to think how we might be saved; and, I believe no mind was ever like mine so replete with inventions and confused with schemes, though how to escape death I knew not. The captain immediately ordered the hatches to be nailed down on the slaves in the hold, where there were above twenty, all of whom must unavoidably have perished if he had been obeyed. When he desired the men to nail down the hatches I thought that my sin was the cause of this, and that God would charge me with these people's blood. This thought rushed upon my mind that instant with such violence, that it quite overpowered me, and I fainted. I recovered just as the people were about to nail down the hatches; perceiving which, I desired them to stop. The captain then said it must be done; I asked him why? He said, that every one would endeavour to get into the boat, which was but small, and thereby we should be drowned; for it would not have carried above ten at the most. I could no longer restrain my emotion, and I told him he deserved drowning for not knowing how to navigate the vessel; and I believe the people would have tossed him overboard if I had given them the least hint of it. However, the hatches were not nailed down; and, as none of us could leave the vessel then on account of the darkness, and as we knew not where to go, and were convinced besides that the boat could not survive the surfs, and besides being broken, we all said we would remain on the dry part of the vessel, and trust to God till day-light appeared, when we should know better what to do.

I then advised to get the boat prepared against morning, and some of us began to set about it; but some abandoned all care of the ship, and themselves, and fell to drinking. Our boat had a piece out of her bottom near two feet long, and we had no materials to mend her; however, necessity being the mother of invention, I took some pump leather and nailed it to the broken part, and plastered it over with tallow-grease. And, thus prepared, with the utmost anxiety of mind, we watched for day-light, and thought every minute an hour, till it appeared. At last it saluted our longing eyes, and kind Providence accompanied its approach with what was no small comfort to us; for the dreadful swell began to subside; and the next thing that we discovered to raise our drooping spirits, was a small key, or desolate island, about five or six miles off; but a barrier soon presented itself; for there was not water enough for our boat to go over the reefs, and this threw us again into a sad consternation; but there was no alternative, we were therefore obliged to put but few things in the boat at once; and, what was still worse, all of us were frequently under the necessity of getting out to drag and lift it over the reefs. This cost us much labour and fatigue; and, what was yet more distressing, we could not avoid having our legs cut and torn very much with the rocks. There were only four people that would work with me at the oars; and they consisted of three black men and a Dutch Creole sailor; and, though we went with the boat five times that day, we had no others to assist us. But, had we not worked in this manner, I really believe the people could not have been saved; for not one of the white men did any thing to preserve their lives; and indeed they soon got so drunk that they were not able, but lay about the deck like swine, so that we were at last obliged to lift them into the boat, and carry them on shore by force. This want of assistance made our labour intolerably severe; insomuch that, by putting on shore so often that day, the skin was partly stript off my hands.

However, we continued all the day to toil and strain our exertions, till we had brought all on board safe to the shore; so that out of thirty-two people we lost not one.

My dream now returned upon my mind with all its force; it was fulfilled in every part; for our danger was the same I had dreamt of; and I could not help looking on myself as the principal instrument in effecting our deliverance: for, owing to some of our people getting drunk, the rest of us were obliged to double our exertions; and it was fortunate we did, for in a very little time longer the patch of leather on the boat would have been worn out, and she would have been no longer fit for service. Situated as we were, who could think that men should be so careless of the danger they were in? for, if the wind had but raised the swell as it was when the vessel struck, we must have bid a final fare-well to all hopes of deliverance; and though I warned the people who were drinking, and entreated them to embrace the moment of deliverance, nevertheless they persisted, as if not possessed of the least spark of reason. I could not help thinking, that if any of these people had been lost, God would charge me with their lives, which, perhaps, was one cause of my labouring so hard for their preservation, and indeed every one of them afterwards seemed so sensible of the service I had rendered them, that while we were on the key, I was a kind of chieftain amongst them. I brought some limes, oranges, and lemons ashore; and, finding it to be a good soil where we were, I planted several of them as a token to any one that might be cast away hereafter. This key, as we afterwards found, was one of the Bahama islands, which consist of a cluster of large islands, with smaller ones or keys, as they are called, interspersed among them. It was about a mile in circumference, with a white sandy beach running in a regular order along it. On that part of it where we first attempted to land, there stood some very large birds, called flamingoes: these, from the reflection of the sun, appeared to us, at a little distance, as large as men; and, when they walked backwards and forwards, we could not conceive what they were: our captain swore they were can-nibals. This created a great panic among us; and we held a consultation how to act. The captain wanted to go to a key that was within sight, but a great way off; but I was against it, as in so doing we should not be able to save all the people; "And therefore," said I, "let us go on shore here, and perhaps these cannibals may take to the water." Accordingly, we steered towards them; and when we approached them, to our very great joy and no less wonder, they walked off one after the other very deliberately; and at last they took flight, and relieved us entirely from our fears. About the key there were turtles and several sorts of fish in such abundance that we caught them without bait, which was a great relief to us after the salt provisions on board. There was also a large rock on the beach, about ten feet high, which was in the form of a punchbowl at the top; this we could not help thinking Providence had ordained to supply us with rain-water; and it was something singular, that, if we did not take the water when it rained, in some little time after it would turn as salt as sea-water.

Our first care, after refreshment, was, to make ourselves tents to lodge in, which we did as well as we could with some sails we had brought from the ship. We then began to think how we might get from this place, which was quite uninhabited; and we determined to repair our boat, which was very much shattered, and to put to sea in quest of a ship, or some inhabited island. It took us up, however, eleven days before we could get the boat ready for sea, in the manner we wanted it, with a sail and other necessaries. When we had got all things prepared, the captain wanted me to stay on shore, while he went to sea in quest of a vessel to take all the people off the key; but this I refused; and the captain and myself, with five more, set off in the boat towards New Providence. We had no more than two musquet loads of gun-powder with us, if any thing should happen; and our stock of provisions consisted of three gallons of rum, four of water, some salt beef, some biscuit; and in this manner we proceeded to sea.

On the second day of our voyage, we came to an island called Abbico, the largest of the Bahama islands. We were much in want of water; for by this time our water was expended, and we were exceedingly fatigued in pulling two days in the heat of the sun; and it being late in the evening, we hauled the boat ashore to try for water, and remain during the night: when we came ashore we searched for water, but could find none. When it was dark, we made a fire around us for fear of the wild beasts, as the place was an entire thick wood, and we took it by turns to watch. In this situation we found very little rest, and waited with impatience for the morning. As soon as the light appeared we set off again with our boat, in hopes of finding assistance during the day. We were now much dejected and weakened by pulling the boat; for our sail was of no use, and we were almost famished for want of fresh water to drink. We had nothing left to eat but salt beef, and that we could not use without water. In this situation we toiled all day in sight of the island, which was very long; in the evening, seeing no relief, we made shore again, and fastened our boat. We then went to look for fresh water, being quite faint for the want of it; and we dug and searched about for some all the remainder of the evening, but could not find one drop, so that our dejection at this period became excessive, and our terror so great, that we expected nothing but death to deliver us. We could not touch our beef, which was as salt as brine, without fresh water; and we were in the greatest terror from the apprehension of wild beasts. When unwelcome night came, we acted as on the night before; and the next morning we set off again from the island in hopes of seeing some vessel. In this manner we toiled as well as we were able till four o'clock, during which we passed several keys, but could not meet with a ship; and, still famishing with thirst, went ashore on one of those keys again in hopes of finding some water. Here we found some leaves with a few drops of water on them, which we lapped with much eagerness; we then dug in several places, but without success. As we were digging holes in search of water, there came forth some very thick and black stuff; but none of us could touch it, except the poor Dutch Creole, who drank above a quart of it, as eagerly as if it had been wine. We tried to catch fish, but could not: and we now began to repine at our fate, and abandon ourselves to despair; when, in the midst of our murmuring, the captain, all at once cried out, "A sail! a sail!

a sail!" This gladdening sound was like a reprieve to a convict, and we all instantly turned to look at it; but in a little time some of us began to be afraid it was not a sail. However, at a venture, we embarked, and steered after it; and, in half an hour, to our unspeakable joy, we plainly saw that it was a vessel. At this our drooping spirits revived, and we made towards her with all the speed imaginable. When we came near to her, we found she was a little sloop, about the size of a Gravesend hoy, and quite full of people; a circumstance which we could not make out the meaning of. Our captain, who was a Welshman, swore that they were pirates, and would kill us. I said, be that as it might, we must board her if we were to die for it; and, if they should not receive us kindly, we must oppose them as well as we could: for there was no alternative between their perishing and ours. This counsel was immediately taken; and I really believe that the captain, myself, and the Dutchman, would then have faced twenty men. We had two cutlasses and a musquet, that I brought in the boat; and in this situation, we rowed alongside, and immediately boarded her. I believe there were about forty hands on board; but how great was our surprise, as soon as we got on board, to find that the major part of them were in the same predicament as ourselves.

They belonged to a whaling schooner that was wrecked two days before us about nine miles to the north of our vessel. When she was wrecked, some of them had taken to their boats, and had left some of their people and property on a key, in the same manner as we had done; and were going, like us, to New Providence in quest of a ship, when they met with this little sloop, called a wrecker; their employment in those seas being to look after wrecks. They were then going to take the remainder of the people belonging to the schooner; for which the wrecker was to have all things belonging to the vessel, and likewise their people's help to get what they could out of her, and were then to carry the crew to New Providence.

We told the people of the wrecker the condition of our vessel, and we made the same agreement with them as the schooner's people; and, on their complying, we begged of them to go to our key directly, because our people were in want of water. They agreed, therefore, to go along with us first; and in two days we arrived at the key, to the inexpressible joy of the people that we had left behind, as they had been reduced to great extremities for want of water in our absence. Luckily for us, the wrecker had now more people on board than she could carry or victual for any moderate length of time; they therefore hired the schooner's people to work on the wreck, and we left them our boat, and embarked for New Providence.

Nothing could have been more fortunate than our meeting with this wrecker, for New Providence was at such a distance that we never could have reached it in our boat. The island of Abbico was much longer than we expected; and it was not till after sailing for three or four days that we got safe to the farther end of it, towards New Providence. When we arrived there we watered, and got a good many lobsters and other shell-fish, which proved a great relief to us, as our provisions and water were almost exhausted. We then proceeded on our voyage; but the day after we left the island, late in the evening and whilst we were yet amongst the Bahama keys, we were overtaken by a violent gale of wind, so that we were obliged to cut away the mast. The vessel was very near foundering; for she parted from her anchors, and struck several times on the shoals. Here we expected every minute that she would have gone to pieces, and each moment to be our last; so much so, that my old captain and sickly useless mate, and several others, fainted; and death stared us in the face on every side. All the swearers on board now began to call on the God of Heaven to assist them: and sure enough beyond our comprehension he did assist us, and in a miraculous manner delivered us! In the very height of our extremity the wind lulled for a few minutes; and, although the swell was high beyond expression, two men, who were expert swimmers, attempted to go to the buoy of the anchor, which we still saw in the water, at some distance, in a little punt that belonged to the wrecker, which was not large enough to carry more than two. She filled at different times in their endeavours to get into her alongside of our vessel; and they saw nothing but death before them, as well as we; but they said they might as well die that way as any other. A coil of very small rope, with a little buoy, was put in along with them; and, at last, with great hazard they got the punt clear from the vessel; and these two intrepid water heroes paddled away for life towards the buoy of the anchor. Our eyes were fixed on them all the time, expecting every minute to be their last; and the prayers of all those that remained in their senses were offered up to God, on their behalf, for a speedy deliverance, and for our own, which depended on them; and he heard and answered us! These two men at last reached the buoy; and having fastened the punt to it, they tied one end of their rope to the small buoy that they had in the punt, and sent it adrift towards the vessel. We on board observing this, threw out boat-hooks and leads fastened to lines, in order to catch the buoy: at last we caught it, and fastened a hawser to the end of the small rope; we then gave them a sign to pull, and they pulled the hawser to them, and fastened it to the buoy: which being done, we hauled for our lives; and, through the mercy of God, we got again from the shoals into deep water, and the punt got safe to the vessel. It is impossible for any to conceive our heartfelt joy at this second deliverance from ruin, but those who have suffered the same hardships. Those whose strength and senses were gone, came to themselves, and were now as elated as they were before depressed. Two days after this the wind ceased, and the water became smooth. The punt then went on shore, and we cut down some trees; and having found our mast and mended it, we brought it on board, and fixed it up. As soon as we had done this we got up the anchor, and away we went once more for New Providence, which in three days more we reached safe, after having been above three weeks in a situation in which we did not expect to escape with life. The inhabitants here were very kind to us; and, when they learned our situation, shewed us a great deal of hospitality and friendship. Soon after this, every one of my old fellow-sufferers that were free, parted from us, and shaped their course where their inclination led them. One merchant, who had a large sloop, seeing our condition, and knowing we wanted to go to Georgia, told four of us that his vessel was going there; and, if we would work on board and load her, he would give us our passage free. As we could not get any wages whatever, and found it very hard to get off the place, we were obliged to consent to his proposal; and we went on board and helped to load the sloop, though we had only our victuals allowed us. When she was entirely loaded, he told us she was going to Jamaica first, where we must go if we went in her. This, however, I refused; but my fellow-sufferers not having any money to help themselves with, necessity obliged them to accept of the offer, and to steer that course, though they did not like it.

We stayed in New Providence about seventeen or eighteen days; during which time I met with many friends, who gave me encouragement to stay there with them, but I declined it; though, had not my heart been fixed on England, I should have stayed, as I liked the place extremely, and there were some free black people here who were very happy, and we passed our time pleasantly together, with the melodious sound of the catguts under the lime and lemon trees. At length Capt. Phillips hired a sloop to carry him and some of the slaves that he could not sell here, to Georgia; and I agreed to go with him in this vessel, meaning now to take my farewell of that place. When the vessel was ready, we all embarked; and I took my leave of New Providence, not without regret. We sailed about four o'clock in the morning, with a fair wind, for Georgia; and, about eleven o'clock the same morning, a sudden and short gale sprung up and blew away most of our sails; and, as we were still among the keys, in a very few minutes it dashed the sloop against the rocks. Luckily for us the water was deep; and the sea was not so angry, but that, after having for some time laboured hard, and being many in number, we were saved through God's mercy: and, by using our greatest exertions, we got the vessel off. The next day we returned to [New] Providence, where we soon got her again refitted. Some of the people swore that we had spells set upon us, by somebody in Montserrat; and others said that we had witches and wizzards amongst the poor helpless slaves; and that we never should arrive safe at Georgia. But these things did not deter me; I said, "Let us again face the winds and seas, and swear not, but trust to God, and he will deliver us." We therefore once more set sail; and with hard labour, in seven days time, arrived safe at Georgia.

After our arrival we went up to the town of Savannah; and the same evening I went to a friend's house to lodge, whose name was Mosa, a black man. We were very happy at meeting each other; and, after supper, we had a light till between nine and ten o'clock at night. About that time the watch or patrole came by, and, discerning a light in the house, they knocked at the door; we opened it, and they came in and sat down, and drank some punch with us; they also begged some limes of me, as they understood I had some, which I readily gave them. A little after this, they told me I must go to the watch-house with them; this surprised me a good deal after our kindness to them, and I asked them, Why so? They said that all negroes, who had a light in their houses after nine o'clock were to be taken into custody, and either pay some dollars, or be flogged. Some of these people knew that I was a free man; but, as the man of the house was not free, and had his master to protect him, they did not take the same liberty with him they did with me. I told them that I was a free man, and just arrived from [New] Providence; that we were not making any noise, and that I was not a stranger in that place, but was very well known there: "Besides," said I, "what will you do with me?"—"That you shall see," replied they; "but you must go to the watch-house with us." Now, whether they meant to get money from me or not, I was at a loss to know; but I thought immediately of the oranges and limes at Santa Cruz: and seeing that nothing would pacify them, I went with them to the watch-house, where I remained during the night. Early the next morning these imposing ruffians flogged a negro man and woman that they had in the watch-house, and then they told me that I must be flogged too; I asked why? and if there was no law for free men? and told them if there was I would have it put in force against them. But this only exasperated them the more, and they instantly swore they would serve me as Doctor Perkins had done; and were going to lay violent hands on me; when one of them, more humane than the rest, said, that as I was a free man they could not justify stripping me by law. I then immediately sent for Dr. Brady, who was known to be a honest and worthy man; and on his coming to my assistance, they let me go.

This was not the only disagreeable incident I met with while I was in this place; for, one day, while I was a little way out of the town of Savannah, I was beset by two white men, who meant to play their usual tricks with me in the way of kidnapping. As soon as these men accosted me, one of them said to the other, "This is the very fellow we are looking for, that you lost": and the other swore immediately that I was the identical person. On this they made up to me, and were about to handle me; but I told them to be still and keep off, for I had seen those tricks played upon other free blacks, and they must not think to serve me so. At this they paused a little, and one said to the other—it will not do; and the other answered that I talked too good English. I replied, I believed I did; and I had also with me a revengeful stick equal to the occasion; and my mind was likewise good. Happily, however, it was not used; and, after we had talked together a little in this manner, the rogues left me.

I stayed in Savannah some time, anxiously trying to get to Montserrat once more to see Mr. King, my old master, and then to take a final farewell of the American quarter of the globe. At last I met with a sloop called the Speedwell, Captain John Bunton, which belonged to Grenada, and was bound to Martinico, a French island, with a cargo of rice; and I shipped myself on board of her.

Before I left Georgia, a black woman who had a child lying dead, being very tenacious of the church burial service, and not able to get any white person to perform it, applied to me for that purpose. I told her I was no parson; and, besides, that the service over the dead did not affect the soul. This however did not satisfy her; she still urged me very hard; I therefore complied with her entreaties, and at last consented to act the parson for the first time in my life. As she was much respected, there was a great company both of white and black people at the grave. I then accordingly assumed my new vocation, and performed the funeral ceremony to the satisfaction of all present; after which I bade adieu to Georgia, and sailed for Martinico.

CHAP. IX.

The Author arrives at Martinico—Meets with new difficulties—
Gets to Montserrat, where he takes leave of his old master, and
sails for England—Meets Capt. Pascal—Learns the French
horn—Hires himself with Doctor Irving, where he learns to
freshen sea water—Leaves the Doctor and goes a voyage to
Turkey and Portugal; & afterwards goes a voyage to Grenada,
and another to Jamaica—Returns to the Doctor, and they em-
bark together on a voyage to the North Pole, with the Hon.
Capt. Phipps—Some account of that voyage, and the dangers
the Author was in—He returns to England.

I THUS took a final leave of Georgia; for the treatment I
had received in it disgusted me very much against the place;
and when I left it and sailed for Martinico, I determined
never more to revisit it. My new captain conducted his vessel safer than my former one; and, after an agreeable voyage, we got safe to our intended port. While I was on this
island I went about a good deal, and found it very pleasant:
in particular, I admired the town of St. Pierre, which is the
principal one in the island, and built more like an European
town than any I had seen in the West Indies. In general also,
slaves were better treated, had more holidays, and looked
better than those in the English islands. After we had done
our business here, I wanted my discharge, which was necessary; for it was then the month of May, and I wished much
to be at Montserrat to bid farewell to Mr. King, and all my
other friends there, in time to sail for Old England in the
July fleet. But, alas! I had put a great stumbling block in my
own way, by which I was near losing my passage that season
to England. I had lent my captain some money, which I now
wanted, to enable me to prosecute my intentions. This I told
him; but when I applied for it, though I urged the necessity
of my occasion, I met with so much shuffling from him, that
I began at last to be afraid of losing my money, as I could
not recover it by law; for I have already mentioned, that

throughout the West Indies no black man's testimony is admitted, on any occasion, against any white person whatever, and therefore my own oath would have been of no use. I was obliged therefore, to remain with him till he might be disposed to return it to me. Thus we sailed from Martinico for the Grenades. I frequently pressing the captain for my money, to no purpose; and, to render my condition worse, when we got there, the captain and his owners quarrelled; so that my situation became daily more irksome: for besides that we on board had little or no victuals allowed us, and I could not get my money nor wages, as I could then have gotten my passage free to Montserrat had I been able to accept it. The worst of all was, that it was growing late in July, and the ships in the islands must sail by the 26th of that month. At last, however, with a great many entreaties, I got my money from the captain, and took the first vessel I could meet with for St. Eustatia. From thence I went in another to Basseterre in St. Kitt's, where I arrived on the 19th of July. On the 22d, having met with a vessel bound to Montserrat, I wanted to go in her; but the captain and others would not take me on board until I should advertise myself, and give notice of my going off the island. I told them of my haste to be in Montserrat; and that the time then would not admit of advertising, it being late in the evening, and the vessel about to sail; but he insisted it was necessary, and otherwise he said he would not take me. This reduced me to great perplexity; for if I should be compelled to submit to this degrading necessity, which every black freeman is under, of advertising himself like a slave, when he leaves an island, and which I thought a gross imposition upon any freedom, I feared I should miss that opportunity of going to Montserrat, and then I could not get to England that year. The vessel was just going off, and no time could be lost; I immediately therefore set about with a heavy heart, to try who I could get to befriend me in complying with the demands of the captain. Luckily I found, in a few minutes, some gentlemen of Montserrat whom I knew; and having told them my situation, I requested their friendly assistance in helping me off the island. Some of them, on this, went with me to the captain, and satisfied him of my freedom;

and, to my very great joy, he desired me to go on board. We then set sail, and the next day, the 23d, I arrived at the wished-for place, after an absence of six months, in which I had more than once experienced the delivering hand of Providence, when all human means of escaping destruction seemed hopeless. I saw my friends with a gladness of heart, which was increased by my absence, and the dangers I had escaped; and I was received with great friendship by them all, but particularly by Mr. King, to whom I related the fate of his sloop, the Nancy, and the causes of her being wrecked. I now learned, with extreme sorrow, that his house was washed away during my absence, by the bursting of a pond at the top of a mountain that was opposite the town of Plymouth. It swept a great part of the town away, and Mr. King lost a great deal of property from the inundation, and nearly his life. When I told him I intended to go to London that season, and that I had come to visit him before my departure, the good man expressed a great deal of affection for me, and sorrow that I should leave him, and warmly advised me to stay there; insisting, as I was much respected by all the gentlemen in the place, that I might do very well, and in a short time have land and slaves of my own. I thanked him for this instance of his friendship; but, as I wished very much to be in London, I declined remaining any longer there, and begged he would excuse me. I then requested he would be kind enough to give me a certificate of my behaviour while in his service, which he very readily complied with, and gave me the following:

Montserrat, 26th of July, 1767.

The bearer hereof, Gustavus Vasa, was my slave for upwards of three years, during which he has always behaved himself well, and discharged his duty with honesty and assiduity.
ROBERT KING.
To all whom this may concern.

Having obtained this, I parted from my kind master, after many sincere professions of gratitude and regard, and prepared for my departure for London. I immediately agreed to go with one Capt. John Hamer, for seven guineas (the passage to London), on board a ship called the Andromache; and on the 24th and 25th, I had free dances, as they are called, with some of my friends and countrymen, previous to my setting off; after which I took leave of all my friends, and on the 26th I embarked for London, exceedingly glad to see myself once more on board of a ship, and still more so, in steering the course I had long wished for. With a light heart I bade Montserrat farewell, and never had my feet on it since; and with it I bade adieu to the sound of the cruel whip, and all other dreadful instruments of torture! adieu to the offensive sight of the violated chastity of the sable females, which has too often accosted my eyes! adieu to oppressions (although to me less severe than to most of my countrymen!) and adieu to the angry howling dashing surfs! I wished for a grateful and thankful heart to praise the Lord God on high for all his mercies! in this extacy I steered the ship all night.

We had a most prosperous voyage, and, at the end of seven weeks, arrived at Cherry-garden stairs. Thus were my longing eyes once more gratified with a sight of London, after having been absent from it above four years. I immediately received my wages, and I never had earned seven guineas so quick in my life before; I had thirty-seven guineas in all, when I got cleared of the ship. I now entered upon a scene quite new to me, but full of hope. In this situation my first thoughts were to look out for some of my former friends, and amongst the first of those were the Miss Guerins. As soon as I had regaled myself I went in quest of those kind ladies, whom I was very impatient to see; and, with some difficulty and perseverance, I found them at May's-hill, Greenwich. They were most agreeably surprised to see me, and I was quite overjoyed at meeting with them. I told them my history, at which they expressed great wonder, and freely acknowledged it did their cousin, Capt. Pascal, no honour. He then visited there frequently; and I met him, four or five days after, in Greenwich-park. When he saw me, he appeared a good deal surprised, and asked me how I came back? I answered, "In a ship." To which he replied dryly, "I suppose you did not walk back to London on the water." As I saw, by his manner, that he did not seem to be sorry for his behaviour to me, and that I had not much reason to expect any favour from him, I told him that he had used me very ill, after I had been such a faithful servant to him for so many years; on which, without saying any more, he turned about and went away. A few days after this I met Capt. Pascal at Miss Guerin's house, and asked him for my prize-money. He said there was none due to me; for if my prize-money had been 10,000£ he had a right to it all. I told him I was informed otherwise, on which he bade me defiance, and, in a bantering tone, desired me to commence a law-suit against him for it: "There are lawyers enough," said he, "that will take the cause in hand, and you had better try it." I told him then that I would try it, which enraged him very much; however, out of regard to the ladies, I remained still, and never made any farther demand of my right. Some time afterwards, these friendly ladies asked me what I meant to do with myself, and how they could assist me. I thanked them, and said, if they pleased, I would be their servant; but if not I had thirty-seven guineas, which would support me for some time, and I would be much obliged to them to recommend me to some person who would teach me a business whereby I might earn my living. They answered me very politely, that they were sorry it did not suit them to take me as their servant, and asked me what business I should like to learn? I said, hair-dressing. They then promised to assist me in this; and soon after, they recommended me to a gentleman, whom I had known before, one Capt. O'Hara, who treated me with much kindness, and procured me a master, a hair-dresser, in Coventry-court, Haymarket, with whom he placed me. I was with this man from September till the February following. In that time we had a neighbour in the same court, who taught the French-horn. He used to blow it so well that I was charmed with it, and agreed with him to teach me to blow it. Accordingly he took me in hand, and began to instruct me, and I soon learned all the three parts. I took great delight in blowing on this instrument, the evenings being long; and besides that I was fond of it, I did not like to be idle, and it filled up my vacant hours innocently. At this time also I agreed with the Rev. Mr. Gregory, who lived in the same court, where he kept an academy and an evening school, to improve me in arithmetic. This he did as far as Barter and Aligation; so that all the time I was here I was entirely employed. In February 1768, I hired myself to Dr. Charles Irving, in Pall-mall, so celebrated for his successful experiments in making sea-water fresh; and here I had plenty of hair-dressing to improve my hand. This gentleman was an excellent master; he was exceedingly kind and good-tempered; and allowed me in the evenings to attend my schools, which I esteemed a great blessing; therefore I thank God and him for it, and used all diligence to improve the opportunity. This diligence and attention recommended me to the notice and care of my three preceptors, who, on their parts, bestowed a great deal of pains in my instruction, and besides were all very kind to me. My wages, however, which were by two-thirds less than ever I had in my life (for I had only 12£. per ann.) I soon found would not be sufficient to defray this extraordinary expence of masters, and my own necessary expences; my old thirty-seven guineas had by this time worn all away to one. I thought it best, therefore, to try the sea again in quest of more money, as I had been bred to it, and had hitherto found the profession of it successful. I had also a very great desire to see Turkey, and I now determined to gratify it. Accordingly, in the month of May, 1768, I told the Doctor of my wish to go to sea again, to which he made no opposition; and we parted on friendly terms. The same day I went into the city in quest of a master. I was extremely fortunate in my enquiry; for I soon heard of a gentleman who had a ship going to Italy and Turkey, and he wanted a man who could dress hair well. I was overjoyed at this, and went immediately on board of his ship, as I had been directed, which I found to be fitted up with great taste, and I already foreboded no small pleasure in sailing in her. Not finding the gentleman on board, I was directed to his lodgings, where I met with him the next day, and gave him a specimen of my dressing. He liked it so well that he hired me immediately, so that I was perfectly happy, for the ship, master, and voyage, were entirely to my mind. The ship was called the Delaware, and my master's name was John Jolly, a neat, smart, good-humoured man, just such a one as I wished to serve. We sailed from England in July following, and our voyage was extremely pleasant. We went to Villa Franca, Nice, and Leghorn; and in all these places I was charmed with the richness and beauty of the countries, and struck with the elegant buildings with which they abound. We had always in them plenty of extraordinary good wines and rich fruits, which I was very fond of; and I had frequent occasions of gratifying both my taste and curiosity; for my captain always lodged on shore in those places, which afforded me opportunities to see the country around. I also learned navigation of the mate, which I was very fond of. When we left Italy, we had delightful sailing among the Archipelago islands, and from thence to Smyrna in Turkey. This is a very ancient city; the houses are built of stone, and most of them have graves adjoining to them; so that they sometimes present the appearance of church-yards. Provisions are very plentiful in this city, and good wine less than a penny a pint. The grapes, pomegranates, and many other fruits, were also the richest and largest I ever saw or tasted. The natives are well-looking and strong made, and treated me always with great civility. In general I believe they are fond of black people; and several of them gave me pressing invitations to stay amongst them, although they keep the Franks, or Christians, separate, and do not suffer them to dwell immediately amongst them. I was astonished in not seeing women in any of their shops, and very rarely any in the streets; and whenever I did they were covered with a veil from head to foot, so that I could not see their faces, except when any of them, out of curiosity, uncovered them to look at me, which they sometimes did. I was surprised to see how the Greeks are, in some measure, kept under by the Turks, as the negroes are in the West-Indies by the white people. The less refined Greeks, as I have already hinted, dance here in the same manner as we do in our nation.

On the whole, during our stay here, which was about five months, I liked the place and the Turks extremely well. I could not help observing one remarkable circumstance there; the tails of the sheep are flat, and so very large, that I have known the tail even of a lamb to weigh from eleven to thirteen pounds. The fat of them is very white and rich, and

is excellent in puddings, for which it is much used. Our ship
being at length richly loaded with silk and other articles, we
sailed for England.

In May 1769, soon after our return from Turkey, our ship
made a delightful voyage to Oporto, in Portugal, where we
arrived at the time of the carnival. On our arrival, there
were sent on board of us thirty-six articles to be observed,
with very heavy penalties if we should break any of them;
and none of us even dared to go on board any other vessel,
or on shore, till the Inquisition had sent on board and
searched for every thing illegal, especially bibles. All we had
were produced, and certain other things were sent on shore
till the ships were going away; and any person, in whose
custody a bible was found concealed, was to be imprisoned
and flogged, and sent into slavery for ten years. I saw here
many magnificent sights, particularly the garden of Eden,
where many of the clergy and laity went in procession in
their several orders with the host, and sung Te Deum. I had
a great curiosity to go into some of their churches, but could
not gain admittance without using the necessary sprinkling
of holy water at my entrance. From curiosity, and a wish to
be holy, I therefore complied with this ceremony, but its virtues were lost upon me, for I found myself nothing the better for it. This place abounds with plenty of all kinds of
provisions. The town is well built and pretty, and commands
a fine prospect. Our ship having taken in a load of wine, and
other commodities, we sailed for London, and arrived there
in July following.

Our next voyage was to the Mediterranean. The ship was
again got ready, and we sailed in September for Genoa. This
is one of the finest cities I ever saw; some of the edifices
were of beautiful marble, and made a most noble appearance; and many had very curious fountains before them.
The churches were rich and magnificent, and curiously
adorned both in the inside and out. But all this grandeur
was, in my eyes, disgraced by the galley-slaves, whose condition, both there and in other parts of Italy, is truly piteous
and wretched. After we had staid there some weeks, during
which we bought many different things we wanted, and got
them very cheap, we sailed to Naples, a charming city, and
remarkably clean. The bay is the most beautiful I ever saw;

the moles for shipping are excellent. I thought it extraordinary to see grand operas acted here on Sunday nights, and even attended by their Majesties. I too, like these great ones, went to those sights, and vainly served God in the day while I thus served mammon effectually at night. While we remained here, there happened an eruption of Mount Vesuvius, of which I had a perfect view. It was extremely awful; and we were so near that the ashes from it used to be thick on our deck. After we had transacted our business at Naples, we sailed with a fair wind once more for Smyrna, where we arrived in December. A seraskier, or officer, took a liking to me here, and wanted me to stay, and offered me two wives; however I refused the temptation, thinking one was as much as some could manage, and more than others would venture on. The merchants here travel in caravans or large companies. I have seen many caravans from India, with some hundreds of camels, laden with different goods. The people of these caravans are quite brown. Among other articles, they brought with them a great quantity of locusts, which are a kind of pulse, sweet and pleasant to the palate, and in shape resembling French beans, but longer. Each kind of goods is sold in a street by itself, and I always found the Turks very honest in their dealings. They let no Christians into their mosques, or churches, for which I was very sorry; as I was always fond of going to see the different modes of worship of the people wherever I went. The plague broke out while we were in Smyrna, and we stopped taking goods into the ship till it was over. She was then richly laden, and we sailed in about March 1770 for England. One day in our passage we met with an accident which was near burning the ship. A black cook, in melting some fat, overset the pan into the fire under the deck, which immediately began to blaze, and the flame went up very high under the foretop. With the fright, the poor cook became almost white, and altogether speechless. Happily, however, we got the fire out without doing much mischief. After various delays in this passage, which was tedious, we arrived in Standgate-creek in July; and at the latter end of the year, some new event occurred, so that my noble captain, the ship, and I, all separated.

In April 1771, I shipped myself as a steward with Capt. William Robertson, of the ship Grenada Planter, once more to try my fortune in the West-Indies; and we sailed from London for Madeira, Barbadoes, and the Grenadas. When we were at this last place, having some goods to sell, I met once more with my former kind of West-India customers.

A white man, an islander, bought some goods of me to the amount of some pounds, and made me many fair promises as usual, but without any intention of paying me. He had likewise bought goods from some more of our people, whom he intended to serve in the same manner; but he still amused us with promises. However, when our ship was loaded and near sailing, this honest buyer discovered no intention or sign of paying for any thing he had bought of us; but, on the contrary, when I asked him for my money, he threatened me and another black man he had bought goods of, so that we found we were like to get more blows than payment. On this we went to complain to one Mr. M'Intosh, a justice of the peace; we told his worship of the man's villainous tricks, and begged that he would be kind enough to see us redressed: but being negroes, although free, we could not get any remedy; and our ship being then just upon the point of sailing, we knew not how to help ourselves, though we thought it hard to lose our property in this manner. Luckily for us, however, this man was also indebted to three white sailors, who could not get a farthing from him; they therefore readily joined us, and we all went together in search of him. When we found where he was, we took him out of a house and threatened him with vengeance; on which, finding he was likely to be handled roughly, the rogue offered each of us some small allowance, but nothing near our demands. This exasperated us much; and some were for cutting his ears off; but he begged hard for mercy, which was at last granted him, after we had entirely stripped him. We then let him go, for which he thanked us, glad to get off so easily, and ran into the bushes, after having wished us a good voyage. We then repaired on board, and shortly after set sail for England. I cannot help remarking here a very narrow escape we had from being blown up, owing to a piece of negligence of mine. Just as our ship was under sail,

I went down under the cabin to do some business, and had a lighted candle in my hand, which, in my hurry, without thinking, I held in a barrel of gunpowder. It remained in the powder until it was near catching fire, when fortunately I observed it, and snatched it out in time and providentially no harm happened; but I was so overcome with terror, that I immediately fainted at the deliverance.

In twenty-eight days time we arrived in England, and I got clear of this ship. But, being still of a roving disposition, and desirous of seeing as many different parts of the world as I could, I shipped myself soon after, in the same year, as steward on board of a fine large ship, called the Jamaica, Captain David Watt; and we sailed from England in December 1771, for Nevis and Jamaica. I found Jamaica to be a very fine, large island, well peopled, and the most considerable of the West-India islands. There were a vast number of negroes here, whom I found, as usual, exceedingly imposed upon by the white people, and the slaves punished as in the other islands. There are negroes whose business it is to flog slaves; they go about to different people for employment, and the usual pay is from one to four bits. I saw many cruel punishments inflicted on the slaves in the short time I staid here. In particular I was present when a poor fellow was tied up and kept hanging by the wrists at some distance from the ground, and then some half hundred weights were fixed to his ancles, in which posture he was flogged most unmercifully. There were also, as I heard, two different masters noted for cruelty on the island, who had staked up two negroes naked, and in two hours the vermin stung them to death. I heard a gentleman, I well knew, tell my captain, that he passed sentence on a negro man to be burnt alive for attempting to poison an overseer. I pass over numerous instances, in order to relieve the reader by a milder scene of roguery. Before I had been long on the island, one Mr. Smith, at Port Morant, bought goods of me to the amount of twenty-five pounds sterling; but when I demanded payment from him, he was each time going to beat me, and threatened that he would put me in gaol. One time he would say I was going to set his house on fire; at another he would swear I was going to run away with his slaves. I was astonished at this usage from a person who was in the situation of a gentleman, but I had no alternative, and was therefore obliged to submit. When I came to Kingston, I was surprised to see the number of Africans, who were assembled together on Sundays; particularly at a large commodious place called Spring Path. Here each different nation of Africa meet and dance, after the manner of their own country. They still retain most of their native customs: they bury their dead, and put victuals, pipes, and tobacco, and other things in the grave with the corpse, in the same manner as in Africa. Our ship having got her loading, we sailed for London, where we arrived in the August following. On my return to London, I waited on my old and good master, Dr. Irving, who made me an offer of his service again. Being now tired of the sea, I gladly accepted it. I was very happy in living with this gentleman once more; during which time we were daily employed in reducing old Neptune's dominions by purifying the briny element, and making it fresh. Thus I went on till May 1773, when I was roused by the sound of fame to seek new adventures, and to find, towards the North Pole, what our Creator never intended we should, a passage to India. An expedition was now fitting out to explore a north-east passage, conducted by the Honourable Constantine John Phipps, late Lord Mulgrave, in his Majesty's sloop of war the Race Horse. My master being anxious for the reputation of this adventure, we therefore prepared every thing for our voyage, and I attended him on board the Race Horse, the 24th day of May 1773. We proceeded to Sheerness, where we were joined by his Majesty's sloop the Carcass, commanded by Capt. Lutwidge. On the 4th of June we sailed towards our destined place, the pole; and on the 15th of the same month we were off Shetland. On this day I had a great and unexpected deliverance from an accident which was near blowing up the ship and destroying the crew, which made me ever after during the voyage uncommonly cautious. The ship was so filled that there was very little room on board for any one, which placed me in a very awkward situation. I had resolved to keep a journal of this singular and interesting voyage; and I had no other place for this purpose but a little cabin, or the doctor's store-room, where I slept. This little place was stuffed with all manner of combustibles, particularly with tow and aquafortis, and many other dangerous things. It happened in the evening, as I was writing my journal, that I had occasion to take the candle out of the lanthorn, and a spark unfortunately having touched a single thread of the tow, all the rest caught the flame, and immediately the whole was in a blaze. I saw nothing but present death before me, and expected to be the first to perish in the flames. In a moment the alarm was spread, and many people who were near ran to assist in putting out the fire. All this time I was in the very midst of the flames; my shirt, and the handkerchief on my neck, were burnt, and I was almost smothered with the smoke. However, through God's mercy, as I was nearly giving up all hopes, some people brought blankets and mattresses, and threw them on the flames, by which means, in a short time, the fire was put out. I was severely reprimanded and menaced by such of the officers who knew it, and strictly charged never more to go there with a light; and, indeed, even my own fears made me give heed to this command for a little time; but at last, not being able to write my journal in any other part of the ship, I was tempted again to venture by stealth with a light in the same cabin, though not without considerable fear and dread on my mind. On the 20th of June we began to use Dr. Irving's apparatus for making salt water fresh; I used to attend the distillery; I frequently purified from twenty-six to forty gallons a day. The water thus distilled was perfectly pure, well tasted, and free from salt; and was used on various occasions on board the ship. On the 28th of June, being in lat[itude]. 78, we made Greenland, where I was surprised to see the sun did not set. The weather now became extremely cold; and as we sailed between north and east, which was our course, we saw many very high and curious mountains of ice; and also a great number of very large whales, which used to come close to our ship, and blow the water up to a very great height in the air. One morning we had vast quantities of sea-horses about the ship, which neighed exactly like any other horses. We fired some harpoon guns amongst them in order to take some, but we could not get any. The 30th, the captain of a Greenland ship came on board, and told us of three ships that were lost in the ice; however we still held on our course till July the 11th, when we were stopt by one compact impenetrable body of ice. We ran along it from east to west above ten degrees; and on the 27th we got as far north as 80, 37; and in 19 or 20 degrees east longitude from London. On the 29th and 30th of July we saw one continued plain of smooth unbroken ice, bounded only by the horizon, and we fastened to a piece of ice that was eight yards eleven inches thick. We had generally sunshine, and constant day-light; which gave cheerfulness and novelty to the whole of this striking, grand, and uncommon scene; and, to heighten it still more, the reflection of the sun from the ice gave the clouds a most beautiful appearance. We killed many different animals at this time, and, among the rest, nine bears. Though they had nothing in their paunches but water yet they were all very fat. We used to decoy them to the ship sometimes by burning feathers or skins. I thought them coarse eating, but some of the ship's company relished them very much. Some of our people once, in a boat, fired at and wounded a sea-horse, which dived immediately; and in a little time after brought up with it a number of others. They all joined in an attack upon the boat, and were with difficulty prevented from staving or oversetting her; but a boat from the Carcass having come to assist ours, & joined it, they dispersed, after having wrested an oar from one of the men. One of the ship's boats had before been attacked in the same manner, but happily no harm was done. Though we wounded several of these animals we never got but one. We remained hereabouts until the 1st of August; when the two ships got completely fastened in the ice, occasioned by the loose ice that set in from the sea. This made our situation very dreadful and alarming; so that on the 7th day we were in very great apprehension of having the ships squeezed to pieces. The officers now held a council to know what was best for us to do in order to save our lives; and it was determined that we should endeavour to escape by dragging our boats along the ice towards the sea; which, however, was farther off than any of us thought. This determination filled us with extreme dejection, and confounded us with despair; for we had very little prospect of escaping with life. However, we sawed some of the ice about the ships, to keep it from hurting them; and thus kept them in a kind of pond. We then began to drag the boats as well as we could towards the sea; but, after two or three days labour, we made very little progress; so that some of our hearts totally failed us, and I really began to give up myself for lost, when I saw our surrounding calamities. While we were at this hard labour I once fell into a pond we had made amongst some loose ice, and was very near being drowned; but providentially some people were near, who gave me immediate assistance, and thereby I escaped drowning. Our deplorable condition, which kept up the constant apprehension of our perishing in the ice, brought me gradually to think of eternity in such a manner as I never had done before. I had the fears of death hourly upon me, and shuddered at the thoughts of meeting the grim king of terrors in the *natural* state I then was in, and was exceedingly doubtful of a happy eternity if I should die in it. I had no hopes of my life being prolonged for any time; for we saw that our existence could not be long on the ice after leaving the ships, which were now out of sight, and some miles from the boats. Our appearance now became truly lamentable; pale dejection seized every countenance; many, who had been before blasphemers, in this our distress began to call on the good God of heaven for his help; and in the time of our utter need he heard us, and against hope, or human probability, delivered us! It was the eleventh day of the ships being thus fastened, and the fourth of our drawing the boats in this manner, that the wind changed to the E. N. E. The weather immediately became mild and the ice broke towards the sea, which was to the S. W. of us. Many of us on this got on board again, and with all our might we hove the ships into every open water we could find, and made all the sail on them in our power: now, having a prospect of success, we made signals for the boats and the remainder of the people. This seemed to us like a reprieve from death; and happy was the man who could first get on board of any ship, or the first boat he could meet. We then proceeded in this manner till we got into the open water again, which we accomplished in about thirty hours, to our infinite joy and gladness of heart. As soon as we were out of danger, we came to anchor and refitted; and on the 19th of August we sailed from this uninhabited extremity of the world, where the inhospitable climate affords neither food nor shelter, and not a tree or shrub of any kind grows amongst its barren rocks, but all is one desolate and expanded waste of ice, which even the constant beams of the sun, for six months in the year, cannot penetrate or dissolve. The sun now being on the decline, the days shortened as we sailed to the southward; and, on the 28th, in latitude 73, it was dark by ten o'clock at night. September the 10th, in latitude 58–59, we met a very severe gale of wind and high seas, and shipped a great deal of water in the space of ten hours. This made us work exceedingly hard at all our pumps a whole day; and one sea, which struck the ship with more force than any thing I ever met with of the kind before, laid her under water for some time, so that we thought she would have gone down. Two boats were washed from the booms, and the long-boat from the chucks; all other moveable things on the deck were also washed away, among which were many curious things of different kinds, which we had brought from Greenland; and we were obliged, in order to lighten the ship, to toss some of our guns overboard. We saw a ship at the same time in very great distress, and her masts were gone; but we were unable to assist her. We now lost sight of the Carcass till the 26th, when we saw land about Orfordness, off which place she joined us. From thence we sailed for London, and on the 30th came up to Deptford. And thus ended our Arctic voyage, to the no small joy of all on board, after having been absent four months; in which time, at the imminent hazard of our lives, we explored nearly as far towards the Pole as 81 degrees north, and 20 degrees east longitude; being much farther, by all accounts, than any navigator had ever ventured before; in which we fully proved the impracticability of finding a passage that way to India.

CHAP. X.

The Author leaves Dr. Irving, and engages on board a Turkey ship—Account of a black man's being kidnapped on board, and sent to the West Indies, and the Author's fruitless endeavours to procure his freedom—Some account of the manner of the Author's conversion to the Faith of Jesus Christ.

OUR voyage to the North Pole being ended, I returned to London with Dr. Irving, with whom I continued for some time, during which I began seriously to reflect on the dangers I had escaped, particularly those of my last voyage, which made a lasting impression on my mind, and, by the grace of God, proved afterwards a mercy to me: it caused me to reflect deeply on my eternal state, and to seek the Lord with full purpose of heart ere it be too late. I rejoiced greatly; and heartily thanked the Lord for directing me to London, where I was determined to work out my own salvation, and, in so doing, procure a title to heaven; being the result of a mind blinded by ignorance and sin.

In process of time I left my master, Doctor Irving, the purifier of waters. I lodged in Coventry-court, Haymarket, where I was continually oppressed and much concerned about the salvation of my soul, and was determined (in my own strength) to be a first-rate Christian. I used every means for this purpose; and, not being able to find any person amongst those with whom I was then acquainted that acquiesced with me in point of religion, or, in scripture language, that would shew me any good, I was much dejected, and knew not where to seek relief; however, I first frequented the neighbouring churches, St. James's and others, two or three times a day, for many weeks: still I came away dissatisfied: something was wanting that I could not obtain, and I really found more heart-felt relief in reading my bible at home than in attending the church; and, being resolved to be saved, I pursued other methods. First I went among the people called Quakers, whose meeting at times was held in silence, and I remained as much in the dark as ever. I then searched into the Roman Catholic principles, but was not in the least edified. I, at length, had recourse to the Jews, which availed me nothing, as the fear of eternity daily harassed my mind and I knew not where to seek shelter from the wrath to come. However, this was my conclusion, at all events, to read the Four Evangelists, and whatever sect or party I found adhering thereto, such I would join. Thus I went on heavily without any guide to direct me the way that leadeth to eternal life. I asked different people questions about the manner of going to heaven, and was told different ways. Here I was much staggered, and could not find any at that time more righteous than myself, or indeed so much inclined to devotion. I thought we should not all be saved (this is agreeable to the holy scriptures), nor would all be damned. I found none among the circle of my acquaintance that kept holy the Ten Commandments. So righteous was I in my own eyes, that I was convinced I excelled many of them in that point, by keeping eight out of ten; and finding those, who in general termed themselves Christians, not so honest or so good in their morals as the Turks. I really thought the Turks were in a safer way of salvation than my neighbours; so that between hopes and fears I went on, and the chief comforts I enjoyed were in the musical French-horn, which I then practised, and also dressing of hair. Such was my situation some months, experiencing the dishonesty of many people here. I determined at last to set out for Turkey, and there to end my days. It was now early in the spring 1774. I sought for a master, and found a Captain John Hughes, commander of a ship called Anglicania, fitting out in the river Thames, and bound to Smyrna in Turkey. I shipped myself with him as a steward; at the same time I recommended to him a very clever black man, John Annis, as a cook. This man was on board the ship near two months doing his duty; he had formerly lived many years with Mr. William Kirkpatrick, a gentleman of the island of St. Kitt's, from whom he parted by consent, though he afterwards tried many schemes to inveigle the poor man. He had applied to many captains, who traded to St. Kitt's, to trepan him; and when all their attempts and schemes of kidnapping proved abortive, Mr. Kirkpatrick came to our ship at Union-stairs, on Easter Monday, April the 4th, with two wherry-boats and six men, having learned that the man was on board; and tied, and forcibly took him away from the ship, in the presence of the crew and the chief mate, who had detained him after he had information to come away. I believe this was a combined piece of business; but, be that as it may, it certainly reflected great disgrace on the mate, and captain also, who, although they had desired the oppressed man to stay on board, yet notwithstanding this vile act on the man who had served him, he did not in the least assist to recover him, or pay me a farthing of his wages, which was about five pounds. I proved the only friend he had, who attempted to regain him his liberty, if possible, having known the want of liberty myself. I sent, as soon as I could, to Gravesend, and got knowledge of the ship in which he was; but unluckily she had sailed the first tide after he was put on board. My intention was then immediately to apprehend Mr. Kirkpatrick, who was about setting off for Scotland; and having obtained a *habeas corpus* for him, and got a tipstaff to go with me to St. Paul's Church yard, where he lived; he, suspecting something of this kind, set a watch to look out. My being known to them obliged me to use the following deception: I whitened my face, that they might not know me, and this had the desired effect. He did not go out of his house that night, and next morning I contrived a well-plotted stratagem, notwithstanding he had a gentleman in his house to personate him. My direction to the tipstaff had the desired effect; he got admittance into the house, and conducted him to a judge, according to the writ. When he came there, his plea was, that he had not the body in custody, on which he was admitted to bail. I proceeded immediately to that well-known philanthropist, Granville Sharp, Esq. who received me with the utmost kindness, and gave me every instruction that was needful on the occasion. I left him in full hopes that I should gain the unhappy man his liberty, with the warmest sense of gratitude towards Mr. Sharp for his kindness. But, alas! my attorney proved unfaithful; he took my money, lost me many months employ, and did not the least good in the cause; and when the poor man arrived at St. Kitt's, he was, according to custom, staked to the ground with four pins through a cord, two on his wrists, and two on his ancles, was cut and flogged most unmercifully, and afterwards loaded cruelly with irons about his neck. I had two very moving letters from him while he was in this situation; and I made attempts to go after him at a great hazard, but was sadly disappointed: I also was told of it by some very respectable families, now in London, who saw him in St. Kitt's, in the same state, in which he remained till kind death released him out of the hands of his tyrants. During this disagreeable business, I was under strong convictions of sin, and thought that my state was worse than any man's; my mind was unaccountably disturbed; I often wished for death, though, at the same time, convinced I was altogether unprepared for that awful summons: suffering much by villains in the late cause, and being much concerned about the state of my soul, these things (but particularly the latter) brought me very low; so that I became a burden to myself, and viewed all things around me as emptiness and vanity, which could give no satisfaction to a troubled conscience. I was again determined to go to Turkey, and resolved, at that time, never more to return to England. I engaged as steward on board a Turkeyman (the Wester Hall, Capt. Lina), but was prevented by means of my late captain, Mr. Hughes, and others. All this appeared to be against me, and the only comfort I then experienced was in reading the Holy Scriptures, where I saw that "there is no new thing under the sun," Eccles[iastes]. i. 9. and what was appointed for me I must submit to. Thus I continued to travel in much heaviness, and frequently murmured against the Almighty, particularly in his providential dealings; and, awful to think! I began to blaspheme, and wished often to be any thing but a human being. In these severe conflicts the Lord answered me by awful "visions of the night, when deep sleep falleth upon men, in slumberings upon the bed," Job xxxiii. 15. He was pleased, in much mercy, to give me to see, and in some measure understand, the great and awful scene of the Judgment-day, that "no unclean person, no unholy thing, can enter into the kingdom of God," Eph[esians]. v. 5. I would then, if it had been possible, have changed my

nature with the meanest worm on the earth, and was ready
to say to the mountains and rocks, "fall on me," Rev[elation].
vi. 16. but all in vain. I then, in the greatest agony, requested
the divine Creator, that he would grant me a small space of
time to repent of my follies and vile iniquities, which I felt
were grievous. The Lord, in his manifold mercies, was
pleased to grant my request, and being yet in a state of time,
the sense of God's mercies was so great on my mind when
I awoke, that my strength entirely failed me for many minutes, and I was exceedingly weak. This was the first spiritual
mercy I ever was sensible of, and being on praying ground,
as soon as I recovered a little strength, and got out of bed
and dressed myself I invoked heaven from my inmost soul,
and fervently begged that God would never again permit
me to blaspheme his most holy name. The Lord, who is
long-suffering, and full of compassion to such poor rebels
as we are, condescended to hear and answer. I felt that I was
altogether unholy, and saw clearly what a bad use I had
made of the faculties I was endowed with: they were given
me to glorify God with; I thought, therefore, I had better
want them here, and enter into life eternal, than abuse them
and be cast into hell fire. I prayed to be directed, if there
were any holier persons than those with whom I was acquainted, that the Lord would point them out to me. I appealed to the searcher of hearts, whether I did not wish to
love him more, and serve him better. Notwithstanding all
this, the reader may easily discern, if a believer, that I was
still in nature's darkness. At length I hated the house in
which I lodged, because God's most holy name was blasphemed in it; then I saw the word of God verified, viz. "Before they call, I will answer; and while they are yet speaking,
I will hear."

I had a great desire to read the Bible the whole day at
home; but not having a convenient place for retirement, I
left the house in the day, rather than stay amongst the
wicked ones; and that day, as I was walking, it pleased God
to direct me to a house where there was an old sea-faring
man, who experienced much of the love of God shed
abroad in his heart. He began to discourse with me; and, as
I desired to love the Lord, his conversation rejoiced me

greatly; and indeed I had never heard before the love of Christ to believers set forth in such a manner, and in so clear a point of view. Here I had more questions to put to the man than his time would permit him to answer: and in that memorable hour there came in a Dissenting Minister; he joined our discourse, and asked me some few questions; among others, where I heard the gospel preached? I knew not what he meant by hearing the gospel; I told him I had read the gospel: and he asked me where I went to church, or whether I went at all, or not? To which I replied, "I attended St. James's, St. Martin's, and St. Ann's, Soho."— "So," said he, "you are a churchman?" I answered, I was. He then invited me to a love feast at his chapel that evening. I accepted the offer, and thanked him; and soon after he went away. I had some further discourse with the old Christian, added to some profitable reading, which made me exceedingly happy. When I left him he reminded me of coming to the feast; I assured him I would be there. Thus we parted, and I weighed over the heavenly conversation that had passed between these two men, which cheered my then heavy and drooping spirit more than any thing I had met with for many months. However, I thought the time long in going to my supposed banquet. I also wished much for the company of these friendly men; their company pleased me much; and I thought the gentleman very kind in asking me, a stranger, to a feast; but how singular did it appear to me, to have it in a chapel! When the wished for hour came I went, and happily the old man was there, who kindly seated me, as he belonged to the place. I was much astonished to see the place filled with people, and no signs of eating and drinking. There were many ministers in the company. At last they began by giving out hymns, and between the singing, the ministers engaged in prayer: in short, I knew not what to make of this sight, having never seen any thing of the kind in my life before now. Some of the guests began to speak their experience, agreeable to what I read in the Scriptures: much was said by every speaker of the providence of God, and his unspeakable mercies to each of them. This I knew in a great measure, and could most heartily join them. But when they spoke of a future state, they seemed to be altogether certain of their calling and election of God; and that no one could ever separate them from the love of Christ, or pluck them out of his hands. This filled me with utter consternation, intermingled with admiration. I was so amazed as not to know what to think of the company; my heart was attracted, and my affections were enlarged; I wished to be as happy as them, and was persuaded in my mind that they were different from the world "that lieth in wickedness," 1 John v. 19. Their language and singing, &c. did well harmonize; I was entirely overcome, and wished to live and die thus. Lastly, some persons produced some neat baskets full of buns, which they distributed about; and each person communicated with his neighbour, and sipped water out of different mugs, which they handed about to all who were present. This kind of Christian fellowship I had never seen, nor ever thought of seeing on earth; it fully reminded me of what I had read in the Holy Scriptures of the primitive Christians, who loved each other and broke bread, in partaking of it, even from house to house. This entertainment (which lasted about four hours) ended in singing and prayer. It was the first soul-feast I ever was present at. These last twenty-four hours produced me things, spiritual and temporal, sleeping and waking, judgment and mercy, that I could not but admire the goodness of God, in directing the blind, blasphemous sinner in the path that he knew not of, even among the just; and instead of judgment he has shewed mercy, and will hear and answer the prayers and supplications of every returning prodigal;

> O! to grace how great a debtor
> Daily I'm constrain'd to be.

After this I was resolved to win heaven, if possible; and if I perished, I thought it should be at the feet of Jesus, in praying to him for salvation. After having been an eyewitness to some of the happiness which attended those who feared God, I knew not how, with any propriety, to return to my lodgings, where the name of God was continually profaned, at which I felt the greatest horror; I paused in my mind for some time, not knowing what to do; whether to hire a bed elsewhere, or go home again. At last, fearing an evil report might arise, I went home, with a farewell to card-playing and vain-jesting, &c. I saw that time was very short, eternity long, and very near; and I viewed those persons alone blessed, who were found ready at midnight-call, or when the Judge of all, both quick and dead, cometh.

The next day I took courage, and went to Holborn, to see my new and worthy acquaintance, the old man, Mr. C——; he, with his wife, a gracious woman, were at work at silk-weaving; they seemed mutually happy, and both quite glad to see me, and I more to see them. I sat down, and we conversed much about soul matters, &c. Their discourse was amazingly delightful, edifying, and pleasant. I knew not at last how to leave this agreeable pair, till time summoned me away. As I was departing, they lent me a little book, entitled "The Conversion of an Indian." It was in questions and answers. The poor man came over the sea to London, to enquire after the Christian's God, who (through rich mercy) he found, and had not his journey in vain. The above book was of great use to me, and at that time was a means of strengthening my faith; however, in parting, they both invited me to call on them when I pleased. This delighted me, and I took care to make all the improvement from it I could: and so far I thanked God for such company and desires. I prayed that the many evils I felt within might be done away, and that I might be weaned from my former carnal acquaintances. This was quickly heard and answered, and I was soon connected with those whom the Scripture calls the excellent of the earth. I heard the gospel preached, and the thoughts of my heart and actions were laid open by the preachers, and the way of salvation by Christ alone was evidently set forth. Thus I went on happily for near two months; and I once heard, during this period, a reverend gentleman, Mr. Green, speak of a man who had departed this life in full assurance of his going to glory. I was much astonished at the assertion; and did very deliberately inquire how he could get at this knowledge. I was answered fully, agreeably to what I read in the oracles of truth; and was told also, that if I did not experience the new birth, and the pardon of my sins, thro' the blood of Christ, before I died, I could not enter the kingdom of heaven. I knew not what to think of this report, as I thought I kept eight commandments out of ten; then my worthy interpreter told me I did not do it, nor could I; and he added, that no man ever did or could keep the commandments, without offending in one point. I thought this sounded very strange, and puzzled me much for many weeks; for I thought it a hard saying. I then asked my friend Mr. L——d, who was clerk in a chapel, why the commandments of God were given, if we could not be saved by them? To which he replied, "The law is a school-master to bring us to Christ," who alone could, and did keep the commandments, and fulfilled all their requirements for his elect people, even those to whom he had given a living faith, and the sins of those chosen vessels *were already* atoned for and forgiven them whilst living; and if I did not experience the same before my exit, the Lord would say at that great day to me, "Go, ye cursed," &c. &c. for God would appear faithful in his judgments to the wicked, as he would be faithful in shewing mercy to those who were ordained to it before the world was; therefore Christ Jesus seemed to be all in all to that man's soul. I was much wounded at this discourse, and brought into such a dilemma as I never expected. I asked him, if *he* was to die that moment, whether he was sure to enter the kingdom of God; and added, "Do you *know* that your sins are forgiven you?" he answered in the affirmative. Then confusion, anger, and discontent seized me, and I staggered much at this sort of doctrine; it brought me to a stand, not knowing which to believe, whether salvation by works, or by faith only in Christ. I requested him to tell me how I might know when my sins were forgiven me. He assured me he could not, and that none but God alone could do this. I told him it was very mysterious; but he said it was really matter of fact, and quoted many portions of Scripture immediately to the point, to which I could make no reply. He then desired me to pray to God to shew me these things. I answered that I prayed to God every day. He said, "I perceive you are a churchman." I answered, I was. He then entreated me to beg of God, to shew me what I was, and the true state of my soul. I thought the prayer very short and odd; so we parted for that time. I weighed all these things over, and could not help thinking how it was possible for a man to know his sins were forgiven him in this life. I wished that God would reveal this self-same thing to me. In a short time after this, I went to Westminster chapel; the late Rev. Dr. Peckwell preached from Lam[entations]. iii. 39. It was a wonderful sermon; he clearly shewed that a living man had no cause to complain for the punishments of his sins; he evidently justified the Lord in all his dealings with the sons of men; he also shewed the justice of God in the eternal punishment of the wicked and impenitent. The discourse seemed to me like a two-edged sword cutting all ways; it afforded me much joy, intermingled with many fears about my soul; and when it was ended, he gave it out that he intended, the ensuing week, to examine all those who meant to attend the Lord's table. Now I thought much of my good works, and, at the same time, was doubtful of my being a proper object to receive the sacrament: I was full of meditation till the day of examining. However, I went to the chapel, and, though much distressed, I addressed the reverend gentleman, thinking, if I was not right, he would endeavour to convince me of it. When I conversed with him, the first thing he asked me was, What I knew of Christ? I told him I believed in him, and had been baptized in his name. "Then," said he, "when were you brought to the knowledge of God; and how were you convinced of sin?" I knew not what he meant by these questions; I told him I kept eight commandments out of ten; but that I sometimes swore on board of ship, and sometimes when on shore, and broke the sabbath. He then asked me if I could read; I answered, "Yes."—"Then," said he, "do you read in the Bible, he that offends in one point is guilty of all?" I said, "Yes." Then he assured me, that one sin unatoned for was as sufficient to damn a soul, as one leak was to sink a ship. Here I was struck with awe; for the minister exhorted me much, and reminded me of the shortness of time, and the length of eternity, and that no unregenerate soul, or any thing unclean, could enter the kingdom of Heaven.

He did not admit me as a communicant; but recommended me to read the scriptures, and hear the word preached; not to neglect fervent prayer to God, who has promised to hear the supplications of those who seek him in godly sincerity; so I took my leave of him, with many thanks, and resolved to follow his advice, so far as the Lord would condescend to enable me. During this time I was out of employ, nor was likely to get a situation suitable for me, which obliged me to go once more to sea. I engaged as steward of a ship called the Hope, Captain Richard Strange, bound from London to Cadiz in Spain. In a short time after I was on board, I heard the name of God much blasphemed, and I feared greatly lest I should catch the horrible infection. I thought if I sinned again, after having life and death set evidently before me, I should certainly go to hell. My mind was uncommonly chagrined, and I murmured much at God's providential dealings with me, and was discontented with the commandments, that I could not be saved by what I had done; I hated all things, and wished I had never been born; confusion seized me, and I wished to be annihilated. One day I was standing on the very edge of the stern of the ship, thinking to drown myself; but this scripture was instantaneously impressed on my mind, "That no murderer hath eternal life abiding in him," I John iii. 15. Then I paused, and thought myself the unhappiest man living. Again, I was convinced that the Lord was better to me than I deserved, and I was better off in the world than many. After this I began to fear death; I fretted, mourned, and prayed, till I became a burden to others, but more so to myself. At length I concluded to beg my bread on shore, rather than go again to sea amongst a people who feared not God, and I entreated the captain three different times to discharge me; he would not, but each time gave me greater encouragement to continue with him, and all on board shewed me very great civility: notwithstanding all this, I was unwilling to embark again. At last some of my religious friends advised me, by saying it was my lawful calling, consequently it was my duty to obey, and that God was not confined to place, &c. particularly Mr. G. Smith, the governor of Tothill-fields, Bridewell, who pitied my case, and read the eleventh chapter of the Hebrews to me, with exhortations. He prayed for me, and I believe that he prevailed on my behalf, as my burden was then greatly removed, and I found a heartfelt resignation to the will of

God. The good man gave me a pocket Bible, and Alleine's Alarm to the Unconverted. We parted, and the next day I went on board again. We sailed for Spain, and I found favour with the captain. It was the fourth of the month of September when we sailed from London, and we had a delightful voyage to Cadiz, where we arrived the twenty-third of the same month. The place is strong, commands a fine prospect, and is very rich. The Spanish galleons frequent that port, and some arrived whilst we were there. I had many opportunities of reading the Scriptures. I wrestled hard with God in fervent prayers, who had declared in his word that he would hear the groanings and deep sighs of the poor in spirit. I found this verified to my utter astonishment and comfort in the following manner: On the morning of the 6th of October (I pray you to attend) all that day, I thought I should see or hear something supernatural. I had a secret impulse on my mind of something that was to take place, which drove me continually for that time to a throne of grace. It pleased God to enable me to wrestle with him, as Jacob did: I prayed that if sudden death were to happen, and I perished, it might be at Christ's feet.

In the evening of the same day, as I was reading and meditating on the fourth chapter of the Acts, twelfth verse, under the solemn apprehensions of eternity, and reflecting on my past actions, I began to think I had lived a moral life, and that I had a proper ground to believe I had an interest in the divine favour; but still meditating on the subject, not knowing whether salvation was to be had partly for our own good deeds, or solely as the sovereign gift of God:—in this deep consternation the Lord was pleased to break in upon my soul with his bright beams of heavenly light; and in an instant, as it were, removing the veil, and letting light into a dark place, Isa[iah]. xxv. 7. I saw clearly, with the eye of faith, the crucified Saviour bleeding on the cross on Mount Calvary: the Scriptures became an unsealed book, I saw myself a condemned criminal under the law, which came with its full force to my conscience, and when "the commandment came sin revived, and I died." I saw the Lord Jesus Christ in his humiliation, loaded and bearing my reproach, sin, and shame. I then clearly perceived, that by the deed of the law no flesh living could be justified. I was then convinced, that by the first Adam sin came, and by the second Adam (the Lord Jesus Christ) all that are saved must be made alive. It was given me at that time to know what it was to be born again, John iii. 5. I saw the eighth chapter to the Romans, and the doctrines of God's decrees verified, agreeable to his eternal, everlasting and unchangeable purposes. The word of God was sweet to my taste, yea sweeter than honey and the honey comb. Christ was revealed to my soul as the chiefest among ten thousand. These heavenly moments were really as life to the dead, and what John calls an earnest of the Spirit. This was indeed unspeakable, and, I firmly believe, undeniable by many. Now every leading providential circumstance that happened to me, from the day I was taken from my parents to that hour, was then, in my view, as if it had but just then occurred. I was sensible of the invisible hand of God, which guided and protected me, when in truth I knew it not: still the Lord pursued me although I slighted and disregarded it; this mercy melted me down. When I considered my poor wretched state, I wept, seeing what a great debtor I was to sovereign free grace. Now the Ethiopian was willing to be saved by Jesus Christ, the sinner's only surety, and also to rely on none other person or thing for salvation. Self was obnoxious, and good works he had none; for it is God that worketh in us both to will and to do. Oh! the amazing things of that hour can never be told—it was joy in the Holy Ghost! I felt an astonishing change; the burden of sin, the gaping jaws of hell, and the fears of death, that weighed me down before, now lost their horror; indeed I thought death would now be the best earthly friend I ever had. Such were my grief and joy, as, I believe, are seldom experienced. I was bathed in tears, and said, What am I, that God should thus look on me, the vilest of sinners? I felt a deep concern for my mother and friends, which occasioned me to pray with fresh ardour; and, in the abyss of thought, I viewed the unconverted people of the world in a very awful state, being without God and without hope.

It pleased God to pour out on me the spirit of prayer and the grace of supplication, so that in loud acclamations I was enabled to praise and glorify his most holy name. When I got out of the cabin, and told some of the people what the Lord had done for me, alas! who could understand me or believe my report! None but to whom the arm of the Lord was revealed. I became a barbarian to them in talking of the love of Christ: his name was to me as ointment poured forth; indeed it was sweet to my soul, but to them a rock of offence. I thought my case singular, and every hour a day until I came to London, for I much longed to be with some to whom I could tell of the wonders of God's love towards me, and join in prayer to him whom my soul loved and thirsted after. I had uncommon commotions within, such as few can tell aught about. Now the Bible was my only companion and comfort; I prized it much, with many thanks to God that I could read it for myself, and was not left to be tossed about or led by man's devices and notions. The worth of a soul cannot be told.—May the Lord give the reader an understanding in this. Whenever I looked in the Bible I saw things new, and many texts were immediately applied to me with great comfort; for I knew that to me was the word of salvation sent. Sure I was that the Spirit which indited the word opened my heart to receive the truth of it as it is in Jesus—that the same Spirit enabled me to act with faith upon the promises which were precious to me, and enabled me to believe to the salvation of my soul. By free grace I was persuaded that I had a part and lot in the first resurrection, and was enlightened with the "light of the living," Job xxxiii. 30. I wished for a man of God, with whom I might converse; my soul was like the chariots of Aminadab, Canticles vi. 12. These, among others, were the precious promises that were so powerfully applied to me: "All things whatsoever ye shall ask in prayer, believing, ye shall receive," Matt[hew]. xxi. 22. "Peace I leave with you, my peace I give unto you," John xiv. 27. I saw the blessed Redeemer to be the fountain of life, and the well of salvation. I experienced him to be all in all; he had brought me by a way that I knew not, and he had made crooked paths straight. Then in his name I set up his Ebenezer, saying, Hitherto He hath helped me: and could say to the sinners about me, Behold what a Saviour I have! Thus I was, by the teaching of that all glorious Deity, the great One in Three, and Three in One, confirmed in the truths of the Bible; those oracles of everlasting truth, on which every soul living must stand or fall eternally, agreeably to Acts iv. 12. "Neither is there salvation in any other, for there is no other name under heaven given among men whereby we must be saved, but only Jesus Christ." May God give the reader a right understanding in these facts! "To him that believeth, all things are possible, but to them that are unbelieving, nothing is pure," Titus i. 15.

During this period we remained at Cadiz until our ship got laden. We sailed about the 4th of November; and, having a good passage, we arrived in London the month following, to my comfort, with heart-felt gratitude to God, for his rich and unspeakable mercies.

On my return, I had but one text which puzzled me, or that the devil endeavoured to buffet me with, viz. Rom[ans]. xi. 6. and as I had heard of the Rev. Mr. Romaine, and his great knowledge in the Scriptures, I wished much to hear him preach. One day I went to Blackfriars church, and, to my great satisfaction and surprise, he preached from that very text. He very clearly shewed the difference between human works and free election, which is according to God's sovereign will and pleasure. These glad tidings set me entirely at liberty, and I went out of the church rejoicing, seeing my spots were those of God's children. I went to Westminster chapel, and saw some of my old friends, who were glad when they perceived the wonderful change that the Lord had wrought in me, particularly Mr. G. Smith, my worthy acquaintance, who was a man of a choice spirit, and had great zeal for the Lord's service. I enjoyed his correspondence till he died in the year 1784. I was again examined in that same chapel, and was received into church-fellowship amongst them: I rejoiced in spirit, making melody in my heart to the God of all my mercies. Now my whole wish was to be dissolved, and to be with Christ—but, alas! I must wait my appointed time.

Miscellaneous Verses;

Or,

Reflections on the State of my Mind during my first Convictions of the Necessity of believing the Truth, and of experiencing the inestimable Benefits of Christianity.

WELL may I say my life has been
One scene of sorrow and of pain;
From early days I griefs have known,
And as I grew my griefs have grown.

Dangers were always in my path,
And fear of wrath and sometimes death;
While pale dejection in me reign'd,
I often wept, by grief constrain'd.

When taken from my native land,
By an unjust and cruel band,
How did uncommon dread prevail!
My sighs no more I could conceal.

To ease my mind I often strove,
And tried my trouble to remove:
I sung and utter'd sighs between—
Assay'd to stifle guilt with sin.

But, O! not all that I could do
Would stop the current of my woe;
Conviction still my vileness shew'd;
How great my guilt—how lost to good.

"Prevented, that I could not die,
Nor could to one sure refuge fly;
An orphan state I had to mourn,—
Forsook by all, and left forlorn."

Those who beheld my downcast mien,
Could not guess at my woes unseen:
They by appearance could not know
The troubles that I waded through.

Lust, anger, blasphemy, and pride,
With legions of such ills beside,
"Troubled my thoughts," while doubts and fears
Clouded and darken'd most my years.

"Sighs now no more would be confin'd—
They breath'd the trouble of my mind:"
I wish'd for death, but check'd the word,
And often pray'd unto the Lord.

Unhappy, more than some on earth,
I thought the place that gave me birth—
Strange thoughts oppress'd—while I replied,
"Why not in Ethiopia died?"

And why thus spar'd, when nigh to hell!—
God only knew—I could not tell!—
"A tott'ring fence, a bowing wall,
I thought myself e'er since the fall."

Oft times I mus'd, and nigh despair,
While birds melodious fill'd the air.
"Thrice happy songsters, ever free,"
How blest were they compar'd to me!

Thus all things added to my pain;
While grief compell'd me to complain;
When sable clouds began to rise,
My mind grew darker than the skies.

The English nation forc'd to leave,
How did my breast with sorrow heave!
I long'd for rest—cried "Help me, Lord!
Some mitigation, Lord, afford!"

Yet on, dejected, still I went—
Heart-throbbing woes within me pent;
Nor land, nor sea, could comfort give,
Nor aught my anxious mind relieve.

Weary with troubles, yet unknown
To all but God and self alone,
Numerous months for peace I strove,
Numerous foes I had to prove.

Inur'd to dangers, grief, and woes,
Train'd up 'midst perils, death, and foes,
I said, "Must it thus ever be?
No quiet is permitted me."

Hard hap, and more than heavy lot!
I pray'd to God, "Forget me not—
What thou ordain'st help me to bear;
But, O! deliver from despair!"

Strivings and wrestling seem'd in vain;
Nothing I did could ease my pain:
Then gave I up my work and will,
Confess'd and own'd my doom was hell!

Like some poor pris'ner at the bar,
Conscious of guilt, of sin, and fear,
Arraign'd, and self-condemn'd, I stood,
"Lost in the world and in my blood!"

Yet here, 'midst blackest clouds confin'd,
A beam from Christ, the day-star, shin'd;
Surely, thought I, if Jesus please,
He can at once sign my release.

I, ignorant of his righteousness,
Set up my labours in its place;
"Forgot for why his blood was shed,
And pray'd and fasted in his stead."

He dy'd for sinners—I am one;
Might not his blood for me atone?
Tho' I am nothing else but sin,
Yet surely he can make me clean!

Thus light came in, and I believ'd;
Myself forgot, and help receiv'd!

My Saviour then I know I found,
For, eas'd from guilt, no more I groan'd.

O, happy hour, in which I ceas'd
To mourn, for then I found a rest!
My soul and Christ were now as one—
Thy light, O Jesus, in me shone!

Bless'd be thy name; for now I know
I and my works can nothing do;
"The Lord alone can ransom man—
For this the spotless Lamb was slain!"

When sacrifices, works, and pray'r,
Prov'd vain, and ineffectual were,
"Lo then I come!" the Saviour cry'd
And, bleeding, bow'd his head and dy'd.

He dy'd for all who ever saw
No help in them, nor by the law:
I this have seen and gladly own
"Salvation is by Christ alone!"

CHAP. XI.

*The Author embarks on board a ship bound for Cadiz—Is near
being shipwrecked—Goes to Malaga—Remarkable for ca-
thedral there—The Author disputes with a Popish priest—
Picks up eleven miserable men at sea in returning to England—Engages again with Doctor Irving to accompany
him to Jamaica and the Musquito shore—Meets with an Indian Prince on board—The Author attempts to instruct him
in the truths of the Gospel—Frustrated by the bad example
of some in the ship—They arrive on the Musquito shore with*

*some slaves they purchased at Jamaica, and begin to cultivate
a Plantation—Some account of the manners and customs of
the Musquito Indians—Successful device of the Author's to
quell a riot among them—Curious entertainment given by
them to Doctor Irving and the Author; he leaves the shore
and goes for Jamaica—Is barbarously treated by a man with
whom he engaged for his passage—Escapes, and goes to the
Musquito admiral, who treats him kindly—He gets another
vessel, and goes on board—Instances of bad treatment—
Meets Dr. Irving—Gets to Jamaica—Is cheated by his
captain—Leaves the Doctor, and sails for England.*

W HEN our ship was got ready for sea again, I was entreated by the captain to go in her once more; but, as I felt
myself as happy as I could wish to be in this life, I for some
time refused; however, the advice of my friends at last prevailed, and in full resignation to the will of God, I again
embarked for Cadiz in March, 1775. We had a very good
passage, without any material accident, until we arrived off
the Bay of Cadiz; when one Sunday, just as we were going
into the harbour, the ship struck against a rock, and knocked
off a garboard plank, which is the next to the keel. In an
instant all hands were in the greatest confusion, and began
with loud cries to call on God to have mercy on them. Although I could not swim, and saw no way of escaping death,
I felt no dread in my then situation, having no desire to live.
I even rejoiced in spirit, thinking this death would be sudden glory. But the fulness of time was not yet come. The
people near to me were very much astonished in seeing me
thus calm and resigned; but I told them of the peace of God,
which, through sovereign grace, I enjoyed, and these words
were that instant in my mind:

Christ is my pilot wise, my compass is his word;
My soul each storm defies, while I have such a Lord.
I trust his faithfulness and power,
To save me in the trying hour.

Though rocks and quicksands deep through all my pas-
    sage lie,
Yet Christ shall safely keep and guide me with his eye.

How can I sink with such a prop,
That bears the world and all things up?

At this time there were many large Spanish flukers or
passage vessels full of people crossing the channel, who,
seeing our condition, a number of them came alongside of
us. As many hands as could be employed began to work;
some at our three pumps, and the rest unloading the ship as
fast as possible. There being only a single rock, called the
Porpus, on which we struck, we soon got off it, and providentially it was then high water; we therefore run the ship
ashore at the nearest place to keep her from sinking. After
many tides, with a great deal of care and industry, we got
her repaired again. When we had dispatched our business
at Cadiz, we went to Gibraltar, and from thence to Malaga,
a very pleasant and rich city, where there is one of the finest
cathedrals I had ever seen. It had been above fifty years in
building, as I had heard, though it was not then quite finished; a great part of the inside, however, was completed,
and highly decorated with the richest marble columns, and
many superb paintings; it was lighted occasionally by an
amazing number of wax tapers of different sizes, some of
which were as thick as a man's thigh; these, however, were
only used on some of their grand festivals.

I was very much shocked at the custom of bull-baiting,
and other diversions which prevailed here on Sunday evenings, to the great scandal of Christianity and morals. I used
to express my abhorrence of it to a priest whom I met with.
I had frequent contests about religion with the reverend
father, in which he took great pains to make a proselyte of
me to his church; and I no less to convert him to mine. On
these occasions I used to produce my bible, and shewed him
in what points his church erred. He then said he had been
in England, and that every person there read the bible,
which was very wrong; but I answered him, that Christ desired us to search the scriptures. In his zeal for my conversion, he solicited me to go to one of the universities in
Spain, and declared that I should have my education free;
and told me, if I got myself made a priest, I might in time
become even Pope; and he said that Pope Benedict was a
black man. As I was ever desirous of learning, I paused

some time upon this temptation, and thought by being crafty (by going to the university), I might catch some with guile; but again I began to think it would only be hypocrisy in me to embrace his offer, as I could not in conscience conform to the opinions of his church. I was therefore enabled to regard the word of God, which says, "Come out from amongst them"; and I refused Father Vincent's offer. So we parted without conviction on either side.

Having taken at this place some fine wines, fruits, and money, we proceeded to Cadiz, where we took about two tons more of money, &c. and then sailed for England in the month of June. When we were about the north latitude 42, we had contrary winds for several days, and the ship did not make in that time above six or seven miles straight course. This made the captain exceedingly fretful and peevish; and I was very sorry to hear God's most holy name often blasphemed by him. One day, as he was in that impious mood, a young gentleman on board, who was a passenger, reproved him, and said, he acted wrong, for we ought to be thankful to God for all things, as we were not in want of any thing on board; and though the wind was contrary for us, yet it was fair for some others, who perhaps stood in more need of it than we. I immediately seconded this young gentleman with some boldness, and said we had not the least cause to murmur, for that the Lord was better to us than we deserved, and that he had done all things well. I expected that the captain would be very angry with me for speaking, but he replied not a word. However, before that time, or hour, on the following day, being the 21st of June, much to our great joy and astonishment, we saw the providential hand of our benign Creator, whose ways with his blind creatures are past finding out. The preceding night I dreamed that I saw a boat immediately off the starboard main shrouds; and exactly at half past one o'clock the following day at noon, while I was below, just as we had dined in the cabin, the man at the helm cried out, A boat! which brought my dream that instant into my mind. I was the first man that jumped on the deck; and looking from the shrouds onward, according to my dream, I descried a little boat at some distance; but, as the waves were high, it was as much as we could do sometimes to discern her; we, however, stopped the ship's way, and the boat which was extremely small, came alongside with eleven miserable men, whom we took on board immediately. To all human appearance, these people must have perished in the course of an hour, or less; the boat being small, it barely contained them. When we took them up they were half drowned, and had no victuals, compass, water, or any other necessary whatsoever, and had only one bit of an oar to stir with, and that right before the wind; so that they were obliged to trust entirely to the mercy of the waves. As soon as we got them all on board, they bowed themselves on their knees, and, with hands and voices lifted up to heaven, thanked God for their deliverance; and I trust that my prayers were not wanting amongst them at the same time. This mercy of the Lord quite melted me, and I recollected his words, which I saw thus verified, in the 107th Psalm, "O give thanks unto the Lord, for he is good, for his mercy endureth for ever. Hungry and thirsty, their souls fainted in them. They cried unto the Lord in their trouble, and he delivered them out of their distresses. And he led them forth by the right way, that they might go to a city of habitation. O that men would praise the Lord for his goodness, and for his wonderful works to the children of men. For he satisfieth the longing soul, and filleth the hungry soul with goodness."

"Such as sit in darkness and in the shadow of death:"

"Then they cried unto the Lord in their trouble, and he saved them out of their distresses. They that go down to the sea in ships; that do business in great waters; these see the works of the Lord, and his wonders in the deep. Whoso is wise and will observe these things, even they shall understand the loving kindness of the Lord."

The poor distressed captain said, "that the Lord is good; for, seeing that I am not fit to die, he therefore gave me a space of time to repent." I was very glad to hear this expression, and took an opportunity, when convenient, of talking to him on the providence of God. They told us they were Portuguese, and were in a brig loaded with corn, which shifted that morning at five o'clock, owing to which the vessel sunk that instant with two of the crew; and how these eleven got into the boat (which was lashed to the deck) not one of them could tell. We provided them with every necessary, and brought them all safe to London: and I hope the Lord gave them repentance unto eternal life.

At our arrival, I was happy once more amongst my friends and brethren till November, when my old friend, the celebrated Dr. Irving, bought a remarkable fine sloop, about 150 tons. He had a mind for a new adventure, in cultivating a plantation at Jamaica and the Musquito Shore; he asked me to go with him, and said that he would trust me with his estate in preference to any one. By the advice, therefore, of my friends, I accepted of the offer, knowing that the harvest was fully ripe in those parts, and I hoped to be an instrument, under God, of bringing some poor sinner to my well-beloved master, Jesus Christ. Before I embarked, I found with the Doctor four Musquito Indians, who were chiefs in their own country, and were brought here by some English traders for some selfish ends. One of them was the Musquito king's son, a youth of about eighteen years of age; and whilst he was here he was baptized by the name of George. They were going back at the government's expence, after having been in England about twelve months, during which they learned to speak pretty good English. When I came to talk to them, about eight days before we sailed, I was very much mortified in finding that they had not frequented any churches since they were here, and were baptized, nor was any attention paid to their morals. I was very sorry for this mock Christianity, and had just an opportunity to take some of them once to church before we sailed. We embarked in the month of November 1775, on board of the sloop Morning Star, Captain David Miller, and sailed for Jamaica. In our passage I took all the pains that I could to instruct the Indian prince in the doctrines of Christianity, of which he was entirely ignorant; and, to my great joy, he was quite attentive, and received with gladness the truths that the Lord enabled me to set forth to him. I taught him in the compass of eleven days all the letters, and he could put even two or three of them together, and spell them. I had Fox's Martyrology with cuts, and he used to be very fond of looking into it, and would ask many questions about the papal cruelties he saw depicted there, which I

explained to him. I made such progress with this youth, especially in religion, that when I used to go to bed at different
hours of the night, if he was in his bed, he would get up on
purpose to go to prayer with me, without any other clothes
than his shirt; and before he would eat any of his meals
amongst the gentlemen in the cabin, he would first come to
me to pray, as he called it. I was well pleased at this, and
took great delight in him, and used much supplication to
God for his conversion. I was in full hope of seeing daily
every appearance of that change which I could wish; not
knowing the devices of Satan, who had many of his emissaries to sow his tares as fast as I sowed the good seed, and pull
down as fast as I built up. Thus we went on nearly four-fifths
of our passage, when Satan at last got the upper hand. Some
of his messengers, seeing this poor heathen much advanced
in piety, began to ask him whether I had converted him to
Christianity, laughed and made their jest at him, for which I
rebuked them as much as I could; but this treatment caused
the prince to halt between two opinions. Some of the true
sons of Belial, who did not believe that there was any hereafter, told him never to fear the devil, for there was none
existing; and if ever he came to the prince, they desired he
might be sent to them. Thus they teazed the poor innocent
youth, so that he would not learn his book any more! He
would not drink nor carouse with these ungodly actors, nor
would he be with me even at prayers. This grieved me very
much. I endeavoured to persuade him as well as I could, but
he would not come; and entreated him very much to tell me
his reasons for acting thus. At last he asked me, "How comes
it that all the white men on board, who can read and write,
observe the sun, and know all things, yet swear, lie, and get
drunk, only excepting yourself?" I answered him, the reason was, that they did not fear God; and that if any one of
them died so, they could not go to, or be happy with God.
He replied, that if a certain person went to hell, he would
go to hell too! I was sorry to hear this; and, as he sometimes
had the tooth-ach, and also some other persons in the ship
at the same time, I asked him if their tooth-ach made him
easy? he said, No. Then I told him, if he and these people
went to hell together, their pains would not make his any

lighter. This had great weight with him, it depressed his spirits much; and he became ever after, during the passage, fond of being alone. When we came into the latitude of Martinico, and near making the land, one morning we had a brisk gale of wind, and, carrying too much sail, the mainmast went over the side. Many people were then all about the deck, and the yards, masts, and rigging, came tumbling all about us, yet there was not one of us in the least hurt, although some were within a hair's breadth of being killed; and, particularly, I saw two men, who, by the providential hand of God, were most miraculously preserved from being smashed to pieces. On the fifth of January we made Antigua and Montserrat, and ran along the rest of the islands: and on the fourteenth we arrived at Jamaica. One Sunday, while we were there, I took the Musquito, prince George, to church, where he saw the sacrament administered. When we came out we saw all kinds of people, almost from the church door for the space of half a mile down to the water-side, buying and selling all kinds of commodities: and these acts afforded me great matter of exhortation to this youth, who was much astonished. Our vessel being ready to sail for the Musquito shore, I went with the Doctor on board a Guineaman, to purchase some slaves to carry with us, and cultivate a plantation; and I chose them all of my own countrymen, some of whom came from Lybia. On the 12th of February we sailed from Jamaica, and on the eighteenth arrived at the Musquito shore, at a place called Dupeupy. All our Indian guests now, after I had admonished them, and a few cases of liquor given them by the Doctor, took an affectionate leave of us, and went ashore, where they were met by the Musquito king, and we never saw one of them afterwards. We then sailed to the southward of the shore, to a place called Cape Gracias a Dios, where there was a large lagoon or lake, which received the emptying of two or three very fine large rivers, and abounded much in fish and land tortoise. Some of the native Indians came on board of us here; and we used them well, and told them we were come to dwell amongst them, which they seemed pleased at. So the Doctor and I, with some others, went with them ashore; and they took us to different places to view the land, in

order to choose a place to make a plantation of. We fixed on
a spot near a river's bank, in a rich soil; and, having got our
necessaries out of the sloop, we began to clear away the
woods, and plant different kinds of vegetables, which had a
quick growth. While we were employed in this manner, our
vessel went northward to Black River to trade. While she
was there, a Spanish guarda costa met with and took her.
This proved very hurtful, and a great embarrassment to us.
However, we went on with the culture of the land. We used
to make fires every night all around us, to keep off wild
beasts, which, as soon as it was dark, set up a most hideous
roaring. Our habitation being far up in the woods, we frequently saw different kinds of animals; but none of them
ever hurt us, except poisonous snakes, the bite of which the
Doctor used to cure by giving to the patient, as soon as possible, about half a tumbler of strong rum, with a good deal
of Cayenne pepper in it. In this manner he cured two natives, and one of his own slaves. The Indians were exceedingly fond of the Doctor, and they had good reason for it;
for I believe they never had such an useful man amongst
them. They came from all quarters to our dwelling; and
some *woolwow*, or flat-headed Indians, who lived fifty or
sixty miles above our river, and this side of the South Sea,
brought us a good deal of silver in exchange for our goods.
The principal articles we could get from our neighbouring
Indians were turtle oil, and shells, little silk grass, and some
provisions; but they would not work at any thing for us,
except fishing; and a few times they assisted to cut some
trees down, in order to build us houses; which they did exactly like the Africans, by the joint labour of men, women,
and children. I do not recollect any of them to have had
more than two wives. These always accompanied their husbands when they came to our dwelling, and then they generally carried whatever they brought to us, and always
squatted down behind their husbands. Whenever we gave
them any thing to eat, the men and their wives ate separate.
I never saw the least sign of incontinence amongst them.
The women are ornamented with beads, and fond of paint-
ing themselves; the men also paint, even to excess, both
their faces and shirts; their favourite colour is red. The
women generally cultivate the ground, and the men are all

fishermen and canoe-makers. Upon the whole, I never met any nation that were so simple in their manners as these people, or had so little ornament in their houses. Neither had they, as I ever could learn, one word expressive of an oath. The worst word I ever heard amongst them when they were quarreling, was one that they had got from the English, which was, "you rascal." I never saw any mode of worship among them; but in this they were not worse than their European brethren or neighbours, for I am sorry to say that there was not one white person in our dwelling, nor any where else, that I saw in different places I was at on the shore, that was better or more pious than those unenlightened Indians; but they either worked or slept on Sundays; and, to my sorrow, working was too much Sunday's employment with ourselves; so much so, that in some length of time we really did not know one day from another. This mode of living laid the foundation of my decamping at last. The natives are well made and warlike; and they particularly boast of having never been conquered by the Spaniards. They are great drinkers of strong liquors when they can get them. We used to distill rum from pine-apples, which were very plentiful here; and then we could not get them away from our place. Yet they seemed to be singular, in point of honesty, above any other nation I was ever amongst. The country being hot, we lived under an open shed, where we had all kinds of goods, without a door or a lock to any one article; yet we slept in safety, and never lost any thing, or were disturbed. This surprised us a good deal; and the Doctor, myself, and others, used to say, if we were to lie in that manner in Europe we should have our throats cut the first night. The Indian governor goes once in a certain time all about the province or district, and has a number of men with him as attendants and assistants. He settles all the differences among the people, like the judges here, and is treated with very great respect. He took care to give us timely notice before he came to our habitation, by sending his stick as a token, for rum, sugar, and gunpowder, which we did not refuse sending; and at the same time we made the utmost preparation to receive his honour and his train. When he came with his tribe, and all our neighbouring chieftains, we expected to find him a grave reverend judge, solid and sagacious; but, instead of that, before he and his gang came in sight, we heard them very clamorous; and they even had plundered some of our good neighbouring Indians, having intoxicated themselves with our liquor. When they arrived we did not know what to make of our new guests, and would gladly have dispensed with the honour of their company. However, having no alternative, we feasted them plentifully all the day till the evening; when the Governor, getting quite drunk, grew very unruly, and struck one of our most friendly chiefs, who was our nearest neighbour, and also took his gold-laced hat from him. At this a great commotion took place; and the Doctor interfered to make peace, as we could all understand one another, but to no purpose; and at last they became so outrageous, that the Doctor, fearing he might get into trouble, left the house, and made the best of his way to the nearest wood, leaving me to do as well as I could among them. I was so enraged with the governor, that I could have wished to have seen him tied fast to a tree, and flogged for his behaviour; but I had not people enough to cope with his party. I therefore thought of a stratagem to appease the riot. Recollecting a passage I had read in the life of Columbus, when he was amongst the Indians in Jamaica, where, on some occasion, he frightened them, by telling them of certain events in the heavens, I had recourse to the same expedient, and it succeeded beyond my most sanguine expectations. When I had formed my determination, I went in the midst of them, and taking hold of the governor, I pointed up to the heavens. I menaced him and the rest: I told them God lived there, and that he was angry with them, and they must not quarrel so; that they were all brothers, and if they did not leave off, and go away quietly, I would take the book (pointing to the bible), read, and *tell* God to make them dead. This was something like magic. The clamour immediately ceased, and I gave them some rum and a few other things; after which they went away peaceably; and the Governor afterwards gave our neighbour, who was called Captain Plasmyah, his hat again. When the Doctor returned, he was exceedingly glad at my success in thus getting rid of our troublesome guests. The Musquito people within our vicinity, out of respect to the

Doctor, myself, and his people, made entertainments of the grand kind, called in their tongue *tourrie* or *drykbot*. The English of this expression is, a feast of drinking about, of which it seems a corruption of language. The drink consisted of pine-apples roasted, and casades chewed or beaten in mortars; which, after lying some time, ferments, and becomes so strong as to intoxicate, when drank in any quantity. We had timely notice given to us of the entertainment. A white family, within five miles of us, told us how the drink was made; I and two others went before the time to the village, where the mirth was appointed to be held, and there we saw the whole art of making the drink and also the kind of animals that were to be eaten there. I cannot say the sight of either the drink or the meat were enticing to me. They had some thousands of pine-apples roasting, which they squeezed, dirt and all, into a canoe they had there for the purpose. The casade drink was in beef barrels and other vessels, and looked exactly like hogwash. Men, women, and children were thus employed in roasting the pine-apples, and squeezing them with their hands. For food they had many land torpins or tortoises, some dried turtle, and three large alligators alive, and tied fast to the trees. I asked the people what they were going to do with these alligators? and I was told they were to be eaten. I was much surprised at this, and went home not a little disgusted at the preparations. When the day of the feast was come, we took some rum with us, and went to the appointed place, where we found a great assemblage of these people, who received us very kindly. The mirth had begun before we came; and they were dancing with music: and the musical instruments were nearly the same as those of any other sable people; but, as I thought, much less melodious than any other nation I ever knew. They had many curious gestures in dancing, and a variety of motions and postures of their bodies, which to me were in no wise attracting. The males danced by themselves, and the females also by themselves, as with us. The Doctor shewed his people the example, by immediately joining the women's party, though not by their choice. On perceiving the women disgusted, he joined the males. At night there were great illuminations, by setting fire to many pine-trees, while the drykbot went round merrily by calabashes or gourds: but the liquor might more justly be called eating than drinking. One Owden, the oldest father in the vicinity, was drest in a strange and terrifying form. Around his body were skins adorned with different kinds of feathers, and he had on his head a very large and high head-piece, in the form of a grenadier's cap, with prickles like a porcupine; and he made a certain noise which resembled the cry of an alligator. Our people skipped amongst them out of complaisance, though some could not drink of their tourrie; but our rum met with customers enough, and was soon gone. The alligators were killed, and some of them roasted. Their manner of roasting is by digging a hole in the earth, and filling it with wood, which they burn to coal, and then they lay sticks across, on which they set the meat. I had a raw piece of the alligator in my hand: it was very rich: I thought it looked like fresh salmon, and it had a most fragrant smell, but I could not eat any of it. This merry-making at last ended without the least discord in any person in the company, although it was made up of different nations and complexions.

The rainy season came on here about the latter end of May, which continued till August very heavily; so that the rivers were overflowed, and our provisions then in the ground were washed away. I thought this was in some measure a judgment upon us for working on Sundays, and it hurt my mind very much. I often wished to leave this place and sail for Europe; for our mode of procedure, and living in this heathenish form was very irksome to me. The word of God saith, "What does it avail a man if he gain the whole world, and lose his own soul?" This was much and heavily impressed on my mind; and, though I did not know how to speak to the Doctor for my discharge, it was disagreeable for me to stay any longer. But about the middle of June I took courage enough to ask him for it. He was very unwilling at first to grant me my request; but I gave him so many reasons for it, that at last he consented to my going, and gave me the following certificate of my behaviour:

The bearer, Gustavus Vassa, has served me several years with strict honesty, sobriety, and fidelity. I can, therefore, with justice recommend him for these qualifications; and indeed in every respect I consider him as an excellent servant. I do hereby certify that he always behaved well, and that he is perfectly trust-worthy.

CHARLES IRVING.

Musquito shore, June 15, 1776

Though I was much attached to the Doctor, I was happy when he consented to my going. I got every thing ready for my departure, and hired some Indians, with a large canoe, to carry me off. All my poor countrymen, the slaves, when they heard of my leaving them, were very sorry, as I had always treated them with care and affection, and did every thing I could to comfort the poor creatures, and render their condition easy. Having taken leave of my old friends and companions, on the 18th of June, accompanied by the Doctor, I left that spot of the world, and went southward above twenty miles along the river. There I found a sloop, the captain of which told me he was going to Jamaica. Having agreed for my passage with him and one of the owners, who was also on board, named Hughes, the Doctor and I parted, not without shedding tears on both sides. The vessel then sailed along the river till night, when she stopped in a lagoon within the same river. During the night a schooner, belonging to the same owners came in, and, as she was in want of hands, Hughes, the owner of the sloop, asked me to go in the schooner as a sailor, and said he would give me wages. I thanked him; but I said I wanted to go to Jamaica. He then immediately changed his tone, and swore, and abused me very much, and asked how I came to be freed! I told him, and said that I came into that vicinity with Dr. Irving, whom he had seen that day. This account was of no use; he still swore exceedingly at me, and cursed the master for a fool that sold me my freedom, and the Doctor for another in letting me go from him. Then he desired me to go in the schooner, or else I should not go out of the sloop as a free man. I said this was very hard, and begged to be put on shore again; but he swore that I should not. I said I had been twice amongst the Turks, yet had never seen any such usage with them, and much less could I have expected any thing of this kind among the Christians. This incensed him exceedingly; and, with a volley of oaths and imprecations, he replied, "Christians! Damn you, you are one of St. Paul's men; but by G——, except you have St. Paul's or St. Peter's faith, and walk upon the water to the shore, you shall not go out of the vessel!" which I now found was going amongst the Spaniards towards Carthagena, where he swore he would sell me. I simply asked him what right he had to sell me? But, without another word, he made some of his people tie ropes round each of my ancles, and also to each wrist, and another rope round my body, and hoisted me up without letting my feet touch or rest upon any thing. Thus I hung, without any crime committed, and without judge or jury, merely because I was a freeman, and could not by the law get any redress from a white person in those parts of the world. I was in great pain from my situation, and cried and begged very hard for some mercy, but all in vain. My tyrant in a rage brought a musquet out of the cabin, and loaded it before me and the crew, and swore that he would shoot me if I cried any more. I had now no alternative; I therefore remained silent, seeing not one white man on board who said a word on my behalf. I hung in that manner from between ten and eleven o'clock at night till about one in the morning; when, finding my cruel abuser fast asleep, I begged some of his slaves to slacken the rope that was round my body, that my feet might rest on something. This they did at the risk of being cruelly used by their master, who beat some of them severely at first for not tying me when he commanded them. Whilst I remained in this condition, till between five and six o'clock next morning, I trusted & prayed to God to forgive this blasphemer, who cared not what he did, but when he got up out of his sleep in the morning was of the very same temper and disposition as when he left me at night. When they got up the anchor, and the vessel was getting under way, I once more cried and begged to be released; and now being fortunately in the way of their hoisting the sails, they loosed me. When I was let down, I spoke to one Mr. Cox, a carpenter, whom I knew on board, on the impropriety of this conduct. He also knew the Doctor, and the good opinion he ever had of me. This man then went to the captain, and told him not to carry me away in that manner; that I was the Doctor's steward, who regarded me very highly, and would resent this usage when he should come to know it. On which he desired a young man to put me ashore in a small canoe I brought with me. This sound gladdened my heart and I got hastily into the canoe, and set off whilst my tyrant was down in the cabin; but he soon spied me out, when I was not above thirty or forty yards from the vessel, and, running upon the deck with a loaded musket in his hand, he presented it at me, and swore heavily and dreadfully, that he would shoot me that instant, if I did not come back on board. As I knew the wretch would have done as he said, without hesitation, I put back to the vessel again; but, as the good Lord would have it, just as I was alongside he was abusing the captain for letting me go from the vessel; which the captain returned, and both of them soon got into a very great heat. The young man that was with me, now got out of the canoe; the vessel was sailing on fast with a smooth sea; and I then thought it was neck or nothing, so at that instant I set off again for my life, in the canoe, towards the shore; and fortunately the confusion was so great amongst them on board, that I got out of the reach of the musket shot, unnoticed, while the vessel sailed on with a fair wind a different way; so that they could not overtake me without tacking: but, even before that could be done, I should have been on shore, which I soon reached, with many thanks to God for this unexpected deliverance. I then went and told the other owner, who lived near that shore (with whom I had agreed for my passage) of the usage I had met with. He was very much astonished, and appeared very sorry for it. After treating me with kindness, he gave me some refreshment, and three heads of roasted Indian corn, for a voyage of about eighteen miles south, to look for another vessel. He then directed me to an Indian chief of a district, who was also the Musquito admiral, and had once been at our dwelling; after which I set off with the canoe across a large lagoon alone (for I could not get any one to assist me) though I was much jaded, and had pains in my bowels, by means of the rope I had hung by the night before. I was therefore at different times unable to manage the canoe, for the paddling was very laborious. However, a little before dark, I got to my destined place,

where some of the Indians knew me, and received me
kindly. I asked for the admiral; and they conducted me to his
dwelling. He was glad to see me, and refreshed me with such
things as the place afforded; and I had a hammock to sleep
in. They acted towards me more like Christians than those
whites I was amongst the last night, though they had been
baptized. I told the admiral I wanted to go to the next port
to get a vessel to carry me to Jamaica; and requested him to
send the canoe back which I then had, for which I was to
pay him. He agreed with me, and sent five able Indians with
a large canoe to carry me and my things to my intended
place, about fifty miles; and we set off the next morning.
When we got out of the lagoon and went along shore, the
sea was so high that the canoe was oftentimes very near
being filled with water. We were obliged to go ashore, and
drag her across different necks of land; we were also two
nights in the swamps, which swarmed with musquito flies,
and they proved troublesome to us. This tiresome journey
of land and water ended, however, on the third day, to my
great joy; and I got on board of a sloop commanded by one
Captain Jenning. She was then partly loaded, and he told
me he was expecting daily to sail for Jamaica; and having
agreed with me to work my passage, I went to work accordingly. I was not many days on board before we sailed; but,
to my sorrow and disappointment, though used to such
tricks, we went to the southward along the Musquito shore,
instead of steering for Jamaica. I was compelled to assist in
cutting a great deal of mahogany wood on the shore as we
coasted along it, and load the vessel with it, before she
sailed. This fretted me much; but, as I did not know how to
help myself among these deceivers, I thought patience was
the only remedy I had left, and even that was forced. There
was much hard work and little victuals on board, except by
good luck we happened to catch turtles. On this coast there
was also a particular kind of fish called manatee, which is
most excellent eating, and the flesh is more like beef than
fish; the scales are as large as a shilling, and the skin thicker
than I ever saw that of any other fish. Within the brackish
waters along shore there were likewise vast numbers of
alligators, which made the fish scarce. I was on board this

sloop sixteen days, during which, in our coasting, we came
to another place, where there was a smaller sloop called the
Indian Queen, commanded by one John Baker. He also was
an Englishman, and had been a long time along the shore
trading for turtle shells and silver, and had got a good quantity of each on board. He wanted some hands very much;
and, understanding I was a freeman, and wanted to go to
Jamaica, he told me if he could get one or two men more,
that he would sail immediately for that Island; he also pretended to show me some marks of attention and respect,
and promised to give me forty-five shillings sterling a month
if I would go with him. I thought this much better than cutting wood for nothing. I therefore told the other captain
that I wanted to go to Jamaica in the other vessel; but he
would not listen to me: and, seeing me resolved to go in a
day or two, he got the vessel under sail, intending to carry
me away against my will. This treatment mortified me extremely. I immediately, according to an agreement I had
made with the captain of the Indian Queen, called for her
boat, which was lying near us, and it came along-side; and
by the means of a north pole shipmate which I met with in
the sloop I was in, I got my things into the boat, and went
on board of the Indian Queen, July the 10th. A few days
after I was there, we got all things ready and sailed; but
again, to my great mortification, this vessel still went to the
south, nearly as far as Carthagena, trading along the coast,
instead of going to Jamaica, as the captain had promised
me: and, what was worst of all, he was a very cruel and
bloody-minded man, and was a horrid blasphemer. Among
others, he had a white pilot, one Stoker, whom he beat
often as severely as he did some negroes he had on board.
One night in particular, after he had beaten this man most
cruelly, he put him into the boat, and made two negroes
row him to a desolate key, or small island; and he loaded
two pistols; and swore bitterly that he would shoot the negroes if they brought Stoker on board again. There was not
the least doubt but that he would do as he said, and the two
poor fellows were obliged to obey the cruel mandate; but,
when the captain was asleep, the two negroes took a blanket, at the risque of their lives, and carried it to the unfor-

tunate Stoker, which I believe was the means of saving his
life from the annoyance of insects. A great deal of entreaty
was used with the captain the next day, before he would
consent to let Stoker come on board; and when the poor
man was brought on board he was very ill, from his situation during the night, and he remained so till he was
drowned a little time after. As we sailed southward we
came to many uninhabited islands, which were overgrown
with fine large cocoa-nut trees. As I was very much in want
of provisions, I brought a boat load of the nuts on board,
which lasted me and others for several weeks, and afforded
us many a delicious repast in our scarcity. One day, before
this, I could not help observing the providential hand of
God, that ever supplies all our wants, though in the ways
and manner we know not. I had been a whole day without
food, and made signals for boats to come off, but in vain. I
therefore earnestly prayed to God for relief in my need;
and at the close of the evening I went off the deck. Just as
I laid down I heard a noise on the deck; and, not knowing
what it meant, I went directly on the deck again, when
what should I see but a fine large fish, about seven or eight
pounds, which had jumped aboard! I took it, and admired,
with thanks, the good hand of God; and what I considered
as not less extraordinary, the captain, who was very avari-
cious, did not attempt to take it from me, there being only
him and I on board; for the rest were all gone ashore trading. Sometimes the people did not come off for some days:
this used to fret the captain, and then he would vent his
fury on me by beating me, or making me feel in other cruel
ways. One day especially, in this wild, wicked, and mad career, after striking me several times with different things,
and once across my mouth, even with a red burning stick
out of the fire, he got a barrel of gunpowder on the deck,
and swore that he would blow up the vessel. I was then at
my wit's end, and earnestly prayed to God to direct me.
The head was out of the barrel; and the captain took a
lighted stick out of the fire to blow himself and me up, because there was a vessel then in sight coming in, which he
supposed was a Spanish Guarda Costa, and he was afraid
of falling into their hands. Seeing this, I got an axe, unnoticed by him, and placed myself between him and the pow-

der, having resolved in myself, as soon as he attempted to
put the fire in the barrel, to chop him down that instant. I
was more than an hour in this situation; during which he
struck me often, still keeping the fire in his hand for this
wicked purpose. I really should have thought myself justifiable in any other part of the world if I had killed him, and
prayed to God, who gave me a mind which rested solely on
himself. I prayed for resignation, that his will might be
done: and the following two portions of his holy word,
which occurred to my mind, buoyed up my hope, and kept
me from taking the life of this wicked man. "He hath determined the times before appointed, and set bounds to
our habitations," Acts xvii. 26. And, "Who is there among
you that feareth the Lord, that obeyeth the voice of his
servant, that walketh in darkness and hath no light? let him
trust in the name of the Lord, and stay upon his God,"
Isaiah l. 10. And this, by the grace of God, I was enabled to
do. I found him a present help in the time of need, and the
captain's fury began to subside as the night approached:
but I found,

> That he who cannot stem his anger's tide
> Doth a wild horse without a bridle ride.

The next morning we discovered that the vessel which had
caused such a fury in the captain was an English sloop. They
soon came to an anchor where we were, and, to my no small
surprise, I learned that Dr. Irving was on board of her on his
way from the Musquito shore to Jamaica. I was for going
immediately to see this old master and friend, but the captain would not suffer me to leave the vessel. I then informed
the Doctor, by letter, how I was treated, and begged that he
would take me out of the sloop: but he informed me that it
was not in his power, as he was a passenger himself; but he
sent me some rum and sugar for my own use. I now learned
that after I had left the estate which I managed for this
gentleman on the Musquito shore, during which the slaves
were well fed and comfortable, a white overseer had supplied my place: this man, through inhumanity and ill-judged
avarice, beat and cut the poor slaves most unmercifully; and
the consequence was, that every one got into a large Pu-

riogua canoe, and endeavoured to escape; but, not knowing where to go, or how to manage the canoe, they were all drowned; in consequence of which the Doctor's plantation was left uncultivated, and he was now returning to Jamaica to purchase more slaves and stock it again.

On the 14th of October, the Indian Queen arrived at Kingston in Jamaica. When we were unloaded I demanded my wages, which amounted to eight pounds five shillings sterling; but Captain Baker refused to give me one farthing, although it was the hardest earned money I ever worked for in my life. I found out Dr. Irving upon this, and acquainted him of the captain's knavery. He did all he could to help me to get my money; and we went to every magistrate in Kingston (and there were nine), but they all refused to do any thing for me, and said my oath could not be admitted against a white man. Nor was this all; for Baker threatened that he would beat me severely if he could catch me, for attempting to demand my money; and this he would have done; but that I got, by means of Dr. Irving, under the protection of Capt. Douglas, of the Squirrel man of war. I thought this exceedingly hard usage; though indeed I found it to be too much the practice there to pay free negro men for their labour in this manner.

One day I went with a free negro tailor, named Joe Diamond, to one Mr. Cochran, who was indebted to him some trifling sum; and the man, not being able to get his money, began to murmur. The other immediately took a horse-whip to pay him with it; but by the help of a good pair of heels, the tailor got off. Such oppressions as these made me seek for a vessel to get off the island as fast as I could: and, by the mercy of God, I found a ship in November bound for England, when I embarked with a convoy, after having taken a last farewell of Dr. Irving. When I left Jamaica he was employed in refining sugars; and offered me a place, but I refused. And some months after my arrival in England I learned, with much sorrow, that this my amiable friend was dead, owing to his having eaten some poisoned fish.

We had many very heavy gales of wind in our passage; in the course of which no material incident occurred, except that an American privateer, falling in with the fleet, was captured and set fire to by his Majesty's ship the Squirrel.

On January the seventh, 1777, we arrived at Plymouth. I was happy once more to tread upon English ground; and, after passing some little time at Plymouth and Exeter among some pious friends, whom I was happy to see, I went to London, with a heart replete with thanks to God for all past mercies.

CHAP. XII.

Different transactions of the Author's life till the present time—His application to the late Bishop of London to be appointed a missionary to Africa—Some account of his share in the conduct of the late expedition to Sierra Leona—Petition to the Queen—His marriage—Conclusion.

Such were the various scenes to which I was a witness, and the fortune I experienced until the year 1777. Since that period, my life has been more uniform, and the incidents of it fewer than in any other equal number of years preceding; I therefore hasten to the conclusion of a narrative, which I fear the reader may think already sufficiently tedious.

I had suffered so many impositions in my commercial transactions in different parts of the world, that I became heartily disgusted with the seafaring life, and was determined not to return to it, at least for some time. I therefore once more engaged in service shortly after my return, and continued for the most part in this situation until 1784.

Soon after my arrival in London, I saw a remarkable circumstance relative to African complexion, which I thought so extraordinary that I shall beg leave just to mention it: A white negro woman, that I had formerly seen in London and other parts, had married a white man, by whom she had three boys, and they were every one mulattoes, and yet they had fine light hair. In 1779, I served Governor Macnamara, who had been a considerable time on the coast of Africa. In the time of my service I used to ask frequently other servants to join me in family prayer; but this only excited their mockery. However, the Governor, understanding that I was of a religious turn, wished to know what religion I was of; I told him I was a protestant of the church of England, agreeable to the thirty-nine articles of that church; and that whomsoever I found to preach according to that doctrine, those I would hear. A few days after this, we had some more discourse on the same subject; when he said he would, if I chose, as he thought I might be of service in converting my countrymen to the Gospel-faith, get me sent out as a missionary to Africa. I at first refused going, and told him how I had been served on a like occasion by some white people the last voyage I went to Jamaica, when I attempted, (if it were the will of God) to be the means of converting the Indian prince; and said I supposed they would serve me worse than Alexander the coppersmith did St. Paul, if I should attempt to go amongst them in Africa. He told me not to fear, for he would apply to the Bishop of London to get me ordained. On these terms I consented to the Governor's proposal to go to Africa, in hope of doing good, if possible, amongst my countrymen; so, in order to have me sent out properly, we immediately wrote the following letters to the late Bishop of London:

To The Right Reverend Father in God, ROBERT, *Lord Bishop of London.*
THE MEMORIAL OF GUSTAVUS VASSA,
    SHEWETH,

    THAT your memorialist is a native of Africa, and has a knowledge of the manners and customs of the inhabitants of that country.

    That your memorialist has resided in different parts of Europe for twenty-two years last past, and embraced the Christian faith in the year 1759.

    That your memorialist is desirous of returning to Africa as a missionary, if encouraged by your Lordship, in hopes of being able to prevail upon his countrymen to become Christians; and your memorialist is the more induced to undertake the same, from the success that has attended the like undertakings when encouraged by the Portuguese through their different settlements on the coast of Africa, and also by the Dutch; both governments encouraged the blacks, who by their education are qualified to undertake the same, and are found more proper than European clergymen, unacquainted with the language and customs of the country.

Your memorialist's only motive for soliciting the office of a missionary is, that he may be a means, under God, of reforming his countrymen and persuading them to embrace the Christian religion. Therefore your memorialist humbly prays your Lordship's encouragement and support in the undertaking.

GUSTAVUS VASSA.

At Mr. Guthrie's, Tailor,
No. 17, Hedge-lane.

MY LORD, I have resided near seven years on the coast of Africa, for most part of the time as commanding officer. From the knowledge I have of the country and its inhabitants, I am inclined to think that the within plan will be attended with great success, if countenanced by your Lordship. I beg further to represent to your Lordship, that the like attempts, when encouraged by other governments, have met with uncommon success; and at this very time I know a very respectable character, a black priest, at Cape Coast Castle. I know the within-named Gustavus Vassa, and believe him a moral good man. I have the honour to be,
My Lord,
Your Lordship's
Humble and obedient Servant,
Grove, 11th March, 1779.
MATT. MACNAMARA.

This letter was also accompanied by the following from Dr. Wallace, who had resided in Africa for many years, and whose sentiments on the subject of the African mission were the same with Governor Macnamara's:

MY LORD,   *March 13, 1779.*
  I have resided near five years in Senegambia, on the
coast of Africa, and have had the honour of filling very
considerable employments in that province. I do approve of the within plan, and think the undertaking very
laudable and proper, and that it deserves your Lordship's protection and encouragement, in which case it
must be attended with the intended success. I am, my
Lord,

                    Your Lordship's
                    humble and obedient Servant,
                    THOMAS WALLACE.

  With these letters I waited on the Bishop, by the Governor's desire, and presented them to his Lordship. He received me with much condescension and politeness; but,
from some certain scruples of delicacy, and saying the Bish-
ops were not of opinion in sending a new missionary to
Africa, he declined to ordain me.
  My sole motive for thus dwelling on this transaction, or
inserting these papers, is the opinion which gentlemen of
sense and education, who are acquainted with Africa, entertain of the probability of converting the inhabitants of it to
the faith of Jesus Christ, if the attempt were countenanced
by the legislature.
  Shortly after this I left the Governor, and served a noble-
man in the Dorsetshire militia, with whom I was encamped
at Coxheath for some time; but the operations there were
too minute and uninteresting to make a detail of.
  In the year 1783, I visited eight counties in Wales, from
motives of curiosity. While I was in that part of the country,
I was led to go down into a coal-pit in Shropshire, but my
curiosity nearly cost me my life; for while I was in the pit the
coals fell in, and buried one poor man, who was not far from
me: upon this I got out as fast as I could, thinking the surface of the earth the safest part of it.
  In the spring of 1784, I thought of visiting old ocean
again. In consequence of this I embarked as steward on
board a fine new ship called the London, commanded by
Martin Hopkins, and sailed for New York. I admired this
city very much; it is large and well-built, and abounds with

provisions of all kinds. [While we lay here, a circumstance happened which I thought extremely singular:—One day a malefactor was to be executed on a gallows; but with condition that if any woman, having nothing on but her shift, married the man under the gallows, his life was to be saved. This extraordinary privilege was claimed; a woman presented herself; and the marriage ceremony was performed.]

Our ship having got laden, we returned to London in January 1785. When she was again ready for another voyage, the captain being an agreeable man, I sailed with him from hence in the spring, March 1785, for Philadelphia. On the 5th of April we took our departure from the land's end, with a pleasant gale; and, about nine o'clock that night the moon shone bright, and the sea was smooth, while our ship was going free by the wind at the rate of about four or five miles an hour.—At this time another ship was going nearly as fast as we on the opposite point, meeting us right in the teeth, yet none on board observed either ship until we struck each other forcibly head and head, to the astonishment and consternation of both crews. She did us much damage, but I believe we did her more; for when we passed by each other, which we did very quickly, they called to us to bring to, and hoist out our boats, but we had enough to do to mind ourselves; and in about eight minutes we saw no more of her. We refitted as well as we could the next day, and proceeded on our voyage, and in May arrived at Philadelphia.

I was very glad to see this favourite old town once more; and my pleasure was much increased in seeing the worthy Quakers, freeing and easing the burthens of many of my oppressed African brethren. It rejoiced my heart when one of these friendly people took me to see a free-school they had erected for every denomination of black people, whose minds are cultivated here, and forwarded to virtue; and thus they are made useful members of the community. Does not the success of this practice say loudly to the planters, in the language of scripture—"Go ye, and do likewise"?

In October 1785, I was accompanied by some of the Africans, and presented this address of thanks to the gentlemen called Friends or Quakers, in Whitehart-court, Lombard-street:

GENTLEMEN,

By reading your book, intitled, A Caution to Great Britain and her Colonies, concerning the Calamitous State of the enslaved Negroes, We, part of the poor, oppressed, needy, and much degraded negroes, desire to approach you, with this address of thanks, with our inmost love and warmest acknowledgments; and with the deepest sense of your benevolence, unwearied labour, and kind interposition, towards breaking the yoke of slavery, and to administer a little comfort and ease to thousands and tens of thousands of very grievously afflicted and too heavy burthened negroes.

Gentlemen, could you, by perseverance, at last be enabled, under God, to lighten in any degree the heavy burthen of the afflicted, no doubt it would, in some measure, be the possible means under God of saving the souls of many of the oppressors; and if so, sure we are that the God, whose eyes are ever upon all his creatures, and always rewards every true act of virtue, and regards the prayers of the oppressed, will give to you and yours those blessings which it is not in our power to express or conceive, but which we, as a part of those captivated, oppressed, and afflicted people, most earnestly wish and pray for.

These gentlemen received us very kindly, with a promise to exert themselves on behalf of the oppressed Africans; and we parted.

While in town, I chanced once to be invited to a Quaker's wedding. The simple and yet expressive mode used at their solemnizations is worthy of note. The following is the true form of it:

Near the close of a meeting for worship, wherein there are frequently seasonable exhortations from some of their ministers, the bride and bridegroom stand up, and, taking each other by the hand in a solemn manner, the man audibly declares to this purpose:

"Friends, in the fear of the Lord, and before this assembly, I take this my friend, M. N. to be my wife; promising, through divine assistance, to be unto her a loving and faithful husband until it shall please the Lord by death to separate us:" And the woman makes the like declaration. Then the man and woman sign their names to the certificate; and as many witnesses as have a mind. I had the honour to subscribe mine to a certificate in Whiteheart-Court, Lombard-Street. This mode I highly recommend.

We returned to London in August, and our ship not going immediately to sea, I shipped as a steward in an American ship called the Harmony, Captain John Willett, and left London in March 1786, bound to Philadelphia. Eleven days after sailing, we carried our foremast away. We had a nine weeks passage, which caused our trip not to succeed well, the market for our goods proving bad; and, to make it worse, my commander began to play me the like tricks as others too often practise on free negroes in the West Indies. But, I thank God, I found many friends here who in some measure prevented him. On my return to London in August, I was very agreeably surprised to find, that the benevolence of government adopted the plan of some philanthropic individuals, to send the Africans from hence to their native quarter, and that some vessels were then engaged to carry them to Sierra Leona; an act which redounded to the honour of all concerned in its promotion, and filled me with prayers and much rejoicing. There was then in the city a select committee of gentlemen for the black poor, to some of whom I had the honour of being known; and as soon as they heard of my arrival, they sent for me to the committee. When I came there, they informed me of the intention of government; and, as they seemed to think me qualified to superintend part of the undertaking, they asked me to go with the black poor to Africa. I pointed out to them many objections to my going; and particularly I expressed some difficulties on the account of the slave-dealers, as I would certainly oppose their traffic in the human species by every means in my power. However, these objections were over-ruled by the gentlemen of the committee, who prevailed on me to consent to go; and recommended me to the honourable Commissioners of his Majesty's Navy, as a proper person to act as commissary for government in the intended expedition; and they accordingly appointed me, in November 1786, to that office, and gave me sufficient power to act for the government in the capacity of commissary; having received my warrant and the following order:

> *By the principal Officers and Commissioners of his Majesty's Navy.*
>
> WHEREAS you are directed, by our warrant of the 4th of last month, to receive into your charge, from Mr. Joseph Irwin, the surplus provisions remaining of what was provided for the voyage, as well as the provisions for the support of the black poor, after the landing at Sierra Leona, with the clothing, tools, and all other articles provided at government's expence; and as the provisions were laid in at the rate of two months for the voyage, and for four months after the landing, but the number embarked being so much less than we expected, whereby there may be a considerable surplus of provisions, clothing, &c. these are, in addition to former orders, to direct and require you to appropriate or dispose of such surplus to the best advantage you can for the benefit of government, keeping and rendering to us a faithful account of what you do therein. And for your guidance in preventing any white persons going, who are not intended to have the indulgence of being carried thither, we send you herewith a list of those recommended by the committee for the black poor, as proper persons to be permitted to embark, and acquaint you that you are not to suffer any others to go who do not produce a certificate from the committee for the black poor, of their having their permission for it. For which this shall be your warrant. Dated at the Navy Office, January 16, 1787.
>
> To Mr. Gustavus Vassa, Commissary of Provisions and Stores for the Black Poor to Sierra Leona.
> J. HINSLOW.
> GEO. MARSH.
> W. PALMER.

I proceeded immediately to the executing of my duty on board the vessels destined for the voyage, where I continued till the March following.

During my continuance in the employment of government I was struck with the flagrant abuses committed by the agent, and endeavoured to remedy them, but without effect. One instance, among many which I could produce, may serve as a specimen. Government had ordered to be provided all necessaries (slops, as they are called, included) for 750 persons; however, not being able to muster more than 426, I was ordered to send the superfluous slops, &c. to the king's stores at Portsmouth; but, when I demanded them for that purpose from the agent, it appeared they had never been bought, though paid for by government. But that was not all, government were not the only objects of peculation; these poor people suffered infinitely more; their accommodations were most wretched; many of them wanted beds, and many more clothing and other necessaries. For the truth of this, and much more, I do not seek credit from my own assertion. I appeal to the testimony of Capt. Thompson, of the Nautilus, who convoyed us, to whom I applied in February 1787 for a remedy, when I had remonstrated to the agent in vain, and even brought him to be a witness of the injustice and oppression I had complained of. I appeal also to a letter written by these wretched people, so early as the beginning of the preceding January, and published in the Morning Herald, on the fourth of that month, signed by twenty of their chiefs.

I could not silently suffer government to be thus cheated, and my countrymen plundered and oppressed, and even left destitute of the necessaries for almost their existence. I therefore informed the Commissioners of the Navy of the agent's proceeding; but my dismission was soon after procured by the unjust means of Samuel Hoare, banker in the city; and he moreover, empowered the same agent to receive on board, at the government expence, a number of persons as passengers, contrary to the orders I received. By this I suffered a considerable loss in my property: however, the Commissioners were satisfied with my conduct, and wrote to Capt. Thompson, expressing their approbation of it.

Thus provided, they proceeded on their voyage; and at last, worn out by treatment, perhaps, not the most mild, and wasted by sickness, brought on by want of medicine, clothes, bedding, &c. they reached Sierra Leona just at the commencement of the rains. At that season of the year it is impossible to cultivate the lands; their provisions therefore were exhausted before they could derive any benefit from agriculture; and it is not surprising that many, especially the Lascars, whose constitutions are very tender, and who had been cooped up in ships from October to June, and accommodated in the manner I have mentioned, should be so wasted by their confinement as not long to survive it.

Thus ended my part of the long-talked of expedition to Sierra Leona; an expedition, which, however unfortunate in the event, was humane and politic in its design, nor was its failure owing to government; every thing was done on their part; but there was evidently sufficient mismanagement attending the conduct and execution of it to defeat its success.

I should not have been so ample in my account of this transaction, had not the share I bore in it been made the subject of partial animadversion, and even my dismission from my employment thought worthy of being made, by Hoare and others, matter of public triumph. The motive which might influence any person to descend to a petty contest with an obscure African, and to seek gratification by his depression, perhaps it is not proper here to enquire into or relate, even if its detection were necessary to my vindication; but I thank Heaven it is not. I wish to stand by my own integrity, and not to shelter myself under the impropriety of another; and I trust the behaviour of the Commissioners of the Navy to me entitles me to make this assertion; for after I had been dismissed, March 24, I drew up a memorial thus:

> *To The Right Honourable the Lords Commissioners*
> *of his Majesty's Treasury.*
> *The Memorial and Petition of* GUSTAVUS VASSA,
> *a black man, late Commissary to the Black Poor,*
> *going to* AFRICA.

HUMBLY SHEWETH,

THAT your Lordships' memorialist was, by the Honourable the Commissioners of his Majesty's Navy, on the 4th of December last, appointed to the above employment by warrant from that board;

That he accordingly proceeded to the execution of his duty on board of the Vernon, being one of the ships appointed to proceed to Africa with the above poor;

That your memorialist, to his great grief and astonishment, received a letter of dismission, from the Honourable Commissioners of the Navy, by your Lordships' orders:

That, conscious of having acted with the most perfect fidelity and the greatest assiduity in discharging the trust reposed in him, he is altogether at a loss to conceive the reasons of your Lordships' having altered the favourable opinion you were pleased to conceive of him, sensible that your Lordships would not proceed to so severe a measure without some apparent good cause; he therefore has every reason to believe that his conduct has been grossly misrepresented to your Lordships, and he is the more confirmed in his opinion, because, by opposing measures of others concerned in the same expedition, which tended to defeat your Lordships' humane intentions, and to put the government to a very considerable additional expence, he created a number of enemies, whose misrepresentations, he has too much reason to believe, laid the foundation of his dismission. Unsupported by friends, and unaided by the advantages of a liberal education, he can only hope for redress from the justice of his cause, in addition to the mortification of having been removed from his employment, and the advantage which he reasonably might have expected to have derived therefrom. He has had the misfortune to have sunk a considerable part of his little property in fitting himself out, and in other expences arising out of his situation, an account of which he here annexes. Your memorialist will not trouble your Lordships with a vindication of any part of his conduct, because he knows not of what crimes he is accused; he, however, earnestly entreats that you will be pleased to direct an enquiry into his behaviour during the time he acted in the public service; and, if it be found that his dismission arose from false representations, he is confident that in your Lordships' justice he shall find redress.

Your petitioner therefore humbly prays that your Lordships will take his case into consideration, and that you will be pleased to order payment of the above referred to account, amounting to 32£.4s. and also the wages intended, which is most humbly submitted. *London, May 12, 1787.*

The above petition was delivered into the hands of their Lordships, who were kind enough, in the space of some few months afterwards, without hearing, to order me 50£. sterling—that is 18£. wages for the time (upwards of four months) I acted a faithful part in their service.—Certainly the sum is more than a free negro would have had in the western colonies!!!

From that period to the present time my life has passed in an even tenor, and great part of my study and attention has been to assist in the cause of my much injured countrymen.

March the 21st, 1788, I had the honour of presenting the Queen with a petition on behalf of my African brethren, which was received most graciously by her Majesty:

To the QUEEN's *Most Excellent Majesty.*
MADAM,

YOUR Majesty's well known benevolence and humanity embolden me to approach your royal presence, trusting that the obscurity of my situation will not prevent your Majesty from attending to the sufferings for which I plead.

Yet I do not solicit your royal pity for my own distress: my sufferings, although numerous, are in a measure forgotten. I supplicate your Majesty's compassion for millions of my African countrymen, who groan under the lash of tyranny in the West Indies.

The oppression and cruelty exercised to the unhappy negroes there, have at length reached the British legislature, and they are now deliberating on its redress; even several persons of property in slaves in the West Indies have petitioned parliament against its continuance, sensible that it is as impolitic as it is unjust and what is inhuman must ever be unwise.

Your majesty's reign has hitherto been distinguished by private acts of benevolence and bounty; surely the more extended the misery is, the greater claim it has to your Majesty's compassion, and the greater must be your Majesty's pleasure in administering to its relief.

I presume, therefore, gracious Queen, to implore your interposition with your royal consort, in favour of the wretched Africans; that, by your Majesty's benevolent influence, a period may now be put to their misery; and that they may be raised from the condition of brutes, to which they are at present degraded, to the rights and situation of men, and be admitted to partake of the blessings of your Majesty's happy government; so shall your Majesty enjoy the heart-felt pleasure of procuring happiness to millions, and be rewarded in the grateful prayers of themselves, and of their posterity.

And may the all-bountiful Creator shower on your Majesty, and the Royal Family, every blessing that this world can afford, and every fulness of joy which divine revelation has promised us in the next.

I am your Majesty's most dutiful and devoted servant to command,
GUSTAVUS VASSA,
The oppressed Ethiopian.

No. 53, Baldwin's-Gardens.

The negro consolidated act, made by the assembly of Jamaica last year, and the new act of amendment now in agitation there, contain a proof of the existence of those charges that have been made against the planters relative to the treatment of their slaves.

I hope to have the satisfaction of seeing the renovation of liberty and justice, resting on the British government, to vindicate the honour of our common nature. These are concerns which do not perhaps belong to any particular office: but, to speak more seriously to every man of sentiment, actions like these are the just and sure foundation of future fame; a reversion, though remote, is coveted by some noble minds as a substantial good. It is upon these grounds that I hope and expect the attention of gentlemen in power. These are designs consonant to the elevation of their rank, and the dignity of their stations; they are ends suitable to the nature of a free and generous government; and, connected with views of empire and dominion, suited to the benevolence and solid merit of the legislature. It is a pursuit of substantial greatness.—May the time come—at least the speculation to me is pleasing—when the sable people shall gratefully commemorate the auspicious aera of extensive freedom: then shall those persons particularly be named with praise and honour, who generously proposed and stood forth in the cause of humanity, liberty, and good policy; and brought to the ear of the legislature designs worthy of royal patronage and adoption. May Heaven make the British senators the dispersers of light, liberty and science, to the uttermost parts of the earth: then will be glory to God on the highest, on earth peace, and good-will to men.—Glory, honour, peace, &c. to every soul of man that worketh good; to the Britons first, (because to them the Gospel is preached), and also to the nations. "Those that honour their Maker have mercy on the poor." "It is righteousness exalteth a nation; but sin is a reproach to any people: destruction shall be to the workers of iniquity, and the wicked shall fall by their own wickedness." May the blessings of the Lord be upon the heads of all those who commiserated the cases of the oppressed negroes, and the fear of God prolong their days; and may their expectations be filled with gladness! "The liberal devise liberal things, and by liberal things shall stand," Isaiah xxxii. 8. They can say with pious Job, "Did not I weep for him that was in trouble; Was not my soul grieved for the poor?" Job xxx. 25.

As the inhuman traffic of slavery is now taken into the consideration of the British legislature, I doubt not, if a system of commerce was established in Africa, the demand for manufactures would most rapidly augment, as the native inhabitants would insensibly adopt the British fashions, manners, customs, &c. In proportion to the civilization, so will be the consumption of British manufactures.

The wear and tear of a continent, nearly twice as large as Europe, and rich in vegetable and mineral productions, is much easier conceived than calculated.

A case in point.—It cost the Aborigines of Britain little or nothing in clothing, &c. The difference between their forefathers and the present generation, in point of consumption, is literally infinite. The supposition is most obvious. It will be equally immense in Africa.—The same cause, viz. civilization, will ever have the same effect.

It is trading upon safe grounds. A commercial intercourse with Africa opens an inexhaustible source of wealth to the manufacturing interests of Great Britain, and to all which the slave-trade is an objection.

If I am not misinformed, the manufacturing interest is equal, if not superior, to the landed interest, as to the value, for reasons which will soon appear. The abolition of slavery, so diabolical, will give a most rapid extension of manufactures, which is totally and diametrically opposite to what some interested people assert.

The manufacturers of this country must and will, in the nature and reason of things, have a full and constant employ, by supplying the African markets.

Population, the bowels and surface of Africa, abound in valuable and useful returns; the hidden treasures of centuries will be brought to light and into circulation. Industry, enterprize, and mining, will have their full scope, proportionably as they civilize. In a word, it lays open an endless field of commerce to the British manufacturers and merchant adventurers. The manufacturing interest and the general interests are synonimous. The abolition of slavery would be in reality an universal good.

Tortures, murder, and every other imaginable barbarity and iniquity are practised upon the poor slaves with impunity. I hope the slave-trade will be abolished. I pray it may be an event at hand. The great body of manufacturers, uniting in the cause, will considerably facilitate and expedite it; and, as I have already stated, it is most substantially their interest and advantage, and as such the nation's at large, (except those persons concerned in manufacturing neck-yokes, collars, chains, hand-cuffs, leg-bolts, drags, thumb-screws, iron-muzzles, and coffins; cats, scourges, and other instruments of torture used in the slave trade). In a short time one sentiment alone will prevail, from motives of interest as well as justice and humanity. Europe contains one hundred and twenty millions of inhabitants. Query.—How many millions doth Africa contain? Supposing the Africans, collectively and individually, to expend 5£ a head in raiment and furniture yearly when civilized, &c. an immensity beyond the reach of imagination!

This I conceive to be a theory founded upon facts, and therefore an infallible one. If the blacks were permitted to remain in their own country, they would double themselves every fifteen years. In proportion to such increase will be the demand for manufactures. Cotton and indigo grow spontaneously in most parts of Africa; a consideration this of no small consequence to the manufacturing towns of Great Britain. It opens a most immense, glorious, and happy prospect—the clothing, &c. of a continent ten thousand miles in circumference, and immensely rich in productions of every denomination in return for manufactures.

Since the first publication of my Narrative, I have been in a great variety of scenes in many parts of Great Britain, Ireland, and Scotland, an account of which might well be added here; but as this would swell the volume too much, I shall only observe in general, that in May 1791, I sailed from Liverpool to Dublin where I was very kindly received, and from thence to Cork, and then travelled over many counties in Ireland. I was every where exceedingly well treated, by persons of all ranks. I found the people extremely hospitable, particularly in Belfast, where I took my passage on board of a vessel for Clyde, on the 29th of January, and arrived at Greenock on the 30th. Soon after I returned to London, where I found persons of note from Holland and Germany, who requested me to go there; and I was glad to hear that an edition of my Narrative had been printed in both places, also in New York. I remained in London till I heard the debate in the house of Commons on the Slave Trade, April the 2d and 3d. I then went to Soham in Cambridgeshire, and was married on the 7th of April to Miss Cullen, daughter of James and Ann Cullen, late of Ely.

I have only therefore to request the reader's indulgence, and conclude. I am far from the vanity of thinking there is any merit in this Narrative; I hope censure will be suspended, when it is considered that it was written by one who was as unwilling as unable to adorn the plainness of truth by the colouring of imagination. My life and fortune have been extremely chequered, and my adventures various. Even those I have related are considerably abridged. If any incident in this little work should appear uninteresting and trifling to most readers, I can only say, as my excuse for mentioning it, that almost every event of my life made an impression on my mind, and influenced my conduct. I early accustomed myself to look at the hand of God in the minutest occurrence, and to learn from it a lesson of morality and religion; and in this light every circumstance I have related was to me of importance. After all, what makes any event important, unless by its observation we become better and wiser, and learn "to do justly, to love mercy, and to walk humbly before God!" To those who are possessed of this spirit, there is scarcely any book or incident so trifling that does not afford some profit, while to others the experience of ages seems of no use; and even to pour out to them the treasures of wisdom is throwing the jewels of instruction away.

THE END.

THE

HISTORY OF MARY PRINCE,

A WEST INDIAN SLAVE.

RELATED BY HERSELF.

———

WITH A SUPPLEMENT BY THE EDITOR.

———

To which is added,

THE NARRATIVE OF ASA-ASA,

A CAPTURED AFRICAN.

———

"By our sufferings, since ye brought us
　　To the man-degrading mart,—
All sustain'd by patience, taught us
　　Only by a broken heart,—
Deem our nation brutes no longer,
　　Till some reason ye shall find
Worthier of regard, and stronger
　　Than the colour of our kind."　　Cowper.

———

LONDON:

PUBLISHED BY F. WESTLEY AND A. H. DAVIS,
Stationers' Hall Court;
And by WAUGH & INNES, EDINBURGH.

———

1831.

PREFACE.

THE idea of writing Mary Prince's history was first suggested by herself. She wished it to be done, she said, that good people in England might hear from a slave what a slave had felt and suffered; and a letter of her late master's, which will be found in the Supplement, induced me to accede to her wish without farther delay. The more immediate object of the publication will afterwards appear.

The narrative was taken down from Mary's own lips by a lady who happened to be at the time residing in my family as a visitor. It was written out fully, with all the narrator's repetitions and prolixities, and afterwards pruned into its present shape; retaining, as far as was practicable, Mary's exact expressions and peculiar phraseology. No fact of importance has been omitted, and not a single circumstance or sentiment has been added. It is essentially her own, without any material alteration farther than was requisite to exclude redundancies and gross grammatical errors, so as to render it clearly intelligible.

After it had been thus written out, I went over the whole, carefully examining her on every fact and circumstance detailed: and in all that relates to her residence in Antigua I had the advantage of being assisted in this scrutiny by Mr. Joseph Phillips, who was a resident in that colony during the same period, and had known her there.

The names of all the persons mentioned by the narrator have been printed in full, except those of Capt. I——and his wife, and that of Mr. D——, to whom conduct of peculiar atrocity is ascribed. These three individuals are now gone to answer at a far more awful tribunal than that of public opinion, for the deeds of which their former bondwoman accuses them; and to hold them up more openly to human reprobation could no longer affect themselves, while it might deeply lacerate the feelings of their surviving and perhaps innocent relatives, without any commensurate public advantage.

Without detaining the reader with remarks on other

points which will be adverted to more conveniently in the Supplement, I shall here merely notice farther, that the Anti-Slavery Society have no concern whatever with this publication, nor are they in any degree responsible for the statements it contains. I have published the tract, not as their Secretary, but in my private capacity; and any profits that may arise from the sale will be exclusively appropriated to the benefit of Mary Prince herself.

THO. PRINGLE.

7, Solly Terrace, Claremont Square,
January 25, 1831.

P.S. Since writing the above, I have been furnished by my friend Mr. George Stephen, with the interesting narrative of Asa-Asa, a captured African, now under his protection; and have printed it as a suitable appendix to this little history.

T.P.

THE

HISTORY OF MARY PRINCE,

A WEST INDIAN SLAVE.

(Related by herself.)

I was born at Brackish-Pond, in Bermuda, on a farm belonging to Mr. Charles Myners. My mother was a household slave; and my father, whose name was Prince, was a sawyer belonging to Mr. Trimmingham, a ship-builder at Crow-Lane. When I was an infant, old Mr. Myners died, and there was a division of the slaves and other property among the family. I was bought along with my mother by old Captain Darrel, and given to his grandchild, little Miss Betsey Williams. Captain Williams, Mr. Darrel's son-in-law, was master of a vessel which traded to several places in America and the West Indies, and he was seldom at home long together.

Mrs. Williams was a kind-hearted good woman, and she treated all her slaves well. She had only one daughter, Miss Betsey, for whom I was purchased, and who was about my own age. I was made quite a pet of by Miss Betsey, and loved her very much. She used to lead me about by the hand, and call me her little nigger. This was the happiest period of my life; for I was too young to understand rightly my condition as a slave, and too thoughtless and full of spirits to look forward to the days of toil and sorrow.

My mother was a household slave in the same family. I was under her own care, and my little brothers and sisters were my play-fellows and companions. My mother had several fine children after she came to Mrs. Williams,—three girls and two boys. The tasks given out to us children were light, and we used to play together with Miss Betsey, with as much freedom almost as if she had been our sister.

My master, however, was a very harsh, selfish man; and we always dreaded his return from sea. His wife was herself much afraid of him; and, during his stay at home, seldom dared to shew her usual kindness to the slaves. He often left her, in the most distressed circumstances, to reside in other female society at some place in the West Indies of which I have forgot the name. My poor mistress bore his ill-treatment with great patience, and all her slaves loved and pitied her. I was truly attached to her, and, next to my own mother, loved her better than any creature in the world. My obedience to her commands was cheerfully given: it sprung solely from the affection I felt for her, and not from fear of the power which the white people's law had given her over me.

I had scarcely reached my twelfth year when my mistress became too poor to keep so many of us at home; and she hired me out to Mrs. Pruden, a lady who lived about five miles off, in the adjoining parish, in a large house near the sea. I cried bitterly at parting with my dear mistress and Miss Betsey, and when I kissed my mother and brothers and sisters, I thought my young heart would break, it pained me so. But there was no help; I was forced to go. Good Mrs. Williams comforted me by saying that I should still be near the home I was about to quit, and might come over and see her and my kindred whenever I could obtain leave of absence from Mrs. Pruden. A few hours after this I was taken to a strange house, and found myself among strange people. This separation seemed a sore trial to me then; but oh! 'twas light, light to the trials I have since endured!—'twas nothing—nothing to be mentioned with them; but I was a child then, and it was according to my strength.

I knew that Mrs. Williams could no longer maintain me; that she was fain to part with me for my food and clothing; and I tried to submit myself to the change. My new mistress was a passionate woman; but yet she did not treat me very unkindly. I do not remember her striking me but once, and that was for going to see Mrs. Williams when I heard she was sick, and staying longer than she had given me leave to do. All my employment at this time was nursing a sweet baby, little Master Daniel; and I grew so fond of my nurseling that it was my greatest delight to walk out with him by the sea-shore, accompanied by his brother and sister, Miss Fanny and Master James.—Dear Miss Fanny! She was a sweet, kind young lady, and so fond of me that she wished me to learn all that she knew herself; and her method of teaching me was as follows:—Directly she had said her lessons to her grandmamma, she used to come running to me, and make me repeat them one by one after her; and in a few months I was able not only to say my letters but to spell many small words. But this happy state was not to last long. Those days were too pleasant to last. My heart always softens when I think of them.

At this time Mrs. Williams died. I was told suddenly of her death, and my grief was so great that, forgetting I had the baby in my arms, I ran away directly to my poor mistress's house; but reached it only in time to see the corpse carried out. Oh, that was a day of sorrow.—a heavy day! All the slaves cried. My mother cried and lamented her sore; and I (foolish creature!) vainly entreated them to bring my dear mistress back to life. I knew nothing rightly about death then, and it seemed a hard thing to bear. When I thought about my mistress I felt as if the world was all gone wrong; and for many days and weeks I could think of nothing else. I returned to Mrs. Pruden's; but my sorrow was too great to be comforted, for my own dear mistress was always in my mind. Whether in the house or abroad, my thoughts were always talking to me about her.

I staid at Mrs. Pruden's about three months after this; I was then sent back to Mr. Williams to be sold. Oh, that was a sad sad time! I recollect the day well. Mrs. Pruden came to me and said, "Mary, you will have to go home directly; your master is going to be married, and he means to sell you and two of your sisters to raise money for the wedding." Hearing this I burst out a crying,—though I was then far from being sensible of the full weight of my misfortune, or of the misery that waited for me. Besides, I did not like to leave Mrs. Pruden, and the dear baby, who had grown very fond of me. For some time I could scarcely believe that Mrs. Pruden was in earnest, till I received orders for my immediate return.—Dear Miss Fanny! how she cried at parting with me, whilst I kissed and hugged the baby, thinking I should never see him again. I left Mrs. Pruden's, and walked home with a heart full of sorrow. The idea of being sold away from my mother and Miss Betsey was so frightful, that I dared not trust myself to think about it. We had been bought of Mr. Myners, as I have mentioned, by Miss Betsey's grandfather, and given to her, so that we were by right *her* property, and I never thought we should be separated or sold away from her.

When I reached the house, I went in directly to Miss Betsey. I found her in great distress; and she cried out as soon as she saw me, "Oh, Mary! my father is going to sell you all to raise money to marry that wicked woman. You are *my* slaves, and he has no right to sell you; but it is all to please her." She then told me that my mother was living with her father's sister at a house close by, and I went there to see her. It was a sorrowful meeting; and we lamented with a great and sore crying our unfortunate situation. "Here comes one of my poor picaninnies!" she said, the moment I came in, "one of the poor slave-brood who are to be sold to-morrow."

Oh dear! I cannot bear to think of that day,—it is too much.—It recalls the great grief that filled my heart, and the woeful thoughts that passed to and fro through my mind, whilst listening to the pitiful words of my poor mother, weeping for the loss of her children. I wish I could find words to tell you all I then felt and suffered. The great God above alone knows the thoughts of the poor slave's heart, and the bitter pains which follow such separations as these. All that we love taken away from us—Oh, it is sad, sad! and sore to be borne!—I got no sleep that night for thinking of the morrow; and dear Miss Betsey was scarcely less distressed. She could not bear to part with her old play-mates, and she cried sore and would not be pacified.

The black morning at length came; it came too soon for my poor mother and us. Whilst she was putting on us the new osnaburgs in which we were to be sold, she said, in a sorrowful voice, (I shall never forget it!) "See, I am *shrouding* my poor children; what a task for a mother!"—She then called Miss Betsey to take leave of us. "I am going to carry my little chickens to market," (these were her very words,) "take your last look of them; may be you will see them no more." "Oh, my poor slaves! my own slaves!" said dear Miss Betsey, "you belong to me; and it grieves my heart to part with you."—Miss Betsey kissed us all, and, when she left us, my mother called the rest of the slaves to bid us good bye. One of them, a woman named Moll, came with her infant in her arms. "Ay!" said my mother, seeing her turn away and look at her child with the tears in her eyes, "your turn will come next." The slaves could say nothing to comfort us; they could only weep and lament with us. When I left my dear little brothers and the house in which I had been brought up, I thought my heart would burst.

Our mother, weeping as she went, called me away with the children Hannah and Dinah, and we took the road that led to Hamble Town, which we reached about four o'clock in the afternoon. We followed my mother to the market-place, where she placed us in a row against a large house, with our backs to the wall and our arms folded across our breasts. I, as the eldest, stood first, Hannah next to me, then Dinah; and our mother stood beside crying over us. My heart throbbed with grief and terror so violently, that I pressed my hands quite tightly across my breast, but I could not keep it still, and it continued to leap as though it would burst out of my body. But who cared for that? Did one of the many by-standers, who were looking at us so carelessly, think of the pain that wrung the hearts of the negro woman and her young ones? No, no! They were not all bad, I dare say, but slavery hardens white people's hearts towards the blacks; and many of them were not slow to make their remarks upon us aloud, without regard to our grief—though their light words fell like cayenne on the fresh wounds of our hearts. Oh those white people have small hearts who can only feel for themselves.

At length the vendue master, who was to offer us for sale like sheep or cattle, arrived, and asked my mother which was the eldest. She said nothing, but pointed to me. He took me by the hand, and led me out into the middle of the street, and, turning me slowly round, exposed me to the view of those who attended the vendue. I was soon surrounded by strange men, who examined and handled me in the same manner that a butcher would a calf or a lamb he was about to purchase, and who talked about my shape and size in like words—as if I could no more understand their meaning than the dumb beasts. I was then put up to sale. The bidding commenced at a few pounds, and gradually rose to fifty-seven,* when I was knocked down to the highest bidder; and the people who stood by said that I had fetched a great sum for so young a slave.

I then saw my sisters led forth, and sold to different owners; so that we had not the sad satisfaction of being partners in bondage. When the sale was over, my mother hugged and kissed us, and mourned over us, begging of us to keep up a good heart, and do our duty to our new masters. It was a sad parting; one went one way, one another, and our poor mammy went home with nothing.†

---

*Bermuda currency; about £38 sterling.

†Let the reader compare the above affecting account, taken down from the mouth of this negro woman, with the following description of a vendue of slaves at the Cape of Good Hope, published by me in 1826, from the letter of a friend,—and mark their similarity in several characteristic circumstances. The resemblance is easily accounted for; slavery wherever it prevails produces similar effects.—"Having heard that there was to be a sale of cattle, farm stock, &c. by auction, at a Veld-Cornet's in the vicinity, we halted our waggon one day for the purpose of procuring a fresh spann of oxen. Among the stock of the farm sold, was a female slave and her three children. The two eldest children were girls, the one about thirteen years of age, and the other about eleven; the youngest was a boy. The whole family were exhibited together, but they were sold separately, and to different purchasers. The farmers examined them as if they had been so many head of cattle. While the sale was going on, the mother and her children were exhibited on a table, that they might be seen by the company, which was very large. There could not have been a finer subject for an able painter than this unhappy group. The tears, the anxiety, the anguish of the mother, while she met the gaze of the multitude, eyed the different countenances of the bidders, or cast a heartrending look upon the children; and the simplicity and touching sorrow of the young ones, while they clung to their distracted parent, wiping their eyes, and half concealing their faces,—contrasted with the marked insensibility and jocular countenances of the spectators and purchasers,—furnished a striking commentary on the miseries of slavery, and its debasing effects upon the hearts of its abettors. While the woman was in this distressed situation she was asked, 'Can you feed sheep?' Her reply was so indistinct that it escaped me; but it was probably in the negative, for her purchaser

My new master was a Captain I——, who lived at Spanish Point. After parting with my mother and sisters, I followed him to his store, and he gave me into the charge of his son, a lad about my own age, Master Benjy, who took me to my new home. I did not know where I was going, or what my new master would do with me. My heart was quite broken with grief, and my thoughts went back continually to those from whom I had been so suddenly parted. "Oh, my mother! my mother!" I kept saying to myself, "Oh, my mammy and my sisters and my brothers, shall I never see you again!"

Oh, the trials! the trials! they make the salt water come into my eyes when I think of the days in which I was afflicted—the times that are gone; when I mourned and grieved with a young heart for those whom I loved.

It was night when I reached my new home. The house was large, and built at the bottom of a very high hill; but I could not see much of it that night. I saw too much of it afterwards. The stones and the timber were the best things in it; they were not so hard as the hearts of the owners.*

Before I entered the house, two slave women, hired from another owner, who were at work in the yard, spoke to me, and asked who I belonged to? I replied, "I am come to live here." "Poor child, poor child!" they both said; "you must keep a good heart, if you are to live here."—When I went in, I stood up crying in a corner. Mrs. I——came and took off my hat, a little black silk hat Miss Pruden made for me, and said in a rough voice, "You are not come here to stand up in corners and cry, you are come here to work." She then put a child into my arms, and, tired as I was, I was forced instantly to take up my old occupation of a nurse.—I could not bear to look at my mistress, her countenance was so stern. She was a stout tall woman with a very dark complexion, and her brows were always drawn together into a

---

rejoined, in a loud and harsh voice, 'Then I will teach you with the sjamboc,' (a whip made of the rhinoceros' hide.) The mother and her three children were sold to three separate purchasers; and they were literally torn from each other."—*Ed.*

*These strong expressions, and all of a similar character in this little narrative, are given verbatim as uttered by Mary Prince.—*Ed.*

frown. I thought of the words of the two slave women when I saw Mrs. I——, and heard the harsh sound of her voice.

The person I took the most notice of that night was a French Black called Hetty, whom my master took in privateering from another vessel, and made his slave. She was the most active woman I ever saw, and she was tasked to her utmost. A few minutes after my arrival she came in from milking the cows, and put the sweet-potatoes on for supper. She then fetched home the sheep, and penned them in the fold; drove home the cattle, and staked them about the pond side;* fed and rubbed down my master's horse, and gave the hog and the fed cow† their suppers; prepared the beds, and undressed the children, and laid them to sleep. I liked to look at her and watch all her doings, for hers was the only friendly face I had as yet seen, and I felt glad that she was there. She gave me my supper of potatoes and milk, and a blanket to sleep upon, which she spread for me in the passage before the door of Mrs. I——'s chamber.

I got a sad fright, that night. I was just going to sleep, when I heard a noise in my mistress's room; and she presently called out to inquire if some work was finished that she had ordered Hetty to do. "No, Ma'am, not yet," was Hetty's answer from below. On hearing this, my master started up from his bed, and just as he was, in his shirt, ran down stairs with a long cow-skin‡ in his hand. I heard immediately after, the cracking of the thong, and the house rang to the shrieks of poor Hetty, who kept crying out, "Oh, Massa! Massa! me dead. Massa! have mercy upon me—don't kill me outright."—This was a sad beginning for me. I sat up upon my blanket, trembling with terror, like a frightened hound, and thinking that my turn would come next. At length the house became still, and I forgot for a little while all my sorrows by falling fast asleep.

The next morning my mistress set about instructing me

---

*The cattle on a small plantation in Bermuda are, it seems, often thus staked or tethered, both night and day, in situations where grass abounds.

†A cow fed for slaughter.

‡A thong of hard twisted hide, known by this name in the West Indies.

in my tasks. She taught me to do all sorts of household work; to wash and bake, pick cotton and wool, and wash floors, and cook. And she taught me (how can I ever forget it!) more things than these; she caused me to know the exact difference between the smart of the rope, the cart-whip, and the cow-skin, when applied to my naked body by her own cruel hand. And there was scarcely any punishment more dreadful than the blows I received on my face and head from her hard heavy fist. She was a fearful woman, and a savage mistress to her slaves.

There were two little slave boys in the house, on whom she vented her bad temper in a special manner. One of these children was a mulatto, called Cyrus, who had been bought while an infant in his mother's arms; the other, Jack, was an African from the coast of Guinea, whom a sailor had given or sold to my master. Seldom a day passed without these boys receiving the most severe treatment, and often for no fault at all. Both my master and mistress seemed to think that they had a right to ill-use them at their pleasure; and very often accompanied their commands with blows, whether the children were behaving well or ill. I have seen their flesh ragged and raw with licks.—Lick—lick—they were never secure one moment from a blow, and their lives were passed in continual fear. My mistress was not contented with using the whip, but often pinched their cheeks and arms in the most cruel manner. My pity for these poor boys was soon transferred to myself; for I was licked, and flogged, and pinched by her pitiless fingers in the neck and arms, exactly as they were. To strip me naked—to hang me up by the wrists and lay my flesh open with the cow-skin, was an ordinary punishment for even a slight offence. My mistress often robbed me too of the hours that belong to sleep. She used to sit up very late, frequently even until morning; and I had then to stand at a bench and wash during the greater part of the night, or pick wool and cotton; and often I have dropped down overcome by sleep and fatigue, till roused from a state of stupor by the whip, and forced to start up to my tasks.

Poor Hetty, my fellow slave, was very kind to me, and I used to call her my Aunt; but she led a most miserable life, and her death was hastened (at least the slaves all believed and said so), by the dreadful chastisement she received from my master during her pregnancy. It happened as follows. One of the cows had dragged the rope away from the stake to which Hetty had fastened it, and got loose. My master flew into a terrible passion, and ordered the poor creature to be stripped quite naked, notwithstanding her pregnancy, and to be tied up to a tree in the yard. He then flogged her as hard as he could lick, both with the whip and cow-skin, till she was all over streaming with blood. He rested, and then beat her again and again. Her shrieks were terrible. The consequence was that poor Hetty was brought to bed before her time, and was delivered after severe labour of a dead child. She appeared to recover after her confinement, so far that she was repeatedly flogged by both master and mistress afterwards; but her former strength never returned to her. Ere long her body and limbs swelled to a great size; and she lay on a mat in the kitchen, till the water burst out of her body and she died. All the slaves said that death was a good thing for poor Hetty; but I cried very much for her death. The manner of it filled me with horror. I could not bear to think about it; yet it was always present to my mind for many a day.

After Hetty died all her labours fell upon me, in addition to my own. I had now to milk eleven cows every morning before sunrise, sitting among the damp weeds; to take care of the cattle as well as the children; and to do the work of the house. There was no end to my toils—no end to my blows. I lay down at night and rose up in the morning in fear and sorrow; and often wished that like poor Hetty I could escape from this cruel bondage and be at rest in the grave. But the hand of God whom then I knew not, was stretched over me; and I was mercifully preserved for better things. It was then, however, my heavy lot to weep, weep, weep, and that for years; to pass from one misery to another, and from one cruel master to a worse. But I must go on with the thread of my story.

One day a heavy squall of wind and rain came on suddenly, and my mistress sent me round the corner of the house to empty a large earthen jar. The jar was already cracked with an old deep crack that divided it in the middle, and in turning it upside down to empty it, it parted in my hand. I could not help the accident, but I was dreadfully frightened, looking forward to a severe punishment. I ran crying to my mistress, "O mistress, the jar has come in two." "You have broken it, have you?" she replied; "come directly here to me." I came trembling; she stripped and flogged me long and severely with the cow-skin; as long as she had strength to use the lash, for she did not give over till she was quite tired.—When my master came home at night, she told him of my fault; and oh, frightful! how he fell a swearing. After abusing me with every ill name he could think of, (too, too bad to speak in England,) and giving me several heavy blows with his hand, he said, "I shall come home tomorrow morning at twelve, on purpose to give you a round hundred." He kept his word—Oh sad for me! I cannot easily forget it. He tied me up upon a ladder, and gave me a hundred lashes with his own hand, and master Benjy stood by to count them for him. When he had licked me for some time he sat down to take breath; then after resting, he beat me again and again, until he was quite wearied, and so hot (for the weather was very sultry), that he sank back in his chair, almost like to faint. While my mistress went to bring him drink, there was a dreadful earthquake. Part of the roof fell down, and every thing in the house went—clatter, clatter, clatter. Oh I thought the end of all things near at hand; and I was so sore with the flogging, that I scarcely cared whether I lived or died. The earth was groaning and shaking; every thing tumbling about; and my mistress and the slaves were shrieking and crying out, "The earthquake! the earthquake!" It was an awful day for us all.

During the confusion I crawled away on my hands and knees, and laid myself down under the steps of the piazza, in front of the house. I was in a dreadful state—my body all blood and bruises, and I could not help moaning piteously. The other slaves, when they saw me, shook their heads and said, "Poor child! poor child!"—I lay there till the morning, careless of what might happen, for life was very weak in me, and I wished more than ever to die. But when we are very young, death always seems a great way off, and it would not come that night to me. The next morning I was forced by my master to rise and go about my usual work, though my body and limbs were so stiff and sore, that I could not move without the greatest pain.—Nevertheless, even after all this severe punishment, I never heard the last of that jar; my mistress was always throwing it in my face.

Some little time after this, one of the cows got loose from the stake, and eat one of the sweet-potato slips. I was milking when my master found it out. He came to me, and without any more ado, stooped down, and taking off his heavy boot, he struck me such a severe blow in the small of my back, that I shrieked with agony, and thought I was killed; and I feel a weakness in that part to this day. The cow was frightened at his violence, and kicked down the pail and spilt the milk all about. My master knew that this accident was his own fault, but he was so enraged that he seemed glad of an excuse to go on with his ill usage. I cannot remember how many licks he gave me then, but he beat me till I was unable to stand, and till he himself was weary.

After this I ran away and went to my mother, who was living with Mr. Richard Darrel. My poor mother was both grieved and glad to see me; grieved because I had been so ill used, and glad because she had not seen me for a long, long while. She dared not receive me into the house, but she hid me up in a hole in the rocks near, and brought me food at night, after every body was asleep. My father, who lived at Crow-Lane, over the salt-water channel, at last heard of my being hid up in the cavern, and he came and took me back to my master. Oh I was loth, loth to go back; but as there was no remedy, I was obliged to submit.

When we got home, my poor father said to Capt. I——, "Sir, I am sorry that my child should be forced to run away from her owner; but the treatment she has received is enough to break her heart. The sight of her wounds has nearly broke mine.—I entreat you, for the love of God, to forgive her for running away, and that you will be a kind master to her in future." Capt. I——said I was used as well as I deserved, and that I ought to be punished for running away. I then took courage and said that I could stand the floggings no longer; that I was weary of my life, and therefore I had run away to my mother; but mothers could only weep and mourn over their children, they could not save them from cruel masters—from the whip, the rope, and the cow-skin. He told me to hold my tongue and go about my work, or he would find a way to settle me. He did not, however, flog me that day.

For five years after this I remained in his house, and almost daily received the same harsh treatment. At length he put me on board a sloop, and to my great joy sent me away to Turk's Island. I was not permitted to see my mother or father, or poor sisters and brothers, to say good bye, though going away to a strange land, and might never see them again. Oh the Buckra people who keep slaves think that black people are like cattle, without natural affection. But my heart tells me it is far otherwise.

We were nearly four weeks on the voyage, which was unusually long. Sometimes we had a light breeze, sometimes a great calm, and the ship made no way; so that our provisions and water ran very low, and we were put upon short allowance. I should almost have been starved had it not been for the kindness of a black man called Anthony, and his wife, who had brought their own victuals, and shared them with me.

When we went ashore at the Grand Quay, the captain sent me to the house of my new master, Mr. D——, to whom Captain I——had sold me. Grand Quay is a small town upon a sandbank; the houses low and built of wood. Such was my new master's. The first person I saw, on my arrival, was Mr. D——, a stout sulky looking man, who carried me through the hall to show me to his wife and children. Next day I was put up by the vendue master to know how much I was worth, and I was valued at one hundred pounds currency.

My new master was one of the owners or holders of the salt ponds, and he received a certain sum for every slave that worked upon his premises, whether they were young or old. This sum was allowed him out of the profits arising from the salt works. I was immediately sent to work in the salt water, with the rest of the slaves. This work was perfectly new to me. I was given a half barrel and a shovel, and had to stand up to my knees in the water, from four o'clock in the morning till nine, when we were given some Indian corn boiled in water, which we were obliged to swallow as fast as we could for fear the rain should come on and melt the salt. We were then called again to our tasks, and worked through the heat of the day; the sun flaming upon our heads like fire, and raising salt blisters in those parts which were not completely covered. Our feet and legs, from standing in the salt water for so many hours, soon became full of dreadful boils, which eat down in some cases to the very bone, afflicting the sufferers with great torment. We came home at twelve; ate our corn soup, called *blawly,* as fast as we could, and went back to our employment till dark at night. We then shovelled up the salt in large heaps, and went down to the sea, where we washed the pickle from our limbs, and cleaned the barrows and shovels from the salt. When we returned to the house, our master gave us each our allowance of raw Indian corn, which we pounded in a mortar and boiled in water for our suppers.

We slept in a long shed, divided into narrow slips, like the stalls used for cattle. Boards fixed upon stakes driven into the ground, without mat or covering, were our only beds. On Sundays, after we had washed the salt bags, and done other work required of us, we went into the bush and cut the long soft grass, of which we made trusses for our legs and feet to rest upon, for they were so full of the salt boils that we could get no rest lying upon the bare boards.

Though we worked from morning till night, there was no satisfying Mr. D——. I hoped, when I left Capt. I——, that I should have been better off, but I found it was but going from one butcher to another. There was this difference between them: my former master used to beat me while raging and foaming with passion; Mr. D——was usually quite calm. He would stand by and give orders for a slave to be cruelly whipped, and assist in the punishment, without moving a muscle of his face; walking about and taking snuff with the greatest composure. Nothing could touch his hard heart—neither sighs, nor tears, nor prayers, nor streaming blood; he was deaf to our cries, and careless of our sufferings.—Mr. D——has often stripped me naked, hung me up by the wrists, and beat me with the cow-skin, with his own hand, till my body was raw with gashes. Yet there was nothing very remarkable in this; for it might serve as a sample of the common usage of the slaves on that horrible island.

Owing to the boils in my feet, I was unable to wheel the barrow fast through the sand, which got into the sores, and made me stumble at every step; and my master, having no pity for my sufferings from this cause, rendered them far more intolerable, by chastising me for not being able to move so fast as he wished me. Another of our employments was to row a little way off from the shore in a boat, and dive for large stones to build a wall round our master's house. This was very hard work; and the great waves breaking over us continually, made us often so giddy that we lost our footing, and were in danger of being drowned.

Ah, poor me!—my tasks were never ended. Sick or well, it was work—work—work!—After the diving season was over, we were sent to the South Creek, with large bills, to cut up mangoes to burn lime with. Whilst one party of slaves were thus employed, another were sent to the other side of the island to break up coral out of the sea.

When we were ill, let our complaint be what it might, the only medicine given to us was a great bowl of hot salt water, with salt mixed with it, which made us very sick. If we could not keep up with the rest of the gang of slaves, we were put in the stocks, and severely flogged the next morning. Yet, not the less, our master expected, after we had thus been kept from our rest, and our limbs rendered stiff and sore with ill usage, that we should still go through the ordinary tasks of the day all the same.—Sometimes we had to work all night, measuring salt to load a vessel; or turning a machine to draw water out of the sea for the salt-making. Then we had no sleep—no rest—but were forced to work as fast as we could, and go on again all next day the same as usual. Work—work—work—Oh that Turk's Island was a horrible place! The people in England, I am sure, have never found out what is carried on there. Cruel, horrible place!

Mr. D——had a slave called old Daniel, whom he used to treat in the most cruel manner. Poor Daniel was lame in the hip, and could not keep up with the rest of the slaves; and our master would order him to be stripped and laid down on the ground, and have him beaten with a rod of rough briar till his skin was quite red and raw. He would

then call for a bucket of salt, and fling upon the raw flesh till
the man writhed on the ground like a worm, and screamed
aloud with agony. This poor man's wounds were never
healed, and I have often seen them full of maggots, which
increased his torments to an intolerable degree. He was an
object of pity and terror to the whole gang of slaves, and in
his wretched case we saw, each of us, our own lot, if we
should live to be as old.

Oh the horrors of slavery!—How the thought of it pains
my heart! But the truth ought to be told of it; and what my
eyes have seen I think it is my duty to relate; for few people
in England know what slavery is. I have been a slave—I
have felt what a slave feels, and I know what a slave knows;
and I would have all the good people in England to know it
too, that they may break our chains, and set us free.

Mr. D——had another slave called Ben. He being very
hungry, stole a little rice one night after he came in from
work, and cooked it for his supper. But his master soon
discovered the theft; locked him up all night; and kept him
without food till one o'clock the next day. He then hung
Ben up by his hands, and beat him from time to time till the
slaves came in at night. We found the poor creature hung up
when we came home; with a pool of blood beneath him, and
our master still licking him. But this was not the worst. My
master's son was in the habit of stealing the rice and rum.
Ben had seen him do this, and thought he might do the
same, and when the master found out that Ben had stolen
the rice and swore to punish him, he tried to excuse himself
by saying that Master Dickey did the same thing every
night. The lad denied it to his father, and was so angry with
Ben for informing against him, that out of revenge he ran
and got a bayonet, and whilst the poor wretch was suspended by his hands and writhing under his wounds, he run
it quite through his foot. I was not by when he did it, but I
saw the wound when I came home, and heard Ben tell the
manner in which it was done.

I must say something more about this cruel son of a cruel
father.—He had no heart—no fear of God; he had been
brought up by a bad father in a bad path, and he delighted
to follow in the same steps. There was a little old woman

among the slaves called Sarah, who was nearly past work; and, Master Dickey being the overseer of the slaves just then, this poor creature, who was subject to several bodily infirmities, and was not quite right in her head, did not wheel the barrow fast enough to please him. He threw her down on the ground, and after beating her severely, he took her up in his arms and flung her among the prickly-pear bushes, which are all covered over with sharp venomous prickles. By this her naked flesh was so grievously wounded, that her body swelled and festered all over, and she died a few days later. In telling my own sorrows, I cannot pass by those of my fellow-slaves—for when I think of my own griefs, I remember theirs.

I think it was about ten years I had worked in the salt ponds at Turk's Island, when my master left off business, and retired to a house he had in Bermuda, leaving his son to succeed him in the island. He took me with him to wait upon his daughters; and I was joyful, for I was sick, sick of Turk's Island, and my heart yearned to see my native place again, my mother, and my kindred.

I had seen my poor mother during the time I was a slave in Turk's Island. One Sunday morning I was on the beach with some of the slaves, and we saw a sloop come in loaded with slaves to work in the salt water. We got a boat and went aboard. When I came upon the deck I asked the black people, "Is there any one here for me?" "Yes," they said, "your mother." I thought they said this in jest—I could scarcely believe them for joy; but when I saw my poor mammy my joy was turned to sorrow, for she had gone from her senses. "Mammy," I said, "is this you?" She did not know me. "Mammy," I said, "what's the matter?" She began to talk foolishly, and said that she had been under the vessel's bottom. They had been overtaken by a violent storm at sea. My poor mother had never been on the sea before, and she was so ill, that she lost her senses, and it was long before she came quite to herself again. She had a sweet child with her—a little sister I had never seen, about four years of age, called Rebecca. I took her on shore with me, for I felt I should love her directly; and I kept her with me a week. Poor little thing! hers has been a sad life, and continues so to this day. My mother worked for some years on the island, but was taken back to Bermuda some time before my master carried me again thither.*

After I left Turk's Island, I was told by some negroes that came over from it, that the poor slaves had built up a place with boughs and leaves, where they might meet for prayers, but the white people pulled it down twice, and would not allow them even a shed for prayers. A flood came down soon after and washed away many houses, filled the place with sand, and overflowed the ponds: and I do think that this was for their wickedness; for the Buckra men† there were very wicked. I saw and heard much that was very very bad at that place.

I was several years the slave of Mr. D——after I returned to my native place. Here I worked in the grounds. My work was planting and hoeing sweet-potatoes, Indian corn, plaintains, bananas, cabbages, pumpkins, onions, &c. I did all the household work, and attended upon a horse and cow besides,—going also upon all errands. I had to curry the horse—to clean and feed him—and sometimes to ride him a little. I had more than enough to do—but still it was not so very bad as Turk's Island.

My old master often got drunk, and then he would get in a fury with his daughter, and beat her till she was not fit to be seen. I remember on one occasion I had gone to fetch water, and when I was coming up the hill I heard a great screaming; I ran as fast as I could to the house, put down the water, and went into the chamber, where I found my master beating Miss D——dreadfully. I strove with all my strength

---

*Of the subsequent lot of her relatives she can tell but little. She says, her father died while she and her mother were at Turk's Island; and that he had been long dead and buried before any of his children in Bermuda knew of it, they being slaves on other estates. Her mother died after Mary went to Antigua. Of the fate of the rest of her kindred, seven brothers and three sisters, she knows nothing further than this— that the eldest sister, who had several children to her master, was taken by him to Trinidad; and that the youngest, Rebecca, is still alive, and in slavery in Bermuda. Mary herself is now about forty-three years of age.—*Ed.*

†Negro term for white people.

to get her away from him; for she was all black and blue with bruises. He had beat her with his fist, and almost killed her. The people gave me credit for getting her away. He turned round and began to lick me. Then I said, "Sir, this is not Turk's Island." I can't repeat his answer, the words were too wicked—too bad to say. He wanted to treat me the same in Bermuda as he had done in Turk's Island.

He had an ugly fashion of stripping himself quite naked, and ordering me then to wash him in a tub of water. This was worse to me than all the licks. Sometimes when he called me to wash him I would not come, my eyes were so full of shame. He would then come to beat me. One time I had plates and knives in my hand, and I dropped both plates and knives, and some of the plates were broken. He struck me so severely for this, that at last I defended myself, for I thought it was high time to do so. I then told him I would not live longer with him, for he was a very indecent man—very spiteful, and too indecent; with no shame for his servants, no shame for his own flesh. So I went away to a neighbouring house and sat down and cried till the next morning, when I went home again, not knowing what else to do.

After that I was hired to work at Cedar Hills, and every Saturday night I paid the money to my master. I had plenty of work to do there—plenty of washing; but yet I made myself pretty comfortable. I earned two dollars and a quarter a week, which is twenty pence a day.

During the time I worked there, I heard that Mr. John Wood was going to Antigua. I felt a great wish to go there, and I went to Mr. D——, and asked him to let me go in Mr. Wood's service. Mr. Wood did not then want to purchase me; it was my own fault that I came under him, I was so anxious to go. It was ordained to be, I suppose; God led me there. The truth is, I did not wish to be any longer the slave of my indecent master.

Mr. Wood took me with him to Antigua, to the town of St. John's, where he lived. This was about fifteen years ago. He did not then know whether I was to be sold; but Mrs. Wood found that I could work, and she wanted to buy me. Her husband then wrote to my master to inquire whether I was to be sold? Mr. D——wrote in reply, "that I should not be sold to any one that would treat me ill." It was strange he should say this, when he had treated me so ill himself. So I was purchased by Mr. Wood for 300 dollars, (or £100 Bermuda currency.)

My work there was to attend the chambers and nurse the child, and to go down to the pond and wash clothes. But I soon fell ill of the rheumatism, and grew so very lame that I was forced to walk with a stick. I got the Saint Anthony's fire, also, in my left leg, and became quite a cripple. No one cared much to come near me, and I was ill a long long time; for several months I could not lift the limb. I had to lie in a little old out-house, that was swarming with bugs and other vermin, which tormented me greatly; but I had no other place to lie in. I got the rheumatism by catching cold at the pond side, from washing in the fresh water; in the salt water I never got cold. The person who lived in next yard, (a Mrs. Greene) could not bear to hear my cries and groans. She was kind, and used to send an old slave woman to help me, who sometimes brought me a little soap. When the doctor found I was so ill, he said I must be put into a bath of hot water. The old slave got the bark of some bush that was good for the pains, which she boiled in the hot water, and every night she came and put me into the bath, and did what she could for me: I don't know what I should have done, or what would have become of me, had it not been for her.—My mistress, it is true, did send me a little food; but no one from our family came near me but the cook, who used to shove my food in at the door, and say, "Molly, Molly, there's your dinner." My mistress did not care to take any trouble about me; and if the Lord had not put it into the hearts of the neighbours to be kind to me, I must, I really think, have lain and died.

It was a long time before I got well enough to work in the house. Mrs. Wood, in the meanwhile, hired a mulatto woman to nurse the child; but she was such a fine lady she wanted to be mistress over me. I thought it very hard for a coloured woman to have rule over me because I was a slave and she was free. Her name was Martha Wilcox: she was a saucy woman, very saucy; and she went and complained of me, without cause, to my mistress, and made her angry with me. Mrs. Wood told me that if I did not mind what I was about, she would get my master to strip me and give me fifty lashes: "You have been used to the whip," she said, "and you shall have it here." This was the first time she threatened to have me flogged; and she gave me the threatening so strong of what she would have done to me, that I thought I should have fallen down at her feet, I was so vexed and hurt by her words. The mulatto woman was rejoiced to have power to keep me down. She was constantly making mischief; there was no living for the slaves—no peace after she came.

I was also sent by Mrs. Wood to be put in the Cage one night, and was next morning flogged, by the magistrate's order, at her desire; and this all for a quarrel I had about a pig with another slave woman. I was flogged on my naked back on this occasion: although I was in no fault after all; for old Justice Dyett, when we came before him, said that I was in the right, and ordered the pig to be given to me. This was about two or three years after I came to Antigua.

When we moved from the middle of the town to the Point, I used to be in the house and do all the work and mind the children, though still very ill with the rheumatism. Every week I had to wash two large bundles of clothes, as much as a boy could help me to lift; but I could give no satisfaction. My mistress was always abusing and fretting after me. It is not possible to tell all her ill language.—One day she followed me foot after foot scolding and rating me. I bore in silence a great deal of ill words: at last my heart was quite full, and I told her that she ought not to use me so;—that when I was ill I might have lain and died for what she cared; and no one would then come near me to nurse me, because they were afraid of my mistress. This was a great affront. She called her husband and told him what I had said. He flew into a passion: but did not beat me then; he only abused and swore at me; and then gave me a note and bade me go and look for an owner. Not that he meant to sell me; but he did this to please his wife and to frighten me. I went to Adam White, a cooper, a free black, who had money, and asked him to buy me. He went directly to Mr. Wood, but was informed that I was not to be sold. The next day my master whipped me.

Another time (about five years ago) my mistress got vexed with me, because I fell sick and I could not keep on with my work. She complained to her husband, and he sent me off again to look for an owner. I went to a Mr. Burchell, showed him the note, and asked him to buy me for my own benefit; for I had saved about 100 dollars, and hoped, with a little help, to purchase my freedom. He accordingly went to my master:—"Mr. Wood," he said, "Molly has brought me a note that she wants an owner. If you intend to sell her, I may as well buy her as another." My master put him off and said that he did not mean to sell me. I was very sorry at this, for I had no comfort with Mrs. Wood, and I wished greatly to get my freedom.

The way in which I made my money was this.—When my master and mistress went from home, as they sometimes did, and left me to take care of the house and premises, I had a good deal of time to myself, and made the most of it. I took in washing, and sold coffee and yams and other provisions to the captains of ships. I did not sit still idling during the absence of my owners; for I wanted, by all honest means, to earn money to buy my freedom. Sometimes I bought a hog cheap on board ship, and sold it for double the money on shore; and I also earned a good deal by selling coffee. By this means I by degrees acquired a little cash. A gentleman also lent me some to help to buy my freedom—but when I could not get free he got it back again. His name was Captain Abbot.

My master and mistress went on one occasion into the country, to Date Hill, for change of air, and carried me with them to take charge of the children, and to do the work of the house. While I was in the country, I saw how the field negroes are worked in Antigua. They are worked very hard and fed but scantily. They are called out to work before daybreak, and come home after dark; and then each has to heave his bundle of grass for the cattle in the pen. Then, on Sunday morning, each slave has to go out and gather a large bundle of grass; and, when they bring it home, they have all to sit at the manager's door and wait till he come out: often have they to wait there till past eleven o'clock, without any breakfast. After that, those that have yams or potatoes, or fire-wood to sell, hasten to market to buy a dog's worth* of salt fish, or pork, which is a great treat for them. Some of them buy a little pickle out of the shad barrels, which they call sauce, to season their yams and Indian corn. It is very wrong, I know, to work on Sunday or go to market; but will not God call the Buckra men to answer for this on the great day of judgment—since they will give the slaves no other day?

While we were at Date Hill Christmas came; and the slave woman who had the care of the place (which then belonged to Mr. Roberts the marshal), asked me to go with her to her husband's house, to a Methodist meeting for prayer, at a plantation called Winthorps. I went; and they were the first prayers I ever understood. One woman prayed; and then they all sung a hymn; then there was another prayer and another hymn; and then they all spoke by turns of their own griefs as sinners. The husband of the woman I went with was a black driver. His name was Henry. He confessed that he had treated the slaves very cruelly; but said that he was compelled to obey the orders of his master. He prayed them all to forgive him, and he prayed that God would forgive him. He said it was a horrid thing for a ranger† to have sometimes to beat his own wife or sister; but he must do so if ordered by his master.

I felt sorry for my sins also. I cried the whole night, but I was too much ashamed to speak. I prayed God to forgive me. This meeting had a great impression on my mind, and led my spirit to the Moravian Church; so that when I got back to town, I went and prayed to have my name put down in the Missionaries' book; and I followed the church earnestly every opportunity. I did not then tell my mistress about it; for I knew that she would not give me leave to go. But I felt I *must* go. Whenever I carried the children their lunch at school, I ran round and went to hear the teachers.

The Moravian ladies (Mrs. Richter, Mrs. Olufsen, and Mrs. Sauter) taught me to read in the class; and I got on

---

* A dog is the 72nd part of a dollar.

† The head negro of an estate—a person who has the chief superintendence under the manager.

very fast. In this class there were all sorts of people, old and young, grey headed folks and children; but most of them were free people. After we had done spelling, we tried to read in the Bible. After the reading was over, the missionary gave out a hymn for us to sing. I dearly loved to go to the church, it was so solemn. I never knew rightly that I had much sin till I went there. When I found out that I was a great sinner, I was very sorely grieved, and very much frightened. I used to pray God to pardon my sins for Christ's sake, and forgive me for every thing I had done amiss; and when I went home to my work, I always thought about what I had heard from the missionaries, and wished to be good that I might go to heaven. After a while I was admitted a candidate for the holy Communion.—I had been baptized long before this, in August 1817, by the Rev. Mr. Curtin, of the English Church, after I had been taught to repeat the Creed and the Lord's Prayer. I wished at that time to attend a Sunday School taught by Mr. Curtin, but he would not receive me without a written note from my master, granting his permission. I did not ask my owner's permission, from the belief that it would be refused; so that I got no farther instruction at that time from the English Church.*

Some time after I began to attend the Moravian Church, I met with Daniel James, afterwards my dear husband. He was a carpenter and cooper to his trade; an honest, hardworking, decent black man, and a widower. He had purchased his freedom of his mistress, old Mrs. Baker, with money he had earned whilst a slave. When he asked me to marry him, I took time to consider the matter over with myself, and would not say yes till he went to church with me

---

*She possesses a copy of Mrs. Trimmer's "Charity School Spelling Book," presented to her by the Rev. Mr. Curtin, and dated August 30, 1817. In this book her name is written "Mary, Princess of Wales"—an appellation which, she says, was given her by her owners. It is a common practice with the colonists to give ridiculous names of this description to their slaves; being, in fact, one of the numberless modes of expressing the habitual contempt with which they regard the negro race.—In printing this narrative we have retained Mary's paternal name of Prince.—*Ed.*

and joined the Moravians. He was very industrious after he bought his freedom; and he had hired a comfortable house, and had convenient things about him. We were joined in marriage, about Christmas 1826, in the Moravian Chapel at Spring Gardens, by the Rev. Mr. Olufsen. We could not be married in the English Church. English marriage is not allowed to slaves; and no free man can marry a slave woman.

When Mr. Wood heard of my marriage, he flew into a great rage, and sent for Daniel, who was helping to build a house for his old mistress. Mr. Wood asked him who gave him a right to marry a slave of his? My husband said, "Sir, I am a free man, and thought I had a right to choose a wife, but if I had known Molly was not allowed to have a husband, I should not have asked her to marry me." Mrs. Wood was more vexed about my marriage than her husband. She could not forgive me for getting married, but stirred up Mr. Wood to flog me dreadfully with the horsewhip. I thought it very hard to be whipped at my time of life for getting a husband—I told her so. She said that she would not have nigger men about the yards and premises, or allow a nigger man's clothes to be washed in the same tub where hers were washed. She was fearful, I think, that I should lose her time, in order to wash and do things for my husband; but I had then no time to wash for myself; I was obliged to put out my own clothes, though I was always at the wash-tub.

I had not much happiness in my marriage, owing to my being a slave. It made my husband sad to see me so ill-treated. Mrs. Wood was always abusing me about him. She did not lick me herself, but she got her husband to do it for her, whilst she fretted the flesh off my bones. Yet for all this she would not sell me. She sold five slaves whilst I was with her; but though she was always finding fault with me, she would not part with me. However, Mr. Wood afterwards allowed Daniel to have a place to live in our yard, which we were very thankful for.

After this, I fell ill again with the rheumatism, and was sick a long time; but whether sick or well, I had my work to do. About this time I asked my master and mistress to let me buy my own freedom. With the help of Mr. Burchell, I could have found the means to pay Mr. Wood; for it was agreed that I should afterwards serve Mr. Burchell a while, for the cash he was to advance for me. I was earnest in the request to my owners; but their hearts were hard—too hard to consent. Mrs. Wood was very angry—she grew quite outrageous—she called me a black devil, and asked me who had put freedom into my head. "To be free is very sweet," I said: but she took good care to keep me a slave. I saw her change colour, and I left the room.

About this time my master and mistress were going to England to put their son to school, and bring their daughters home; and they took me with them to take care of the child. I was willing to come to England; I thought that by going there I should probably get cured of my rheumatism, and should return with my master and mistress, quite well, to my husband. My husband was willing for me to come away, for he had heard that my master would free me,—and I also hoped this might prove true; but it was all a false report.

The steward of the ship was very kind to me. He and my husband were in the same class in the Moravian Church. I was thankful that he was so friendly, for my mistress was not kind to me on the passage; and she told me, when she was angry, that she did not intend to treat me any better in England than in the West Indies—that I need not expect it. And she was as good as her word.

When we drew near to England, the rheumatism seized all my limbs worse than ever, and my body was dreadfully swelled. When we landed at the Tower, I shewed my flesh to my mistress, but she took no great notice of it. We were obliged to stop at the tavern till my master got a house; and a day or two after, my mistress sent me down into the washhouse to learn to wash in the English way. In the West Indies we wash with cold water—in England with hot. I told my mistress I was afraid that putting my hands first into the hot water and then into the cold, would increase the pain in my limbs. The doctor had told my mistress long before I came from the West Indies, that I was a sickly body and the washing did not agree with me. But Mrs. Wood would not release me from the tub, so I was forced to do as I could. I grew worse, and could not stand to wash. I was then forced to sit down with the tub before me, and often through pain and weakness was reduced to kneel or to sit down on the floor, to finish my task. When I complained to my mistress of this, she only got into a passion as usual, and said washing in hot water could not hurt any one;—that I was lazy and insolent, and wanted to be free of my work; but that she would make me do it. I thought her very hard on me, and my heart rose up within me. However I kept still at that time, and went down again to wash the child's things; but the English washerwomen who were at work there, when they saw that I was so ill, had pity upon me and washed them for me.

After that, when we came up to live in Leigh Street, Mrs. Wood sorted out five bags of clothes which we had used at sea, and also such as had been worn since we came on shore, for me and the cook to wash. Elizabeth the cook told her, that she did not think that I was able to stand to the tub, and that she had better hire a woman. I also said myself, that I had come over to nurse the child, and that I was sorry I had come from Antigua, since mistress would work me so hard, without compassion for my rheumatism. Mr. and Mrs. Wood, when they heard this, rose up in a passion against me. They opened the door and bade me get out. But I was a stranger, and did not know one door in the street from another, and was unwilling to go away. They made a dreadful uproar, and from that day they constantly kept cursing and abusing me. I was obliged to wash, though I was very ill. Mrs. Wood, indeed once hired a washerwoman, but she was not well treated, and would come no more.

My master quarrelled with me another time, about one of our great washings, his wife having stirred him up to do so. He said he would compel me to do the whole of the washing given out to me, or if I again refused, he would take a short course with me: he would either send me down to the brig in the river, to carry me back to Antigua, or he would turn me at once out of doors, and let me provide for myself. I said I would willingly go back, if he would let me purchase my own freedom. But this enraged him more than all the rest: he cursed and swore at me dreadfully, and said he would never sell my freedom—if I wished to be free, I was free in England, and I might go and try what freedom would do for me, and be d——d. My heart was very sore with this treatment, but I had to go on. I continued to do my work, and did all I could to give satisfaction, but all would not do.

Shortly after, the cook left them, and then matters went on ten times worse. I always washed the child's clothes without being commanded to do it, and any thing else that was wanted in the family; though still I was very sick—very sick indeed. When the great washing came round, which was every two months, my mistress got together again a great many heavy things, such as bed-ticks, bed-coverlets, &c. for me to wash. I told her I was too ill to wash such heavy things that day. She said, she supposed I thought myself a free woman, but I was not; and if I did not do it directly I should be instantly turned out of doors. I stood a long time before I could answer, for I did not know well what to do. I knew that I was free in England, but I did not know where to go, or how to get my living; and therefore, I did not like to leave the house. But Mr. Wood said he would send for a constable to thrust me out; and at last I took courage and resolved that I would not be longer thus treated, but would go and trust to Providence. This was the fourth time they had threatened to turn me out, and go where I might, I was determined now to take them at their word; though I thought it very hard, after I had lived with them for thirteen years, and worked for them like a horse, to be driven out in this way, like a beggar. My only fault was being sick, and therefore unable to please my mistress, who thought she never could get work enough out of her slaves; and I told them so: but they only abused me and drove me out. This took place from two to three months, I think, after we came to England.

When I came away, I went to the man (one Mash) who used to black the shoes of the family, and asked his wife to get somebody to go with me to Hatton Garden to the Moravian Missionaries: these were the only persons I knew in England. The woman sent a young girl with me to the mission house, and I saw there a gentleman called Mr. Moore. I told him my whole story, and how my owners had treated me, and asked him to take in my trunk with what few clothes I had. The missionaries were very kind to me— they were sorry for my destitute situation, and gave me leave to bring my things to be placed under their care. They were very good people, and they told me to come to the church.

When I went back to Mr. Wood's to get my trunk, I saw a lady, Mrs. Pell, who was on a visit to my mistress. When Mr. and Mrs. Wood heard me come in, they set this lady to stop me, finding that they had gone too far with me. Mrs. Pell came out to me, and said, "Are you really going to leave, Molly? Don't leave, but come into the country with me." I believe she said this because she thought Mrs. Wood would easily get me back again. I replied to her, "Ma'am, this is the fourth time my master and mistress have driven me out, or threatened to drive me—and I will give them no more occasion to bid me go. I was not willing to leave them, for I am a stranger in this country, but now I must go—I can stay no longer to be so used." Mrs. Pell then went up stairs to my mistress, and told that I would go, and that she could not stop me. Mrs. Wood was very much hurt and frightened when she found I was determined to go out that day. She said, "If she goes the people will rob her, and then turn her adrift." She did not say this to me, but she spoke it loud enough for me to hear; that it might induce me not to go, I suppose. Mr. Wood also asked me where I was going to. I told him where I had been, and that I should never have gone away had I not been driven out by my owners. He had given me a written paper some time before, which said that I had come with them to England by my own desire; and that was true. It said also that I left them of my own free will, because I was a free woman in England; and that I was idle and would not do my work—which was not true. I gave this paper afterwards to a gentleman who inquired into my case.*

I went into the kitchen and got my clothes out. The nurse and the servant girl were there, and I said to the man who was going to take out my trunk, "Stop, before you take up this trunk, and hear what I have to say before these people. I am going out of this house, as I was ordered; but I have done no wrong at all to my owners, neither here nor in the West Indies. I always worked very hard to please them, both by night and day; but there was no giving satisfaction, for

*See page 266.

my mistress could never be satisfied with reasonable service. I told my mistress I was sick, and yet she has ordered me out of doors. This is the fourth time; and now I am going out."

And so I came out, and went and carried my trunk to the Moravians. I then returned back to Mash the shoe-black's house, and begged his wife to take me in. I had a little West Indian money in my trunk; and they got it changed for me. This helped to support me for a little while. The man's wife was very kind to me. I was very sick, and she boiled nourishing things up for me. She also sent for a doctor to see me, and he sent me medicine, which did me good, though I was ill for a long time with the rheumatic pains. I lived a good many months with these poor people, and they nursed me, and did all that lay in their power to serve me. The man was well acquainted with my situation, as he used to go to and fro to Mr. Wood's house to clean shoes and knives; and he and his wife were sorry for me.

About this time, a woman of the name of Hill told me of the Anti-Slavery Society, and went with me to their office, to inquire if they could do any thing to get me my freedom, and send me back to the West Indies. The gentlemen of the Society took me to a lawyer, who examined very strictly into my case; but told me that the laws of England could do nothing to make me free in Antigua.* However, they did all they could for me: they gave me a little money from time to time to keep me from want; and some of them went to Mr. Wood to try to persuade him to let me return a free woman to my husband; but though they offered him, as I have heard, a large sum for my freedom, he was sulky and obstinate, and would not consent to let me go free.

This was the first winter I spent in England, and I suffered much from the severe cold, and from the rheumatic pains, which still at times torment me. However, Providence was very good to me, and I got many friends—especially some Quaker ladies, who hearing of my case, came and

---

*She came first to the Anti-Slavery Office in Aldermanbury, about the latter end of November 1828; and her case was referred to Mr. George Stephen to be investigated. More of this hereafter.—*Ed.*

sought me out, and gave me good warm clothing and money. Thus I had great cause to bless God in my affliction.

When I got better I was anxious to get some work to do, as I was unwilling to eat the bread of idleness. Mrs. Mash, who was a laundress, recommended me to a lady for a char-woman. She paid me very handsomely for what work I did, and I divided the money with Mrs. Mash; for though very poor, they gave me food when my own money was done, and never suffered me to want.

In the spring, I got into service with a lady, who saw me at the house where I sometimes worked as a charwoman. This lady's name was Mrs. Forsyth. She had been in the West Indies, and was accustomed to Blacks, and liked them. I was with her six months, and went with her to Margate. She treated me well, and gave me a good character when she left London.*

After Mrs. Forsyth went away, I was again out of place, and went to lodgings, for which I paid two shillings a week, and found coals and candle. After eleven weeks, the money I had saved in service was all gone, and I was forced to go back in the Anti-Slavery office to ask a supply, till I could get another situation. I did not like to go back—I did not like to be idle. I would rather work for my living than get it for nothing. They were very good to give me a supply, but I felt shame at being obliged to apply for relief whilst I had strength to work.

At last I went into the service of Mr. and Mrs. Pringle, where I have been ever since, and am as comfortable as I can be while separated from my dear husband, and away from my own country and all old friends and connections. My dear mistress teaches me daily to read the word of God, and takes great pains to make me understand it. I enjoy the great privilege of being enabled to attend church three times on the Sunday; and I have met with many kind friends since I have been here, both clergymen and others. The Rev. Mr. Young, who lives in the next house, has shown me much kindness, and taken much pains to instruct me, particularly while my master and mistress were absent in Scotland. Nor must I forget, among my friends, the Rev. Mr. Mortimer, the

---

*She refers to a written certificate which will be inserted afterwards.

good clergyman of the parish, under whose ministry I have now sat for upwards of twelve months. I trust in God I have profited by what I have heard from him. He never keeps back the truth, and I think he has been the means of opening my eyes and ears much better to understand the word of God. Mr. Mortimer tells me that he cannot open the eyes of my heart, but that I must pray to God to change my heart, and make me to know the truth, and the truth will make me free.

I still live in the hope that God will find a way to give me my liberty, and give me back to my husband. I endeavour to keep down my fretting, and to leave all to Him, for he knows what is good for me better than I know myself. Yet, I must confess, I find it a hard and heavy task to do so.

I am often much vexed, and I feel great sorrow when I hear some people in this country say, that the slaves do not need better usage, and do not want to be free.* They believe the foreign people,† who deceive them, and say slaves are happy. I say, Not so. How can slaves be happy when they have the halter round their neck and the whip upon their back? and are disgraced and thought no more of than beasts?—and are separated from their mothers, and husbands, and children, and sisters, just as cattle are sold and separated? Is it happiness for a driver in the field to take down his wife or sister or child, and strip them, and whip them in such a disgraceful manner?—women that have had children exposed in the open field to shame! There is no modesty or decency shown by the owner to his slaves; men, women, and children are exposed alike. Since I have been here I have often wondered how English people can go out into the West Indies and act in such a beastly manner. But when they go to the West Indies, they forget God and all feeling of shame, I think, since they can see and do such things. They tie up slaves like hogs—moor‡ them up like cattle, and they lick them, so as hogs, or cattle, or horses

---

*The whole of this paragraph especially, is given as nearly as was possible in Mary's precise words.

†She means West Indians.

‡A West Indian phrase: to fasten or tie up.

never were flogged;—and yet they come home and say, and make some good people believe, that slaves don't want to get out of slavery. But they put a cloak about the truth. It is not so. All slaves want to be free—to be free is very sweet. I will say the truth to English people who may read this history that my good friend, Miss S——, is now writing down for me. I have been a slave myself—and I know what slaves feel—I can tell by myself what other slaves feel, and by what they have told me. The man that says slaves be quite happy in slavery—that they don't want to be free—that man is either ignorant or a lying person. I never heard a slave say so. I never heard a Buckra man say so, till I heard tell of it in England. Such people ought to be ashamed of themselves. They can't do without slaves, they say. What's the reason they can't do without slaves as well as in England? No slaves here—no whips—no stocks—no punishment, except for wicked people. They hire servants in England, and if they don't like them, they send them away: they can't lick them. Let them work ever so hard in England, they are far better off than slaves. If they get a bad master, they give warning and go hire to another. They have their liberty. That's just what *we* want. We don't mind hard work, if we had proper treatment, and proper wages like English servants, and proper time given in the week to keep us from breaking the Sabbath. But they won't give it: they will have work—work—work, night and day, sick or well, till we are quite done up; and we must not speak up nor look amiss, however much we be abused. And then when we are quite done up, who cares for us, more than for a lame horse? This is slavery. I tell it, to let English people know the truth; and I hope they will never leave off to pray God, and call loud to the great King of England, till all the poor blacks be given free, and slavery done up for evermore.

SUPPLEMENT

TO THE

HISTORY OF MARY PRINCE

BY THE EDITOR

LEAVING Mary's narrative, for the present, without comment to the reader's reflections, I proceed to state some circumstances connected with her case which have fallen more particularly under my own notice, and which I consider it incumbent now to lay fully before the public.

About the latter end of November, 1828, this poor woman found her way to the office of the Anti-Slavery Society in Aldermanbury, by the aid of a person who had become acquainted with her situation, and had advised her to apply there for advice and assistance. After some preliminary examination into the accuracy of the circumstances related by her, I went along with her to Mr. George Stephen, solicitor, and requested him to investigate and draw up a statement of her case, and have it submitted to counsel, in order to ascertain whether or not, under the circumstances, her freedom could be legally established on her return to Antigua. On this occasion, in Mr. Stephen's presence and mine, she expressed, in very strong terms, her anxiety to return thither if she could go as a free person, and, at the same time, her extreme apprehensions of the fate that would probably await her if she returned as a slave. Her words were, "I would rather go into my grave than go back a slave to Antigua, though I wish to go back to my husband very much—very much—very much! I am much afraid my owners would separate me from my husband, and use me very hard, or perhaps sell me for a field negro;—and slavery is too too bad. I would rather go into my grave!"

The paper which Mr. Wood had given her before she left his house, was placed by her in Mr. Stephen's hands. It was expressed in the following terms:—

> I have already told Molly, and now give it her in writing, in order that there may be no misunderstanding on her part, that as I brought her from Antigua at her own request and entreaty, and that she is consequently now free, she is of course at liberty to take her baggage and go where she pleases. And, in consequence of her late conduct, she must do one of two things—either quit the house, or return to Antigua by the earliest opportunity, as she does not evince a disposition to make herself useful. As she is a stranger in London, I do not wish to turn her out, or would do so, as two female servants are sufficient for my establishment. If after this she does remain, it will be only during her good behaviour; but on no consideration will I allow her wages or any other remuneration for her services.
> JOHN A. WOOD.
>
> *London, August 18, 1828.*

This paper, though not devoid of inconsistencies, which will be apparent to any attentive reader, is craftily expressed; and was well devised to serve the purpose which the writer had obviously in view, namely, to frustrate any appeal which the friendless black woman might make to the sympathy of strangers, and thus prevent her from obtaining an asylum, if she left his house, from any respectable family. As she had no one to refer to for a character in this country except himself, he doubtless calculated securely on her being speedily driven back, as soon as the slender fund she had in her possession was expended, to throw herself unconditionally upon his tender mercies; and his disappointment in this expectation appears to have exasperated his feelings of resentment towards the poor woman, to a degree which few persons alive to the claims of common justice, not to speak of Christianity or common humanity, could easily have anticipated. Such, at least, seems the only intelligible inference that can be drawn from his subsequent conduct.

The case having been submitted, by desire of the Anti-Slavery Committee, to the consideration of Dr. Lushington and Mr. Sergeant Stephen, it was found that there existed no legal means of compelling Mary's master to grant her manumission; and that if she returned to Antigua, she would inevitably fall again under his power, or that of his attorneys, as a slave. It was, however, resolved to try what could be affected for her by amicable negotiation; and with this view Mr. Ravenscroft, a solicitor, (Mr. Stephen's relative,) called upon Mr. Wood, in order to ascertain whether he would consent to Mary's manumission on any reasonable terms, and to refer, if required, the amount of compensation for her value to arbitration. Mr. Ravenscroft with some difficulty obtained one or two interviews, but found Mr. Wood so full of animosity against the woman, and so firmly bent against any arrangement having her freedom for its object, that the negotiation was soon broken off as hopeless. The angry slave-owner declared "that he would not move a finger about her in this country, or grant her manumission on any terms whatever; and that if she went back to the West Indies, she must take the consequences."

This unreasonable conduct of Mr. Wood, induced the Anti-Slavery Committee, after several other abortive attempts to effect a compromise, to think of bringing the case under the notice of Parliament. The heads of Mary's statement were accordingly engrossed in a Petition, which Dr. Lushington offered to present, and to give notice at the same time of his intention to bring in a Bill to provide for the entire emancipation of all slaves brought to England with the owner's consent. But before this step was taken, Dr. Lushington again had recourse to negotiation with the master; and, partly through the friendly intervention of Mr. Manning, partly by personal conference, used every persuasion in his power to induce Mr. Wood to relent and let the bondwoman go free. Seeing the matter thus seriously taken up, Mr. Wood became at length alarmed,—not relishing, it appears, the idea of having the case publicly discussed in the House of Commons; and to avert this result he submitted to temporize—assumed a demeanour of unwonted civility, and even hinted to Mr. Manning (as I was given to understand) that if he was not driven to utter hostility by the threatened exposure, he would probably meet our wishes "in his own time and way." Having gained time by these manœuvres, he adroitly endeavoured to cool the ardour of Mary's new friends, in her cause, by representing her as an abandoned and worthless woman, ungrateful towards him, and undeserving of sympathy from others; allegations which he supported by the ready affirmation of some of his West India friends, and by one or two plausible letters procured from Antigua. By these and like artifices he appears completely to have imposed on Mr. Manning, the respectable West India merchant whom Dr. Lushington had asked to negotiate with him; and he prevailed so far as to induce Dr. Lushington himself (actuated by the benevolent view of thereby best serving Mary's cause,) to abstain from any remarks upon his conduct when the petition was at last presented in Parliament. In this way he dextrously contrived to neutralize all our efforts, until the close of the Session of 1829; soon after which he embarked with his family for the West Indies.

Every exertion for Mary's relief having thus failed; and being fully convinced from a twelvemonth's observation of her conduct, that she was really a well-disposed and respectable woman; I engaged her, in December 1829, as a domestic servant in my own family. In this capacity she has remained ever since; and I am thus enabled to speak of her conduct and character with a degree of confidence I could not have otherwise done. The importance of this circumstance will appear in the sequel.

From the time of Mr. Wood's departure to Antigua, in 1829, till June or July last, no farther effort was attempted for Mary's relief. Some faint hope was still cherished that this unconscionable man would at length relent, and "in his own time and way," grant the prayer of the exiled negro woman. After waiting, however, nearly twelve months longer, and seeing the poor woman's spirits daily sinking under the sickening influence of hope deferred, I resolved on a final attempt in her behalf, through the intervention of the Moravian Missionaries, and of the Governor of Antigua. At my request, Mr. Edward Moore, agent of the Moravian

Brethren in London, wrote to the Rev. Joseph Newby, their Missionary in that island, empowering him to negotiate in his own name with Mr. Wood for Mary's manumission, and to procure his consent, if possible, upon terms of ample pecuniary compensation. At the same time the excellent and benevolent William Allen, of the Society of Friends, wrote to Sir Patrick Ross, the Governor of the Colony, with whom he was on terms of friendship, soliciting him to use his influence in persuading Mr. Wood to consent: and I confess I was sanguine enough to flatter myself that we should thus at length prevail. The result proved, however, that I had not yet fully appreciated the character of the man we had to deal with.

Mr. Newby's answer arrived early in November last, mentioning that he had done all in his power to accomplish our purpose, but in vain; and that if Mary's manumission could not be obtained without Mr. Wood's consent, he believed there was no prospect of its ever being effected.

A few weeks afterwards I was informed by Mr. Allen, that he had received a letter from Sir Patrick Ross, stating that he also had used his best endeavours in the affair, but equally without effect. Sir Patrick at the same time inclosed a letter, addressed by Mr. Wood to his Secretary, Mr. Taylor, assigning his reasons for persisting in this extraordinary course. This letter requires our special attention. Its tenor is as follows:—

My dear Sir,

In reply to your note relative to the woman Molly, I beg you will have the kindness to oblige me by assuring his Excellency that I regret exceedingly my inability to comply with his request, which under other circumstances would afford me very great pleasure.

There are many and powerful reasons for inducing me to refuse my sanction to her returning here in the way she seems to wish. It would be to reward the worst species of ingratitude, and subject myself to insult whenever she came in my way. Her moral character is very bad, as the police records will shew; and she would be a very troublesome character should she come here without any restraint. She is not a native of this country, and I know of no relation she has here. I induced her to take a husband, a short time before she left this, by providing a comfortable house in my yard for them, and prohibiting her going out after 10 to 12 o'clock (our bed-time) without special leave. This she considered the greatest, and indeed the only, grievance she ever complained of, and all my efforts could not prevent it. In hopes of inducing her to be steady to her husband, who was a free man, I gave him the house to occupy during our absence; but it appears the attachment was too loose to bind her, and he has taken another wife; so on that score I do her no injury.—In England she made her election, and quitted my family. This I had no right to object to; and I should have thought no more of it, but not satisfied to leave quietly, she gave every trouble and annoyance in her power, and endeavoured to injure the character of my family by the most vile and infamous falsehoods, which was embodied in a petition to the House of Commons, and would have been presented, had not my friends from this island, particularly the Hon. Mr. Byam and Dr. Coull, come forward, and disproved what she had asserted.

It would be beyond the limits of an ordinary letter to detail her baseness, though I will do so should his Excellency wish it; but you may judge of her depravity by one circumstance, which came out before Mr. Justice Dyett, in a quarrel with another female.

*   *   *   *   *   *   *   *   *   *

Such a thing I could not have believed possible.*

Losing her value as a slave in a pecuniary point of view I consider of no consequence; for it was our intention, had she conducted herself properly and returned with us, to have given her freedom. She has taken her freedom; and all I wish is, that she would enjoy it without meddling with me.

Let me again repeat, if his Excellency wishes it, it will afford me great pleasure to state such particulars of her, and which will be incontestably proved by numbers here, that I am sure will acquit me in his opinion of acting unkind or ungenerous

---

*I omit the circumstance here mentioned, because it is too indecent to appear in a publication likely to be perused by females. It is, in all probability, a vile calumny; but even if it were perfectly true, it would not serve Mr. Wood's case one straw.—Any reader who wishes it, may see the passage referred to, in the autograph letter in my possession. T.P.

towards her. I'll say nothing of the liability I should incur, under the Consolidated Slave Law, of dealing with a free person as a slave.

My only excuse for entering so much into detail must be that of my anxious wish to stand justified in his Excellency's opinion.

> I am, my dear Sir,
> Yours very truly,
> JOHN A. WOOD.
> *20th Oct. 1830.*

Charles Taylor, Esq.
  &C.&C.&C.

I forgot to mention that it was at her own special request that she accompanied me to England—and also that she had a considerable sum of money with her, which she had saved in my service. I knew of £36 to £40, at least, for I had some trouble to recover it from a white man, to whom she had lent it.

> J.A.W.

Such is Mr. Wood's justification of his conduct in thus obstinately refusing manumission to the Negro-woman who had escaped from his "house of bondage."

Let us now endeavour to estimate the validity of the excuses assigned, and the allegations advanced by him, for the information of Governor Sir Patrick Ross, in this deliberate statement of his case.

1. To allow the woman to return home free, would, he affirms "be to reward the worst species of ingratitude."

He assumes, it seems, the sovereign power of pronouncing a virtual sentence of banishment, for the alleged crime of ingratitude. Is this then a power which any man ought to possess over his fellow-mortal? or which any good man would ever wish to exercise? And, besides, there is no evidence whatever, beyond Mr. Wood's mere assertion, that Mary Prince owed him or his family the slightest mark of gratitude. Her account of the treatment she received in his service, *may* be incorrect; but her simple statement is at least supported by minute and feasible details, and, unless rebutted by positive facts, will certainly command credence from impartial minds more readily than his angry accusation, which has something absurd and improbable in its very front. Moreover, is it not absurd to term the assertion of her *natural rights* by a slave,—even supposing her to have been kindly dealt with by her "owners," and treated in every respect the reverse of what Mary affirms to have been her treatment by Mr. Wood and his wife,—"the *worst* species of ingratitude"? This may be West Indian ethics, but it will scarcely be received as sound doctrine in Europe.

2. To permit her return would be "to subject himself to insult whenever she came in his way."

This is a most extraordinary assertion. Are the laws of Antigua then so favourable to the free blacks, or the colonial police so feebly administered, that there are no sufficient restraints to protect a rich colonist like Mr. Wood,—a man who counts among his familiar friends the Honourable Mr. Byam, and Mr. Taylor the Government Secretary,—from being insulted by a poor Negro-woman? It is preposterous.

3. Her moral character is so bad, that she would prove very troublesome should she come to the colony "without any restraint."

"Any restraint"? Are there no restraints (supposing them necessary) short of absolute slavery to keep "troublesome characters" in order? But this, I suppose, is the *argumentum ad gubernatorem*—to frighten the governor. She is such a termagant, it seems, that if she once gets back to the colony *free*, she will not only make it too hot for poor Mr. Wood, but the police and courts of justice will scarce be a match for her! Sir Patrick Ross, no doubt, will take care how he intercedes farther for so formidable a virago! How can one treat such arguments seriously?

4. She is not a native of the colony, and he knows of no relation she has there.

True: But was it not her home (so far as a slave can have a home) for thirteen or fourteen years? Were not the connexions, friendships, and associations of her mature life formed there? Was it not there she hoped to spend her latter years in domestic tranquillity with her husband, free from the lash of the taskmaster? These considerations may appear light to Mr. Wood, but they are every thing to this poor woman.

5. He induced her, he says, to take a husband, a short

time before she left Antigua, and gave them a comfortable house in his yard, &c. &c.

This paragraph merits attention. He "*Induced her to take a husband*"? If the fact were true, what brutality of mind and manners does it not indicate among these slave-holders? They refuse to legalize the marriages of their slaves, but *induce* them to form such temporary connexions as may suit the owner's conveniency, just as they would pair the lower animals; and this man has the effrontery to tell us so! Mary, however, tells a very different story [see page 254] and her assertion, independently of other proof, is at least as credible as Mr. Wood's. The reader will judge for himself as to the preponderance of internal evidence in the conflict-ing statements.

6. He alleges that she was, before marriage, licentious, and even depraved in her conduct, and unfaithful to her husband afterwards.

These are serious charges. But if true, or even partially true, how comes it that a person so correct in his family hours and arrangements as Mr. Wood professes to be, and who expresses so edifying a horror of licentiousness, could reconcile it to his conscience to keep in the bosom of his family so *depraved,* as well as so *troublesome* a character for at least thirteen years, and confide to her for long periods too the charge of his house and the care of his children—for such I shall shew to have been the facts? How can he ac-count for not having rid himself with all speed, of so dis-reputable an inmate—he who values her loss so little "in a pecuniary point of view"? How can he account for having sold *five other slaves* in that period, and yet have retained this shocking woman—nay, even have refused to sell her, on more than one occasion, when offered her full value? It could not be from ignorance of her character, for the cir-cumstance which he adduces as a proof of her shameless depravity, and which I have omitted on account of its inde-cency, occurred, it would appear, not less than *ten years ago.* Yet, notwithstanding her alleged ill qualities and habits of gross immorality, he has not only constantly refused to part with her; but after thirteen long years, brings her to England as an attendant on his wife and children, with the avowed intention of carrying her back along with his maiden daughter, a young lady returning from school! Such are the extraordinary facts; and until Mr. Wood shall reconcile these singular inconsistencies between his actions and his allegations, he must not be surprised if we in England prefer giving credit to the former rather than the latter; although at present it appears somewhat difficult to say which side of the alternative is the more creditable to his own character.

7. Her husband, he says, has taken another wife; "so that on that score," he adds, "he does her no injury."

Supposing this fact be true, (which I doubt, as I doubt every mere assertion from so questionable a quarter) I shall take leave to put a question or two to Mr. Wood's conscience. Did he not write from England to his friend Mr. Darrel, soon after Mary left his house, directing him to turn her husband, Daniel James, off his premises, on account of her offence; telling him to inform James at the same time that his wife had *taken up* with another man, who had robbed her of all she had—a calumny as groundless as it was cruel? I further ask if the person who invented this story (whoever he may be) was not likely enough to impose similar fabrications on the poor negro man's credulity, until he may have been induced to prove false to his marriage vows, and to "take another wife," as Mr. Wood coolly expresses it? But withal, I strongly doubt the fact of Daniel James' infidelity; for there is now before me a letter from himself to Mary, dated in April 1830, couched in strong terms of conjugal affection; expressing his anxiety for her speedy return, and stating that he had lately "received a grace" (a token of religious advancement) in the Moravian church, a circumstance altogether incredible if the man were living in open adultery, as Mr. Wood's assertion implies.

8. Mary, he says, endeavoured to injure the character of his family by infamous falsehoods, which were embodied in a petition to the House of Commons, and would have been presented, had not his friends from Antigua, the Hon. Mr. Byam, and Dr. Coull, disproved her assertions.

I can say something on this point from my own knowledge. Mary's petition contained simply a brief statement of her case, and, among other things, mentioned the treatment she had received from Mr. and Mrs. Wood. Now the principal facts are corroborated by other evidence, and Mr. Wood must bring forward very different testimony from that of Dr. Coull before well-informed persons will give credit to his contradiction. The value of that person's evidence in such cases will be noticed presently. Of the Hon. Mr. Byam I know nothing, and shall only at present remark that it is not likely to redound greatly to his credit to appear in such company. Furthermore, Mary's petition was presented, as Mr. Wood ought to know; though it was not discussed, nor his conduct exposed as it ought to have been.

9. He speaks of the liability he should incur, under the Consolidated Slave Law, of dealing with a free person as a slave.

Is not this pretext hypocritical in the extreme? What liability could he possibly incur by voluntarily resigning the power, conferred on him by an iniquitous colonial law, of reimposing the shackles of slavery on the bondwoman from whose limbs they had fallen when she touched the free soil of England?—There exists no liability from which he might not have been easily secured, or for which he would not have been fully compensated.

He adds in a postscript that Mary had a considerable sum of money with her,—from £36 to £40 at least, which she had saved in his service. The fact is, that she had at one time 113 dollars in cash; but only a very small portion of that sum appears to have been brought by her to England, the rest having been partly advanced, as she states, to assist her husband, and partly lost by being lodged in unfaithful custody.

Finally, Mr. Wood repeats twice that it will afford him great pleasure to state for the governor's satisfaction, if required, such particulars of "the woman Molly," upon incontestable evidence, as he is sure will acquit him in his Excellency's opinion "of acting unkind or ungenerous towards her."

This is well: and I now call upon Mr. Wood to redeem his pledge;—to bring forward facts and proofs fully to elucidate the subject;—to reconcile, if he can, the extraordinary discrepancies which I have pointed out between his assertions and the actual facts, and especially between his account of Mary Prince's character and his own conduct in regard to her. He has now to produce such a statement as will acquit him not only in the opinion of Sir Patrick Ross, but of the British public. And in this position he has spontaneously placed himself, in attempting to destroy, by his deliberate criminatory letter, the poor woman's fair fame and reputation,—an attempt but for which the present publication would probably never have appeared.

Here perhaps we might safely leave the case to the judgment of the public, but as this negro woman's character, not the less valuable to her because her condition is so humble, has been so unscrupulously blackened by her late master, a party so much interested and inclined to place her in the worst point of view,—it is incumbent on me, as her advocate with the public, to state such additional testimony in her behalf as I can fairly and conscientiously adduce.

My first evidence is Mr. Joseph Phillips, of Antigua. Having submitted to his inspection Mr. Wood's letter and Mary Prince's narrative, and requested his candid and deliberate sentiments in regard to the actual facts of the case, I have been favoured with the following letter from him on the subject:—

London, January 18, 1831.

Dear Sir,

In giving you my opinion of Mary Prince's narrative, and of Mr. Wood's letter respecting her, addressed to Mr. Taylor, I shall first mention my opportunities of forming a proper estimate of the conduct and character of both parties.

I have known Mr. Wood since his first arrival in Antigua in 1803. He was then a poor young man, who had been brought up as a ship carpenter in Bermuda. He was afterwards raised to be a clerk in the Commissariat department, and realised sufficient capital to commence business as a merchant. This last profession he has followed successfully for a good many years, and is understood to have accumulated very considerable wealth. After he entered into trade, I had constant intercourse with him in the way of business; and in 1824 and 1825, I was regularly employed on his premises as his clerk; consequently, I had opportunities of seeing a good deal of his character both as a merchant and as a master of slaves. The former topic I pass over as irrelevant to the present subject; in reference to the latter, I shall merely observe that he was not, in regard to ordinary matters, more severe than the ordinary run of slave owners; but, if seriously offended, he was not of a disposition to be easily appeased, and would spare no cost or sacrifice to gratify his vindictive feelings. As regards the exaction of work from domestic slaves, his wife was probably more severe than himself—it was almost impossible for the slaves ever to give her entire satisfaction.

Of their slave Molly (or Mary) I know less than of Mr. and Mrs. Wood; but I saw and heard enough of her, both while I was constantly employed on Mr. Wood's premises, and while I was there occasionally on business, to be quite certain that she was viewed by her owners as their most respectable and trustworthy female slave. It is within my personal knowledge that she had usually the charge of the house in their absence, was entrusted with the keys, &c.; and was always considered by the neighbours and visitors as their confidential household servant, and as a person in whose integrity they placed unlimited confidence,—although when Mrs. Wood was at home, she was no doubt kept pretty closely at washing and other hard work. A decided proof of the estimation to which she was held by her owners exists in the fact that Mr. Wood uniformly refused to part with her, whereas he sold five other slaves while she was with them. Indeed, she always appeared to me to be a slave of superior intelligence and respectability; and I always understood such to be her general character in the place.

As to what Mr. Wood alleges about her being frequently before the police, &c. I can only say I never heard of the circumstance before; and as I lived for twenty years in the same small town, and in the vicinity of their residence, I think I could scarcely have failed to become acquainted with it, had such been the fact. She might, however, have been occasionally before the magistrate in consequence of little disputes among the slaves, without any serious imputation on her general respectability. She says she was twice summoned to appear as a witness on such occasions; and that she was once sent by her mistress to be confined in the Cage, and was afterwards flogged by her desire. This cruel practice is very common in Antigua; and, in my opinion, is but little creditable to the slave owners and magistrates by whom such arbitrary punishments are inflicted, frequently for very trifling faults. Mr. James Scotland is the only magistrate in the colony who invariably refuses to sanction this reprehensible practice.

Of the immoral conduct ascribed to Molly by Mr. Wood, I can say nothing further than this—that I have heard she had at a former period (previous to her marriage) a connexion with a white person, a Capt.——, which I have no doubt was broken off when she became seriously impressed with religion. But, at any rate, such connexions are so common, I might almost say universal, in our slave colonies, that except by the missionaries and a few serious persons, they are considered, if faults at all, so very venial as scarcely to deserve the name of immorality. Mr. Wood knows this colonial estimate of such connexions as well as I do; and, however false such an estimate must be allowed to be, especially when applied to their own conduct by persons of education, pretending to adhere to the pure Christian rule of morals,—yet when he ascribes to a negro slave, to whom legal marriage was denied, such great criminality for laxity of this sort, and professes to be so exceedingly shocked and amazed at the tale he himself relates, he must, I am confident, have had a farther object in view than the information of Mr. Taylor or Sir Patrick Ross. He must, it is evident, have been aware that his letter would be sent to Mr. Allen, and accordingly adapted it, as more important documents from the colonies are often adapted, *for effect in England.* The tale of the slave Molly's immoralities, be assured, was not intended for Antigua so much as for Stoke Newington, and Peckham, and Aldermanbury.

In regard to Mary's narrative generally, although I cannot speak to the accuracy of the details, except in a few recent particulars, I can with safety declare that I see no reason to question the truth of a single fact stated by her, or even to suspect her in any instance of intentional exaggeration. It bears in my judgment the genuine stamp of truth and nature. Such is my unhesitating opinion, after a residence of twenty-seven years in the West Indies.

To T. Pringle, Esq.   I remain, &c.   JOSEPH PHILLIPS.

P.S. As Mr. Wood refers to the evidence of Dr. T. Coull in opposition to Mary's assertions, it may be proper to enable you justly to estimate the worth of that person's evidence in cases connected with the condition and treatment of slaves. You are aware that in 1829, Mr. M'Queen of Glasgow, in noticing a Report of the "Ladies' Society of Birmingham for the relief of British Negro Slaves," asserted with his characteristic audacity, that the statement which it contained respecting distressed and deserted slaves in Antigua was "an abominable falsehood." Not contented with this, and with insinuating that I, as agent of the society in the distribution of their charity in Antigua, had fraudulently duped them out of their money by a fabricated tale of distress, Mr. M'Queen proceeded to libel me in the most opprobrious terms, as "a man of the most worthless and abandoned character.* Now I know from good authority that it was

---

*In elucidation of the circumstances above referred to, I subjoin the following extracts from the Report of the Birmingham Ladies' Society for 1830:—

As a portion of the funds of this association has been appropriated to assist the benevolent efforts of a society which has for fifteen years afforded relief to distressed and deserted slaves in Antigua, it may not be uninteresting to our friends to learn the manner in which the agent of this society has been treated for simply obeying the command of our Saviour, by ministering, like the good Samaritan, to the distresses of the helpless and the desolate. The society's proceedings being adverted to by a friend of Africa, at one of the public meetings held in this country, a West Indian planter, who was present, wrote over to his friends in Antigua, and represented the conduct of the distributors of this charity in such a light, that it was deemed worthy of the cognizance of the House of Assembly. Mr. Joseph Phillips, a resident of the island, who had most kindly and disinterestedly exerted himself in the distribution of the money from England among the poor deserted slaves, was brought before the Assembly, and most severely interrogated: on his refusing to deliver up his private correspondence with his friends in England, he was thrown into a loathsome jail, where he was kept for nearly five months; while his loss of business, and the oppressive proceedings instituted against him, were involving him in poverty and ruin. On his discharge by the House of Assembly, he was seized in their lobby for debt, and again imprisoned.

In our report for the year 1826, we quoted a passage from the 13th Report of the Society for the relief of deserted Slaves in the island of Antigua, in reference to a case of great distress. This statement fell into

upon Dr. Coull's information that Mr. M'Queen founded this impudent contradiction of notorious facts, and this audacious libel of my personal character. From this single circumstance you may judge of the value of his evidence in the case of Mary Prince. I can furnish further information respecting Dr. Coull's

---

the hands of Mr. M'Queen, the Editor of the Glasgow Courier. Of the consequences resulting from this circumstance we only gained information through the Leicester Chronicle, which had copied an article from the Weekly Register of Antigua, dated St. John's, September 22, 1829. We find from this that Mr. M'Queen affirms, that 'with the exception of the fact that the society is, as it deserves to be, duped out of its money, the whole tale' (of the distress above referred to) 'is an abominable falsehood.' This statement, which we are informed has appeared in many of the public papers, is COMPLETELY REFUTED in our Appendix, No. 4, to which we refer our readers. Mr. M'Queen's statements, we regret to say, would lead many to believe that there are no deserted Negroes to assist; and that the case mentioned was a perfect fabrication. He also distinctly avers, that the disinterested and humane agent of the society, Mr. Joseph Phillips, is 'a man of the most worthless and abandoned character.' In opposition to this statement, we learn the good character of Mr. Phillips from those who have long been acquainted with his laudable exertions in the cause of humanity, and from the Editor of the Weekly Register of Antigua, who speaks, on his own knowledge, of more than twenty years back; confidently appealing at the same time to the inhabitants of the colony in which he resides for the truth of his averments, and producing a testimonial to Mr. Phillips's good character signed by two members of the Antigua House of Assembly, and by Mr. Wyke, the collector of his Majesty's customs, and by Antigua merchants, as follows—'that they have been acquainted with him the last four years and upwards, and he has always conducted himself in an upright becoming manner—his character we know to be unimpeached, and his morals unexceptionable.'

(Signed)	Thomas Sanderson	John D. Taylor
	John A. Wood	George Wyke
	Samuel L. Darrel	Giles S. Musson
	Robert Grant	

St. John's, Antigua, June 28, 1825.

In addition to the above testimonies, Mr. Phillips has brought over to England with him others of a more recent date, from some of the most respectable persons in Antigua—sufficient to cover with confusion all his unprincipled calumniators. See also his account of his own case in the Anti-Slavery Reporter, No. 74, p. 69.

colonial proceedings, both private and judicial, should circumstances require it.

J.P.

I leave the preceding letter to be candidly weighed by the reader in opposition to the inculpatory allegations of Mr. Wood—merely remarking that Mr. Wood will find it somewhat difficult to impugn the evidence of Mr. Phillips, whose "upright," "unimpeached," and "unexceptionable" character, he has himself vouched for in unqualified terms, by affixing his signature to the testimonial published in the Weekly Register of Antigua in 1825. (See Note, p. 279.)

The next testimony in Mary's behalf is that of Mrs. Forsyth, a lady in whose service she spent the summer of 1829. [See page 261.] This lady, on leaving London to join her husband, voluntarily presented Mary with a certificate, which, though it relates only to a recent and short period of her history, is a strong corroboration of the habitual respectability of her character. It is in the following terms:—

Mrs. Forsyth states, that the bearer of this paper (Mary James,) has been with her for the last six months: that she has found her an excellent character, being honest, industrious, and sober; and that she parts with her on no other account than this—that being obliged to travel with her husband, who has lately come from abroad in bad health, she has no farther need of a servant. Any person wishing to engage her, can have her character in full from Miss Robson, 4, Keppel Street, Russel Square, whom Mrs. Forsyth has requested to furnish particulars to any one desiring them.

4, Keppel Street, 28th Sept. 1829.

In the last place, I add my own testimony in behalf of this negro woman. Independently of the scrutiny, which, as Secretary of the Anti-Slavery Society, I made into her case when she first applied for assistance, at 18, Aldermanbury, and the watchful eye I kept upon her conduct for the insuing twelve months, while she was the occasional pensioner of the Society, I have now had the opportunity of closely observing her conduct for fourteen months, in the situation of a domestic servant in my own family; and the following is the deliberate opinion of Mary's character, formed not only by myself, but also by my wife and sister-in-law, after this ample period of observation. We have found her perfectly honest and trustworthy in all respects; so that we have no hesitation in leaving every thing in the house at her disposal. She had the entire charge of the house during our absence in Scotland for three months last autumn, and conducted herself in that charge with the utmost discretion and fidelity. She is not, it is true, a very expert housemaid, nor capable of much hard work, (for her constitution appears to be a good deal broken) but she is careful, industrious, and anxious to do her duty and to give satisfaction. She is capable of strong attachments, and feels deep, though unobtrusive, gratitude for real kindness shown her. She possesses considerable natural sense, and has much quickness of observation and discrimination of character. She is remarkable for *decency* and *propriety* of conduct—and her *delicacy*, even in trifling minutiæ, has been a trait of special remark by the females of my family. This trait, which is obviously quite unaffected, would be a most inexplicable anomaly, if her former habits had been so indecent and depraved as Mr. Wood alleges. Her chief faults, so far as we have discovered them, are, a somewhat violent and hasty temper, and a considerable share of natural pride and self-importance; but these defects have been but rarely and transiently manifested, and have scarcely occasioned an hour's uneasiness at any time in our household. Her religious knowledge, notwithstanding the pious care of her Moravian instructors in Antigua, is still but very limited, and her views of christianity indistinct; but her profession, whatever it may have of imperfection, I am convinced, has nothing of insincerity. In short, we consider her on the whole as respectable and well-behaved a person in her station, as any domestic, white or black, (and we have had ample experience of both colours,) that we have ever had in our service.

But after all, Mary's character, important though its exculpation be to her, is not really the point of chief practical interest in this case. Suppose all Mr. Wood's defamatory allegations to be true—suppose him to be able to rake up against her out of the records of the Antigua police, or from the veracious testimony of his brother colonists, twenty stories as bad or worse than what he insinuates—suppose the whole of her own statement to be false, and even the whole of her conduct since she came under our observation of her to be a tissue of hypocrisy;—suppose all this—and leave the negro woman as black in character as in complexion,*—yet it would affect not the main facts—which are these.—1. Mr. Wood, not daring in England to punish this woman arbitrarily, as he would have done in the West Indies, drove her out of his house, or, left her, at least, only the alternative of returning instantly to Antigua, with the certainty of severe treatment there, or submitting in silence to what she considered intolerable usage in his household. 2. He has since obstinately persisted in refusing her manumission, to enable her to return home in security, though repeatedly offered more than ample compensation for her value as a slave; and this on various frivolous pretexts, but really, and indeed not unavowedly, in order to *punish* her for leaving his service in England, though he himself had professed to give her that option. These unquestionable facts speak volumes.†

---

*If it even were so, how strong a plea of palliation might not the poor negro bring, by adducing the neglect of her various owners to afford religious instruction or moral discipline, and the habitual influence of their evil *example* (to say the very least,) before her eyes? What moral good could she possibly learn—what moral evil could she easily escape, while under the uncontrolled power of such masters as she describes Captain I—— and Mr. D—— of Turk's Island? All things considered, it is indeed wonderful to find her such as she now is. But as she has herself piously expressed it, "that God whom then she knew not mercifully preserved her for better things."

†Since the preceding pages were printed off, I have been favoured with a communication from the Rev. J. Curtin, to whom among other acquaintances of Mr. Wood's in this country, the entire proof sheets of this pamphlet had been sent for inspection. Mr. Curtin corrects some omissions and inaccuracies in Mary Prince's narrative [See page 254] by stating, 1. That she was baptized, not in August, but on the 6th of April, 1817; 2. That sometime before her baptism, on her being admitted a catechumen, preparatory to that holy ordinance, she brought a note from her owner, Mr. Wood, recommending her for religious instruction, &c. 3. That it was his usual practice, when any adult slaves came

on *week days* to school, to require their owner's permission for their attendance; but that on *Sundays* the chapel was open indiscriminately to all.—Mary, after a personal interview with Mr. Curtin, and after hearing his letter read by me, still maintains that Mr. Wood's note recommended her for baptism merely, and that she never received any religious instruction whatever from Mr. and Mrs. Wood, or from any one else at that period beyond what she has stated in her narrative. In regard to her non-admission to the Sunday school without permission from her owners, she admits that she may possibly have mistaken the clergyman's meaning on that point, but says that such was certainly her impression at the time, and the actual cause of her non-attendance.

Mr. Curtin finds in his books some reference to Mary's connection with a Captain——, (the individual, I believe, alluded to by Mr. Phillips [page 278,]; but he states that when she attended his chapel she was always decently and becomingly dressed, and appeared to him to be in a situation of trust in her mistress's family.

Mr. Curtin offers no comment on any other part of Mary's statement; but he speaks in very favourable, though general terms of the respectability of Mr. Wood, whom he had known for many years in Antigua; and of Mrs. Wood, though she was not personally known to him, he says, that he had "heard her spoken of by those of her acquaintance, as a lady of very mild and amiable manners."

Another friend of Mr. and Mrs. Wood, a lady who had been their guest both in Antigua and England, alleges that Mary has grossly misrepresented them in her narrative; and says that she "can vouch for their being the most benevolent, kind-hearted people that can possibly live." She has declined, however, to furnish me with any written correction of the misrepresentations she complains of, although I offered to insert her testimony in behalf of her friends, if sent to me in time. And having already kept back the publication a fortnight waiting for communications of this sort, I will not delay it longer. Those who have withheld their strictures have only themselves to blame.

Of the general character of Mr. and Mrs. Wood, I would not designedly give any *unfair* impression. Without implicitly adopting either the *ex parte* view of Mary Prince, or the unmeasured encomiums of their friends, I am willing to believe them to be, on the whole, fair, perhaps favourable, specimens of colonial character. Let them even be rated, if you will, in the very highest and most benevolent class of slaveholders; and, laying every thing else entirely out of view, let Mr. Wood's conduct in this affair be tried exclusively by the facts established beyond dispute, and by his own statement of the case in his letter to Mr. Taylor. But then, I ask, if the very *best* and *mildest* of your slave-owners can act as Mr. Wood is proved to have acted, what is to be expected of persons whose mildness, or equity, or common humanity no one will

The case affords a most instructive illustration of the true spirit of the slave system, and of the pretensions of the slaveholders to assert, not merely their claims to a "vested right" in the labour of their bondmen, but to an indefeasible property in them as their "absolute chattels." It furnishes a striking practical comment on the assertions of the West Indians that self-interest is a sufficient check to the indulgence of vindictive feelings in the master; for here is a case where a man (a *respectable* and *benevolent* man as his friends aver) prefers losing entirely the full price of the slave, for the mere satisfaction of preventing a poor black woman from returning home to her husband! If the pleasure of thwarting the benevolent wishes of the Anti-Slavery Society in behalf of the deserted negro, be an additional motive with Mr. Wood, it will not much mend his wretched plea.

I may here add a few words respecting the earlier portion of Mary Prince's narrative. The facts there stated must necessarily rest entirely,—since we have no collateral evidence,—upon their intrinsic claims to probability, and upon the reliance the reader may feel disposed, after perusing the foregoing pages, to place on her veracity. To my judgment, the internal evidence of the truth of her narrative appears remarkably strong. The circumstances are related in a tone of natural sincerity, and are accompanied in almost every case with characteristic and minute details, which must, I conceive, carry with them full conviction to every candid mind that this negro woman has actually seen, felt, and suffered all that she so impressively describes; and that the picture she has given of West Indian slavery is not less true than it is revolting.

But there may be some persons into whose hands this tract may fall, so imperfectly acquainted with the real character of Negro Slavery, as to be shocked into partial, if not absolute incredulity, by the acts of inhuman oppression and

---

dare to vouch for? If such things are done in the green tree, what will be done in the dry?—And what else then can Colonial Slavery possibly be, even in its best estate, but a system incurably evil and iniquitous?—I require no other data—I need add no further comment.

brutality related of Capt. I——and his wife, and of Mr.
D——, the salt manufacturer of Turk's Island. Here, at least,
such persons may be disposed to think, there surely must be
some exaggeration; the facts are too shocking to be credible. The facts are indeed shocking, but unhappily not the
less credible on that account. Slavery is a curse to the oppressor scarcely less than to the oppressed; its natural tendency is to brutalize both. After a residence myself of six
years in a slave colony, I am inclined to doubt whether, as
regards its *demoralizing* influence, the master is not even a
greater object of compassion than his bondman. Let those
who are disposed to doubt the atrocities related in this narrative, on the testimony of a sufferer, examine the details of
many cases of similar barbarity that have lately come before the public, on unquestionable evidence. Passing over
the reports of the Fiscal of Berbice,* and the Mauritius horrors recently unveiled,† let them consider the case of Mr.
and Mrs. Moss, of the Bahamas, and their slave Kate, so
justly denounced by the Secretary for the Colonies;‡ the
cases of Eleanor Mead,§—of Henry Williams,¶ and of the
Rev. Mr. Bridges and Kitty Hylton,** in Jamaica. These cases
alone might suffice to demonstrate the inevitable tendency
of slavery as it exists in our colonies, to brutalize the master
to a truly frightful degree—a degree which would often cast
into the shade even the atrocities related in the narrative of
Mary Prince; and which are sufficient to prove, independently of all other evidence, that there is nothing in the revolting character of the facts to affect their credibility; but
that on the contrary, similar deeds are at this very time of
frequent occurrence in almost every one of our slave colonies. The system of coercive labour may vary in different
places; it may be more destructive to human life in the cane
culture of Mauritius and Jamaica, than in the predial and

---

*See Anti-Slavery Reporter, Nos. 5 and 16.

†Ibid, No. 44.

‡Ibid, No. 47.

§Ibid, No. 64, p. 345; No. 71, p. 481.

¶Ibid, No. 65, p. 356; No. 69, p. 431.

**Anti-Slavery Reporter, Nos. 66, 69 and 76.

domestic bondage of Bermuda or the Bahamas,—but the spirit and character of slavery are every where the same, and cannot fail to produce similar effects. Wherever slavery prevails, there will inevitably be found cruelty and oppression. Individuals who have preserved humane, and amiable, and tolerant dispositions towards their black dependents, may doubtless be found among slaveholders; but even where a happy instance of this sort occurs, such as Mary's first mistress, the kindhearted Mrs. Williams, the favoured condition of the slave is still as precarious as it is rare: it is every moment at the mercy of events; and must always be held by a tenure so proverbially uncertain as that of human prosperity, or human life. Such examples, like a feeble and flickering streak of light in a gloomy picture, only serve by contrast to exhibit the depth of the prevailing shades. Like other exceptions, they only prove the general rule; the unquestionable tendency of the system is to vitiate the best tempers, and to harden the most feeling hearts. "Never be kind, nor speak kindly to a slave," said an accomplished English lady in South Africa to my wife: "I have now," she added, "been for some time a slave-owner, and have found, from vexatious experience in my own household, that nothing but harshness and hauteur will do with slaves."

I might perhaps not inappropriately illustrate this point more fully by stating many cases which fell under my own personal observation, or became known to me through authentic sources, at the Cape of Good Hope—a colony where slavery assumes, as it is averred, a milder aspect than in any other dependency of the empire where it exists; and I could shew, from the judicial records of that colony, received by me within these few weeks, cases scarcely inferior in barbarity to the worst of those to which I have just specially referred; but to do so would lead me too far from the immediate purpose of this pamphlet, and extend it to an inconvenient length. I shall therefore content myself with quoting a single short passage from the excellent work of my friend Dr. Walsh, entitled "Notices of Brazil,"——a work which, besides its other merits, has vividly illustrated the true spirit of Negro Slavery, as it displays itself not merely in that country, but wherever it has been permitted to open its Pandora's box of misery and crime.

Let the reader ponder on the following just remarks, and compare the facts stated by the Author in illustration of them, with the circumstances related at pages 238 to 240 of Mary's narrative:—

If then we put out of the question the injury inflicted on others, and merely consider the deterioration of feeling and principle with which it operates on ourselves, ought it not to be a sufficient, and, indeed, unanswerable argument, against the permission of Slavery?

The exemplary manner in which the paternal duties are performed at home, may mark people as the most fond and affectionate parents; but let them once go abroad, and come within the contagion of slavery, and it seems to alter the very nature of a man; and the father has sold, and still sells, the mother and her children, with as little compunction as he would a sow and her litter of pigs; and he often disposes of them together.

This deterioration of feeling is conspicuous in many ways among the Brazilians. They are naturally a people of a humane and good-natured disposition, and much indisposed to cruelty or severity of any kind. Indeed, the manner in which many of them treat their slaves is a proof of this, as it is really gentle and considerate; but the natural tendency to cruelty and oppression in the human heart, is continually evolved by the impunity and uncontrolled licence in which they are exercised. I never walked through the streets of Rio, that some house did not present to me the semblance of a bridewell, where the moans and the cries of the sufferers, and the sounds of whips and scourges within, announced to me that corporal punishment was being inflicted. Whenever I remarked this to a friend, I was always answered that the refractory nature of the slave rendered it necessary, and no house could properly be conducted unless it was practised. But this is certainly not the case; and the chastisement is constantly applied in the very wantonness of barbarity, and would not, and dared not, be inflicted on the humblest wretch in society, if he was not a slave, and so put out of the pale of pity.

Immediately joining our house was one occupied by

a mechanic, from which the most dismal cries and moans constantly proceeded. I entered the shop one day, and found it was occupied by a saddler, who had two negro boys working at his business. He was a tawny, cadaverous-looking man, with a dark aspect; and he had cut from his leather a scourge like a Russian knout, which he held in his hand, and was in the act of exercising on one of the naked children in an inner room: and this was the cause of the moans and cries we heard every day, and almost all day long.

In the rear of our house was another, occupied by some women of bad character, who kept, as usual, several negro slaves. I was awoke early one morning by dismal cries, and looking out of the window, I saw in the back yard of the house, a black girl of about fourteen years old; before her stood her mistress, a white woman, with a large stick in her hand. She was undressed except her petticoat and chemise, which had fallen down and left her shoulders and bosom bare. Her hair was streaming behind, and every fierce and malevolent passion was depicted in her face. She too, like my hostess at Governo [another striking illustration of the *dehumanizing* effects of Slavery,] was the very representation of a fury. She was striking the poor girl, whom she had driven up into a corner, where she was on her knees appealing for mercy. She shewed her none, but continued to strike her on the head and thrust the stick into her face, till she was herself exhausted, and her poor victim covered with blood. This scene was renewed every morning, and the cries and moans of the poor suffering blacks, announced that they were enduring the penalty of slavery, in being the objects on which the irritable and malevolent passions of the whites are allowed to vent themselves with impunity; nor could I help deeply deploring that state of society in which the vilest characters in the community are allowed an almost uncontrolled power of life and death, over their innocent, and far more estimable fellow-creatures.—(Notices of Brazil, vol. ii. pp. 354–356.)

In conclusion, I may observe that the history of Mary Prince furnishes a corollary to Lord Stowell's decision in the case of the slave Grace, and that it is most valuable on this account. Whatever opinions may be held by some readers on the grave question of immediately abolishing Colonial Slavery, nothing assuredly can be more repugnant to the feelings of Englishmen than that the system should be permitted to extend its baneful influence to this country. Yet such is the case, when the slave landed in England still only possesses that qualified degree of freedom, that a change of domicile will determine it. Though born a British subject, and resident within the shores of England, he is cut off from his dearest natural rights by the sad alternative of regaining them at the expence of liberty, and the certainty of severe treatment. It is true that he has the option of returning; but it is a cruel mockery to call it a voluntary choice, when upon his return depend his means of subsistence and his re-union with all that makes life valuable. Here he has tasted "the sweets of freedom," to quote the words of the unfortunate Mary Prince; but if he desires to restore himself to his family, or to escape from suffering and destitution, and the other evils of a climate uncongenial to his constitution and habits, he must abandon the enjoyment of his late-acquired liberty, and again subject himself to the arbitrary power of a vindictive master.

The case of Mary Prince is by no means a singular one; many of the same kind are daily occurring; and even if the case were singular, it would still loudly call for the interference of the legislature. In instances of this kind no injury can possibly be done to the owner by confirming to the slave his resumption of his natural rights. It is the master's spontaneous act to bring him to this country; he knows when he brings him that he divests himself of his property; and it is, in fact, a minor species of slave trading, when he has thus enfranchised his slave, to *re-capture* that slave by the necessities of his condition, or by working upon the better feelings of his heart. Abstractedly from all legal technicalities, there is no real difference between thus compelling the return of the enfranchised negro, and trepanning a free native of England by delusive hopes into perpetual slavery. The most ingenious casuist could not point out any essential distinction between the two cases. Our boasted liberty is the dream of imagination, and no longer the characteristic of our country, if its bulwarks can thus be thrown down by colonial special pleading. It would well become the character of the present Government to introduce a Bill into the Legislature making perpetual that freedom which the slave has acquired by his passage here, and thus to declare, in the most ample sense of the words, (what indeed we had long fondly believed to be the fact, though it now appears that we have been mistaken) THAT NO SLAVE CAN EXIST WITHIN THE SHORES OF GREAT BRITAIN.

NARRATIVE OF LOUIS ASA-ASA,

A CAPTURED AFRICAN.

THE following interesting narrative is a convenient supplement to the history of Mary Prince. It is given, like hers, as nearly as possible in the narrator's words, with only so much correction as was necessary to connect the story, and render it grammatical. The concluding passage in inverted commas, is entirely his own.

While Mary's narrative shews the disgusting character of colonial slavery, this little tale explains with equal force the horrors in which it originates.

It is necessary to explain that Louis came to this country about five years ago, in a French vessel called the Pearl. She had lost her reckoning, and was driven by stress of weather into the port of St. Ives, in Cornwall. Louis and his four companions were brought to London upon a writ of Habeas Corpus at the instance of Mr. George Stephen; and, after some trifling opposition on the part of the master of the vessel, were discharged by Lord Wynford. Two of his unfortunate fellow-sufferers died of the measles at Hampstead; the other two returned to Sierra Leone; but poor Louis, when offered the choice of going back to Africa, replied, "Me no father, no mother now; me stay with you." And here he has ever since remained; conducting himself in a way to gain the good will and respect of all who know him. He is remarkably intelligent, understands our language perfectly, and can read and write well. The last sentences of the following narrative will seem almost too peculiar to be his own; but it is not the first time that in conversation with Mr. George Stephen, he has made similar remarks. On one occasion in particular, he was heard saying to himself in the kitchen, while sitting by the fire apparently in deep thought, "Me think,—me think——" A fellow-servant inquired what he meant; and he added, "Me think what a good thing I came to England! Here, I know what God is, and read my Bible; in my country they have no God, no Bible."

How severe and just a reproof to the guilty wretches who visit his country only with fire and sword! How deserved a censure upon the not less guilty men, who dare to vindicate the state of slavery, on the lying pretext, that its victims are of an inferior nature! And scarcely less deserving of reprobation are those who have it in their power to prevent these crimes, but who remain inactive from indifference, or are dissuaded from throwing the shield of British power over the victim of oppression, by the sophistry, and the clamour, and the avarice of the oppressor. It is the reproach and the sin of England. May God avert from our country the ruin which this national guilt deserves!

We lament to add, that the Pearl which brought these negroes to our shore, was restored to its owners at the instance of the French Government, instead of being condemned as a prize to Lieut. Rye, who, on his own responsibility, detained her, with all her manacles and chains and other detestable proofs of her piratical occupation on board. We trust it is not yet too late to demand investigation into the reasons for restoring her.

THE NEGRO BOY'S NARRATIVE.

My father's name was Clashoquin; mine is Asa-Asa. He lived in a country called Bycla, near Egie, a large town. Egie is as large as Brighton; it was some way from the sea. I had five brothers and sisters. We all lived together with my father and mother; he kept a horse, and was respectable, but not one of the great men. My uncle was one of the great men at Egie: he could make men come and work for him: his name was Otou. He had a great deal of land and cattle. My father sometimes worked on his own land, and used to make charcoal. I was too little to work; my eldest brother used to work on the land; and we were all very happy.

A great many people, whom we called Adinyés, set fire to Egie in the morning before daybreak; there were some thousands of them. They killed a great many, and burnt all their houses. They staid two days, and then carried away all the people whom they did not kill.

They came again every now and then for a month, as long as they could find people to carry away. They used to tie them by the feet, except when they were taking them off, and then they let them loose; but if they offered to run away, they would shoot them. I lost a great many friends and relations at Egie; about a dozen. They sold all they carried away, to be slaves. I know this because I afterwards saw them as slaves on the other side of the sea. They took away brothers, and sisters, and husbands, and wives; they did not care about this. They were sold for cloth or gunpowder, sometimes for salt or guns; sometimes they got four or five guns for a man: they were English guns, made like my master's that I clean for his shooting. The Adinyés burnt a great many places besides Egie. They burnt all the country wherever they found villages; they used to shoot men, women, and children, if they ran away.

They came to us about eleven o'clock one day, and directly they came they set our house on fire. All of us had run away. We kept together, and went into the woods, and stopped there two days. The Adinyés then went away, and we returned home and found every thing burnt. We tried to build a little shed, and were beginning to get comfortable again. We found several of our neighbours lying about wounded; they had been shot. I saw the bodies of four or five little children whom they had killed with blows on the head. They had carried away their fathers and mothers, but the children were too small for slaves, so they killed them. They had killed several others, but these were all that I saw. I saw them lying in the street like dead dogs.

In about a week after we got back, the Adinyés returned, and burnt all the sheds and houses they had left standing. We all ran away again; we went to the woods as we had done before.—They followed us the next day. We went farther into the woods, and staid there about four days and nights; we were half starved; we only got a few potatoes. My uncle Otou was with us. At the end of this time, the Adinyés found us. We ran away. They called my uncle to go to them; but he refused, and they shot him immediately: they killed him. The rest of us ran on, and they did not get at us till the next day. I ran up into a tree: they followed me and brought me down. They tied my feet. I do not know if they found my father and mother, and brothers and sisters: they had run faster than me, and were half a mile farther when I got up into the tree: I have never seen them since. There was a man who ran up into the tree with me: I believe they shot him, for I never saw him again.

They carried away about twenty besides me. They carried us to the sea. They did not beat us; they only killed one man, who was very ill and too weak to carry his load: they made all of us carry chickens and meat for our food; but this poor man could not carry his load, and they ran him through the body with a sword.—He was a neighbour of ours. When we got to the sea they sold all of us, but not to the same person. They sold us for money; and I was sold six times over, sometimes for money, sometimes for cloth, and sometimes for a gun. I was about thirteen years old. It was about half a year from the time I was taken, before I saw the white people.

We were taken in a boat from place to place, and sold at every place we stopped at. In about six months we got to a ship, in which we first saw white people: they were French. They bought us. We found here a great many other slaves; there were about eighty, including women and children. The Frenchmen sent away all but five of us into another very large ship. We five staid on board till we got to England, which was about five or six months. The slaves we saw on board the ship were chained together by the legs below deck, so close they could not move. They were flogged very cruelly; I saw one of them flogged till he died; we could not tell what for. They gave them enough to eat. The place they were confined in below deck was so hot and nasty I could not bear to be in it. A great many of the slaves were ill, but they were not attended to. They used to flog me very bad on board the ship: the captain cut my head very bad one time.

I am very happy to be in England, as far as I am very well;—but I have no friend belonging to me, but God, who will take care of me as he has done already. I am very glad

I have come to England, to know who God is. I should like much to see my friends again, but I do not now wish to go back to them: for if I go back to my own country, I might be taken as a slave again. I would rather stay here, where I am free, than go back to my country to be sold. I shall stay in England as long as (please God) I shall live. I wish the King of England could know all I have told you. I wish it that he may see how cruelly we are used. We had no king in our country, or he would have stopt it. I think the King of England might stop it, and this is why I wish him to know it all. I have heard say he is good; and if he is, he will stop it if he can. I am well off myself, for I am well taken care of, and have good bed and good clothes; but I wish my own people to be as comfortable.

LOUIS ASA-ASA.

London, January 31, 1831.

NARRATIVE

OF THE

LIFE

OF

FREDERICK DOUGLASS,

AN

AMERICAN SLAVE.

WRITTEN BY HIMSELF.

BOSTON:

PUBLISHED AT THE ANTI-SLAVERY OFFICE,

NO. 25 CORNHILL

1845.

PREFACE.

In the month of August, 1841, I attended an anti-slavery convention in Nantucket, at which it was my happiness to become acquainted with FREDERICK DOUGLASS, the writer of the following Narrative. He was a stranger to nearly every member of that body; but, having recently made his escape from the southern prison-house of bondage, and feeling his curiosity excited to ascertain the principles and measures of the abolitionists,—of whom he had heard a somewhat vague description while he was a slave,—he was induced to give his attendance, on the occasion alluded to, though at that time a resident in New Bedford.

Fortunate, most fortunate occurrence!—fortunate for the millions of his manacled brethren, yet panting for deliverance from their awful thraldom!—fortunate for the cause of negro emancipation, and of universal liberty!—fortunate for the land of his birth, which he has already done so much to save and bless!—fortunate for a large circle of friends and acquaintances, whose sympathy and affection he has strongly secured by the many sufferings he has endured, by his virtuous traits of character, by his ever-abiding remembrance of those who are in bonds, as being bound with them!—fortunate for the multitudes, in various parts of our republic, whose minds he has enlightened on the subject of slavery, and who have been melted to tears by his pathos, or roused to virtuous indignation by his stirring eloquence against the enslavers of men!—fortunate for himself, as it at once brought him into the field of public usefulness, "gave the world assurance of a MAN," quickened the slumbering energies of his soul, and consecrated him to the great work of breaking the rod of the oppressor, and letting the oppressed go free!

I shall never forget his first speech at the convention—the extraordinary emotion it excited in my own mind—the powerful impression it created upon a crowded auditory, completely taken by surprise—the applause which followed from the beginning to the end of his felicitous remarks. I think I never hated slavery so intensely as at that moment; certainly, my perception of the enormous outrage which is inflicted by it, on the godlike nature of its victims, was rendered far more clear than ever. There stood one, in physical proportion and stature commanding and exact—in intellect richly endowed—in natural eloquence a prodigy—in soul manifestly "created but a little lower than the angels"—yet a slave, ay, a fugitive slave,—trembling for his safety, hardly daring to believe that on the American soil, a single white person could be found who would befriend him at all hazards, for the love of God and humanity! Capable of high attainments as an intellectual and moral being—needing nothing but a comparatively small amount of cultivation to make him an ornament to society and a blessing to his race—by the law of the land, by the voice of the people, by the terms of the slave code, he was only a piece of property, a beast of burden, a chattel personal, nevertheless!

A beloved friend from New Bedford prevailed on Mr. DOUGLASS to address the convention. He came forward to the platform with a hesitancy and embarrassment, necessarily the attendants of a sensitive mind in such a novel position. After apologizing for his ignorance, and reminding the audience that slavery was a poor school for the human intellect and heart, he proceeded to narrate some of the facts in his own history as a slave, and in the course of his speech gave utterance to many noble thoughts and thrilling reflections. As soon as he had taken his seat, filled with hope and admiration, I rose, and declared that PATRICK HENRY, of revolutionary fame, never made a speech more eloquent in the cause of liberty, than the one we had just listened to from the lips of that hunted fugitive. So I believed at that time—such is my belief now. I reminded the audience of the peril which surrounded this self-emancipated young man at the North—even in Massachusetts, on the soil of the Pilgrim Fathers, among the descendants of revolutionary sires; and I appealed to them, whether they would ever allow him to be carried back into slavery,—law or no law, constitution or no constitution. The response was unanimous and in thunder-tones—"NO!" "Will you succor and protect him as a brother-man—a resident of the Bay State?" "YES!" shouted the whole mass, with an energy so startling, that the ruthless ty-rants south of Mason and Dixon's line might almost have heard the mighty burst of feeling, and recognized it as the pledge of an invincible determination, on the part of those who gave it, never to betray him that wanders, but to hide the outcast, and firmly to abide the consequences.

It was at once deeply impressed upon my mind, that, if Mr. DOUGLASS could be persuaded to consecrate his time and talents to the promotion of the anti-slavery enterprise, a powerful impetus would be given to it, and a stunning blow at the same time inflicted on northern prejudice against a colored complexion. I therefore endeavored to instil hope and courage into his mind, in order that he might dare to engage in a vocation so anomalous and responsible for a person in his situation; and I was seconded in this ef-fort by warm-hearted friends, especially by the late General Agent of the Massachusetts Anti-Slavery Society, Mr. JOHN A. COLLINS, whose judgment in this instance entirely coin-cided with my own. At first, he could give no encourage-ment; with unfeigned diffidence, he expressed his conviction that he was not adequate to the performance of so great a task; the path marked out was wholly an untrodden one; he was sincerely apprehensive that he should do more harm than good. After much deliberation, however, he consented to make a trial; and ever since that period, he has acted as a lecturing agent, under the auspices either of the American or the Massachusetts Anti-Slavery Society. In labors he has been most abundant; and his success in combating preju-dice, in gaining proselytes, in agitating the public mind, has far surpassed the most sanguine expectations that were raised at the commencement of his brilliant career. He has borne himself with gentleness and meekness, yet with true manliness of character. As a public speaker, he excels in pathos, wit, comparison, imitation, strength of reasoning, and fluency of language. There is in him that union of head and heart, which is indispensable to an enlightenment of the heads and a winning of the hearts of others. May his strength continue to be equal to his day! May he continue to "grow in grace, and in the knowledge of God," that he may be increasingly serviceable in the cause of bleeding humanity, whether at home or abroad!

It is certainly a very remarkable fact, that one of the most efficient advocates of the slave population, now before the public, is a fugitive slave, in the person of FREDERICK DOUGLASS; and that the free colored population of the United States are as ably represented by one of their own number, in the person of CHARLES LENOX REMOND, whose eloquent appeals have extorted the highest applause of multitudes on both sides of the Atlantic. Let the calumniators of the colored race despise themselves for their baseness and illiberality of spirit, and henceforth cease to talk of the natural inferiority of those who require nothing but time and opportunity to attain to the highest point of human excellence.

It may, perhaps, be fairly questioned, whether any other portion of the population of the earth could have endured the privations, sufferings and horrors of slavery, without having become more degraded in the scale of humanity than the slaves of African descent. Nothing has been left undone to cripple their intellects, darken their minds, debase their moral nature, obliterate all traces of their relationship to mankind; and yet how wonderfully they have sustained the mighty load of a most frightful bondage, under which they have been groaning for centuries! To illustrate the effect of slavery on the white man,—to show that he has no powers of endurance, in such a condition, superior to those of his black brother,—DANIEL O'CONNELL, the distinguished advocate of universal emancipation, and the mightiest champion of prostrate but not conquered Ireland, relates the following anecdote in a speech delivered by him in the Conciliation Hall, Dublin, before the Loyal National Repeal Association, March 31, 1845. "No matter," said Mr. O'CONNELL, "under what specious term it may disguise itself, slavery is still hideous. *It has a natural, an inevitable tendency to brutalize every noble faculty of man.* An American sailor, who was cast away on the shore of Africa, where he was kept in slavery for three years, was at the expiration of that period, found to be imbruted and stultified—he had lost all reasoning power; and having forgotten his native language, could only utter some savage gibberish between Arabic and English, which nobody could understand, and which even he himself found difficulty in pronouncing. So much for the humanizing influence of THE DOMESTIC INSTITUTION!" Admitting this to have been an extraordinary case of mental deterioration, it proves at least that the white slave can sink as low in the scale of humanity as the black one.

Mr. DOUGLASS has very properly chosen to write his own Narrative, in his own style, and according to the best of his ability, rather than to employ some one else. It is, therefore, entirely his own production; and, considering how long and dark was the career he had to run as a slave,—how few have been his opportunities to improve his mind since he broke his iron fetters,—it is, in my judgment, highly creditable to his head and heart. He who can peruse it without a tearful eye, a heaving breast, an afflicted spirit,—without being filled with an unutterable abhorrence of slavery and all its abettors, and animated with a determination to seek the immediate overthrow of that execrable system,—without trembling for the fate of this country in the hands of a righteous God, who is ever on the side of the oppressed, and whose arm is not shortened that it cannot save,—must have a flinty heart, and be qualified to act the part of a trafficker "in slaves and the souls of men." I am confident that it is essentially true in all its statements; that nothing has been set down in malice, nothing exaggerated, nothing drawn from the imagination; that it comes short of the reality, rather than overstates a single fact in regard to SLAVERY AS IT IS. The experience of FREDERICK DOUGLASS, as a slave, was not a peculiar one; his lot was not especially a hard one; his case may be regarded as a very fair specimen of the treatment of slaves in Maryland, in which State it is conceded that they are better fed and less cruelly treated than in Georgia, Alabama, or Louisiana. Many have suffered incomparably more, while very few on the plantations have suffered less, than himself. Yet how deplorable was his situation! what terrible chastisements were inflicted upon his person! what still more shocking outrages were perpetrated upon his mind! with all his noble powers and sublime aspirations, how like a brute was he treated, even by those professing to have the same mind in them that was in Christ Jesus! to what dreadful liabilities was he continually subjected! how destitute of friendly counsel and aid, even in his greatest extremities! how heavy was the midnight of woe which shrouded in blackness the last ray of hope, and filled the future with terror and gloom! what longings after freedom took possession of his breast, and how his misery augmented, in proportion as he grew reflective and intelligent,—thus demonstrating that a happy slave is an extinct man! how he thought, reasoned, felt, under the lash of the driver, with the chains upon his limbs! what perils he encountered in his endeavors to escape from his horrible doom! and how signal have been his deliverance and preservation in the midst of a nation of pitiless enemies!

This Narrative contains many affecting incidents, many passages of great eloquence and power; but I think the most thrilling one of them all is the description DOUGLASS gives of his feelings, as he stood soliloquizing respecting his fate, and the chances of his one day being a freeman, on the banks of the Chesapeake Bay—viewing the receding vessels as they flew with their white wings before the breeze, and apostrophizing them as animated by the living spirit of freedom. Who can read that passage, and be insensible to its pathos and sublimity? Compressed into it is a whole Alexandrian library of thought, feeling, and sentiment—all that can, all that need be, urged, in the form of expostulation, entreaty, rebuke, against that crime of crimes,—making man the property of his fellow-man! O, how accursed is that system, which entombs the godlike mind of man, defaces the divine image, reduces those who by creation were crowned with glory and honor to a level with four-footed beasts, and exalts the dealer in human flesh above all that is called God! Why should its existence be prolonged one hour? Is it not evil, only evil, and that continually? What does its presence imply but the absence of all fear of God, all regard for man, on the part of the people of the United States? Heaven speed its eternal overthrow!

So profoundly ignorant of the nature of slavery are many persons, that they are stubbornly incredulous whenever they read or listen to any recital of the cruelties which are daily inflicted on its victims. They do not deny that the slaves are held as property; but that terrible fact seems to convey to their minds no idea of injustice, exposure to outrage, or savage barbarity. Tell them of cruel scourgings, of mutilations and brandings, of scenes of pollution and blood, of the banishment of all light and knowledge, and they affect to be greatly indignant at such enormous exaggerations, such wholesale misstatements, such abominable libels on the character of the southern planters! As if all these direful outrages were not the natural results of slavery! As if it were less cruel to reduce a human being to the condition of a thing, than to give him a severe flagellation, or to deprive him of necessary food and clothing! As if whips, chains, thumb-screws, paddles, bloodhounds, overseers, drivers, patrols, were not all indispensable to keep the slaves down, and to give protection to their ruthless oppressors! As if, when the marriage institution is abolished, concubinage, adultery, and incest, must not necessarily abound; when all the rights of humanity are annihilated, any barrier remains to protect the victim from the fury of the spoiler; when absolute power is assumed over life and liberty, it will not be wielded with destructive sway! Skeptics of this character abound in society. In some few instances, their incredulity arises from a want of reflection; but, generally, it indicates a hatred of the light, a desire to shield slavery from the assaults of its foes, a contempt of the colored race, whether bond or free. Such will try to discredit the shocking tales of slaveholding cruelty which are recorded in this truthful Narrative; but they will labor in vain. Mr. DOUGLASS has frankly disclosed the place of his birth, the names of those who claimed ownership in his body and soul, and the names also of those who committed the crimes which he has alleged against them. His statements, therefore, may easily be disproved, if they are untrue.

In the course of his Narrative, he relates two instances of murderous cruelty,—in one of which a planter deliberately shot a slave belonging to a neighboring plantation, who had unintentionally gotten within his lordly domain in quest of fish; and in the other, an overseer blew out the brains of a slave who had fled to a stream of water to escape a bloody scourging. Mr. DOUGLASS states that in neither of these instances was any thing done by way of legal arrest or judicial investigation. The Baltimore American, of March 17, 1845, relates a similar case of atrocity, perpetrated with similar impunity—as follows:—"*Shooting a Slave.*—We learn, upon the authority of a letter from Charles county, Maryland, received by a gentleman of this city, that a young man, named Matthews, a nephew of General Matthews, and whose father, it is believed, holds an office at Washington, killed one of the slaves upon his father's farm by shooting him. The letter states that young Matthews had been left in charge of the farm; that he gave an order to the servant, which was disobeyed, when he proceeded to the house, *obtained a gun, and, returning, shot the servant.* He immediately, the letter continues, fled to his father's residence, where he still remains unmolested."—Let it never be forgotten, that no slaveholder or overseer can be convicted of any outrage perpetrated on the person of a slave, however diabolical it may be, on the testimony of colored witnesses, whether bond or free. By the slave code, they are adjudged to be as incompetent to testify against a white man, as though they were indeed a part of the brute creation. Hence, there is no legal protection in fact, whatever there may be in form, for the slave population; and any amount of cruelty may be inflicted on them with impunity. Is it possible for the human mind to conceive of a more horrible state of society?

The effect of a religious profession on the conduct of southern masters is vividly described in the following Narrative, and shown to be any thing but salutary. In the nature of the case, it must be in the highest degree pernicious. The testimony of Mr. DOUGLASS, on this point, is sustained by a cloud of witnesses, whose veracity is unimpeachable. "A slaveholder's profession of Christianity is a palpable imposture. He is a felon of the highest grade. He is a man-stealer. It is of no importance what you put in the other scale."

Reader! are you with the man-stealers in sympathy and purpose, or on the side of their down-trodden victims? If with the former, then are you the foe of God and man. If with the latter, what are you prepared to do and dare in their behalf? Be faithful, be vigilant, be untiring in your efforts to break every yoke, and let the oppressed go free. Come what may—cost what it may—inscribe on the banner which you unfurl to the breeze, as your religious and political motto—"No Compromise with Slavery! No Union with Slaveholders!"

WM. LLOYD GARRISON.

Boston, May 1, 1845.

LETTER
FROM WENDELL PHILLIPS, ESQ.

Boston, April 22, 1845.

My Dear Friend:

You remember the old fable of "The Man and the Lion," where the lion complained that he should not be so misrepresented "when the lions wrote history."

I am glad the time has come when the "lions write history." We have been left long enough to gather the character of slavery from the involuntary evidence of the masters. One might, indeed, rest sufficiently satisfied with what, it is evident, must be, in general, the results of such a relation, without seeking farther to find whether they have followed in every instance. Indeed, those who stare at the half-peck of corn a week, and love to count the lashes on the slave's back, are seldom the "stuff" out of which reformers and abolitionists are to be made. I remember that, in 1838, many were waiting for the results of the West India experiment, before they could come into our ranks. Those "results" have come long ago; but, alas! few of that number have come with them, as converts. A man must be disposed to judge of emancipation by other tests than whether it has increased the produce of sugar,—and to hate slavery for other reasons than because it starves men and whips women,— before he is ready to lay the first stone of his anti-slavery life.

I was glad to learn, in your story, how early the most neglected of God's children waken to a sense of their rights, and of the injustice done them. Experience is a keen teacher; and long before you had mastered your A B C, or knew where the "white sails" of the Chesapeake were bound, you began, I see, to gauge the wretchedness of the slave, not by his hunger and want, not by his lashes and toil, but by the cruel and blighting death which gathers over his soul.

In connection with this, there is one circumstance which makes your recollections peculiarly valuable, and renders your early insight the more remarkable. You come from that part of the country where we are told slavery appears with its fairest features. Let us hear, then, what it is at its best estate—gaze on its bright side, if it has one; and then imagination may task her powers to add dark lines to the picture, as she travels southward to that (for the colored man) Valley of the Shadow of Death, where the Mississippi sweeps along.

Again, we have known you long, and can put the most entire confidence in your truth, candor, and sincerity. Every one who has heard you speak has felt, and, I am confident, every one who reads your book will feel, persuaded that you give them a fair specimen of the whole truth. No one-sided portrait,—no wholesale complaints,—but strict justice done, whenever individual kindliness has neutralized, for a moment, the deadly system with which it was strangely allied. You have been with us, too, some years, and can fairly compare the twilight of rights, which your race enjoy at the North, with that "noon of night" under which they labor south of Mason and Dixon's line. Tell us whether, after all, the half-free colored man of Massachusetts is worse off than the pampered slave of the rice swamps!

In reading your life, no one can say that we have unfairly picked out some rare specimens of cruelty. We know that the bitter drops, which even you have drained from the cup, are no incidental aggravations, no individual ills, but such as must mingle always and necessarily in the lot of every slave. They are the essential ingredients, not the occasional results, of the system.

After all, I shall read your book with trembling for you. Some years ago, when you were beginning to tell me your real name and birthplace, you may remember I stopped you, and preferred to remain ignorant of all. With the exception of a vague description, so I continued, till the other day, when you read me your memoirs. I hardly knew, at the time, whether to thank you or not for the sight of them, when I reflected that it was still dangerous, in Massachusetts, for honest men to tell their names! They say the fathers, in 1776, signed the Declaration of Independence with the halter about their necks. You, too, publish your declaration of freedom with danger compassing you around. In all the broad lands which the Constitution of the United States overshadows, there is no single spot,—

however narrow or desolate,—where a fugitive slave can plant himself and say, "I am safe." The whole armory of Northern Law has no shield for you. I am free to say that, in your place, I should throw the MS. into the fire.

You, perhaps, may tell your story in safety, endeared as you are to so many warm hearts by rare gifts, and a still rarer devotion of them to the service of others. But it will be owing only to your labors, and the fearless efforts of those who, trampling the laws and Constitution of the country under their feet, are determined that they will "hide the outcast," and that their hearths shall be, spite of the law, an asylum for the oppressed, if, some time or other, the humblest may stand in our streets, and bear witness in safety against the cruelties of which he has been the victim.

Yet it is sad to think, that these very throbbing hearts which welcome your story, and form your best safeguard in telling it, are all beating contrary to the "statute in such case made and provided." Go on, my dear friend, till you, and those who, like you, have been saved, so as by fire, from the dark prison-house, shall stereotype these free, illegal pulses into statutes; and New England, cutting loose from a blood-stained Union, shall glory in being the house of refuge for the oppressed;—till we no longer merely "*hide* the outcast," or make a merit of standing idly by while he is hunted in our midst; but, consecrating anew the soil of the Pilgrims as an asylum for the oppressed, proclaim our *welcome* to the slave so loudly, that the tones shall reach every hut in the Carolinas, and make the brokenhearted bondman leap up at the thought of old Massachusetts.

God Speed the day!

Till then, and ever,

Yours truly,

WENDELL PHILLIPS.

FREDERICK DOUGLASS.

NARRATIVE

OF THE

LIFE OF
FREDERICK DOUGLASS.

CHAPTER I.

I was born in Tuckahoe, near Hillsborough, and about twelve miles from Easton, in Talbot county, Maryland. I have no accurate knowledge of my age, never having seen any authentic record containing it. By far the larger part of the slaves know as little of their ages as horses know of theirs, and it is the wish of most masters within my knowledge to keep their slaves thus ignorant. I do not remember to have ever met a slave who could tell of his birthday. They seldom come nearer to it than planting-time, harvest-time, cherry-time, spring-time, or fall-time. A want of information concerning my own was a source of unhappiness to me even during childhood. The white children could tell their ages. I could not tell why I ought to be deprived of the same privilege. I was not allowed to make any inquiries of my master concerning it. He deemed all such inquiries on the part of a slave improper and impertinent, and evidence of a restless spirit. The nearest estimate I can give makes me now between twenty-seven and twenty-eight years of age. I come to this, from hearing my master say, some time during 1835, I was about seventeen years old.

My mother was named Harriet Bailey. She was the daughter of Isaac and Betsey Bailey, both colored, and quite dark. My mother was of a darker complexion than either my grandmother or grandfather.

My father was a white man. He was admitted to be such by all I ever heard speak of my parentage. The opinion was also whispered that my master was my father; but of the correctness of this opinion, I know nothing; the means of knowing was withheld from me. My mother and I were separated when I was but an infant—before I knew her as my mother. It is a common custom, in the part of Maryland from which I ran away, to part children from their mothers at a very early age. Frequently, before the child has reached its twelfth month, its mother is taken from it, and hired out on some farm a considerable distance off, and the child is placed under the care of an old woman, too old for field labor. For what this separation is done, I do not know, unless it be to hinder the development of the child's affection toward its mother, and to blunt and destroy the natural affection of the mother for the child. This is the inevitable result.

I never saw my mother, to know her as such, more than four or five times in my life; and each of these times was very short in duration, and at night. She was hired by a Mr. Stewart, who lived about twelve miles from my home. She made her journeys to see me in the night, travelling the whole distance on foot, after the performance of her day's work. She was a field hand, and a whipping is the penalty of not being in the field at sunrise, unless a slave has special permission from his or her master to the contrary—a permission which they seldom get, and one that gives to him that gives it the proud name of being a kind master. I do not recollect of ever seeing my mother by the light of day. She was with me in the night. She would lie down with me, and get me to sleep, but long before I waked she was gone. Very little communication ever took place between us. Death soon ended what little we could have while she lived, and with it her hardships and suffering. She died when I was about seven years old, on one of my master's farms, near Lee's Mill. I was not allowed to be present during her illness, at her death, or burial. She was gone long before I knew any thing about it. Never having enjoyed, to any considerable extent, her soothing presence, her tender and watchful care, I received the tidings of her death with much the same emotions I should have probably felt at the death of a stranger.

Called thus suddenly away, she left me without the slightest intimation of who my father was. The whisper that my master was my father, may or may not be true; and, true or false, it is of but little consequence to my purpose whilst the fact remains, in all its glaring odiousness, that slaveholders have ordained, and by law established, that the children of slave women shall in all cases follow the condition of their mothers, and this is done too obviously to administer to their own lusts, and make a gratification of their wicked desires profitable as well as pleasurable; for by this cunning arrangement, the slaveholder, in cases not a few, sustains to his slaves the double relation of master and father.

I know of such cases; and it is worthy of remark that such slaves invariably suffer greater hardships, and have more to contend with, than others. They are, in the first place, a constant offence to their mistress. She is ever disposed to find fault with them; they can seldom do any thing to please her; she is never better pleased than when she sees them under the lash, especially when she suspects her husband of showing to his mulatto children favors which he withholds from his black slaves. The master is frequently compelled to sell this class of his slaves, out of deference to the feelings of his white wife; and, cruel as the deed may strike any one to be, for a man to sell his own children to human flesh-mongers, it is often the dictate of humanity for him to do so; for, unless he does this, he must not only whip them himself, but must stand by and see one white son tie up his brother, of but few shades darker complexion than himself, and ply the gory lash to his naked back; and if he lisp one word of disapproval, it is set down to his parental partiality, and only makes a bad matter worse, both for himself and the slave whom he would protect and defend.

Every year brings with it multitudes of this class of slaves. It was doubtless in consequence of a knowledge of this fact, that one great statesman of the south predicted the downfall of slavery by the inevitable laws of population. Whether this prophecy is ever fulfilled or not, it is nevertheless plain that a very different-looking class of people are springing up at the south, and are now held in slavery, from those originally brought to this country from Africa; and if their increase will do no other good, it will do away the force of the argument, that God cursed Ham, and therefore American slavery is right. If the lineal descendants of Ham are alone to be scripturally enslaved, it is certain that slavery at the south must soon become unscriptural; for thousands are ushered into the world, annually, who, like myself, owe their existence to white fathers, and those fathers most frequently their own masters.

I have had two masters. My first master's name was Anthony. I do not remember his first name. He was generally called Captain Anthony—a title which, I presume, he acquired by sailing a craft on the Chesapeake Bay. He was not considered a rich slaveholder. He owned two or three farms, and about thirty slaves. His farms and slaves were under the care of an overseer. The overseer's name was Plummer. Mr. Plummer was a miserable drunkard, a profane swearer, and a savage monster. He always went armed with a cowskin and a heavy cudgel. I have known him to cut and slash the women's heads so horribly, that even master would be enraged at his cruelty, and would threaten to whip him if he did not mind himself. It required extraordinary barbarity on the part of an overseer to affect him. He was a cruel man, hardened by a long life of slaveholding. He would at times seem to take great pleasure in whipping a slave. I have often been awakened at the dawn of day by the most heart-rending shrieks of an own aunt of mine, whom he used to tie up to a joist, and whip upon her naked back till she was literally covered with blood. No words, no tears, no prayers, from his gory victim, seemed to move his iron heart from its bloody purpose. The louder she screamed, the harder he whipped; and where the blood ran fastest, there he whipped longest. He would whip her to make her scream, and whip her to make her hush; and not until overcome by fatigue, would he cease to swing the blood-clotted cowskin. I remember the first time I ever witnessed this horrible exhibition. I was quite a child, but I well remember it. I never shall forget it whilst I remember any thing. It was the first of a long series of such outrages, of which I was doomed to be a witness and a participant. It struck me with awful force. It was the blood-stained gate, the entrance to the hell of slavery, through which I was about to pass. It was a most terrible spectacle. I wish I could commit to paper the feelings with which I beheld it.

This occurrence took place very soon after I went to live with my old master, and under the following circumstances. Aunt Hester went out one night,—where or for what I do not know,—and happened to be absent when my master desired her presence. He had ordered her not to go out evenings, and warned her that she must never let him catch her in company with a young man, who was paying attention to her, belonging to Colonel Lloyd. The young man's name was Ned Roberts, generally called Lloyd's Ned. Why master was so careful of her, may be safely left to conjecture. She was a woman of noble form, and of graceful proportions, having very few equals, and fewer superiors, in personal appearance, among the colored or white women of our neighborhood.

Aunt Hester had not only disobeyed his orders in going out, but had been found in company with Lloyd's Ned; which circumstance, I found, from what he said while whipping her, was the chief offence. Had he been a man of pure morals himself, he might have been thought interested in protecting the innocence of my aunt; but those who knew him will not suspect him of any such virtue. Before he commenced whipping Aunt Hester, he took her into the kitchen, and stripped her from neck to waist, leaving her neck, shoulders, and back, entirely naked. He then told her to cross her hands, calling her at the same time a d——d b——h. After crossing her hands, he tied them with a strong rope, and led her to a stool under a large hook in the joist, put in for the purpose. He made her get upon the stool, and tied her hands to the hook. She now stood fair for his infernal purpose. Her arms were stretched up at their full length, so that she stood upon the ends of her toes. He then said to her, "Now, you d——d b——h, I'll learn you how to disobey my orders!" and after rolling up his sleeves, he commenced to lay on the heavy cowskin, and soon the warm, red blood (amid heartrending shrieks from her, and horrid oaths from him) came dripping to the floor. I was so terrified and horror-stricken at the sight, that I hid myself in a closet, and dared not venture out till long after the bloody transaction was over. I expected it would be my turn next. It was all new to me. I had never seen anything like it before. I had always lived with my grandmother on the outskirts of the plantation, where she was put to raise the children of the younger women. I had therefore been, until now, out of the way of the bloody scenes that often occurred on the plantation.

CHAPTER II.

My master's family consisted of two sons, Andrew and Richard, one daughter, Lucretia, and her husband, Captain Thomas Auld. They lived in one house, upon the home plantation of Colonel Edward Lloyd. My master was Colonel Lloyd's clerk and superintendent. He was what might be called the overseer of the overseers. I spent two years of childhood on this plantation in my old master's family. It was here that I witnessed the bloody transaction recorded in the first chapter; and as I received my first impressions of slavery on this plantation, I will give some description of it, and of slavery as it there existed. The plantation is about twelve miles north of Easton, in Talbot county, and is situated on the border of Miles River. The principal products raised upon it were tobacco, corn, and wheat. These were raised in great abundance; so that, with the products of this and the other farms belonging to him, he was able to keep in almost constant employment a large sloop, in carrying them to market at Baltimore. This sloop was named Sally Lloyd, in honor of one of the colonel's daughters. My master's son-in-law, Captain Auld, was master of the vessel; she was otherwise manned by the colonel's own slaves. Their names were Peter, Isaac, Rich, and Jake. These were esteemed very highly by the other slaves, and looked upon as the privileged ones of the plantation; for it was no small affair, in the eyes of the slaves, to be allowed to see Baltimore.

Colonel Lloyd kept from three to four hundred slaves on his home plantation, and owned a large number more on the neighboring farms belonging to him. The names of the farms nearest to the home plantation were Wye Town and New Design. "Wye Town" was under the overseership of a man named Noah Willis. New Design was under the overseership of a Mr. Townsend. The overseers of these, and all the rest of the farms, numbering over twenty, received advice and direction from the managers of the home plantation. This was the great business place. It was the seat of government for the whole twenty farms. All disputes among the overseers were settled here. If a slave was convicted of any high misdemeanor, became unmanageable, or evinced a determination to run away, he was brought immediately here, severely whipped, put on board the sloop, carried to Baltimore, and sold to Austin Woolfolk, or some other slave-trader, as a warning to the slaves remaining.

Here, too, the slaves of all the other farms received their monthly allowance of food, and their yearly clothing. The men and women slaves received, as their monthly allowance of food, eight pounds of pork, or its equivalent in fish, and one bushel of corn meal. Their yearly clothing consisted of two coarse linen shirts, one pair of linen trousers, like the shirts, one jacket, one pair of trousers for winter, made of coarse negro cloth, one pair of stockings, and one pair of shoes; the whole of which could not have cost more than seven dollars. The allowance of the slave children was given to their mothers, or the old women having the care of them. The children unable to work in the field had neither shoes, stockings, jackets, nor trousers, given to them; their clothing consisted of two coarse linen shirts per year. When these failed them, they went naked until the next allowance-day. Children from seven to ten years old, of both sexes, almost naked, might be seen at all seasons of the year.

There were no beds given the slaves, unless one coarse blanket be considered such, and none but the men and women had these. This, however, is not considered a very great privation. They find less difficulty from the want of beds, than from the want of time to sleep; for when their day's work in the field is done, the most of them having their washing, mending, and cooking to do, and having few or none of the ordinary facilities for doing either of these, very many of their sleeping hours are consumed in preparing for the field the coming day; and when this is done, old and young, male and female, married and single, drop down side by side, on one common bed,—the cold, damp floor,—each covering himself or herself with their miserable blankets; and here they sleep till they are summoned to the field by the driver's horn. At the sound of this, all must rise, and be off to the field. There must be no halting; every one must be at his or her post; and woe betides them who hear not this morning summons to the field; for if they are not awakened by the sense of hearing, they are by the sense of feeling: no age nor sex finds any favor. Mr. Severe, the overseer, used to stand by the door of the quarter, armed with a large hickory stick and heavy cowskin, ready to whip any one who was so unfortunate as not to hear, or, from any other cause, was prevented from being ready to start for the field at the sound of the horn.

Mr. Severe was rightly named: he was a cruel man. I have seen him whip a woman, causing the blood to run half an hour at the time; and this, too, in the midst of her crying children, pleading for their mother's release. He seemed to take pleasure in manifesting his fiendish barbarity. Added to his cruelty, he was a profane swearer. It was enough to chill the blood and stiffen the hair of an ordinary man to hear him talk. Scarce a sentence escaped him but that was commenced or concluded by some horrid oath. The field was the place to witness his cruelty and profanity. His presence made it both the field of blood and blasphemy. From the rising till the going down of the sun, he was cursing, raving, cutting, and slashing among the slaves of the field, in the most frightful manner. His career was short. He died very soon after I went to Colonel Lloyd's; and he died as he lived, uttering, with his dying groans, bitter curses and horrid oaths. His death was regarded by the slaves as the result of a merciful providence.

Mr. Severe's place was filled by a Mr. Hopkins. He was a very different man. He was less cruel, less profane, and made less noise, than Mr. Severe. His course was characterized by no extraordinary demonstrations of cruelty. He whipped, but seemed to take no pleasure in it. He was called by the slaves a good overseer.

The home plantation of Colonel Lloyd wore the appearance of a country village. All the mechanical operations for all the farms were performed here. The shoemaking and mending, the blacksmithing, cartwrighting, coopering, weaving, and grain-grinding, were all performed by the slaves on the home plantation. The whole place wore a business-like aspect very unlike the neighboring farms. The number of houses, too, conspired to give it advantage over the neighboring farms. It was called by the slaves the *Great House Farm*. Few privileges were esteemed higher, by the slaves of the out-farms, than that of being selected to do errands at the Great House Farm. It was associated in their minds with greatness. A representative could not be prouder of his election to a seat in the American Congress, than a slave on one of the out-farms would be of his election to do errands at the Great House Farm. They regarded it as evidence of great confidence reposed in them by their overseers; and it was on this account, as well as a constant desire to be out of the field from under the driver's lash, that they esteemed it a high privilege, one worth careful living for. He was called the smartest and most trusty fellow, who had this honor conferred upon him the most frequently. The competitors for this office sought as diligently to please their overseers, as the office-seekers in the political parties seek to please and deceive the people. The same traits of character might be seen in Colonel Lloyd's slaves, as are seen in the slaves of the political parties.

The slaves selected to go to the Great House Farm, for the monthly allowance for themselves and their fellow-slaves, were peculiarly enthusiastic. While on their way, they would make the dense old woods, for miles around, reverberate with their wildsongs, revealing at once the highest joy and the deepest sadness. They would compose and sing as they went along, consulting neither time nor tune. The thought that came up, came out—if not in the word, in the sound;—and as frequently in the one as in the other. They would sometimes sing the most pathetic sentiment in the most rapturous tone, and the most rapturous sentiment in the most pathetic tones. Into all of their songs they would manage to weave something of the Great House Farm. Especially would they do this, when leaving home. They would then sing most exultingly the following words:—

I am going away to the Great House Farm!
O, yea! O, yea! O!

This they would sing, as a chorus, to words which to many would seem unmeaning jargon, but which, nevertheless, were full of meaning to themselves. I have sometimes thought that the mere hearing of those songs would do more to impress some minds with the horrible character of slavery, than the reading of whole volumes of philosophy on the subject could do.

I did not, when a slave, understand the deep meaning of those rude and apparently incoherent songs. I was myself within the circle; so that I neither saw nor heard as those without might see and hear. They told a tale of woe which was then altogether beyond my feeble comprehension; they were tones loud, long, and deep; they breathed the prayer and complaint of souls boiling over with the bitterest anguish. Every tone was a testimony against slavery, and a prayer to God for deliverance from chains. The hearing of those wild notes always depressed my spirit, and filled me with ineffable sadness. I have frequently found myself in tears while hearing them. The mere recurrence to those songs, even now, afflicts me; and while I am writing these lines, an expression of feeling has already found its way down my cheek. To those songs I trace my first glimmering conception of the dehumanizing character of slavery. I can never get rid of that conception. Those songs still follow me, to deepen my hatred of slavery, and quicken my sympathies for my brethren in bonds. If any one wishes to be impressed with the soul-killing effects of slavery, let him go to Colonel Lloyd's plantation, and, on allowance-day, place himself in the deep pine woods, and there let him, in silence, analyze the sounds that shall pass through the chambers of his soul,—and if he is not thus impressed, it will only be because "there is no flesh in his obdurate heart."

I have often been utterly astonished, since I came to the

north, to find persons who could speak of the singing, among slaves, as evidence of their contentment and happiness. It is impossible to conceive of a greater mistake. Slaves sing most when they are most unhappy. The songs of the slave represent the sorrows of his heart; and he is relieved by them, only as an aching heart is relieved by its tears. At least, such is my experience. I have often sung to drown my sorrow, but seldom to express my happiness. Crying for joy, and singing for joy, were alike uncommon to me while in the jaws of slavery. The singing of a man cast away upon a desolate island might be as appropriately considered as evidence of contentment and happiness, as the singing of a slave; the songs of the one and of the other are prompted by the same emotion.

CHAPTER III.

COLONEL Lloyd kept a large and finely cultivated garden, which afforded almost constant employment for four men, besides the chief gardener, (Mr. M'Durmond.) This garden was probably the greatest attraction of the place. During the summer months, people came from far and near—from Baltimore, Easton, and Annapolis—to see it. It abounded in fruits of almost every description, from the hardy apple of the north to the delicate orange of the south. This garden was not the least source of trouble on the plantation. Its excellent fruit was quite a temptation to the hungry swarms of boys, as well as the older slaves, belonging to the colonel, few of whom had the virtue or the vice to resist it. Scarcely a day passed, during the summer, but that some slave had to take the lash for stealing fruit. The colonel had to resort to all kinds of stratagems to keep his slaves out of the garden. The last and most successful one was that of tarring his fence all around; after which, if a slave was caught with any tar upon his person, it was deemed sufficient proof that he had either been into the garden, or had tried to get in. In either case, he was severely whipped by the chief gardener. This plan worked well; the slaves became as fearful of tar as of the lash. They seemed to realize the impossibility of touching *tar* without being defiled.

The colonel also kept a splendid riding equipage. His stable and carriage-house presented the appearance of some of our large city livery establishments. His horses were of the finest form and noblest blood. His carriage-house contained three splendid coaches, three or four gigs, besides dearborns and barouches of the most fashionable style.

This establishment was under the care of two slaves—old Barney and young Barney—father and son. To attend to this establishment was their sole work. But it was by no means an easy employment; for in nothing was Colonel Lloyd more particular than in the management of his horses. The slightest inattention to these was unpardonable, and was visited upon those, under whose care they were placed, with the severest punishment; no excuse could shield them, if the colonel only suspected any want of attention to his horses—a supposition which he frequently indulged, and one which, of course, made the office of old and young Barney a very trying one. They never knew when they were safe from punishment. They were frequently whipped when least deserving, and escaped whipping when most deserving it. Every thing depended upon the looks of the horses, and the state of Colonel Lloyd's own mind when his horses were brought to him for use. If a horse did not move fast enough, or hold his head high enough, it was owing to some fault of his keepers. It was painful to stand near the stable-door, and hear the various complaints against the keepers when a horse was taken out for use. "This horse has not had proper attention. He has not been sufficiently rubbed and curried, or he has not been properly fed; his food was too wet or too dry; he got it too soon or too late; he was too hot or too cold; he had too much hay, and not enough of grain; or he had too much grain, and not enough of hay; instead of old Barney's attending to the horse, he had very improperly left it to his son." To all these complaints, no matter how unjust, the slave must answer never a word. Colonel Lloyd could not brook any contradiction from a slave. When he spoke, a slave must stand, listen, and tremble; and such was literally the case. I have seen Colonel Lloyd make old Barney, a man between fifty and sixty years of age, uncover his bald head, kneel down upon the cold, damp ground, and receive upon his naked and toil-worn shoulders more than thirty lashes at the time. Colonel Lloyd had three sons—Edward, Murray, and Daniel,—and three sons-in-law, Mr. Winder, Mr. Nicholson, and Mr. Lowndes. All of these lived at the Great House Farm, and enjoyed the luxury of whipping the servants when they pleased, from old Barney down to William Wilkes, the coach-driver. I have seen Winder make one of the house-servants stand off from him a suitable distance to be touched with the end of his whip, and at every stroke raise great ridges upon his back.

To describe the wealth of Colonel Lloyd would be almost equal to describing the riches of Job. He kept from ten to fifteen house-servants. He was said to own a thousand slaves, and I think this estimate quite within the truth. Colonel Lloyd owned so many that he did not know them when he saw them; nor did all the slaves of the out-farms know him. It is reported of him, that, while riding along the road one day, he met a colored man, and addressed him in the usual manner of speaking to colored people on the public highways of the south: "Well, boy, whom do you belong to?" "To Colonel Lloyd," replied the slave. "Well, does the colonel treat you well?" "No, sir," was the ready reply. "What, does he work you too hard?" "Yes, sir." "Well, don't he give you enough to eat?" "Yes, sir, he gives me enough, such as it is."

The colonel, after ascertaining where the slave belonged, rode on; the man also went on about his business, not dreaming that he had been conversing with his master. He thought, said, and heard nothing more of the matter, until two or three weeks afterwards. The poor man was then informed by his overseer that, for having found fault with his master, he was now to be sold to a Georgia trader. He was immediately chained and handcuffed; and thus, without a moment's warning, he was snatched away, and forever sundered, from his family and friends, by a hand more unrelenting than death. This is the penalty of telling the truth, of telling the simple truth, in answer to a series of plain questions.

It is partly in consequence of such facts, that slaves, when inquired of as to their condition and the character of their masters, almost universally say they are contented, and that their masters are kind. The slaveholders have been known to send in spies among their slaves, to ascertain their views and feelings in regard to their condition. The frequency of this has had the effect to establish among the slaves the maxim, that a still tongue makes a wise head. They suppress the truth rather than take the consequences of telling it, and in so doing prove themselves a part of the human family. If they have any thing to say of their masters, it is generally in their masters' favor, especially when speaking to an untried man. I have been frequently asked, when a slave, if I had a kind master, and do not remember ever to have given a negative answer; nor did I, in pursuing this course, consider myself as uttering what was absolutely false; for I always measured the kindness of my master by the standard of kindness set up among slaveholders around us. Moreover, slaves are like other people, and imbibe prejudices quite common to others. They think their own better than that of others. Many, under the influence of this prejudice, think their own masters are better than the masters of other slaves; and this, too, in some cases, when the very reverse is true. Indeed, it is not uncommon for slaves even to fall out and quarrel among themselves about the relative goodness of their masters, each contending for the superior goodness of his own over that of the others. At the very same time, they mutually execrate their masters when viewed separately. It was so on our plantation. When Colonel Lloyd's slaves met the slaves of Jacob Jepson, they seldom parted without a quarrel about their masters; Colonel Lloyd's slaves contending that he was the richest, and Mr. Jepson's slaves that he was the smartest, and most of a man. Colonel Lloyd's slaves would boast his ability to buy and sell Jacob Jepson. Mr. Jepson's slaves would boast his ability to whip Colonel Lloyd. These quarrels would almost always end in a fight between the parties, and those that whipped were supposed to have gained the point at issue. They seemed to think that the greatness of their masters was transferable to themselves. It was considered as being bad enough to be a slave; but to be a poor man's slave was deemed a disgrace indeed!

CHAPTER IV.

Mr. Hopkins remained but a short time in the office of overseer. Why his career was so short, I do not know, but suppose he lacked the necessary severity to suit Colonel Lloyd. Mr. Hopkins was succeeded by Mr. Austin Gore, a man possessing, in an eminent degree, all those traits of character indispensable to what is called a first-rate overseer. Mr. Gore had served Colonel Lloyd, in the capacity of overseer, upon one of the out-farms, and had shown himself worthy of the high station of overseer upon the home or Great House Farm.

Mr. Gore was proud, ambitious, and persevering. He was artful, cruel, and obdurate. He was just the man for such a place, and it was just the place for such a man. It afforded scope for the full exercise of all his powers, and he seemed to be perfectly at home in it. He was one of those who could torture the slightest look, word, or gesture, on the part of the slave, into impudence, and would treat it accordingly. There must be no answering back to him; no explanation was allowed a slave, showing himself to have been wrongfully accused. Mr. Gore acted fully up to the maxim laid down by slaveholders,—"It is better that a dozen slaves suffer under the lash, than that the overseer should be convicted, in the presence of the slaves, of having been at fault." No matter how innocent a slave might be—it availed him nothing, when accused by Mr. Gore of any misdemeanor. To be accused was to be convicted, and to be convicted was to be punished; the one always following the other with immutable certainty. To escape punishment was to escape accusation; and few slaves had the fortune to do either, under the overseership of Mr. Gore. He was just proud enough to demand the most debasing homage of the slave, and quite servile enough to crouch, himself, at the feet of the master. He was ambitious enough to be contented with nothing short of the highest rank of overseers, and persevering enough to reach the height of his ambition. He was cruel enough to inflict the severest punishment, artful enough to descend to the lowest trickery, and obdurate enough to be insensible to the voice of a reproving conscience. He was, of all the overseers, the most dreaded by the slaves. His presence was painful; his eye flashed confusion; and seldom was his sharp, shrill voice heard, without producing horror and trembling in their ranks.

Mr. Gore was a grave man, and, though a young man, he indulged in no jokes, said no funny words, seldom smiled. His words were in perfect keeping with his looks, and his looks were in perfect keeping with his words. Overseers will sometimes indulge in a witty word, even with the slaves; not so with Mr. Gore. He spoke but to command, and commanded but to be obeyed; he dealt sparingly with his words, and bountifully with his whip, never using the former where the latter would answer as well. When he whipped, he seemed to do so from a sense of duty, and feared no consequences. He did nothing reluctantly, no matter how disagreeable; always at his post, never inconsistent. He never promised but to fulfill. He was, in a word, a man of the most inflexible firmness and stone-like coolness.

His savage barbarity was equalled only by the consummate coolness with which he committed the grossest and most savage deeds upon the slaves under his charge. Mr. Gore once undertook to whip one of Colonel Lloyd's slaves, by the name of Demby. He had given Demby but few stripes, when, to get rid of the scourging, he ran and plunged himself into a creek, and stood there at the depth of his shoulders, refusing to come out. Mr. Gore told him that he would give him three calls, and that, if he did not come out at the third call, he would shoot him. The first call was given. Demby made no response, but stood his ground. The second and third calls were given with the same result. Mr. Gore then, without consultation or deliberation with any one, not even giving Demby an additional call, raised his musket to his face, taking deadly aim at his standing victim, and in an instant poor Demby was no more. His mangled body sank out of sight, and blood and brains marked the water where he had stood.

A thrill of horror flashed through every soul upon the plantation, excepting Mr. Gore. He alone seemed cool and collected. He was asked by Colonel Lloyd and my old master, why he resorted to this extraordinary expedient. His reply was, (as well as I can remember,) that Demby had become unmanageable. He was setting a dangerous example to the other slaves,—one which, if suffered to pass without some such demonstration on his part, would finally lead to the total subversion of all rule and order upon the plantation. He argued that if one slave refused to be corrected, and escaped with his life, the other slaves would soon copy the example; the result of which would be, the freedom of the slaves, and the enslavement of the whites. Mr. Gore's defence was satisfactory. He was continued in his station as overseer upon the home plantation. His fame as an overseer went abroad. His horrid crime was not even submitted to judicial investigation. It was committed in the presence of slaves, and they of course could neither institute a suit, nor testify against him; and thus the guilty perpetrator of one of the bloodiest and most foul murders goes unwhipped of justice, and uncensured by the community in which he lives. Mr. Gore lived in St. Michael's, Talbot county, Maryland, when I left there; and if he is still alive, he very probably lives there now; and if so, he is now, as he was then, as highly esteemed and as much respected as though his guilty soul had not been stained with his brother's blood.

I speak advisedly when I say this,—that killing a slave, or any colored person, in Talbot county, Maryland, is not treated as a crime, either by the courts or the community. Mr. Thomas Lanman, of St. Michael's, killed two slaves, one of whom he killed with a hatchet, by knocking his brains out. He used to boast of the commission of the awful and bloody deed. I have heard him do so laughingly, saying, among other things, that he was the only benefactor of his country in the company, and that when others would do as much as he had done, we should be relieved of "the d——d niggers."

The wife of Mr. Giles Hicks, living but a short distance from where I used to live, murdered my wife's cousin, a young girl between fifteen and sixteen years of age, mangling her person in the most horrible manner, breaking her nose and breastbone with a stick, so that the poor girl expired in a few hours afterward. She was immediately buried, but had not been in her untimely grave but a few hours before she was taken up and examined by the coroner, who decided that she had come to her death by severe beating. The offence for which this girl was thus murdered was this:—She had been set that night to mind Mrs. Hicks's baby, and during the night she fell asleep, and the baby cried. She, having lost her rest for several nights previous, did not hear the crying. They were both in the room with Mrs. Hicks. Mrs. Hicks, finding the girl slow to move, jumped from her bed, seized an oak stick of wood by the fireplace, and with it broke the girl's nose and breastbone, and thus ended her life. I will not say that this most horrid murder produced no sensation in the community. It did produce sensation, but not enough to bring the murderess to punishment. There was a warrant issued for her arrest, but it was never served. Thus she escaped not only punishment, but even the pain of being arraigned before a court for her horrid crime.

Whilst I am detailing bloody deeds which took place during my stay on Colonel Lloyd's plantation, I will briefly narrate another, which occurred about the same time as the murder of Demby by Mr. Gore.

Colonel Lloyd's slaves were in the habit of spending a part of their nights and Sundays in fishing for oysters, and in this way made up the deficiency of their scanty allowance. An old man belonging to Colonel Lloyd, while thus engaged, happened to get beyond the limits of Colonel Lloyd's, and on the premises of Mr. Beal Bondly. At this trespass, Mr. Bondly took offence, and with his musket came down to the shore, and blew its deadly contents into the poor old man.

Mr. Bondly came over to see Colonel Lloyd the next day, whether to pay him for his property, or to justify himself in what he had done, I know not. At any rate, this whole fiendish transaction was soon hushed up. There was very little said about it at all, and nothing done. It was a common saying, even among little white boys, that it was worth a half-cent to kill a "nigger," and a half-cent to bury one.

CHAPTER V.

As to my own treatment while I lived on Colonel Lloyd's plantation, it was very similar to that of the other slave children. I was not old enough to work in the field, and there being little else than field work to do, I had a great deal of leisure time. The most I had to do was to drive up the cows at evening, keep the fowls out of the garden, keep the front yard clean, and run of errands for my old master's daughter, Mrs. Lucretia Auld. The most of my leisure time I spent in helping Master Daniel Lloyd in finding his birds, after he had shot them. My connection with Master Daniel was of some advantage to me. He became quite attached to me, and was a sort of protector of me. He would not allow the older boys to impose upon me, and would divide his cakes with me.

I was seldom whipped by my old master, and suffered little from any thing else than hunger and cold. I suffered much from hunger, but much more from cold. In hottest summer and coldest winter, I was kept almost naked—no shoes, no stockings, no jacket, no trousers, nothing on but a coarse tow linen shirt, reaching only to my knees. I had no bed. I must have perished with cold, but that, the coldest nights, I used to steal a bag which was used for carrying corn to the mill. I would crawl into this bag, and there sleep on the cold, damp, clay floor, with my head in and feet out. My feet have been so cracked with the frost, that the pen with which I am writing might be laid in the gashes.

We were not regularly allowanced. Our food was coarse

corn meal boiled. This was called *mush*. It was put into a large wooden tray or trough, and set down upon the ground. The children were then called like so many pigs, and like so many pigs they would come and devour the mush; some with oystershells, others with pieces of shingle, some with naked hands, and none with spoons. He that ate fastest got most; he that was strongest secured the best place; and few left the trough satisfied.

I was probably between seven and eight years old when I left Colonel Lloyd's plantation. I left it with joy. I shall never forget the ecstasy with which I received the intelligence that my old master (Anthony) had determined to let me go to Baltimore, to live with Mr. Hugh Auld, brother to my old master's son-in-law, Captain Thomas Auld. I received this information about three days before my departure. They were three of the happiest days I ever enjoyed. I spent the most part of all these three days in the creek, washing off the plantation scurf, and preparing myself for my departure.

The pride of appearance which this would indicate was not my own. I spent the time in washing, not so much because I wished to, but because Mrs. Lucretia had told me I must get all the dead skin off my feet and knees before I could go to Baltimore; for the people in Baltimore were very cleanly, and would laugh at me if I looked dirty. Besides, she was going to give me a pair of trousers, which I should not put on unless I got all the dirt off me. The thought of owning a pair of trousers was great indeed! It was almost a sufficient motive, not only to make me take off what would be called by pig-drovers the mange, but the skin itself. I went at it in good earnest, working for the first time with the hope of reward.

The ties that ordinarily bind children to their homes were all suspended in my case. I found no severe trial in my departure. My home was charmless; it was not home to me; on parting from it, I could not feel that I was leaving any thing which I could have enjoyed by staying. My mother was dead, my grandmother lived far off, so that I seldom saw her. I had two sisters and one brother, that lived in the same house with me; but the early separation of us from our mother had well nigh blotted the fact of our relationship from our memories. I looked for home elsewhere, and was confident of finding none which I should relish less than the one which I was leaving. If, however, I found in my new home hardship, hunger, whipping, and nakedness, I had the consolation that I should not have escaped any one of them by staying. Having already had more than a taste of them in the house of my old master, and having endured them there, I very naturally inferred my ability to endure them elsewhere, and especially at Baltimore; for I had something of the feeling about Baltimore that is expressed in the proverb, that "being hanged in England is preferable to dying a natural death in Ireland." I had the strongest desire to see Baltimore. Cousin Tom, though not fluent in speech, had inspired me with that desire by his eloquent description of the place. I could never point out any thing at the Great House, no matter how beautiful or powerful, but that he had seen something at Baltimore far exceeding, both in beauty and strength, the object which I pointed out to him. Even the Great House itself, with all its pictures, was far inferior to many buildings in Baltimore. So strong was my desire, that I thought a gratification of it would fully compensate for whatever loss of comforts I should sustain by the exchange. I left without a regret, and with the highest hopes of future happiness.

We sailed out of Miles River for Baltimore on a Saturday morning. I remember only the day of the week, for at that time I had no knowledge of the days of the month, nor the months of the year. On setting sail, I walked aft, and gave to Colonel Lloyd's plantation what I hoped would be the last look. I then placed myself in the bows of the sloop, and there spent the remainder of the day in looking ahead, interesting myself in what was in the distance rather than in things near by or behind.

In the afternoon of that day, we reached Annapolis, the capital of the State. We stopped but a few moments, so that I had no time to go on shore. It was the first large town that I had ever seen, and though it would look small compared with some of our New England factory villages, I thought it a wonderful place for its size—more imposing even than the Great House Farm!

We arrived at Baltimore early on Sunday morning, landing at Smith's Wharf, not far from Bowley's Wharf. We had on board the sloop a large flock of sheep; and after aiding in driving them to the slaughterhouse of Mr. Curtis on Louden Slater's Hill, I was conducted by Rich, one of the hands belonging on board of the sloop, to my new home in Alliciana Street, near Mr. Gardner's ship-yard, on Fells Point.

Mr. and Mrs. Auld were both at home, and met me at the door with their little son Thomas, to take care of whom I had been given. And here I saw what I had never seen before; it was a white face beaming with the most kindly emotions; it was the face of my new mistress, Sophia Auld. I wish I could describe the rapture that flashed through my soul as I beheld it. It was a new and strange sight to me, brightening up my pathway with the light of happiness. Little Thomas was told, there was his Freddy,—and I was told to take care of little Thomas; and thus I entered upon the duties of my new home with the most cheering prospect ahead.

I look upon my departure from Colonel Lloyd's plantation as one of the most interesting events of my life. It is possible, and even quite probable, that but for the mere circumstance of being removed from that plantation to Baltimore, I should have to-day, instead of being here seated by my own table, in the enjoyment of freedom and the happiness of home, writing this Narrative, been confined in the galling chains of slavery. Going to live at Baltimore laid the foundation, and opened the gateway, to all my subsequent prosperity. I have ever regarded it as the first plain manifestation of that kind providence which has ever since attended me, and marked my life with so many favors. I regarded the selection of myself as being somewhat remarkable. There were a number of slave children that might have been sent from the plantation to Baltimore. There were those younger, those older, and those of the same age. I was chosen from among them all, and was the first, last, and only choice.

I may be deemed superstitious, and even egotistical, in regarding this event as a special interposition of divine Providence in my favor. But I should be false to the earliest sentiments of my soul, if I suppressed the opinion. I prefer to be true to myself, even at the hazard of incurring the ridicule of others, rather than to be false, and incur my own abhorrence. From my earliest recollection, I date the entertainment of a deep conviction that slavery would not always be able to hold me within its foul embrace; and in the darkest hours of my career in slavery, this living word of faith and spirit of hope departed not from me, but remained like ministering angels to cheer me through the gloom. This good spirit was from God, and to him I offer thanksgiving and praise.

CHAPTER VI.

My new mistress proved to be all she appeared when I first met her at the door,—a woman of the kindest heart and finest feelings. She had never had a slave under her control previously to myself, and prior to her marriage she had been dependent upon her own industry for a living. She was by trade a weaver; and by constant application to her business, she had been in a good degree preserved from the blighting and dehumanizing effects of slavery. I was utterly astonished at her goodness. I scarcely knew how to behave towards her. She was entirely unlike any other white woman I had ever seen. I could not approach her as I was accustomed to approach other white ladies. My early instruction was all out of place. The crouching servility, usually so acceptable a quality in a slave, did not answer when manifested toward her. Her favor was not gained by it; she seemed to be disturbed by it. She did not deem it impudent or unmannerly for a slave to look her in the face. The meanest slave was put fully at ease in her presence, and none left without feeling better for having seen her. Her face was made of heavenly smiles, and her voice of tranquil music.

But, alas! this kind heart had but a short time to remain such. The fatal poison of irresponsible power was already in her hands, and soon commenced its infernal work. That cheerful eye, under the influence of slavery, soon became red with rage; that voice, made all of sweet accord, changed to one of harsh and horrid discord; and that angelic face gave place to that of a demon.

Very soon after I went to live with Mr. and Mrs. Auld, she very kindly commenced to teach me the A, B, C. After I had learned this, she assisted me in learning to spell words of three or four letters. Just at this point of my progress, Mr. Auld found out what was going on, and at once forbade Mrs. Auld to instruct me further, telling her, among other things, that it was unlawful, as well as unsafe, to teach a slave to read. To use his own words, further, he said, "If you give a nigger an inch, he will take an ell. A nigger should know nothing but to obey his master—to do as he is told to do. Learning would *spoil* the best nigger in the world. Now," said he, "if you teach that nigger (speaking of myself) how to read, there would be no keeping him. It would forever unfit him to be a slave. He would at once become unmanageable, and of no value to his master. As to himself, it could do him no good, but a great deal of harm. It would make him discontented and unhappy." These words sank deep into my heart, stirred up sentiments within that lay slumbering, and called into existence an entirely new train of thought. It was a new and special revelation, explaining dark and mysterious things, with which my youthful understanding had struggled, but struggled in vain. I now understood what had been to me a most perplexing difficulty—to wit, the white man's power to enslave the black man. It was a grand achievement, and I prized it highly. From that moment, I understood the pathway from slavery to freedom. It was just what I wanted, and I got it at a time when I the least expected it. Whilst I was saddened by the thought of losing the aid of my kind mistress, I was gladdened by the invaluable instruction which, by the merest accident, I had gained from my master. Though conscious of the difficulty of learning without a teacher, I set out with high hope, and a fixed purpose, at whatever cost of trouble, to learn how to read. The very decided manner with which he spoke, and strove to impress his wife with the evil consequences of giving me instruction, served to convince me that he was deeply sensible of the truths he was uttering. It gave me the best assurance that I might rely with the utmost confidence on the results which, he said, would flow from teaching me to read. What he most dreaded, that I most desired. What he most loved, that I most hated. That which to him was a great evil, to be carefully shunned, was to me a great good, to be diligently sought; and the argument which he so warmly urged, against my learning to read, only served to inspire me with a desire and determination to learn. In learning to read, I owe almost as much to the bitter opposition of my master, as to the kindly aid of my mistress. I acknowledge the benefit of both.

I had resided but a short time in Baltimore before I observed a marked difference, in the treatment of slaves, from that which I had witnessed in the country. A city slave is almost a freeman, compared with a slave on the plantation. He is much better fed and clothed, and enjoys privileges altogether unknown to the slave on the plantation. There is a vestige of decency, a sense of shame, that does much to curb and check those outbreaks of atrocious cruelty so commonly enacted upon the plantation. He is a desperate slaveholder, who will shock the humanity of his nonslaveholding neighbors with the cries of his lacerated slave. Few are willing to incur the odium attaching to the reputation of being a cruel master; and above all things, they would not be known as not giving a slave enough to eat. Every city slaveholder is anxious to have it known of him, that he feeds his slaves well; and it is due to them to say, that most of them do give their slaves enough to eat. There are, however, some painful exceptions to this rule. Directly opposite to us, on Philpot Street, lived Mr. Thomas Hamilton. He owned two slaves. Their names were Henrietta and Mary. Henrietta was about twenty-two years of age, Mary was about fourteen; and of all the mangled and emaciated creatures I ever looked upon, these two were the most so. His heart must be harder than stone, that could look upon these unmoved. The head, neck, and shoulders of Mary were literally cut to pieces. I have frequently felt her head, and found its nearly covered with festering sores, caused by the lash of her cruel mistress. I do not know that her master ever whipped her, but I have been an eye-witness to the cruelty of Mrs. Hamilton. I used to be in Mr. Hamilton's house nearly every day. Mrs. Hamilton used to sit in a large chair in the middle of the room, with a heavy cowskin always by her side, and scarce an hour passed during the day but was marked by the blood of one of these slaves. The girls seldom passed her without her saying, "Move faster, you *black gip!*" at the same time giving them a blow with the cowskin over the head or shoulders, often drawing the blood. She would then say, "Take that, *you black gip!*"—continuing, "If you don't move faster, I'll move you!" Added to the cruel lashings to which these slaves were subjected, they were kept nearly half-starved. They seldom knew what it was to eat a full meal. I have seen Mary contending with the pigs for the offal thrown into the street. So much was Mary kicked and cut to pieces, that she was oftener called *"pecked"* than by her name.

CHAPTER VII.

I LIVED in Master Hugh's family about seven years. During this time, I succeeded in learning to read and write. In accomplishing this, I was compelled to resort to various stratagems. I had no regular teacher. My mistress, who had kindly commenced to instruct me, had, in compliance with the advice and direction of her husband, not only ceased to instruct, but had set her face against my being instructed by any one else. It is due, however, to my mistress to say of her, that she did not adopt this course of treatment immediately. She at first lacked the depravity indispensable to shutting me up in mental darkness. It was at least necessary for her to have some training in the exercise of irresponsible power, to make her equal to the task of treating me as though I were a brute.

My mistress was, as I have said, a kind and tenderhearted woman; and in the simplicity of her soul she commenced, when I first went to live with her, to treat me as she supposed one human being ought to treat another. In entering upon the duties of a slaveholder, she did not seem to perceive that I sustained to her the relation of a mere chattel, and that for her to treat me as a human being was not only wrong, but dangerously so. Slavery proved as injurious to her as it did to me. When I went there, she was a pious, warm, and tender-hearted woman. There was no sorrow or suffering for which she had not a tear. She had bread for the hungry, clothes for the naked, and comfort for every mourner that came within her reach. Slavery soon proved its ability to divest her of these heavenly qualities. Under its influence, the tender heart became stone, and the lamblike disposition gave way to one of tiger-like fierceness. The first step in her downward course was in her ceasing to instruct me. She now commenced to practise her husband's precepts. She finally became even more violent in her opposition than her husband himself. She was not satisfied with simply doing as well as he had commanded; she seemed anxious to do better. Nothing seemed to make her more angry than to see me with a newspaper. She seemed to think that here lay the danger. I have had her rush at me with a face made all up of fury, and snatch from me a newspaper, in a manner that fully revealed her apprehension. She was an apt woman; and a little experience soon demonstrated, to her satisfaction, that education and slavery were incompatible with each other.

From this time I was most narrowly watched. If I was in a separate room any considerable length of time, I was sure to be suspected of having a book, and was at once called to give an account of myself. All this, however, was too late. The first step had been taken. Mistress, in teaching me the alphabet, had given me the *inch,* and no precaution could prevent me from taking the *ell.*

The plan which I adopted, and the one by which I was most successful, was that of making friends of all the little white boys whom I met in the street. As many of these as I could, I converted into teachers. With their kindly aid, obtained at different times and in different places, I finally succeeded in learning to read. When I was sent of errands, I always took my book with me, and by going one part of my errand quickly, I found time to get a lesson before my return. I used also to carry bread with me, enough of which was always in the house, and to which I was always welcome; for I was much better off in this regard than many of the poor white children in our neighborhood. This bread I used to bestow upon the hungry little urchins, who, in return, would give me that more valuable bread of knowledge. I am strongly tempted to give the names of two or three of those little boys, as a testimonial of the gratitude and affection I bear them; but prudence forbids;—not that it would injure me, but it might embarrass them; for it is almost an unpardonable offence to teach slaves to read in this Christian country. It is enough to say of the dear little fellows, that they lived on Philpot Street, very near Durgin and Bailey's ship-yard. I used to talk this matter of slavery over with them. I would sometimes say to them, I wished I could be as free as they would be when they got to be men. "You will be free as soon as you are twenty-one, *but I am a slave for life!* Have not I as good a right to be free as you have?" These words used to trouble them; they would express for me the liveliest sympathy, and console me with the hope that something would occur by which I might be free.

I was now about twelve years old, and the thought of being *a slave for life* began to bear heavily upon my heart. Just about this time, I got hold of a book entitled "The Columbian Orator." Every opportunity I got, I used to read this book. Among much of other interesting matter, I found in it a dialogue between a master and his slave. The slave was represented as having run away from his master three times. The dialogue represented the conversation which took place between them, when the slave was retaken the third time. In this dialogue, the whole argument in behalf of slavery was brought forward by the master, all of which was disposed of by the slave. The slave was made to say some very smart as well as impressive things in reply to his master—things which had the desired though unexpected effect; for the conversation resulted in the voluntary emancipation of the slave on the part of the master.

In the same book, I met with one of Sheridan's mighty speeches on and in behalf of Catholic emancipation. These were choice documents to me. I read them over and over again with unabated interest. They gave tongue to interesting thoughts of my own soul, which had frequently flashed through my mind, and died away for want of utterance. The moral which I gained from the dialogue was the power of truth over the conscience of even a slaveholder. What I got from Sheridan was a bold denunciation of slavery, and a powerful vindication of human rights. The reading of these documents enabled me to utter my thoughts, and to meet the arguments brought forward to sustain slavery; but while they relieved me of one difficulty, they brought on another even more painful than the one of which I was relieved. The more I read, the more I was led to abhor and detest my enslavers. I could regard them in no other light than a band of successful robbers, who had left their homes, and gone to Africa, and stolen us from our homes, and in a strange land reduced us to slavery. I loathed them as being the meanest as well as the most wicked of men. As I read and contemplated the subject, behold! that very discontentment which Master Hugh had predicted would follow my learning to read had already come, to torment and sting my soul to unutterable anguish. As I writhed under it, I would at times feel that learning to read had been a curse rather than a blessing. It had given me a view of my wretched condition, without the remedy. It opened my eyes to the horrible pit, but to no ladder upon which to get out. In moments of agony, I envied my fellow-slaves for their stupidity, I have often wished myself a beast. I preferred the condition of the meanest reptile to my own. Any thing, no matter what, to get rid of thinking! It was this everlasting thinking of my condition that tormented me. There was no getting rid of it. It was pressed upon me by every object within sight or hearing, animate or inanimate. The silver trump of freedom had roused my soul to eternal wakefulness. Freedom now appeared, to disappear no more forever. It was heard in every sound, and seen in every thing. It was ever present to torment me with a sense of my wretched condition. I saw nothing without seeing it, I heard nothing without hearing it, and felt nothing without feeling it. It looked from every star, it smiled in every calm, breathed in every wind, and moved in every storm.

I often found myself regretting my own existence, and wishing myself dead; and but for the hope of being free, I have no doubt but that I should have killed myself, or done something for which I should have been killed. While in this state of mind, I was eager to hear any one speak of slavery. I was a ready listener. Every little while, I could hear something about the abolitionists. It was some time before I found what the word meant. It was always used in such connections as to make it an interesting word to me. If a slave ran away and succeeded in getting clear, or if a slave killed his master, set fire to a barn, or did any thing very wrong in the mind of a slaveholder, it was spoken of as the fruit of *abolition*. Hearing the word in this connection very often, I set about learning what it meant. The dictionary afforded me little or no help. I found it was "the act of abolishing;" but then I did not know what was to be abolished. Here I was perplexed. I did not dare to ask any one about its meaning, for I was satisfied that it was something they wanted me to know very little about. After a patient waiting, I got one of our city papers, containing an account of the number of petitions from the north, praying for the abolition of slavery in the District of Columbia, and of the slave trade between the States. From this time I understood the words *abolition* and *abolitionist,* and always drew near when that word was spoken, expecting to hear something of importance to myself and fellow-slaves. The light broke in upon me by degrees. I went one day down on the wharf of Mr. Waters; and seeing two Irishmen unloading a scow of stone, I went, unasked, and helped them. When we had finished, one of them came to me and asked me if I were a slave. I told him I was. He asked, "Are ye a slave for life?" I told him that I was. The good Irishman seemed to be deeply affected by the statement. He said to the other that it was a pity so fine a little fellow as myself should be a slave for life. He said it was a shame to hold me. They both advised me to run away to the north; that I should find friends there, and that I should be free. I pretended not to be interested in what they said, and treated them as if I did not understand them; for I feared they might be treacherous. White men have been known to encourage slaves to escape, and then, to get the reward, catch them and return them to their masters. I was afraid that these seemingly good men might use me so; but I nevertheless remembered their advice, and from that time

I resolved to run away. I looked forward to a time at which it would be safe for me to escape. I was too young to think of doing so immediately; besides, I wished to learn how to write, as I might have occasion to write my own pass. I consoled myself with the hope that I should one day find a good chance. Meanwhile, I would learn to write.

The idea as to how I might learn to write was suggested to me by being in Durgin and Bailey's ship-yard, and frequently seeing the ship carpenters, after hewing, and getting a piece of timber ready for use, write on the timber the name of that part of the ship for which it was intended. When a piece of timber was intended for the larboard side, it would be marked thus—"L." When a piece was for the starboard side, it would be marked thus—"S." A piece for the larboard side forward, would be marked thus—"L. F." When a piece was for starboard side forward, it would be marked thus—"S. F." For larboard aft, it would be marked thus—"L. A." For starboard aft, it would be marked thus— "S.A." I soon learned the names of these letters, and for what they were intended when placed upon a piece of timber in the ship-yard. I immediately commenced copying them, and in a short time was able to make the four letters named. After that, when I met with any boy who I knew could write, I would tell him I could write as well as he. The next word would be, "I don't believe you. Let me see you try it." I would then make the letters which I had been so fortunate as to learn, and ask him to beat that. In this way I got a good many lessons in writing, which it is quite possible I should never have gotten in any other way. During this time, my copy-book was the board fence, brick wall, and pavement; my pen and ink was a lump of chalk. With these, I learned mainly how to write. I then commenced and continued copying the Italics in Webster's Spelling Book, until I could make them all without looking on the book. By this time, my little Master Thomas had gone to school, and learned how to write, and had written over a number of copybooks. These had been brought home, and shown to some of our near neighbors, and then laid aside. My mistress used to go to class meeting at the Wilk Street meeting-house every Monday afternoon, and leave me to take care of the house. When left thus, I used to spend the time in writing in the spaces left in Master Thomas's copy-book, copying what he had written. I continued to do this until I could write a hand very similar to that of Master Thomas. Thus, after a long, tedious effort for years, I finally succeeded in learning how to write.

CHAPTER VIII.

In a very short time after I went to live at Baltimore, my old master's youngest son Richard died; and in about three years and six months after his death, my old master, Captain Anthony, died, leaving only his son, Andrew, and daughter, Lucretia, to share his estate. He died while on a visit to see his daughter at Hillsborough. Cut off thus unexpectedly, he left no will as to the disposal of his property. It was therefore necessary to have a valuation of the property, that it might be equally divided between Mrs. Lucretia and Master Andrew. I was immediately sent for, to be valued with the other property. Here again my feelings rose up in detestation of slavery. I had now a new conception of my degraded condition. Prior to this, I had become, if not insensible to my lot, at least partly so. I left Baltimore with a young heart overborne with sadness, and a soul full of apprehension. I took passage with Captain Rowe, in the schooner Wild Cat, and, after a sail of about twenty-four hours, I found myself near the place of my birth. I had now been absent from it almost, if not quite, five years. I, however, remembered the place very well. I was only about five years old when I left it, to go and live with my old master on Colonel Lloyd's plantation; so that I was now between ten and eleven years old.

We were all ranked together at the valuation. Men and women, old and young, married and single, were ranked with horses, sheep, and swine. There were horses and men, cattle and women, pigs and children, all holding the same rank in the scale of being, and were all subjected to the same narrow examination. Silvery-headed age and sprightly youth, maids and matrons, had to undergo the same indelicate inspection. At this moment, I saw more clearly than ever the brutalizing effects of slavery upon both slave and slaveholder.

After the valuation, then came the division. I have no language to express the high excitement and deep anxiety which were felt among us poor slaves during this time. Our fate for life was now to be decided. We had no more voice in that decision than the brutes among whom we were ranked. A single word from the white men was enough— against all our wishes, prayers, and entreaties—to sunder forever the dearest friends, dearest kindred, and strongest ties known to human beings. In addition to the pain of separation, there was the horrid dread of falling into the hands of Master Andrew. He was known to us all as being a most cruel wretch,—a common drunkard, who had, by his reckless mismanagement and profligate dissipation, already wasted a large portion of his father's property. We all felt that we might as well be sold at once to the Georgia traders, as to pass into his hands; for we knew that that would be our inevitable condition,—a condition held by us all in the utmost horror and dread.

I suffered more anxiety than most of my fellow-slaves. I had known what it was to be kindly treated; they had known nothing of the kind. They had seen little or nothing of the world. They were in very deed men and women of sorrow, and acquainted with grief. Their backs had been made familiar with the bloody lash, so that they had become callous; mine was yet tender; for while at Baltimore I got few whippings, and few slaves could boast of a kinder master and mistress than myself; and the thought of passing out of their hands into those of Master Andrew—a man who, but a few days before, to give me a sample of his bloody disposition, took my little brother by the throat, threw him on the ground, and with the heel of his boot stamped upon his head till the blood gushed from his nose and ears—was well calculated to make me anxious as to my fate. After he had committed this savage outrage upon my brother, he turned to me, and said that was the way he meant to serve me one of these days,—meaning, I suppose, when I came into his possession.

Thanks to a kind Providence, I fell to the portion of Mrs. Lucretia, and was sent immediately back to Baltimore, to live again in the family of Master Hugh. Their joy at my return equalled their sorrow at my departure. It was a glad day to me. I had escaped a [fate] worse than lion's jaws. I was absent from Baltimore, for the purpose of valuation and division, just about one month, and it seemed to have been six.

Very soon after my return to Baltimore, my mistress, Lucretia, died, leaving her husband and one child, Amanda; and in a very short time after her death, Master Andrew died. Now all the property of my old master, slaves included, was in the hands of strangers,—strangers who had had nothing to do with accumulating it. Not a slave was left free. All remained slaves, from the youngest to the oldest. If any one thing in my experience, more than another, served to deepen my conviction of the infernal character of slavery, and to fill me with unutterable loathing of slaveholders, it was their base ingratitude to my poor old grandmother. She had served my old master faithfully from youth to old age. She had been the source of all his wealth; she had peopled his plantation with slaves; she had become a great-grandmother in his service. She had rocked him in infancy, attended him in childhood, served him through life, and at his death wiped from his icy brow the cold death-sweat, and closed his eyes forever. She was nevertheless left a slave—a slave for life—a slave in the hands of strangers; and in their hands she saw her children, her grandchildren, and her great-grandchildren, divided, like so many sheep, without being gratified with the small privilege of a single word, as to their or her own destiny. And, to cap the climax of their base ingratitude and fiendish barbarity, my grandmother, who was now very old, having outlived my old master and all his children, having seen the beginning and end of all of them, and her present owners finding she was of but little value, her frame already racked with the pains of old age, and complete helplessness fast stealing over her once active limbs, they took her to the woods, built her a little hut, put up a little mud-chimney, and then made her welcome to the privilege of supporting herself there in perfect loneliness; thus virtually turning her out to die! If my poor old grandmother now lives, she lives to suffer in utter loneliness; she lives to remember and mourn over the loss of children, the loss of grandchildren, and the loss of great-grandchildren. They are, in the language of the slave's poet, Whittier,—

> Gone, gone, sold and gone
> To the rice swamp dank and lone,
> Where the slave-whip ceaseless swings,
> Where the noisome insect stings,
> Where the fever-demon strews
> Poison with the falling dews,
> Where the sickly sunbeams glare
> Through the hot and misty air:
>> Gone, gone, sold and gone
>> To the rice swamp—dank and lone,
>> From Virginia hills and waters—
>> Woe is me, my stolen daughters

The hearth is desolate. The children, the unconscious children, who once sang and danced in her presence, are gone. She gropes her way, in the darkness of age, for a drink of water. Instead of the voices of her children, she hears by day the moans of the dove, and by night the screams of the hideous owl. All is gloom. The grave is at the door. And now, when weighed down by the pains and aches of old age, when the head inclines to the feet, when the beginning and ending of human existence meet, and helpless infancy and painful old age combine together—at this time, this most needful time, the time for the exercise of that tenderness and affection which children only can exercise towards a declining parent—my poor old grandmother, the devoted mother of twelve children, is left all alone, in yonder little hut, before a few dim embers. She stands—she sits—she staggers—she falls—she groans—she dies—and there are none of her children or grandchildren present, to wipe from her wrinkled brow the cold sweat of death, or to place beneath the sod her fallen remains. Will not a righteous God visit for these things?

In about two years after the death of Mrs. Lucretia, Mas-

ter Thomas married his second wife. Her name was Rowena
Hamilton. She was the eldest daughter of Mr. William
Hamilton. Master now lived in St. Michael's. Not long after
his marriage, a misunderstanding took place between himself and Master Hugh; and as a means of punishing his
brother, he took me from him to live with himself at St.
Michael's. Here I underwent another most painful separation. It, however, was not so severe as the one I dreaded at
the division of property; for, during this interval, a great
change had taken place in Master Hugh and his once kind
and affectionate wife. The influence of brandy upon him,
and of slavery upon her, had effected a disastrous change in
the characters of both; so that, as far as they were concerned, I thought I had little to lose by the change. But it
was not to them that I was attached. It was to those little
Baltimore boys that I felt the strongest attachment. I had
received many good lessons from them, and was still receiving them, and the thought of leaving them was painful indeed. I was leaving, too, without the hope of ever being
allowed to return. Master Thomas had said he would never
let me return again. The barrier betwixt himself and brother
he considered impassable.

I then had to regret that I did not at least make the attempt to carry out my resolution to run away; for the
chances of success are tenfold greater from the city than
from the country.

I sailed from Baltimore for St. Michael's in the sloop
Amanda, Captain Edward Dodson. On my passage, I paid
particular attention to the direction which the steamboats
took to go to Philadelphia. I found, instead of going down,
on reaching North Point they went up the bay, in a north-
easterly direction. I deemed this knowledge of the utmost
importance. My determination to run away was again revived. I resolved to wait only so long as the offering of a
favorable opportunity. When that came, I was determined
to be off.

CHAPTER IX.

I HAVE now reached a period of my life when I can give dates. I left Baltimore, and went to live with Master Thomas Auld, at St. Michael's, in March, 1832. It was now more than seven years since I lived with him in the family of my old master, on Colonel Lloyd's plantation. We of course were now almost entire strangers to each other. He was to me a new master, and I to him a new slave. I was ignorant of his temper and disposition; he was equally so of mine. A very short time, however, brought us into full acquaintance with each other. I was made acquainted with his wife not less than with himself. They were well matched, being equally mean and cruel. I was now, for the first time during a space of more than seven years, made to feel the painful gnawings of hunger—a something which I had not experienced before since I left Colonel Lloyd's plantation. It went hard enough with me then, when I could look back to no period at which I had enjoyed a sufficiency. It was tenfold harder after living in Master Hugh's family, where I had always had enough to eat, and of that which was good. I have said Master Thomas was a mean man. He was so. Not to give a slave enough to eat, is regarded as the most aggravated development of meanness even among slaveholders. The rule is, no matter how coarse the food, only let there be enough of it. This is the theory; and in the part of Maryland from which I came, it is the general practice,—though there are many exceptions. Master Thomas gave us enough of neither coarse nor fine food. There were four slaves of us in the kitchen—my sister Eliza, my aunt Priscilla, Henny, and myself; and we were allowed less than a half of a bushel of corn-meal per week, and very little else, either in the shape of meat or vegetables. It was not enough for us to subsist upon. We were therefore reduced to the wretched necessity of living at the expense of our neighbors. This we did by begging and stealing, whichever came handy in the time of need, the one being considered as legitimate as the other. A great many times have we poor creatures been nearly perishing with hunger, when food in abundance lay smouldering in the safe and smoke-house, and our pious mistress was aware of the fact; and yet that mistress and her husband would kneel every morning, and pray that God would bless them in basket and store!

Bad as all slaveholders are, we seldom meet one destitute of every element of character commanding respect. My master was one of this rare sort. I do not know of one single noble act ever performed by him. The leading trait in his character was meanness; and if there were any other element in his nature, it was made subject to this. He was mean; and, like most other mean men, he lacked the ability to conceal his meanness. Captain Auld was not born a slaveholder. He had been a poor man, master only of a Bay craft. He came into possession of all his slaves by marriage; and of all men, adopted slaveholders are the worst. He was cruel, but cowardly. He commanded without firmness. In the enforcement of his rules, he was at times rigid, and at times lax. At times, he spoke to his slaves with the firmness of Napoleon and the fury of a demon; at other times, he might well be mistaken for an inquirer who had lost his way. He did nothing of himself. He might have passed for a lion, but for his ears. In all things noble which he attempted, his own meanness shone most conspicuous. His airs, words, and actions were the airs, words, and actions of born slaveholders, and, being assumed, were awkward enough. He was not even a good imitator. He possessed all the disposition to deceive, but wanted the power. Having no resources within himself, he was compelled to be the copyist of many, and being such, he was forever the victim of inconsistency; and of consequence he was an object of contempt, and was held as such even by his slaves. The luxury of having slaves of his own to wait upon him was something new and unprepared for. He was a slaveholder without the ability to hold slaves. He found himself incapable of managing his slaves either by force, fear, or fraud. We seldom called him "master;" we generally called him "Captain Auld," and were hardly disposed to title him at all. I doubt not that our conduct had much to do with making him appear awkward, and of consequence fretful. Our want of reverence for him must have perplexed him greatly. He wished to have us call him master, but lacked the firmness necessary to command us to do so. His wife used to insist upon our calling him so, but to no purpose. In August, 1832, my master attended a Methodist camp-meeting held in the Bay-side, Talbot county, and there experienced religion. I indulged a faint hope that his conversion would lead him to emancipate his slaves, and that, if he did not do this, it would, at any rate, make him more kind and humane. I was disappointed in both these respects. It neither made him to be humane to his slaves, nor to emancipate them. If it had any effect on his character, it made him more cruel and hateful in all his ways; for I believe him to have been a much worse man after his conversion than before. Prior to his conversion, he relied upon his own depravity to shield and sustain him in his savage barbarity; but after his conversion, he found religious sanction and support for his slaveholding cruelty. He made the greatest pretensions to piety. His house was the house of prayer. He prayed morning, noon, and night. He very soon distinguished himself among his brethren, and was soon made a class-leader and exhorter. His activity in revivals was great, and he proved himself an instrument in the hands of the church in converting many souls. His house was the preachers' home. They used to take great pleasure in coming there to put up; for while he starved us, he stuffed them. We have had three or four preachers there at a time. The names of those who used to come most frequently while I lived there, were Mr. Storks, Mr. Ewery, Mr. Humphry, and Mr. Hickey. I have also seen Mr. George Cookman at our house. We slaves loved Mr. Cookman. We believed him to be a good man. We thought him instrumental in getting Mr. Samuel Harrison, a very rich slaveholder, to emancipate his slaves; and by some means got the impression that he was laboring to effect the emancipation of all the slaves. When he was at our house, we were sure to be called in to prayers. When the others were there, we were sometimes called in and sometimes not. Mr. Cookman took more notice of us than either of the other ministers. He could not come among us without betraying his sympathy for us, and, stupid as we were, we had the sagacity to see it.

While I lived with my master in St. Michael's, there was a white young man, a Mr. Wilson, who proposed to keep a Sabbath school for the instruction of such slaves as might be disposed to learn to read the New Testament. We met but three times, when Mr. West and Mr. Fairbanks, both class-leaders, with many others, came upon us with sticks and other missiles, drove us off, and forbade us to meet again. Thus ended our little Sabbath school in the pious town of St. Michael's.

I have said my master found religious sanction for his cruelty. As an example, I will state one of many facts going to prove the charge. I have seen him tie up a lame young woman, and whip her with a heavy cowskin upon her naked shoulders, causing the warm red blood to drip; and, in justification of the bloody deed, he would quote this passage of Scripture—"He that knoweth his master's will, and doeth it not, shall be beaten with many stripes."

Master would keep this lacerated young woman tied up in this horrid situation four or five hours at a time. I have known him to tie her up early in the morning, and whip her before breakfast; leave her, go to his store, return at dinner, and whip her again, cutting her in the places already made raw with his cruel lash. The secret of master's cruelty toward "Henny" is found in the fact of her being almost helpless. When quite a child, she fell into the fire, and burned herself horribly. Her hands were so burnt that she never got the use of them. She could do very little but bear heavy burdens. She was to master a bill of expense; and as he was a mean man, she was a constant offence to him. He seemed desirous of getting the poor girl out of existence. He gave her away once to his sister; but, being a poor gift, she was not disposed to keep her. Finally, my benevolent master, to use his own words, "set her adrift to take care of herself." Here was a recently-converted man, holding on upon the mother, and at the same time turning out her helpless child, to starve and die! Master Thomas was one of the many pious slaveholders who hold slaves for the very charitable purpose of taking care of them.

My master and myself had quite a number of differences. He found me unsuitable to his purpose. My city life, he said, had had a very pernicious effect upon me. It had almost ruined me for every good purpose, and fitted me for every thing which was bad. One of my greatest faults was that of letting his horse run away, and go down to his father-in-law's farm, which was about five miles from St. Michael's. I would then have to go after it. My reason for this kind of carelessness, or carefulness, was, that I could always get something to eat when I went there. Master William Hamilton, my master's father-in-law, always gave his slaves enough to eat. I never left there hungry, no matter how great the need of my speedy return. Master Thomas at length said he would stand it no longer. I had lived with him nine months, during which time he had given me a number of severe whippings, all to no good purpose. He resolved to put me out, as he said, to be broken; and, for this purpose, he let me for one year to a man named Edward Covey. Mr. Covey was a poor man, a farm-renter. He rented the place upon which he lived, as also the hands with which he tilled it. Mr. Covey had acquired a very high reputation for breaking young slaves, and this reputation was of immense value to him. It enabled him to get his farm tilled with much less expense to himself than he could have had it done without such a reputation. Some slaveholders thought it not much loss to allow Mr. Covey to have their slaves one year, for the sake of the training to which they were subjected, without any other compensation. He could hire young help with great ease, in consequence of this reputation. Added to the natural good qualities of Mr. Covey, he was a professor of religion—a pious soul—a member and a class-leader in the Methodist church. All of this added weight to his reputation as a "nigger-breaker." I was aware of all the facts, having been acquainted with them by a young man who had lived there. I nevertheless made the change gladly; for I was sure of getting enough to eat, which is not the smallest consideration to a hungry man.

CHAPTER X.

I LEFT Master Thomas's house, and went to live with Mr. Covey, on the 1st of January, 1833. I was now, for the first time in my life, a field hand. In my new employment, I found myself even more awkward than a country boy appeared to be in a large city. I had been at my new home but one week before Mr. Covey gave me a very severe whipping, cutting my back, causing the blood to run, and raising ridges on my flesh as large as my little finger. The details of this affair are as follows: Mr. Covey sent me, very early in the morning of one of our coldest days in the month of January, to the woods, to get a load of wood. He gave me a team of unbroken oxen. He told me which was the in-hand ox, and which the off-hand one. He then tied the end of a large rope around the horns of the in-hand ox, and gave me the other end of it, and told me, if the oxen started to run, that I must hold on upon the rope. I had never driven oxen before, and of course I was very awkward. I, however, succeeded in getting to the edge of the woods with little difficulty; but I had got a very few rods into the woods, when the oxen took fright, and started full tilt, carrying the cart against trees, and over stumps, in the most frightful manner. I expected every moment that my brains would be dashed out against the trees. After running thus for a considerable distance, they finally upset the cart, dashing it with great force against a tree, and threw themselves into a dense thicket. How I escaped death, I do not know. There I was, entirely alone, in a thick wood, in a place new to me. My cart was upset and shattered, my oxen were entangled among the young trees, and there was none to help me. After a long spell of effort, I succeeded in getting my cart righted, my oxen disentangled, and again yoked to the cart. I now proceeded with my team to the place where I had, the day before, been chopping wood, and loaded my cart pretty heavily, thinking in this way to tame my oxen. I then proceeded on my way home. I had now consumed one half of the day. I got out of the woods safely, and now felt out of danger. I stopped my oxen to open the woods gate; and just as I did so, before I could get hold of my ox-rope, the oxen again started, rushed through the gate, catching it between the wheel and the body of the cart, tearing it to pieces, and coming within a few inches of crushing me against the gate-post. Thus twice, in one short day, I escaped death by the merest chance. On my return, I told Mr. Covey what had happened, and how it happened. He ordered me to return to the woods again immediately. I did so, and he followed on after me. Just as I got into the woods, he came up and told me to stop my cart, and that he would teach me how to trifle away my time, and break gates. He then went to a large gum-tree, and with his axe cut three large switches, and, after trimming them up neatly with his pocket-knife, he ordered me to take off my clothes. I made him no answer, but stood with my clothes on. He repeated his order. I still made him no answer, nor did I move to strip myself. Upon this he rushed at me with the fierceness of a tiger, tore off my clothes, and lashed me till he had worn out his switches, cutting me so savagely as to leave the marks visible for a long time after. This whipping was the first of a number just like it, and for similar offences.

I lived with Mr. Covey one year. During the first six months, of that year, scarce a week passed without his whipping me. I was seldom free from a sore back. My awkwardness was almost always his excuse for whipping me. We were worked fully up to the point of endurance. Long before day we were up, our horses fed, and by the first approach of day we were off to the field with our hoes and ploughing teams. Mr. Covey gave us enough to eat, but scarce time to eat it. We were often less than five minutes taking our meals. We were often in the field from the first approach of day till its last lingering ray had left us, and at saving-fodder time, midnight often caught us in the field binding blades.

Covey would be out with us. The way he used to stand it, was this. He would spend the most of his afternoons in bed. He would then come out fresh in the evening, ready to urge us on with his words, example, and frequently with the whip. Mr. Covey was one of the few slaveholders who could and did work with his hands. He was a hard-working man. He knew by himself just what a man or a boy could do. There was no deceiving him. His work went on in his absence almost as well as in his presence; and he had the faculty of making us feel that he was ever present with us. This he did by surprising us. He seldom approached the spot where we were at work openly, if he could do it secretly. He always aimed at taking us by surprise. Such was his cunning, that we used to call him, among ourselves, "the snake." When we were at work in the cornfield, he would sometimes crawl on

his hands and knees to avoid detection, and all at once he
would rise nearly in our midst, and scream out, "Ha, ha!
Come, come! Dash on, dash on!" This being his mode of
attack, it was never safe to stop a single minute. His com-
ings were like a thief in the night. He appeared to us as
being ever at hand. He was under every tree, behind every
stump, in every bush, and at every window, on the plantation. He would sometimes mount his horse, as if bound to
St. Michael's, a distance of seven miles, and in half an hour
afterwards you would see him coiled up in the corner of the
wood-fence, watching every motion of the slaves. He would,
for this purpose, leave his horse tied up in the woods. Again,
he would sometimes walk up to us, and give us orders as
though he was upon the point of starting on a long journey,
turn his back upon us, and make as though he was going to
the house to get ready; and, before he would get half way
thither, he would turn short and crawl into a fence-corner,
or behind some tree, and there watch us till the going down
of the sun.

   Mr. Covey's *forte* consisted in his power to deceive. His
life was devoted to planning and perpetrating the grossest
deceptions. Every thing he possessed in the shape of learning or religion, he made conform to his disposition to deceive. He seemed to think himself equal to deceiving the
Almighty. He would make a short prayer in the morning,
and a long prayer at night; and, strange as it may seem, few
men would at times appear more devotional than he. The
exercises of his family devotions were always commenced
with singing; and, as he was a very poor singer himself, the
duty of raising the hymn generally came upon me. He
would read his hymn, and nod at me to commence. I would
at times do so; at others, I would not. My non-compliance
would almost always produce much confusion. To show
himself independent of me, he would start and stagger
through with his hymn in the most discordant manner. In
this state of mind, he prayed with more than ordinary spirit.
Poor man! such was his disposition, and success at deceiving, I do verily believe that he sometimes deceived himself
into the solemn belief, that he was a sincere worshipper of
the most high God; and this, too, at a time when he may be
said to have been guilty of compelling his woman slave to

commit the sin of adultery. The facts in the case are these: Mr. Covey was a poor man; he was just commencing in life; he was only able to buy one slave; and, shocking as is the fact, he bought her, as he said, for a *breeder*. This woman was named Caroline. Mr. Covey bought her from Mr. Thomas Lowe, about six miles from St. Michael's. She was a large, able-bodied woman, about twenty years old. She had already given birth to one child, which proved her to be just what he wanted. After buying her, he hired a married man of Mr. Samuel Harrison, to live with him one year; and him he used to fasten up with her every night! The result was, that, at the end of the year, the miserable woman gave birth to twins. At this result Mr. Covey seemed to be highly pleased, both with the man and the wretched woman. Such was his joy, and that of his wife, that nothing they could do for Caroline during her confinement was too good, or too hard, to be done. The children were regarded as being quite an addition to his wealth.

If at any one time of my life more than another, I was made to drink the bitterest dregs of slavery, that time was during the first six months of my stay with Mr. Covey. We were worked in all weathers. It was never too hot or too cold; it could never rain, blow, hail, or snow, too hard for us to work in the field. Work, work, work, was scarcely more the order of the day than of the night. The longest days were too short for him, and the shortest nights too long for him. I was somewhat unmanageable when I first went there, but a few months of this discipline tamed me. Mr. Covey succeeded in breaking me. I was broken in body, soul, and spirit. My natural elasticity was crushed, my intellect languished, the disposition to read departed, the cheerful spark that lingered about my eye died; the dark night of slavery closed in upon me; and behold a man transformed into a brute!

Sunday was my only leisure time. I spent this in a sort of beast-like stupor, between sleep and wake, under some large tree. At times I would rise up, a flash of energetic freedom would dart through my soul, accompanied with a faint beam of hope, that flickered for a moment, and then vanished. I sank down again, mourning over my wretched condition. I was sometimes prompted to take my life, and that of Covey, but was prevented by a combination of hope and fear. My sufferings on this plantation seem now like a dream rather than a stern reality.

Our house stood within a few rods of the Chesapeake Bay, whose broad bosom was ever white with sails from every quarter of the habitable globe. Those beautiful vessels, robed in purest white, so delightful to the eye of freemen, were to me so many shrouded ghosts, to terrify and torment me with thoughts of my wretched condition. I have often, in the deep stillness of a summer's Sabbath, stood all alone upon the lofty banks of that noble bay, and traced, with saddened heart and tearful eye, the countless number of sails moving off to the mighty ocean. The sight of these always affected me powerfully. My thoughts would compel utterance; and there, with no audience but the Almighty, I would pour out my soul's complaint, in my rude way, with an apostrophe to the moving multitude of ships:—

"You are loosed from your moorings, and are free; I am fast in my chains, and am a slave! You move merrily before the gentle gale, and I sadly before the bloody whip! You are freedom's swift-winged angels, that fly around the world; I am confined in bands of iron! O that I were free! O, that I were on one of your gallant decks, and under your protecting wing! Alas! betwixt me and you, the turbid waters roll. Go on, go on. O that I could also go! Could I but swim! If I could fly! O, why was I born a man, of whom to make a brute! The glad ship is gone; she hides in the dim distance. I am left in the hottest hell of unending slavery. O God, save me! God, deliver me! Let me be free! Is there any God? Why am I a slave? I will run away. I will not stand it. Get caught, or get clear, I'll try it. I had as well die with ague as the fever. I have only one life to lose. I had as well be killed running as die standing. Only think of it; one hundred miles straight north, and I am free! Try it? Yes! God helping me, I will. It cannot be that I shall live and die a slave. I will take to the water. This very bay shall yet bear me into freedom. The steamboats steered in a north-east course from North Point. I will do the same; and when I get to the head of the bay, I will turn my canoe adrift, and walk straight through Delaware into Pennsylvania. When I get there, I shall not be required to have a pass; I can travel without being disturbed. Let but the first opportunity offer, and, come what will, I am off. Meanwhile, I will try to bear up under the yoke. I am not the only slave in the world. Why should I fret? I can bear as much as any of them. Besides, I am but a boy, and all boys are bound to some one. It may be that my misery in slavery will only increase my happiness when I get free. There is a better day coming."

Thus I used to think, and thus I used to speak to myself; goaded almost to madness at one moment, and at the next reconciling myself to my wretched lot.

I have already intimated that my condition was much worse, during the first six months of my stay at Mr. Covey's, than in the last six. The circumstances leading to the change in Mr. Covey's course toward me form an epoch in my humble history. You have seen how a man was made a slave; you shall see how a slave was made a man. On one of the hottest days of the month of August, 1833, Bill Smith, William Hughes, a slave named Eli, and myself, were engaged in fanning wheat. Hughes was clearing the fanned wheat from before the fan, Eli was turning, Smith was feeding, and I was carrying wheat to the fan. The work was simple, requiring strength rather than intellect; yet, to one entirely unused to such work, it came very hard. About three o'clock of that day, I broke down; my strength failed me; I was seized with a violent aching of the head, attended with extreme dizziness; I trembled in every limb. Finding what was coming, I nerved myself up, feeling it would never do to stop work. I stood as long as I could stagger to the hopper with grain. When I could stand no longer, I fell, and felt as if held down by an immense weight. The fan of course stopped; every one had his own work to do; and no one could do the work of the other, and have his own go on at the same time.

Mr. Covey was at the house, about one hundred yards from the treading-yard where we were fanning. On hearing the fan stop, he left immediately, and came to the spot where we were. He hastily inquired what the matter was. Bill answered that I was sick, and there was no one to bring wheat to the fan. I had by this time crawled away under the side of the post and rail-fence by which the yard was enclosed, hoping to find relief by getting out of the sun. He then asked where I was. He was told by one of the hands.

He came to the spot, and, after looking at me awhile, asked me what was the matter. I told him as well as I could, for I scarce had strength to speak. He then gave me a savage kick in the side, and told me to get up. I tried to do so, but fell back in the attempt. He gave me another kick, and again told me to rise. I again tried, and succeeded in gaining my feet; but, stooping to get the tub with which I was feeding the fan, I again staggered and fell. While down in this situation, Mr. Covey took up the hickory slat with which Hughes had been striking off the half-bushel measure, and with it gave me a heavy blow upon the head, making a large wound, and the blood ran freely; and with this again told me to get up. I made no effort to comply, having now made up my mind to let him do his worst. In a short time after receiving this blow, my head grew better. Mr. Covey had now left me to my fate. At this moment I resolved, for the first time, to go to my master, enter a complaint, and ask his protection. In order to this, I must that afternoon walk seven miles; and this, under the circumstances, was truly a severe undertaking. I was exceedingly feeble; made so as much by the kicks and blows which I received, as by the severe fit of sickness to which I had been subjected. I, however, watched my chance, while Covey was looking in an opposite direction, and started for St. Michael's. I succeeded in getting a considerable distance on my way to the woods, when Covey discovered me, and called after me to come back, threatening what he would do if I did not come. I disregarded both his calls and his threats, and made my way to the woods as fast as my feeble state would allow; and thinking I might be overhauled by him if I kept the road, I walked through the woods, keeping far enough from the road to avoid detection, and near enough to prevent losing my way. I had not gone far before my little strength again failed me. I could go no farther. I fell down, and lay for a considerable time. The blood was yet oozing from the wound on my head. For a time I thought I should bleed to death; and think now that I should have done so, but that the blood so matted my hair as to stop the wound. After lying there about three quarters of an hour, I nerved myself up again, and started on my way, through bogs and briers, barefooted and bareheaded, tearing my feet sometimes at nearly every step; and after a journey of about seven miles, occupying some five hours to perform it, I arrived at master's store. I then presented an appearance enough to affect any but a heart of iron. From the crown of my head to my feet, I was covered with blood. My hair was all clotted with dust and blood; my shirt was stiff with blood. My legs and feet were torn in sundry places with briers and thorns, and were also covered with blood. I suppose I looked like a man who had escaped a den of wild beasts, and barely escaped them. In this state I appeared before my master, humbly entreating him to interpose his authority for my protection. I told him all the circumstances as well as I could, and it seemed, as I spoke, at times to affect him. He would then walk the floor, and seek to justify Covey by saying he expected I deserved it. He asked me what I wanted. I told him, to let me get a new home; that as sure as I lived with Mr. Covey again, I should live with but to die with him; that Covey would surely kill me; he was in a fair way for it. Master Thomas ridiculed the idea that there was any danger of Mr. Covey's killing me, and said that he knew Mr. Covey; that he was a good man, and that he could not think of taking me from him; that, should he do so, he would lose the whole year's wages; that I belonged to Mr. Covey for one year, and that I must go back to him, come what might; and that I must not trouble him with any more stories, or that he would himself *get hold of me.* After threatening me thus, he gave me a very large dose of salts, telling me that I might remain in St. Michael's that night, (it being quite late,) but that I must be off back to Mr. Covey's early in the morning; and that if I did not, he would *get hold of me*, which meant that he would whip me. I remained all night, and, according to his orders, I started off to Covey's in the morning, (Saturday morning,) wearied in body and broken in spirit. I got no supper that night, or breakfast that morning. I reached Covey's about nine o'clock; and just as I was getting over the fence that divided Mrs. Kemp's fields from ours, out ran Covey with his cowskin, to give me another whipping. Before he could reach me, I succeeded in getting to the cornfield; and as the corn was very high, it afforded me the means of hiding. He seemed very angry, and searched for me a long time. My behavior was altogether unaccountable. He finally gave up the chase, thinking, I suppose, that I must come home for something to eat; he would give himself no further trouble in looking for me. I spent that day mostly in the woods, having the alternative before me,—to go home and be whipped to death, or stay in the woods and be starved to death. That night, I fell in with Sandy Jenkins, a slave with whom I was somewhat acquainted. Sandy had a free wife who lived about four miles from Mr. Covey's; and it being Saturday, he was on his way to see her. I told him my circumstances, and he very kindly invited me to go home with him. I went home with him, and talked this whole matter over, and got his advice as to what course it was best for me to pursue. I found Sandy an old adviser. He told me, with great solemnity, I must go back to Covey; but that before I went, I must go with him into another part of the woods, where there was a certain *root*, which, if I would take some of it with me, carrying it *always on my right side*, would render it impossible for Mr. Covey, or any other white man, to whip me. He said he had carried it for years; and since he had done so, he had never received a blow, and never expected to while he carried it. I at first rejected the idea, that the simple carrying of a root in my pocket would have any such effect as he had said, and was not disposed to take it; but Sandy impressed the necessity with much earnestness, telling me it could do no harm, if it did no good. To please him, I at length took the root, and, according to his direction, carried it upon my right side. This was Sunday morning. I immediately started for home; and upon entering the yard gate, out came Mr. Covey on his way to meeting. He spoke to me very kindly, bade me drive the pigs from a lot near by, and passed on towards the church. Now, this singular conduct of Mr. Covey really made me begin to think that there was something in the *root* which Sandy had given me; and had it been on any other day than Sunday, I could have attributed the conduct to no other cause than the influence of that root; and as it was, I was half inclined to think the *root* to be something more than I at first had taken it to be. All went well till Monday morning. On this morning, the virtue of the *root* was fully tested. Long before daylight, I was called to go and rub, curry, and feed, the horses. I obeyed, and was glad to obey. But whilst thus engaged, whilst in the act of throwing down some blades from the loft, Mr. Covey entered the stable with a long rope; and just as I was half out of the loft, he caught hold of my legs, and was about tying me. As soon as I found what he was up to, I gave a sudden spring, and as I did so, he holding to my legs, I was brought sprawling on the stable floor. Mr. Covey seemed now to think he had me, and could do what he pleased; but at this moment—from whence came the spirit I don't know—I resolved to fight; and, suiting my action to the resolution, I seized Covey hard by the throat; and as I did so, I rose. He held on to me, and I to him. My resistance was so entirely unexpected, that Covey seemed taken all aback. He trembled like a leaf. This gave me assurance, and I held him uneasy, causing the blood to run where I touched him with the ends of my fingers. Mr. Covey soon called out to Hughes for help. Hughes came, and, while Covey held me, attempted to tie my right hand. While he was in the act of doing so, I watched my chance, and gave him a heavy kick close under the ribs. This kick fairly sickened Hughes, so that he left me in the hands of Mr. Covey. This kick had the effect of not only weakening Hughes, but Covey also. When he saw Hughes bending over with pain, his courage quailed. He asked me if I meant to persist in my resistance. I told him I did, come what might; that he had used me like a brute for six months, and that I was determined to be used so no longer. With that, he strove to drag me to a stick that was lying just out of the stable door. He meant to knock me down. But just as he was leaning over to get the stick, I seized him with both hands by his collar, and brought him by a sudden snatch to the ground. By this time, Bill came. Covey called upon him for assistance. Bill wanted to know what he could do. Covey said, "Take hold of him, take hold of him!" Bill said his master hired him out to work, and not to help to whip me; so he left Covey and myself to fight our own battle out. We were at it for nearly two hours. Covey at length let me go, puffing and blowing at a great rate, saying that if I had not resisted, he would not have whipped me half so much. The truth was, that he had not whipped me at all. I considered him as getting entirely the worst end of the bargain; for he had drawn no blood from me, but I had from him. The whole six months afterwards, that I spent with Mr. Covey, he never laid the weight of his finger upon me in anger. He would occasionally say, he didn't want to get hold of me again. "No," thought I, "you need not; for you will come off worse than you did before."

This battle with Mr. Covey was the turning-point in my career as a slave. It rekindled the few expiring embers of freedom, and revived within me a sense of my own manhood. It recalled the departed self-confidence, and inspired me again with a determination to be free. The gratification afforded by the triumph was a full compensation for whatever else might follow, even death itself. He only can understand the deep satisfaction which I experienced, who has himself repelled by force the bloody arm of slavery. I felt as I never felt before. It was a glorious resurrection, from the tomb of slavery, to the heaven of freedom. My long-crushed spirit rose, cowardice departed, bold defiance took its place; and I now resolved that, however long I might remain a slave in form, the day had passed forever when I could be a slave in fact. I did not hesitate to let it be known of me, that the white man who expected to succeed in whipping, must also succeed in killing me.

From this time I was never again what might be called fairly whipped, though I remained a slave four years afterwards. I had several fights, but was never whipped.

It was for a long time a matter of surprise to me why Mr. Covey did not immediately have me taken by the constable to the whipping-post, and there regularly whipped for the crime of raising my hand against a white man in defence of myself. And the only explanation I can now think of does not entirely satisfy me; but such as it is, I will give it. Mr. Covey enjoyed the most unbounded reputation for being a first-rate overseer and negro-breaker. It was of considerable importance to him. That reputation was at stake; and had he sent me—a boy about sixteen years old—to the public whipping-post, his reputation would have been lost; so, to save his reputation, he suffered me to go unpunished.

My term of actual service to Mr. Edward Covey ended on Christmas day, 1833. The days between Christmas and New Year's day are allowed as holidays; and, accordingly, we were not required to perform any labor, more than to feed and take care of the stock. This time we regarded as our own, by the grace of our masters; and we therefore used or abused it nearly as we pleased. Those of us who had families at a distance, were generally allowed to spend the whole six days in their society. This time, however, was spent in various ways. The staid, sober, thinking and industrious ones of our number would employ themselves in making corn-brooms, mats, horse-collars, and baskets; and another class of us would spend the time in hunting opossums, hares, and coons. But by far the larger part engaged in such sports and merriments as playing ball, wrestling, running foot-races, fiddling, dancing, and drinking whisky; and this latter mode of spending the time was by far the most agreeable to the feelings of our masters. A slave who would work during the holidays was considered by our masters as scarcely deserving them. He was regarded as one who rejected the favor of his master. It was deemed a disgrace not to get drunk at Christmas; and he was regarded as lazy indeed, who had not provided himself with the necessary means, during the year, to get whisky enough to last him through Christmas.

From what I know of the effect of these holidays upon the slave, I believe them to be among the most effective means in the hands of the slaveholder in keeping down the spirit of insurrection. Were the slaveholders at once to abandon this practice, I have not the slightest doubt it would lead to an immediate insurrection among the slaves. These holidays serve as conductors, or safety-valves, to carry off the rebellious spirit of enslaved humanity. But for these, the slave would be forced up to the wildest desperation; and woe betide the slaveholder, the day he ventures to remove or hinder the operation of those conductors! I warn him that, in such an event, a spirit will go forth in their midst, more to be dreaded than the most appalling earthquake.

The holidays are part and parcel of the gross fraud, wrong, and inhumanity of slavery. They are professedly a custom established by the benevolence of the slaveholders; but I undertake to say, it is the result of selfishness, and one of the grossest frauds committed upon the down-trodden slave. They do not give the slaves this time because they would not like to have their work during its continuance, but because they know it would be unsafe to deprive them of it. This will be seen by the fact, that the slaveholders like to have their slaves spend those days just in such a manner as to make them as glad of their ending as of their beginning. Their object seems to be, to disgust their slaves with freedom, by plunging them into the lowest depths of dissipation. For instance, the slaveholders not only like to see the slave drink of his own accord, but will adopt various plans to make him drunk. One plan is, to make bets on their slaves, as to who can drink the most whisky without getting drunk; and in this way they succeed in getting whole multitudes to drink to excess. Thus, when the slave asks for virtuous freedom, the cunning slaveholder, knowing his ignorance, cheats him with a dose of vicious dissipation, artfully labelled with the name of liberty. The most of us used to drink it down, and the result was just what might be supposed: many of us were led to think that there was little to choose between liberty and slavery. We felt, and very properly too, that we had almost as well be slaves to man as to rum. So, when the holidays ended, we staggered up from the filth of our wallowing, took a long breath, and marched to the field,—feeling, upon the whole, rather glad to go, from what our master had deceived us into a belief was freedom, back to the arms of slavery.

I have said that this mode of treatment is a part of the whole system of fraud and inhumanity of slavery. It is so. The mode here adopted to disgust the slave with freedom, by allowing him to see only the abuse of it, is carried out in other things. For instance, a slave loves molasses; he steals some. His master, in many cases, goes off to town, and buys a large quantity; he returns, takes his whip, and commands the slave to eat the molasses, until the poor fellow is made sick at the very mention of it. The same mode is sometimes adopted to make the slaves refrain from asking for more food than their regular allowance. A slave runs through his allowance, and applies for more. His master is enraged at him; but, not willing to send him off without food, gives him more than is necessary, and compels him to eat it within a given time. Then, if he complains that he cannot eat it, he is said to be satisfied neither full nor fasting, and is whipped for being hard to please! I have an abundance of such illustrations of the same principle, drawn from my own observation, but think the cases I have cited sufficient. The practice is a very common one.

On the first of January, 1834, I left Mr. Covey, and went to live with Mr. William Freeland, who lived about three miles from St. Michael's. I soon found Mr. Freeland a very different man from Mr. Covey. Though not rich, he was what would be called an educated southern gentleman. Mr. Covey, as I have shown, was a well-trained negro-breaker and slave-driver. The former (slaveholder though he was) seemed to possess some regard for honor, some reverence for justice, and some respect for humanity. The latter seemed totally insensible to all such sentiments. Mr. Freeland had many of the faults peculiar to slaveholders, such as being very passionate and fretful; but I must do him the justice to say, that he was exceedingly free from those degrading vices to which Mr. Covey was constantly addicted. The one was open and frank, and we always knew where to find him. The other was a most artful deceiver, and could be understood only by such as were skillful enough to detect his cunningly-devised frauds. Another advantage I gained in my new master was, he made no pretensions to, or profession of, religion; and this, in my opinion, was truly a great advantage. I assert most unhesitatingly, that the religion of the south is a mere covering for the most horrid crimes,—a justifier of the most appalling barbarity,—a sanctifier of the most hateful frauds,—and a dark shelter under which the darkest, foulest, grossest, and most infernal deeds of slaveholders find the strongest protection. Were I to be again reduced to the chains of slavery, next to that enslavement, I should regard being the slave of a religious master the greatest calamity that could befall me. For of all slaveholders with whom I have ever met, religious slaveholders are the worst. I have ever found them the meanest and basest, the most cruel and cowardly, of all others. It was my unhappy lot not only to belong to a religious slaveholder, but to live in a community of such religionists. Very near Mr. Freeland lived the Rev. Daniel Weeden, and in the same neighborhood lived the Rev. Rigby Hopkins. These were members and ministers in the Reformed Methodist Church. Mr. Weeden owned, among others, a woman slave, whose name I have forgotten. This woman's back, for weeks, was kept literally raw, made so by the lash of this merciless, *religious* wretch. He used to hire hands. His maxim was, Behave well or behave ill, it is the duty of a master occasionally to whip a slave, to remind him of his master's authority. Such was his theory, and such his practice.

Mr. Hopkins was even worse than Mr. Weeden. His chief boast was his ability to manage slaves. The peculiar feature of his government was that of whipping slaves in advance of deserving it. He always managed to have one or more of his slaves to whip every Monday morning. He did this to alarm their fears, and strike terror into those who escaped. His plan was to whip for the smallest offences, to prevent the commission of large ones. Mr. Hopkins could always find some excuse for whipping a slave. It would astonish one, unaccustomed to a slaveholding life, to see with what wonderful ease a slaveholder can find things, of which to make occasion to whip a slave. A mere look, word, or motion,—a mistake, accident, or want of power,—are all matters for which a slave may be whipped at any time. Does a slave look dissatisfied? It is said, he has the devil in him, and it must be whipped out. Does he speak loudly when spoken to by his master? Then he is getting high-minded, and should be taken down a button-hole lower. Does he forget to pull off his hat at the approach of a white person? Then he is wanting in reverence, and should be whipped for it. Does he ever venture to vindicate his conduct, when censured for it? Then he is guilty of impudence,—one of the greatest crimes of which a slave can be guilty. Does he ever venture to suggest a different mode of doing things from that pointed out by his master? He is indeed presumptuous, and getting above himself; and nothing less than a flogging will do for him. Does he, while ploughing, break a plough,—or, while hoeing, break a hoe? It is owing to his carelessness, and for it a slave must always be whipped. Mr. Hopkins could always find something of this sort to justify the use of the lash, and he seldom failed to embrace such opportunities. There was not a man in the whole county, with whom the slaves who had the getting their own home, would not prefer to live, rather than with this Rev. Mr. Hopkins. And yet there was not a man any where round, who made higher professions of religion, or was more active in revivals—more attentive to the class, love-feast, prayer and preaching meetings, or more devotional in his family,—that prayed earlier, later, louder, and longer,—than this same reverend slave-driver, Rigby Hopkins.

But to return to Mr. Freeland, and to my experience while in his employment. He, like Mr. Covey, gave us enough to eat; but, unlike Mr. Covey, he also gave us sufficient time to take our meals. He worked us hard, but always between sunrise and sunset. He required a good deal of work to be done, but gave us good tools with which to work. His farm was large, but he employed hands enough to work it, and with ease, compared with many of his neighbors. My treatment, while in his employment, was heavenly, compared with what I experienced at the hands of Mr. Edward Covey.

Mr. Freeland was himself the owner of but two slaves. Their names were Henry Harris and John Harris. The rest of his hands he hired. These consisted of myself, Sandy Jenkins,* and Handy Caldwell. Henry and John were quite intelligent, and in a very little while after I went there, I succeeded in creating in them a strong desire to learn how to read. This desire soon sprang up in the others also. They very soon mustered up some old spelling-books, and nothing would do but that I must keep a Sabbath school. I agreed to do so, and accordingly devoted my Sundays to teaching these my loved fellow-slaves how to read. Neither of them knew his letters when I went there. Some of the slaves of the neighboring farms found what was going on, and also availed themselves of this little opportunity to learn to read. It was understood, among all who came, that there must be as little display about it as possible. It was necessary to keep our religious masters at St. Michael's unacquainted with the fact, that, instead of spending the Sab-

---

*This is the same man who gave me the roots to prevent my being whipped by Mr. Covey. He was "a clever soul." We used frequently to talk about the fight with Covey, and as often as we did so, he would claim my success as the result of the roots which he gave me. This superstition is very common among the more ignorant slaves. A slave seldom dies but that his death is attributed to trickery.

bath in wrestling, boxing, and drinking whisky, we were trying to learn how to read the will of God; for they had much rather see us engaged in those degrading sports, than to see us behaving like intellectual, moral, and accountable beings. My blood boils as I think of the bloody manner in which Messrs. Wright Fairbanks and Garrison West, both class-leaders, in connection with many others, rushed in upon us with sticks and stones, and broke up our virtuous little Sabbath school, at St. Michael's—all calling themselves Christians! humble followers of the Lord Jesus Christ! But I am again digressing.

I held my Sabbath school at the house of a free colored man, whose name I deem it imprudent to mention; for should it be known, it might embarrass him greatly, though the crime of holding the school was committed ten years ago. I had at one time over forty scholars, and those of the right sort, ardently desiring to learn. They were of all ages, though mostly men and women. I look back to those Sundays with an amount of pleasure not to be expressed. They were great days to my soul. The work of instructing my dear fellow-slaves was the sweetest engagement with which I was ever blessed. We loved each other, and to leave them at the close of the Sabbath was a severe cross indeed. When I think that these precious souls are to-day shut up in the prison-house of slavery, my feelings overcome me, and I am almost ready to ask, "Does a righteous God govern the universe? and for what does he hold the thunders in his right hand, if not to smite the oppressor, and deliver the spoiled out of the hand of the spoiler?" These dear souls came not to Sabbath school because it was popular to do so, nor did I teach them because it was reputable to be thus engaged. Every moment they spent in that school, they were liable to be taken up, and given thirty-nine lashes. They came because they wished to learn. Their minds had been starved by their cruel masters. They had been shut up in mental darkness. I taught them, because it was the delight of my soul to be doing something that looked like bettering the condition of my race. I kept up my school nearly the whole year I lived with Mr. Freeland; and, beside my Sabbath school, I devoted three evenings in the week, during the winter, to teaching the slaves at home. And I have the happiness to know, that several of those who came to Sabbath school learned how to read; and that one, at least, is now free through my agency.

The year passed off smoothly. It seemed only about half as long as the year which preceded it. I went through it without receiving a single blow. I will give Mr. Freeland the credit of being the best master I ever had, *till I became my own master.* For the ease with which I passed the year, I was, however, somewhat indebted to the society of my fellow-slaves. They were noble souls; they not only possessed loving hearts, but brave ones. We were linked and inter-linked with each other. I loved them with a love stronger than any thing I have experienced since. It is sometimes said that we slaves do not love and confide in each other. In answer to this assertion, I can say, I never loved any or confided in any people more than my fellow-slaves, and especially those with whom I lived at Mr. Freeland's. I believe we would have died for each other. We never undertook to do any thing, of any importance, without a mutual consultation. We never moved separately. We were one; and as much so by our tempers and dispositions, as by the mutual hardships to which we were necessarily subjected by our condition as slaves.

At the close of the year 1834, Mr. Freeland again hired me of my master, for the year of 1835. But, by this time, I began to want to live *upon free land* as well as *with Freeland*; and I was no longer content, therefore, to live with him or any other slaveholder. I began, with the commencement of the year, to prepare myself for a final struggle, which should decide my fate one way or the other. My tendency was upward. I was fast approaching manhood, and year after year had passed, and I was still a slave. These thoughts roused me—I must do something. I therefore resolved that 1835 should not pass without witnessing an attempt, on my part, to secure my liberty. But I was not willing to cherish this determination alone. My fellow-slaves were dear to me. I was anxious to have them participate with me in this, my life-giving determination. I therefore, though with great prudence, commenced early to ascertain their views and feelings in regard to their condition, and to imbue their minds with thoughts of freedom. I bent myself to devising ways and means for our escape, and meanwhile strove, on all fitting occasions, to impress them with the gross fraud and inhumanity of slavery. I went first to Henry, next to John, then to the others. I found, in them all, warm hearts and noble spirits. They were ready to hear, and ready to act when a feasible plan should be proposed. This was what I wanted. I talked to them of our want of manhood, if we submitted to our enslavement without at least one noble effort to be free. We met often, and consulted frequently, and told our hopes and fears, recounted the difficulties, real and imagined, which we should be called on to meet. At times we were almost disposed to give up, and try to content ourselves with our wretched lot; at others, we were firm and unbending in our determination to go. Whenever we suggested any plan, there was shrinking—the odds were fearful. Our path was beset with the greatest obstacles; and if we succeeded in gaining the end of it, our right to be free was yet questionable—we were yet liable to be returned to bondage. We could see no spot, this side of the ocean, where we could be free. We knew nothing about Canada. Our knowledge of the north did not extend farther than New York; and to go there, and be forever harassed with the frightful liability of being returned to slavery—with the certainty of being treated tenfold worse than before—the thought was truly a horrible one, and one which it was not easy to overcome. The case sometimes stood thus: At every gate through which we were to pass, we saw a watchman—at every ferry a guard—on every bridge a sentinel—and in every wood a patrol. We were hemmed in upon every side. Here were the difficulties, real or imagined—the good to be sought, and the evil to be shunned. On the one hand, there stood slavery, a stern reality, glaring frightfully upon us,—its robes already crimsoned with the blood of millions, and even now feasting itself greedily upon our own flesh. On the other hand, away back in the dim distance, under the flickering light of the north star, behind some craggy hill or snow-covered mountain, stood a doubtful freedom—half frozen—beckoning us to come and share its hospitality. This in itself was sometimes enough to stagger us; but when we permitted ourselves to survey the road, we were frequently appalled. Upon either side we saw grim death, assuming the most horrid shapes. Now it was starvation, causing us to eat our own flesh;—now we were contending with the waves, and were drowned;—now we were overtaken, and torn to pieces by the fangs of the terrible bloodhound. We were stung by scorpions, chased by wild beasts, bitten by snakes, and finally, after having nearly reached the desired spot,— after swimming rivers, encountering wild beasts, sleeping in the woods, suffering hunger and nakedness,—we were overtaken by our pursuers, and, in our resistance, we were shot dead upon the spot! I say, this picture sometimes appalled us, and made us

> rather bear those ills we had,
> Than fly to others, that we knew not of.

In coming to a fixed determination to run away, we did more than Patrick Henry, when he resolved upon liberty or death. With us it was a doubtful liberty at most, and almost certain death if we failed. For my part, I should prefer death to hopeless bondage.

Sandy, one of our number, gave up the notion, but still encouraged us. Our company then consisted of Henry Harris, John Harris, Henry Bailey, Charles Roberts, and myself. Henry Bailey was my uncle, and belonged to my master. Charles married my aunt: he belonged to my master's father-in-law, Mr. William Hamilton.

The plan we finally concluded upon was, to get a large canoe belonging to Mr. Hamilton, and upon the Saturday night previous to Easter holidays, paddle directly up the Chesapeake Bay. On our arrival at the head of the bay, a distance of seventy or eighty miles from where we lived, it was our purpose to turn our canoe adrift, and follow the guidance of the north star till we got beyond the limits of Maryland. Our reason for taking the water route was, that we were less liable to be suspected as runaways; we hoped to be regarded as fishermen; whereas, if we should take the land route, we should be subjected to interruptions of almost every kind. Any one having a white face, and being so disposed, could stop us, and subject us to examination.

The week before our intended start, I wrote several protections, one for each of us. As well as I can remember, they were in the following words, to wit:—

This is to certify that I, the undersigned, have given the bearer, my servant, full liberty to go to Baltimore, and spend the Easter holidays. Written with mine own hand, &c., 1835.

WILLIAM HAMILTON,
Near St. Michael's, in Talbot county, Maryland.

We were not going to Baltimore; but, in going up the bay, we went toward Baltimore, and these protections were only intended to protect us while on the bay.

As the time drew near for our departure, our anxiety became more and more intense. It was truly a matter of life and death with us. The strength of our determination was about to be fully tested. At this time, I was very active in explaining every difficulty, removing every doubt, dispelling every fear, and inspiring all with the firmness indispensable to success in our undertaking; assuring them that half was gained the instant we made the move; we had talked long enough; we were now ready to move; if not now, we never should be; and if we did not intend to move now, we had as well fold our arms, sit down, and acknowledge ourselves fit only to be slaves. This, none of us were prepared to acknowledge. Every man stood firm; and at our last meeting, we pledged ourselves afresh, in the most solemn manner, that, at the time appointed, we would certainly start in pursuit of freedom. This was in the middle of the week, at the end of which we were to be off. We went, as usual, to our several fields of labor, but with bosoms highly agitated with thoughts of our truly hazardous undertaking. We tried to conceal our feelings as much as possible; and I think we succeeded very well.

After a painful waiting, the Saturday morning, whose night was to witness our departure, came. I hailed it with joy, bring what of sadness it might. Friday night was a sleepless one for me. I probably felt more anxious than the rest, because I was, by common consent, at the head of the whole affair. The responsibility of success or failure lay heavily upon me. The glory of the one, and the confusion of the other, were alike mine. The first two hours of that morning were such as I never experienced before, and hope never to again. Early in the morning, we went, as usual, to the field. We were spreading manure; and all at once, while thus engaged, I was overwhelmed with an indescribable feeling, in the fulness of which I turned to Sandy, who was near by, and said, "We are betrayed!" "Well," said he, "that thought has this moment struck me." We said no more. I was never more certain of any thing.

The horn was blown as usual, and we went up from the field to the house for breakfast. I went for the form, more than for want of any thing to eat that morning. Just as I got to the house, in looking out at the lane gate, I saw four white men, with two colored men. The white men were on horseback, and the colored ones were walking behind, as if tied. I watched them a few moments till they got up to our lane gate. Here they halted, and tied the colored men to the gatepost. I was not yet certain as to what the matter was. In a few moments, in rode Mr. Hamilton, with a speed betokening great excitement. He came to the door, and inquired if Master William was in. He was told he was at the barn. Mr. Hamilton, without dismounting, rode up to the barn with extraordinary speed. In a few moments, he and Mr. Freeland returned to the house. By this time, the three constables rode up and in great haste dismounted, tied their horses, and met Master William and Mr. Hamilton returning from the barn; and after talking awhile, they all walked up to the kitchen door. There was no one in the kitchen but myself and John. Henry and Sandy were up at the barn. Mr. Freeland put his head in at the door, and called me by name, saying, there were some gentlemen at the door who wished to see me. I stepped to the door, and inquired what they wanted. They at once seized me, and, without giving me any satisfaction, tied me—lashing my hands closely together. I insisted upon knowing what the matter was. They at length said, that they had learned I had been in a "scrape," and that I was to be examined before my master; and if their information proved false, I should not be hurt.

In a few moments, they succeeded in tying John. They then turned to Henry, who had by this time returned, and commanded him to cross his hands. "I won't!" said Henry, in a firm tone, indicating his readiness to meet the consequences of his refusal. "Won't you?" said Tom Graham, the constable. "No, I won't!" said Henry, in a still stronger tone. With this, two of the constables pulled out their shining pistols, and swore, by their Creator, that they would make him cross his hands or kill him. Each cocked his pistol, and, with fingers on the trigger, walked up to Henry, saying, at the same time, if he did not cross his hands, they would blow his damned heart out. "Shoot me, shoot me!" said Henry; "you can't kill me but once. Shoot, shoot,—and be damned! *I won't be tied!*" This he said in a tone of loud defiance; and at the same time, with a motion as quick as lightning, he with one single stroke dashed the pistols from the hand of each constable. As he did this, all hands fell upon him, and, after beating him some time, they finally overpowered him, and got him tied.

During the scuffle, I managed, I know not how, to get my pass out, and, without being discovered, put it into the fire. We were all now tied; and just as we were to leave for Easton jail, Betsy Freeland, mother of William Freeland, came to the door with her hands full of biscuits, and divided them between Henry and John. She then delivered herself of a speech, to the following effect: —addressing herself to me, she said, "*You devil! You yellow devil!* it was you that put it into the heads of Henry and John to run away. But for you, you long-legged mulatto devil! Henry nor John would never have thought of such a thing." I made no reply, and was immediately hurried off towards St. Michael's. Just a moment previous to the scuffle with Henry, Mr. Hamilton suggested the propriety of making a search for the protections which he had understood Frederick had written for himself and the rest. But, just at the moment he was about carrying his proposal into effect, his aid was needed in helping to tie Henry; and the excitement attending the scuffle caused them either to forget, or to deem it unsafe, under the circumstances, to search. So we were not yet convicted of the intention to run away.

When we got about half way to St. Michael's, while the constables having us in charge were looking ahead, Henry inquired of me what he should do with his pass. I told him to eat it with his biscuit, and own nothing; and we passed the word around, "*Own nothing*;" and "*Own nothing!*" said we all. Our confidence in each other was unshaken. We were resolved to succeed or fail together, after the calamity had befallen us as much as before. We were now prepared for any thing. We were to be dragged that morning fifteen miles behind horses, and then to be placed in the Easton jail. When we reached St. Michael's, we underwent a sort of examination. We all denied that we ever intended to run away. We did this more to bring out the evidence against us, than from any hope of getting clear of being sold; for, as I have said, we were ready for that. The fact was, we cared but little where we went, so we went together. Our greatest concern was about separation. We dreaded that more than any thing this side of death. We found the evidence against us to be the testimony of one person; our master would not tell who it was; but we came to a unanimous decision among ourselves as to who their informant was. We were sent off to the jail at Easton. When we got there, we were delivered up to the sheriff, Mr. Joseph Graham, and by him placed in jail. Henry, John, and myself, were placed in one room together— Charles, and Henry Bailey, in another. Their object in separating us was to hinder concert.

We had been in jail scarcely twenty minutes, when a swarm of slave traders, and agents for slave traders, flocked into jail to look at us, and to ascertain if we were for sale. Such a set of beings I never saw before! I felt myself surrounded by so many fiends from perdition. A band of pirates never looked more like their father, the devil. They laughed and grinned over us, saying, "Ah, my boys! we have got you, haven't we?" And after taunting us in various ways, they one by one went into an examination of us, with intent to ascertain our value. They would impudently ask us if we would not like to have them for our masters. We would make them no answer, and leave them to find out as best they could. Then they would curse and swear at us, telling us that they could take the devil out of us in a very little while, if we were only in their hands.

While in jail, we found ourselves in much more comfortable quarters than we expected when we went there. We did not get much to eat, nor that which was very good; but we had a good clean room, from the windows of which we could see what was going on in the street, which was very much better than though we had been placed in one of the dark, damp cells. Upon the whole, we got along very well, so far as the jail and its keeper were concerned. Immediately after the holidays were over, contrary to all our expectations, Mr. Hamilton and Mr. Freeland came up to Easton, and took Charles, the two Henrys, and John, out of jail, and carried them home, leaving me alone. I regarded this separation as a final one. It caused me more pain than any thing else in the whole transaction. I was ready for any thing rather than separation. I supposed that they had consulted together, and had decided that, as I was the whole cause of the intention of the others to run away, it was hard to make the innocent suffer with the guilty; and that they had, therefore, concluded to take the others home, and sell me, as a warning to the others that remained. It is due to the noble Henry to say, he seemed almost as reluctant at leaving the prison as at leaving home to come to the prison. But we knew we should, in all probability, be separated, if we were sold; and since he was in their hands, he concluded to go peaceably home.

I was now left to my fate. I was all alone, and within the walls of a stone prison. But a few days before, and I was full of hope. I expected to have been safe in a land of freedom; but now I was covered with gloom, sunk down to the utmost despair. I thought the possibility of freedom was gone. I was kept in this way about one week, at the end of which, Captain Auld, my master, to my surprise and utter astonishment, came up, and took me out, with the intention of sending me, with a gentleman of his acquaintance, into Alabama. But, from some cause or other, he did not send me to Alabama, but concluded to send me back to Baltimore, to live again with his brother Hugh, and to learn a trade.

Thus, after an absence of three years and one month, I was once more permitted to return to my old home at Baltimore. My master sent me away, because there existed against me a very great prejudice in the community, and he feared I might be killed.

In a few weeks after I went to Baltimore, Master Hugh hired me to Mr. William Gardner, an extensive ship-builder, on Fell's Point. I was put there to learn how to calk. It, however, proved a very unfavorable place for the accomplishment of this object. Mr. Gardner was engaged that spring in building two large man-of-war brigs, professedly for the Mexican government. The vessels were to be launched in the July of that year, and in failure thereof, Mr. Gardner was to lose a considerable sum; so that when I entered, all was hurry. There was no time to learn any thing. Every man had to do that which he knew how to do. In entering the ship-yard, my orders from Mr. Gardner were, to do whatever the carpenters commanded me to do. This was placing me at the beck and call of about seventy-five men. I was to regard all these as masters. Their word was to be my law. My situation was a most trying one. At times I needed a dozen pair of hands. I was called a dozen ways in the space of a single minute. Three or four voices would strike my ear at the same moment. It was—"Fred., come help me to cant this timber here."—"Fred., come carry this timber yonder."—"Fred., bring that roller here."—"Fred., go get a fresh can of water."—"Fred., come help saw off the end of this timber." —"Fred., go quick, and get the crowbar."—"Fred., hold on the end of this fall."—"Fred., go to the blacksmith's shop, and get a new punch."—"Hurra, Fred.! run and bring me a cold chisel."—"I say, Fred., bear a hand, and get up a fire as quick as lightning under that steam-box."—"Halloo, nigger! come, turn this grindstone."—"Come, come! move, move! and *bowse* this timber forward."—"I say, darky, blast your eyes why don't you heat up some pitch?"—"Halloo! halloo! halloo!" (Three voices at the same time.) "Come here!—Go there!—Hold on where you are! Damn you, if you move, I'll knock your brains out!"

This was my school for eight months; and I might have remained there longer, but for a most horrid fight I had with four of the white apprentices, in which my left eye was nearly knocked out, and I was horribly mangled in other respects. The facts in the case were these: Until a very little while after I went there, white and black ship-carpenters worked side by side, and no one seemed to see any impropriety in it. All hands seemed to be very well satisfied. Many of the black carpenters were freemen. Things seemed to be going on very well. All at once, the white carpenters knocked off, and said they would not work with free colored workmen. Their reason for this, as alleged, was, that if free colored carpenters were encouraged, they would soon take the trade into their own hands, and poor white men would be thrown out of employment. They therefore felt called upon at once to put a stop to it. And, taking advantage of Mr.

Gardner's necessities, they broke off, swearing they would work no longer, unless he would discharge his black carpenters. Now, though this did not extend to me in form, it did reach me in fact. My fellow-apprentices very soon began to feel it degrading to them to work with me. They began to put on airs, and talk about the "niggers" taking the country, saying we all ought to be killed; and, being encouraged by the journeymen, they commenced making my condition as hard as they could, by hectoring me around, and sometimes striking me. I, of course, kept the vow I made after the fight with Mr. Covey, and struck back again, regardless of consequences; and while I kept them from combining, I succeeded very well; for I could whip the whole of them, taking them separately. They, however, at length combined, and came upon me, armed with sticks, stones, and heavy handspikes. One came in front with a half brick. There was one at each side of me, and one behind. While I was attending to those in front, and on either side, the one behind ran up with the handspike, and struck me a heavy blow upon the head. It stunned me. I fell, and with this they all ran upon me, and fell to beating me with their fists. I let them lay on for a while, gathering strength. In an instant, I gave a sudden surge, and rose to my hands and knees. Just as I did that, one of their number gave me, with his heavy boot, a powerful kick in the left eye. My eyeball seemed to have burst. When they saw my eye closed, and badly swollen, they left me. With this I seized the handspike, and for a time pursued them. But here the carpenters interfered, and I thought I might as well give it up. It was impossible to stand my hand against so many. All this took place in sight of not less than fifty white ship-carpenters, and not one interposed a friendly word; but some cried, "Kill the damned nigger! Kill him! kill him! He struck a white person." I found my only chance for life was in flight. I succeeded in getting away without an additional blow, and barely so; for to strike a white man is death by Lynch law,—and that was the law in Mr. Gardner's ship-yard; nor is there much of any other out of Mr. Gardner's ship-yard.

I went directly home, and told the story of my wrong to Master Hugh; and I am happy to say of him, irreligious as he was, his conduct was heavenly, compared with that of his brother Thomas under similar circumstances. He listened attentively to my narration of the circumstances leading to the savage outrage, and gave many proofs of his strong indignation at it. The heart of my once overkind mistress was again melted into pity. My puffed-out eye and blood-covered face moved her to tears. She took a chair by me, washed the blood from my face, and, with a mother's tenderness, bound up my head, covering the wounded eye with a lean piece of fresh beef. It was almost compensation for my suffering to witness, once more, a manifestation of kindness from this, my once affectionate old mistress. Master Hugh was very much enraged. He gave expression to his feelings by pouring out curses upon the heads of those who did the deed. As soon as I got a little the better of my bruises, he took me with him to Esquire Watson's, on Bond Street, to see what could be done about the matter. Mr. Watson inquired who saw the assault committed. Master Hugh told him it was done in Mr. Gardner's ship-yard, at midday, where there were a large company of men at work. "As to that," he said, "the deed was done, and there was no question as to who did it." His answer was, he could do nothing in the case, unless some white man would come forward and testify. He could issue no warrant on my word. If I had been killed in the presence of a thousand colored people, their testimony combined would have been insufficient to have arrested one of the murderers. Master Hugh, for once, was compelled to say this state of things was too bad. Of course, it was impossible to get any white man to volunteer his testimony in my behalf, and against the white young men. Even those who may have sympathized with me were not prepared to do this. It required a degree of courage unknown to them to do so; for just at that time, the slightest manifestation of humanity toward a colored person was denounced as abolitionism, and that name subjected its bearer to frightful liabilities. The watchwords of the bloody-minded in that region, and in those days, were, "Damn the abolitionists!" and "Damn the niggers!" There was nothing done, and probably nothing would have been done if I had been killed. Such was, and such remains, the state of things in the Christian city of Baltimore.

Master Hugh, finding he could get no redress, refused to

let me go back again to Mr. Gardner. He kept me himself, and his wife dressed my wound till I was again restored to health. He then took me into the ship-yard of which he was foreman, in the employment of Mr. Walter Price. There I was immediately set to calking, and very soon learned the art of using my mallet and irons. In the course of one year from the time I left Mr. Gardner's, I was able to command the highest wages given to the most experienced calkers. I was now of some importance to my master. I was bringing him from six to seven dollars per week. I sometimes brought him nine dollars per week: my wages were a dollar and a half a day. After learning how to calk, I sought my own employment, made my own contracts, and collected the money which I earned. My pathway became much more smooth than before; my condition was now much more comfortable. When I could get no calking to do, I did nothing. During these leisure times, those old notions about freedom would steal over me again. When in Mr. Gardner's employment, I was kept in such a perpetual whirl of excitement, I could think of nothing, scarcely, but my life; and in thinking of my life, I almost forgot my liberty. I have observed this in my experience of slavery,—that whenever my condition was improved, instead of its increasing my contentment, it only increased my desire to be free, and set me to thinking of plans to gain my freedom. I have found that, to make a contented slave, it is necessary to make a thoughtless one. It is necessary to darken his moral and mental vision, and, as far as possible, to annihilate the power of reason. He must be able to detect no inconsistencies in slavery; he must be made to feel that slavery is right; and he can be brought to that only when he ceases to be a man.

I was now getting, as I have said, one dollar and fifty cents per day. I contracted for it; I earned it; it was paid to me; it was rightfully my own; yet, upon each returning Saturday night, I was compelled to deliver every cent of that money to Master Hugh. And why? Not because he earned it,—not because he had any hand in earning it,—not because I owed it to him,—nor because he possessed the slightest shadow of a right to it; but solely because he had the power to compel me to give it up. The right of the grim-visaged pirate upon the high seas is exactly the same.

CHAPTER XI.

I NOW come to that part of my life during which I planned, and finally succeeded in making my escape from slavery. But before narrating any of the peculiar circumstances, I deem it proper to make known my intention not to state all the facts connected with the transaction. My reasons for pursuing this course may be understood from the following: First, were I to give a minute statement of all the facts, it is not only possible, but quite probable, that others would thereby be involved in the most embarrassing difficulties. Secondly, such a statement would most undoubtedly induce greater vigilance on the part of slaveholders than has existed heretofore among them; which would, of course, be the means of guarding a door whereby some dear brother bondman might escape his galling chains. I deeply regret the necessity that impels me to suppress any thing of importance connected with my experience in slavery. It would afford me great pleasure indeed, as well as materially add to the interest of my narrative, were I at liberty to gratify a curiosity, which I know exists in the minds of many, by an accurate statement of all the facts pertaining to my most fortunate escape. But I must deprive myself of this pleasure, and the curious of the gratification which such a statement would afford. I would allow myself to suffer under the greatest imputations which evil-minded men might suggest, rather than exculpate myself, and thereby run the hazard of closing the slightest avenue by which a brother slave might clear himself of the chains and fetters of slavery.

I have never approved of the very public manner in which some of our western friends have conducted what they call the *underground railroad,* but which, I think, by their open declarations, has been made most emphatically the *upper-ground railroad.* I honor those good men and women for their noble daring, and applaud them for willingly subjecting themselves to bloody persecution, by openly avowing their participation in the escape of slaves. I, however, can see very little good resulting from such a course, either to themselves or the slaves escaping; while, upon the other hand, I see and feel assured that those open declarations are a positive evil to the slaves remaining, who are seeking to escape. They do nothing towards enlightening the slave, whilst they do much towards enlightening the master. They stimulate him to greater watchfulness, and enhance his power to capture his slave. We owe something to the slaves south of the line as well as to those north of it; and in aiding the latter on their way to freedom, we should be careful to do nothing which would be likely to hinder the former from escaping from slavery. I would keep the merciless slaveholder profoundly ignorant of the means of flight adopted by the slave. I would leave him to imagine himself surrounded by myriads of invisible tormentors, ever ready to snatch from his infernal grasp his trembling prey. Let him be left to feel his way in the dark; let darkness commensurate with his crime hover over him; and let him feel that at every step he takes, in pursuit of the flying bondman, he is running the frightful risk of having his hot brains dashed out by an invisible agency. Let us render the tyrant no aid; let us not hold the light by which he can trace the footprints of our flying brother. But enough of this. I will now proceed to the statement of those facts, connected with my escape, for which I am alone responsible, and for which no one can be made to suffer but myself.

In the early part of the year 1838, I became quite restless. I could see no reason why I should, at the end of each week, pour the reward of my toil into the purse of my master. When I carried to him my weekly wages, he would, after counting the money, look me in the face with a robber-like fierceness, and ask, "Is this all?" He was satisfied with nothing less than the last cent. He would, however, when I made him six dollars, sometimes give me six cents, to encourage me. It had the opposite effect. I regarded it as a sort of admission of my right to the whole. The fact that he gave me any part of my wages was proof, to my mind, that he believed me entitled to the whole of them. I always felt worse for having received any thing; for I feared that the giving me a few cents would ease his conscience, and make him feel himself to be a pretty honorable sort of robber. My discontent grew upon me. I was ever on the look-out for means of escape; and, finding no direct means, I determined to try to hire my time, with a view of getting money with which to make my escape. In the spring of 1838, when Master Thomas came to Baltimore to purchase his spring goods, I got an opportunity, and applied to him to allow me to hire my time. He unhesitatingly refused my request, and told me this was another stratagem by which to escape. He told me I could go nowhere but that he could get me; and that, in the event of my running away, he should spare no pains in his efforts to catch me. He exhorted me to content myself, and be obedient. He told me, if I would be happy, I must lay out no plans for the future. He said, if I behaved myself properly, he would take care of me. Indeed, he advised me to complete thoughtlessness of the future, and taught me to depend solely upon him for happiness. He seemed to see fully the pressing necessity of setting aside my intellectual nature, in order to [ensure] contentment in slavery. But in spite of him, and even in spite of myself, I continued to think, and to think about the injustice of my enslavement, and the means of escape.

About two months after this, I applied to Master Hugh for the privilege of hiring my time. He was not acquainted with the fact that I had applied to Master Thomas, and had been refused. He too, at first, seemed disposed to refuse; but, after some reflection, he granted me the privilege, and proposed the following terms: I was to be allowed all my time, make all contracts with those for whom I worked, and find my own employment; and, in return for this liberty, I was to pay him three dollars at the end of each week; find myself in calking tools, and in board and clothing. My board was two dollars and a half per week. This, with the wear and tear of clothing and calking tools, made my regular expenses about six dollars per week. This amount I was compelled to make up, or relinquish the privilege of hiring my time. Rain or shine, work or no work, at the end of each week the money must be forthcoming, or I must give up my privilege. This arrangement, it will be perceived, was decidedly in my master's favor. It relieved him of all need of looking after me. His money was sure. He received all the benefits of slaveholding without its evils; while I endured all the evils of a slave, and suffered all the care and anxiety of a freeman. I found it a hard bargain. But, hard as it was, I thought it better than the old mode of getting along. It was a step towards freedom to be allowed to bear the responsibilities of a freeman, and I was determined to hold on upon it. I bent myself to the work of making money. I was ready to work at night as well as day, and by the most untiring perseverance and industry, I made enough to meet my expenses, and lay up a little money every week. I went on thus from May till August. Master Hugh then refused to allow me to hire my time longer. The ground for his refusal was a failure on my part, one Saturday night, to pay him for my week's time. This failure was occasioned by my attending a camp meeting about ten miles from Baltimore. During the week, I had entered into an engagement with a number of young friends to start from Baltimore to the camp ground early Saturday evening; and being detained by my employer, I was unable to get down to Master Hugh's without disappointing the company. I knew that Master Hugh was in no special need of the money that night. I therefore decided to go to the camp meeting, and upon my return pay him the three dollars. I staid at the camp meeting one day longer than I intended when I left. But as soon as I returned, I called upon him to pay him what he considered his due. I found him very angry; he could scarce restrain his wrath. He said he had a great mind to give me a severe whipping. He wished to know how I dared go out of the city without asking his permission. I told him I hired my time, and while I paid him the price which he asked for it, I did not know that I was bound to ask him when and where I should go. This reply troubled him; and, after reflecting a few moments, he turned to me, and said I should hire my time no longer; that the next thing he should know of, I would be running away. Upon the same plea, he told me to bring my tools and clothing home forthwith. I did so; but instead of seeking work, as I had been accustomed to do previously to hiring my time, I spent the whole week without the performance of a single stroke of work. I did this in retaliation. Saturday night, he called upon me as usual for my week's wages. I told him I had no wages; I had done no work that week. Here we were upon the point of coming to blows. He raved, and swore his determination to get hold of me. I did not allow myself a single word; but was resolved, if he laid the weight of his hand upon me, it should be blow for blow. He did not strike me, but told me that he would find me in constant employment in future. I thought the matter over during the next day, Sunday, and finally resolved upon the third day of September, as the day upon which I would make a second attempt to secure my freedom. I now had three weeks during which to prepare for my journey. Early on Monday morning, before Master Hugh had time to make any engagement for me, I went out and got employment of Mr. Butler, at his ship-yard near the drawbridge, upon what is called the City Block, thus making it unnecessary for him to seek employment for me. At the end of the week, I brought him between eight and nine dollars. He seemed very well pleased, and asked me why I did not do the same the week before. He little knew what my plans were. My object in working steadily was to remove any suspicion he might entertain of my intent to run away; and in this I succeeded admirably. I suppose he thought I was never better satisfied with my condition than at the very time during which I was planning my escape. The second week passed, and again I carried him my full wages; and so well pleased was he, that he gave me twenty-five cents, (quite a large sum for a slaveholder to give a slave) and bade me to make a good use of it. I told him I would.

Things went on without very smoothly indeed, but within there was trouble. It is impossible for me to describe my feelings as the time of my contemplated start drew near. I had a number of warm-hearted friends in Baltimore,— friends that I loved almost as I did my life,—and the thought of being separated from them forever was painful beyond expression. It is my opinion that thousands would escape from slavery, who now remain, but for the strong cords of affection that bind them to their friends. The thought of leaving my friends was decidedly the most painful thought with which I had to contend. The love of them was my tender point, and shook my decision more than all things else. Besides the pain of separation, the dread and apprehension of a failure exceeded what I had experienced at my first attempt. The appalling defeat I then sustained returned to torment me. I felt assured that, if I failed in this attempt, my case would be a hopeless one—it would seal my fate as a slave forever. I could not hope to get off with any thing less than the severest punishment, and being placed beyond the means of escape. It required no very vivid imagination to depict the most frightful scenes through which I should have to pass, in case I failed. The wretchedness of slavery, and the blessedness of freedom, were perpetually before me. It was life and death with me. But I remained firm, and, according to my resolution, on the third day of September, 1838, I left my chains, and succeeded in reaching New York without the slightest interruption of any kind. How I did so,—what means I adopted,—what direction I travelled, and by what mode of conveyance—I must leave unexplained, for the reasons before mentioned.

I have been frequently asked how I felt when I found myself in a free State. I have never been able to answer the question with any satisfaction to myself. It was a moment of the highest excitement I ever experienced. I suppose I felt as one may imagine the unarmed mariner to feel when he is rescued by a friendly man-of-war from the pursuit of a pirate. In writing to a dear friend, immediately after my arrival at New York, I said I felt like one who had escaped a den of hungry lions. This state of mind, however, very soon subsided; and I was again seized with a feeling of great insecurity and loneliness. I was yet liable to be taken back, and subjected to all the tortures of slavery. This in itself was enough to damp the ardor of my enthusiasm. But the loneliness overcame me. There I was in the midst of thousands, and yet a perfect stranger; without home and without friends, in the midst of thousands of my own brethren—children of a common Father, and yet I dared not to unfold to any one of them my sad condition. I was afraid to speak to any one for fear of speaking to the wrong one, and thereby falling into the hands of money-loving kidnappers, whose business it was to lie in wait for the panting fugitive, as the ferocious beasts of the forest lie in wait for their prey. The motto which I adopted when I started from slavery was this—"Trust no man!" I saw in every white man an enemy, and in almost every colored man cause for distrust. It was a most painful situation; and, to understand it, one must needs experience it, or imagine himself in similar circumstances. Let him be a fugitive slave in a strange land—a land given up to be the hunting-ground for slaveholders—whose inhabitants are legalized kidnappers—where he is every moment subjected to the terrible liability of being seized upon by his fellowmen, as the hideous crocodile seizes upon his prey!—I say, let him place himself in my situation—without home or friends—without money or credit—wanting shelter, and no one to give it—wanting bread, and no money to buy it,—and at the same time let him feel that he is pursued by merciless men-hunters, and in total darkness as to what to do, where to go, or where to stay,—perfectly helpless both as to the means of defence and means of escape,—in the midst of plenty, yet suffering the terrible gnawings of hunger,—in the midst of houses, yet having no home,—among fellow-men, yet feeling as if in the midst of wild beasts, whose greediness to swallow up the trembling and half-famished fugitive is only equalled by that with which the monsters of the deep swallow up the helpless fish upon which they subsist,—I say, let him be placed in this most trying situation,—the situation in which I was placed,—then, and not till then, will he fully appreciate the hardships of, and know how to sympathize with, the toil-worn and whip-scarred fugitive slave.

Thank Heaven, I remained but a short time in this distressed situation. I was relieved from it by the humane hand of Mr. DAVID RUGGLES, whose vigilance, kindness, and perseverance, I shall never forget. I am glad of an opportunity to express, as far as words can, the love and gratitude I bear him. Mr. Ruggles is now afflicted with blindness, and is himself in need of the same kind offices which he was once so forward in the performance of toward others. I had been in New York but a few days, when Mr. Ruggles sought me out, and very kindly took me to his boarding-house at the corner of Church and Lespenard Streets. Mr. Ruggles was then very deeply engaged in the memorable *Darg* case, as well as attending to a number of other fugitive slaves, devising ways and means for their successful escape; and, though watched and hemmed in on almost every side, he seemed to be more than a match for his enemies.

Very soon after I went to Mr. Ruggles, he wished to know of me where I wanted to go; as he deemed it unsafe for me to remain in New York. I told him I was a calker, and should like to go where I could get work. I thought of going to Canada; but he decided against it, and in favor of my going to New Bedford, thinking I should be able to get work there at my trade. At this time, Anna,* my intended wife, came on; for I wrote to her immediately after my arrival at New York, (notwithstanding my homeless, houseless, and helpless condition,) informing her of my successful flight, and wishing her to come on forthwith. In a few days after her arrival, Mr. Ruggles called in the Rev. J. W. C. Pennington, who, in the presence of Mr. Ruggles, Mrs. Michaels, and two or three others, performed the marriage ceremony, and gave us a certificate, of which the following is an exact copy:—

This may certify, that I joined together in holy matrimony Frederick Johnson† and Anna Murray, as man and wife, in the presence of Mr. David Ruggles and Mrs. Michaels.

JAMES W. C. PENNINGTON.

New York, Sept. 15, 1838.

Upon receiving this certificate, and a five-dollar bill from Mr. Ruggles, I shouldered one part of our baggage, and Anna took up the other, and we set out forthwith to take passage on board of the steamboat John W. Richmond for Newport, on our way to New Bedford. Mr. Ruggles gave me a letter to a Mr. Shaw in Newport, and told me, in case my money did not serve me to New Bedford, to stop in Newport and obtain further assistance; but upon our arrival at Newport, we were so anxious to get to a place of safety, that, notwithstanding we lacked the necessary money to pay our fare, we decided to take seats in the stage, and promise to pay when we got to New Bedford. We were encouraged to do this by two excellent gentlemen, residents of New Bedford, whose names I afterward ascertained to be Joseph Ricketson and William C. Taber. They seemed at once to understand our circumstances, and gave us such assurance of their friendliness as put us fully at ease in their presence.

---

*She was free.

†I had changed my name from Frederick *Bailey* to that of *Johnson*.

It was good indeed to meet with such friends, at such a time. Upon reaching New Bedford, we were directed to the house of Mr. Nathan Johnson, by whom we were kindly received, and hospitably provided for. Both Mr. and Mrs. Johnson took a deep and lively interest in our welfare. They proved themselves quite worthy of the name of abolitionists. When the stage-driver found us unable to pay our fare, he held on upon our baggage as security for the debt. I had but to mention the fact to Mr. Johnson, and he forthwith advanced the money.

We now began to feel a degree of safety, and to prepare ourselves for the duties and responsibilities of a life of freedom. On the morning after our arrival at New Bedford, while at the breakfast-table, the question arose as to what name I should be called by. The name given me by my mother was, "Frederick Augustus Washington Bailey." I, however, had dispensed with the two middle names long before I left Maryland so that I was generally known by the name of "Frederick Bailey." I started from Baltimore bearing the name of "Stanley." When I got to New York, I again changed my name to "Frederick Johnson," and thought that would be the last change. But when I got to New Bedford, I found it necessary again to change my name. The reason of this necessity was, that there were so many Johnsons in New Bedford, it was already quite difficult to distinguish between them. I gave Mr. Johnson the privilege of choosing me a name, but told him he must not take from me the name of "Frederick." I must hold on to that, to preserve a sense of my identity. Mr. Johnson had just been reading the "Lady of the Lake," and at once suggested that my name be "Douglass." From that time until now I have been called "Frederick Douglass;" and as I am more widely known by that name than by either of the others, I shall continue to use it as my own.

I was quite disappointed at the general appearance of things in New Bedford. The impression which I had received respecting the character and condition of the people of the north, I found to be singularly erroneous. I had very strangely supposed, while in slavery, that few of the comforts, and scarcely any of the luxuries, of life were enjoyed at the north, compared with what were enjoyed by the slaveholders of the south. I probably came to this conclusion from the fact that northern people owned no slaves. I supposed that they were about upon a level with the non-slaveholding population of the south. I knew they were exceedingly poor, and I had been accustomed to regard their poverty as the necessary consequence of their being non-slaveholders. I had somehow imbibed the opinion that, in the absence of slaves, there could be no wealth, and very little refinement. And upon coming to the north, I expected to meet with a rough, hard-handed, and uncultivated population, living in the most Spartan-like simplicity, knowing nothing of the ease, luxury, pomp, and grandeur of southern slaveholders. Such being my conjectures, any one acquainted with the appearance of New Bedford may very readily infer how palpably I must have seen my mistake.

In the afternoon of the day when I reached New Bedford, I visited the wharves, to take a view of the shipping. Here I found myself surrounded with the strongest proofs of wealth. Lying at the wharves, and riding in the stream, I saw many ships of the finest model, in the best order, and of the largest size. Upon the right and left, I was walled in by granite warehouses of the widest dimensions, stowed to their utmost capacity with the necessaries and comforts of life. Added to this, almost every body seemed to be at work, but noiselessly so, compared with what I had been accustomed to in Baltimore. There were no loud songs heard from those engaged in loading and unloading ships. I heard no deep oaths or horrid curses on the laborer. I saw no whipping of men; but all seemed to go smoothly on. Every man appeared to understand his work, and went at it with a sober, yet cheerful earnestness, which betokened the deep interest which he felt in what he was doing, as well as a sense of his own dignity as a man. To me this looked exceedingly strange. From the wharves I strolled around and over the town, gazing with wonder and admiration at the splendid churches, beautiful dwellings, and finely-cultivated gardens; evincing an amount of wealth, comfort, taste, and refinement, such as I had never seen in any part of slaveholding Maryland.

Every thing looked clean, new, and beautiful. I saw few or no dilapidated houses, with poverty-stricken inmates; no half-naked children and barefooted women, such as I had been accustomed to see in Hillsborough, Easton, St. Michael's, and Baltimore. The people looked more able, stronger, healthier, and happier, than those of Maryland. I was for once made glad by a view of extreme wealth, without being saddened by seeing extreme poverty. But the most astonishing as well as the most interesting thing to me was the condition of the colored people, a great many of whom, like myself, had escaped thither as a refuge from the hunters of men. I found many, who had not been seven years out of their chains, living in finer houses, and evidently enjoying more of the comforts of life, than the average of slaveholders in Maryland. I will venture to assert that my friend Mr. Nathan Johnson (of whom I can say with a grateful heart, "I was hungry, and he gave me meat; I was thirsty, and he gave me drink; I was a stranger, and he took me in") lived in a neater house; dined at a better table; took, paid for, and read, more newspapers; better understood the moral, religious, and political character of the nation,—than nine tenths of the slaveholders in Talbot county, Maryland. Yet Mr. Johnson was a working man. His hands were hardened by toil, and not his alone, but those also of Mrs. Johnson. I found the colored people much more spirited than I had supposed they would be. I found among them a determination to protect each other from the blood-thirsty kidnapper, at all hazards. Soon after my arrival, I was told of a circumstance which illustrated their spirit. A colored man and a fugitive slave were on unfriendly terms. The former was heard to threaten the latter with informing his master of his whereabouts. Straightway a meeting was called among the colored people, under the stereotyped notice, "Business of importance!" The betrayer was invited to attend. The people came at the appointed hour, and organized the meeting by appointing a very religious old gentleman as president, who, I believe, made a prayer, after which he addressed the meeting as follows: *"Friends, we have got him here, and I would recommend that you young men just take him outside the door, and kill him!"* With this, a number of them bolted at him; but they were intercepted by some more timid than themselves, and the betrayer escaped their vengeance, and has not been seen in New Bedford since. I believe there have been no more such threats, and should there be here-after, I doubt not that death would be the consequence.

I found employment, the third day after my arrival, in stowing a sloop with a load of oil. It was new, dirty, and hard work for me; but I went at it with a glad heart and a willing hand. I was now my own master. It was a happy moment, the rapture of which can be understood only by those who have been slaves. It was the first work, the reward of which was to be entirely my own. There was no Master Hugh standing ready, the moment I earned the money, to rob me of it. I worked that day with a pleasure I had never before experienced. I was at work for myself and newly-married wife. It was to me the starting-point of a new existence. When I got through with that job, I went in pursuit of a job of calking; but such was the strength of prejudice against color, among the white calkers, that they refused to work with me, and of course I could get no employment.* Finding my trade of no immediate benefit, I threw off my calking habiliments, and prepared myself to do any kind of work I could get to do. Mr. Johnson kindly let me have his wood-horse and saw, and I very soon found myself plenty of work. There was no work too hard—none too dirty. I was ready to saw wood, shovel coal, carry the hod, sweep the chimney, or roll oil casks,—all of which I did for nearly three years in New Bedford, before I became known to the anti-slavery world.

In about four months after I went to New Bedford, there came a young man to me, and inquired if I did not wish to take the "Liberator." I told him I did; but, just having made my escape from slavery, I remarked that I was unable to pay for it then. I, however, finally became a subscriber to it. The paper came, and I read it from week to week with such feel-ings as it would be quite idle for me to attempt to describe. The paper became my meat and my drink. My soul was set all on fire. Its sympathy for my brethren in bonds—its scath-ing denunciations of slaveholders—its faithful exposures of slavery—and its powerful attacks upon the upholders of the

---

*I am told that colored persons can now get employment at calking in New Bedford—a result of anti-slavery effort.

institution—sent a thrill of joy through my soul, such as I had never felt before!

I had not long been a reader of the "Liberator," before I got a pretty correct idea of the principles, measures and spirit of the anti-slavery reform. I took right hold of the cause. I could do but little; but what I could, I did with a joyful heart, and never felt happier than when in an anti-slavery meeting. I seldom had much to say at the meetings, because what I wanted to say was said so much better by others. But, while attending an anti-slavery convention at Nantucket, on the 11th of August, 1841, I felt strongly moved to speak, and was at the same time much urged to do so by Mr. William C. Coffin, a gentleman who had heard me speak in the colored people's meeting at New Bedford. It was a severe cross, and I took it up reluctantly. The truth was, I felt myself a slave, and the idea of speaking to white people weighed me down. I spoke but a few moments, when I felt a degree of freedom, and said what I desired with considerable ease. From that time until now, I have been engaged in pleading the cause of my brethren—with what success, and with what devotion, I leave those acquainted with my labors to decide.

APPENDIX.

I FIND, since reading over the foregoing Narrative, that I have, in several instances, spoken in such a tone and manner, respecting religion, as may possibly lead those unacquainted with my religious views to suppose me an opponent of all religion. To remove the liability of such misapprehension, I deem it proper to append the following brief explanation. What I have said respecting and against religion, I mean strictly to apply to the *slaveholding religion* of this land, and with no possible reference to Christianity proper; for, between the Christianity of this land, and the Christianity of

Christ, I recognize the widest possible difference—so wide, that to receive the one as good, pure, and holy, is of necessity to reject the other as bad, corrupt, and wicked. To be the friend of the one, is of necessity to be the enemy of the other. I love the pure, peaceable, and impartial Christianity of Christ: I therefore hate the corrupt, slaveholding, women-whipping, cradle-plundering, partial and hypocritical Christianity of this land. Indeed, I can see no reason, but the most deceitful one, for calling the religion of this land Christianity. I look upon it as the climax of all misnomers, the boldest of all frauds, and the grossest of all libels. Never was there a clearer case of "stealing the livery of the court of heaven to serve the devil in." I am filled with unutterable loathing when I contemplate the religious pomp and show, together with the horrible inconsistencies, which every where surround me. We have men-stealers for ministers, women-whippers for missionaries, and cradle-plunderers for church members. The man who wields the blood-clotted cowskin during the week fills the pulpit on Sunday, and claims to be a minister of the meek and lowly Jesus. The man who robs me of my earnings at the end of each week meets me as a class-leader on Sunday morning, to show me the way of life, and the path of salvation. He who sells my sister, for purposes of prostitution, stands forth as the pious advocate of purity. He who proclaims it a religious duty to read the Bible denies me the right of learning to read the name of the God who made me. He who is the religious advocate of marriage robs whole millions of its sacred influence, and leaves them to the ravages of wholesale pollution. The warm defender of the sacredness of the family relation is the same that scatters whole families,—sundering husbands and wives, parents and children, sisters and brothers,—leaving the hut vacant, and the hearth desolate. We see the thief preaching against theft, and the adulterer against adultery. We have men sold to build churches, women sold to support the gospel, and babes sold to purchase Bibles for the *poor heathen! all for the glory of God and the good of souls!* The slave auctioneer's bell and the church-going bell chime in with each other, and the bitter cries of the heart-broken slave are drowned in the religious shouts of his pious master. Revivals of religion and revivals in the slave-trade go hand in hand together. The slave prison and the church stand near each other. The clanking of fetters and the rattling of chains in the prison, and the pious psalm and solemn prayer in the church, may be heard at the same time. The dealers in the bodies and souls of men erect their stand in the presence of the pulpit, and they mutually help each other. The dealer gives his blood-stained gold to support the pulpit, and the pulpit, in return, covers his infernal business with the garb of Christianity. Here we have religion and robbery the allies of each other—devils dressed in angels' robes, and hell presenting the semblance of paradise.

> Just God! and these are they,
>   Who minister at thine altar, God of right!
> Men who their hands, with prayer and blessing, lay
>   On Israel's ark of light.
>
> What! preach, and kidnap men?
>   Give thanks, and rob thy own afflicted poor?
> Talk of thy glorious liberty, and then
>   Bolt hard the captive's door?
>
> What! servants of thy own
>   Merciful Son, who came to seek and save
> The homeless and the outcast, fettering down
>   The tasked and plundered slave!
>
> Pilate and Herod friends!
>   Chief priests and rulers, as of old, combine!
> Just God and holy! is that church which lends
>   Strength to the spoiler thine?

The Christianity of America is a Christianity, of whose votaries it may be as truly said, as it was of the ancient scribes and Pharisees, "They bind heavy burdens, and grievous to be borne, and lay them on men's shoulders, but they themselves will not move them with one of their fingers. All their works they do for to be seen of men.—They love the uppermost rooms at feasts, and the chief seats in the synagogues, . . . and to be called of men, Rabbi, Rabbi.—But woe unto you, scribes and Pharisees, hypocrites! for ye shut up the kingdom of heaven against men; for ye neither go in yourselves, neither suffer ye them that are entering to go in. Ye devour widows' houses, and for a pretence make long prayers; therefore ye shall receive the greater damnation. Ye compass sea and land to make one proselyte, and when he is made, ye make him twofold more the child of hell than yourselves.—Woe unto you, scribes and Pharisees, hypocrites! for ye pay tithe of mint, and anise, and cumin, and have omitted the weightier matters of the law, judgment, mercy, and faith; these ought ye to have done, and not to leave the other undone. Ye blind guides! which strain at a gnat, and swallow a camel. Woe unto you, scribes and Pharisees, hypocrites! for ye make clean the outside of the cup and of the platter; but within, they are full of extortion and excess.—Woe unto you, scribes and Pharisees, hypocrites! for ye are like unto whited sepulchres, which indeed appear beautiful outward, but are within full of dead men's bones, and of all uncleanness. Even so ye also outwardly appear righteous unto men, but within ye are full of hypocrisy and iniquity."

Dark and terrible as is this picture, I hold it to be strictly true of the overwhelming mass of professed Christians in America. They strain at a gnat, and swallow a camel. Could any thing be more true of our churches? They would be shocked at the proposition of fellowshipping a *sheep*-stealer; and at the same time they hug to their communion a *man*-stealer, and brand me with being an infidel, if I find fault with them for it. They attend with Pharisaical strictness to the outward forms of religion, and at the same time neglect the weightier matters of the law, judgment, mercy, and faith. They are always ready to sacrifice, but seldom to show mercy. They are they who are represented as professing to love God whom they have not seen, whilst they hate their brother whom they have seen. They love the heathen on the other side of the globe. They can pray for him, pay money to have the Bible put into his hand, and missionaries to instruct him; while they despise and totally neglect the heathen at their own doors.

Such is, very briefly, my view of the religion of this land; and to avoid any misunderstanding, growing out of the use of general terms, I mean, by the religion of this land, that which is revealed in the words, deeds, and actions, of those bodies, north and south, calling themselves Christian churches, and yet in union with slaveholders. It is against religion, as presented by these bodies, that I have felt it my duty to testify.

I conclude these remarks by copying the following portrait of the religion of the south, (which is, by communion and fellowship, the religion of the north,) which I soberly affirm is "true to the life," and without caricature or the slightest exaggeration. It is said to have been drawn, several years before the present anti-slavery agitation began, by a northern Methodist preacher, who, while residing at the south, had an opportunity to see slaveholding morals, manners, and piety, with his own eyes. "Shall I not visit for these things? saith the Lord. Shall not my soul be avenged on such a nation as this?"

A PARODY.

Come, saints and sinners, hear me tell
How pious priests whip Jack and Nell,
And women buy and children sell,
And preach all sinners down to hell,
 And sing of heavenly union.

They'll bleat and baa, dona like goats,
Gorge down black sheep, and strain at motes,
Array their backs in fine black coats,
Then seize their negroes by their throats,
 And choke, for heavenly union.

They'll church you if you sip a dram,
And damn you if you steal a lamb;
Yet rob old Tony, Doll, and Sam,
Of human rights, and bread and ham;
 Kidnapper's heavenly union.

They'll loudly talk of Christ's reward,
And bind his image with a cord,
And scold, and swing the lash abhorred,

And sell their brother in the Lord
   To handcuffed heavenly union.

They'll read and sing a sacred song,
And make a prayer both loud and long,
And teach the right and do the wrong,
Hailing the brother, sister throng,
   With words, of heavenly union.

We wonder how such saints can sing,
Or praise the Lord upon the wing,
Who roar, and scold, and whip, and sting,
And to their slaves and mammon cling,
   In guilty conscience union.

They'll raise tobacco, corn, and rye,
And drive, and thieve, and cheat, and lie,
And lay up treasures in the sky,
By making switch and cowskin fly,
   In hope of heavenly union.

They'll crack old Tony on the skull,
And preach and roar like Bashan bull,
Or braying ass, of mischief full,
Then seize old Jacob by the wool,
   And pull for heavenly union.

A roaring, ranting, sleek man-thief,
Who lived on mutton, veal, and beef,
Yet never would afford relief
To needy, sable sons of grief,
   Was big with heavenly union.

'Love not the world,' the preacher said,
And winked his eye, and shook his head;
He seized on Tom, and Dick, and Ned,
Cut short their meat, and clothes, and bread,
   Yet still loved heavenly union.

Another preacher whining spoke
Of One whose heart for sinners broke:

He tied old Nanny to an oak,
And drew the blood at every stroke,
    And prayed for heavenly union.

Two others oped their iron jaws,
And waved their children-stealing paws;
There sat their children in gewgaws;
By stinting negroes' backs and maws,
    They kept up heavenly union.

All good from Jack another takes,
And entertains their flirts and rakes,
Who dress as sleek as glossy snakes,
And cram their mouths with sweetened cakes;
    And this goes down for union.

Sincerely and earnestly hoping that this little book may
do something toward throwing light on the American slave
system, and hastening the glad day of deliverance to the
millions of my brethren in bonds—faithfully relying upon
the power of truth, love, and justice, for success in my humble efforts—and solemnly pledging my self anew to the sacred cause,—I subscribe myself,

                              FREDERICK DOUGLASS.

Lynn, Mass., April 28, 1845.

                    THE END.

INCIDENTS

IN THE

LIFE OF A SLAVE GIRL.

WRITTEN BY HERSELF.

Linda Brent

"Northerners know nothing at all about Slavery. They think it is perpetual
bondage only. They have no conception of the depth of *degradation* involved in
that word, SLAVERY ; if they had, they would never cease their efforts until so horrible a system was overthrown."

A WOMAN OF NORTH CAROLINA.

"Rise up, ye women that are at ease! Hear my voice, ye careless daughters! Give
ear unto my speech."

ISAIAH xxxii. 9.

———

EDITED BY L. MARIA CHILD.

———

BOSTON:
PUBLISHED FOR THE AUTHOR.
1861.

PREFACE BY THE AUTHOR.

READER, be assured this narrative is no fiction. I am aware that some of my adventures may seem incredible; but they are, nevertheless, strictly true. I have not exaggerated the wrongs inflicted by Slavery; on the contrary, my descriptions fall far short of the facts. I have concealed the names of places, and given persons fictitious names. I had no motive for secrecy on my own account, but I deemed it kind and considerate towards others to pursue this course.

I wish I were more competent to the task I have undertaken. But I trust my readers will excuse deficiencies in consideration of circumstances. I was born and reared in Slavery; and I remained in a Slave State twenty-seven years. Since I have been at the North, it has been necessary for me to work diligently for my own support, and the education of my children. This has not left me much leisure to make up for the loss of early opportunities to improve myself; and it has compelled me to write these pages at irregular intervals, whenever I could snatch an hour from household duties.

When I first arrived in Philadelphia, Bishop Paine advised me to publish a sketch of my life, but I told him I was altogether incompetent to such an undertaking. Though I have improved my mind somewhat since that time, I still remain of the same opinion; but I trust my motives will excuse what might otherwise seem presumptuous. I have not written my experiences in order to attract attention to myself; on the contrary, it would have been more pleasant to me to have been silent about my own history. Neither do I care to excite sympathy for my own sufferings. But I do earnestly desire to arouse the women of the North to a realizing sense of the condition of two millions of women at the South, still in bondage, suffering what I suffered, and most of them far worse. I want to add my testimony to that of abler pens to convince the people of the Free States what Slavery really is. Only by experience can any one realize how deep, and dark, and foul is that pit of abominations. May the blessing of God rest on this imperfect effort in behalf of my persecuted people!

LINDA BRENT.

INTRODUCTION BY THE EDITOR.

THE author of the following autobiography is personally known to me, and her conversation and manners inspire me with confidence. During the last seventeen years, she has lived the greater part of the time with a distinguished family in New York, and has so deported herself as to be highly esteemed by them. This fact is sufficient, without further credentials of her character. I believe those who know her will not be disposed to doubt her veracity, though some incidents in her story are more romantic than fiction.

At her request, I have revised her manuscript; but such changes as I have made have been mainly for purposes of condensation and orderly arrangement. I have not added any thing to the incidents, or changed the import of her very pertinent remarks. With trifling exceptions, both the ideas and the language are her own. I pruned excrescences a little, but otherwise I had no reason for changing her lively and dramatic way of telling her own story. The names of both persons and places are known to me; but for good reasons I suppress them.

It will naturally excite surprise that a woman reared in Slavery should be able to write so well. But circumstances will explain this. In the first place, nature endowed her with quick perceptions. Secondly, the mistress, with whom she lived till she was twelve years old, was a kind, considerate friend, who taught her to read and spell. Thirdly, she was placed in favorable circumstances after she came to the North; having frequent intercourse with intelligent persons, who felt a friendly interest in her welfare, and were disposed to give her opportunities for self-improvement.

I am well aware that many will accuse me of indecorum for presenting these pages to the public; for the experiences of this intelligent and much-injured woman belong to a class which some call delicate subjects, and others indelicate. This peculiar phase of Slavery has generally been kept veiled; but the public ought to be made acquainted with its monstrous features, and I willingly take the responsibility of presenting them with the veil withdrawn. I do this for the sake of my sisters in bondage, who are suffering wrongs so foul, that our ears are too delicate to listen to them. I do it with the hope of arousing conscientious and reflecting women at the North to a sense of their duty in the exertion of moral influence on the question of Slavery, on all possible occasions. I do it with the hope that every man who reads this narrative will swear solemnly before God that, so far as he has power to prevent it, no fugitive from Slavery shall ever be sent back to suffer in that loathsome den of corruption and cruelty.

L. MARIA CHILD.

CONTENTS.

INCIDENTS

IN THE

LIFE OF A SLAVE GIRL,

SEVEN YEARS CONCEALED.

I.

CHILDHOOD.

I was born a slave; but I never knew it till six years of happy childhood had passed away. My father was a carpenter, and considered so intelligent and skilful in his trade, that, when buildings out of the common line were to be erected, he was sent for from long distances, to be head workman. On condition of paying his mistress two hundred dollars a year, and supporting himself, he was allowed to work at his trade, and manage his own affairs. His strongest wish was to purchase his children; but, though he several times offered his hard earnings for that purpose, he never succeeded. In complexion my parents were a light shade of brownish yellow, and were termed mulattoes. They lived together in a comfortable home; and, though we were all slaves, I was so fondly shielded that I never dreamed I was a piece of merchandise, trusted to them for safe keeping, and liable to be demanded of them at any moment. I had one brother, William, who was two years younger than myself—a bright, affectionate child. I had also a great treasure in my maternal grandmother, who was a remarkable woman in many respects. She was the daughter of a planter in South Carolina, who, at his death, left her mother and his three children free, with money to go to St. Augustine, where they had relatives. It was during the Revolutionary War; and they were captured on their passage, carried back, and sold to different purchasers. Such was the story my grandmother used to tell me; but I do not remember all the particulars. She was a little girl when she was captured and sold to the keeper of a large hotel. I have often heard her tell how hard she fared during childhood. But as she grew older she evinced so much intelligence, and was so faithful, that her master and mistress could not help seeing it was for their interest to take care of such a valuable piece of property. She became an indispensable personage in the household, officiating in all capacities, from cook and wet nurse to seamstress. She was much praised for her cooking; and her nice crackers became so famous in the neighborhood that many people were desirous of obtaining them. In consequence of numerous requests of this kind, she asked permission of her mistress to bake crackers at night, after all the household work was done; and she obtained leave to do it, provided she would clothe herself and her children from the profits. Upon these terms, after working hard all day for her mistress, she began her midnight bakings, assisted by her two oldest children. The business proved profitable; and each year she laid by a little, which was saved for a fund to purchase her children. Her master died, and the property was divided among his heirs. The widow had her dower in the hotel which she continued to keep open. My grandmother remained in her service as a slave; but her children were divided among her master's children. As she had five, Benjamin, the youngest one, was sold, in order that each heir might have an equal portion of dollars and cents. There was so little difference in our ages that he seemed more like my brother than my uncle. He was a bright, handsome lad, nearly white; for he inherited the complexion my grandmother had derived from Anglo-Saxon ancestors. Though only ten years old, seven hundred and twenty dollars were paid for him. His sale was a terrible blow to my grandmother, but she was naturally hopeful, and she went to work with renewed energy, trusting in time to be able to purchase some of her children. She had laid up three hundred dollars, which her mistress one day begged as a loan, promising to pay her soon. The reader probably knows that no promise or writing given to a slave is legally binding; for, according to Southern laws, a slave, *being* property, can *hold* no property. When my grandmother lent her hard earnings to her mistress, she trusted solely to her honor. The honor of a slaveholder to a slave!

To this good grandmother I was indebted for many comforts. My brother Willie and I often received portions of the crackers, cakes, and preserves, she made to sell; and after we ceased to be children we were indebted to her for many more important services.

Such were the unusually fortunate circumstances of my early childhood. When I was six years old, my mother died; and then, for the first time, I learned, by the talk around me, that I was a slave. My mother's mistress was the daughter of my grandmother's mistress. She was the foster sister of my mother; they were both nourished at my grandmother's breast. In fact, my mother had been weaned at three months old, that the babe of the mistress might obtain sufficient food. They played together as children; and, when they became women, my mother was a most faithful servant to her whiter foster sister. On her death-bed her mistress promised that her children should never suffer for any thing; and during her lifetime she kept her word. They all spoke kindly of my dead mother, who had been a slave merely in name, but in nature was noble and womanly. I grieved for her, and my young mind was troubled with the thought who would now take care of me and my little brother. I was told that my home was now to be with her mistress; and I found it a happy one. No toilsome or disagreeable duties were imposed on me. My mistress was so kind to me that I was always glad to do her bidding, and proud to labor for her as much as my young years would permit. I would sit by her side for hours, sewing diligently, with a heart as free from care as that of any free-born white child. When she thought I was tired, she would send me out to run and jump; and away I bounded, to gather berries or flowers to decorate her room. Those were happy days—too happy to last. The slave child had no thought for the morrow; but there came that blight, which too surely waits on every human being born to be a chattel.

When I was nearly twelve years old, my kind mistress sickened and died. As I saw the cheek grow paler, and the eye more glassy, how earnestly I prayed in my heart that she might live! I loved her; for she had been almost like a mother to me. My prayers were not answered. She died, and they buried her in the little churchyard, where, day after day, my tears fell upon her grave.

I was sent to spend a week with my grandmother. I was now old enough to begin to think of the future; and again and again I asked myself what they would do with me. I felt sure I should never find another mistress so kind as the one who was gone. She had promised my dying mother that her children should never suffer for any thing; and when I remembered that, and recalled her many proofs of attachment to me, I could not help having some hopes that she had left me free. My friends were almost certain it would be so. They thought she would be sure to do it, on account of my mother's love and faithful service. But, alas! we all know that the memory of a faithful slave does not avail much to save her children from the auction block.

After a brief period of suspense, the will of my mistress was read, and we learned that she had bequeathed me to her sister's daughter, a child of five years old. So vanished our hopes. My mistress had taught me the precepts of God's Word: "Thou shalt love thy neighbor as thyself." "Whatsoever ye would that men should do unto you, do ye even so unto them." But I was her slave, and I suppose she did not recognize me as her neighbor. I would give much to blot out from my memory that one great wrong. As a child, I loved my mistress; and, looking back on the happy days I spent with her, I try to think with less bitterness of this act of injustice. While I was with her, she taught me to read and spell; and for this privilege, which so rarely falls to the lot of a slave, I bless her memory.

She possessed but few slaves; and at her death those were all distributed among her relatives. Five of them were my grandmother's children, and had shared the same milk that nourished her mother's children. Notwithstanding my grandmother's long and faithful service to her owners, not one of her children escaped the auction block. These God-breathing machines are no more, in the sight of their masters, than the cotton they plant, or the horses they tend.

II.

THE NEW MASTER AND MISTRESS.

Dr. Flint, a physician in the neighborhood, had married the sister of my mistress, and I was now the property of their little daughter. It was not without murmuring that I prepared for my new home; and what added to my unhappiness, was the fact that my brother William was purchased by the same family. My father, by his nature, as well as by the habit of transacting business as a skillful mechanic, had more of the feelings of a freeman than is common among slaves. My brother was a spirited boy; and being brought up under such influences, he daily detested the name of master and mistress. One day, when his father and his mistress both happened to call him at the same time, he hesitated between the two; being perplexed to know which had the strongest claim upon his obedience. He finally concluded to go to his mistress. When my father reproved him for it, he said, "You both called me, and I didn't know which I ought to go to first."

"You are *my* child," replied our father, "and when I call you, you should come immediately, if you have to pass through fire and water."

Poor Willie! He was now to learn his first lesson of obedience to a master. Grandmother tried to cheer us with hopeful words, and they found an echo in the credulous hearts of youth.

When we entered our new home we encountered cold

looks, cold words, and cold treatment. We were glad when the night came. On my narrow bed I moaned and wept, I felt so desolate and alone.

I had been there nearly a year, when a dear little friend of mine was buried. I heard her mother sob, as the clods fell on the coffin of her only child, and I turned away from the grave, feeling thankful that I still had something left to love. I met my grandmother, who said, "Come with me, Linda;" and from her tone I knew that something sad had happened. She led me apart from the people, and then said, "My child, your father is dead." Dead! How could I believe it? He had died so suddenly I had not even heard that he was sick. I went home with my grandmother. My heart rebelled against God, who had taken from me mother, father, mistress, and friend. The good grandmother tried to comfort me. "Who knows the ways of God?" said she. "Perhaps they have been kindly taken from the evil days to come." Years afterwards I often thought of this. She promised to be a mother to her grandchildren, so far as she might be permitted to do so; and strengthened by her love, I returned to my master's. I thought I should be allowed to go to my father's house the next morning; but I was ordered to go for flowers, that my mistress's house might be decorated for an evening party. I spent the day gathering flowers and weaving them into festoons, while the dead body of my father was lying within a mile of me. What cared my owners for that? He was merely a piece of property. Moreover, they thought he had spoiled his children, by teaching them to feel that they were human beings. This was blasphemous doctrine for a slave to teach; presumptuous in him, and dangerous to the masters.

The next day I followed his remains to a humble grave beside that of my dear mother. There were those who knew my father's worth, and respected his memory.

My home now seemed more dreary than ever. The laugh of the little slave-children sounded harsh and cruel. It was selfish to feel so about the joy of others. My brother moved about with a very grave face. I tried to comfort him, by saying, "Take courage, Willie; brighter days will come by and by."

"You don't know any thing about it, Linda," he replied.

"We shall have to stay here all our days; we shall never be free."

I argued that we were growing older and stronger, and that perhaps we might, before long, be allowed to hire our own time, and then we could earn money to buy our freedom. William declared this was much easier to say than to do; moreover, he did not intend to *buy* his freedom. We held daily controversies upon this subject.

Little attention was paid to the slaves' meals in Dr. Flint's house. If they could catch a bit of food while it was going, well and good. I gave myself no trouble on that score, for on my various errands I passed my grandmother's house, where there was always something to spare for me. I was frequently threatened with punishment if I stopped there; and my grandmother, to avoid detaining me, often stood at the gate with something for my breakfast or dinner. I was indebted to *her* for all my comforts, spiritual or temporal. It was *her* labor that supplied my scanty wardrobe. I have a vivid recollection of the linsey-woolsey dress given me every winter by Mrs. Flint. How I hated it! It was one of the badges of slavery.

While my grandmother was thus helping to support me from her hard earnings, the three hundred dollars she had lent her mistress were never repaid. When her mistress died, her son-in-law, Dr. Flint, was appointed executor. When grandmother applied to him for payment, he said the estate was insolvent, and the law prohibited payment. It did not, however, prohibit him from retaining the silver candelabra, which had been purchased with that money. I presume they will be handed down in the family, from generation to generation.

My grandmother's mistress had always promised her that, at her death, she should be free; and it was said that in her will she made good the promise. But when the estate was settled, Dr. Flint told the faithful old servant that, under existing circumstances, it was necessary she should be sold.

On the appointed day, the customary advertisement was posted up, proclaiming that there would be a "public sale of negroes, horses, &c." Dr. Flint called to tell my grandmother that he was unwilling to wound her feelings by putting her up at auction, and that he would prefer to dispose of her at private sale. My grandmother saw through his hypocrisy; she understood very well that he was ashamed of the job. She was a very spirited woman, and if he was base enough to sell her, when her mistress intended she should be free, she was determined the public should know it. She had for a long time supplied many families with crackers and preserves; consequently, "Aunt Marthy," as she was called, was generally known, and every body who knew her respected her intelligence and good character. Her long and faithful service in the family was also well known, and the intention of her mistress to leave her free. When the day of sale came, she took her place among the chattels, and at the first call she sprang upon the auction-block. Many voices called out, "Shame! Shame! Who is going to sell you, aunt Marthy? Don't stand there! That is no place for *you*." Without saying a word, she quietly awaited her fate. No one bid for her. At last, a feeble voice said, "Fifty dollars." It came from a maiden lady, seventy years old, the sister of my grandmother's deceased mistress. She had lived forty years under the same roof with my grandmother; she knew how faithfully she had served her owners, and how cruelly she had been defrauded of her rights; and she resolved to protect her. The auctioneer waited for a higher bid; but her wishes were respected; no one bid above her. She could neither read nor write; and when the bill of sale was made out, she signed it with a cross. But what consequence was that, when she had a big heart overflowing with human kindness? She gave the old servant her freedom.

At that time, my grandmother was just fifty years old. Laborious years had passed since then; and now my brother and I were slaves to the man who had defrauded her of her money, and tried to defraud her of her freedom. One of my mother's sisters, called Aunt Nancy, was also a slave in his family. She was a kind, good aunt to me; and supplied the place of both housekeeper and waiting maid to her mistress. She was, in fact, at the beginning and end of every thing.

Mrs. Flint, like many southern women, was totally deficient in energy. She had not strength to superintend her household affairs; but her nerves were so strong, that she could sit in her easy chair and see a woman whipped, till the blood trickled from every stroke of the lash. She was a member of the church; but partaking of the Lord's supper did not seem to put her in a Christian frame of mind. If dinner was not served at the exact time on that particular Sunday, she would station herself in the kitchen, and wait till it was dished, and then spit in all the kettles and pans that had been used for cooking. She did this to prevent the cook and her children from eking out their meagre fare with the remains of the gravy and other scrapings. The slaves could get nothing to eat except what she chose to give them. Provisions were weighed out by the pound and ounce, three times a day. I can assure you she gave them no chance to eat wheat bread from her flour barrel. She knew how many biscuits a quart of flour would make, and exactly what size they ought to be.

Dr. Flint was an epicure. The cook never sent a dinner to his table without fear and trembling; for if there happened to be a dish not to his liking, he would either order her to be whipped, or compel her to eat every mouthful of it in his presence. The poor, hungry creature might not have objected to eating it; but she did not object to having her master cram it down her throat till she choked.

They had a pet dog, that was a nuisance in the house. The cook was ordered to make some Indian mush for him. He refused to eat, and when his head was held over it, the froth flowed from his mouth into the basin. He died a few minutes after. When Dr. Flint came in, he said the mush had not been well cooked, and that was the reason the animal would not eat it. He sent for the cook, and compelled her to eat it. He thought that the woman's stomach was stronger than the dog's; but her sufferings afterwards proved that he was mistaken. This poor woman endured many cruelties from her master and mistress; sometimes she was locked up, away from her nursing baby, for a whole day and night.

When I had been in the family a few weeks, one of the plantation slaves was brought to town, by order of his master. It was near night when he arrived, and Dr. Flint ordered him to be taken to the work house, and tied up to the joist, so that his feet would just escape the ground. In that situation he was to wait till the doctor had taken his tea. I shall never forget that night. Never before, in my life, had I heard hundreds of blows fall, in succession, on a human being. His piteous groans, and his "O, pray don't, massa," rang in my ear for months afterwards. There were many conjectures as to the cause of this terrible punishment. Some said master accused him of stealing corn; others said the slave had quarrelled with his wife, in presence of the overseer, and had accused his master of being the father of her child. They were both black, and the child was very fair.

I went into the work house next morning, and saw the cowhide still wet with blood, and the boards all covered with gore. The poor man lived, and continued to quarrel with his wife. A few months afterwards Dr. Flint handed them both over to a slave-trader. The guilty man put their value into his pocket, and had the satisfaction of knowing that they were out of sight and hearing. When the mother was delivered into the trader's hands, she said. "You promised to treat me well." To which he replied, "You have let your tongue run too far; damn you!" She had forgotten that it was a crime for a slave to tell who was the father of her child.

From others than the master persecution also comes in such cases. I once saw a young slave girl dying soon after the birth of a child nearly white. In her agony she cried out, "O Lord, come and take me!" Her mistress stood by, and mocked at her like an incarnate fiend. "You suffer, do you?" she exclaimed. "I am glad of it. You deserve it all, and more too."

The girl's mother said, "The baby is dead, thank God; and I hope my poor child will soon be in heaven, too."

"Heaven!" retorted the mistress. "There is no such place for the like of her and her bastard."

The poor mother turned away, sobbing. Her dying daughter called her, feebly, and as she bent over her, I heard her say, "Don't grieve so, mother; God knows all about it; and HE will have mercy upon me."

Her sufferings, afterwards, became so intense, that her mistress felt unable to stay; but when she left the room, the scornful smile was still on her lips. Seven children called her mother. The poor black woman had but the one child, whose eyes she saw closing in death, while she thanked God for taking her away from the greater bitterness of life.

III.

THE SLAVES' NEW YEAR'S DAY.

Dr. Flint owned a fine residence in town, several farms, and about fifty slaves, besides hiring a number by the year.

Hiring-day at the south takes place on the 1st of January. On the 2d, the slaves are expected to go to their new masters. On a farm, they work until the corn and cotton are laid. They then have two holidays. Some masters give them a good dinner under the trees. This over, they work until Christmas eve. If no heavy charges are meantime brought against them, they are given four or five holidays, whichever the master or overseer may think proper. Then comes New Year's eve; and they gather together their little alls, or more properly speaking, their little nothings, and wait anxiously for the dawning of day. At the appointed hour the grounds are thronged with men, women, and children, waiting, like criminals, to hear their doom pronounced. The slave is sure to know who is the most humane, or cruel master, within forty miles of him.

It is easy to find out, on that day, who clothes and feeds his slaves well; for he is surrounded by a crowd, begging, "Please, massa, hire me this year. I will work very hard, massa."

If a slave is unwilling to go with his new master, he is whipped, or locked up in jail, until he consents to go, and promises not to run away during the year. Should he chance to change his mind, thinking it justifiable to violate an extorted promise, woe unto him if he is caught! The whip is used till the blood flows at his feet; and his stiffened limbs are put in chains, to be dragged in the field for days and days!

If he lives until the next year, perhaps the same man will hire him again, without even giving him an opportunity of going to the hiring-ground. After those for hire are disposed of, those for sale are called up.

O, you happy free women, contrast *your* New Year's day with that of the poor bond-woman! With you it is a pleasant season, and the light of the day is blessed. Friendly wishes meet you every where, and gifts are showered upon you. Even hearts that have been estranged from you soften at this season, and lips that have been silent echo back, "I wish you a happy New Year." Children bring their little offerings, and raise their rosy lips for a caress. They are your own, and no hand but that of death can take them from you.

But to the slave mother New Year's day comes laden with peculiar sorrows. She sits on her cold cabin floor, watching the children who may all be torn from her the next morning; and often does she wish that she and they might die before the day dawns. She may be an ignorant creature, degraded by the system that has brutalized her from childhood; but she has a mother's instincts, and is capable of feeling a mother's agonies.

On one of these sale days, I saw a mother lead seven children to the auction-block. She knew that *some* of them would be taken from her; but they took *all*. The children were sold to a slave-trader, and their mother was bought by a man in her own town. Before night her children were all far away. She begged the trader to tell her where he intended to take them; this he refused to do. How *could* he, when he knew he would sell them, one by one, wherever he could command the highest price? I met that mother in the street, and her wild, haggard face lives to-day in my mind. She wrung her hands in anguish, and exclaimed, "Gone! All gone! Why *don't* God kill me?" I had no words wherewith to comfort her. Instances of this kind are of daily, yea, of hourly occurrence.

Slaveholders have a method, peculiar to their institution, of getting rid of *old* slaves, whose lives have been worn out in their service. I knew an old woman, who for seventy years faithfully served her master. She had become almost helpless, from hard labor and disease. Her owners moved to Alabama, and the old black woman was left to be sold to any body who would give twenty dollars for her.

IV.

THE SLAVE WHO DARED TO
FEEL LIKE A MAN.

Two years had passed since I entered Dr. Flint's family, and those years had brought much of the knowledge that comes from experience, though they had afforded little opportunity for any other kinds of knowledge.

My grandmother had, as much as possible, been a mother to her orphan grandchildren. By perseverance and unwearied industry, she was now mistress of a snug little home, surrounded with the necessaries of life. She would have been happy could her children have shared them with her. There remained but three children and two grandchildren, all slaves. Most earnestly did she strive to make us feel that it was the will of God: that He had seen fit to place us under such circumstances; and though it seemed hard, we ought to pray for contentment.

It was a beautiful faith, coming from a mother who could not call her children her own. But I, and Benjamin, her youngest boy, condemned it. We reasoned that it was much more the will of God that we should be situated as she was. We longed for a home like hers. There we always found sweet balsam for our troubles. She was so loving, so sympathizing! She always met us with a smile, and listened with patience to all our sorrows. She spoke so hopefully, that unconsciously the clouds gave place to sunshine. There was a grand big oven there, too, that baked bread and nice things for the town, and we knew there was always a choice bit in store for us.

But, alas! Even the charms of the old oven failed to reconcile us to our hard lot. Benjamin was now a tall, handsome lad, strongly and gracefully made, and with a spirit too bold and daring for a slave. My brother William, now twelve years old, had the same aversion to the word master that he had when he was an urchin of seven years. I was his confidant. He came to me with all his troubles. I remember one instance in particular. It was on a lovely spring morning, and when I marked the sunlight dancing here and there, its beauty seemed to mock my sadness. For my master, whose restless, craving, vicious nature roved about day and night, seeking whom to devour, had just left me, with stinging, scorching words; words that scathed ear and brain like fire. O, how I despised him! I thought how glad I should be, if some day when he walked the earth, it would open and swallow him up, and disencumber the world of a plague.

When he told me that I was made for his use, made to obey his command in *every* thing; that I was nothing but a slave, whose will must and should surrender to his, never before had my puny arm felt half so strong.

So deeply was I absorbed in painful reflections afterwards, that I neither saw nor heard the entrance of any one, till the voice of William sounded close beside me. "Linda," said he, "what makes you look so sad? I love you. O, Linda, isn't this a bad world? Every body seems so cross and unhappy. I wish I had died when poor father did."

I told him that every body was *not* cross, or unhappy; that those who had pleasant homes, and kind friends, and who were not afraid to love them, were happy. But we, who were slave-children, without father or mother, could not expect to be happy. We must be good; perhaps that would bring us contentment.

"Yes," he said, "I try to be good; but what's the use? They are all the time troubling me." Then he proceeded to relate his afternoon's difficulty with young master Nicholas. It seemed that the brother of master Nicholas had pleased himself with making up stories about William. Master Nicholas said he should be flogged, and he would do it. Whereupon he went to work; but William fought bravely, and the young master, finding he was getting the better of him, undertook to tie his hands behind him. He failed in that likewise. By dint of kicking and fisting, William came out of the skirmish none the worse for a few scratches.

He continued to discourse, on his young master's *meanness*; how he whipped the *little* boys, but was a perfect coward when a tussle ensued between him and white boys of his own size. On such occasions he always took to his legs. William had other charges to make against him. One was his rubbing up pennies with quicksilver, and passing them off for quarters of a dollar on an old man who kept a fruit stall. William was often sent to buy fruit, and he earnestly inquired of me what he ought to do under such circumstances. I told him it was certainly wrong to deceive the old man, and that it was his duty to tell him of the impositions practised by his young master. I assured him the old man would not be slow to comprehend the whole, and there the matter would end. William thought it might with the old man, but not with *him*. He said he did not mind the smart of the whip, but he did not like the *idea* of being whipped.

While I advised him to be good and forgiving I was not unconscious of the beam in my own eye. It was the very knowledge of my own shortcomings that urged me to retain, if possible, some sparks of my brother's God-given nature. I had not lived fourteen years in slavery for nothing. I had felt, seen, and heard enough, to read the characters, and question the motives, of those around me. The war of my life had begun; and though one of God's most powerless creatures, I resolved never to be conquered. Alas, for me!

If there was one pure, sunny spot for me, I believed it to be in Benjamin's heart, and in another's, whom I loved with all the ardor of a girl's first love. My owner knew of it, and sought in every way to render me miserable. He did not resort to corporal punishment, but to all the petty, tyrannical ways that human ingenuity could devise.

I remember the first time I was punished. It was in the month of February. My grandmother had taken my old shoes, and replaced them with a new pair. I needed them; for several inches of snow had fallen, and it still continued to fall. When I walked through Mrs. Flint's room, their creaking grated harshly on her refined nerves. She called me to her, and asked what I had about me that made such a horrid noise. I told her it was my new shoes. "Take them off," said she; "and if you put them on again, I'll throw them into the fire."

I took them off, and my stockings also. She then sent me a long distance, on an errand. As I went through the snow, my bare feet tingled. That night I was very hoarse; and I went to bed thinking the next day would find me sick, perhaps dead. What was my grief on waking to find myself quite well!

I had imagined if I died, or was laid up for some time, that my mistress would feel a twinge of remorse that she had so hated "the little imp," as she styled me. It was my ignorance of that mistress that gave rise to such extravagant imaginings.

Dr. Flint occasionally had high prices offered for me; but he always said, "She don't belong to me. She is my daughter's property, and I have no right to sell her." Good, honest man! My young mistress was still a child, and I could look for no protection from her. I loved her, and she returned my affection. I once heard her father allude to her attachment to me, and his wife promptly replied that it proceeded from fear. This put unpleasant doubts into my mind. Did the child feign what she did not feel? or was her mother jealous of the mite of love she bestowed on me? I concluded it must be the latter. I said to myself, "Surely, little children are true."

One afternoon I sat at my sewing, feeling unusual depression of spirits. My mistress had been accusing me of an offence, of which I assured her I was perfectly innocent; but I saw, by the contemptuous curl of her lip, that she believed I was telling a lie.

I wondered for what wise purpose God was leading me through such thorny paths, and whether still darker days were in store for me. As I sat musing thus, the door opened softly, and William came in. "Well, brother," said I, "what is the matter this time?"

"O Linda, Ben and his master have had a dreadful time!" said he.

My first thought was that Benjamin was killed. "Don't be frightened, Linda," said William; "I will tell you all about it."

It appeared that Benjamin's master had sent for him, and he did not immediately obey the summons. When he did, his master was angry, and began to whip him. He resisted. Master and slave fought, and finally the master was thrown. Benjamin had cause to tremble; for he had thrown to the ground his master—one of the richest men in town. I anxiously awaited the result.

That night I stole to my grandmother's house; and Benjamin also stole thither from his master's. My grandmother had gone to spend a day or two with an old friend living in the country.

"I have come," said Benjamin, "to tell you good by. I am going away."

I inquired where.

"To the north," he replied.

I looked at him to see whether he was in earnest. I saw it all in his firm, set mouth. I implored him not to go, but he paid no heed to my words. He said he was no longer a boy, and every day made his yoke more galling. He had raised his hand against his master, and was to be publicly whipped for the offence. I reminded him of the poverty and hardships he must encounter among strangers. I told him he might be caught and brought back; and that was terrible to think of.

He grew vexed, and asked if poverty and hardships with freedom, were not preferable to our treatment in slavery. "Linda," he continued, "we are dogs here; foot-balls, cattle, every thing that's mean. No, I will not stay. Let them bring me back. We don't die but once."

He was right; but it was hard to give him up. "Go," said I, "and break your mother's heart."

I repented of my words ere they were out.

"Linda," said he, speaking as I had not heard him speak that evening, "how *could* you say that? Poor mother! be kind to her, Linda; and you, too, cousin Fanny."

Cousin Fanny was a friend who had lived some years with us.

Farewells were exchanged, and the bright, kind boy, endeared to us by so many acts of love, vanished from our sight.

It is not necessary to state how he made his escape. Suffice it to say, he was on his way to New York when a violent storm overtook the vessel. The captain said he must put into the nearest port. This alarmed Benjamin, who was aware that he would be advertised in every port near his own town. His embarrassment was noticed by the captain. To port they went. There the advertisement met the captain's eye. Benjamin so exactly answered its description, that the captain laid hold on him, and bound him in chains. The storm passed, and they proceeded to New York. Before reaching that port Benjamin managed to get off his chains and throw them overboard. He escaped from the vessel, but was pursued, captured, and carried back to his master.

When my grandmother returned home and found her youngest child had fled, great was her sorrow; but, with characteristic piety, she said, "God's will be done." Each morning, she inquired if any news had been heard from her boy. Yes, news *was* heard. The master was rejoicing over a letter, announcing the capture of his human chattel.

That day seems but as yesterday, so well do I remember it. I saw him led through the streets in chains, to jail. His face was ghastly pale, yet full of determination. He had begged one of the sailors to go to his mother's house and ask her not to meet him. He said the sight of her distress would take from him all self-control. She yearned to see him, and she went; but she screened herself in the crowd, that it might be as her child had said.

We were not allowed to visit him; but we had known the jailer for years, and he was a kind-hearted man. At midnight he opened the jail door for my grandmother and myself to enter, in disguise. When we entered the cell not a sound broke the stillness. "Benjamin, Benjamin!" whispered my grandmother. No answer. "Benjamin!" she again faltered. There was a jingle of chains. The moon had just risen, and cast an uncertain light through the bars of the window. We knelt down and took Benjamin's cold hands in ours. We did not speak. Sobs were heard, and Benjamin's lips were unsealed; for his mother was weeping on his neck. How vividly does memory bring back that sad night! Mother and son talked together. He asked her pardon for the suffering he had caused her. She said she had nothing to forgive; she could not blame his desire for freedom. He told her that when he was captured, he broke away, and was about casting himself into the river, when thoughts of *her* came over him, and he desisted. She asked if he did not also think of God. I fancied I saw his face grow fierce in the moonlight. He answered, "No, I did not think of him. When a man is hunted like a wild beast he forgets there is a God, a heaven. He forgets every thing in his struggle to get beyond the reach of the bloodhounds."

"Don't talk so, Benjamin," said she. "Put your trust in God. Be humble, my child, and your master will forgive you."

"Forgive me for *what,* mother? For not letting him treat me like a dog? No! I will never humble myself to him. I have worked for him for nothing all my life, and I am repaid with stripes and imprisonment. Here I will stay till I die, or till he sells me."

The poor mother shuddered at his words. I think he felt it; for when he next spoke, his voice was calmer. "Don't fret about me, mother. I ain't worth it," said he. "I wish I had some of your goodness. You bear every thing patiently, just as though you thought it was all right. I wish I could."

She told him she had not always been so; once, she was like him; but when sore troubles came upon her, and she had no arm to lean upon, she learned to call on God, and he lightened her burdens. She besought him to do likewise.

We overstaid our time, and were obliged to hurry from the jail.

Benjamin had been imprisoned three weeks, when my grandmother went to intercede for him with his master. He was immovable. He said Benjamin should serve as an example to the rest of his slaves; he should be kept in jail till he was subdued, or be sold if he got but one dollar for him. However, he afterwards relented in some degree. The chains were taken off, and we were allowed to visit him.

As his food was of the coarsest kind, we carried him as often as possible a warm supper, accompanied with some little luxury for the jailer.

Three months elapsed, and there was no prospect of release or of a purchaser. One day he was heard to sing and laugh. This piece of indecorum was told to his master, and the overseer was ordered to re-chain him. He was now confined in an apartment with other prisoners, who were covered with filthy rags. Benjamin was chained near them, and was soon covered with vermin. He worked at his chains till he succeeded in getting out of them. He passed them through the bars of the window, with a request that they should be taken to his master, and he should be informed that he was covered with vermin.

This audacity was punished with heavier chains, and prohibition of our visits.

My grandmother continued to send him fresh changes of clothes. The old ones were burned up. The last night we saw him in jail his mother still begged him to send for his master, and beg his pardon. Neither persuasion nor argument could turn him from his purpose. He calmly answered, "I am waiting his time."

Those chains were mournful to hear.

Another three months passed, and Benjamin left his prison walls. We that loved him waited to bid him a long and last farewell. A slave trader had bought him. You remember, I told you what price he brought when ten years of age. Now he was more than twenty years old, and sold for three hundred dollars. The master had been blind to his own interest. Long confinement had made his face too pale, his form too thin; moreover, the trader had heard something of his character, and it did not strike him as suitable for a slave. He said he would give any price if the handsome lad was a girl. We thanked God that he was not.

Could you have seen that mother clinging to her child, when they fastened the irons upon his wrists; could you have heard her heartrending groans, and seen her bloodshot eyes wander wildly from face to face, vainly pleading for mercy; could you have witnessed that scene as I saw it, you would exclaim, *Slavery is damnable!*

Benjamin, her youngest, her pet, was forever gone! She could not realize it. She had had an interview with the trader for the purpose of ascertaining if Benjamin could be purchased. She was told it was impossible, as he had given bonds not to sell him till he was out of the state. He promised that he would not sell him till he reached New Orleans.

With a strong arm and unvaried trust, my grandmother began her work of love. Benjamin must be free. If she succeeded, she knew they would still be separated; but the sacrifice was not too great. Day and night she labored. The trader's price would treble that he gave; but she was not discouraged.

She employed a lawyer to write to a gentleman, whom she knew, in New Orleans. She begged him to interest himself for Benjamin, and he willingly favored her request.

When he saw Benjamin, and stated his business, he thanked him; but said he preferred to wait a while before making the trader an offer. He knew he had tried to obtain a high price for him, and had invariably failed. This encouraged him to make another effort for freedom. So one morning, long before day, Benjamin was missing. He was riding over the blue billows, bound for Baltimore.

For once his white face did him a kindly service. They had no suspicion that it belonged to a slave; otherwise, the law would have been followed out to the letter, and the *thing* rendered back to slavery. The brightest skies are often overshadowed by the darkest clouds. Benjamin was taken sick, and compelled to remain in Baltimore three weeks. His strength was slow in returning; and his desire to continue his journey seemed to retard his recovery. How could he get strength without air and exercise? He resolved to venture on a short walk. A by-street was selected, where he thought himself secure of not being met by any one that knew him; but a voice called out, "Halloo, Ben, my boy! what are you doing *here*?"

His first impulse was to run; but his legs trembled so that he could not stir. He turned to confront his antagonist, and behold, there stood his old master's next door neighbor! He thought it was all over with him now; but it proved otherwise. That man was a miracle. He possessed a goodly number of slaves, and yet was not quite deaf to that mystic clock, whose ticking is rarely heard in the slaveholder's breast.

"Ben, you are sick," said he. "Why, you look like a ghost. I guess I gave you something of a start. Never mind, Ben, I am not going to touch you. You had a pretty tough time of it, and you may go on your way rejoicing for all me. But I would advise you to get out of this place plaguy quick, for there are several gentlemen here from our town." He described the nearest and safest route to New York, and added, "I shall be glad to tell your mother I have seen you. Good by, Ben."

Benjamin turned away, filled with gratitude, and surprised that the town he hated contained such a gem—a gem worthy of a purer setting.

This gentleman was a Northerner by birth, and had married a southern lady. On his return, he told my grandmother that he had seen her son, and of the service he had rendered him.

Benjamin reached New York safely, and concluded to stop there until he had gained strength enough to proceed further. It happened that my grandmother's only remaining son had sailed for the same city on business for his mistress. Through God's providence, the brothers met. You may be sure it was a happy meeting. "O Phil," exclaimed Benjamin, "I am here at last." Then he told him how near he came to dying, almost in sight of free land, and how he prayed that he might live to get one breath of free air. He said life was worth something now, and it would be hard to die. In the old jail he had not valued it; once, he was tempted to destroy it; but something, he did not know what, had prevented him; perhaps it was fear. He had heard those who profess to be religious declare there was no heaven for self-murderers; and as his life had been pretty hot here, he did not desire a continuation of the same in another world. "If I die now," he exclaimed, "thank God, I shall die a freeman!"

He begged my uncle Phillip not to return south; but stay and work with him, till they earned enough to buy those at home. His brother told him it would kill their mother if he deserted her in her trouble. She had pledged her house, and with difficulty had raised money to buy him. Would he be bought?

"No, never!" he replied. "Do you suppose, Phil, when I have got so far out of their clutches, I will give them one red cent? No! And do you suppose I would turn mother out of her home in her old age? That I would let her pay all those hard-earned dollars for me, and never to see me? For you know she will stay south as long as her other children are slaves. What a good mother! Tell her to buy *you,* Phil. You have been a comfort to her, and I have been a trouble. And Linda, poor Linda; what'll become of her? Phil, you don't know what a life they lead her. She has told me something about it, and I wish old Flint was dead, or a better man. When I was in jail, he asked her if she didn't want *him* to ask my master to forgive me, and take me home again. She told him, No; that I didn't want to go back. He got mad, and said we were all alike. I never despised my own master half as much as I do that man. There is many a worse slave-holder than my master; but for all that I would not be his slave."

While Benjamin was sick, he had parted with nearly all his clothes to pay necessary expenses. But he did not part with a little pin I fastened in his bosom when we parted. It was the most valuable thing I owned, and I thought none more worthy to wear it. He had it still.

His brother furnished him with clothes, and gave him what money he had.

They parted with moistened eyes; and as Benjamin turned away, he said, "Phil, I part with all my kindred." And so it proved. We never heard from him again.

Uncle Phillip came home; and the first words he uttered when he entered the house were, "Mother, Ben is free! I have seen him in New York." She stood looking at him with a bewildered air. "Mother, don't you believe it?" he said, laying his hand softly upon her shoulder. She raised her hands, and exclaimed, "God be praised! Let us thank him." She dropped on her knees, and poured forth her heart in prayer. Then Phillip must sit down and repeat to her every word Benjamin had said. He told her all; only he forbore to mention how sick and pale her darling looked. Why should he distress her when she could do him no good?

The brave old woman still toiled on, hoping to rescue some of her other children. After a while she succeeded in buying Phillip. She paid eight hundred dollars, and came home with the precious document that secured his freedom. The happy mother and son sat together by the old hearthstone that night, telling how proud they were of each other, and how they would prove to the world that they could take care of themselves, as they had long taken care of others. We all concluded by saying, "He that is *willing* to be a slave, let him be a slave."

V.

THE TRIALS OF GIRLHOOD.

During the first years of my service in Dr. Flint's family, I was accustomed to share some indulgences with the children of my mistress. Though this seemed to me no more than right, I was grateful for it, and tried to merit the kindness by the faithful discharge of my duties. But I now entered on my fifteenth year—a sad epoch in the life of a slave girl. My master began to whisper foul words in my ear. Young as I was, I could not remain ignorant of their import. I tried to treat them with indifference or contempt. The master's age, my extreme youth, and the fear that his conduct would be reported to my grandmother, made me bear this treatment for many months. He was a crafty man, and resorted to many means to accomplish his purposes. Sometimes he had stormy, terrific ways, that made his victims tremble; sometimes he assumed a gentleness that he thought must surely subdue. Of the two, I preferred his stormy moods, although they left me trembling. He tried his utmost to corrupt the pure principles my grandmother had instilled. He peopled my young mind with unclean images, such as only a vile monster could think of. I turned from him with disgust and hatred. But he was my master. I was compelled to live under the same roof with him—where I saw a man forty years my senior daily violating the most sacred commandments of nature. He told me I was his property; that I must be subject to his will in all things. My soul revolted against the mean tyranny. But where could I turn for protection? No matter whether the slave girl be as black as ebony or as fair as her mistress. In either case, there is no shadow of law to protect her from insult, from violence, or even from death; all these are inflicted by fiends who bear the shape of men. The mistress, who ought to protect the helpless victim, has no other feelings towards her but those of jealousy and rage. The degradation, the wrongs, the vices, that grow out of slavery, are more than I can describe. They are greater than you would willingly believe.

Surely, if you credited one half the truths that are told you concerning the helpless millions suffering in this cruel bondage, you at the north would not help to tighten the yoke. You surely would refuse to do for the master, on your own soil, the mean and cruel work which trained bloodhounds and the lowest class of whites do for him at the south.

Every where the years bring to all enough of sin and sorrow; but in slavery the very dawn of life is darkened by these shadows. Even the little child, who is accustomed to wait on her mistress and her children, will learn, before she is twelve years old, why it is that her mistress hates such and such a one among the slaves. Perhaps the child's own mother is among those hated ones. She listens to violent outbreaks of jealous passion, and cannot help understanding what is the cause. She will become prematurely knowing in evil things. Soon she will learn to tremble when she hears her master's footfall. She will be compelled to realize that she is no longer a child. If God has bestowed beauty upon her, it will prove her greatest curse. That which commands admiration in the white woman only hastens the degradation of the female slave. I know that some are too much brutalized by slavery to feel the humiliation of their position; but many slaves feel it most acutely, and shrink from the memory of it. I cannot tell how much I suffered in the presence of these wrongs, nor how I am still pained by the retrospect. My master met me at every turn, reminding me that I belonged to him, and swearing by heaven and earth that he would compel me to submit to him. If I went out for a breath of fresh air, after a day of unwearied toil, his footsteps dogged me. If I knelt by my mother's grave, his dark shadow fell on me even there. The light heart which nature had given me became heavy with sad forebodings. The other slaves in my master's house noticed the change. Many of them pitied me; but none dared to ask the cause. They had no need to inquire. They knew too well the guilty practices under that roof; and they were aware that to speak of them was an offence that never went unpunished.

I longed for some one to confide in. I would have given the world to have laid my head on my grandmother's faithful bosom, and told her all my troubles. But Dr. Flint swore he would kill me, if I was not as silent as the grave. Then, although my grandmother was all in all to me, I feared her as well as loved her. I had been accustomed to look up to her with a respect bordering upon awe. I was very young, and felt shamefaced about telling her such impure things, especially as I knew her to be very strict on such subjects. Moreover, she was a woman of a high spirit. She was usually very quiet in her demeanor; but if her indignation was once roused, it was not very easily quelled. I had been told that she once chased a white gentleman with a loaded pistol, because he insulted one of her daughters. I dreaded the consequences of a violent outbreak; and both pride and fear kept me silent. But though I did not confide in my grandmother, and even evaded her vigilant watchfulness and inquiry, her presence in the neighborhood was some protection to me. Though she had been a slave, Dr. Flint was afraid of her. He dreaded her scorching rebukes. Moreover, she was known and patronized by many people; and he did not wish to have his villany made public. It was lucky for me that I did not live on a distant plantation, but in a town not so large that the inhabitants were ignorant of each other's affairs. Bad as are the laws and customs in a slave-holding community, the doctor, as a professional man, deemed it prudent to keep up some outward show of decency.

O, what days and nights of fear and sorrow that man caused me! Reader, it is not to awaken sympathy for myself that I am telling you truthfully what I suffered in slavery. I do it to kindle a flame of compassion in your hearts for my sisters who are still in bondage, suffering as I once suffered.

I once saw two beautiful children playing together. One was a fair white child; the other was her slave, and also her sister. When I saw them embracing each other, and heard their joyous laughter, I turned sadly away from the lovely sight. I foresaw the inevitable blight that would fall on the little slave's heart. I knew how soon her laughter would be changed to sighs. The fair child grew up to be a still fairer woman. From childhood to womanhood her pathway was blooming with flowers, and overarched by a sunny sky. Scarcely one day of her life had been clouded when the sun rose on her happy bridal morning.

How had those years dealt with her slave sister, the little playmate of her childhood? She, also, was very beautiful; but the flowers and sunshine of love were not for her. She drank the cup of sin, and shame, and misery, whereof her persecuted race are compelled to drink.

In view of these things, why are ye silent, ye free men and women of the north? Why do your tongues falter in maintenance of the right? Would that I had more ability! But my heart is so full, and my pen is so weak! There are noble men and women who plead for us, striving to help those who cannot help themselves. God bless them! God give them strength and courage to go on! God bless those, every where, who are laboring to advance the cause of humanity!

VI.

THE JEALOUS MISTRESS.

I WOULD ten thousand times rather that my children should be the half-starved paupers of Ireland than to be the most pampered among the slaves of America. I would rather drudge out my life on a cotton plantation, till the grave opened to give me rest, than to live with an unprincipled master and a jealous mistress. The felon's home in a penitentiary is preferable. He may repent, and turn from the error of his ways, and so find peace; but it is not so with a favorite slave. She is not allowed to have any pride of character. It is deemed a crime in her to wish to be virtuous.

Mrs. Flint possessed the key to her husband's character before I was born. She might have used this knowledge to counsel and to screen the young and the innocent among her slaves; but for them she had no sympathy. They were the objects of her constant suspicion and malevolence. She watched her husband with unceasing vigilance; but he was well practised in means to evade it. What he could not find opportunity to say in words he manifested in signs. He invented more than were ever thought of in a deaf and dumb asylum. I let them pass, as if I did not understand what he meant; and many were the curses and threats bestowed on me for my stupidity. One day he caught me teaching myself to write. He frowned, as if he was not well pleased; but I suppose he came to the conclusion that such an accomplishment might help to advance his favorite scheme. Before long, notes were often slipped into my hand. I would return them, saying, "I can't read them, sir." "Can't you?" he replied; "then I must read them to you." He always finished the reading by asking, "Do you understand?" Sometimes he would complain of the heat of the tea room, and order his supper to be placed on a small table in the piazza. He would seat himself there with a well-satisfied smile, and tell me to stand by and brush away the flies. He would eat very slowly, pausing between the mouthfuls. These intervals were employed in describing the happiness I was so foolishly throwing away, and in threatening me with the penalty that finally awaited my stubborn disobedience. He boasted much of the forbearance he had exercised towards me, and reminded me that there was a limit to his patience. When I succeeded in avoiding opportunities for him to talk to me at home, I was ordered to come to his office, to do some errand. When there, I was obliged to stand and listen to such language as he saw fit to address to me. Sometimes I so openly expressed my contempt for him that he would become violently enraged, and I wondered why he did not strike me. Circumstanced as he was, he probably thought it was better policy to be forbearing. But the state of things grew worse and worse daily. In desperation I told him that I must and would apply to my grandmother for protection. He threatened me with death, and worse than death, if I made any complaint to her. Strange to say, I did not despair. I was naturally of a buoyant disposition, and always I had a hope of somehow getting out of his clutches. Like many a poor, simple slave before me, I trusted that some threads of joy would yet be woven into my dark destiny.

I had entered my sixteenth year, and every day it became more apparent that my presence was intolerable to

Mrs. Flint. Angry words frequently passed between her and her husband. He had never punished me himself, and he would not allow any body else to punish me. In that respect, she was never satisfied; but, in her angry moods, no terms were too vile for her to bestow upon me. Yet I, whom she detested so bitterly, had far more pity for her than he had, whose duty it was to make her life happy. I never wronged her, or wished to wrong her; and one word of kindness from her would have brought me to her feet.

After repeated quarrels between the doctor and his wife, he announced his intention to take his youngest daughter, then four years old, to sleep in his apartment. It was necessary that a servant should sleep in the same room, to be on hand if the child stirred. I was selected for that office, and informed for what purpose that arrangement had been made. By managing to keep within sight of people, as much as possible, during the day time, I had hitherto succeeded in eluding my master, though a razor was often held to my throat to force me to change this line of policy. At night I slept by the side of my great aunt, where I felt safe. He was too prudent to come into her room. She was an old woman, and had been in the family many years. Moreover, as a married man, and a professional man, he deemed it necessary to save appearances in some degree. But he resolved to remove the obstacle in the way of his scheme; and he thought he had planned it so that he should evade suspicion. He was well aware how much I prized my refuge by the side of my old aunt, and he determined to dispossess me of it. The first night the doctor had the little child in his room alone. The next morning, I was ordered to take my station as nurse the following night. A kind Providence interposed in my favor. During the day Mrs. Flint heard of this new arrangement, and a storm followed. I rejoiced to hear it rage.

After a while my mistress sent for me to come to her room. Her first question was, "Did you know you were to sleep in the doctor's room?"

"Yes, ma'am."

"Who told you?"

"My master."

"Will you answer truly all the questions I ask?"

"Yes, ma'am."

"Tell me, then, as you hope to be forgiven, are you innocent of what I have accused you?"

"I am."

She handed me a Bible, and said, "Lay your hand on your heart, kiss this holy book, and swear before God that you tell me the truth."

I took the oath she required, and I did it with a clear conscience.

"You have taken God's holy word to testify your innocence," said she. "If you have deceived me, beware! Now take this stool, sit down, look me directly in the face, and tell me all that has passed between your master and you."

I did as she ordered. As I went on with my account her color changed frequently, she wept, and sometimes groaned. She spoke in tones so sad, that I was touched by her grief. The tears came to my eyes; but I was soon convinced that her emotions arose from anger and wounded pride. She felt that her marriage vows were desecrated, her dignity insulted; but she had no compassion for the poor victim of her husband's perfidy. She pitied herself as a martyr; but she was incapable of feeling for the condition of shame and misery in which her unfortunate, helpless slave was placed.

Yet perhaps she had some touch of feeling for me; for when the conference was ended, she spoke kindly, and promised to protect me. I should have been much comforted by this assurance if I could have had confidence in it; but my experiences in slavery had filled me with distrust. She was not a very refined woman, and had not much control over her passions. I was an object of her jealousy, and, consequently, of her hatred; and I knew I could not expect kindness or confidence from her under the circumstances in which I was placed. I could not blame her. Slaveholders' wives feel as other women would under similar circumstances. The fire of her temper kindled from small sparks, and now the flame became so intense that the doctor was obliged to give up his intended arrangement.

I knew I had ignited the torch, and I expected to suffer for it afterwards; but I felt too thankful to my mistress for the timely aid she rendered me to care much about that. She now took me to sleep in a room adjoining her own.

There I was an object of her especial care, though not to her especial comfort, for she spent many a sleepless night to watch over me. Sometimes I woke up, and found her bending over me. At other times she whispered in my ear, as though it was her husband who was speaking to me, and listened to hear what I would answer. If she startled me, on such occasions, she would glide stealthily away; and the next morning she would tell me I had been talking in my sleep, and ask who I was talking to. At last, I began to be fearful for my life. It had been often threatened; and you can imagine, better than I can describe, what an unpleasant sensation it must produce to wake up in the dead of night and find a jealous woman bending over you. Terrible as this experience was, I had fears that it would give place to one more terrible.

My mistress grew weary of her vigils; they did not prove satisfactory. She changed her tactics. She now tried the trick of accusing my master of crime, in my presence, and gave my name as the author of the accusation. To my utter astonishment, he replied, "I don't believe it; but if she did acknowledge it, you tortured her into exposing me." Tortured into exposing him! Truly, Satan had no difficulty in distinguishing the color of his soul! I understood his object in making this false representation. It was to show me that I gained nothing by seeking the protection of my mistress; that the power was still all in his own hands. I pitied Mrs. Flint. She was a second wife, many years the junior of her husband; and the hoary-headed miscreant was enough to try the patience of a wiser and better woman. She was completely foiled, and knew not how to proceed. She would gladly have had me flogged for my supposed false oath; but, as I have already stated, the doctor never allowed any one to whip me. The old sinner was politic. The application of the lash might have led to remarks that would have exposed him in the eyes of his children and grandchildren. How often did I rejoice that I lived in a town where all the inhabitants knew each other! If I had been on a remote plantation, or lost among the multitude of a crowded city, I should not be a living woman at this day.

The secrets of slavery are concealed like those of the Inquisition. My master was, to my knowledge, the father of eleven slaves. But did the mothers dare to tell who was the father of their children? Did the other slaves dare to allude to it, except in whispers among themselves? No, indeed! They knew too well the terrible consequences.

My grandmother could not avoid seeing things which excited her suspicions. She was uneasy about me, and tried various ways to buy me; but the never-changing answer was always repeated: "Linda does not belong to *me*. She is my daughter's property, and I have no legal right to sell her." The conscientious man! He was too scrupulous to *sell* me; but he had no scruples whatever about committing a much greater wrong against the helpless young girl placed under his guardianship, as his daughter's property. Sometimes my persecutor would ask me whether I would like to be sold. I told him I would rather be sold to any body than to lead such a life as I did. On such occasions he would assume the air of a very injured individual, and reproach me for my ingratitude. "Did I not take you into the house, and make you the companion of my own children?" he would say. "Have I ever treated you like a negro? I have never allowed you to be punished, not even to please your mistress. And this is the recompense I get, you ungrateful girl!" I answered that he had reasons of his own for screening me from punishment, and that the course he pursued made my mistress hate me and persecute me. If I wept, he would say, "Poor child! Don't cry! don't cry! I will make peace for you with your mistress. Only let me arrange matters in my own way. Poor, foolish girl! you don't know what is for your own good. I would cherish you. I would make a lady of you. Now go, and think of all I have promised you."

I did think of it.

Reader, I draw no imaginary pictures of southern homes. I am telling you the plain truth. Yet when victims make their escape from the wild beast of Slavery, northerners consent to act the part of bloodhounds, and hunt the poor fugitive back into his den, "full of dead men's bones, and all uncleanness." Nay, more, they are not only willing, but proud, to give their daughters in marriage to slaveholders. The poor girls have romantic notions of a sunny clime, and of the flowering vines that all the year round shade a happy home. To what disappointments are they destined! The young wife soon learns that the husband in whose hands she has placed her happiness pays no regard to his marriage vows. Children of every shade of complexion play with her own fair babies, and too well she knows that they are born unto him of his own household. Jealousy and hatred enter the flowery home, and it is ravaged of its loveliness.

Southern women often marry a man knowing that he is the father of many little slaves. They do not trouble themselves about it. They regard such children as property, as marketable as the pigs on the plantation; and it is seldom that they do not make them aware of this by passing them into the slave-trader's hands as soon as possible, and thus getting them out of their sight. I am glad to say there are some honorable exceptions.

I have myself known two southern wives who exhorted their husbands to free those slaves towards whom they stood in a "parental relation;" and their request was granted. These husbands blushed before the superior nobleness of their wives' natures. Though they had only counselled them to do that which it was their duty to do, it commanded their respect, and rendered their conduct more exemplary. Concealment was at an end, and confidence took the place of distrust.

Though this bad institution deadens the moral sense, even in white women, to a fearful extent, it is not altogether extinct. I have heard southern ladies say of Mr. Such a one, "He not only thinks it no disgrace to be the father of those little niggers, but he is not ashamed to call himself their master. I declare, such things ought not to be tolerated in any decent society!"

VII.

THE LOVER.

WHY does the slave ever love? Why allow the tendrils of the heart to twine around objects which may at any moment be wrenched away by the hand of violence? When separations come by the hand of death, the pious soul can bow in resignation, and say, "Not my will, but thine be done, O Lord!" But when the ruthless hand of man strikes the blow, regardless of the misery he causes, it is hard to be submissive. I did not reason thus when I was a young girl. Youth will be youth. I loved and I indulged the hope that the dark clouds around me would turn out a bright lining. I forgot that in the land of my birth the shadows are too dense for light to penetrate. A land

Where laughter is not mirth; nor thought the mind;
Nor words a language; nor e'en men mankind.
Where cries reply to curses, shrieks to blows,
And each is tortured in his separate hell.

There was in the neighborhood a young colored carpenter; a free born man. We had been well acquainted in childhood, and frequently met together afterwards. We became mutually attached, and he proposed to marry me. I loved him with all the ardor of a young girl's first love. But when I reflected that I was a slave, and that the laws gave no sanction to the marriage of such, my heart sank within me. My lover wanted to buy me; but I knew that Dr. Flint was too wilful and arbitrary a man to consent to that arrangement. From him, I was sure of experiencing all sort of opposition, and I had nothing to hope from my mistress. She would have been delighted to have got rid of me, but not in that way. It would have relieved her mind of a burden if she could have seen me sold to some distant state, but if I was married near home I should be just as much in her husband's power as I had previously been,—for the husband of a slave has no power to protect her. Moreover, my mistress, like many others, seemed to think that slaves had no right to any family ties of their own; that they were created merely to wait upon the family of the mistress. I once heard her abuse a young slave girl, who told her that a colored man wanted to make her his wife. "I will have you peeled and pickled, my lady," said she, "if I ever hear you mention that subject again. Do you suppose that I will have you tending *my* children with the children of that nigger?" The girl to whom she said this had a mulatto child, of course not acknowledged by its father. The poor black man who loved her would have been proud to acknowledge his helpless offspring.

Many and anxious were the thoughts I revolved in my mind. I was at a loss what to do. Above all things, I was desirous to spare my lover the insults that had cut so deeply into my own soul. I talked with my grandmother about it, and partly told her my fears. I did not dare to tell her the worst. She had long suspected all was not right, and if I confirmed her suspicions I knew a storm would rise that would prove the overthrow of all my hopes.

This love-dream had been my support through many trials; and I could not bear to run the risk of having it suddenly dissipated. There was a lady in the neighborhood, a particular friend of Dr. Flint's, who often visited the house. I had a great respect for her, and she had always manifested a friendly interest in me. Grandmother thought she would have great influence with the doctor. I went to this lady, and told her my story. I told her I was aware that my lover's being a free-born man would prove a great objection; but he wanted to buy me; and if Dr. Flint would consent to that arrangement, I felt sure he would be willing to pay any reasonable price. She knew that Mrs. Flint disliked me; therefore, I ventured to suggest that perhaps my mistress would approve of my being sold, as that would rid her of me. The lady listened with kindly sympathy, and promised to do her utmost to promote my wishes. She had an interview with the doctor, and I believe she pleaded my cause earnestly; but it was all to no purpose.

How I dreaded my master now! Every minute I expected to be summoned to his presence; but the day passed, and I heard nothing from him. The next morning, a message was brought to me: "Master wants you in his study." I found the door ajar, and I stood a moment gazing at the hateful man who claimed a right to rule me, body and soul. I entered, and tried to appear calm. I did not want him to know how my heart was bleeding. He looked fixedly at me, with an expression which seemed to say, "I have half a mind to kill you on the spot." At last he broke the silence, and that was a relief to both of us.

"So you want to be married, do you?" said he, "and to a free nigger."

"Yes, sir."

"Well, I'll soon convince you whether I am your master, or the nigger fellow you honor so highly. If you *must* have a husband, you may take up with one of my slaves."

What a situation I should be in, as the wife of one of *his* slaves, even if my heart had been interested!

I replied, "Don't you suppose, sir, that a slave can have some preference about marrying? Do you suppose that all men are alike to her?"

"Do you love this nigger?" said he, abruptly.

"Yes, sir."

"How dare you tell me so!" he exclaimed, in great wrath. After a slight pause, he added, "I supposed you thought more of yourself; that you felt above the insults of such puppies."

I replied, "If he is a puppy, I am a puppy, for we are both of the negro race. It is right and honorable for us to love each other. The man you call a puppy never insulted me, sir; and he would not love me if he did not believe me to be a virtuous woman."

He sprang upon me like a tiger, and gave me a stunning blow. It was the first time he had ever struck me; and fear did not enable me to control my anger. When I had recovered a little from the effects, I exclaimed, "You have struck me for answering you honestly. How I despise you!"

There was silence for some minutes. Perhaps he was deciding what should be my punishment; or, perhaps, he wanted to give me time to reflect on what I had said, and to whom I had said it. Finally, he asked, "Do you know what you have said?"

"Yes, sir; but your treatment drove me to it."

"Do you know that I have a right to do as I like with you,—that I can kill you, if I please?"

"You have tried to kill me, and I wish you had; but you have no right to do as you like with me."

"Silence!" he exclaimed, in a thundering voice. "By heavens, girl, you forget yourself too far! Are you mad? If you are, I will soon bring you to your senses. Do you think any other master would bear what I have borne from you this morning? Many masters would have killed you on the spot. How would you like to be sent to jail for your insolence?"

"I know I have been disrespectful, sir," I replied; "but you drove me to it; I couldn't help it. As for the jail, there would be more peace for me there than there is here."

"You deserve to go there," said he, "and to be under such treatment, that you would forget the meaning of the word *peace*. It would do you good. It would take some of your high notions out of you. But I am not ready to send you there yet, notwithstanding your ingratitude for all my kindness and forbearance. You have been the plague of my life. I have wanted to make you happy, and I have been repaid with the basest ingratitude; but though you have proved yourself incapable of appreciating my kindness, I will be lenient towards you, Linda. I will give you one more chance to redeem your character. If you behave yourself and do as I require, I will forgive you and treat you as I always have done; but if you disobey me, I will punish you as I would the meanest slave on my plantation. Never let me hear that fellow's name mentioned again. If I ever know of your speaking to him, I will cowhide you both; and if I catch him lurking about my premises, I will shoot him as soon as I would a dog. Do you hear what I say? I'll teach you a lesson about marriage and free niggers! Now go, and let this be the last time I have occasion to speak to you on this subject."

Reader, did you ever hate? I hope not. I never did but once; and I trust I never shall again. Somebody has called it "the atmosphere of hell;" and I believe it is so.

For a fortnight the doctor did not speak to me. He thought to mortify me; to make me feel that I had disgraced myself by receiving the honorable addresses of a respectable colored man, in preference to the base proposals of a white man. But though his lips disdained to address me, his eyes were very loquacious. No animal ever watched its prey more narrowly than he watched me. He knew that I could write, though he had failed to make me read his letters; and he was now troubled lest I should exchange letters with another man. After a while he became weary of silence; and I was sorry for it. One morning, as he passed through the hall, to leave the house, he contrived to thrust a note into my hand. I thought I had better read it, and spare myself the vexation of having him read it to me. It expressed regret for the blow he had given me, and reminded me that I myself was wholly to blame for it. He hoped I had become convinced of the injury I was doing myself by incurring his displeasure. He wrote that he had made up his mind to go to Louisiana; that he should take several slaves with him, and intended I should be one of the number. My mistress would remain where she was; therefore I should have nothing to fear from that quarter. If I merited kindness from him, he assured me that it would be lavishly bestowed. He begged me to think over the matter, and answer the following day.

The next morning I was called to carry a pair of scissors to his room. I laid them on the table, with the letter beside them. He thought it was my answer, and did not call me back. I went as usual to attend my young mistress to and from school. He met me in the street, and ordered me to stop at his office on my way back. When I entered, he showed me his letter, and asked me why I had not answered it. I replied, "I am your daughter's property, and it is in your power to send me, or take me, wherever you please." He said he was very glad to find me so willing to go, and that we should start early in the autumn. He had a large practice in the town, and I rather thought he had made up the story merely to frighten me. However that might be, I was determined that I would never go to Louisiana with him.

Summer passed away, and early in the autumn Dr. Flint's eldest son was sent to Louisiana to examine the country, with a view to emigrating. That news did not disturb me. I knew very well that I should not be sent with *him*. That I had not been taken to the plantation before this time, was owing to the fact that his son was there. He was jealous of his son; and jealousy of the overseer had kept him from punishing me by sending me into the fields to work. Is it strange that I was not proud of these protectors? As for the overseer, he was a man for whom I had less respect than I had for a bloodhound.

Young Mr. Flint did not bring back a favorable report of Louisiana, and I heard no more of that scheme. Soon after this, my lover met me at the corner of the street, and I stopped to speak to him. Looking up, I saw my master watching us from his window. I hurried home, trembling with fear. I was sent for, immediately, to go to his room. He met me with a blow. "When is mistress to be married?" said he, in a sneering tone. A shower of oaths and imprecations followed. How thankful I was that my lover was a free man! that my tyrant had no power to flog him for speaking to me in the street!

Again and again I revolved in my mind how all this would end. There was no hope that the doctor would consent to sell me on any terms. He had an iron will, and was determined to keep me, and to conquer me. My lover was an intelligent and religious man. Even if he could have obtained permission to marry me while I was a slave, the marriage would give him no power to protect me from my master. It would have made him miserable to witness the insults I should have been subjected to. And then, if we had children, I knew they must "follow the condition of the mother." What a terrible blight that would be on the heart of a free, intelligent father! For *his* sake, I felt that I ought not to link his fate with my own unhappy destiny. He was going to Savannah to see about a little property left him by an uncle; and hard as it was to bring my feelings to it, I earnestly entreated him not to come back. I advised him to go to the Free States, where his tongue would not be tied, and where his intelligence would be of more avail to him. He left me, still hoping the day would come when I could be bought. With me the lamp of hope had gone out. The dream of my girlhood was over. I felt lonely and desolate.

Still I was not stripped of all. I still had my good grandmother, and my affectionate brother. When he put his arms round my neck, and looked into my eyes, as if to read there the troubles I dared not tell, I felt that I still had something to love. But even that pleasant emotion was chilled by the reflection that he might be torn from me at any moment, by some sudden freak of my master. If he had known how we loved each other, I think he would have exulted in separating us. We often planned together how we could get to the north. But, as William remarked, such things are easier said than done. My movements were very closely watched, and we had no means of getting any money to defray our expenses. As for grandmother, she was strongly opposed to her children's undertaking any such project. She had not forgotten poor Benjamin's sufferings, and she was afraid that if another child tried to escape, he would have a similar or a worse fate. To me, nothing seemed more dreadful than my present life. I said to myself, "William must be free. He shall go to the north, and I will follow him." Many a slave sister has formed the same plans.

VIII.

WHAT SLAVES ARE TAUGHT TO THINK OF THE NORTH.

SLAVEHOLDERS pride themselves upon being honorable men; but if you were to hear the enormous lies they tell their slaves, you would have small respect for their veracity. I have spoken plain English. Pardon me. I cannot use a milder term. When they visit the north, and return home, they tell their slaves of the runaways they have seen, and describe them to be in the most deplorable condition. A slaveholder once told me that he had seen a runaway friend of mine in New York, and that she besought him to take her back to her master, for she was literally dying of starvation; that many days she had only one cold potato to eat, and at other times could get nothing at all. He said he refused to take her, because he knew her master would not thank him for bringing such a miserable wretch to his house. He ended by saying to me, "This is the punishment she brought on herself for running away from a kind master."

This whole story was false. I afterwards staid with that friend in New York, and found her in comfortable circumstances. She had never thought of such a thing as wishing to go back to slavery. Many of the slaves believe such stories, and think it is not worth while to exchange slavery for such a hard kind of freedom. It is difficult to persuade such that freedom could make them useful men, and enable them to protect their wives and children. If those heathen in our Christian land had as much teaching as some Hindoos, they would think otherwise. They would know that liberty is more valuable than life. They would begin to understand their own capabilities, and exert themselves to become men and women.

But while the Free States sustain a law which hurls fugitives back into slavery, how can the slaves resolve to become men? There are some who strive to protect wives and daughters from the insults of their masters; but those who have such sentiments have had advantages above the general mass of slaves. They have been partially civilized and Christianized by favorable circumstances. Some are bold enough to *utter* such sentiments to their masters. O, that there were more of them!

Some poor creatures have been so brutalized by the lash that they will sneak out of the way to give their masters free access to their wives and daughters. Do you think this proves the black man to belong to an inferior order of beings? What would *you* be, if you had been born and brought up a slave, with generations of slaves for ancestors? I admit that the black man *is* inferior. But what is it that makes him so? It is the ignorance in which white men compel him to live; it is the torturing whip that lashes manhood out of him;

it is the fierce bloodhounds of the south, and the scarcely less cruel human bloodhounds of the north, who enforce the Fugitive Slave Law. *They* do the work.

Southern gentlemen indulge in the most contemptuous expressions about the Yankees, while they, on their part, consent to do the vilest work for them, such as the ferocious bloodhounds and the despised negro-hunters are employed to do at home. When southerners go to the north, they are proud to do them honor; but the northern man is not welcome south of Mason and Dixon's line, unless he suppresses every thought and feeling at variance with their "peculiar institution." Nor is it enough to be silent. The masters are not pleased, unless they obtain a greater degree of subservience than that; and they are generally accommodated. Do they respect the northerner for this? I trow not. Even the slaves despise "a northern man with southern principles;" and that is the class they generally see. When northerners go to the south to reside, they prove very apt scholars. They soon imbibe the sentiments and disposition of their neighbors, and generally go beyond their teachers. Of the two, they are proverbially the hardest masters.

They seem to satisfy their consciences with the doctrine that God created the Africans to be slaves. What a libel upon the heavenly Father, who "made of one blood all nations of men!" And then who *are* Africans? Who can measure the amount of Anglo-Saxon blood coursing in the veins of American slaves?

I have spoken of the pains slaveholders take to give their slaves a bad opinion of the north; but, notwithstanding this, intelligent slaves are aware that they have many friends in the Free States. Even the most ignorant have some confused notions about it. They knew that I could read; and I was often asked if I had seen any thing in the newspapers about white folks over in the big north, who were trying to get their freedom for them. Some believe that the abolitionists have already made them free, and that it is established by law, but that their masters prevent the law from going into effect. One woman begged me to get a newspaper and read it over. She said her husband told her that the black people had sent word to the queen of 'Merica that they were all slaves; that she didn't believe it, and went to Washington city to see the president about it. They quarrelled; she drew her sword upon him, and swore that he should help her to make them all free.

That poor, ignorant woman thought that America was governed by a Queen, to whom the President was subordinate. I wish the President was subordinate to Queen Justice.

IX.

SKETCHES OF NEIGHBORING SLAVEHOLDERS.

THERE was a planter in the country, not far from us, whom I will call Mr. Litch. He was an ill-bred, uneducated man, but very wealthy. He had six hundred slaves, many of whom he did not know by sight. His extensive plantation was managed by well-paid overseers. There was a jail and a whipping post on his grounds; and whatever cruelties were perpetrated there, they passed without comment. He was so effectually screened by his great wealth that he was called to no account for his crimes, not even for murder.

Various were the punishments resorted to. A favorite one was to tie a rope round a man's body, and suspend him from the ground. A fire was kindled over him, from which was suspended a piece of fat pork. As this cooked, the scalding drops of fat continually fell on the bare flesh. On his own plantation, he required very strict obedience to the eighth commandment. But depredations on the neighbors were allowable, provided the culprit managed to evade detection or suspicion. If a neighbor brought a charge of theft against any of his slaves, he was browbeaten by the master, who assured him that his slaves had enough of every thing at home, and had no inducement to steal. No sooner was the neighbor's back turned, than the accused was sought out, and whipped for his lack of discretion. If a slave stole from him even a pound of meat or a peck of corn, if detection followed, he was put in chains and imprisoned, and so kept till his form was attentuated by hunger and suffering.

A freshet once bore his wine cellar and meat house miles away from the plantation. Some slaves followed, and secured bits of meat and bottles of wine. Two were detected; a ham and some liquor being found in their huts. They were summoned by their master. No words were used, but a club felled them to the ground. A rough box was their coffin, and their interment was a dog's burial. Nothing was said.

Murder was so common on his plantation that he feared to be alone after nightfall. He might have believed in ghosts.

His brother, if not equal in wealth, was at least equal in cruelty. His bloodhounds were well trained. Their pen was spacious, and a terror to the slaves. They were let loose on a runway, and, if they tracked him, they literally tore the flesh from his bones. When this slaveholder died, his shrieks and groans were so frightful that they appalled his own friends. His last words were, "I am going to hell; bury my money with me."

After death his eyes remained open. To press the lids down, silver dollars were laid on them. These were buried with him. From this circumstance, a rumor went abroad that his coffin was filled with money. Three times his grave was opened, and his coffin taken out. The last time, his body was found on the ground, and a flock of buzzards were pecking at it. He was again interred, and a sentinel set over his grave. The perpetrators were never discovered.

Cruelty is contagious in uncivilized communities. Mr. Conant, a neighbor of Mr. Litch, returned from town one evening in a partial state of intoxication. His body servant gave him some offence. He was divested of his clothes, except his shirt, whipped, and tied to a large tree in front of the house. It was a stormy night in winter. The wind blew bitterly cold, and the boughs of the old tree crackled under falling sleet. A member of the family, fearing he would freeze to death, begged that he might be taken down; but the master would not relent. He remained there three hours; and, when he was cut down, he was more dead than alive. Another slave, who stole a pig from this master, to appease his hunger, was terribly flogged. In desperation, he tried to run away. But at the end of two miles, he was so faint with loss of blood, he thought he was dying. He had a wife, and he longed to see her once more. Too sick to walk, he crept back that long distance on his hands and knees. When he reached his master's, it was night. He had not strength to rise and open the gate. He moaned, and tried to call for help. I had a friend living in the same family. At last his cry reached her. She went out and found the prostrate man at the gate. She ran back to the house for assistance, and two men returned with her. They carried him in, and laid him on the floor. The back of his shirt was one clot of blood. By means of lard, my friend loosened it from the raw flesh. She bandaged him, gave him cool drink, and left him to rest. The master said he deserved a hundred more lashes. When his own labor was stolen from him, he had stolen food to appease his hunger. This was his crime.

Another neighbor was a Mrs. Wade. At no hour of the day was there cessation of the lash on her premises. Her labors began with the dawn, and did not cease till long after nightfall. The barn was her particular place of torture. There she lashed the slaves with the might of a man. An old slave of hers once said to me, "It is hell in missis's house. 'Pears I can never get out. Day and night I prays to die."

The mistress died before the old woman, and, when dying, entreated her husband not to permit any one of her slaves to look on her after death. A slave who had nursed her children, and had still a child in her care, watched her chance, and stole with it in her arms to the room where lay her dead mistress. She gazed a while on her, then raised her hand and dealt two blows on her face, saying, as she did so, "The devil is got you now!" She forgot that the child was looking on. She had just begun to talk; and she said to her father, "I did see ma, and mammy did strike ma, so," striking her own face with her little hand. The master was startled. He could not imagine how the nurse could obtain access to the room where the corpse lay; for he kept the door locked. He questioned her. She confessed that what the child had said was true, and told how she had procured the key. She was sold to Georgia.

In my childhood I knew a valuable slave, named Charity,

and loved her, as all children did. Her young mistress married, and took her to Louisiana. Her little boy, James, was sold to a good sort of master. He became involved in debt, and James was sold again to a wealthy slaveholder, noted for his cruelty. With this man he grew up to manhood, receiving the treatment of a dog. After a severe whipping, to save himself from further infliction of the lash, with which he was threatened, he took to the woods. He was in a most miserable condition—cut by the cowskin, half naked, half starved, and without the means of procuring a crust of bread.

Some weeks after his escape, he was captured, tied, and carried back to his master's plantation. This man considered punishment in his jail, on bread and water, after receiving hundreds of lashes, too mild for the poor slave's offence. Therefore he decided, after the overseer should have whipped him to his satisfaction, to have him placed between the screws of the cotton gin, to stay as long as he had been in the woods. This wretched creature was cut with the whip from his head to his feet, then washed with strong brine, to prevent the flesh from mortifying, and make it heal sooner than it otherwise would. He was then put into the cotton gin, which was screwed down, only allowing him room to turn on his side when he could not lie on his back. Every morning a slave was sent with a piece of bread and a bowl of water, which was placed within reach of the poor fellow. The slave was charged, under penalty of severe punishment, not to speak to him.

Four days passed, and the slave continued to carry the bread and water. On the second morning, he found the bread gone, but the water untouched. When he had been in the press four days and five nights, the slave informed his master that the water had not been used for four mornings, and that a horrible stench came from the gin house. The overseer was sent to examine into it. When the press was unscrewed, the dead body was found partly eaten by rats and vermin. Perhaps the rats that devoured his bread had gnawed him before life was extinct. Poor Charity! Grandmother and I often asked each other how her affectionate heart would bear the news, if she should ever hear of the murder of her son. We had known her husband, and knew that James was like him in manliness and intelligence. These were the qualities that made it so hard for him to be a plantation slave. They put him into a rough box, and buried him with less feeling than would have been manifested for an old house dog. Nobody asked any questions. He was a slave; and the feeling was that the master had a right to do what he pleased with his own property. And what did *he* care for the value of a slave? He had hundreds of them. When they had finished their daily toil, they must hurry to eat their little morsels, and be ready to extinguish their pine knots before nine o'clock, when the overseer went his patrol rounds. He entered every cabin, to see that men and their wives had gone to bed together, lest the men, from over-fatigue, should fall asleep in the chimney corner, and remain there till the morning horn called them to their daily task. Women are considered of no value, unless they continually increase their owner's stock. They are put on a par with animals. This same master shot a woman through the head, who had run away and been brought back to him. No one called him to account for it. If a slave resisted being whipped, the bloodhounds were unpacked, and set upon him, to tear his flesh from his bones. The master who did these things was highly educated, and styled a perfect gentleman. He also boasted the name and standing of a Christian, though Satan never had a truer follower.

I could tell of more slaveholders as cruel as those I have described. They are not exceptions to the general rule. I do not say there are no humane slaveholders. Such characters do exist, notwithstanding the hardening influences around them. But they are "like angels' visits—few and far between."

I knew a young lady who was one of these rare specimens. She was an orphan, and inherited as slaves a woman and her six children. Their father was a free man. They had a comfortable home of their own, parents and children living together. The mother and eldest daughter served their mistress during the day, and at night returned to their dwelling, which was on the premises. The young lady was very pious, and there was some reality in her religion. She taught her slaves to lead pure lives, and wished them to enjoy the fruit of their own industry. *Her* religion was not a garb put on for Sunday, and laid aside till Sunday returned again. The eldest daughter of the slave mother was promised in marriage to a free man; and the day before the wedding this good mistress emancipated her, in order that her marriage might have the sanction of *law*.

Report said that this young lady cherished an unrequited affection for a man who had resolved to marry for wealth. In the course of time a rich uncle of hers died. He left six thousand dollars to his two sons by a colored woman, and the remainder of his property to this orphan niece. The metal soon attracted the magnet. The lady and her weighty purse became his. She offered to manumit her slaves— telling them that her marriage might make unexpected changes in their destiny, and she wished to insure their happiness. They refused to take their freedom, saying that she had always been their best friend, and they could not be so happy any where as with her. I was not surprised. I had often seen them in their comfortable home, and thought that the whole town did not contain a happier family. They had never felt slavery; and, when it was too late, they were convinced of its reality.

When the new master claimed this family as his property, the father became furious, and went to his mistress for protection. "I can do nothing for you now, Harry," said she. "I no longer have the power I had a week ago. I have succeeded in obtaining the freedom of your wife; but I cannot obtain it for your children." The unhappy father swore that nobody should take his children from him. He concealed them in the woods for some days; but they were discovered and taken. The father was put in jail, and the two oldest boys sold to Georgia. One little girl, too young to be of service to her master, was left with the wretched mother. The other three were carried to their master's plantation. The eldest soon became a mother; and when the slaveholder's wife looked at the babe, she wept bitterly. She knew that her own husband had violated the purity she had so carefully inculcated. She had a second child by her master, and then he sold her and his offspring to his brother. She bore two children to the brother, and was sold again. The next sister went crazy. The life she was compelled to lead drove her mad. The third one became the mother of five daughters. Before the birth of the fourth the pious mistress died. To the last, she rendered every kindness to the slaves that her unfortunate circumstances permitted. She passed away peacefully, glad to close her eyes on a life which had been made so wretched by the man she loved.

This man squandered the fortune he had received, and sought to retrieve his affairs by a second marriage; but, having retired after a night of drunken debauch, he was found dead in the morning. He was called a good master; for he fed and clothed his slaves better than most masters, and the lash was not heard on his plantation so frequently as on many others. Had it not been for slavery, he would have been a better man, and his wife a happier woman.

No pen can give an adequate description of the all-pervading corruption produced by slavery. The slave girl is reared in an atmosphere of licentiousness and fear. The lash and the foul talk of her master and his sons are her teachers. When she is fourteen or fifteen, her owner, or his sons, or the overseer, or perhaps all of them, begin to bribe her with presents. If these fail to accomplish their purpose, she is whipped or starved into submission to their will. She may have had religious principles inculcated by some pious mother or grandmother, or some good mistress; she may have a lover, whose good opinion and peace of mind are dear to her heart; or the profligate men who have power over her may be exceedingly odious to her. But resistance is hopeless.

> The poor worm
> Shall prove her contest vain. Life's little day
> Shall pass, and she is gone!

The slaveholder's sons are, of course, vitiated, even while boys, by the unclean influences every where around them. Nor do the master's daughters always escape. Severe retributions sometimes come upon him for the wrongs he does to the daughters of the slaves. The white daughters early hear their parents quarrelling about some female slave. Their curiosity is excited, and they soon learn the cause. They are attended by the young slave girls whom their father has corrupted; and they hear such talk as should never meet youthful ears, or any other ears. They know that the woman slaves are subject to their father's authority in all things; and in some cases they exercise the same authority over the men slaves. I have myself seen the master of such a household whose head was bowed down in shame; for it was known in the neighborhood that his daughter had selected one of the meanest slaves on his plantation to be the father of his first grandchild. She did not make her advances to her equals, nor even to her father's more intelligent servants. She selected the most brutalized, over whom her authority could be exercised with less fear of exposure. Her father, half frantic with rage, sought to revenge himself on the offending black man; but his daughter, foreseeing the storm that would arise, had given him free papers, and sent him out of the state.

In such cases the infant is smothered, or sent where it is never seen by any who know its history. But if the white parent is the *father,* instead of the mother, the offspring are unblushingly reared for the market. If they are girls, I have indicated plainly enough what will be their inevitable destiny.

You may believe what I say; for I write only that whereof I know. I was twenty-one years in that cage of obscene birds. I can testify, from my own experience and observation, that slavery is a curse to the whites as well as to the blacks. It makes white fathers cruel and sensual; the sons violent and licentious; it contaminates the daughters, and makes the wives wretched. And as for the colored race, it needs an abler pen than mine to describe the extremity of their sufferings, the depth of their degradation.

Yet few slaveholders seem to be aware of the widespread moral ruin occasioned by this wicked system. Their talk is of blighted cotton crops—not of the blight on their children's souls.

If you want to be fully convinced of the abominations of slavery, go on a southern plantation, and call yourself a negro trader. Then there will be no concealment; and you will see and hear things that will seem to you impossible among human beings with immortal souls.

X.

A PERILOUS PASSAGE IN THE SLAVE GIRL'S LIFE.

After my lover went away, Dr. Flint contrived a new plan. He seemed to have an idea that my fear of my mistress was his greatest obstacle. In the blandest tones, he told me that he was going to build a small house for me, in a secluded place, four miles away from the town. I shuddered; but I was constrained to listen, while he talked of his intention to give me a home of my own, and to make a lady of me. Hitherto, I had escaped my dreaded fate, by being in the midst of people. My grandmother had already had high words with my master about me. She had told him pretty plainly what she thought of his character, and there was considerable gossip in the neighborhood about our affairs, to which the open-mouthed jealousy of Mrs. Flint contributed not a little. When my master said he was going to build a house for me, and that he could do it with little trouble and expense, I was in hopes something would happen to frustrate his scheme; but I soon heard that the house was actually begun. I vowed before my Maker that I would never enter it: I had rather toil on the plantation from dawn till dark; I had rather live and die in jail, than drag on, from day to day, through such a living death. I was determined that the master, whom I so hated and loathed, who had blighted the prospects of my youth, and made my life a desert, should not, after my long struggle with him, succeed at last in trampling his victim under his feet. I would do any thing, every thing, for the sake of defeating him. What *could* I do? I thought and thought, till I became desperate, and made a plunge into the abyss.

And now, reader, I come to a period in my unhappy life, which I would gladly forget if I could. The remembrance fills me with sorrow and shame. It pains me to tell you of it; but I have promised to tell you the truth, and I will do it honestly, let it cost me what it may. I will not try to screen myself behind the plea of compulsion from a master; for it was not so. Neither can I plead ignorance or thoughtlessness. For years, my master had done his utmost to pollute my mind with foul images, and to destroy the pure principles inculcated by my grandmother, and the good mistress of my childhood. The influences of slavery had had the same effect on me that they had on other young girls; they had made me prematurely knowing, concerning the evil ways of the world. I knew what I did, and I did it with deliberate calculation.

But, O, ye happy women, whose purity has been sheltered from childhood, who have been free to choose the objects of your affection, whose homes are protected by law, do not judge the poor desolate slave girl too severely! If slavery had been abolished, I, also, could have married the man of my choice; I could have had a home shielded by the laws; and I should have been spared the painful task of confessing what I am now about to relate; but all my prospects had been blighted by slavery. I wanted to keep myself pure; and, under the most adverse circumstances, I tried hard to preserve my self-respect; but I was struggling alone in the powerful grasp of the demon Slavery; and the monster proved too strong for me. I felt as if I was forsaken by God and man; as if all my efforts must be frustrated; and I became reckless in my despair.

I have told you that Dr. Flint's persecutions and his wife's jealousy had given rise to some gossip in the neighborhood. Among others, it chanced that a white unmarried gentleman had obtained some knowledge of the circumstances in which I was placed. He knew my grandmother, and often spoke to me in the street. He became interested for me, and asked questions about my master, which I answered in part. He expressed a great deal of sympathy, and a wish to aid me. He constantly sought opportunities to see me, and wrote to me frequently. I was a poor slave girl, only fifteen years old.

So much attention from a superior person was, of course, flattering; for human nature is the same in all. I also felt grateful for his sympathy, and encouraged by his kind words. It seemed to me a great thing to have such a friend. By degrees, a more tender feeling crept into my heart. He was an educated and eloquent gentleman; too eloquent, alas, for the poor slave girl who trusted in him. Of course I saw whither all this was tending. I knew the impassable gulf between us; but to be an object of interest to a man who is not married, and who is not her master, is agreeable to the pride and feelings of a slave, if her miserable situation has left her any pride or sentiment. It seems less degrading to give one's self, than to submit to compulsion. There is something akin to freedom in having a lover who has no control over you, except that which he gains by kindness and attachment. A master may treat you as rudely as he pleases, and you dare not speak; moreover, the wrong does not seem so great with an unmarried man, as with one who has a wife to be made unhappy. There may be sophistry in all this; but the condition of a slave confuses all principles of morality, and, in fact, renders the practice of them impossible.

When I found that my master had actually begun to build the lonely cottage, other feelings mixed with those I have described. Revenge, and calculations of interest, were added to flattered vanity and sincere gratitude for kindness. I knew nothing would enrage Dr. Flint so much as to know that I favored another, and it was something to triumph over my tyrant even in that small way. I thought he would revenge himself by selling me, and I was sure my friend, Mr. Sands, would buy me. He was a man of more generosity and feeling than my master, and I thought my freedom could be easily obtained from him. The crisis of my fate now came so near that I was desperate. I shuddered to think of being the mother of children that should be owned by my old tyrant. I knew that as soon as a new fancy took him, his victims were sold far off to get rid of them; especially if they had children. I had seen several women sold, with babies at the breast. He never allowed his offspring by slaves to remain long in sight of himself and his wife. Of a man who was not my master I could ask to have my children well supported; and in this case, I felt confident I should obtain the boon. I also felt quite sure that they would be made free. With all these thoughts revolving in my mind, and seeing no other way of escaping the doom I so much dreaded, I made a headlong plunge. Pity me, and pardon me, O virtuous reader! You never knew what it is to be a slave; to be en-

tirely unprotected by law or custom; to have the laws reduce you to the condition of a chattel, entirely subject to
the will of another. You never exhausted your ingenuity in
avoiding the snares, and eluding the power of a hated tyrant; you never shuddered at the sound of his footsteps, and
trembled within hearing of his voice. I know I did wrong.
No one can feel it more sensibly than I do. The painful and
humiliating memory will haunt me to my dying day. Still, in
looking back, calmly, on the events of my life, I feel that the
slave woman ought not to be judged by the same standard
as others.

The months passed on. I had many unhappy hours. I secretly mourned over the sorrow I was bringing on my
grandmother, who had so tried to shield me from harm. I
knew that I was the greatest comfort of her old age, and
that it was a source of pride to her that I had not degraded
myself, like most of the slaves. I wanted to confess to her
that I was no longer worthy of her love; but I could not
utter the dreaded words.

As for Dr. Flint, I had a feeling of satisfaction and triumph in the thought of telling *him*. From time to time he
told me of his intended arrangements, and I was silent. At
last, he came and told me the cottage was completed, and
ordered me to go to it. I told him I would never enter it. He
said, "I have heard enough of such talk as that. You shall go,
if you are carried by force; and you shall remain there."

I replied, "I will never go there. In a few months I shall
be a mother."

He stood and looked at me in dumb amazement, and left
the house without a word. I thought I should be happy in
my triumph over him. But now that the truth was out, and
my relatives would hear of it, I felt wretched. Humble as
were their circumstances, they had pride in my good character. Now, how could I look at them in the face? My self-
respect was gone! I had resolved that I would be virtuous,
though I was a slave. I had said, "Let the storm beat! I will
brave it till I die." And now, how humiliated I felt!

I went to my grandmother. My lips moved to make con-
fession, but the words stuck in my throat. I sat down in the
shade of a tree at her door and began to sew. I think she saw
something unusual was the matter with me. The mother of

slaves is very watchful. She knows there is no security for her children. After they have entered their teens she lives in daily expectation of trouble. This leads to many questions. If the girl is of a sensitive nature, timidity keeps her from answering truthfully, and this well-meant course has a tendency to drive her from maternal counsels. Presently, in came my mistress, like a mad woman, and accused me concerning her husband. My grandmother, whose suspicions had been previously awakened, believed what she said. She exclaimed, "O Linda! Has it come to this? I had rather see you dead than to see you as you now are. You are a disgrace to your dead mother." She tore from my fingers my mother's wedding ring and her silver thimble. "Go away!" she exclaimed, "and never come to my house again." Her reproaches fell so hot and heavy, that they left me no chance to answer. Bitter tears, such as the eyes never shed but once, were my only answer. I rose from my seat, but fell back again, sobbing. She did not speak to me; but the tears were running down her furrowed cheeks, and they scorched me like fire. She had always been so kind to me! *So* kind! How I longed to throw myself at her feet, and tell her all the truth! But she had ordered me to go, and never to come there again. After a few minutes, I mustered strength, and started to obey her. With what feelings did I now close that little gate, which I used to open with such an eager hand in my childhood! It closed upon me with a sound I never heard before.

Where could I go? I was afraid to return to my master's. I walked on recklessly, not caring where I went, or what would become of me. When I had gone four or five miles, fatigue compelled me to stop. I sat down on the stump of an old tree. The stars were shining through the boughs above me. How they mocked me, with their bright, calm light! The hours passed by, and as I sat there alone a chilliness and deadly sickness came over me. I sank on the ground. My mind was full of horrid thoughts. I prayed to die; but the prayer was not answered. At last, with great effort I roused myself, and walked some distance further, to the house of a woman who had been a friend of my mother. When I told her why I was there, she spoke soothingly to me; but I could not be comforted. I thought I could bear my shame if I could only be reconciled to my grandmother. I longed to open my heart to her. I thought if she could know the real state of the case, and all I had been bearing for years, she would perhaps judge me less harshly. My friend advised me to send for her. I did so; but days of agonizing suspense passed before she came. Had she utterly forsaken me? No. She came at last. I knelt before her, and told her the things that had poisoned my life; how long I had been persecuted; that I saw no way of escape; and in an hour of extremity I had become desperate. She listened in silence. I told her I would bear any thing and do any thing, if in time I had hopes of obtaining her forgiveness. I begged of her to pity me, for my dead mother's sake. And she did pity me. She did not say, "I forgive you;" but she looked at me lovingly, with her eyes full of tears. She laid her old hand gently on my head, and murmured, "Poor child! Poor child!"

XI.

THE NEW TIE TO LIFE.

I RETURNED to my good grandmother's house. She had an interview with Mr. Sands. When she asked him why he could not have left her one ewe lamb,—whether there were not plenty of slaves who did not care about character,—he made no answer, but he spoke kind and encouraging words. He promised to care for my child, and to buy me, be the conditions what they might.

I had not seen Dr. Flint for five days. I had never seen him since I made the avowal to him. He talked of the disgrace I had brought on myself; how I had sinned against my master, and mortified my old grandmother. He intimated that if I had accepted his proposals, he, as a physician, could have saved me from exposure. He even condescended to pity me. Could he have offered wormwood more bitter? He, whose persecutions had been the cause of my sin!

"Linda," said he, "though you have been criminal towards me, I feel for you, and I can pardon you if you obey my wishes. Tell me whether the fellow you wanted to marry is the father of your child. If you deceive me, you shall feel the fires of hell."

I did not feel as proud as I had done. My strongest weapon with him was gone. I was lowered in my own estimation, and had resolved to bear his abuse in silence. But when he spoke contemptuously of the lover who had always treated me honorably; when I remembered that but for *him* I might have been a virtuous, free, and happy wife, I lost my patience. "I have sinned against God and myself," I replied; "but not against you."

He clinched his teeth, and muttered, "Curse you!" He came towards me, with ill-suppressed rage, and exclaimed, "You obstinate girl! I could grind your bones to powder! You have thrown yourself away on some worthless rascal. You are weak-minded, and have been easily persuaded by those who don't care a straw for you. The future will settle accounts between us. You are blinded now; but hereafter you will be convinced that your master was your best friend. My lenity towards you is a proof of it. I might have punished you in many ways. I might have whipped till you fell dead under the lash. But I wanted you to live; I would have bettered your condition. Others cannot do it. You are my slave. Your mistress, disgusted by your conduct, forbids you to return to the house; therefore I leave you here for the present; but I shall see you often. I will call tomorrow."

He came with frowning brows, that showed a dissatisfied state of mind. After asking about my health, he inquired whether my board was paid, and who visited me. He then went on to say that he had neglected his duty; that as a physician there were certain things that he ought to have explained to me. Then followed talk such as would have made the most shameless blush. He ordered me to stand up before him. I obeyed. "I command you," said he, "to tell me whether the father of your child is white or black." I hesitated. "Answer me this instant!" he exclaimed. I did answer. He sprang upon me like a wolf, and grabbed my arm as if he would have broken it. "Do you love him?" said he, in a hissing tone.

"I am thankful that I do not despise him," I replied.

He raised his hand to strike me; but it fell again. I don't know what it is that arrested the blow. He sat down, with lips tightly compressed. At last he spoke. "I came here," said he, "to make you a friendly proposition; but your ingratitude chafes me beyond endurance. You turn aside all my good intentions towards you. I don't know what it is that keeps me from killing you." Again he rose, as if he had a mind to strike me.

But he resumed. "On one condition I will forgive your insolence and crime. You must henceforth have no communication of any kind with the father of your child. You must not ask any thing from him, or receive any thing from him. I will take care of you and your child. You had better promise this at once, and not wait till you are deserted by him. This is the last act of mercy I shall show towards you."

I said something about being unwilling to have my child supported by a man who had cursed it and me also. He rejoined, that a woman who had sunk to my level had no right to expect any thing else. He asked, for the last time, would I accept his kindness? I answered that I would not.

"Very well," said he; "then take the consequences of your wayward course. Never look to me for help. You are my slave, and shall always be my slave. I will never sell you, that you may depend upon."

Hope died away in my heart as he closed the door after him. I had calculated that in his rage he would sell me to a slave-trader; and I knew the father of my child was on the watch to buy me.

About this time my uncle Phillip was expected to return from a voyage. The day before his departure I had officiated as bridesmaid to a young friend. My heart was then ill at ease, but my smiling countenance did not betray it. Only a year had passed; but what fearful changes it had wrought! My heart had grown gray in misery. Lives that flash in sunshine, and lives that are born in tears, receive their hue from circumstances. None of us know what a year may bring forth.

I felt no joy when they told me my uncle had come. He wanted to see me, though he knew what had happened. I shrank from him at first; but at last consented that he should come to my room. He received me as he always had done. O, how my heart smote me when I felt his tears on my burning cheeks! The words of my grandmother came to my mind,—"Perhaps your mother and father are taken from the evil days to come." My disappointed heart could now praise God that it was so. But why, thought I, did my relatives ever cherish hopes for me? What was there to save me from the usual fate of slave girls? Many more beautiful and more intelligent than I had experienced a similar fate, or a far worse one. How could they hope that I should escape?

My uncle's stay was short, and I was not sorry for it. I was too ill in mind and body to enjoy my friends as I had done. For some weeks I was unable to leave my bed. I could not have any doctor but my master, and I would not have him sent for. At last, alarmed by my increasing illness, they sent for him. I was very weak and nervous; and as soon as he entered the room, I began to scream. They told him my state was very critical. He had no wish to hasten me out of the world, and he withdrew.

When my babe was born, they said it was premature. It weighed only four pounds; but God let it live. I heard the doctor say I could not survive till morning. I had often prayed for death; but now I did not want to die, unless my child could die too. Many weeks passed before I was able to leave my bed. I was a mere wreck of my former self. For a year there was scarcely a day when I was free from chills and fever. My babe also was sickly. His little limbs were often racked with pain. Dr. Flint continued his visits, to look after my health; and he did not fail to remind me that my child was an addition to his stock of slaves.

I felt too feeble to dispute with him, and listened to his remarks in silence. His visits were less frequent; but his busy spirit could not remain quiet. He employed my brother in his office; and he was made the medium of frequent notes and messages to me. William was a bright lad, and of much use to the doctor. He had learned to put up medicines, to leech, cup, and bleed. He had taught himself to read and spell. I was proud of my brother, and the old doctor suspected as much. One day, when I had not seen him for several weeks, I heard his steps approaching the door. I dreaded the encounter, and hid myself. He inquired for me, of course; but I was nowhere to be found. He went to his office, and despatched William with a note. The color mounted to my brother's face when he gave it to me; and he said, "Don't you hate me, Linda, for bringing you these things?" I told him I could not blame him; he was a slave, and obliged to obey his master's will. The note ordered me to come to his office. I went. He demanded to know where I was when he called. I told him I was at home. He flew into a passion, and said he knew better. Then he launched out upon his usual themes,—my crimes against him, and my ingratitude for his forbearance. The laws were laid down to me anew, and I was dismissed. I felt humiliated that my brother should stand by, and listen to such language as would be addressed only to a slave. Poor boy! He was powerless to defend me; but I saw the tears, which he vainly strove to keep back. The manifestation of feeling irritated the doctor. William could do nothing to please him. One morning he did not arrive at the office so early as usual; and that circumstance afforded his master an opportunity to vent his spleen. He was put in jail. The next day my brother sent a trader to the doctor, with a request to be sold. His master was greatly incensed at what he called his insolence. He said he had put him there to reflect upon his bad conduct, and he certainly was not giving any evidence of repentance. For two days he harassed himself to find somebody to do his office work; but every thing went wrong without William. He was released, and ordered to take his old stand, with many threats, if he was not careful about his future behavior.

As the months passed on, my boy improved in health. When he was a year old, they called him beautiful. The little vine was taking deep root in my existence, though its clinging fondness excited a mixture of love and pain. When I was most sorely oppressed I found a solace in his smiles. I loved to watch his infant slumbers; but always there was a dark cloud over my enjoyment. I could never forget that he was a slave. Sometimes I wished that he might die in infancy.

God tried me. My darling became very ill. The bright eyes grew dull, and the little feet and hands were so icy cold that I thought death had already touched them. I had prayed for his death, but never so earnestly as I now prayed for his life; and my prayer was heard. Alas, what mockery it is for a slave mother to try to pray back her dying child to life! Death is better than slavery. It was a sad thought that I had no name to give my child. His father caressed him and treated him kindly, whenever he had a chance to see him. He was not unwilling that he should bear his name; but he had no legal claim to it; and if I had bestowed it upon him, my master would have regarded it as a new crime, a new piece of insolence, and would, perhaps, revenge it on the boy. O, the serpent of Slavery has many and poisonous fangs!

XII.

FEAR OF INSURRECTION.

Not far from this time Nat Turner's insurrection broke out; and the news threw our town into great commotion. Strange that they should be alarmed, when their slaves were so "contented and happy"! But so it was.

It was always the custom to have a muster every year. On that occasion every white man shouldered his musket. The citizens and the so-called country gentlemen wore military uniforms. The poor whites took their places in the ranks in every-day dress, some without shoes, some without hats. This grand occasion had already passed; and when the slaves were told there was to be another muster, they were surprised and rejoiced. Poor creatures! They thought it was going to be a holiday. I was informed of the true state of affairs, and imparted it to the few I could trust. Most gladly would I have proclaimed it to every slave; but I dared not.

All could not be relied on. Mighty is the power of the torturing lash.

By sunrise, people were pouring in from every quarter within twenty miles of the town. I knew the houses were to be searched; and I expected it would be done by country bullies and the poor whites. I knew nothing annoyed them so much as to see colored people living in comfort and respectability; so I made arrangements for them with especial care. I arranged every thing in my grandmother's house as neatly as possible. I put white quilts on the beds, and decorated some of the rooms with flowers. When all was arranged, I sat down at the window to watch. Far as my eye could reach, it rested on a motley crowd of soldiers. Drums and fifes were discoursing martial music. The men were divided into companies of sixteen, each headed by a captain. Orders were given, and the wild scouts rushed in every direction, wherever a colored face was to be found.

It was a grand opportunity for the low whites, who had no negroes of their own to scourge. They exulted in such a chance to exercise a little brief authority, and show their subserviency to the slaveholders; not reflecting that the power which trampled on the colored people also kept themselves in poverty, ignorance, and moral degradation. Those who never witnessed such scenes can hardly believe what I know was inflicted at this time on innocent men, women, and children, against whom there was not the slightest ground for suspicion. Colored people and slaves who lived in remote parts of the town suffered in an especial manner. In some cases the searchers scattered powder and shot among their clothes, and then sent other parties to find them, and bring them forward as proof that they were plotting insurrection. Every where men, women, and children were whipped till the blood stood in puddles at their feet. Some received five hundred lashes; others were tied hands and feet, and tortured with a bucking paddle, which blisters the skin terribly. The dwellings of the colored people, unless they happened to be protected by some influential white person, who was nigh at hand, were robbed of clothing and every thing else the marauders thought worth carrying away. All day long these unfeeling wretches went round, like a troop of demons, terrifying and tormenting the helpless. At night, they formed themselves into patrol bands, and went wherever they chose among the colored people, acting out their brutal will. Many women hid themselves in woods and swamps, to keep out of their way. If any of the husbands or fathers told of these outrages, they were tied up to the public whipping post, and cruelly scourged for telling lies about white men. The consternation was universal. No two people that had the slightest tinge of color in their faces dared to be seen talking together.

I entertained no positive fears about our household, because we were in the midst of white families who would protect us. We were ready to receive the soldiers whenever they came. It was not long before we heard the tramp of feet and the sound of voices. The door was rudely pushed open; and in they tumbled, like a pack of hungry wolves. They snatched at every thing within their reach. Every box, trunk, closet, and corner underwent a thorough examination. A box in one of the drawers containing some silver change was eagerly pounced upon. When I stepped forward to take it from them, one of the soldiers turned and said angrily, "What d'ye foller us fur? D'ye s'pose white folks is come to steal?"

I replied, "You have come to search; but you have searched that box, and I will take it, if you please."

At that moment I saw a white gentleman who was friendly to us; and I called to him, and asked him to have the goodness to come in and stay till the search was over. He readily complied. His entrance into the house brought in the captain of the company, whose business it was to guard the outside of the house, and see that none of the inmates left it. This officer was Mr. Litch, the wealthy slaveholder whom I mentioned, in the account of neighboring planters, as being notorious for his cruelty. He felt above soiling his hands with the search. He merely gave orders; and, if a bit of writing was discovered, it was carried to him by his ignorant followers, who were unable to read.

My grandmother had a large trunk of bedding and table cloths. When that was opened, there was a great shout of surprise; and one exclaimed, "Where'd the damned niggers git all dis sheet an' table clarf?"

My grandmother, emboldened by the presence of our

white protector said, "You may be sure we didn't pilfer 'em from *your* houses."

"Look here, mammy," said a grim-looking fellow without any coat, "you seem to feel mighty gran' 'cause you got all them 'ere fixens. White folks oughter have 'em all."

His remarks were interrupted by a chorus of voices shouting, "We's got 'em! We's got 'em! Dis 'ere yaller gal's got letters!"

There was a general rush for the supposed letter, which, upon examination, proved to be some verses written to me by a friend. In packing away my things, I had overlooked them. When their captain informed them of their contents, they seemed much disappointed. He inquired of me who wrote them. I told him it was one of my friends. "Can you read them?" he asked. When I told him I could, he swore, and raved, and tore the paper into bits. "Bring me all your letters!" said he, in commanding tone. I told him I had none. "Don't be afraid," he continued, in an insinuating way. "Bring them all to me. Nobody shall do you any harm." Seeing I did not move to obey him, his pleasant tone changed to oaths and threats. "Who writes to you? half free niggers?" inquired he. I replied, "O, no; most of my letters are from white people. Some request me to burn them after they are read, and some I destroy without reading."

An exclamation of surprise from some of the company put a stop to our conversation. Some silver spoons which ornamented an old-fashioned buffet had just been discovered. My grandmother was in the habit of preserving fruit for many ladies in the town, and of preparing suppers for parties; consequently she had many jars of preserves. The closet that contained these was next invaded, and the contents tasted. One of them, who was helping himself freely, tapped his neighbor on the shoulder, and said, "Wal done! Don't wonder de niggers want to kill all de white folks, when dey live on 'sarves" [meaning preserves]. I stretched out my hand to take the jar, saying, "You were not sent here to search for sweetmeats."

"And what *were* we sent for?" said the captain, bristling up to me. I evaded the question.

The search of the house was completed, and nothing found to condemn us. They next proceeded to the garden, and knocked about every bush and vine, with no better success. The captain called his men together, and, after a short consultation, the order to march was given. As they passed out of the gate, the captain turned back, and pronounced a malediction on the house. He said it ought to be burned to the ground, and each of its inmates receive thirty-nine lashes. We came out of this affair very fortunately; not losing any thing except some wearing apparel.

Towards evening the turbulence increased. The soldiers, stimulated by drink, committed still greater cruelties. Shrieks and shouts continually rent the air. Not daring to go to the door, I peeped under the window curtain. I saw a mob dragging along a number of colored people, each white man, with his musket upraised, threatening instant death if they did not stop their shrieks. Among the prisoners was a respectable old colored minister. They had found a few parcels of shot in his house, which his wife had for years used to balance her scales. For this they were going to shoot him on Court House Green. What a spectacle was that for a civilized country! A rabble, staggering under intoxication, assuming to be the administrators of justice!

The better class of the community exerted their influence to save the innocent, persecuted people; and in several instances they succeeded, by keeping them shut up in jail till the excitement abated. At last the white citizens found that their own property was not safe from the lawless rabble they had summoned to protect them. They rallied the drunken swarm, drove them back into the country, and set a guard over the town.

The next day, the town patrols were commissioned to search colored people that lived out of the city; and the most shocking outrages were committed with perfect impunity. Every day for a fortnight, if I looked out, I saw horsemen with some poor panting negro tied to their saddles, and compelled by the lash to keep up with their speed, till they arrived at the jail yard. Those who had been whipped too unmercifully to walk were washed with brine, tossed into a cart, and carried to jail. One black man, who had not fortitude to endure scourging, promised to give information about the conspiracy. But it turned out that he knew nothing at all. He had not even heard the name of

Nat Turner. The poor fellow had, however, made up a story, which augmented his own sufferings and those of the colored people.

The day patrol continued for some weeks, and at sundown a night guard was substituted. Nothing at all was proved against the colored people, bond or free. The wrath of the slaveholders was somewhat appeased by the capture of Nat Turner. The imprisoned were released. The slaves were sent to their masters, and the free were permitted to return to their ravaged homes. Visiting was strictly forbidden on the plantations. The slaves begged the privilege of again meeting at their little church in the woods, with their burying ground around it. It was built by the colored people, and they had no higher happiness than to meet there and sing hymns together, and pour out their hearts in spontaneous prayer. Their request was denied, and the church was demolished. They were permitted to attend the white churches, a certain portion of the galleries being appropriated to their use. There, when every body else had partaken of the communion, and the benediction had been pronounced, the minister said, "Come down, now, my colored friends." They obeyed the summons, and partook of the bread and wine, in commemoration of the meek and lowly Jesus, who said, "God is your Father, and all ye are brethren."

XIII.

THE CHURCH AND SLAVERY.

AFTER the alarm caused by Nat Turner's insurrection had subsided, the slaveholders came to the conclusion that it would be well to give the slaves enough of religious instruction to keep them from murdering their masters. The Episcopal clergyman offered to hold a separate service on

Sundays for their benefit. His colored members were very few, and also very respectable—a fact which I presume had some weight with him. The difficulty was to decide on a suitable place for them to worship. The Methodist and Baptist churches admitted them in the afternoon; but their carpets and cushions were not so costly as those at the Episcopal church. It was at last decided that they should meet at the house of a free colored man, who was a member.

I was invited to attend, because I could read. Sunday evening came, and, trusting to the cover of night, I ventured out. I rarely ventured out by daylight, for I always went with fear, expecting at every turn to encounter Dr. Flint, who was sure to turn me back, or order me to his office to inquire where I got my bonnet, or some other article of dress. When the Rev. Mr. Pike came, there were some twenty persons present. The reverend gentleman knelt in prayer, then seated himself, and requested all present, who could read, to open their books, while he gave out the portions he wished them to repeat or respond to.

His text was, "Servants, be obedient to them that are your masters according to the flesh, with fear and trembling, in singleness of your heart, as unto Christ."

Pious Mr. Pike brushed up his hair till it stood upright, and, in deep, solemn tones, began: "Hearken, ye servants! Give strict heed unto my words. You are rebellious sinners. Your hearts are filled with all manner of evil. 'Tis the devil who tempts you. God is angry with you, and will surely punish you, if you don't forsake your wicked ways. You that live in town are eye-servants behind your master's back. Instead of serving your masters faithfully, which is pleasing in the sight of your heavenly Master, you are idle, and shirk your work. God sees you. You tell lies. God hears you. Instead of being engaged in worshipping him, you are hidden away somewhere, feasting on your master's substance; tossing coffee-grounds with some wicked fortuneteller, or cutting cards with another old hag. Your masters may not find you out, but God sees you, and will punish you. O, the depravity of your hearts! When your master's work is done, are you quietly together, thinking of the goodness of God to such sinful creatures? No; you are quarrelling, and tying up little bags of roots to bury under the door-steps to poison each other with. God sees you. You men steal away to every grog shop to sell your master's corn, that you may buy rum to drink. God sees you. You sneak into the back streets, or among the bushes, to pitch coppers. Although your masters may not find you out, God sees you; and he will punish you. You must forsake your sinful ways, and be faithful servants. Obey your old master and your young master—your old mistress and your young mistress. If you disobey your earthly master, you offend your heavenly Master. You must obey God's commandments. When you go from here, don't stop at the corners of the streets to talk, but go directly home, and let your master and mistress see that you have come."

The benediction was pronounced. We went home, highly amused at brother Pike's gospel teaching, and we determined to hear him again. I went the next Sabbath evening, and heard pretty much a repetition of the last discourse. At the close of the meeting, Mr. Pike informed us that he found it very inconvenient to meet at the friend's house, and he should be glad to see us, every Sunday evening, at his own kitchen.

I went home with the feeling that I had heard the Reverend Mr. Pike for the last time. Some of his members repaired to his house, and found that the kitchen sported two tallow candles; the first time, I am sure, since its present occupant owned it, for the servants never had any thing but pine knots. It was so long before the reverend gentleman descended from his comfortable parlor that the slaves left, and went to enjoy a Methodist shout. They never seem so happy as when shouting and singing at religious meetings. Many of them are sincere, and nearer to the gate of heaven than sanctimonious Mr. Pike, and other long-faced Christians, who see wounded Samaritans, and pass by on the other side.

The slaves generally compose their own songs and hymns; and they do not trouble their heads much about the measure. They often sing the following verses:

> Old Satan is one busy ole man;
>   He rolls dem blocks all in my way;
> But Jesus is my bosom friend;
>   He rolls dem blocks away.

If I had died, when I was young,
  Den how my stam'ring tongue would have sung;
But I am ole, and now I stand
  A narrow chance for to tread dat heavenly land.

I well remember one occasion when I attended a Methodist class meeting. I went with a burdened spirit, and happened to sit next a poor, bereaved mother, whose heart was still heavier than mine. The class leader was the town constable—a man who bought and sold slaves, who whipped his brethren and sisters of the church at the public whipping post, in jail or out of jail. He was ready to perform that Christian office any where for fifty cents. This white-faced, black-hearted brother came near us, and said to the stricken woman, "Sister, can't you tell us how the Lord deals with your soul? Do you love him as you did formerly?"

She rose to her feet, and said, in piteous tones, "My Lord and Master, help me! My load is more than I can bear. God has hid himself from me, and I am left in darkness and misery." Then, striking her breast, she continued, "I can't tell you what is in here! They've got all my children. Last week they took the last one. God only knows where they've sold her. They let me have her sixteen years, and then—O! O! Pray for her brothers and sisters! I've got nothing to live for now. God make my time short!"

She sat down, quivering in every limb. I saw that constable class leader become crimson in the face with suppressed laughter, while he held up his handkerchief, that those who were weeping for the poor woman's calamity might not see his merriment. Then, with assumed gravity, he said to the bereaved mother, "Sister, pray to the Lord that every dispensation of his divine will may be sanctified to the good of your poor needy soul!"

The congregation struck up a hymn, and sung as though they were as free as the birds that warbled round us,—

Ole Satan thought he had a mighty aim;
He missed my soul, and caught my sins.
Cry Amen, cry Amen, cry Amen to God!

He took my sins upon his back;
Went muttering and grumbling down to hell.
Cry Amen, cry Amen, cry Amen to God!

Ole Satan's church is here below.
Up to God's free church I hope to go.
Cry Amen, cry Amen, cry Amen to God!

Precious are such moments to the poor slaves. If you were to hear them at such times, you might think they were happy. But can that hour of singing and shouting sustain them through the dreary week, toiling without wages, under constant dread of the lash?

The Episcopal clergyman, who, ever since my earliest recollection, had been a sort of god among the slaveholders, concluded, as his family was large, that he must go where money was more abundant. A very different clergyman took his place. The change was very agreeable to the colored people, who said, "God has sent us a good man this time." They loved him, and their children followed him for a smile or a kind word. Even the slaveholders felt his influence. He brought to the rectory five slaves. His wife taught them to read and write, and to be useful to her and themselves. As soon as he was settled, he turned his attention to the needy slaves around him. He urged upon his parishioners the duty of having a meeting expressly for them every Sunday, with a sermon adapted to their comprehension. After much argument and importunity, it was finally agreed that they might occupy the gallery of the church on Sunday evenings. Many colored people, hitherto unaccustomed to attend church, now gladly went to hear the gospel preached. The sermons were simple, and they understood them. Moreover, it was the first time they had ever been addressed as human beings. It was not long before his white parishioners began to be dissatisfied. He was accused of preaching better sermons to the negroes than he did to them. He honestly confessed that he bestowed more pains upon those sermons than upon any others; for the slaves were reared in such ignorance that it was a difficult task to adapt himself to their comprehension. Dissensions arose in the parish. Some wanted he should preach to them in the evening, and to the slaves in the afternoon. In the midst of these disputings his wife died, after a very short illness. Her slaves gathered round her dying bed in great sorrow. She said, "I have tried to do you good and promote your happiness; and if I have failed, it has not been for want of interest in your welfare. Do not weep for me; but prepare for the new duties that lie before you. I leave you all free. May we meet in a better world." Her liberated slaves were sent away, with funds to establish them comfortably. The colored people will long bless the memory of that truly Christian woman. Soon after her death her husband preached his farewell sermon, and many tears were shed at his departure.

Several years after, he passed through our town and preached to his former congregation. In his afternoon sermon he addressed the colored people. "My friends," said he, "it affords me great happiness to have an opportunity of speaking to you again. For two years I have been striving to do something for the colored people of my own parish; but nothing is yet accomplished. I have not even preached a sermon to them. Try to live according to the word of God, my friends. Your skin is darker than mine; but God judges men by their hearts, not by the color of their skins." This was strange doctrine from a southern pulpit. It was very offensive to slaveholders. They said he and his wife had made fools of their slaves, and that he preached like a fool to the negroes.

I knew an old black man, whose piety and childlike trust in God were beautiful to witness. At fifty-three years old he joined the Baptist church. He had a most earnest desire to learn to read. He thought he should know how to serve God better if he could only read the Bible. He came to me, and begged me to teach him. He said he could not pay me, for he had no money; but he would bring me nice fruit when the season for it came. I asked him if he didn't know it was contrary to law; and that slaves were whipped and imprisoned for teaching each other to read. This brought the tears into his eyes. "Don't be troubled, uncle Fred," said I. "I have no thoughts of refusing to teach you. I only told you of the law, that you might know the danger, and be on your guard." He thought he could plan to come three times a week without its being suspected. I selected a quiet nook, where no intruder was likely to penetrate, and there I taught him his A, B, C. Considering his age, his progress was astonishing. As soon as he could spell in two syllables he wanted to spell out words in the Bible. The happy smile that illuminated his face put joy into my heart. After spelling out a few words, he paused, and said, "Honey, it 'pears when I can read dis good book I shall be nearer to God. White man is got all de sense. He can larn easy. It ain't easy for ole black man like me. I only wants to read dis book, dat I may know how to live; den I hab no fear 'bout dying."

I tried to encourage him by speaking of the rapid progress he had made. "Hab patience, child," he replied. "I larns slow."

I had no need of patience. His gratitude, and the happiness I imparted, were more than a recompense for all my trouble.

At the end of six months he had read through the New Testament, and could find any text in it. One day, when he had recited unusually well, I said, "Uncle Fred, how do you manage to get your lessons so well?"

"Lord bress you, chile," he replied. "You nebber gibs me a lesson dat I don't pray to God to help me to understan' what I spells and what I reads. And he *does* help me, chile. Bress his holy name!"

There are thousands, who, like good uncle Fred, are thirsting for the water of life; but the law forbids it, and the churches withhold it. They send the Bible to the heathen abroad, and neglect the heathen at home. I am glad that missionaries go out to the dark corners of the earth; but I ask them not to overlook the dark corners at home. Talk to American slaveholders as you talk to savages in Africa. Tell *them* it was wrong to traffic in men. Tell them it is sinful to sell their own children, and atrocious to violate their own daughters. Tell them that all men are brethren, and that man has no right to shut out the light of knowledge from his brother. Tell them they are answerable to God for sealing up the Fountain of Life from souls that are thirsting for it.

There are men who would gladly undertake such missionary work as this; but, alas! their number is small. They are hated by the south, and would be driven from its soil, or dragged to prison to die, as others have been before them.

The field is ripe for the harvest, and awaits the reapers. Perhaps the great grandchildren of uncle Fred may have freely imparted to them the divine treasures, which he sought by stealth, at the risk of the prison and the scourge.

Are doctors of divinity blind, or are they hypocrites? I suppose some are the one, and some the other; but I think if they felt the interest in the poor and the lowly, that they ought to feel, they would not be so *easily* blinded. A clergyman who goes to the south, for the first time, has usually some feeling, however vague, that slavery is wrong. The slaveholder suspects this, and plays his game accordingly. He makes himself as agreeable as possible; talks on theology, and other kindred topics. The reverend gentleman is asked to invoke a blessing on a table loaded with luxuries. After dinner he walks round the premises, and sees the beautiful groves and flowering vines, and the comfortable huts of favored household slaves. The southerner invites him to talk with those slaves. He asks them if they want to be free, and they say, "O, no, massa." This is sufficient to satisfy him. He comes home to publish a "South Side View of Slavery," and to complain of the exaggerations of abolitionists. He assures people that he has been to the south, and seen slavery for himself; that it is a beautiful "patriarchal institution;" that the slaves don't want their freedom; that they have hallelujah meetings, and other religious privileges.

What does *he* know of the half-starved wretches toiling from dawn till dark on the plantations? of mothers shrieking for their children, torn from their arms by slave traders? of young girls dragged down into moral filth? of pools of blood around the whipping post? of hounds trained to tear human flesh? of men screwed into cotton gins to die? The slaveholder showed him none of these things, and the slaves dared not tell of them if he had asked them.

There is a great difference between Christianity and religion at the south. If a man goes to the communion table, and pays money into the treasury of the church, no matter if it be the price of blood, he is called religious. If a pastor has offspring by a woman not his wife, the church dismiss him, if she is a white woman; but if she is colored, it does not hinder his continuing to be their good shepherd.

When I was told that Dr. Flint had joined the Episcopal church, I was much surprised. I supposed that religion had a purifying effect on the character of men; but the worst persecutions I endured from him were after he was a communicant. The conversation of the doctor, the day after he had been confirmed, certainly gave *me* no indication that he had "renounced the devil and all his works." In answer to some of his usual talk, I reminded him that he had just joined the church. "Yes, Linda," said he. "It was proper for me to do so. I am getting in years, and my position in society requires it, and it puts an end to all the damned slang. You would do well to join the church, too, Linda."

"There are sinners enough in it already," rejoined I. "If I could be allowed to live like a Christian, I should be glad."

"You can do what I require; and if you are faithful to me, you will be as virtuous as my wife," he replied.

I answered that the Bible didn't say so.

His voice became hoarse with rage. "How dare you preach to me about your infernal Bible!" he exclaimed. "What right have you, who are my negro, to talk to me about what you would like and what you wouldn't like? I am your master, and you shall obey me."

No wonder the slaves sing,—

> Ole Satan's church is here below;
> Up to God's free church I hope to go.

XIV.

ANOTHER LINK TO LIFE.

I HAD not returned to my master's house since the birth of my child. The old man raved to have me thus removed from his immediate power; but his wife vowed, by all that was good and great, she would kill me if I came back; and he did not doubt her word. Sometimes he would stay away for a season. Then he would come and renew the old threadbare discourse about his forbearance and my ingratitude. He labored, most unnecessarily, to convince me that I had lowered myself. The venomous old reprobate had no need of descanting on that theme. I felt humiliated enough. My unconscious babe was the ever-present witness of my shame. I listened with silent contempt when he talked about my having forfeited *his* good opinion; but I shed bitter tears that I was no longer worthy of being respected by the good and pure. Alas! slavery still held me in its poisonous grasp. There was no chance for me to be respectable. There was no prospect of being able to lead a better life.

Sometimes, when my master found that I still refused to accept what he called his kind offers, he would threaten to sell my child. "Perhaps that will humble you," said he.

Humble *me*! Was I not already in the dust? But his threat lacerated my heart. I knew the law gave him power to fulfil it; for slaveholders have been cunning enough to enact that "the child shall follow the condition of the *mother*," not of the *father*; thus taking care that licentiousness shall not interfere with avarice. This reflection made me clasp my innocent babe all the more firmly to my heart. Horrid visions passed through my mind when I thought of his liability to fall into the slave trader's hands. I wept over him, and said, "O my child! perhaps they will leave you in some cold cabin to die, and then throw you into a hole, as if you were a dog."

When Dr. Flint learned that I was again to be a mother, he was exasperated beyond measure. He rushed from the house, and returned with a pair of shears. I had a fine head of hair; and he often railed about my pride of arranging it nicely. He cut every hair close to my head, storming and swearing all the time. I replied to some of his abuse, and he struck me. Some months before, he had pitched me down stairs in a fit of passion; and the injury I received was so serious that I was unable to turn myself in bed for many days. He then said, "Linda, I swear by God I will never raise my hand against you again;" but I knew that he would forget his promise.

After he discovered my situation, he was like a restless spirit from the pit. He came every day; and I was subjected to such insults as no pen can describe. I would not describe them if I could; they were too low, too revolting. I tried to keep them from my grandmother's knowledge as much as I could. I knew she had enough to sadden her life, without having my troubles to bear. When she saw the doctor treat me with violence, and heard him utter oaths terrible enough to palsy a man's tongue, she could not always hold her peace. It was natural and motherlike that she should try to defend me; but it only made matters worse.

When they told me my new-born babe was a girl, my heart was heavier than it had ever been before. Slavery is terrible for men; but it is far more terrible for women. Superadded to the burden common to all, *they* have wrongs, and sufferings, and mortifications peculiarly their own.

Dr. Flint had sworn that he would make me suffer, to my last day, for this new crime against *him,* as he called it; and as long as he had me in his power he kept his word. On the fourth day after the birth of my babe, he entered my room suddenly, and commanded me to rise and bring my baby to him. The nurse who took care of me had gone out of the room to prepare some nourishment, and I was alone. There was no alternative. I rose, took up my babe, and crossed the room to where he sat. "Now stand there," said he, "till I tell you to go back!" My child bore a strong resemblance to her father, and to the deceased Mrs. Sands, her grandmother. He noticed this; and while I stood before him, trembling with weakness, he heaped upon me and my little one every vile epithet he could think of. Even the grandmother in her grave did not escape his curses. In the midst of his vituperations I fainted at his feet. This recalled him to his senses. He took the baby from my arms, laid it on the bed, dashed cold water in my face, took me up, and shook me violently, to restore my consciousness before any one entered the room. Just then my grandmother came in, and he hurried out of the house. I suffered in consequence of this treatment; but I begged my friends to let me die, rather than send for the doctor. There was nothing I dreaded so much as his presence. My life was spared; and I was glad for the sake of my little ones. Had it not been for these ties to life, I should have been glad to be released by death, though I had lived only nineteen years.

Always it gave me a pang that my children had no lawful

claim to a name. Their father offered his; but, if I had wished to accept the offer, I dared not while my master lived. Moreover, I knew it would not be accepted at their baptism. A Christian name they were at least entitled to; and we resolved to call my boy for our dear good Benjamin, who had gone far away from us.

My grandmother belonged to the church; and she was very desirous of having the children christened. I knew Dr. Flint would forbid it, and I did not venture to attempt it. But chance favored me. He was called to visit a patient out of town, and was obliged to be absent during Sunday. "Now is the time," said my grandmother; "we will take the children to church, and have them christened."

When I entered the church, recollections of my mother came over me, and I felt subdued in spirit. There she had presented me for baptism, without any reason to feel ashamed. She had been married, and had such legal rights as slavery allows to a slave. The vows had at least been sacred to *her,* and she had never violated them. I was glad she was not alive, to know under what different circumstances her grandchildren were presented for baptism. Why had my lot been so different from my mother's? *Her* master had died when she was a child; and she remained with her mistress till she married. She was never in the power of any master; and thus she escaped one class of the evils that generally fall upon slaves.

When my baby was about to be christened, the former mistress of my father stepped up to me, and proposed to give it her Christian name. To this I added the surname of my father, who had himself no legal right to it; for my grandfather on the paternal side was a white gentleman. What tangled skeins are the genealogies of slavery! I loved my father; but it mortified me to be obliged to bestow his name on my children.

When we left the church, my father's old mistress invited me to go home with her. She clasped a gold chain round my baby's neck. I thanked her for this kindness; but I did not like the emblem. I wanted no chain to be fastened on my daughter, not even if its links were of gold. How earnestly I prayed that she might never feel the weight of slavery's chain, whose iron entereth into the soul!

XV.

CONTINUED PERSECUTIONS.

My children grew finely; and Dr. Flint would often say to me, with an exulting smile, "These brats will bring me a handsome sum of money one of these days."

I thought to myself that, God being my helper, they should never pass into his hands. It seemed to me I would rather see them killed than have them given up to his power. The money for the freedom of myself and my children could be obtained; but I derived no advantage from that circumstance. Dr. Flint loved money, but he loved power more. After much discussion, my friends resolved on making another trial. There was a slaveholder about to leave for Texas, and he was commissioned to buy me. He was to begin with nine hundred dollars, and go up to twelve. My master refused his offers. "Sir," said he, "she don't belong to me. She is my daughter's property, and I have no right to sell her. I mistrust that you come from her paramour. If so, you may tell him that he cannot buy her for any money; neither can he buy her children."

The doctor came to see me the next day, and my heart beat quicker as he entered. I never had seen the old man tread with so majestic a step. He seated himself and looked at me with withering scorn. My children had learned to be afraid of him. The little one would shut her eyes and hide her face on my shoulder whenever she saw him; and Benny, who was now nearly five years old, often inquired, "What makes that bad man come here so many times? Does he want to hurt us?" I would clasp the dear boy in my arms, trusting that he would be free before he was old enough to solve the problem. And now, as the doctor sat there so grim and silent, the child left his play and came and nestled up by me. At last my tormentor spoke. "So you are left in disgust, are you?" said he. "It is no more than I expected. You remember I told you years ago that you would be treated so. So he is tired of you? Ha! ha! ha! The virtuous madam don't like to hear about it, does she? Ha! ha! ha!" There was a sting in his calling me virtuous madam. I no longer had the power of answering him as I had formerly done. He continued: "So it seems you are trying to get up another intrigue. Your new paramour came to me, and offered to buy you; but you may be assured you will not succeed. You are mine; and you shall be mine for life. There lives no human being that can take you out of slavery. I would have done it; but you rejected my kind offer."

I told him I did not wish to get up any intrigue; that I had never seen the man who offered to buy me.

"Do you tell me I lie?" exclaimed he, dragging me from my chair. "Will you say again that you never saw that man?"

I answered, "I do say so."

He clinched my arm with a volley of oaths. Ben began to scream, and I told him to go to his grandmother.

"Don't you stir a step, you little wretch!" said he. The child drew nearer to me, and put his arms round me, as if he wanted to protect me. This was too much for my enraged master. He caught him up and hurled him across the room. I thought he was dead, and rushed towards him to take him up.

"Not yet!" exclaimed the doctor. "Let him lie there till he comes to."

"Let me go! Let me go!" I screamed, "or I will raise the whole house." I struggled and got away; but he clinched me again. Somebody opened the door, and he released me. I picked up my insensible child, and when I turned my tormentor was gone. Anxiously, I bent over the little form, so pale and still; and when the brown eyes at last opened, I don't know whether I was very happy.

All the doctor's former persecutions were renewed. He came morning, noon, and night. No jealous lover ever watched a rival more closely than he watched me and the unknown slaveholder, with whom he accused me of wishing to get up an intrigue. When my grandmother was out of the way he searched every room to find him.

In one of his visits, he happened to find a young girl, whom he had sold to a trader a few days previous. His statement was, that he sold her because she had been too familiar with the overseer. She had had a bitter life with him, and was glad to be sold. She had no mother, and no near ties.

She had been torn from all her family years before. A few friends had entered into bonds for her safety, if the trader would allow her to spend with them the time that intervened between her sale and the gathering up of his human stock. Such a favor was rarely granted. It saved the trader the expense of board and jail fees, and though the amount was small, it was a weighty consideration in a slave-trader's mind.

Dr. Flint always had an aversion to meeting slaves after he had sold them. He ordered Rose out of the house; but he was no longer her master, and she took no notice of him. For once the crushed Rose was the conqueror. His gray eyes flashed angrily upon her; but that was the extent of his power. "How came this girl here?" he exclaimed. "What right had you to allow it, when you knew I had sold her?"

I answered, "This is my grandmother's house, and Rose came to see her. I have no right to turn any body out of doors, that comes here for honest purposes."

He gave me the blow that would have fallen upon Rose if she had still been his slave. My grandmother's attention had been attracted by loud voices, and she entered in time to see a second blow dealt. She was not a woman to let such an outrage, in her own house, go unrebuked. The doctor undertook to explain that I had been insolent. Her indignant feelings rose higher and higher, and finally boiled over in words. "Get out of my house!" she exclaimed. "Go home, and take care of your wife and children, and you will have enough to do, without watching my family."

He threw the birth of my children in her face, and accused her of sanctioning the life I was leading. She told him I was living with her by compulsion of his wife; that he needn't accuse her, for he was the one to blame; he was the one who had caused all the trouble. She grew more and more excited as she went on. "I tell you what, Dr. Flint," said she, "you ain't got many more years to live, and you'd better be saying your prayers. It will take 'em all, and more too, to wash the dirt off your soul."

"Do you know whom you are talking to?" he exclaimed.

She replied, "Yes, I know very well who I am talking to."

He left the house in a great rage. I looked at my grandmother. Our eyes met. Their angry expression had passed away, but she looked sorrowful and weary—weary of incessant strife. I wondered that it did not lessen her love for me; but if it did she never showed it. She was always kind, always ready to sympathize with my troubles. There might have been peace and contentment in that humble home if it had not been for the demon Slavery.

The winter passed undisturbed by the doctor. The beautiful spring came; and when Nature resumes her loveliness, the human soul is apt to revive also. My drooping hopes came to life again with the flowers. I was dreaming of freedom again; more for my children's sake than my own. I planned and I planned. Obstacles hit against plans. There seemed no way of overcoming them; and yet I hoped.

Back came the wily doctor. I was not at home when he called. A friend had invited me to a small party, and to gratify her I went. To my great consternation, a messenger came in haste to say that Dr. Flint was at my grandmother's, and insisted on seeing me. They did not tell him where I was, or he would have come and raised a disturbance in my friend's house. They sent me a dark wrapper; I threw it on and hurried home. My speed did not save me; the doctor had gone away in anger. I dreaded the morning, but I could not delay it; it came, warm and bright. At an early hour the doctor came and asked me where I had been last night. I told him. He did not believe me, and sent to my friend's house to ascertain the facts. He came in the afternoon to assure me he was satisfied that I had spoken the truth. He seemed to be in a facetious mood, and I expected some jeers were coming. "I suppose you need some recreation," said he, "but I am surprised at your being there, among those negroes. It was not the place for you. Are you *allowed* to visit such people?"

I understood this covert fling at the white gentleman who was my friend; but I merely replied, "I went to visit my friends, and any company they keep is good enough for me."

He went on to say, "I have seen very little of you of late, but my interest in you is unchanged. When I said I would have no more mercy on you I was rash. I recall my words. Linda, you desire freedom for yourself and your children, and you can obtain it only through me. If you agree to what

I am about to propose, you and they shall be free. There must be no communication of any kind between you and their father. I will procure a cottage, where you and the children can live together. Your labor shall be light, such as sewing for my family. Think what is offered you, Linda—a home and freedom! Let the past be forgotten. If I have been harsh with you at times, your wilfulness drove me to it. You know I exact obedience from my own children, and I consider you as yet a child."

He paused for an answer, but I remained silent.

"Why don't you speak?" said he. "What more do you wait for?"

"Nothing, sir."

"Then you accept my offer?"

"No, sir."

His anger was ready to break loose; but he succeeded in curbing it, and replied, "You have answered without thought. But I must let you know there are two sides to my proposition; if you reject the bright side, you will be obliged to take the dark one. You must either accept my offer, or you and your children shall be sent to your young master's plantation, there to remain till your young mistress is married; and your children shall fare like the rest of the negro children. I give you a week to consider it."

He was shrewd; but I knew he was not to be trusted. I told him I was ready to give my answer now.

"I will not receive it now," he replied. "You act too much from impulse. Remember that you and your children can be free a week from to-day if you choose."

On what a monstrous chance hung the destiny of my children! I knew that my master's offer was a snare, and that if I entered it escape would be impossible. As for his promise, I knew him so well that I was sure if he gave me free papers, they would be so managed as to have no legal value. The alternative was inevitable. I resolved to go to the plantation. But then I thought how completely I should be in his power, and the prospect was appalling. Even if I should kneel before him, and implore him to spare me, for the sake of my children, I knew he would spurn me with his foot, and my weakness would be his triumph.

Before the week expired, I heard that young Mr. Flint

was about to be married to a lady of his own stamp. I foresaw the position I should occupy in his establishment. I had once been sent to the plantation for punishment, and fear of the son had induced the father to recall me very soon. My mind was made up; I was resolved that I would foil my master and save my children, or I would perish in the attempt. I kept my plans to myself; I knew that friends would try to dissuade me from them, and I would not wound their feelings by rejecting their advice.

On the decisive day the doctor came, and said he hoped I had made a wise choice.

"I am ready to go to the plantation, sir," I replied.

"Have you thought how important your decision is to your children?" said he.

I told him I had.

"Very well. Go to the plantation, and my curse go with you," he replied. "Your boy shall be put to work, and he shall soon be sold; and your girl shall be raised for the purpose of selling as well. Go your own ways!" He left the room with curses, not to be repeated.

As I stood rooted to the spot, my grandmother came and said, "Linda, child, what did you tell him?"

I answered that I was going to the plantation.

"*Must* you go?" said she. "Can't something be done to stop it?"

I told her it was useless to try; but she begged me not to give up. She said she would go to the doctor, and remind him how long and how faithfully she had served in the family, and how she had taken her own baby from her breast to nourish his wife. She would tell him I had been out of the family so long they would not miss me; that she would pay them for my time, and the money would procure a woman who had more strength for the situation than I had. I begged her not to go; but she persisted in saying, "He will listen to *me*, Linda." She went, and was treated as I expected. He coolly listened to what she said, but denied her request. He told her that what he did was for my good, that my feelings were entirely above my situation, and that on the plantation I would receive treatment that was suitable to my behavior.

My grandmother was much cast down. I had my secret

hopes; but I must fight my battle alone. I had a woman's pride, and a mother's love for my children; and I resolved that out of the darkness of this hour a brighter dawn should rise for them. My master had power and law on his side; I had a determined will. There is might in each.

XVI.

SCENES AT THE PLANTATION.

Eᴀʀʟʏ the next morning I left my grandmother's with my youngest child. My boy was ill, and I left him behind. I had many sad thoughts as the old wagon jolted on. Hitherto, I had suffered alone; now, my little one was to be treated as a slave. As we drew near the great house, I thought of the time when I was formerly sent there out of revenge. I wondered for what purpose I was now sent. I could not tell. I resolved to obey orders so far as duty required; but within myself, I determined to make my stay as short as possible. Mr. Flint was waiting to receive us, and told me to follow him up stairs to receive orders for the day. My little Ellen was left below in the kitchen. It was a change for her, who had always been so carefully tended. My young master said she might amuse herself in the yard. This was kind of him, since the child was hateful to his sight. My task was to fit up the house for the reception of the bride. In the midst of sheets, tablecloths, towels, drapery, and carpeting, my head was as busy planning, as were my fingers with the needle. At noon I was allowed to go to Ellen. She had sobbed herself to sleep. I heard Mr. Flint say to a neighbor, "I've got her down here, and I'll soon take the town notions out of her head. My father is partly to blame for her nonsense. He ought to have broke her in long ago." The remark was made within my hearing, and it would have been quite as manly to have made it to my face. He *had* said things to my face which might, or might not, have surprised his neighbor if he had known of them. He was "a chip off the old block."

I resolved to give him no cause to accuse me of being too much of a lady, so far as work was concerned. I worked day and night, with wretchedness before me. When I lay down beside my child, I felt how much easier it would be to see her die than to see her master beat her about, as I daily saw him beat other little ones. The spirit of the mothers was so crushed by the lash, that they stood by, without courage to remonstrate. How much more must I suffer, before I should be "broke in" to that degree?

I wished to appear as contented as possible. Sometimes I had an opportunity to send a few lines home; and this brought up recollections that made it difficult, for a time, to seem calm and indifferent to my lot. Notwithstanding my efforts, I saw that Mr. Flint regarded me with a suspicious eye. Ellen broke down under the trials of her new life. Separated from me, with no one to look after her, she wandered about, and in a few days cried herself sick. One day, she sat under the window where I was at work, crying that weary cry which makes a mother's heart bleed. I was obliged to steel myself to bear it. After a while it ceased. I looked out, and she was gone. As it was near noon, I ventured to go down in search of her. The great house was raised two feet above the ground. I looked under it, and saw her about midway, fast asleep. I crept under and drew her out. As I held her in my arms, I thought how well it would be for her if she never waked up; and I uttered my thought aloud. I was startled to hear some one say, "Did you speak to me?" I looked up, and saw Mr. Flint standing beside me. He said nothing further, but turned, frowning, away. That night he sent Ellen a biscuit and a cup of sweetened milk. This generosity surprised me. I learned afterwards, that in the afternoon he had killed a large snake, which crept from under the house; and I supposed that incident had prompted his unusual kindness.

The next morning the old cart was loaded with shingles for town. I put Ellen into it, and sent her to her grandmother. Mr. Flint said I ought to have asked his permission. I told him the child was sick, and required attention which

I had no time to give. He let it pass; for he was aware that I had accomplished much work in a little time.

I had been three weeks on the plantation, when I planned a visit home. It must be at night, after every body was in bed. I was six miles from town, and the road was very dreary. I was to go with a young man, who, I knew, often stole to town to see his mother. One night, when all was quiet, we started. Fear gave speed to our steps, and we were not long in performing the journey. I arrived at my grandmother's. Her bed room was on the first floor, and the window was open, the weather being warm. I spoke to her and she awoke. She let me in and closed the window, lest some late passer-by should see me. A light was brought, and the whole household gathered round me, some smiling and some crying. I went to look at my children, and thanked God for their happy sleep. The tears fell as I leaned over them. As I moved to leave, Benny stirred. I turned back, and whispered, "Mother is here." After digging at his eyes with his little fists, they opened, and he sat up in bed, looking at me curiously. Having satisfied himself that it was I, he exclaimed, "O mother! you ain't dead, are you? They didn't cut off your head at the plantation, did they?"

My time was up too soon, and my guide was waiting for me. I laid Benny back in his bed, and dried his tears by a promise to come again soon. Rapidly we retraced our steps back to the plantation. About half way we were met by a company of four patrols. Luckily we heard their horses' hoofs before they came in sight, and we had time to hide behind a large tree. They passed, hallooing and shouting in a manner that indicated a recent carousal. How thankful we were that they had not their dogs with them! We hastened our footsteps, and when we arrived on the plantation we heard the sound of the hand-mill. The slaves were grinding their corn. We were safely in the house before the horn summoned them to their labor. I divided my little parcel of food with my guide, knowing that he had lost the chance of grinding his corn, and must toil all day in the field.

Mr. Flint often took an inspection of the house, to see that no one was idle. The entire management of the work was trusted to me, because he knew nothing about it; and rather than hire a superintendent he contented himself with my arrangements. He had often urged upon his father the necessity of having me at the plantation to take charge of his affairs, and make clothes for the slaves; but the old man knew him too well to consent to that arrangement.

When I had been working a month at the plantation, the great aunt of Mr. Flint came to make him a visit. This was the good old lady who paid fifty dollars for my grandmother, for the purpose of making her free, when she stood on the auction block. My grandmother loved this old lady, whom we all called Miss Fanny. She often came to take tea with us. On such occasions the table was spread with a snow-white cloth, and the china cups and silver spoons were taken from the old-fashioned buffet. There were hot muffins, tea rusks, and delicious sweetmeats. My grandmother kept two cows, and the fresh cream was Miss Fanny's delight. She invariably declared that it was the best in town. The old ladies had cosey times together. They would work and chat, and sometimes, while talking over old times, their spectacles would get dim with tears, and would have to be taken off and wiped. When Miss Fanny bade us good by, her bag was filled with grandmother's best cakes, and she was urged to come again soon.

There had been a time when Dr. Flint's wife came to take tea with us, and when her children were also sent to have a feast of "Aunt Marthy's" nice cooking. But after I became an object of her jealousy and spite, she was angry with grandmother for giving a shelter to me and my children. She would not even speak to her in the street. This wounded my grandmother's feelings, for she could not retain ill will against the woman whom she had nourished with her milk when a babe. The doctor's wife would gladly have prevented our intercourse with Miss Fanny if she could have done it, but fortunately she was not dependent on the bounty of the Flints. She had enough to be independent; and that is more than can ever be gained from charity, however lavish it may be.

Miss Fanny was endeared to me by many recollections, and I was rejoiced to see her at the plantation. The warmth of her large, loyal heart made the house seem pleasanter while she was in it. She staid a week, and I had many talks with her. She said her principal object in coming was to see how I was treated, and whether any thing could be done for me. She inquired whether she could help me in any way. I told her I believed not. She condoled with me in her own peculiar way; saying she wished that I and all my grandmother's family were at rest in our graves, for not until then should she feel any peace about us. The good old soul did not dream that I was planning to bestow peace upon her, with regard to myself and my children; not by death, but by securing our freedom.

Again and again I had traversed those dreary twelve miles, to and from the town; and all the way, I was meditating upon some means of escape for myself and my children. My friends had made every effort that ingenuity could devise to effect our purchase, but all their plans had proved abortive. Dr. Flint was suspicious, and determined not to loosen his grasp upon us. I could have made my escape alone; but it was more for my helpless children than for myself that I longed for freedom. Though the boon would have been precious to me, above all price, I would not have taken it at the expense of leaving them in slavery. Every trial I endured, every sacrifice I made for their sakes, drew them closer to my heart, and gave me fresh courage to beat back the dark waves that rolled and rolled over me in a seemingly endless night of storms.

The six weeks were nearly completed, when Mr. Flint's bride was expected to take possession of her new home. The arrangements were all completed, and Mr. Flint said I had done well. He expected to leave home on Saturday, and return with his bride the following Wednesday. After receiving various orders from him, I ventured to ask permission to spend Sunday in town. It was granted; for which favor I was thankful. It was the first I had ever asked of him, and I intended it should be the last. I needed more than one night to accomplish the project I had in view; but the whole of Sunday would give me an opportunity. I spent the Sabbath with my grandmother. A calmer, more beautiful day never came down out of heaven. To me it was a day of conflicting emotions. Perhaps it was the last day I should ever spend under that dear, old sheltering roof! Perhaps these were the last talks I should ever have with the faithful old friend of my whole life! Perhaps it was the last time I and my children should be together! Well, better so, I thought, than that they should be slaves. I knew the doom that awaited my fair baby in slavery, and I determined to save her from it, or perish in the attempt. I went to make this vow at the graves of my poor parents, in the burying-ground of the slaves. "There the wicked cease from troubling, and there the weary be at rest. There the prisoners rest together; they hear not the voice of the oppressor; the servant is free from his master." I knelt by the graves of my parents, and thanked God, as I had often done before, that they had not lived to witness my trials, or to mourn over my sins. I had received my mother's blessing when she died; and in many an hour of tribulation I had seemed to hear her voice, sometimes chiding me, sometimes whispering loving words into my wounded heart. I have shed many and bitter tears, to think that when I am gone from my children they cannot remember me with such entire satisfaction as I remembered my mother.

The graveyard was in the woods, and twilight was coming on. Nothing broke the death-like stillness except the occasional twitter of a bird. My spirit was overawed by the solemnity of the scene. For more than ten years I had frequented this spot, but never had it seemed to me so sacred as now. A black stump, at the head of my mother's grave, was all that remained of a tree my father had planted. His grave was marked by a small wooden board, bearing his name, the letters of which were nearly obliterated. I knelt down and kissed them, and poured forth a prayer to God for guidance and support in the perilous step I was about to take. As I passed the wreck of the old meeting house, where, before Nat Turner's time, the slaves had been allowed to meet for worship, I seemed to hear my father's voice come from it, bidding me not to tarry till I reached freedom or the grave. I rushed on with renovated hopes. My trust in God had been strengthened by that prayer among the graves.

My plan was to conceal myself at the house of a friend, and remain there a few weeks till the search was over. My hope was that the doctor would get discouraged, and, for fear of losing my value, and also of subsequently finding my children among the missing, he would consent to sell us; and I knew somebody would buy us. I had done all in my power to make my children comfortable during the time I expected to be separated from them. I was packing my things, when grandmother came into the room, and asked what I was doing. "I am putting my things in order," I replied. I tried to look and speak cheerfully; but her watchful eye detected something beneath the surface. She drew me towards her, and asked me to sit down. She looked earnestly at me, and said, "Linda, do you want to kill your old grandmother? Do you mean to leave your little, helpless children? I am old now, and cannot do for your babies as I once did for you."

I replied, that if I went away, perhaps their father would be able to secure their freedom.

"Ah, my child," said she, "don't trust too much to him. Stand by your own children, and suffer with them till death. Nobody respects a mother who forsakes her children; and if you leave them, you will never have a happy moment. If you go, you will make me miserable the short time I have to live. You would be taken and brought back, and your sufferings would be dreadful. Remember poor Benjamin. Do give it up, Linda. Try to bear a little longer. Things may turn out better than we expect."

My courage failed me, in view of the sorrow I should bring on that faithful, loving old heart. I promised that I would try longer, and that I would take nothing out of her house without her knowledge.

Whenever the children climbed on my knee, or laid their heads on my lap, she would say, "Poor little souls! what would you do without a mother? She don't love you, as I do." And she would hug them to her own bosom, as if to reproach me for my want of affection; but she knew all the while that I loved them better than my life. I slept with her that night, and it was the last time. The memory of it haunted me for many a year.

On Monday I returned to the plantation, and busied myself with preparations for the important day. Wednesday came. It was a beautiful day, and the faces of the slaves were as bright as the sunshine. The poor creatures were merry. They were expecting little presents from the bride, and hoping for better times under her administration. I had no such hopes for them. I knew that the young wives of slaveholders often thought their authority and importance would be best established and maintained by cruelty; and what I had heard of young Mrs. Flint gave me no reason to expect that her rule over them would be less severe than that of the master and overseer. Truly, the colored race are the most cheerful and forgiving people on the face of the earth. That their masters sleep in safety is owing to their superabundance of heart; and yet they look upon their sufferings with less pity than they would bestow on those of a horse or a dog.

I stood at the door with others to receive the bridegroom and bride. She was a handsome, delicate-looking girl, and her face flushed with emotion at sight of her new home. I thought it likely that visions of a happy future were rising before her. It made me sad; for I knew how soon clouds would come over her sunshine. She examined every part of the house, and told me she was delighted with the arrangements I had made. I was afraid old Mrs. Flint had tried to prejudice her against me, and I did my best to please her.

All passed off smoothly for me until dinner time arrived. I did not mind the embarrassment of waiting on a dinner party, for the first time in my life, half so much as I did the meeting with Dr. Flint and his wife, who would be among the guests. It was a mystery to me why Mrs. Flint had not made her appearance at the plantation during all the time I was putting the house in order. I had not met her, face to face, for five years, and I had no wish to see her now. She was a praying woman, and, doubtless, considered my present position a special answer to her prayers. Nothing could please her better than to see me humbled and trampled upon. I was just where she would have me—in the power of a hard, unprincipled master. She did not speak to me when she took her seat at table; but her satisfied, triumphant smile, when I handed her her plate, was more eloquent than words. The old doctor was not so quiet in his demonstrations. He ordered me here and there, and spoke with peculiar emphasis when he said "your *mistress*." I was drilled like a disgraced soldier. When all was over, and the last key turned, I sought my pillow, thankful that God had appointed a season of rest for the weary.

The next day my new mistress began her housekeeping. I was not exactly appointed maid of all work; but I was to do whatever I was told. Monday evening came. It was always a busy time. On that night the slaves received their weekly allowance of food. Three pounds of meat, a peck of corn, and perhaps a dozen herring were allowed to each man. Women received a pound and a half of meat, a peck of corn, and the same number of herring. Children over twelve years old had half the allowance of the women. The meat was cut and weighed by the foreman of the field hands, and piled on planks before the meat house. Then the second foreman went behind the building, and when the first foreman called out, "Who takes this piece of meat?" he answered by calling somebody's name. This method was resorted to as a means of preventing partiality in distributing the meat. The young mistress came out to see how things were done on her plantation, and she soon gave a specimen of her character. Among those in waiting for their allowance was a very old slave, who had faithfully served the Flint family through three generations. When he hobbled up to get his bit of meat, the mistress said he was too old to have any allowance; that when niggers were too old to work, they ought to be fed on grass. Poor old man! He suffered much before he found rest in the grave.

My mistress and I got along very well together. At the end of a week, old Mrs. Flint made us another visit, and was closeted a long time with her daughter-in-law. I had my suspicions what was the subject of the conference. The old doctor's wife had been informed that I could leave the plantation on one condition, and she was very desirous to keep me there. If she had trusted me, as I deserved to be trusted by her, she would have had no fears of my accepting that condition. When she entered her carriage to return home, she said to young Mrs. Flint, "Don't neglect to send for them as quick as possible." My heart was on the watch all the time, and I at once concluded that she spoke of my children. The doctor came the next day, and as I entered the room to spread the tea table, I heard him say, "Don't wait any longer. Send for them to-morrow." I saw through the plan. They thought my children's being there would fetter me to the spot, and that it was a good place to break us all in to abject submission to our lot as slaves. After the doctor left, a gentleman called, who had always manifested friendly feelings towards my grandmother and her family. Mr. Flint carried him over the plantation to show him the results of labor performed by men and women who were unpaid, miserably clothed, and half famished. The cotton crop was all they thought of. It was duly admired, and the gentleman returned with specimens to show his friends. I was ordered to carry water to wash his hands. As I did so, he said, "Linda, how do you like your new home?" I told him I liked it as well as I expected. He replied, "They don't think you are contented, and to-morrow they are going to bring your children to be with you. I am sorry for you, Linda. I hope they will treat you kindly." I hurried from the room, unable to thank him. My suspicions were correct. My children were to be brought to the plantation to be "broke in."

To this day I feel grateful to the gentleman who gave me this timely information. It nerved me to immediate action.

XVII.

THE FLIGHT.

Mʀ. Flint was hard pushed for house servants, and rather than lose me he had restrained his malice. I did my work faithfully, though not, of course, with a willing mind. They were evidently afraid I should leave them. Mr. Flint wished that I should sleep in the great house instead of the servants' quarters. His wife agreed to the proposition, but said I mustn't bring my bed into the house, because it would scatter feathers on her carpet. I knew when I went there

that they would never think of such a thing as furnishing a
bed of any kind for me and my little ones. I therefore carried my own bed, and now I was forbidden to use it. I did as
I was ordered. But now that I was certain my children were
to be put in their power, in order to give them a stronger
hold on me, I resolved to leave them that night. I remembered the grief this step would bring upon my dear old
grandmother; and nothing less than the freedom of my children would have induced me to disregard her advice. I went
about my evening work with trembling steps. Mr. Flint
twice called from his chamber door to inquire why the
house was not locked up. I replied that I had not done my
work. "You have had time enough to do it," said he. "Take
care how you answer me!"

I shut all the windows, locked all the doors, and went up
to the third story, to wait till midnight. How long those
hours seemed, and how fervently I prayed that God would
not forsake me in this hour of utmost need! I was about to
risk every thing on the throw of a die; and if I failed, O what
would become of me and my poor children? They would be
made to suffer for my fault.

At half past twelve I stole softly down stairs. I stopped
on the second floor, thinking I heard a noise. I felt my way
down into the parlor, and looked out of the window. The
night was so intensely dark that I could see nothing. I raised
the window very softly and jumped out. Large drops of rain
were falling, and the darkness bewildered me. I dropped on
my knees, and breathed a short prayer to God for guidance
and protection. I groped my way to the road, and rushed
towards the town with almost lightning speed. I arrived at
my grandmother's house, but dared not see her. She would
say, "Linda, you are killing me;" and I knew that would un-
nerve me. I tapped softly at the window of a room, occupied
by a woman, who had lived in the house several years. I
knew she was a faithful friend, and could be trusted with my
secret. I tapped several times before she heard me. At last
she raised the window, and I whispered, "Sally, I have run
away. Let me in, quick." She opened the door softly, and
said in low tones, "For God's sake, don't. Your grandmother
is trying to buy you and de chillern. Mr. Sands was here last
week. He tole her he was going away on business, but he

wanted her to go ahead about buying you and de chillern, and he would help her all he could. Don't run away, Linda. Your grandmother is all bowed down wid trouble now."

I replied, "Sally, they are going to carry my children to the plantation to-morrow; and they will never sell them to any body so long as they have me in their power. Now, would you advise me to go back?"

"No, chile, no," answered she. "When dey finds you is gone, dey won't want de plague ob de chillern; but where is you going to hide? Dey knows ebery inch ob dis house."

I told her I had a hiding-place, and that was all it was best for her to know. I asked her to go into my room as soon as it was light, and take all my clothes out of my trunk, and pack them in hers; for I knew Mr. Flint and the constable would be there early to search my room. I feared the sight of my children would be too much for my full heart; but I could not go into the uncertain future without one last look. I bent over the bed where lay my little Benny and baby Ellen. Poor little ones! fatherless and motherless! Memories of their father came over me. He wanted to be kind to them; but they were not all to him, as they were to my womanly heart. I knelt and prayed for the innocent little sleepers. I kissed them lightly, and turned away.

As I was about to open the street door, Sally laid her hand on my shoulder, and said, "Linda, is you gwine all alone? Let me call your uncle."

"No, Sally," I replied, "I want no one to be brought into trouble on my account."

I went forth into the darkness and rain. I ran on till I came to the house of the friend who was to conceal me.

Early the next morning Mr. Flint was at my grandmother's inquiring for me. She told him she had not seen me, and supposed I was at the plantation. He watched her face narrowly, and said, "Don't you know any thing about her running off?" She assured him that she did not. He went on to say, "Last night she ran off without the least provocation. We had treated her very kindly. My wife liked her. She will soon be found and brought back. Are her children with you?" When told that they were, he said, "I am very glad to hear that. If they are here, she cannot be far off. If I find out that any of my niggers have had any thing to do with this damned business, I'll give 'em five hundred lashes." As he started to go to his father's, he turned round and added, persuasively, "Let her be brought back, and she shall have her children to live with her."

The tidings made the old doctor rave and storm at a furious rate. It was a busy day for them. My grandmother's house was searched from top to bottom. As my trunk was empty, they concluded I had taken my clothes with me. Before ten o'clock every vessel northward bound was thoroughly examined, and the law against harboring fugitives was read to all on board. At night a watch was set over the town. Knowing how distressed my grandmother would be, I wanted to send her a message; but it could not be done. Every one who went in or out of her house was closely watched. The doctor said he would take my children, unless she became responsible for them; which of course she willingly did. The next day was spent in searching. Before night, the following advertisement was posted at every corner, and in every public place for miles round:—

$300 REWARD! Ran away from the subscriber, an intelligent, bright, mulatto girl, named Linda, 21 years of age. Five feet four inches high. Dark eyes, and black hair inclined to curl; but it can be made straight. Has a decayed spot on a front tooth. She can read and write, and in all probability will try to get to the Free States. All persons are forbidden, under penalty of law, to harbor or employ said slave. $150 will be given to whoever takes her in the state, and $300 if taken out of the state and delivered to me, or lodged in jail.

DR. FLINT.

XVIII.
MONTHS OF PERIL.

THE search for me was kept up with more persever-
ence than I had anticipated. I began to think that escape
was impossible. I was in great anxiety lest I should implicate
the friend who harbored me. I knew the consequences
would be frightful; and much as I dreaded being caught,
even that seemed better than causing an innocent person to
suffer for kindness to me. A week had passed in terrible
suspense, when my pursuers came into such close vicinity
that I concluded they had tracked me to my hiding-place. I
flew out of the house, and concealed myself in a thicket of
bushes. There I remained in an agony of fear for two hours.
Suddenly, a reptile of some kind seized my leg. In my fright,
I struck a blow which loosened its hold, but I could not tell
whether I had killed it; it was so dark, I could not see what
it was; I only knew it was something cold and slimy. The
pain I felt soon indicated that the bite was poisonous. I was
compelled to leave my place of concealment, and I groped
my way back into the house. The pain had become intense,
and my friend was startled by my look of anguish. I asked
her to prepare a poultice of warm ashes and vinegar, and I
applied it to my leg, which was already much swollen. The
application gave me some relief, but the swelling did not
abate. The dread of being disabled was greater than the
physical pain I endured. My friend asked an old woman,
who doctored among the slaves, what was good for the bite
of a snake or a lizard. She told her to steep a dozen coppers
in vinegar, over night, and apply the cankered vinegar to
the inflamed part.*

I had succeeded in cautiously conveying some messages
to my relatives. They were harshly threatened, and despair-

---

*The poison of a snake is a powerful acid, and is counteracted by pow-
erful alkalies, such as potash, ammonia, &c. The Indians are accustomed to apply wet ashes, or plunge the limb into strong lye. White
men, employed to lay out railroads in snaky places, often carry ammonia with them as an antidote.—EDITOR.

ing of my having a chance to escape, they advised me to return to my master, ask his forgiveness, and let him make an example of me. But such counsel had no influence with me. When I started upon this hazardous undertaking, I had resolved that, come what would, there should be no turning back. "Give me liberty, or give me death," was my motto. When my friend contrived to make known to my relatives the painful situation I had been in for twenty-four hours, they said no more about my going back to my master. Something must be done, and that speedily; but where to turn for help, they knew not. God in his mercy raised up "a friend in need."

Among the ladies who were acquainted with my grandmother, was one who had known her from childhood, and always been very friendly to her. She had also known my mother and her children, and felt interested for them. At this crisis of affairs she called to see my grandmother, as she not unfrequently did. She observed the sad and troubled expression of her face, and asked if she knew where Linda was, and whether she was safe. My grandmother shook her head, without answering. "Come, Aunt Martha," said the kind lady, "tell me all about it. Perhaps I can do something to help you." The husband of this lady held many slaves, and bought and sold slaves. She also held a number in her own name; but she treated them kindly, and would never allow any of them to be sold. She was unlike the majority of slaveholders' wives. My grandmother looked earnestly at her. Something in the expression of her face said "Trust me!" and she did trust her. She listened attentively to the details of my story, and sat thinking for a while. At last she said, "Aunt Martha, I pity you both. If you think there is any chance of Linda's getting to the Free States, I will conceal her for a time. But first you must solemnly promise that my name shall never be mentioned. If such a thing should become known, it would ruin me and my family. No one in my house must know of it, except the cook. She is so faithful that I would trust my own life with her; and I know she likes Linda. It is a great risk; but I trust no harm will come of it. Get word to Linda to be ready as soon as it is dark, before the patrols are out. I will send the housemaids on errands, and Betty shall go to meet Linda." The place where we were to meet was designated and agreed upon. My grandmother was unable to thank the lady for this noble deed; overcome by her emotions, she sank on her knees and sobbed like a child.

I received a message to leave my friend's house at such an hour, and go to a certain place where a friend would be waiting for me. As a matter of prudence no names were mentioned. I had no means of conjecturing who I was to meet, or where I was going. I did not like to move thus blindfolded, but I had no choice. It would not do for me to remain where I was. I disguised myself, summoned up courage to meet the worst, and went to the appointed place. My friend Betty was there; she was the last person I expected to see. We hurried along in silence. The pain in my leg was so intense that it seemed as if I should drop, but fear gave me strength. We reached the house and entered unobserved. Her first words were: "Honey, now you is safe. Dem devils ain't coming to search *dis* house. When I get you into missis' safe place, I will bring some nice hot supper. I specs you need it after all dis skeering." Betty's vocation led her to think eating the most important thing in life. She did not realize that my heart was too full for me to care much about supper.

The mistress came to meet us, and led me up stairs to a small room over her own sleeping apartment. "You will be safe here, Linda," said she; "I keep this room to store away things that are out of use. The girls are not accustomed to be sent to it, and they will not suspect any thing unless they hear some noise. I always keep it locked, and Betty shall take care of the key. But you must be very careful, for my sake as well as your own; and you must never tell my secret; for it would ruin me and my family. I will keep the girls busy in the morning, that Betty may have a chance to bring your breakfast; but it will not do for her to come to you again till night. I will come to see you sometimes. Keep up your courage. I hope this state of things will not last long." Betty came with the "nice hot supper," and the mistress hastened down stairs to keep things straight till she returned. How my heart overflowed with gratitude! Words choked in my throat; but I could have kissed the feet of my benefactress. For that deed of Christian womanhood, may God forever bless her!

I went to sleep that night with the feeling that I was for the present the most fortunate slave in town. Morning came and filled my little cell with light. I thanked the heavenly Father for this safe retreat. Opposite my window was a pile of feather beds. On the top of these I could lie perfectly concealed, and command a view of the street through which Dr. Flint passed to his office. Anxious as I was, I felt a gleam of satisfaction when I saw him. Thus far I had outwitted him, and I triumphed over it. Who can blame slaves for being cunning? They are constantly compelled to resort to it. It is the only weapon of the weak and oppressed against the strength of their tyrants.

I was daily hoping to hear that my master had sold my children; for I knew who was on the watch to buy them. But Dr. Flint cared even more for revenge than he did for money. My brother William and the good aunt who had served in his family twenty years, and my little Benny, and Ellen, who was a little over two years old, were thrust into jail, as a means of compelling my relatives to give some information about me. He swore my grandmother should never see one of them again till I was brought back. They kept these facts from me for several days. When I heard that my little ones were in a loathsome jail, my first impulse was to go to them. I was encountering dangers for the sake of freeing them, and must I be the cause of their death? The thought was agonizing. My benefactress tried to soothe me by telling me that my aunt would take good care of the children while they remained in jail. But it added to my pain to think that the good old aunt, who had always been so kind to her sister's orphan children, should be shut up in prison for no other crime than loving them. I suppose my friends feared a reckless movement on my part, knowing, as they did, that my life was bound up in my children. I received a note from my brother William. It was scarcely legible, and ran thus: "Wherever you are, dear sister, I beg of you not to come here. We are all much better off than you are. If you come, you will ruin us all. They would force you to tell where you had been, or they would kill you. Take the advice of your friends; if not for the sake of me and your children, at least for the sake of those you would ruin."

Poor William! He also must suffer for being my brother. I took his advice and kept quiet. My aunt was taken out of jail at the end of a month, because Mrs. Flint could not spare her any longer. She was tired of being her own housekeeper. It was quite too fatiguing to order her dinner and eat it too. My children remained in jail, where brother William did all he could for their comfort. Betty went to see them sometimes, and brought me tidings. She was not permitted to enter the jail; but William would hold them up to the grated window while she chatted with them. When she repeated their prattle, and told me how they wanted to see their ma, my tears would flow. Old Betty would exclaim, "Lors, chile! what's you crying 'bout? Dem young uns vil kill you dead. Don't be so chick'n hearted! If you does, you vil nebber git thro' dis world."

Good old soul! She had gone through the world childless. She had never had little ones to clasp their arms round her neck; she had never seen their soft eyes looking into hers; no sweet little voices had called her mother; she had never pressed her own infants to her heart, with the feeling that even in fetters there was something to live for. How could she realize my feelings? Betty's husband loved children dearly, and wondered why God had denied them to him. He expressed great sorrow when he came to Betty with the tidings that Ellen had been taken out of jail and carried to Dr. Flint's. She had the measles a short time before they carried her to jail, and the disease had left her eyes affected. The doctor had taken her home to attend to them. My children had always been afraid of the doctor and his wife. They had never been inside of their house. Poor little Ellen cried all day to be carried back to prison. The instincts of childhood are true. She knew she was loved in the jail. Her screams and sobs annoyed Mrs. Flint. Before night she called one of the slaves, and said, "Here, Bill, carry this brat back to the jail. I can't stand her noise. If she would be quiet I should like to keep the little minx. She would make a handy waiting-maid for my daughter by and by. But if she staid here, with her white face, I suppose I should either kill her or spoil her. I hope the doctor will sell them as far as wind and water can carry them. As for their mother, her ladyship will find out yet what she gets by running away. She hasn't so much feeling for her children as a cow has for its calf. If she had, she would have come back long ago, to get them out of jail, and save all this expense and trouble. The good-for-nothing hussy! When she is caught, she shall stay in jail, in irons, for six months, and then be sold to a sugar plantation. I shall see her broke in yet. What do you stand there for, Bill? Why don't you go off with the brat? Mind, now, that you don't let any of the niggers speak to her in the street!"

When these remarks were reported to me, I smiled at Mrs. Flint's saying that she should either kill my child or spoil her. I thought to myself there was very little danger of the latter. I have always considered it as one of God's special providences that Ellen screamed till she was carried back to jail.

That same night Dr. Flint was called to a patient, and did not return till near morning. Passing my grandmother's, he saw a light in the house, and thought to himself, "Perhaps this has something to do with Linda." He knocked, and the door was opened. "What calls you up so early?" said he. "I saw your light, and I thought I would just stop and tell you that I have found out where Linda is. I know where to put my hands on her, and I shall have her before twelve o'clock." When he had turned away, my grandmother and my uncle looked anxiously at each other. They did not know whether or not it was merely one of the doctor's tricks to frighten them. In their uncertainty, they thought it was best to have a message conveyed to my friend Betty. Unwilling to alarm her mistress, Betty resolved to dispose of me herself. She came to me, and told me to rise and dress quickly. We hurried down stairs, and across the yard, into the kitchen. She locked the door, and lifted up a plank in the floor. A buffalo skin and a bit of carpet were spread for me to lie on, and a quilt thrown over me. "Stay dar," said she, "till I sees if dey know 'bout you. Dey say dey vil put thar hans on you afore twelve o'clock. If dey *did* know whar you are, dey won't know *now*. Dey'll be disapinted dis time. Dat's all I got to say. If dey comes rummagin 'mong *my* tings, de'll get one bressed sarssin from dis 'ere nigger." In my shallow bed I had but just room enough to bring my hands to my face to keep the dust out of my eyes; for Betty walked over me twenty times in an hour, passing from the dresser to the fireplace. When she was alone, I could hear her pronouncing anathemas over Dr. Flint and all his tribe, every now and then saying, with a chuckling laugh, "Dis nigger's too cute for 'em dis time." When the housemaids were about, she had sly ways of drawing them out, that I might hear what they would say. She would repeat stories she had heard about my being in this, or that, or the other place. To which they would answer, that I was not fool enough to be staying round there; that I was in Philadelphia or New York before this time. When all were abed and asleep, Betty raised the plank, and said, "Come out, chile; come out. Dey don't know nottin 'bout you. 'Twas only white folks' lies, to skeer de niggers."

Some days after this adventure I had a much worse fright. As I sat very still in my retreat above stairs, cheerful visions floated through my mind. I thought Dr. Flint would soon get discouraged, and would be willing to sell my children, when he lost all hopes of making them the means of my discovery. I knew who was ready to buy them. Suddenly I heard a voice that chilled my blood. The sound was too familiar to me, it had been too dreadful, for me not to recognize at once my old master. He was in the house, and I at once concluded he had come to seize me. I looked round in terror. There was no way of escape. The voice receded. I supposed the constable was with him, and they were searching the house. In my alarm I did not forget the trouble I was bringing on my generous benefactress. It seemed as if I were born to bring sorrow on all who befriended me, and that was the bitterest drop in the bitter cup of my life. After a while I heard approaching footsteps; the key was turned in my door. I braced myself against the wall to keep from falling. I ventured to look up, and there stood my kind benefactress alone. I was too much overcome to speak, and sunk down upon the floor.

"I thought you would hear your master's voice," she said; "and knowing you would be terrified, I came to tell you there is nothing to fear. You may even indulge in a laugh at the old gentleman's expense. He is so sure you are in New

York, that he came to borrow five hundred dollars to go in pursuit of you. My sister had some money to loan on interest. He has obtained it, and proposes to start for New York to-night. So, for the present, you see you are safe. The doctor will merely lighten his pocket hunting after the bird he has left behind."

XIX.

THE CHILDREN SOLD.

THE doctor came back from New York, of course without accomplishing his purpose. He had expended considerable money, and was rather disheartened. My brother and the children had now been in jail two months, and that also was some expense. My friends thought it was a favorable time to work on his discouraged feelings. Mr. Sands sent a speculator to offer him nine hundred dollars for my brother William, and eight hundred for the two children. These were high prices, as slaves were then selling; but the offer was rejected. If it had been merely a question of money, the doctor would have sold any boy of Benny's age for two hundred dollars; but he could not bear to give up the power of revenge. But he was hard pressed for money, and he revolved the matter in his mind. He knew that if he could keep Ellen till she was fifteen, he could sell her for a high price; but I presume he reflected that she might die, or might be stolen away. At all events, he came to the conclusion that he had better accept the slave-trader's offer. Meeting him in the street, he inquired when he would leave town. "To-day, at ten o'clock," he replied. "Ah, do you go so soon?" said the doctor. "I have been reflecting upon your proposition, and I have concluded to let you have the three negroes if you will say nineteen hundred dollars." After some parley, the trader agreed to his terms. He wanted the bill of sale drawn up and signed immediately, as he had a great deal to attend to during the short time he remained in town. The doctor went to the jail and told William he would take him back into his service if he would promise to behave himself; but he replied that he would rather be sold. "And you *shall* be sold, you ungrateful rascal!" exclaimed the doctor. In less than an hour the money was paid, the papers were signed, sealed, and delivered, and my brother and children were in the hands of the trader.

It was a hurried transaction; and after it was over, the doctor's characteristic caution returned. He went back to the speculator, and said, "Sir, I have come to lay you under obligations of a thousand dollars not to sell any of those negroes in this state." "You come too late," replied the trader; "our bargain is closed." He had, in fact, already sold them to Mr. Sands, but he did not mention it. The doctor required him to put irons on "that rascal, Bill," and to pass through the back streets when he took his gang out of town. The trader was privately instructed to concede to his wishes. My good old aunt went to the jail to bid the children good by, supposing them to be the speculator's property, and that she should never see them again. As she held Benny in her lap, he said, "Aunt Nancy, I want to show you something." He led her to the door and showed her a long row of marks, saying, "Uncle Will taught me to count. I have made a mark for every day I have been here, and it is sixty days. It is a long time; and the speculator is going to take me and Ellen away. He's a bad man. It's wrong for him to take grandmother's children. I want to go to my mother."

My grandmother was told that the children would be restored to her, but she was requested to act as if they were really to be sent away. Accordingly, she made up a bundle of clothes and went to the jail. When she arrived, she found William handcuffed among the gang, and the children in the trader's cart. The scene seemed too much like reality. She was afraid there might have been some deception or mistake. She fainted, and was carried home.

When the wagon stopped at the hotel, several gentlemen came out and proposed to purchase William, but the trader refused their offers, without stating that he was already sold. And now came the trying hour for that drove of human beings, driven away like cattle, to be sold they knew not where. Husbands were torn from wives, parents from children, never to look upon each other again this side of the grave. There was wringing of hands and cries of despair.

Dr. Flint had the supreme satisfaction of seeing the wagon leave town, and Mrs. Flint had the gratification of supposing that my children were going "as far as wind and water would carry them." According to agreement, my uncle followed the wagon some miles, until they came to an old farm house. There the trader took the irons from William, and as he did so, he said, "You are a damned clever fellow. I should like to own you myself. Them gentlemen that wanted to buy you said you was a bright, honest chap, and I must git you a good home. I guess your old master will swear to-morrow, and call himself an old fool for selling the children. I reckon he'll never git their mammy back again. I expect she's made tracks for the north. Good by, old boy. Remember, I have done you a good turn. You must thank me by coaxing all the pretty gals to go with me next fall. That's going to be my last trip. This trading in niggers is a bad business for a fellow that's got any heart. Move on, you fellows!" And the gang went on, God alone knows where.

Much as I despise and detest the class of slave-traders, whom I regard as the vilest wretches on earth, I must do this man the justice to say that he seemed to have some feeling. He took a fancy to William in the jail, and wanted to buy him. When he heard the story of my children, he was willing to aid them in getting out of Dr. Flint's power, even without charging the customary fee.

My uncle procured a wagon and carried William and the children back to town. Great was the joy in my grandmother's house! The curtains were closed, and the candles lighted. The happy grandmother cuddled the little ones to her bosom. They hugged her, and kissed her, and clapped their hands, and shouted. She knelt down and poured forth one of her heartfelt prayers of thanksgiving to God. The father was present for a while; and though such a "parental relation" as existed between him and my children takes slight hold on the hearts or consciences of slaveholders, it must be that he experienced some moments of pure joy in witnessing the happiness he had imparted.

I had no share in the rejoicings of that evening. The events of the day had not come to my knowledge. And now I will tell you something that happened to me; though you will, perhaps, think it illustrates the superstition of slaves. I sat in my usual place on the floor near the window, where I could hear much that was said in the street without being seen. The family had retired for the night, and all was still. I sat there thinking of my children, when I heard a low strain of music. A band of serenaders were under the window, playing "Home, sweet home." I listened till the sounds did not seem like music, but like the moaning of children. It seemed as if my heart would burst. I rose from my sitting posture, and knelt. A streak of moonlight was on the floor before me, and in the midst of it appeared the forms of my two children. They vanished; but I had seen them distinctly. Some will call it a dream, others a vision. I know not how to account for it, but it made a strong impression on my mind, and I felt certain something had happened to my little ones.

I had not seen Betty since morning. Now I heard her softly turning the key. As soon as she entered, I clung to her, and begged her to let me know whether my children were dead, or whether they were sold; for I had seen their spirits in my room, and I was sure something had happened to them. "Lor, chile," said she, putting her arms round me, "you's got de high-sterics. I'll sleep wid you to-night, 'cause you'll make a noise, and ruin missis. Something has stirred you up mightily. When you is done cryin, I'll talk wid you. De chillern is well, and mighty happy. I seed 'em myself. Does dat satisfy you? Dar, chile, be still! Somebody vill hear you." I tried to obey her. She lay down, and was soon sound asleep; but no sleep would come to my eyelids.

At dawn, Betty was up and off to the kitchen. The hours passed on, and the vision of the night kept constantly recurring to my thoughts. After a while I heard the voices of two women in the entry. In one of them I recognized the house-maid. The other said to her, "Did you know Linda Brent's children was sold to the speculator yesterday. They say ole massa Flint was mighty glad to see 'em drove out of town; but they say they've come back agin. I 'spect it's all their daddy's doings. They say he's bought William too. Lor! how it will take hold of ole massa Flint! I'm going roun' to aunt Marthy's to see 'bout it."

I bit my lips till the blood came to keep from crying out. Were my children with their grandmother, or had the speculator carried them off? The suspense was dreadful. Would Betty *never* come, and tell me the truth about it? At last she came, and I eagerly repeated what I had overheard. Her face was one broad, bright smile. "Lor, you foolish ting!" said she. "I'se gwine to tell you all 'bout it. De gals is eating thar breakfast, and missus tole me to let her tell you; but, poor creeter! t'aint right to keep you waitin', and I'se gwine to tell you. Brudder, chillen, all is bought by de daddy! I'se laugh more dan nuff, tinking 'bout ole massa Flint. Lor, how he *vill* swar! He's got ketched dis time, any how; but I must be getting out o' dis, or dem gals vill come and ketch *me*."

Betty went off laughing; and I said to myself, "Can it be true that my children are free? I have not suffered for them in vain. Thank God!"

Great surprise was expressed when it was known that my children had returned to their grandmother's. The news spread through the town, and many a kind word was bestowed on the little ones.

Dr. Flint went to my grandmother's to ascertain who was the owner of my children, and she informed him. "I expected as much," said he. "I am glad to hear it. I have had news from Linda lately, and I shall soon have her. You need never expect to see *her* free. She shall be my slave as long as I live, and when I am dead she shall be the slave of my children. If I ever find out that you or Phillip had anything to do with her running off I'll kill him. And if I meet William in the street, and he presumes to look at me, I'll flog him within an inch of his life. Keep those brats out of my sight!"

As he turned to leave, my grandmother said something to remind him of his own doings. He looked back upon her, as if he would have been glad to strike her to the ground.

I had my season of joy and thanksgiving. It was the first time since my childhood that I had experienced any real happiness. I heard of the old doctor's threats, but they no longer had the same power to trouble me. The darkest cloud that hung over my life had rolled away. Whatever slavery might do to me, it could not shackle my children. If I felt a sacrifice, my little ones were saved. It was well for me that my simple heart believed all that had been promised for their welfare. It is always better to trust than to doubt.

XX.

NEW PERILS.

THE doctor, more exasperated than ever, again tried to revenge himself on my relatives. He arrested uncle Phillip on the charge of having aided my flight. He was carried before a court, and swore truly that he knew nothing of my intention to escape, and that he had not seen me since I left my master's plantation. The doctor then demanded that he should give bail for five hundred dollars that he would have nothing to do with me. Several gentlemen offered to be security for him; but Mr. Sands told him he had better go back to jail, and he would see that he came out without giving bail.

The news of his arrest was carried to my grandmother, who conveyed it to Betty. In the kindness of her heart, she again stowed me away under the floor; and as she walked back and forth, in the performance of her culinary duties, she talked apparently to herself, but with the intention that I should hear what was going on. I hoped that my uncle's imprisonment would last but a few days; still I was anxious. I thought it likely Dr. Flint would do his utmost to taunt and insult him, and I was afraid my uncle might lose control of himself, and retort in some way that would be construed into a punishable offence; and I was well aware that in court his word would not be taken against any white man's. The search for me was renewed. Something had excited suspicions that I was in the vicinity. They searched the house I was in. I heard their steps and their voices. At night, when all were asleep, Betty came to release me from my place of confinement. The fright I had undergone, the constrained posture, and the dampness of the ground, made me ill for several days. My uncle was soon after taken out of prison; but the movements of all my relatives, and of all our friends, were very closely watched.

We all saw that I could not remain where I was much longer. I had already staid longer than was intended, and I knew my presence must be a source of perpetual anxiety to my kind benefactress. During this time, my friends had laid many plans for my escape, but the extreme vigilance of my persecutors made it impossible to carry them into effect.

One morning I was much startled by hearing somebody trying to get into my room. Several keys were tried, but none fitted. I instantly conjectured it was one of the house-maids; and I concluded she must either have heard some noise in the room, or have noticed the entrance of Betty. When my friend came, at her usual time, I told her what had happened. "I knows who it was," said she. " 'Pend upon it, 'twas dat Jenny. Dat nigger allers got de debble in her." I suggested that she might have seen or heard something that excited her curiosity.

"Tut! tut! chile!" exclaimed Betty, "she ain't seen notin', nor hearn notin'. She only 'spects something. Dat's all. She wants to fine out who hab cut and make my gownd. But she won't nebber know. Dat's sartin. I'll git missis to fix her."

I reflected a moment, and said, "Betty, I must leave here to-night."

"Do as you tink best, poor chile," she replied. "I'se mighty 'fraid dat 'ere nigger vill pop on you some time."

She reported the incident to her mistress, and received orders to keep Jenny busy in the kitchen till she could see my uncle Phillip. He told her he would send a friend for me that very evening. She told him she hoped I was going to the north, for it was very dangerous for me to remain any where in the vicinity. Alas, it was not an easy thing, for one in my situation, to go to the north. In order to leave the coast quite clear for me, she went into the country to spend the day with her brother, and took Jenny with her. She was afraid to come and bid me good by, but she left a kind message with Betty. I heard her carriage roll from the door, and I never again saw her who had so generously befriended the poor, trembling fugitive! Though she was a slaveholder, to this day my heart blesses her!

I had not the slightest idea where I was going. Betty brought me a suit of sailor's clothes,—jacket, trowsers, and tarpaulin hat. She gave me a small bundle, saying I might need it where I was going. In cheery tones, she exclaimed, "I'se *so* glad you is gwine to free parts! Don't forget ole Betty. P'raps I'll come 'long by and by."

I tried to tell her how grateful I felt for all her kindness. But she interrupted me. "I don't want no tanks, honey. I'se glad I could help you, and I hope de good Lord vill open de path for you. I'se gwine wid you to de lower gate. Put your hands in your pockets, and walk ricketty, like de sailors."

I performed to her satisfaction. At the gate I found Peter, a young colored man, waiting for me. I had known him for years. He had been an apprentice to my father, and had always borne a good character. I was not afraid to trust to him. Betty bade me a hurried good by, and we walked off. "Take courage, Linda," said my friend Peter. "I've got a dagger, and no man shall take you from me, unless he passes over my dead body."

It was a long time since I had taken a walk out of doors, and the fresh air revived me. It was also pleasant to hear a human voice speaking to me above a whisper. I passed several people whom I knew, but they did not recognize me in my disguise. I prayed internally that, for Peter's sake, as well as my own, nothing might occur to bring out his dagger. We walked on till we came to the wharf. My aunt Nancy's husband was a seafaring man, and it had been deemed necessary to let him into our secret. He took me into his boat, rowed out to a vessel not far distant, and hoisted me on board. We three were the only occupants of the vessel. I now ventured to ask what they proposed to do with me. They said I was to remain on board till near dawn, and then they would hide me in Snaky Swamp, till my uncle Phillip had prepared a place of concealment for me. If the vessel had been bound north, it would have been of no avail to me, for it would certainly have been searched. About four o'clock, we were again seated in the boat, and rowed three miles to the swamp. My fear of snakes had been increased by the venomous bite I had received, and I dreaded to enter this hiding place. But I was in no situation to choose, and I gratefully accepted the best that my poor, persecuted friends could do for me.

Peter landed first, and with a large knife cut a path through bamboos and briers of all descriptions. He came back, took me in his arms, and carried me to a seat made among the bamboos. Before we reached it, we were covered with hundreds of mosquitos. In an hour's time they had so poisoned my flesh that I was a pitiful sight to behold. As the light increased, I saw snake after snake crawling round us. I had been accustomed to the sight of snakes all my life, but these were larger than any I had ever seen. To this day I shudder when I remember that morning. As evening approached, the number of snakes increased so much that we were continually obliged to thrash them with sticks to keep them from crawling over us. The bamboos were so high and so thick that it was impossible to see beyond a very short distance. Just before it became dark we procured a seat nearer to the entrance of the swamp, being fearful of losing our way back to the boat. It was not long before we heard the paddle of oars, and the low whistle, which had been agreed upon as a signal. We made haste to enter the boat, and were rowed back to the vessel. I passed a wretched night; for the heat of the swamp, the mosquitos, and the constant terror of snakes, had brought on a burning fever. I had just dropped asleep, when they came and told me it was time to go back to that horrid swamp. I could scarcely summon courage to rise. But even those large, venomous snakes were less dreadful to my imagination than the white men in that community called civilized. This time Peter took a quantity of tobacco to burn, to keep off the mosquitos. It produced the desired effect on them, but gave me nausea and severe headache. At dark we returned to the vessel. I had been so sick during the day, that Peter declared I should go home that night, if the devil himself was on patrol. They told me a place of concealment had been provided for me at my grandmother's. I could not imagine how it was possible to hide me in her house, every nook and corner of which was known to the Flint family. They told me to wait and see. We were rowed ashore, and went boldly through the streets, to my grandmother's. I wore my sailor's clothes, and had blackened my face with charcoal. I passed several people whom I knew. The father of my children came so near that I brushed against his arm; but he had no idea who it was.

"You must make the most of this walk," said my friend Peter, "for you may not have another very soon."

I thought his voice sounded sad. It was kind of him to conceal from me what a dismal hole was to be my home for a long, long time.

XXI.

THE LOOPHOLE OF RETREAT.

A SMALL shed had been added to my grandmother's house years ago. Some boards were laid across the joists at the top, and between these boards and the roof was a very small garret, never occupied by any thing but rats and mice. It was a pent roof, covered with nothing but shingles, according to the southern custom for such buildings. The garret was only nine feet long and seven wide. The highest part was three feet high, and sloped down abruptly to the loose board floor. There was no admission for either light or air. My uncle Phillip, who was a carpenter, had very skilfully made a concealed trap-door, which communicated with the storeroom. He had been doing this while I was waiting in the swamp. The storeroom opened upon a piazza. To this hole I was conveyed as soon as I entered the house. The air was stifling; the darkness total. A bed had been spread on the floor. I could sleep quite comfortably on one side; but the slope was so sudden that I could not turn on the other without hitting the roof. The rats and mice ran over my bed; but I was weary, and I slept such sleep as the wretched may, when a tempest has passed over them. Morning came. I knew it only by the noises I heard; for in my small den day and night were all the same. I suffered for air even more than for light. But I was not comfortless. I heard the voices of my children. There was joy and there was sadness in the sound. It made my tears flow. How I longed to speak to them! I was eager to look on their faces; but there was no hole, no crack, through which I could peep. This continued darkness was oppressive. It seemed horrible to sit or lie in a cramped position day after day, without one gleam of light. Yet I would have chosen this, rather than my lot as a slave, though white people considered it an easy one; and it was so compared with the fate of others. I was never cruelly overworked; I was never lacerated with the whip from head to foot; I was never so beaten and bruised that I could not turn from one side to the other; I never had my heel-strings cut to prevent my running away; I was never chained to a log and forced to drag it about, while I toiled in the fields from morning till night; I was never branded with hot iron, or torn by bloodhounds. On the contrary, I had always been kindly treated, and tenderly cared for, until I came into the hands of Dr. Flint. I had never wished for freedom till then. But though my life in slavery was comparatively devoid of hardships, God pity the woman who is compelled to lead such a life!

My food was passed up to me through the trap-door my uncle had contrived; and my grandmother, my uncle Phillip, and aunt Nancy would seize such opportunities as they could, to mount up there and chat with me at the opening. But of course this was not safe in the daytime. It must all be done in darkness. It was impossible for me to move in an erect position, but I crawled about my den for exercise. One day I hit my head against something, and found it was a gimlet. My uncle had left it sticking there when he made the trap-door. I was as rejoiced as Robinson Crusoe could have been at finding such a treasure. It put a lucky thought into my head. I said to myself, "Now I will have some light. Now I will see my children." I did not dare to begin my work during the daytime, for fear of attracting attention. But I groped round; and having found the side next the street, where I could frequently see my children, I stuck the gimlet in and waited for evening. I bored three rows of holes, one above another; then I bored out the interstices between. I thus succeeded in making one hole about an inch long and an inch broad. I sat by it till late into the night, to enjoy the little whiff of air that floated in. In the morning I watched for my children. The first person I saw in the street was Dr. Flint. I had a shuddering, superstitious feeling that it was a bad omen. Several familiar faces passed by. At last I heard the merry laugh of children, and presently two sweet little faces were looking up at me, as though they knew I was there, and were conscious of the joy they imparted. How I longed to *tell* them I was there!

My condition was now a little improved. But for weeks I was tormented by hundreds of little red insects, fine as a needle's point, that pierced through my skin, and produced an intolerable burning. The good grandmother gave me herb teas and cooling medicines, and finally I got rid of them. The heat of my den was intense, for nothing but thin shingles protected me from the scorching summer's sun. But I had my consolations. Through my peeping-hole I could watch the children, and when they were near enough, I could hear their talk. Aunt Nancy brought me all the news she could hear at Dr. Flint's. From her I learned that the doctor had written to New York to a colored woman, who had been born and raised in our neighborhood, and had breathed his contaminating atmosphere. He offered her a reward if she could find out any thing about me. I know not what was the nature of her reply; but he soon after started for New York in haste, saying to his family that he had business of importance to transact. I peeped at him as he passed on his way to the steamboat. It was a satisfaction to have miles of land and water between us, even for a little while; and it was a still greater satisfaction to know that he believed me to be in the Free States. My little den seemed less dreary than it had done. He returned, as he did from his former journey to New York, without obtaining any satisfactory information. When he passed our house next morning, Benny was standing at the gate. He had heard them say that he had gone to find me, and he called out, "Dr. Flint, did you bring my mother home? I want to see her." The doctor stamped his foot at him in a rage, and exclaimed,

"Get out of the way, you little damned rascal! If you don't, I'll cut off your head."

Benny ran terrified into the house, saying, "You can't put me in jail again. I don't belong to you now." It was well that the wind carried the words away from the doctor's ear. I told my grandmother of it, when we had our next conference at the trap-door, and begged of her not to allow the children to be impertinent to the irascible old man.

Autumn came, with a pleasant abatement of heat. My eyes had become accustomed to the dim light, and by holding my book or work in a certain position near the aperture I contrived to read and sew. That was a great relief to the tedious monotony of my life. But when winter came, the cold penetrated through the thin shingle roof, and I was dreadfully chilled. The winters there are not so long, or so severe, as in northern latitudes; but the houses are not built to shelter from cold, and my little den was peculiarly comfortless. The kind grandmother brought me bedclothes and warm drinks. Often I was obliged to lie in bed all day to keep comfortable; but with all my precautions, my shoulders and feet were frostbitten. O, those long, gloomy days, with no object for my eye to rest upon, and no thoughts to occupy my mind, except the dreary past and the uncertain future! I was thankful when there came a day sufficiently mild for me to wrap myself up and sit at the loophole to watch the passers by. Southerners have the habit of stopping and talking in the streets, and I heard many conversations not intended to meet my ears. I heard slave-hunters planning how to catch some poor fugitive. Several times I heard allusions to Dr. Flint, myself, and the history of my children, who, perhaps, were playing near the gate. One would say, "I wouldn't move my little finger to catch her, as old Flint's property." Another would say, "I'll catch *any* nigger for the reward. A man ought to have what belongs to him, if he *is* a damned brute." The opinion was often expressed that I was in the Free States. Very rarely did any one suggest that I might be in the vicinity. Had the least suspicion rested on my grandmother's house, it would have been burned to the ground. But it was the last place they thought of. Yet there was no place, where slavery existed,

that could have afforded me so good a place of concealment.

Dr. Flint and his family repeatedly tried to coax and
bribe my children to tell something they had heard said
about me. One day the doctor took them into a shop, and
offered them some bright little silver pieces and gay hand-
kerchiefs if they would tell where their mother was. Ellen
shrank away from him, and would not speak; but Benny
spoke up, and said, "Dr. Flint, I don't know where my
mother is. I guess she's in New York; and when you go there
again, I wish you'd ask her to come home, for I want to see
her; but if you put her in jail, or tell her you'll cut her head
off, I'll tell her to go right back."

XXII.

CHRISTMAS FESTIVITIES.

CHRISTMAS was approaching. Grandmother brought
me materials, and I busied myself making some new garments and little playthings for my children. Were it not that
hiring day is near at hand, and many families are fearfully
looking forward to the probability of separation in a few
days, Christmas might be a happy season for the poor
slaves. Even slave mothers try to gladden the hearts of their
little ones on that occasion. Benny and Ellen had their
Christmas stockings filled. Their imprisoned mother could
not have the privilege of witnessing their surprise and joy.
But I had the pleasure of peeping at them as they went into
the street with their new suits on. I heard Benny ask a little
playmate whether Santa Claus brought him any thing.
"Yes," replied the boy; "but Santa Claus ain't a real man.
It's the children's mothers that put things into the stockings." "No, that can't be," replied Benny, "for Santa Claus

brought Ellen and me these new clothes, and my mother has been gone this long time."

How I longed to tell him that his mother made those garments, and that many a tear fell on them while she worked!

Every child rises early on Christmas morning to see the Johnkannaus. Without them, Christmas would be shorn of its greatest attraction. They consist of companies of slaves from the plantations, generally of the lower class. Two athletic men, in calico wrappers, have a net thrown over them, covered with all manner of bright-colored stripes. Cows' tails are fastened to their backs, and their heads are decorated with horns. A box, covered with sheepskin, is called the gumbo box. A dozen beat on this, while others strike triangles and jawbones, to which bands of dancers keep time. For a month previous they are composing songs, which are sung on this occasion. These companies, of a hundred each, turn out early in the morning, and are allowed to go round till twelve o'clock, begging for contributions. Not a door is left unvisited where there is the least chance of obtaining a penny or a glass of rum. They do not drink while they are out, but carry the rum home in jugs, to have a carousal. These Christmas donations frequently amount to twenty or thirty dollars. It is seldom that any white man or child refuses to give them a trifle. If he does, they regale his ears with the following song:—

> Poor massa, so dey say;
> Down in de heel, so dey say;
> Got no money, so dey say;
> Not one shillin, so dey say;
> God A'mighty bress you, so dey say.

Christmas is a day of feasting, both with white and colored people. Slaves, who are lucky enough to have a few shillings, are sure to spend them for good eating; and many a turkey and pig is captured, without saying, "By your leave, sir." Those who cannot obtain these, cook a 'possum, or a raccoon, from which savory dishes can be made. My grandmother raised poultry and pigs for sale and it was her established custom to have both a turkey and a pig roasted for Christmas dinner.

On this occasion, I was warned to keep extremely quiet, because two guests had been invited. One was the town constable, and the other was a free colored man, who tried to pass himself off for white, and who was always ready to do any mean work for the sake of currying favor with white people. My grandmother had a motive for inviting them. She managed to take them all over the house. All the rooms on the lower floor were thrown open for them to pass in and out; and after dinner, they were invited up stairs to look at a fine mocking bird my uncle had just brought home. There, too, the rooms were all thrown open that they might look in. When I heard them talking on the piazza, my heart almost stood still. I knew this colored man had spent many nights hunting for me. Every body knew he had the blood of a slave father in his veins; but for the sake of passing himself off for white, he was ready to kiss the slaveholders' feet. How I despised him! As for the constable, he wore no false colors. The duties of his office were despicable, but he was superior to his companion, inasmuch as he did not pretend to be what he was not. Any white man, who could raise money enough to buy a slave, would have considered himself degraded by being a constable; but the office enabled its possessor to exercise authority. If he found any slave out after nine o'clock, he could whip him as much as he liked; and that was a privilege to be coveted. When the guests were ready to depart, my grandmother gave each of them some of her nice pudding, as a present for their wives. Through my peep-hole I saw them go out of the gate, and I was glad when it closed after them. So passed the first Christmas in my den.

XXIII.

STILL IN PRISON.

W HEN spring returned, and I took in the little patch of green the aperture commanded, I asked myself how many more summers and winters I must be condemned to spend thus. I longed to draw in a plentiful draught of fresh air, to stretch my cramped limbs, to have room to stand erect, to feel the earth under my feet again. My relatives were constantly on the lookout for a chance of escape; but none offered that seemed practicable, and even tolerably safe. The hot summer came again, and made the turpentine drop from the thin roof over my head.

During the long nights I was restless for want of air, and I had no room to toss and turn. There was but one compensation; the atmosphere was so stifled that even mosquitos would not condescend to buzz in it. With all my detestation of Dr. Flint, I could hardly wish him a worse punishment, either in this world or that which is to come, than to suffer what I suffered in one single summer. Yet the laws allowed *him* to be out in the free air, while I, guiltless of crime, was pent up here, as the only means of avoiding the cruelties the laws allowed him to inflict upon me! I don't know what kept life within me. Again and again, I thought I should die before long; but I saw the leaves of another autumn whirl through the air, and felt the touch of another winter. In summer the most terrible thunder storms were acceptable, for the rain came through the roof, and I rolled up my bed that it might cool the hot boards under it. Later in the season, storms sometimes wet my clothes through and through, and that was not comfortable when the air grew chilly. Moderate storms I could keep out by filling the chinks with oakum.

But uncomfortable as my situation was, I had glimpses of things out of doors, which made me thankful for my wretched hiding-place. One day I saw a slave pass our gate, muttering, "It's his own, and he can kill it if he will." My grandmother told me that woman's history. Her mistress had that day seen her baby for the first time, and in the lineaments of its fair face she saw a likeness to her husband. She turned the bondwoman and her child out of doors, and forbade her ever to return. The slave went to her master, and told him what had happened. He promised to talk with her mistress, and make it all right. The next day she and her baby were sold to a Georgia trader.

Another time I saw a woman rush wildly by, pursued by two men. She was a slave, the wet nurse of her mistress's children. For some trifling offence her mistress ordered her to be stripped and whipped. To escape the degradation and the torture, she rushed to the river, jumped in, and ended her wrongs in death.

Senator Brown, of Mississippi, could not be ignorant of many such facts as these, for they are of frequent occurrence in every Southern State. Yet he stood up in the Congress of the United States, and declared that slavery was "a great moral, social, and political blessing; a blessing to the master, and a blessing to the slave!"

I suffered much more during the second winter than I did during the first. My limbs were benumbed by inaction, and the cold filled them with cramp. I had a very painful sensation of coldness in my head; even my face and tongue stiffened, and I lost the power of speech. Of course it was impossible, under the circumstances, to summon any physician. My brother William came and did all he could for me. Uncle Phillip also watched tenderly over me; and poor grandmother crept up and down to inquire whether there were any signs of returning life. I was restored to consciousness by the dashing of cold water in my face, and found myself leaning against my brother's arm, while he bent over me with streaming eyes. He afterwards told me he thought I was dying, for I had been in an unconscious state sixteen hours. I next became delirious, and was in great danger of betraying myself and my friends. To prevent this, they stupefied me with drugs. I remained in bed six weeks, weary in body and sick at heart. How to get medical advice was the question. William finally went to a Thompsonian doctor, and described himself as having all my pains and aches. He returned with herbs, roots, and ointment. He was especially charged to rub on the ointment by a fire; but how could a fire be made in my little den? Charcoal in a furnace was tried, but there was no outlet for the gas, and it nearly cost me my life. Afterwards coals, already kindled, were brought up in an iron pan, and placed on bricks. I was so weak, and it was so long since I had enjoyed the warmth of a fire, that those few coals actually made me weep. I think the medicines did me some good; but my recovery was very slow. Dark thoughts passed through my mind as I lay there day after day. I tried to be thankful for my little cell, dismal as it was, and even to love it, as part of the price I had paid for the redemption of my children. Sometimes I thought God was a compassionate Father, who would forgive my sins for the sake of my sufferings. At other times, it seemed to me there was no justice or mercy in the divine government. I asked why the curse of slavery was permitted to exist, and why I had been so persecuted and wronged from youth upward. These things took the shape of mystery, which is to this day not so clear to my soul as I trust it will be hereafter.

In the midst of my illness, grandmother broke down under the weight and anxiety and toil. The idea of losing her, who had always been my best friend and a mother to my children, was the sorest trial I had yet had. O, how earnestly I prayed that she might recover! How hard it seemed, that I could not tend upon her, who had so long and so tenderly watched over me!

One day the screams of a child nerved me with strength to crawl to my peeping-hole, and I saw my son covered with blood. A fierce dog, usually kept chained, had seized and bitten him. A doctor was sent for, and I heard the groans and screams of my child while the wounds were being sewed up. O, what torture to a mother's heart, to listen to this and be unable to go to him!

But childhood is like a day in spring, alternately shower and sunshine. Before night Benny was bright and lively, threatening the destruction of the dog; and great was his delight when the doctor told him the next day that the dog had bitten another boy and been shot. Benny recovered from his wounds; but it was long before he could walk.

When my grandmother's illness became known, many ladies, who were her customers, called to bring her some little comforts, and to inquire whether she had every thing she wanted. Aunt Nancy one night asked permission to watch with her sick mother, and Mrs. Flint replied, "I don't see any need of your going. I can't spare you." But when she found other ladies in the neighborhood were so attentive, not wishing to be outdone in Christian charity, she also sallied forth, in magnificent condescension, and stood by the bedside of her who had loved her in her infancy, and who had been repaid by such grievous wrongs. She seemed surprised to find her so ill, and scolded uncle Phillip for not sending for Dr. Flint. She herself sent for him immediately, and he came. Secure as I was in my retreat, I should have been terrified if I had known he was so near me. He pronounced my grandmother in a very critical situation, and said if her attending physician wished it, he would visit her. Nobody wished to have him coming to the house at all hours, and we were not disposed to give him a chance to make out a long bill.

As Mrs. Flint went out, Sally told her the reason Benny was lame was, that a dog had bitten him. "I'm glad of it," replied she. "I wish he had killed him. It would be good news to send to his mother. *Her* day will come. The dogs will grab *her* yet." With these Christian words she and her husband departed, and, to my great satisfaction, returned no more.

I learned from uncle Phillip, with feelings of unspeakable joy and gratitude, that the crisis was passed and grandmother would live. I could now say from my heart, "God is merciful. He has spared me the anguish of feeling that I caused her death."

XXIV.

THE CANDIDATE FOR CONGRESS.

THE summer had nearly ended, when Dr. Flint made a third visit to New York, in search of me. Two candidates were running for Congress, and he returned in season to vote. The father of my children was the Whig candidate. The doctor had hitherto been a stanch Whig; but now he exerted all his energies for the defeat of Mr. Sands. He invited large parties of men to dine in the shade of his trees, and supplied them with plenty of rum and brandy. If any poor fellow drowned his wits in the bowl, and, in the openness of his convivial heart, proclaimed that he did not mean to vote the Democratic ticket, he was shoved into the street without ceremony.

The doctor expended his liquor in vain. Mr. Sands was elected; an event which occasioned me some anxious thoughts. He had not emancipated my children, and if he should die they would be at the mercy of his heirs. Two little voices, that frequently met my ear, seemed to plead with me not to let their father depart without striving to make their freedom secure. Years had passed since I had spoken to him. I had not even seen him since the night I passed him, unrecognized, in my disguise of a sailor. I supposed he would call before he left, to say something to my grandmother concerning the children, and I resolved what course to take.

The day before his departure for Washington I made arrangements, toward evening, to get from my hiding-place into the storeroom below. I found myself so stiff and clumsy that it was with great difficulty I could hitch from one resting place to another. When I reached the storeroom my ankles gave way under me, and I sank exhausted on the floor. It seemed as if I could never use my limbs again. But the purpose I had in view roused all the strength I had. I crawled on my hands and knees to the window, and, screened behind a barrel, I waited for his coming. The clock struck nine, and I knew the steamboat would leave between ten and eleven. My hopes were failing. But presently I heard his voice, saying to some one, "Wait for me a moment. I wish to see aunt Martha." When he came out, as he passed the window, I said, "Stop one moment, and let me speak for my children." He started, hesitated, and then passed on, and went out of the gate. I closed the shutter I had partially opened, and sank down behind the barrel. I had suffered much; but seldom had I experienced a keener pang than I then felt. Had my children, then, become of so little consequence to him? And had he so little feeling for their wretched mother that he would not listen a moment while she pleaded for them? Painful memories were so busy within me, that I forgot I had not hooked the shutter, till I heard some one opening it. I looked up. He had come back. "Who called me?" said he, in a low tone. "I did," I replied. "Oh, Linda," said he, "I knew your voice; but I was afraid to answer, lest my friend should hear me. Why do you come here? Is it possible you risk yourself in this house? They are mad to allow it. I shall expect to hear that you are all ruined." I did not wish to implicate him, by letting him know my place of concealment; so I merely said, "I thought you would come to bid grandmother good by, and so I came here to speak a few words to you about emancipating my children. Many changes may take place during the six months you are gone to Washington, and it does not seem right for you to expose them to the risk of such changes. I want nothing for myself; all I ask is, that you will free my children, or authorize some friend to do it, before you go."

He promised he would do it, and also expressed a readiness to make any arrangements whereby I could be purchased.

I heard footsteps approaching, and closed the shutter hastily. I wanted to crawl back to my den, without letting the family know what I had done; for I knew they would deem it very imprudent. But he stepped back into the house, to tell my grandmother that he had spoken with me at the storeroom window, and to beg of her not to allow me to remain in the house over night. He said it was the height of madness for me to be there; that we should certainly all be ruined. Luckily, he was in too much of a hurry to wait for a reply, or the dear old woman would surely have told him all.

I tried to go back to my den, but found it more difficult to go up than I had to come down. Now that my mission was fulfilled, the little strength that had supported me through it was gone, and I sank helpless on the floor. My grandmother, alarmed at the risk I had run, came into the storeroom in the dark, and locked the door behind her. "Linda," she whispered, "where are you?"

"I am here by the window," I replied. "I *couldn't* have him go away without emancipating the children. Who knows what may happen?"

"Come, come, child," said she, "it won't do for you to stay here another minute. You've done wrong; but I can't blame you, poor thing!"

I told her I could not return without assistance, and she must call my uncle. Uncle Phillip came, and pity prevented him from scolding me. He carried me back to my dungeon, laid me tenderly on the bed, gave me some medicine, and asked me if there was any thing more he could do. Then he went away, and I was left with my own thoughts—starless as the midnight darkness around me.

My friends feared I should become a cripple for life; and I was so weary of my long imprisonment that, had it not been for the hope of serving my children, I should have been thankful to die; but, for their sakes, I was willing to bear on.

XXV.

COMPETITION IN CUNNING.

Dr. Flint had not given me up. Every now and then he would say to my grandmother that I would yet come back, and voluntarily surrender myself; and that when I did, I could be purchased by my relatives, or any one who wished to buy me. I knew his cunning nature too well not to perceive that this was a trap laid for me; and so all my friends understood it. I resolved to match my cunning against his cunning. In order to make him believe that I was in New York, I resolved to write him a letter dated from that place. I sent for my friend Peter, and asked him if he knew any trustworthy seafaring person, who would carry such a letter to New York, and put it in the post office there. He said he knew one that he would trust with his own life to the ends of the world. I reminded him that it was a hazardous thing for him to undertake. He said he knew it, but he was willing to do any thing to help me. I expressed a wish for a New York paper, to ascertain the names of some of the streets. He ran his hand into his pocket, and said, "Here is half a one, that was round a cap I bought of a peddler yesterday." I told him the letter would be ready the next evening. He bade me good by, adding, "Keep up your spirits, Linda; brighter days will come by and by."

My uncle Phillip kept watch over the gate until our brief interview was over. Early the next morning, I seated myself near the little aperture to examine the newspaper. It was a piece of the New York Herald; and, for once, the paper that systematically abuses the colored people, was made to render them a service. Having obtained what information I wanted concerning streets and numbers, I wrote two letters, one to my grandmother, the other to Dr. Flint. I reminded him how he, a gray-headed man, had treated a helpless child, who had been placed in his power, and what years of misery he had brought upon her. To my grandmother, I expressed a wish to have my children sent to me at the north, where I could teach them to respect themselves, and set them a virtuous example; which a slave mother was not allowed to do at the south. I asked her to direct her answer to a certain street in Boston, as I did not live in New York, though I went there sometimes. I dated these letters ahead, to allow for the time it would take to carry them, and sent a memorandum of the date to the messenger. When my friend came for the letters, I said, "God bless and reward you, Peter, for this disinterested kindness. Pray be careful. If you are detected, both you and I will have to suffer dreadfully. I have not a relative who would dare to do it for me." He replied, "You may trust to me, Linda. I don't forget that your father was my best friend, and I will be a friend to his children so long as God lets me live."

It was necessary to tell my grandmother what I had done, in order that she might be ready for the letter, and prepared to hear what Dr. Flint might say about my being at the north. She was sadly troubled. She felt sure mischief would come of it. I also told my plan to aunt Nancy, in order that she might report to us what was said at Dr. Flint's house. I whispered it to her through a crack, and she whispered back, "I hope it will succeed. I shan't mind being a slave all my life, if I can only see you and the children free."

I had directed that my letters should be put into the New York post office on the 20th of the month. On the evening of the 24th my aunt came to say that Dr. Flint and his wife had been talking in a low voice about a letter he had received, and that when he went to his office he promised to bring it when he came to tea. So I concluded I should hear my letter read the next morning. I told my grandmother Dr. Flint would be sure to come, and asked her to have him sit near a certain door, and leave it open, that I might hear what he said. The next morning I took my station within sound of that door, and remained motionless as a statue. It was not long before I heard the gate slam, and the well-known footsteps enter the house. He seated himself in the chair that was placed for him, and said, "Well, Martha, I've brought you a letter from Linda. She has sent me a letter, also. I know exactly where to find her; but I don't choose to go to Boston for her. I had rather she would come back of her own accord, in a respectable manner. Her uncle Phillip is the best person to go for her. With *him,* she would feel perfectly free to act. I am willing to pay his expenses going and returning. She shall be sold to her friends. Her children are free; at least I suppose they are; and when you obtain her freedom, you'll make a happy family. I suppose, Martha, you have no objection to my reading to you the letter Linda has written to you."

He broke the seal, and I heard him read it. The old villain! He had suppressed the letter I wrote to grandmother, and prepared a substitute of his own, the purport of which was as follows:—

Dear Grandmother: I have long wanted to write to you; but the disgraceful manner in which I left you and my children made me ashamed to do it. If you knew how much I have suffered since I ran away, you would pity and forgive me. I have purchased freedom at a dear rate. If any arrangement could be made for me to return to the south without being a slave, I would gladly come. If not, I beg of you to send my children to the north. I cannot live any longer without them. Let me know in time, and I will meet them in New York or Philadelphia, whichever place best suits my uncle's convenience. Write as soon as possible to your unhappy daughter,

LINDA.

"It is very much as I expected it would be," said the old hypocrite, rising to go. "You see the foolish girl has repented of her rashness, and wants to return. We must help her to do it, Martha. Talk with Phillip about it. If he will go for her, she will trust to him, and come back. I should like an answer tomorrow. Good morning, Martha."

As he stepped out on the piazza, he stumbled over my little girl. "Ah, Ellen, is that you?" he said, in his most gracious manner. "I didn't see you. How do you do?"

"Pretty well, sir," she replied. "I heard you tell grandmother that my mother is coming home. I want to see her."

"Yes, Ellen, I am going to bring her home very soon," rejoined he; "and you shall see her as much as you like, you little curly-headed nigger."

This was as good as a comedy to me, who had heard it all; but grandmother was frightened and distressed, because the doctor wanted my uncle to go for me.

The next evening Dr. Flint called to talk the matter over. My uncle told him that from what he had heard of Massachusetts, he judged he should be mobbed if he went there after a runaway slave. "All stuff and nonsense, Phillip!" replied the doctor. "Do you suppose I want you to kick up a row in Boston? The business can all be done quietly. Linda writes that she wants to come back. You are her relative, and she would trust *you*. The case would be different if I went. She might object to coming with *me;* and the damned abolitionists, if they knew I was her master, would not believe me, if I told them she had begged to go back. They would get up a row; and I should not like to see Linda dragged through the streets like a common negro. She has been very ungrateful to me for all my kindness; but I forgive her, and want to act the part of a friend towards her. I have no wish to hold her as my slave. Her friends can buy her as soon as she arrives here."

Finding that his arguments failed to convince my uncle, the doctor "let the cat out of the bag," by saying that he had written to the mayor of Boston, to ascertain whether there was a person of my description at the street and number from which my letter was dated. He had omitted this date in the letter he had made up to read to my grandmother. If I had dated from New York, the old man would probably have made another journey to that city. But even in that dark region, where knowledge is so carefully excluded from the slave, I had heard enough about Massachusetts to come to the conclusion that slaveholders did not consider it a comfortable place to go in search of a runaway. That was before the Fugitive Slave Law was passed; before Massachusetts had consented to become a "nigger hunter" for the south.

My grandmother, who had become skittish by seeing her family always in danger, came to me with a very distressed countenance, and said, "What will you do if the mayor of Boston sends him word that you haven't been there? Then he will suspect the letter was a trick; and maybe he'll find out something about it, and we shall all get into trouble. O Linda, I wish you had never sent the letters."

"Don't worry yourself, Grandmother," said I. "The mayor of Boston won't trouble himself to hunt niggers for Dr. Flint. The letters will do good in the end. I shall get out of this dark hole some time or other."

"I hope you will, child," replied the good, patient old friend. "You have been here a long time; almost five years; but whenever you do go, it will break your old grandmother's heart. I should be expecting every day to hear that you were brought back in irons and put in jail. God help you, poor child! Let us be thankful that some time or other we shall go 'where the wicked cease from troubling, and the weary are at rest.' " My heart responded, Amen.

The fact that Dr. Flint had written to the mayor of Boston convinced me that he believed my letter to be genuine, and of course that he had no suspicion of my being any where in the vicinity. It was a great object to keep up this delusion, for it made me and my friends feel less anxious, and it would be very convenient whenever there was a chance to escape. I resolved, therefore, to continue to write letters from the north from time to time.

Two or three weeks passed, and as no news came from the mayor of Boston, grandmother began to listen to my entreaty to be allowed to leave my cell, sometimes, and exercise my limbs to prevent my becoming a cripple. I was allowed to slip down into the small storeroom, early in the morning, and remain there a little while. The room was all filled up with barrels, except a small open space under my trap-door. This faced the door, the upper part of which was of glass, and purposely left uncurtained, that the curious might look in. The air of this place was close; but it was so much better than the atmosphere of my cell, that I dreaded to return. I came down as soon as it was light, and remained till eight o'clock, when people began to be about, and there was danger that some one might come on the piazza. I had tried various applications to bring warmth and feeling into my limbs, but without avail. They were so numb and stiff that it was a painful effort to move; and had my enemies come upon me during the first mornings I tried to exercise them a little in the small unoccupied space of the storeroom, it would have been impossible for me to have escaped.

XXVI.

IMPORTANT ERA IN MY BROTHER'S LIFE.

I MISSED the company and kind attentions of my brother William, who had gone to Washington with his master, Mr. Sands. We received several letters from him, written without any allusion to me, but expressed in such a manner that I knew he did not forget me. I disguised my hand, and wrote to him in the same manner. It was a long session; and when it closed, William wrote to inform us that Mr. Sands was going to the north, to be gone some time, and that he was to accompany him. I knew that his master had promised to give him his freedom, but no time had been specified. Would William trust to a slave's chances? I remembered how we used to talk together, in our young days, about obtaining our freedom, and I thought it very doubtful whether he would come back to us.

Grandmother received a letter from Mr. Sands, saying that William had proved a most faithful servant, and he would also say a valued friend; that no mother had ever trained a better boy. He said he had travelled through the Northern States and Canada; and though the abolitionists had tried to decoy him away, they had never succeeded. He ended by saying they should be at home shortly.

We expected letters from William, describing the novelties of his journey, but none came. In time, it was reported that Mr. Sands would return late in the autumn, accompanied by a bride. Still no letters from William. I felt almost sure I should never see him again on southern soil; but had he no word of comfort to send to his friends at home? to the poor captive in her dungeon? My thoughts wandered through the dark past, and over the uncertain future. Alone in my cell, where no eye but God's could see me, I wept bitter tears. How earnestly I prayed to him to restore me to my children, and enable me to be a useful woman and a good mother!

At last the day arrived for the return of the travellers. Grandmother had made loving preparations to welcome her absent boy back to the old hearthstone. When the dinner table was laid, William's place occupied its old place. The stage coach went by empty. My grandmother waited dinner. She thought perhaps he was necessarily detained by his master. In my prison I listened anxiously, expecting every moment to hear my dear brother's voice and step. In the course of the afternoon a lad was sent by Mr. Sands to tell grandmother that William did not return with him; that the abolitionists had decoyed him away. But he begged her not to feel troubled about it, for he felt confident she would see William in a few days. As soon as he had time to reflect he would come back, for he could never expect to be so well off at the north as he had been with him.

If you had seen the tears, and heard the sobs, you would have thought the messenger had brought tidings of death instead of freedom. Poor old grandmother felt that she should never see her darling boy again. And I was selfish. I thought more of what I had lost, than of what my brother had gained. A new anxiety began to trouble me. Mr. Sands had expended a good deal of money, and would naturally feel irritated by the loss he had incurred. I greatly feared this might injure the prospects of my children, who were now becoming valuable property. I longed to have their emancipation made certain. The more so, because their master and father was now married. I was too familiar with slavery not to know that promises made to slaves, though with kind intentions, and sincere at the time, depend upon many contingencies for their fulfillment.

Much as I wished William to be free, the step he had taken made me sad and anxious. The following Sabbath was calm and clear; so beautiful that it seemed like a Sabbath in the eternal world. My grandmother brought the children out on the piazza, that I might hear their voices. She thought it would comfort me in my despondency; and it did. They chatted merrily, as only children can. Benny said, "Grandmother, do you think uncle Will has gone for good? Won't he ever come back again? May be he'll find mother. If he does, *won't* she be glad to see him! Why don't you and uncle Phillip, and all of us, go and live where mother is? I should like it; wouldn't you, Ellen?"

"Yes, I should like it," replied Ellen; "but how could we

find her? Do you know the place, grandmother? I don't remember how mother looked—do you, Benny?"

Benny was just beginning to describe me when they were interrupted by an old slave woman, a near neighbor, named Aggie. This poor creature had witnessed the sale of her children, and seen them carried off to parts unknown, without any hopes of ever hearing from them again. She saw that my grandmother had been weeping, and she said, in a sympathizing tone, "What's the matter, aunt Marthy?"

"O Aggie," she replied, "it seems as if I shouldn't have any of my children or grandchildren left to hand me a drink when I'm dying, and lay my old body in the ground. My boy didn't come back with Mr. Sands. He staid at the north."

Poor old Aggie clapped her hands for joy. "Is *dat* what you's crying fur?" she exclaimed. "Git down on your knees and bress de Lord! I don't know whar my poor chillern is, and I nebber 'spect to know. You don't know whar poor Linda's gone to; but you *do* know whar her brudder is. He's in free parts; and dat's de right place. Don't murmur at de Lord's doings, but git down on your knees and tank him for his goodness."

My selfishness was rebuked by what poor Aggie said. She rejoiced over the escape of one who was merely her fellow-bondman, while his own sister was only thinking what his good fortune might cost her children. I knelt and prayed God to forgive me; and I thanked him from my heart, that one of my family was saved from the grasp of slavery.

It was not long before we received a letter from William. He wrote that Mr. Sands had always treated him kindly, and that he had tried to do his duty to him faithfully. But ever since he was a boy, he had longed to be free; and he had already gone through enough to convince him he had better not lose the chance that offered. He concluded by saying, "Don't worry about me, dear grandmother. I shall think of you always; and it will spur me on to work hard and try to do right. When I have earned money enough to give you a home, perhaps you will come to the north, and we can all live happy together."

Mr. Sands told my uncle Phillip the particulars about William's leaving him. He said, "I trusted him as if he were my own brother, and treated him as kindly. The abolitionists talked to him in several places; but I had no idea they could tempt him. However, I don't blame William. He's young and inconsiderate, and those Northern rascals decoyed him. I must confess the scamp was very bold about it. I met him coming down the steps of the Astor House with his trunk on his shoulder, and I asked him where he was going. He said he was going to change his old trunk. I told him it was rather shabby, and asked if he didn't need some money. He said, No, thanked me, and went off. He did not return so soon as I expected; but I waited patiently. At last I went to see if our trunks were packed, ready for our journey. I found them locked, and a sealed note on the table informed me where I could find the keys. The fellow even tried to be religious. He wrote that he hoped God would always bless me, and reward me for my kindness; that he was not unwilling to serve me; but he wanted to be a free man; and that if I thought he did wrong, he hoped I would forgive him. I intended to give him his freedom in five years. He might have trusted me. He has shown himself ungrateful; but I shall not go for him, or send for him. I feel confident that he will soon return to me."

I afterwards heard an account of the affair from William himself. He had not been urged away by abolitionists. He needed no information they could give him about slavery to stimulate his desire for freedom. He looked at his hands, and remembered that they were once in irons. What security had he that they would not be so again? Mr. Sands was kind to him; but he might indefinitely postpone the promise he had made to give him his freedom. He might come under pecuniary embarrassments, and his property be seized by creditors; or he might die, without making any arrangements in his favor. He had too often known such accidents to happen to slaves who had kind masters, and he wisely resolved to make sure of the present opportunity to own himself. He was scrupulous about taking any money from his master on false pretences; so he sold his best clothes to pay for his passage to Boston. The slaveholders pronounced him a base, ungrateful wretch, for thus requiting his master's indulgence. What would *they* have done under similar circumstances?

When Dr. Flint's family heard that William had deserted Mr. Sands, they chuckled greatly over the news. Mrs. Flint made her usual manifestations of Christian feeling, by saying, "I'm glad of it. I hope he'll never get him again. I like to see people paid back in their own coin. I reckon Linda's children will have to pay for it. I should be glad to see them in the speculator's hands again, for I'm tired of seeing those little niggers march about the streets."

XXVII.

NEW DESTINATION FOR THE CHILDREN.

Mrs. Flint proclaimed her intention of informing Mrs. Sands who was the father of my children. She likewise proposed to tell her what an artful devil I was; that I had made a great deal of trouble in her family; that when Mr. Sands was at the north, she didn't doubt I had followed him in disguise, and persuaded William to run away. She had some reason to entertain such an idea; for I had written from the north, from time to time, and I dated my letters from various places. Many of them fell into Dr. Flint's hands, as I expected they would; and he must have come to the conclusion that I travelled about a good deal. He kept a close watch over my children, thinking they would eventually lead to my detection.

A new and unexpected trial was in store for me. One day, when Mr. Sands and his wife were walking in the street, they met Benny. The lady took a fancy to him, and exclaimed, "What a pretty little negro! Whom does he belong to?"

Benny did not hear the answer; but he came home very indignant with the stranger lady, because she had called him a negro. A few days afterwards, Mr. Sands called on my grandmother, and told her he wanted her to take the children to his house. He said he had informed his wife of his relation to them, and told her they were motherless; and she wanted to see them.

When he had gone, my grandmother came and asked what I would do. The question seemed a mockery. What *could* I do? They were Mr. Sands's slaves, and their mother was a slave, whom he had represented to be dead. Perhaps he thought I was. I was too much pained and puzzled to come to any decision; and the children were carried without my knowledge.

Mrs. Sands had a sister from Illinois staying with her. This lady, who had no children of her own, was so much pleased with Ellen, that she offered to adopt her, and bring her up as she would a daughter. Mrs. Sands wanted to take Benjamin. When grandmother reported this to me, I was tried almost beyond endurance. Was this all I was to gain by what I had suffered for the sake of having my children free? True, the prospect *seemed* fair; but I knew too well how lightly slaveholders held such "parental relations." If pecuniary troubles should come, or if the new wife required more money than could conveniently be spared, my children might be thought of as a convenient means of raising funds. I had no trust in thee, O Slavery! Never should I know peace till my children were emancipated with all due formalities of law.

I was too proud to ask Mr. Sands to do any thing for my own benefit; but I could bring myself to become a supplicant for my children. I resolved to remind him of the promise he had made me, and to throw myself upon his honor for the performance of it. I persuaded my grandmother to go to him, and tell him I was not dead, and that I earnestly entreated him to keep the promise he had made me; that I had heard of the recent proposals concerning my children, and did not feel easy to accept them; that he had promised to emancipate them, and it was time for him to redeem his pledge. I knew there was some risk in thus betraying that I was in the vicinity; but what will not a mother do for her children? He received the message with surprise, and said, "The children are free. I have never intended to claim them as slaves. Linda may decide their fate. In my opinion, they had better be sent to the north. I don't think they are quite safe here. Dr. Flint boasts that they are still in his power. He says they were his daughter's property, and as she was not of age when they were sold, the contract is not legally binding."

So, then, after all I had endured for their sakes, my poor children were between two fires; between my old master and their new master! And I was powerless. There was no protecting arm of the law for me to invoke. Mr. Sands proposed that Ellen should go, for the present, to some of his relatives, who had removed to Brooklyn, Long Island. It was promised that she should be well taken care of, and sent to school. I consented to it, as the best arrangement I could make for her. My grandmother, of course, negotiated it all; and Mrs. Sands knew of no other person in the transaction. She proposed that they should take Ellen with them to Washington, and keep her till they had a good chance of sending her, with friends, to Brooklyn. She had an infant daughter. I had had a glimpse of it, as the nurse passed with it in her arms. It was not a pleasant thought to me, that the bondwoman's child should tend her free-born sister; but there was no alternative. Ellen was made ready for the journey. O, how it tried my heart to send her away, so young, alone, among strangers! Without a mother's love to shelter her from the storms of life; almost without memory of a mother! I doubted whether she and Benny would have for me the natural affection that children feel for a parent. I thought to myself that I might perhaps never see my daughter again, and I had a great desire that she should look upon me, before she went, that she might take my image with her in her memory. It seemed to me cruel to have her brought to my dungeon. It was sorrow enough for her young heart to know that her mother was a victim of slavery, without seeing the wretched hiding-place to which it had driven her. I begged permission to pass the last night in one of the open chambers, with my little girl. They thought I was crazy to think of trusting such a young child with my perilous secret. I told them I had watched her character, and I felt sure she would not betray me; that I was determined to have an interview, and if they would not facilitate it, I would take my own way to obtain it. They remonstrated against the rashness of such a proceeding; but finding they could not change my purpose, they yielded. I slipped through the trap-door into the storeroom, and my uncle kept watch at the gate, while I passed into the piazza and went up stairs, to the room I used to occupy. It was more than five years since I had seen it; and how the memories crowded on me! There I had taken shelter when my mistress drove me from her house; there came my old tyrant, to mock, insult, and curse me; there my children were first laid in my arms; there I had watched over them, each day with a deeper and sadder love; there I had knelt to God, in anguish of heart, to forgive the wrong I had done. How vividly it all came back! And after this long, gloomy interval, I stood there such a wreck!

In the midst of these meditations, I heard footsteps on the stairs. The door opened, and my uncle Phillip came in, leading Ellen by the hand. I put my arms round her, and said, "Ellen, my dear child, I am your mother." She drew back a little, and looked at me; then, with sweet confidence, she laid her cheek against mine, and I folded her to the heart that had been so long desolated. She was the first to speak. Raising her head, she said, inquiringly, "You really *are* my mother?" I told her I really was; that during all the long time she had not seen me, I had loved her most tenderly; and that now she was going away, I wanted to see her and talk with her, that she might remember me. With a sob in her voice, she said, "I'm glad you've come to see me; but why didn't you ever come before? Benny and I have wanted so much to see you! He remembers you, and sometimes he tells me about you. Why didn't you come home when Dr. Flint went to bring you?"

I answered, "I couldn't come before, dear. But now that I am with you, tell me whether you like to go away." "I don't know," said she, crying. "Grandmother says I ought not to cry; that I am going to a good place, where I can learn to read and write, and that by and by I can write her a letter. But I shan't have Benny, or grandmother, or uncle Phillip, or any body to love me. Can't you go with me? O, *do* go, dear mother!"

I told her I couldn't go now; but sometime I would come to her, and then she and Benny and I would live together, and have happy times. She wanted to run and bring Benny

to see me now. I told her he was going to the north, before
long, with uncle Phillip, and then I would come to see him
before he went away. I asked if she would like to have me
stay all night and sleep with her. "O, yes," she replied. Then,
turning to her uncle, she said, pleadingly, "*May* I stay?
Please, uncle! She is my own mother." He laid his hand on
her head, and said, solemnly, "Ellen, this is the secret you
have promised grandmother never to tell. If you ever speak
of it to any body, they will never let you see your grandmother again, and your mother can never come to Brooklyn." "Uncle," she replied, "I will never tell." He told her she
might stay with me; and when he had gone, I took her in my
arms and told her I was a slave, and that was the reason she
must never say she had seen me. I exhorted her to be a good
child, to try to please the people where she was going, and
that God would raise her up friends. I told her to say her
prayers, and remember always to pray for her poor mother,
and that God would permit us to meet again. She wept, and
I did not check her tears. Perhaps she would never again
have a chance to pour her tears into a mother's bosom. All
night she nestled in my arms, and I had no inclination to
slumber. The moments were too precious to lose any of
them. Once, when I thought she was asleep, I kissed her
forehead softly, and she said, "I am not asleep, dear mother."

Before dawn they came to take me back to my den. I
drew aside the window curtain, to take a last look of my
child. The moonlight shone on her face, and I bent over her,
as I had done years before, that wretched night when I ran
away. I hugged her close to my throbbing heart; and tears,
too sad for such young eyes to shed, flowed down her
cheeks, as she gave her last kiss, and whispered in my ear,
"Mother, I will never tell." And she never did.

When I got back to my den, I threw myself on the bed
and wept there alone in the darkness. It seemed as if my
heart would burst. When the time for Ellen's departure
drew nigh, I could hear neighbors and friends saying to her,
"Good by, Ellen. I hope your poor mother will find you out.
Won't you be glad to see her!" She replied, "Yes, ma'am;"
and they little dreamed of the weighty secret that weighed
down her young heart. She was an affectionate child, but

naturally very reserved, except with those she loved, and I felt secure that my secret would be safe with her. I heard the gate close after her, with such feelings as only a slave mother can experience. During the day my meditations were very sad. Sometimes I feared I had been very selfish not to give up all claim to her, and let her go to Illinois, to be adopted by Mrs. Sands's sister. It was my experience of slavery that decided me against it. I feared that circumstances might arise that would cause her to be sent back. I felt confident that I should go to New York myself; and then I should be able to watch over her, and in some degree protect her.

Dr. Flint's family knew nothing of the proposed arrangement till after Ellen was gone, and the news displeased them greatly. Mrs. Flint called on Mrs. Sands's sister to inquire into the matter. She expressed her opinion very freely as to the respect Mr. Sands showed for his wife, and for his own character, in acknowledging those "young niggers." And as for sending Ellen away, she pronounced it to be just as much stealing as it would be for him to come and take a piece of furniture out of her parlor. She said her daughter was not of age to sign the bill of sale, and the children were her property; and when she became of age, or was married, she could take them, wherever she could lay hands on them.

Miss Emily Flint, the little girl to whom I had been bequeathed, was now in her sixteenth year. Her mother considered it all right and honorable for her, or her future husband, to steal my children; but she did not understand how any body could hold up their heads in respectable society, after they had purchased their own children, as Mr. Sands had done. Dr. Flint said very little. Perhaps he thought that Benny would be less likely to be sent away if he kept quiet. One of my letters, that fell into his hands, was dated from Canada; and he seldom spoke of me now. This state of things enabled me to slip down into the storeroom more frequently, where I could stand upright, and move my limbs more freely.

Days, weeks, and months passed, and there came no news of Ellen. I sent a letter to Brooklyn, written in my grandmother's name, to inquire whether she had arrived there. Answer was returned that she had not. I wrote to her in Washington; but no notice was taken of it. There was one person there, who ought to have had some sympathy with the anxiety of the child's friends at home; but the links of such relations as he had formed with me, are easily broken and cast away as rubbish. Yet how protectingly and persuasively he once talked to the poor, helpless slave girl! And how entirely I trusted him! But now suspicions darkened my mind. Was my child dead, or had they deceived me, and sold her?

If the secret memoirs of many members of Congress should be published, curious details would be unfolded. I once saw a letter from a member of Congress to a slave, who was the mother of six of his children. He wrote to request that she would send her children away from the great house before his return, as he expected to be accompanied by friends. The woman could not read, and was obliged to employ another to read the letter. The existence of the colored children did not trouble this gentleman, it was only the fear that friends might recognize in their features a resemblance to him.

At the end of six months, a letter came to my grandmother, from Brooklyn. It was written by a young lady in the family, and announced that Ellen had just arrived. It contained the following message from her: "I do try to do just as you told me to, and I pray for you every night and morning." I understood that these words were meant for me; and they were a balsam to my heart. The writer closed her letter by saying, "Ellen is a nice little girl, and we shall like to have her with us. My cousin, Mr. Sands, has given her to me, to be my little waiting maid. I shall send her to school, and I hope some day she will write to you herself." This letter perplexed and troubled me. Had my child's father merely placed her there till she was old enough to support herself? Or had he given her to his cousin, as a piece of property? If the last idea was correct, his cousin might return to the south at any time, and hold Ellen as a slave. I tried to put away from me the painful thought that such a foul wrong could have been done to us. I said to myself, "Surely there must be *some* justice in man;" then I remembered, with a sigh, how slavery perverted all the natural feelings of the human heart. It gave me a pang to look on my light-hearted boy. He believed himself free; and to have him brought under the yoke of slavery, would be more than I could bear. How I longed to have him safely out of the reach of its power!

XXVIII.

AUNT NANCY.

I HAVE mentioned my great-aunt, who was a slave in Dr. Flint's family, and who had been my refuge during the shameful persecutions I suffered from him. This aunt had been married at twenty years of age; that is, as far as slaves *can* marry. She had the consent of her master and mistress, and a clergyman performed the ceremony. But it was a mere form, without any legal value. Her master or mistress could annul it any day they pleased. She had always slept on the floor in the entry, near Mrs. Flint's chamber door, that she might be within call. When she was married, she was told she might have the use of a small room in an out-house. Her mother and her husband furnished it. He was a seafaring man, and was allowed to sleep there when he was at home. But on the wedding evening, the bride was ordered to her old post on the entry floor.

Mrs. Flint, at that time, had no children; but she was expecting to be a mother, and if she should want a drink of water in the night, what could she do without her slave to bring it? So my aunt was compelled to lie at her door, until one midnight she was forced to leave, to give premature birth to a child. In a fortnight she was required to resume her place on the entry floor, because Mrs. Flint's babe needed her attentions. She kept her station there through summer and winter, until she had given premature birth to six children; and all the while she was employed as night-nurse to Mrs. Flint's children. Finally, toiling all day, and being deprived of rest at night, completely broke down her constitution, and Dr. Flint declared it was impossible she could ever become the mother of a living child. The fear of losing so valuable a servant by death, now induced them to allow her to sleep in her little room in the out-house, except when there was sickness in the family. She afterwards had two feeble babes, one of whom died in a few days, and the other in four weeks. I well remember her patient sorrow as she held the last dead baby in her arms. "I wish it could have lived," she said; "it is not the will of God that any of my children should live. But I will try to be fit to meet their little spirits in heaven."

Aunt Nancy was housekeeper and waiting-maid in Dr. Flint's family. Indeed, she was the *factotum* of the household. Nothing went on well without her. She was my mother's twin sister, and, as far as was in her power, she supplied a mother's place to us orphans. I slept with her all the time I lived in my old master's house, and the bond between us was very strong. When my friends tried to discourage me from running away, she always encouraged me. When they thought I had better return and ask my master's pardon, because there was no possibility of escape, she sent me word never to yield. She said if I persevered I might, perhaps, gain the freedom of my children; and even if I perished in doing it, that was better than to leave them to groan under the same persecutions that had blighted my own life. After I was shut up in my dark cell, she stole away, whenever she could, to bring me the news and say something cheering. How often did I kneel down to listen to her words of consolation, whispered through a crack! "I am old, and have not long to live," she used to say; "and I could die happy if I could only see you and the children free. You must pray to God, Linda, as I do for you, that he will lead you out of this darkness." I would beg her not to worry herself on my account; that there was an end of all suffering sooner or later, and that whether I lived in chains or in freedom, I should always remember her as the good friend who had been the comfort of my life. A word from her always strengthened me; and not me only. The whole family relied upon her judgment, and were guided by her advice.

I had been in my cell six years when my grandmother was summoned to the bedside of this, her last remaining daughter. She was very ill, and they said she would die. Grandmother had not entered Dr. Flint's house for several years. They had treated her cruelly, but she thought nothing of that now. She was grateful for permission to watch by the death-bed of her child. They had always been devoted to each other; and now they sat looking into each other's eyes, longing to speak of the secret that had weighed so much on the hearts of both. My aunt had been stricken with paralysis. She lived but two days, and the last day she was speechless. Before she lost the power of utterance, she told her mother not to grieve if she could not speak to her; that she would try to hold up her hand, to let her know that all was well with her. Even the hard-hearted doctor was a little softened when he saw the dying woman try to smile on the aged mother, who was kneeling by her side. His eyes moistened for a moment, as he said she had always been a faithful servant, and they should never be able to supply her place. Mrs. Flint took to her bed, quite overcome by the shock. While my grandmother sat alone with the dead, the doctor came in, leading his youngest son, who had always been a great pet with aunt Nancy, and was much attached to her. "Martha," said he, "aunt Nancy loved this child, and when he comes where you are, I hope you will be kind to him, for her sake." She replied, "Your wife was my foster-child, Dr. Flint, the foster-sister of my poor Nancy, and you little know me if you think I can feel any thing but good will for her children."

"I wish the past could be forgotten, and that we might never think of it," said he; "and that Linda would come to supply her aunt's place. She would be worth more to us than all the money that could be paid for her. I wish it for your sake also, Martha. Now that Nancy is taken away from you, she would be a great comfort to your old age."

He knew he was touching a tender chord. Almost choking with grief, my grandmother replied, "It was not I that drove Linda away. My grandchildren are gone; and of my nine children only one is left. God help me!"

To me, the death of this kind relative was an inexpressible sorrow. I knew that she had been slowly murdered; and

I felt that my troubles had helped to finish the work. After I heard of her illness, I listened constantly to hear what news was brought from the great house; and the thought that I could not go to her made me utterly miserable. At last, as uncle Phillip came into the house, I heard some one inquire, "How is she?" and he answered, "She is dead." My little cell seemed whirling round, and I knew nothing more till I opened my eyes and found uncle Phillip bending over me. I had no need to ask any questions. He whispered, "Linda, she died happy." I could not weep. My fixed gaze troubled him. "Don't look *so*," he said. "Don't add to my poor mother's trouble. Remember how much she has to bear, and that we ought to do all we can to comfort her." Ah, yes, that blessed old grandmother, who for seventy-three years had borne the pelting storms of a slave-mother's life. She did indeed need consolation!

Mrs. Flint had rendered her poor foster-sister childless, apparently without any compunction; and with cruel selfishness had ruined her health by years of incessant, unrequited toil, and broken rest. But now she became very sentimental. I suppose she thought it would be a beautiful illustration of the attachment existing between slaveholder and slave, if the body of her old worn-out servant was buried at her feet. She sent for the clergyman and asked if he had any objection to burying aunt Nancy in the doctor's family burial-place. No colored person had ever been allowed interment in the white people's burying-ground, and the minister knew that all the deceased of our family reposed together in the old graveyard of the slaves. He therefore replied, "I have no objection to complying with your wish; but perhaps aunt Nancy's *mother* may have some choice as to where her remains shall be deposited."

It had never occurred to Mrs. Flint that slaves could have any feelings. When my grandmother was consulted, she at once said she wanted Nancy to lie with all the rest of her family, and where her own old body would be buried. Mrs. Flint graciously complied with her wish, though she said it was painful to her to have Nancy buried away from *her*. She might have added with touching pathos, "I was so long *used* to sleep with her lying near me, on the entry floor."

My uncle Phillip asked permission to bury his sister at

his own expense; and slaveholders are always ready to grant *such* favors to slaves and their relatives. The arrangements were very plain, but perfectly respectable. She was buried on the Sabbath, and Mrs. Flint's minister read the funeral service. There was a large concourse of colored people, bond and free, and a few white persons who had always been friendly to our family. Dr. Flint's carriage was in the procession; and when the body was deposited in its humble resting place, the mistress dropped a tear, and returned to her carriage, probably thinking she had performed her duty nobly.

It was talked of by the slaves as a mighty grand funeral. Northern travellers, passing through the place, might have described this tribute of respect to the humble dead as a beautiful feature in the "patriarchal institution;" a touching proof of the attachment between slaveholders and their servants; and tender-hearted Mrs. Flint would have confirmed this impression, with handkerchief at her eyes. *We* could have told them a different story. We could have given them a chapter of wrongs and sufferings, that would have touched their hearts, if they *had* any hearts to feel for the colored people. We could have told them how the poor old slave-mother had toiled, year after year, to earn eight hundred dollars to buy her son Phillip's right to his own earnings; and how that same Phillip paid the expenses of the funeral, which they regarded as doing so much credit to the master. We could also have told them of a poor, blighted young creature, shut up in a living grave for years, to avoid the tortures that would be inflicted on her, if she ventured to come out and look on the face of her departed friend.

All this, and much more, I thought of, as I sat at my loop-hole, waiting for the family to return from the grave; sometimes weeping, sometimes falling asleep, dreaming strange dreams of the dead and the living.

It was sad to witness the grief of my bereaved grandmother. She had always been strong to bear, and now, as ever, religious faith supported her. But her dark life had become still darker, and age and trouble were leaving deep traces on her withered face. She had four places to knock for me to come to the trap-door, and each place had a different meaning. She now came oftener than she had done, and talked to me of her dead daughter, while tears trickled slowly down her furrowed cheeks. I said all I could to comfort her; but it was a sad reflection, that instead of being able to help her, I was a constant source of anxiety and trouble. The poor old back was fitted to its burden. It bent under it, but did not break.

XXIX.

PREPARATIONS FOR ESCAPE.

I HARDLY expect that the reader will credit me, when I affirm that I lived in that little dismal hole, almost deprived of light and air, and with no space to move my limbs, for nearly seven years. But it is a fact; and to me a sad one, even now; for my body still suffers from the effects of that long imprisonment, to say nothing of my soul. Members of my family, now living in New York and Boston, can testify to the truth of what I say.

Countless were the nights that I sat late at the little loophole scarcely large enough to give me a glimpse of one twinkling star. There, heard the patrols and slave-hunters conferring together about the capture of runaways, well knowing how rejoiced they would be to catch me.

Season after season, year after year, I peeped at my children's faces, and heard their sweet voices, with a heart yearning all the while to say, "Your mother is here." Sometimes it appeared to me as if ages had rolled away since I entered upon that gloomy, monotonous existence. At times, I was stupefied and listless; at other times I became very impatient to know when these dark years would end, and I should again be allowed to feel the sunshine, and breathe the pure air.

After Ellen left us, this feeling increased. Mr. Sands had agreed that Benny might go to the north whenever his

uncle Phillip could go with him; and I was anxious to be
there also, to watch over my children, and protect them so
far as I was able. Moreover, I was likely to be drowned out
of my den, if I remained much longer; for the slight roof was
getting badly out of repair, and uncle Phillip was afraid to
remove the shingles, lest some one should get a glimpse of
me. When storms occurred in the night, they spread mats
and bits of carpet, which in the morning appeared to have
been laid out to dry; but to cover the roof in the daytime
might have attracted attention. Consequently, my clothes
and bedding were often drenched; a process by which the
pains and aches in my cramped and stiffened limbs were
greatly increased. I revolved various plans of escape in my
mind, which I sometimes imparted to my grandmother,
when she came to whisper with me at the trap-door. The
kind-hearted old woman had an intense sympathy for runaways. She had known too much of the cruelties inflicted on
those who were captured. Her memory always flew back at
once to the sufferings of her bright and handsome son, Benjamin, the youngest and dearest of her flock. So, whenever
I alluded to the subject, she would groan out, "O, don't
think of it, child. You'll break my heart." I had no good old
aunt Nancy now to encourage me; but my brother William
and my children were continually beckoning me to the
north.

And now I must go back a few months in my story. I
have stated that the first of January was the time for selling
slaves, or leasing them out to new masters. If time were
counted by heart-throbs, the poor slaves might reckon years
of suffering during that festival so joyous to the free. On the
New Year's day preceding my aunt's death, one of my
friends, named Fanny, was to be sold at auction, to pay her
master's debts. My thoughts were with her during all the
day, and at night I anxiously inquired what had been her
fate. I was told that she had been sold to one master, and
her four little girls to another master, far distant; that she
had escaped from her purchaser, and was not to be found.
Her mother was the old Aggie I have spoken of. She lived
in a small tenement belonging to my grandmother, and
built on the same lot with her own house. Her dwelling was
searched and watched, and that brought the patrols so near

me that I was obliged to keep very close in my den. The hunters were somehow eluded; and not long afterwards Benny accidentally caught sight of Fanny in her mother's hut. He told his grandmother, who charged him never to speak of it, explaining to him the frightful consequences; and he never betrayed the trust. Aggie little dreamed that my grandmother knew where her daughter was concealed, and that the stooping form of her old neighbor was bending under a similar burden of anxiety and fear; but these dangerous secrets deepened the sympathy between the two old persecuted mothers.

My friend Fanny and I remained many weeks hidden within call of each other; but she was unconscious of the fact. I longed to have her share my den, which seemed a more secure retreat than her own; but I had brought so much trouble on my grandmother, that it seemed wrong to ask her to incur greater risks. My restlessness increased. I had lived too long in bodily pain and anguish of spirit. Always I was in dread that by some accident, or some contrivance, slavery would succeed in snatching my children from me. This thought drove me nearly frantic, and I determined to steer for the North Star at all hazards. At this crisis, Providence opened an unexpected way for me to escape. My friend Peter came one evening, and asked to speak with me. "Your day has come, Linda," said he. "I have found a chance for you to go to the Free States. You have a fortnight to decide." The news seemed too good to be true; but Peter explained his arrangements, and told me all that was necessary was for me to say I would go. I was going to answer him with a joyful yes, when the thought of Benny came to my mind. I told him the temptation was exceedingly strong, but I was terribly afraid of Dr. Flint's alleged power over my child, and that I could not go and leave him behind. Peter remonstrated earnestly. He said such a good chance might never occur again; that Benny was free, and could be sent to me; and that for the sake of my children's welfare I ought not to hesitate a moment. I told him I would consult with uncle Phillip. My uncle rejoiced in the plan, and bade me go by all means. He promised, if his life was spared, that he would either bring or send my son to me as soon as I reached a place of safety. I resolved to go, but thought nothing had better be said to my grandmother till very near the time of departure. But my uncle thought she would feel it more keenly if I left here so suddenly. "I will reason with her," said he, "and convince her how necessary it is, not only for your sake, but for hers also. You cannot be blind to the fact that she is sinking under her burdens." I was not blind to it. I knew that my concealment was an ever-present source of anxiety, and that the older she grew the more nervously fearful she was of discovery. My uncle talked with her, and finally succeeded in persuading her that it was absolutely necessary for me to seize the chance so unexpectedly offered.

The anticipation of being a free woman proved almost too much for my weak frame. The excitement stimulated me, and at the same time bewildered me. I made busy preparations for my journey, and for my son to follow me. I resolved to have an interview with him before I went, that I might give him cautions and advice, and tell him how anxiously I should be waiting for him at the north. Grandmother stole up to me as often as possible to whisper words of counsel. She insisted upon writing to Dr. Flint, as soon as I arrived in the Free States, and asking him to sell me to her. She said she would sacrifice her house, and all she had in the world, for the sake of having me safe with my children in any part of the world. If she could only live to know *that* she could die in peace. I promised the dear old faithful friend that I would write to her as soon as I arrived, and put the letter in a safe way to reach her; but in my own mind I resolved that not another cent of her hard earnings should be spent to pay rapacious slaveholders for what they called their property. And even if I had not been unwilling to buy what I had already a right to possess, common humanity would have prevented me from accepting the generous offer, at the expense of turning my aged relative out of house and home, when she was trembling on the brink of the grave.

I was to escape in a vessel; but I forbear to mention any further particulars. I was in readiness, but the vessel was unexpectedly detained several days. Meantime, news came to town of a most horrible murder committed on a fugitive slave, named James. Charity, the mother of this unfortunate young man, had been an old acquaintance of ours. I have told the shocking particulars of his death, in my description of some of the neighboring slaveholders. My grandmother, always nervously sensitive about runaways, was terribly frightened. She felt sure that a similar fate awaited me, if I did not desist from my enterprise. She sobbed, and groaned, and entreated me not to go. Her excessive fear was somewhat contagious, and my heart was not proof against her extreme agony. I was grievously disappointed, but I promised to relinquish my project.

When my friend Peter was apprised of this, he was both disappointed and vexed. He said, that judging from our past experience, it would be a long time before I had such another chance to throw away. I told him it need not be thrown away; that I had a friend concealed near by, who would be glad enough to take the place that had been provided for me. I told him about poor Fanny, and the kindhearted, noble fellow, who never turned his back upon anybody in distress, white or black, expressed his readiness to help her. Aggie was much surprised when she found that we knew her secret. She was rejoiced to hear of such a chance for Fanny, and arrangements were made for her to go on board the vessel the next night. They both supposed that I had long been at the north, therefore my name was not mentioned in the transaction. Fanny was carried on board at the appointed time, and stowed away in a very small cabin. This accommodation had been purchased at a price that would pay for a voyage to England. But when one proposes to go to fine old England, they stop to calculate whether they can afford the cost of the pleasure; while in making a bargain to escape from slavery, the trembling victim is ready to say, "Take all I have, only don't betray me!"

The next morning I peeped through my loophole, and saw that it was dark and cloudy. At night I received news that the wind was ahead, and the vessel had not sailed. I was exceedingly anxious about Fanny, and Peter too, who was running a tremendous risk at my instigation. Next day the wind and weather remained the same. Poor Fanny had been half dead with fright when they carried her on board, and I could readily imagine how she must be suffering now. Grandmother came often to my den, to say how thankful she was I did not go. On the third morning she rapped for me to come down to the storeroom. The poor old sufferer was breaking down under her weight of trouble. She was easily flurried now. I found her in a nervous, excited state, but I was not aware that she had forgotten to lock the door behind her, as usual. She was exceedingly worried about the detention of the vessel. She was afraid all would be discovered, and then Fanny, and Peter, and I, would all be tortured to death, and Phillip would be utterly ruined, and her house would be torn down. Poor Peter! If he should die such a horrible death as the poor slave James had lately done, and all for his kindness in trying to help me, how dreadful it would be for us all! Alas, the thought was familiar to me, and had sent many a sharp pang through my heart. I tried to suppress my own anxiety, and speak soothingly to her. She brought in some allusion to aunt Nancy, the dear daughter she had recently buried, and then she lost all control of herself. As she stood there, trembling and sobbing, a voice from the piazza called out, "Whar is you, aunt Marthy?" Grandmother was startled, and in her agitation opened the door, without thinking of me. In stepped Jenny, the mischievous housemaid, who had tried to enter my room, when I was concealed in the house of my white benefactress. "I's bin huntin ebery whar for you, aunt Marthy," said she. "My missis wants you to send her some crackers." I had slunk down behind a barrel, which entirely screened me, but I imagined that Jenny was looking directly at the spot, and my heart beat violently. My grandmother immediately thought what she had done, and went out quickly with Jenny to count the crackers, locking the door after her. She returned to me, in a few minutes, the perfect picture of despair. "Poor child!" she exclaimed, "my carelessness has ruined you. The boat ain't gone yet. Get ready immediately, and go with Fanny. I ain't got another word to say against it now; for there's no telling what may happen this day."

Uncle Phillip was sent for, and he agreed with his mother in thinking that Jenny would inform Dr. Flint in less than twenty-four hours. He advised getting me on board the boat, if possible; if not, I had better keep very still in my den, where they could not find me without tearing the house down. He said it would not do for him to move in the matter, because suspicion would be immediately excited; but he promised to communicate with Peter. I felt reluctant to apply to him again, having implicated him too much already; but there seemed to be no alternative. Vexed as Peter had been by my indecision, he was true to his generous nature, and said at once that he would do his best to help me, trusting I should show myself a stronger woman this time.

He immediately proceeded to the wharf, and found that the wind had shifted, and the vessel was slowly beating down stream. On some pretext of urgent necessity, he offered two boatmen a dollar apiece to catch up with her. He was of lighter complexion than the boatmen he hired, and when the captain saw them coming so rapidly, he thought officers were pursuing his vessel in search of the runaway slave he had on board. They hoisted sails, but the boat gained upon them, and the indefatigable Peter sprang on board.

The captain at once recognized him. Peter asked him to go below, to speak about a bad bill he had given him. When he told his errand, the captain replied, "Why, the woman's here already; and I've put her where you or the devil would have a tough job to find her."

"But it is another woman I want to bring," said Peter. "*She* is in great distress, too, and you shall be paid any thing within reason, if you'll stop and take her."

"What's her name?" inquired the captain.

"Linda," he replied.

"That's the name of the woman already here," rejoined the captain. "By George! I believe you mean to betray me."

"O!" exclaimed Peter, "God knows I wouldn't harm a hair of your head. I am too grateful to you. But there really *is* another woman in great danger. Do have the humanity to stop and take her!"

After a while they came to an understanding. Fanny, not dreaming I was any where about in that region, had assumed my name, though she called herself Johnson. "Linda is a common name," said Peter, "and the woman I want to bring is Linda Brent."

The captain agreed to wait at a certain place till evening, being handsomely paid for his detention.

Of course, the day was an anxious one for us all. But we

concluded that if Jenny had seen me, she would be too wise to let her mistress know of it; and that she probably would not get a chance to see Dr. Flint's family till evening, for I knew very well what were the rules in that household. I afterwards believed that she did not see me; for nothing ever came of it, and she was one of those base characters that would have jumped to betray a suffering fellow being for the sake of thirty pieces of silver.

I made all my arrangements to go on board as soon as it was dusk. The intervening time I resolved to spend with my son. I had not spoken to him for seven years, though I had been under the same roof, and seen him every day, when I was well enough to sit at the loophole. I did not dare to venture beyond the storeroom; so they brought him there, and locked us up together, in a place concealed from the piazza door. It was an agitating interview for both of us. After we had talked and wept together for a little while, he said, "Mother, I'm glad you're going away. I wish I could go with you. I knew you was here; and I have been *so* afraid they would come and catch you!"

I was greatly surprised, and asked him how he had found it out.

He replied, "I was standing under the eaves, one day, before Ellen went away, and I heard somebody cough up over the wood shed. I don't know what made me think it was you, but I did think so. I missed Ellen, the night before she went away; and grandmother brought her back into the room in the night; and I thought maybe she'd been to see *you,* before she went, for I heard grandmother whisper to her, 'Now go to sleep; and remember never to tell.' "

I asked him if he ever mentioned his suspicions to his sister. He said he never did; but after he heard the cough, if he saw her playing with other children on that side of the house, he always tried to coax her round to the other side, for fear they would hear me cough, too. He said he had kept a close lookout for Dr. Flint, and if he saw him speak to a constable, or a patrol, he always told grandmother. I now recollected that I had seen him manifest uneasiness, when people were on that side of the house, and I had at the time been puzzled to conjecture a motive for his actions. Such prudence may seem extraordinary in a boy of twelve years, but slaves, being surrounded by mysteries, deceptions, and dangers, early learn to be suspicious and watchful, and prematurely cautious and cunning. He had never asked a question of grandmother, or uncle Phillip, and I had often heard him chime in with other children, when they spoke of my being at the north.

I told him I was now really going to the Free States, and if he was a good, honest boy, and a loving child to his dear old grandmother, the Lord would bless him, and bring him to me, and we and Ellen would live together. He began to tell me that grandmother had not eaten any thing all day. While he was speaking, the door was unlocked, and she came in with a small bag of money, which she wanted me to take. I begged her to keep a part of it, at least, to pay for Benny's being sent to the north; but she insisted, while her tears were falling fast, that I should take the whole. "You may be sick among strangers," she said, "and they would send you to the poorhouse to die." Ah, that good grandmother!

For the last time I went up to my nook. Its desolate appearance no longer chilled me, for the light of hope had risen in my soul. Yet, even with the blessed prospect of freedom before me, I felt very sad at leaving forever that old homestead, where I had been sheltered so long by the dear old grandmother; where I had dreamed my first young dream of love; and where, after that had faded away, my children came to twine themselves so closely round my desolate heart. As the hour approached for me to leave, I again descended to the storeroom. My grandmother and Benny were there. She took me by the hand, and said, "Linda, let us pray." We knelt down together, with my child pressed to my heart, and my other arm round the faithful, loving old friend I was about to leave forever. On no other occasion has it ever been my lot to listen to so fervent a supplication for mercy and protection. It thrilled through my heart, and inspired me with trust in God.

Peter was waiting for me in the street. I was soon by his side, faint in body, but strong of purpose. I did not look back upon the old place, though I felt that I should never see it again.

XXX.

NORTHWARD BOUND.

I NEVER could tell how we reached the wharf. My brain was all of a whirl, and my limbs tottered under me. At an appointed place we met my uncle Phillip, who had started before us on a different route, that he might reach the wharf first, and give us timely warning if there was any danger. A row-boat was in readiness. As I was about to step in, I felt something pull me gently, and turning round I saw Benny, looking pale and anxious. He whispered in my ear, "I've been peeping into the doctor's window, and he's at home. Good by, mother. Don't cry; I'll come." He hastened away. I clasped the hand of my good uncle, to whom I owed so much, and of Peter, the brave, generous friend who had volunteered to run such terrible risks to secure my safety. To this day I remember how his bright face beamed with joy, when he told me he had discovered a safe method for me to escape. Yet that intelligent, enterprising, noble-hearted man was a chattel! liable, by the laws of a country that calls itself civilized, to be sold with horses and pigs! We parted in silence. Our hearts were all too full for words!

Swiftly the boat glided over the water. After a while, one of the sailors said, "Don't be down-hearted, madam. We will take you safely to your husband, in——." At first I could not imagine what he meant; but I had presence of mind to think that it probably referred to something the captain had told him; so I thanked him, and said I hoped we should have pleasant weather.

When I entered the vessel the captain came forward to meet me. He was an elderly man, with a pleasant countenance. He showed me to a little box of a cabin, where sat my friend Fanny. She started as if she had seen a spectre. She gazed on me in utter astonishment, and exclaimed, "Linda, can this be *you*? or is it your ghost?" When we were locked in each other's arms, my overwrought feelings could no longer be restrained. My sobs reached the ears of the captain, who came and very kindly reminded us, that for his safety, as well as our own, it would be prudent for us not to attract any attention. He said that when there was a sail in sight he wished us to keep below; but at other times, he had no objection to our being on deck. He assured us that he would keep a good lookout, and if we acted prudently, he thought we should be in no danger. He had represented us as women going to meet our husbands in——. We thanked him, and promised to observe carefully all the directions he gave us.

Fanny and I now talked by ourselves, low and quietly, in our little cabin. She told me of the suffering she had gone through in making her escape, and of her terrors while she was concealed in her mother's house. Above all, she dwelt on the agony of separation from all her children on that dreadful auction day. She could scarcely credit me, when I told her of the place where I had passed nearly seven years. "We have the same sorrows," said I. "No," replied she, "you are going to see your children soon, and there is no hope that I shall ever even hear from mine."

The vessel was soon under way, but we made slow progress. The wind was against us. I should not have cared for this, if we had been out of sight of the town; but until there were miles of water between us and our enemies, we were filled with constant apprehensions that the constables would come on board. Neither could I feel quite at ease with the captain and his men. I was an entire stranger to that class of people, and I had heard that sailors were rough, and sometimes cruel. We were so completely in their power, that if they were bad men, our situation would be dreadful. Now that the captain was paid for our passage, might he not be tempted to make more money by giving us up to those who claimed us as property? I was naturally of a confiding disposition, but slavery had made me suspicious of every body. Fanny did not share my distrust of the captain or his men. She said she was afraid at first, but she had been on board three days while the vessel lay in the dock, and nobody had betrayed her, or treated her otherwise than kindly.

The captain soon came to advise us to go on deck for fresh air. His friendly and respectful manner, combined with Fanny's testimony, reassured me, and we went with him. He placed us in a comfortable seat, and occasionally entered into conversation. He told us he was a Southerner by birth, and had spent the greater part of his life in the Slave States, and that he had recently lost a brother who traded in slaves. "But," said he, "it is a pitiable and degrading business, and I always felt ashamed to acknowledge my brother in connection with it." As we passed Snaky Swamp, he pointed to it, and said, "There is a slave territory that defies all the laws." I thought of the terrible days I had spent there, and though it was not called Dismal Swamp, it made me feel very dismal as I looked at it.

I shall never forget that night. The balmy air of spring was so refreshing! And how shall I describe my sensations when we were fairly sailing on Chesapeake Bay? O, the beautiful sunshine! the exhilarating breeze! And I could enjoy them without fear or restraint. I had never realized what grand things air and sunlight are till I had been deprived of them.

Ten days after we left land we were approaching Philadelphia. The captain said we should arrive there in the night, but he thought we had better wait till morning, and go on shore in broad daylight, as the best way to avoid suspicion.

I replied, "You know best. But will you stay on board and protect us?"

He saw that I was suspicious, and he said he was sorry, now that he had brought us to the end of our voyage, to find I had so little confidence in him. Ah, if he had ever been a slave he would have known how difficult it was to trust a white man. He assured us that we might sleep through the night without fear; that he would take care we were not left unprotected. Be it said to the honor of this captain, Southerner as he was, that if Fanny and I had been white ladies, and our passage lawfully engaged, he could not have treated us more respectfully. My intelligent friend, Peter, had rightly estimated the character of the man to whose honor he had intrusted us.

The next morning I was on deck as soon as the day dawned. I called Fanny to see the sun rise, for the first time in our lives, on free soil; for such I *then* believed it to be. We watched the reddening sky, and saw the great orb come up slowly out of the water, as it seemed. Soon the waves began to sparkle, and every thing caught the beautiful glow. Before us lay the city of strangers. We looked at each other, and the eyes of both were moistened with tears. We had escaped from slavery, and we supposed ourselves to be safe from the hunters. But we were alone in the world, and we had left dear ties behind us; ties cruelly sundered by the demon Slavery.

XXXI.

INCIDENTS IN PHILADELPHIA.

I HAD heard that the poor slave had many friends at the north. I trusted we should find some of them. Meantime, we would take it for granted that all were friends, till they proved to the contrary. I sought out the kind captain, thanked him for his attentions, and told him I should never cease to be grateful for the service he had rendered us. I gave him a message to the friends I had left at home, and he promised to deliver it. We were placed in a row-boat, and in about fifteen minutes were landed on a wood wharf in Philadelphia. As I stood looking round, the friendly captain touched me on the shoulder, and said, "There is a respectable-looking colored man behind you. I will speak to him about the New York trains, and tell him you wish to go directly on." I thanked him, and asked him to direct me to some shops where I could buy gloves and veils. He did so, and said he would talk with the colored man till I returned. I made what haste I could. Constant exercise on board the vessel, and frequent rubbing with salt water, had nearly restored the use of my limbs. The noise of the great city confused me, but I found the shops, and bought some double veils and gloves for Fanny and myself. The shopman told me they were so many levies. I had never heard the word before, but I did not tell him so. I thought if he knew I was a stranger he might ask me where I came from. I gave him a gold piece, and when he returned the change, I counted it, and found out how much a levy was. I made my way back to the wharf, where the captain introduced me to the colored man, as the Rev. Jeremiah Durham, minister of Bethel church. He took me by the hand, as if I had been an old friend. He told us we were too late for the morning cars to New York, and must wait until the evening, or the next morning. He invited me to go home with him, assuring me that his wife would give me a cordial welcome; and for my friend he would provide a home with one of his neighbors. I thanked him for so much kindness to strangers, and told him if I must be detained, I should like to hunt up some people who formerly went from our part of the country. Mr. Durham insisted that I should dine with him, and then he would assist me in finding my friends. The sailors came to bid us good by. I shook their hardy hands, with tears in my eyes. They had all been kind to us, and they had rendered us a greater service than they could possibly conceive of.

I had never seen so large a city, or been in contact with so many people in the streets. It seemed as if those who passed looked at us with an expression of curiosity. My face was so blistered and peeled, by sitting on deck, in wind and sunshine, that I thought they could not easily decide to what nation I belonged.

Mrs. Durham met me with a kindly welcome, without asking any questions. I was tired, and her friendly manner was a sweet refreshment. God bless her! I was sure that she had comforted other weary hearts, before I received her sympathy. She was surrounded by her husband and children, in a home made sacred by protecting laws. I thought of my own children, and sighed.

After dinner Mr. Durham went with me in quest of the friends I had spoken of. They went from my native town, and I anticipated much pleasure in looking on familiar faces. They were not at home, and we retraced our steps through streets delightfully clean. On the way, Mr. Durham observed that I had spoken to him of a daughter I expected to meet; that he was surprised, for I looked so young he had taken me for a single woman. He was approaching a subject on which I was extremely sensitive. He would ask about my husband next, I thought, and if I answered him truly, what would he think of me? I told him I had two children, one in New York, the other at the south. He asked some further questions, and I frankly told him some of the most important events of my life. It was painful for me to do it; but I would not deceive him. If he was desirous of being my friend, I thought he ought to know how far I was worthy of it. "Excuse me, if I have tried your feelings," said he. "I did not question you from idle curiosity. I wanted to understand your situation, in order to know whether I could be of any service to you, or your little girl. Your straightforward answers do you credit; but don't answer every body so openly. It might give some heartless people a pretext for treating you with contempt."

That word *contempt* burned me like coals of fire. I replied, "God alone knows how I have suffered; and He, I trust, will forgive me. If I am permitted to have my children, I intend to be a good mother, and to live in such a manner that people cannot treat me with contempt."

"I respect your sentiments," said he. "Place your trust in God, and be governed by good principles, and you will not fail to find friends."

When we reached home, I went to my room, glad to shut out the world for a while. The words he had spoken made an indelible impression upon me. They brought up great shadows from the mournful past. In the midst of my meditations I was startled by a knock at the door. Mrs. Durham entered, her face all beaming with kindness, to say that there was an anti-slavery friend down stairs, who would like to see me. I overcame my dread of encountering strangers, and went with her. Many questions were asked concerning my experiences, and my escape from slavery; but I observed how careful they all were not to say any thing that might wound my feelings. How gratifying this was, can be fully understood only by those who have been accustomed to be treated as if they were not included within the pale of human beings. The anti-slavery friend had come to inquire into my plans, and to offer assistance, if needed. Fanny was comfortably established, for the present, with a friend of Mr. Durham. The Anti-Slavery Society agreed to pay her expenses to New York. The same was offered to me, but I declined to accept it, telling them that my grandmother had given me sufficient to pay my expenses to the end of my journey. We were urged to remain in Philadelphia a few days, until some suitable escort could be found for us. I gladly accepted the proposition, for I had a dread of meeting slaveholders, and some dread also of railroads. I had never entered a railroad car in my life, and it seemed to me quite an important event.

That night I sought my pillow with feelings I had never carried to it before. I verily believed myself to be a free woman. I was wakeful for a long time, and I had no sooner fallen asleep, than I was roused by fire-bells. I jumped up, and hurried on my clothes. Where I came from, every body hastened to dress themselves on such occasions. The white people thought a great fire might be used as a good opportunity for insurrection, and that it was best to be in readiness; and the colored people were ordered out to labor in extinguishing the flames. There was but one engine in our town, and colored women and children were often required to drag it to the river's edge and fill it. Mrs. Durham's daughter slept in the same room with me, and seeing that she slept through all the din, I thought it was my duty to wake her. "What's the matter?" said she, rubbing her eyes.

"They're screaming fire in the streets, and the bells are ringing," I replied.

"What of that?" said she, drowsily. "We are used to it. We never get up, without the fire is very near. What good would it do?"

I was quite surprised that it was not necessary for us to go and help fill the engine. I was an ignorant child, just beginning to learn how things went on in great cities.

At daylight, I heard women crying fresh fish, berries, radishes, and various other things. All this was new to me. I dressed myself at an early hour, and sat at the window to watch that unknown tide of life. Philadelphia seemed to me a wonderfully great place. At the breakfast table, my idea of going out to drag the engine was laughed over, and I joined in the mirth.

I went to see Fanny, and found her so well contented among her new friends that she was in no haste to leave. I was also very happy with my kind hostess. She had had advantages for education, and was vastly my superior. Every day, almost every hour, I was adding to my little stock of knowledge. She took me out to see the city as much as she deemed prudent. One day she took me to an artist's room, and showed me the portraits of some of her children. I had never seen any paintings of colored people before, and they seemed to be beautiful.

At the end of five days, one of Mrs. Durham's friends offered to accompany us to New York the following morning. As I held the hand of my good hostess in a parting clasp, I longed to know whether her husband had repeated to her what I had told him. I supposed he had, but she never made any allusion to it. I presume it was the delicate silence of womanly sympathy.

When Mr. Durham handed us our tickets, he said, "I am afraid you will have a disagreeable ride; but I could not procure tickets for the first-class cars."

Supposing I had not given him money enough, I offered more. "O, no," said he, "they could not be had for any money. They don't allow colored people to go in the first-class cars."

This was the first chill to my enthusiasm about the Free States. Colored people were allowed to ride in a filthy box, behind white people, at the south, but there they were not required to pay for the privilege. It made me sad to find how the north aped the customs of slavery.

We were stowed away in a large, rough car, with windows on each side, too high for us to look out without standing up. It was crowded with people, apparently of all nations. There were plenty of beds and cradles, containing screaming and kicking babies. Every other man had a cigar or pipe in his mouth, and jugs of whiskey were handed round freely. The fumes of the whiskey and the dense tobacco smoke were sickening to my senses, and my mind was equally nauseated by the coarse jokes and ribald songs around me. It was a very disagreeable ride. Since that time there has been some improvement in these matters.

XXXII.

THE MEETING OF MOTHER
AND DAUGHTER.

WHEN we arrived in New York, I was half crazed by the crowd of coachmen calling out, "Carriage, ma'am?" We bargained with one to take us to Sullivan Street for twelve shillings. A burly Irishman stepped up and said, "I'll tak' ye for sax shillings." The reduction of half the price was an object to us, and we asked if he could take us right away. "Troth an I will, ladies," he replied. I noticed that the hackmen smiled at each other, and I inquired whether his conveyance was decent. "Yes, it's dacent it is, marm. Devil a bit would I be after takin' ladies in a cab that was not dacent." We gave him our checks. He went for the baggage, and soon reappeared, saying, "This way, if you plase, ladies." We followed, and found our trunks on a truck, and we were invited to take our seats on them. We told him that was not what we bargained for, and he must take the trunks off. He swore they should not be touched till we had paid him six shillings. In our situation it was not prudent to attract attention, and I was about to pay him what he required, when a man near by shook his head for me not to do it. After a great ado we got rid of the Irishman, and had our trunks fastened on a hack. We had been recommended to a boarding-house in Sullivan Street, and thither we drove. There Fanny and I separated. The Anti-Slavery Society provided a home for her, and I afterwards heard of her in prosperous circumstances. I sent for an old friend from my part of the country, who had for some time been doing business in New York. He came immediately. I told him I wanted to go to my daughter, and asked him to aid me in procuring an interview.

I cautioned him not to let it be known to the family that I had just arrived from the south, because they supposed I had been at the north seven years. He told me there was a colored woman in Brooklyn who came from the same town I did, and I had better go to her house, and have my daughter meet me there. I accepted the proposition thankfully, and he agreed to escort me to Brooklyn. We crossed Fulton ferry, went up Myrtle Avenue, and stopped at the house he designated. I was just about to enter, when two girls passed. My friend called my attention to them. I turned, and recognized in the eldest, Sarah, the daughter of a woman who used to live with my grandmother, but who had left the south years ago. Surprised and rejoiced at this unexpected meeting, I threw my arms round her, and inquired concerning her mother.

"You take no notice of the other girl," said my friend. I turned, and there stood my Ellen! I pressed her to my heart, then held her away from me to take a look at her. She had changed a good deal in the two years since I parted from her. Signs of neglect could be discerned by eyes less observing than a mother's. My friend invited us all to go into the house; but Ellen said she had been sent of an errand, which she would do as quickly as possible, and go home and ask Mrs. Hobbs to let her come and see me. It was agreed that I should send for her the next day. Her companion, Sarah, hastened to tell her mother of my arrival. When I entered the house, I found the mistress of it absent, and I waited for her return. Before I saw her, I heard her saying, "Where is Linda Brent? I used to know her father and mother." Soon Sarah came with her mother. So there was quite a company of us, all from my grandmother's neighborhood. These friends gathered round me and questioned me eagerly. They laughed, they cried, and they shouted. They thanked God that I had got away from my persecutors and was safe on Long Island. It was a day of great excitement. How different from the silent days I had passed in my dreary den!

The next morning was Sunday. My first waking thoughts were occupied with the note I was to send to Mrs. Hobbs, the lady with whom Ellen lived. That I had recently come into that vicinity was evident; otherwise I should have sooner inquired for my daughter. It would not do to let them know I had just arrived from the south, for that would involve the suspicion of my having been harbored there, and might bring trouble, if not ruin, on several people.

I like a straightforward course, and am always reluctant to resort to subterfuges. So far as my ways have been crooked,

I charge them all upon slavery. It was that system of violence and wrong which now left me no alternative but to enact a falsehood. I began my note by stating that I had recently arrived from Canada, and was very desirous to have my daughter come to see me. She came and brought a message from Mrs. Hobbs, inviting me to her house, and assuring me that I need not have any fears. The conversation I had with my child did not leave my mind at ease. When I asked if she was well treated, she answered yes; but there was no heartiness in the tone, and it seemed to me that she said it from an unwillingness to have me troubled on her account. Before she left me, she asked very earnestly, "Mother, will you take me to live with you?" It made me sad to think that I could not give her a home till I went to work and earned the means; and that might take me a long time. When she was placed with Mrs. Hobbs, the agreement was that she should be sent to school. She had been there two years, and was now nine years old, and she scarcely knew her letters. There was no excuse for this, for there were good public schools in Brooklyn, to which she could have been sent without expense.

She staid with me till dark, and I went home with her. I was received in a friendly manner by the family, and all agreed in saying that Ellen was a useful, good girl. Mrs. Hobbs looked me coolly in the face, and said, "I suppose you know that my cousin, Mr. Sands, has *given* her to my eldest daughter. She will make a nice waiting-maid for her when she grows up." I did not answer a word. How *could* she, who knew by experience the strength of a mother's love, and who was perfectly aware of the relation Mr. Sands bore to my children,—how *could* she look me in the face, while she thrust such a dagger into my heart?

I was no longer surprised that they had kept her in such a state of ignorance. Mr. Hobbs had formerly been wealthy, but he had failed, and afterwards obtained a subordinate situation in the Custom House. Perhaps they expected to return to the south some day; and Ellen's knowledge was quite sufficient for a slave's condition. I was impatient to go to work and earn money, that I might change the uncertain position of my children. Mr. Sands had not kept his promise to emancipate them. I had also been deceived about Ellen.

What security had I with regard to Benjamin? I felt that I had none.

I returned to my friend's house in an uneasy state of mind. In order to protect my children, it was necessary that I should own myself. I called myself free, and sometimes felt so; but I knew I was insecure. I sat down that night and wrote a civil letter to Dr. Flint, asking him to state the lowest terms on which he would sell me; and as I belonged by law to his daughter, I wrote to her also, making a similar request.

Since my arrival at the north I had not been unmindful of my dear brother William. I had made diligent inquiries for him, and having heard of him in Boston, I went thither. When I arrived there, I found he had gone to New Bedford. I wrote to that place, and was informed he had gone on a whaling voyage, and would not return for some months. I went back to New York to get employment near Ellen. I received an answer from Dr. Flint, which gave me no encouragement. He advised me to return and submit myself to my rightful owners, and then any request I might make would be granted. I lent this letter to a friend, who lost it; otherwise I would present a copy to my readers.

XXXIII.

A HOME FOUND.

My greatest anxiety now was to obtain employment. My health was greatly improved, though my limbs continued to trouble me with swelling whenever I walked much. The greatest difficulty in my way was, that those who employed strangers required a recommendation; and in my peculiar position, I could, of course, obtain no certificates from the families I had so faithfully served.

One day an acquaintance told me of a lady who wanted

a nurse for her babe, and I immediately applied for the situation. The lady told me she preferred to have one who had been a mother, and accustomed to the care of infants. I told her I had nursed two babes of my own. She asked me many questions, but, to my great relief, did not require a recommendation from my former employers. She told me she was an English woman, and that was a pleasant circumstance to me, because I had heard they had less prejudice against color than Americans entertained. It was agreed that we should try each other for a week. The trial proved satisfactory to both parties, and I was engaged for a month.

The heavenly Father had been most merciful to me in leading me to this place. Mrs. Bruce was a kind and gentle lady, and proved a true and sympathizing friend. Before the stipulated month expired, the necessity of passing up and down stairs frequently, caused my limbs to swell so painfully, that I became unable to perform my duties. Many ladies would have thoughtlessly discharged me; but Mrs. Bruce made arrangements to save me steps, and employed a physician to attend upon me. I had not yet told her that I was a fugitive slave. She noticed that I was often sad, and kindly inquired the cause. I spoke of being separated from my children, and from relatives who were dear to me; but I did not mention the constant feeling of insecurity which oppressed my spirits. I longed for some one to confide it; but I had been so deceived by white people, that I had lost all confidence in them. If they spoke kind words to me, I thought it was for some selfish purpose. I had entered this family with the distrustful feelings I had brought with me out of slavery; but ere six months had passed, I found that the gentle deportment of Mrs. Bruce and the smiles of her lovely babe were thawing my chilled heart. My narrow mind also began to expand under the influences of her intelligent conversation, and the opportunities for reading, which were gladly allowed me whenever I had leisure from my duties. I gradually became more energetic and more cheerful.

The old feeling of insecurity, especially with regard to my children, often threw its dark shadow across my sunshine. Mrs. Bruce offered me a home for Ellen; but pleasant as it would have been, I did not dare to accept it, for fear of

offending the Hobbs family. Their knowledge of my precarious situation placed me in their power; and I felt that it
was important for me to keep on the right side of them, till,
by dint of labor and economy, I could make a home for my
children. I was far from feeling satisfied with Ellen's situation. She was not well cared for. She sometimes came to
New York to visit me; but she generally brought a request
from Mrs. Hobbs that I would buy her a pair of shoes, or
some article of clothing. This was accompanied by a promise of payment when Mr. Hobbs's salary at the Custom
House became due; but some how or other the pay-day
never came. Thus many dollars of my earnings were expended to keep my child comfortably clothed. That, however, was a slight trouble, compared with the fear that their
pecuniary embarrassments might induce them to sell my
precious young daughter. I knew they were in constant
communication with Southerners, and had frequent opportunities to do it. I have stated that when Dr. Flint put Ellen
in jail, at two years old, she had an inflammation of the eyes,
occasioned by measles. This disease still troubled her; and
kind Mrs. Bruce proposed that she should come to New
York for a while, to be under the care of Dr. Elliott, a well
known oculist. It did not occur to me that there was any
thing improper in a mother's making such a request; but
Mrs. Hobbs was very angry, and refused to let her go. Situated as I was, it was not politic to insist upon it. I made no
complaint, but I longed to be entirely free to act a mother's
part towards my children. The next time I went over to
Brooklyn, Mrs. Hobbs, as if to apologize for her anger, told
me she had employed her own physician to attend to Ellen's eyes, and that she had refused my request because she
did not consider it safe to trust her in New York. I accepted
the explanation in silence; but she had told me that my child
belonged to her daughter, and I suspected that her real motive was a fear of my conveying her property away from
her. Perhaps I did her injustice; but my knowledge of Southerners made it difficult for me to feel otherwise.

Sweet and bitter were mixed in the cup of my life, and I
was thankful that it had ceased to be entirely bitter. I loved
Mrs. Bruce's babe. When it laughed and crowed in my face,

and twined its little tender arms confidingly about my neck, it made me think of the time when Benny and Ellen were babies, and my wounded heart was soothed. One bright morning, as I stood at the window, tossing baby in my arms, my attention was attracted by a young man in sailor's dress, who was closely observing every house as he passed. I looked at him earnestly. Could it be my brother William? It *must* be he—and yet, how changed! I placed the baby safely, flew down stairs, opened the front door, beckoned to the sailor, and in less than a minute I was clasped in my brother's arms. How much we had to tell each other! How we laughed, and how we cried, over each other's adventures! I took him to Brooklyn, and again saw him with Ellen, the dear child whom he had loved and tended so carefully, while I was shut up in my miserable den. He staid in New York a week. His old feelings of affection for me and Ellen were as lively as ever. There are no bonds so strong as those which are formed by suffering together.

XXXIV.

THE OLD ENEMY AGAIN.

My young mistress, Miss Emily Flint, did not return any answer to my letter requesting her to consent to my being sold. But after a while, I received a reply, which purported to be written by her younger brother. In order rightly to enjoy the contents of this letter, the reader must bear in mind that the Flint family supposed I had been at the north many years. They had no idea that I knew of the doctor's three excursions to New York in search of me; that I had heard his voice, when he came to borrow five hundred dollars for that purpose; and that I had seen him pass on his way to the steamboat. Neither were they aware that all the particulars of aunt Nancy's death and burial were conveyed to me at the time they occurred. I have kept the letter, of which I herewith subjoin a copy:—

Your letter to sister was received a few days ago. I gather from it that you are desirous of returning to your native place, among your friends and relatives. We were all gratified with the contents of your letter; and let me assure you that if any members of the family have had any feeling of resentment towards you, they feel it no longer. We all sympathize with you in your unfortunate condition, and are ready to do all in our power to make you contented and happy. It is difficult for you to return home as a free person. If you were purchased by your grandmother, it is doubtful whether you would be permitted to remain, although it would be lawful for you to do so. If a servant should be allowed to purchase herself, after absenting herself so long from her owners, and return free, it would have an injurious effect. From your letter, I think your situation must be hard and uncomfortable. Come home. You have it in your power to be reinstated in our affections. We would receive you with open arms and tears of joy. You need not apprehend any unkind treatment, as we have not put ourselves to any trouble or expense to get you. Had we done so, perhaps we should feel otherwise. You know my sister was always attached to you, and that you were never treated as a slave. You were never put to hard work, nor exposed to field labor. On the contrary, you were taken into the house, and treated as one of us, and almost as free; and we, at least, felt that you were above disgracing yourself by running away. Believing you may be induced to come home voluntarily has induced me to write for my sister. The family will be rejoiced to see you; and your poor old grandmother expressed a great desire to have you come, when she heard your letter read. In her old age she needs the consolation of having her children round her. Doubtless you have heard of the death of your aunt. She was a faithful servant, and a faithful member of the Episcopal church. In her Christian life she taught us how to live—and, O, too high the price of knowledge, she taught us how to die! Could you have seen us round her death bed, with her mother, all mingling our tears in one common stream, you would have thought the same heartfelt tie existed between a master and his servant, as between a mother and her child. But this subject is too painful to dwell upon. I must bring my letter to a close. If you are contented to stay away from your old grandmother, your child, and the friends who love you, stay where you are. We shall never trouble ourselves to apprehend you. But should you prefer to come home, we will do all that we can to make you happy. If you do not wish to remain in the family, I know that father, by our persuasion, will be induced to let you be purchased by any person you may choose in our community. You will please answer this as soon as possible, and let us know your decision. Sister sends much love to you. In the mean time believe me your sincere friend and well wisher.

This letter was signed by Emily's brother, who was as yet a mere lad. I knew, by the style, that it was not written by a person of his age, and though the writing was disguised, I had been made too unhappy by it, in former years, not to recognize at once the hand of Dr. Flint. O, the hypocrisy of slaveholders! Did the old fox suppose I was goose enough to go into such a trap? Verily, he relied too much on "the stupidity of the African race." I did not return the family of Flints any thanks for their cordial invitation—a remissness for which I was, no doubt, charged with base ingratitude.

Not long afterwards I received a letter from one of my friends at the south, informing me that Dr. Flint was about to visit the north. The letter had been delayed, and I supposed he might be already on the way. Mrs. Bruce did not know I was a fugitive. I told her that important business called me to Boston, where my brother then was, and asked permission to bring a friend to supply my place as nurse, for a fortnight. I started on my journey immediately; and as soon as I arrived, I wrote to my grandmother that if Benny came, he must be sent to Boston. I knew she was only waiting for a good chance to send him north, and, fortunately, she had the legal power to do so, without asking leave of any body. She was a free woman; and when my children were purchased, Mr. Sands preferred to have the bill of sale drawn up in her name. It was conjectured that he advanced the money, but it was not known. At the south, a gentleman may have a shoal of colored children without any disgrace; but if he is known to purchase them, with the view of setting them free, the example is thought to be dangerous to their "peculiar institution," and he becomes unpopular.

There was a good opportunity to send Benny in a vessel coming directly to New York. He was put on board with a letter to a friend, who was requested to see him off to Boston. Early one morning, there was a loud rap at my door, and in rushed Benjamin, all out of breath. "O mother!" he exclaimed, "here I am! I run all the way; and I come all alone. How d'you do?"

O reader, can you imagine my joy? No, you cannot, unless you have been a slave mother. Benjamin rattled away as fast as his tongue could go. "Mother, why don't you bring Ellen here? I went over to Brooklyn to see her, and she felt very bad when I bid her good by. She said, 'O Ben, I wish I was going too.' I thought she'd know ever so much; but she don't know so much as I do; for I can read, and she can't. And, mother, I lost all my clothes coming. What can I do to get some more? I 'spose free boys can get along here at the north as well as white boys."

I did not like to tell the sanguine, happy little fellow how much he was mistaken. I took him to a tailor, and procured a change of clothes. The rest of the day was spent in mutual asking and answering of questions, with the wish constantly repeated that the good old grandmother was with us, and frequent injunctions from Benny to write to her immediately, and be sure to tell her every thing about his voyage, and his journey to Boston.

Dr. Flint made his visit to New York, and made every exertion to call upon me, and invite me to return with him; but not being able to ascertain where I was, his hospitable intentions were frustrated, and the affectionate family, who were waiting for me with "open arms," were doomed to disappointment.

As soon as I knew he was safely at home, I placed Benjamin in the care of my brother William, and returned to Mrs. Bruce. There I remained through the winter and spring, endeavoring to perform my duties faithfully, and finding a good degree of happiness in the attractions of baby Mary, the considerate kindness of her excellent mother, and occasional interviews with my darling daughter.

But when summer came, the old feeling of insecurity

haunted me. It was necessary for me to take little Mary out daily, for exercise and fresh air, and the city was swarming with Southerners, some of whom might recognize me. Hot weather brings out snakes and slaveholders, and I like one class of the venomous creatures as little as I do the other. What a comfort it is, to be free to *say* so!

XXXV.

PREJUDICE AGAINST COLOR.

It was a relief to my mind to see preparations for leaving the city. We went to Albany in the steamboat Knickerbocker. When the gong sounded for tea, Mrs. Bruce said, "Linda, it is late, and you and baby had better come to the table with me." I replied, "I know it is time baby had her supper, but I had rather not go with you, if you please. I am afraid of being insulted." "O no, not if you are with *me*," she said. I saw several white nurses go with their ladies, and I ventured to do the same. We were at the extreme end of the table. I was no sooner seated, than a gruff voice said, "Get up! You know you are not allowed to sit here." I looked up, and, to my astonishment and indignation, saw that the speaker was a colored man. If his office required him to enforce the by-laws of the boat, he might, at least, have done it politely. I replied, "I shall not get up, unless the captain comes and takes me up." No cup of tea was offered me, but Mrs. Bruce handed me hers and called for another. I looked to see whether the other nurses were treated in a similar manner. They were all properly waited on.

Next morning, when we stopped at Troy for breakfast, every body was making a rush for the table. Mrs. Bruce said, "Take my arm, Linda, and we'll go in together." The landlord heard her, and said, "Madam, will you allow your nurse and baby to take breakfast with my family?" I knew this was to be attributed to my complexion; but he spoke courteously, and therefore I did not mind it.

At Saratoga we found the United States Hotel crowded, and Mr. Bruce took one of the cottages belonging to the hotel. I had thought, with gladness, of going to the quiet of the country, where I should meet few people, but here I found myself in the midst of a swarm of Southerners. I looked round me with fear and trembling, dreading to see some one who would recognize me. I was rejoiced to find that we were to stay but a short time.

We soon returned to New York, to make arrangements for spending the remainder of the summer at Rockaway. While the laundress was putting the clothes in order, I took an opportunity to go over to Brooklyn to see Ellen. I met her going to a grocery store, and the first words she said were, "O, mother, don't go to Mrs. Hobbs's. Her brother, Mr. Thorne, has come from the south, and may be he'll tell where you are." I accepted the warning. I told her I was going away with Mrs. Bruce the next day, and would try to see her when I came back.

Being in servitude to the Anglo-Saxon race, I was not put into a "Jim Crow car," on our way to Rockaway, neither was I invited to ride through the streets on the top of trunks in a truck; but every where I found the same manifestations of that cruel prejudice, which so discourages the feelings, and represses the energies of the colored people. We reached Rockaway before dark, and put up at the Pavilion—a large hotel, beautifully situated by the sea-side—a great resort of the fashionable world. Thirty or forty nurses were there, of a great variety of nations. Some of the ladies had colored waiting-maids and coachmen, but I was the only nurse tinged with the blood of Africa. When the tea bell rang, I took little Mary and followed the other nurses. Supper was served in a long hall. A young man, who had the ordering of things, took the circuit of the table two or three times, and finally pointed me to a seat at the lower end of it. As there was but one chair, I sat down and took the child in my lap. Whereupon the young man came to me and said, in the blandest manner possible, "Will you please to seat the little girl in the chair, and stand behind it and feed her? After they have done, you will be shown to the kitchen, where you will have a good supper."

This was the climax! I found it hard to preserve my self-control, when I looked round, and saw women who were nurses, as I was, and only one shade lighter in complexion, eyeing me with a defiant look, as if my presence were a contamination. However, I said nothing. I quietly took the child in my arms, went to our room, and refused to go to the table again. Mr. Bruce ordered meals to be sent to the room for little Mary and I. This answered for a few days; but the waiters of the establishment were white, and they soon began to complain, saying they were not hired to wait on negroes. The landlord requested Mr. Bruce to send me down to my meals, because his servants rebelled against bringing them up, and the colored servants of other boarders were dissatisfied because all were not treated alike.

My answer was that the colored servants ought to be dissatisfied with *themselves,* for not having too much self-respect to submit to such treatment; that there was no difference in the price of board for colored and white servants, and there was no justification for difference of treatment. I staid a month after this, and finding I was resolved to stand up for my rights, they concluded to treat me well. Let every colored man and woman do this, and eventually we shall cease to be trampled under foot by our oppressors.

XXXVI.

THE HAIRBREADTH ESCAPE.

After we returned to New York, I took the earliest opportunity to go and see Ellen. I asked to have her called down stairs; for I supposed Mrs. Hobbs's southern brother might still be there, and I was desirous to avoid seeing him, if possible. But Mrs. Hobbs came to the kitchen, and in-sisted on my going up stairs. "My brother wants to see you," said she, "and he is sorry you seem to shun him. He knows you are living in New York. He told me to say to you that he owes thanks to good old aunt Martha for too many little acts of kindness for him to be base enough to betray her grandchild."

This Mr. Thorne had become poor and reckless long be-fore he left the south, and such persons had much rather go to one of the faithful old slaves to borrow a dollar, or get a good dinner, than to go to one whom they consider an equal. It was such acts of kindness as these for which he professed to feel grateful to my grandmother. I wished he had kept at a distance, but as he was here, and knew where I was, I concluded there was nothing to be gained by trying to avoid him; on the contrary, it might be the means of ex-citing his ill will. I followed his sister up stairs. He met me in a very friendly manner, congratulated me on my escape from slavery, and hoped I had a good place, where I felt happy.

I continued to visit Ellen as often as I could. She, good thoughtful child, never forgot my hazardous situation, but always kept a vigilant lookout for my safety. She never made any complaint about her own inconveniences and troubles; but a mother's observing eye easily perceived that she was not happy. On the occasion of one of my visits I found her unusually serious. When I asked her what was the matter, she said nothing was the matter. But I insisted upon knowing what made her look so very grave. Finally, I ascer-tained that she felt troubled about the dissipation that was continually going on in the house. She was sent to the store very often for rum and brandy, and she felt ashamed to ask for it so often; and Mr. Hobbs and Mr. Thorne drank a great deal, and their hands trembled so that they had to call her to pour out the liquor for them. "But for all that," said she, "Mr. Hobbs is good to me, and I can't help liking him. I feel sorry for him." I tried to comfort her, by telling her that I had laid up a hundred dollars, and that before long I hoped to be able to give her and Benjamin a home, and send them to school. She was always desirous not to add to my trou-bles more than she could help, and I did not discover till years afterwards that Mr. Thorne's intemperance was not the only annoyance she suffered from him. Though he professed too much gratitude to my grandmother to injure any of her descendants, he had poured vile language into the ears of her innocent great-grandchild.

I usually went to Brooklyn to spend Sunday afternoon. One Sunday, I found Ellen anxiously waiting for me near the house. "O, mother," said she, "I've been waiting for you this long time. I'm afraid Mr. Thorne has written to tell Dr. Flint where you are. Make haste and come in. Mrs. Hobbs will tell you all about it!"

The story was soon told. While the children were playing in the grape-vine arbor, the day before, Mr. Thorne came out with a letter in his hand, which he tore up and scattered about. Ellen was sweeping the yard at the time, and having her mind full of suspicions of him, she picked up the pieces and carried them to the children, saying, "I wonder who Mr. Thorne has been writing to."

"I'm sure I don't know, and don't care," replied the oldest of the children; "and I don't see how it concerns you."

"But it does concern me," replied Ellen; "for I'm afraid he's been writing to the south about my mother."

They laughed at her, and called her a silly thing, but good-naturedly put the fragments of writing together, in order to read them to her. They were no sooner arranged, than the little girl exclaimed, "I declare, Ellen, I believe you are right."

The contents of Mr. Thorne's letter, as nearly as I can remember, were as follows: "I have seen your slave, Linda, and conversed with her. She can be taken very easily, if you manage prudently. There are enough of us here to swear to her identity as your property. I am a patriot, a lover of my country, and I do this as an act of justice to the laws." He concluded by informing the doctor of the street and number where I lived. The children carried the pieces to Mrs. Hobbs, who immediately went to her brother's room for an explanation. He was not to be found. The servants said they saw him go out with a letter in his hand, and they supposed he had gone to the post office. The natural inference was, that he had sent to Dr. Flint a copy of those fragments. When he returned, his sister accused him of it, and he did not deny the charge. He went immediately to his room, and the next morning he was missing. He had gone over to New York, before any of the family were astir.

It was evident that I had no time to lose; and I hastened back to the city with a heavy heart. Again I was to be torn from a comfortable home, and all my plans for the welfare of my children were to be frustrated by that demon Slavery! I now regretted that I never told Mrs. Bruce my story. I had not concealed it merely on account of being a fugitive; that would have made her anxious, but it would have excited sympathy in her kind heart. I valued her good opinion, and I was afraid of losing it, if I told her all the particulars of my sad story. But now I felt that it was necessary for her to know how I was situated. I had once left her abruptly, without explaining the reason, and it would not be proper to do it again. I went home resolved to tell her in the morning. But the sadness of my face attracted her attention, and, in answer to her kind inquiries, I poured out my full heart to her, before bed time. She listened with true womanly sympathy, and told me she would do all she could to protect me. How my heart blessed her!

Early the next morning, Judge Vanderpool and Lawyer Hopper were consulted. They said I had better leave the city at once, as the risk would be great if the case came to trial. Mrs. Bruce took me in a carriage to the house of one of her friends, where she assured me I should be safe until my brother could arrive, which would be in a few days. In the interval my thoughts were much occupied with Ellen. She was mine by birth, and she was also mine by Southern law, since my grandmother held the bill of sale that made her so. I did not feel that she was safe unless I had her with me. Mrs. Hobbs, who felt badly about her brother's treachery, yielded to my entreaties, on condition that she should return in ten days. I avoided making any promise. She came to me clad in very thin garments, all outgrown, and with a school satchel on her arm, containing a few articles. It was late in October, and I knew the child must suffer; and not daring to go out in the streets to purchase any thing, I took off my own flannel skirt and converted it into one for her. Kind Mrs. Bruce came to bid me good by, and when she saw that I had taken off my clothing for my child, the tears came to her eyes. She said, "Wait for me, Linda," and went out. She soon returned with a nice warm shawl and hood for Ellen. Truly, of such souls as hers are the kingdom of heaven.

My brother reached New York on Wednesday. Lawyer Hopper advised us to go to Boston by the Stonington route, as there was less Southern travel in that direction. Mrs. Bruce directed her servants to tell all inquirers that I formerly lived there, but had gone from the city.

We reached the steamboat Rhode Island in safety. That boat employed colored hands, but I knew that colored passengers were not admitted to the cabin. I was very desirous for the seclusion of the cabin, not only on account of exposure to the night air, but also to avoid observation. Lawyer Hopper was waiting on board for us. He spoke to the stewardess, and asked, as a particular favor, that she would treat us well. He said to me, "Go and speak to the captain yourself by and by. Take your little girl with you, and I am sure that he will not let her sleep on deck." With these kind words and a shake of the hand he departed.

The boat was soon on her way, bearing me rapidly from the friendly home where I had hoped to find security and rest. My brother had left me to purchase the tickets, thinking that I might have better success than he would. When the stewardess came to me, I paid what she asked, and she gave me three tickets with clipped corners. In the most unsophisticated manner I said, "You have made a mistake; I asked you for cabin tickets. I cannot possibly consent to sleep on deck with my little daughter." She assured me there was no mistake. She said on some of the routes colored people were allowed to sleep in the cabin, but not on this route, which was much travelled by the wealthy. I asked her to show me to the captain's office, and she said she would after tea. When the time came, I took Ellen by the hand and went to the captain, politely requesting him to change our tickets, as we should be very uncomfortable on deck. He said it was contrary to their custom, but he would see that we had berths below; he would also try to obtain comfortable seats for us in the cars; of that he was not certain, but he would speak to the conductor about it, when the boat arrived. I thanked him, and returned to the ladies' cabin. He came afterwards and told me that the conductor of the cars was on board, that he had spoken to him, and he had promised to take care of us. I was very much surprised at receiving so much kindness. I don't know whether the pleasing face of my little girl had won his heart, or whether the stewardess inferred from Lawyer Hopper's manner that I was a fugitive, and had pleaded with him in my behalf.

When the boat arrived at Stonington, the conductor kept his promise, and showed us to seats in the first car, nearest the engine. He asked us to take seats next the door, but as he passed through, we ventured to move on toward the other end of the car. No incivility was offered us, and we reached Boston in safety.

The day after my arrival was one of the happiest of my life. I felt as if I was beyond the reach of the bloodhounds; and, for the first time during many years, I had both my children together with me. They greatly enjoyed their reunion, and laughed and chatted merrily. I watched them with a swelling heart. Their every motion delighted me.

I could not feel safe in New York, and I accepted the offer of a friend, that we should share expenses and keep house together. I represented to Mrs. Hobbs that Ellen must have some schooling, and must remain with me for that purpose. She felt ashamed of being unable to read or spell at her age, so instead of sending her to school with Benny, I instructed her myself till she was fitted to enter an intermediate school. The winter passed pleasantly, while I was busy with my needle, and my children with their books.

XXXVII.

A VISIT TO ENGLAND.

In the spring, sad news came to me. Mrs. Bruce was dead. Never again, in this world, should I see her gentle face, or hear her sympathizing voice. I had lost an excellent friend, and little Mary had lost a tender mother. Mr. Bruce wished the child to visit some of her mother's relatives in England, and he was desirous that I should take charge of her. The little motherless one was accustomed to me, and attached to me, and I thought she would be happier in my care than in that of a stranger. I could also earn more in this way than I could by my needle. So I put Benny to a trade, and left Ellen to remain in the house with my friend and go to school.

We sailed from New York, and arrived in Liverpool after a pleasant voyage of twelve days. We proceeded directly to London, and took lodgings at the Adelaide Hotel. The supper seemed to me less luxurious than those I had seen in American hotels; but my situation was indescribably more pleasant. For the first time in my life I was in a place where I was treated according to my deportment, without reference to my complexion. I felt as if a great millstone had been lifted from my breast. Ensconced in a pleasant room, with my dear little charge, I laid my head on my pillow, for the first time, with the delightful consciousness of pure, unadulterated freedom.

As I had constant care of the child, I had little opportunity to see the wonders of that great city; but I watched the tide of life that flowed through the streets, and found it a strange contrast to the stagnation in our Southern towns. Mr. Bruce took his little daughter to spend some days with friends in Oxford Crescent, and of course it was necessary for me to accompany her. I had heard much of the systematic method of English education, and I was very desirous that my dear Mary should steer straight in the midst of so much propriety. I closely observed her little playmates and their nurses, being ready to take any lessons in the science of good management. The children were more rosy than American children, but I did not see that they differed materially in other respects. They were like all children—sometimes docile and sometimes wayward.

We next went to Steventon, in Berkshire. It was a small town, said to be the poorest in the county. I saw men working in the fields for six shillings, and seven shillings, a week, and women for sixpence, and sevenpence, a day, out of which they boarded themselves. Of course they lived in the most primitive manner; it could not be otherwise, where a woman's wages for an entire day were not sufficient to buy a pound of meat. They paid very low rents, and their clothes were made of the cheapest fabrics, though much better than could have been procured in the United States for the same money. I had heard much about the oppression of the poor in Europe. The people I saw around me were, many of them, among the poorest poor. But when I visited them in their little thatched cottages, I felt that the condition of even the meanest and most ignorant among them was vastly superior to the condition of the most favored slaves in America. They labored hard; but they were not ordered out to toil while the stars were in the sky, and driven and slashed by an overseer, through heat and cold, till the stars shone out again. Their homes were very humble; but they were protected by law. No insolent patrols could come, in the dead of night, and flog them at their pleasure. The father, when he closed his cottage door, felt safe with his family around him. No master or overseer could come and take from him his wife, or his daughter. They must separate to earn their living; but the parents knew where their children were going, and could communicate with them by letters. The relations of husband and wife, parent and child, were too sacred for the richest noble in the land to violate with impunity. Much was being done to enlighten these poor people. Schools were established among them, and benevolent societies were active in efforts to ameliorate their condition. There was no law forbidding them to learn to read and write; and if they helped each other in spelling out the Bible, they were in no danger of thirty-nine lashes, as was the case with myself and poor, pious, old uncle Fred. I repeat that the most ignorant and the most destitute of these peasants was a thousand fold better off than the most pampered American slave.

I do not deny that the poor are oppressed in Europe. I am not disposed to paint their condition so rose-colored as the Hon. Miss Murray paints the condition of the slaves in the United States. A small portion of *my* experience would enable her to read her own pages with anointed eyes. If she were to lay aside her title, and, instead of visiting among the fashionable, become domesticated, as a poor governess, on some plantation in Louisiana or Alabama, she would see and hear things that would make her tell quite a different story.

My visit to England is a memorable event in my life, from the fact of my having there received strong religious impressions. The contemptuous manner in which the communion had been administered to colored people, in my native place; the church membership of Dr. Flint, and others like him; and the buying and selling of slaves, by professed ministers of the gospel, had given me a prejudice against the Episcopal church. The whole service seemed to me a mockery and a sham. But my home in Steventon was in the family of a clergyman, who was a true disciple of Jesus. The beauty of his daily life inspired me with faith in the genuineness of Christian professions. Grace entered my heart, and I knelt at the communion table, I trust, in true humility of soul.

I remained abroad ten months, which was much longer than I had anticipated. During all that time, I never saw the slightest symptom of prejudice against color. Indeed, I entirely forgot it, till the time came for us to return to America.

XXXVIII.

RENEWED INVITATIONS TO GO SOUTH.

We had a tedious winter passage, and from the distance spectres seemed to rise up on the shores of the United States. It is a sad feeling to be afraid of one's native country. We arrived in New York safely, and I hastened to Boston to look after my children. I found Ellen well, and improving at her school; but Benny was not there to welcome me. He had been left at a good place to learn a trade, and for several months every thing worked well. He was liked by the master, and was a favorite with his fellow-apprentices; but one day they accidentally discovered a fact they had never before suspected— that he was colored! This at once transformed him into a different being. Some of the apprentices were Americans, others American-born Irish; and it was offensive to their dignity to have a "nigger" among them, after they had been told that he *was* a "nigger." They began by treating him with silent scorn, and finding that he returned the same, they resorted to insults and abuse. He was too spirited a boy to stand that, and he went off. Being desirous to do something to support himself, and having no one to advise him, he shipped for a whaling voyage. When I received these tidings I shed many tears, and bitterly reproached myself for having left him so long. But I had done it for the best, and now all I could do was to pray to the heavenly Father to guide and protect him.

Not long after my return, I received the following letter from Miss Emily Flint, now Mrs. Dodge:—

In this you will recognize the hand of your friend and mistress. Having heard that you had gone with a family to Europe, I have waited to hear of your return to write to you. I should have answered the letter you wrote to me long since, but as I could not then act independently of my father, I knew there could be nothing done satisfactory to you. There were persons here who were willing to buy you and run the risk of getting you. To this I would not consent. I have always been attached to you, and would not like to see you the slave of another, or have unkind treatment. I am married now, and can protect you. My husband expects to move to Virginia this spring, where we think of settling. I am very anxious that you should come and live with me. If you are not willing to come, you may purchase yourself; but I should prefer having you live with me. If you come, you may, if you like, spend a month with your grandmother and friends, then come to me in Norfolk, Virginia. Think this over, and write as soon as possible, and let me know the conclusion. Hoping that your children are well, I remain your friend and mistress.

Of course I did not write to return thanks for this cordial invitation. I felt insulted to be thought stupid enough to be caught by such professions.

> "Come up into my parlor," said the spider to the fly;
> " 'Tis the prettiest little parlor that ever you did spy."

It was plain that Dr. Flint's family were apprised of my movements, since they knew of my voyage to Europe. I expected to have further trouble from them; but having eluded them thus far, I hoped to be as successful in future. The money I had earned, I was desirous to devote to the education of my children, and to secure a home for them. It seemed not only hard, but unjust, to pay for myself. I could not possibly regard myself as a piece of property. Moreover, I had worked many years without wages, and during that time had been obliged to depend on my grandmother for many comforts in food and clothing. My children certainly belonged to me; but though Dr. Flint had incurred no expense for their support, he had received a large sum of money for them. I knew the law would decide that I was his property, and would probably still give his daughter a claim to my children; but I regarded such laws as the regulations of robbers, who had no rights that I was bound to respect.

The Fugitive Slave Law had not then passed. The judges of Massachusetts had not then stooped under chains to enter her courts of justice, so called. I knew my old master was rather skittish of Massachusetts. I relied on her love of freedom, and felt safe on her soil. I am now aware that I honored the old Commonwealth beyond her deserts.

XXXIX.

THE CONFESSION.

For two years my daughter and I supported ourselves comfortably in Boston. At the end of that time, my brother William offered to send Ellen to a boarding school. It required a great effort for me to consent to part with her, for I had few near ties, and it was her presence that made my two little rooms seem home-like. But my judgment prevailed over my selfish feelings. I made preparations for her departure. During the two years we had lived together I had often resolved to tell her something about her father; but I had never been able to muster sufficient courage. I had a shrinking dread of diminishing my child's love. I knew she must have curiosity on the subject, but she had never asked a question. She was always very careful not to say any thing to remind me of my troubles. Now that she was going from me, I thought if I should die before she returned, she might hear my story from some one who did not understand the palliating circumstances; and that if she were entirely ignorant on the subject, her sensitive nature might receive a rude shock.

When we retired for the night, she said, "Mother, it is very hard to leave you alone. I am almost sorry I am going, though I do want to improve myself. But you will write to me often; won't you, mother?"

I did not throw my arms round her. I did not answer her. But in a calm, solemn way, for it cost me great effort, I said, "Listen to me, Ellen; I have something to tell you!" I recounted my early sufferings in slavery, and told her how nearly they had crushed me. I began to tell her how they had driven me into a great sin, when she clasped me in her arms, and exclaimed, "O, don't, mother! Please don't tell me any more."

I said, "But, my child, I want you to know about your father."

"I know all about it, mother," she replied; "I am nothing to my father, and he is nothing to me. All my love is for you.

I was with him five months in Washington, and he never cared for me. He never spoke to me as he did to his little Fanny. I knew all the time he was my father, for Fanny's nurse told me so; but she said I must never tell any body, and I never did. I used to wish he would take me in his arms and kiss me, as he did Fanny; or that he would sometimes smile at me, as he did at her. I thought if he was my own father, he ought to love me. I was a little girl then, and didn't know any better. But now I never think any thing about my father. All my love is for you." She hugged me closer as she spoke, and I thanked God that the knowledge I had so much dreaded to impart had not diminished the affection of my child. I had not the slightest idea she knew that portion of my history. If I had, I should have spoken to her long before; for my pent-up feelings had often longed to pour themselves out to some one I could trust. But I loved the dear girl better for the delicacy she had manifested towards her unfortunate mother.

The next morning, she and her uncle started on their journey to the village in New York, where she was to be placed at school. It seemed as if all the sunshine had gone away. My little room was dreadfully lonely. I was thankful when a message came from a lady, accustomed to employ me, requesting me to come and sew in her family for several weeks. On my return, I found a letter from brother William. He thought of opening an anti-slavery reading room in Rochester, and combining with it the sale of some books and stationery; and he wanted me to unite with him. We tried it, but it was not successful. We found warm anti-slavery friends there, but the feeling was not general enough to support such an establishment. I passed nearly a year in the family of Isaac and Amy Post, practical believers in the Christian doctrine of human brotherhood. They measure a man's worth by his character, not by his complexion. The memory of those beloved and honored friends will remain with me to my latest hour.

XL.

THE FUGITIVE SLAVE LAW.

My brother, being disappointed in his project, concluded to go to California; and it was agreed that Benjamin should go with him. Ellen liked her school, and was a great favorite there. They did not know her history, and she did not tell it, because she had no desire to make capital out of their sympathy. But when it was accidentally discovered that her mother was a fugitive slave, every method was used to increase her advantages and diminish her expenses.

I was alone again. It was necessary for me to be earning money, and I preferred that it should be among those who knew me. On my return from Rochester, I called at the house of Mr. Bruce, to see Mary, the darling little babe that had thawed my heart, when it was freezing into a cheerless distrust of all my fellow-beings. She was growing a tall girl now, but I loved her always. Mr. Bruce had married again, and it was proposed that I should become nurse to a new infant. I had but one hesitation, and that was my feeling of insecurity in New York, now greatly increased by the passage of the Fugitive Slave Law. However, I resolved to try the experiment. I was again fortunate in my employer. The new Mrs. Bruce was an American, brought up under aristocratic influences, and still living in the midst of them; but if she had any prejudice against color, I was never made aware of it; and as for the system of slavery, she had a most hearty dislike of it. No sophistry of Southerners could blind her to its enormity. She was a person of excellent principles and a noble heart. To me, from that hour to the present, she has been a true and sympathizing friend. Blessings be with her and hers!

About the time that I reentered the Bruce family, an event occurred of disastrous import to the colored people. The slave Hamlin, the first fugitive that came under the new law, was given up by the bloodhounds of the north to the bloodhounds of the south. It was the beginning of a reign of terror to the colored population. The great city rushed on in its whirl of excitement, taking no note of the "short and simple annals of the poor." But while fashionables were listening to the thrilling voice of Jenny Lind in Metropolitan Hall, the thrilling voices of poor hunted colored people went up, in an agony of supplication, to the Lord, from Zion's church. Many families, who had lived in the city for twenty years, fled from it now. Many a poor washerwoman, who, by hard labor, had made herself a comfortable home, was obliged to sacrifice her furniture, bid a hurried farewell to friends, and seek her fortune among strangers in Canada. Many a wife discovered a secret she had never known before—that her husband was a fugitive, and must leave her to insure his own safety. Worse still, many a husband discovered that his wife had fled from slavery years ago, and as "the child follows the condition of its mother," the children of his love were liable to be seized and carried into slavery. Every where, in those humble homes, there was consternation and anguish. But what cared the legislators of the "dominant race" for the blood they were crushing out of trampled hearts?

When my brother William spent his last evening with me, before he went to California, we talked nearly all the time of the distress brought on our oppressed people by the passage of this iniquitous law; and never had I seen him manifest such bitterness of spirit, such stern hostility to our oppressors. He was himself free from the operation of the law; for he did not run from any Slaveholding State, being brought into the Free States by his master. But I was subject to it; and so were hundreds of intelligent and industrious people all around us. I seldom ventured into the streets; and when it was necessary to do an errand for Mrs. Bruce, or any of the family, I went as much as possible through back streets and by-ways. What a disgrace to a city calling itself free, that inhabitants, guiltless of offence, and seeking to perform their duties conscientiously, should be condemned to live in such incessant fear, and have nowhere to turn for protection! This state of things, of course, gave rise to many impromptu vigilance committees. Every colored person, and every friend of their persecuted race, kept their eyes wide open. Every evening I examined the newspapers carefully, to see what Southerners had put up at the hotels. I did this for my own sake, thinking my young mistress and her husband might be among the list; I wished also to give information to others, if necessary; for if many were "running to and fro," I resolved that "knowledge should be increased."

This brings up one of my Southern reminiscences, which I will here briefly relate. I was somewhat acquainted with a slave named Luke, who belonged to a wealthy man in our vicinity. His master died, leaving a son and daughter heirs to his large fortune. In the division of the slaves, Luke was included in the son's portion. This young man became a prey to the vices growing out of the "patriarchal institution," and when he went to the north, to complete his education, he carried his vices with him. He was brought home, deprived of the use of his limbs, by excessive dissipation. Luke was appointed to wait upon his bed-ridden master, whose despotic habits were greatly increased by exasperation at his own helplessness. He kept a cowhide beside him, and, for the most trivial occurrence, he would order his attendant to bare his back, and kneel beside the couch, while he whipped him till his strength was exhausted. Some days he was not allowed to wear any thing but his shirt, in order to be in readiness to be flogged. A day seldom passed without his receiving more or less blows. If the slightest resistance was offered, the town constable was sent for to execute the punishment, and Luke learned from experience how much more the constable's strong arm was to be dreaded than the comparatively feeble one of his master. The arm of his tyrant grew weaker, and was finally palsied; and then the constable's services were in constant requisition. The fact that he was entirely dependent on Luke's care, and was obliged to be tended like an infant, instead of inspiring any gratitude or compassion towards his poor slave, seemed only to increase his irritability and cruelty. As he lay there on his bed, a mere degraded wreck of manhood, he took into his head the strangest freaks of despotism; and if Luke hesitated to submit to his orders, the constable was immediately sent for. Some of these freaks were of a nature too filthy to be repeated. When I fled from the house of bondage, I left poor Luke still chained to the bedside of this cruel and disgusting wretch.

One day, when I had been requested to do an errand for Mrs. Bruce, I was hurrying through back streets, as usual, when I saw a young man approaching, whose face was familiar to me. As he came nearer, I recognized Luke. I always rejoiced to see or hear of any one who had escaped from the black pit; but, remembering this poor fellow's extreme hardships, I was peculiarly glad to see him on Northern soil, though I no longer called it *free* soil. I well remembered what a desolate feeling it was to be alone among strangers, and I went up to him and greeted him cordially. At first, he did not know me; but when I mentioned my name, he remembered all about me. I told him of the Fugitive Slave Law, and asked him if he did not know that New York was a city of kidnappers.

He replied, "De risk ain't so bad for me, as 'tis fur you. 'Cause I runned away from de speculator, and you runned away from de massa. Dem speculators vont spen dar money to come here fur a runaway, if dey ain't sartin sure to put dar hans right on him. An I tell you I's tuk good car 'bout dat. I had too hard times down dar, to let 'em ketch dis nigger."

He then told me of the advice he had received, and the plans he had laid. I asked if he had money enough to take him to Canada. " 'Pend upon it, I hab," he replied. "I tuk car far dat. I'd bin workin all my days fur dem cussed whites, an got no pay but kicks and cuffs. So I tought dis nigger had a right to money nuff to bring him to de Free States. Massa Henry he lib till ebery body vish him dead; an ven he did die, I knowed de debbil would hab him, an vouldn't vant him to bring his money 'long too. So I tuk some of his bills, and put 'em in de pocket of his ole trousers. An ven he was buried, dis nigger ask fur dem ole trousers, an dey gub 'em to me." With a low, chuckling laugh, he added, "You see I didn't *steal* it; dey *gub* it to me. I tell you, I had mighty hard time to keep de speculator from findin it; but he didn't git it."

This is a fair specimen of how the moral sense is educated by slavery. When a man has his wages stolen from him, year after year, and the laws sanction and enforce the theft, how can he be expected to have more regard to honesty than has the man who robs him? I have become somewhat enlightened, but I confess that I agree with poor, ignorant, much-abused Luke, in thinking he had a *right* to that money, as a portion of his unpaid wages. He went to Canada forthwith, and I have not since heard from him.

All that winter I lived in a state of anxiety. When I took the children out to breathe the air, I closely observed the countenances of all I met. I dreaded the approach of summer, when snakes and slaveholders make their appearance. I was, in fact, a slave in New York, as subject to slave laws as I had been in a Slave State. Strange incongruity in a State called free!

Spring returned, and I received warning from the south that Dr. Flint knew of my return to my old place, and was making preparations to have me caught. I learned afterwards that my dress, and that of Mrs. Bruce's children, had been described to him by some of the Northern tools, which slaveholders employ for their base purposes, and then indulge in sneers at their cupidity and mean servility.

I immediately informed Mrs. Bruce of my danger, and she took prompt measures for my safety. My place as nurse could not be supplied immediately, and this generous, sympathizing lady proposed that I should carry her baby away. It was a comfort to me to have the child with me; for the heart is reluctant to be torn away from every object it loves. But how few mothers would have consented to have one of their own babes become a fugitive, for the sake of a poor, hunted nurse, on whom the legislators of the country had let loose the bloodhounds! When I spoke of the sacrifice she was making, in depriving herself of her dear baby, she replied, "It is better for you to have baby with you, Linda; for if they get on your track, they will be obliged to bring the child to me; and then, if there is a possibility of saving you, you shall be saved."

This lady had a very wealthy relative, a benevolent gentleman in many respects, but aristocratic and pro-slavery. He remonstrated with her for harboring a fugitive slave; told her she was violating the laws of her country; and asked her if she was aware of the penalty. She replied, "I am very well aware of it. It is imprisonment and one thousand dollars fine. Shame on my country that it *is* so! I am ready to incur the penalty. I will go to the state's prison, rather than have any poor victim torn from my house, to be carried back to slavery."

The noble heart! The brave heart! The tears are in my eyes while I write of her. May the God of the helpless reward her for her sympathy with my persecuted people!

I was sent into New England, where I was sheltered by the wife of a senator, whom I shall always hold in grateful remembrance. This honorable gentleman would not have voted for the Fugitive Slave Law, as did the senator in "Uncle Tom's Cabin;" on the contrary, he was strongly opposed to it; but he was enough under its influence to be afraid of having me remain in his house many hours. So I was sent into the country, where I remained a month with the baby. When it was supposed that Dr. Flint's emissaries had lost track of me, and given up the pursuit for the present, I returned to New York.

XLI.

FREE AT LAST.

Mrs. Bruce, and every member of her family, were exceedingly kind to me. I was thankful for the blessings of my lot, yet I could not always wear a cheerful countenance. I was doing harm to no one; on the contrary, I was doing all the good I could in my small way; yet I could never go out to breathe God's free air without trepidation at my heart. This seemed hard; and I could not think it was a right state of things in any civilized country.

From time to time I received news from my good old grandmother. She could not write; but she employed others to write for her. The following is an extract from one of her last letters:—

Dear Daughter: I cannot hope to see you again on earth; but I pray to God to unite us above, where pain will no more rack this feeble body of mine; where sorrow and parting from my children will be no more. God has promised these things if we are faithful unto the end. My age and feeble health deprive me of going to church now; but God is with me here at home. Thank your brother for his kindness. Give much love to him, and tell him to remember the Creator in the days of his youth, and strive to meet me in the Father's kingdom. Love to Ellen and Benjamin. Don't neglect him. Tell him for me, to be a good boy. Strive, my child, to train them for God's children. May he protect and provide for you, is the prayer of your loving old mother.

These letters both cheered and saddened me. I was always glad to have tidings from the kind, faithful old friend of my unhappy youth; but her messages of love made my heart yearn to see her before she died, and I mourned over the fact that it was impossible. Some months after I returned from my flight to New England, I received a letter from her, in which she wrote, "Dr. Flint is dead. He has left a distressed family. Poor old man! I hope he made his peace with God."

I remembered how he had defrauded my grandmother of the hard earnings she had loaned; how he had tried to cheat her out of the freedom her mistress had promised her, and how he had persecuted her children; and I thought to myself that she was a better Christian than I was, if she could entirely forgive him. I cannot say, with truth, that the news of my old master's death softened my feelings towards him. There are wrongs which even the grave does not bury. The man was odious to me while he lived, and his memory is odious now.

His departure from this world did not diminish my danger. He had threatened my grandmother that his heirs should hold me in slavery after he was gone; that I never should be free so long as a child of his survived. As for Mrs. Flint, I had seen her in deeper afflictions than I supposed the loss of her husband would be, for she had buried several children; yet I never saw any signs of softening in her heart.

The doctor had died in embarrassed circumstances, and had little to will to his heirs, except such property as he was unable to grasp. I was well aware what I had to expect from the family of Flints; and my fears were confirmed by a letter from the south, warning me to be on my guard, because Mrs. Flint openly declared that her daughter could not afford to lose so valuable a slave as I was.

I kept close watch of the newspapers for arrivals; but one Saturday night, being much occupied, I forgot to examine the Evening Express as usual. I went down into the parlor for it, early in the morning, and found the boy about to kindle a fire with it. I took it from him and examined the list of arrivals. Reader, if you have never been a slave, you cannot imagine the acute sensation of suffering at my heart, when I read the names of Mr. and Mrs. Dodge, at a hotel in Courtland Street. It was a third-rate hotel, and that circumstance convinced me of the truth of what I had heard, that they were short of funds and had need of my value, as *they* valued me; and that was by dollars and cents. I hastened with the paper to Mrs. Bruce. Her heart and hand were always open to every one in distress, and she always warmly sympathized with mine. It was impossible to tell how near the enemy was. He might have passed and repassed the house while we were sleeping. He might at that moment be waiting to pounce upon me if I ventured out of doors. I had never seen the husband of my young mistress, and therefore I could not distinguish him from any other stranger. A carriage was hastily ordered; and, closely veiled, I followed Mrs. Bruce, taking the baby again with me into exile. After various turnings and crossings, and returnings, the carriage stopped at the house of one of Mrs. Bruce's friends, where I was kindly received. Mrs. Bruce returned immediately, to instruct the domestics what to say if any one came to inquire for me.

It was lucky for me that the evening paper was not burned up before I had a chance to examine the list of arrivals. It was not long after Mrs. Bruce's return to her house, before several people came to inquire for me. One inquired for me, another asked for my daughter Ellen, and another said he had a letter from my grandmother, which he was requested to deliver in person.

They were told, "She *has* lived here, but she has left."

"How long ago?"

"I don't know, sir."

"Do you know where she went?"

"I do not, sir." And the door was closed.

This Mr. Dodge, who claimed me as his property, was originally a Yankee peddler in the south; then he became a merchant, and finally a slaveholder. He managed to get introduced into what was called the first society, and married Miss Emily Flint. A quarrel arose between him and her brother, and the brother cowhided him. This led to a family feud, and he proposed to remove to Virginia. Dr. Flint left him no property, and his own means had become circumscribed, while a wife and children depended upon him for support. Under these circumstances, it was very natural that he should make an effort to put me into his pocket.

I had a colored friend, a man from my native place, in whom I had the most implicit confidence. I sent for him, and told him that Mr. and Mrs. Dodge had arrived in New York. I proposed that he should call upon them to make inquiries about his friends at the south, with whom Dr. Flint's family were well acquainted. He thought there was no impropriety in his doing so, and he consented. He went to the hotel, and knocked at the door of Mr. Dodge's room, which was opened by the gentleman himself, who gruffly inquired, "What brought you here? How came you to know I was in the city?"

"Your arrival was published in the evening papers, sir; and I called to ask Mrs. Dodge about my friends at home. I didn't suppose it would give any offence."

"Where's that negro girl, that belongs to my wife?"

"What girl, sir?"

"You know well enough. I mean Linda, that ran away from Dr. Flint's plantation, some years ago. I dare say you've seen her, and know where she is."

"Yes, sir, I've seen her, and know where she is. She is out of your reach, sir."

"Tell me where she is, or bring her to me, and I will give her a chance to buy her freedom."

"I don't think it would be of any use, sir. I have heard her say she would go to the ends of the earth, rather than pay any man or woman for her freedom, because she thinks she has a right to it. Besides, she couldn't do it, if she would, for she has spent her earnings to educate her children."

This made Mr. Dodge very angry, and some high words passed between them. My friend was afraid to come where I was; but in the course of the day I received a note from him. I supposed they had not come from the south, in the winter, for a pleasure excursion; and now the nature of their business was very plain.

Mrs. Bruce came to me and entreated me to leave the city the next morning. She said her house was watched, and it was possible that some clew to me might be obtained. I refused to take her advice. She pleaded with an earnest tenderness, that ought to have moved me; but I was in a bitter, disheartened mood. I was weary of flying from pillar to post. I had been chased during half my life, and it seemed as if the chase was never to end. There I sat, in that great city, guiltless of crime, yet not daring to worship God in any of the churches. I heard the bells ringing for afternoon service, and, with contemptuous sarcasm, I said, "Will the preachers take for their text, 'Proclaim liberty to the captive, and the opening of prison doors to them that are bound'? or will they preach from the text, 'Do unto others as ye would they should do unto you'?" Oppressed Poles and Hungarians could find a safe refuge in that city; John Mitchell was free to proclaim in the City Hall his desire for "a plantation well stocked with slaves;" but there I sat, an oppressed American, not daring to show my face. God forgive the black and bitter thoughts I indulged on that Sabbath day! The Scripture says, "Oppression makes even a wise man mad;" and I was not wise.

I had been told that Mr. Dodge said his wife had never signed away her right to my children, and if he could not get me, he would take them. This it was, more than any thing else, that roused such a tempest in my soul. Benjamin was with his uncle William in California, but my innocent young daughter had come to spend a vacation with me. I thought of what I had suffered in slavery at her age, and my heart was like a tiger's when a hunter tries to seize her young.

Dear Mrs. Bruce! I seem to see the expression of her face, as she turned away discouraged by my obstinate mood.

Finding her expostulations unavailing, she sent Ellen to entreat me. When ten o'clock in the evening arrived and Ellen had not returned, this watchful and unwearied friend became anxious. She came to us in a carriage, bringing a well-filled trunk for my journey—trusting that by this time I would listen to reason. I yielded to her, as I ought to have done before.

The next day, baby and I set out in a heavy snow storm, bound for New England again. I received letters from the City of Iniquity, addressed to me under an assumed name. In a few days one came from Mrs. Bruce, informing me that my new master was still searching for me, and that she intended to put an end to this persecution by buying my freedom. I felt grateful for the kindness that prompted this offer, but the idea was not so pleasant to me as might have been expected. The more my mind had become enlightened, the more difficult it was for me to consider myself an article of property; and to pay money to those who had so grievously oppressed me seemed like taking from my sufferings the glory of triumph. I wrote to Mrs. Bruce, thanking her, but saying that being sold from one owner to another seemed too much like slavery; that such a great obligation could not be easily cancelled; and that I preferred to go to my brother in California.

Without my knowledge, Mrs. Bruce employed a gentleman in New York to enter into negotiations with Mr. Dodge. He proposed to pay three hundred dollars down, if Mr. Dodge would sell me, and enter into obligations to relinquish all claim to me or my children forever after. He who called himself my master said he scorned so small an offer for such a valuable servant. The gentleman replied, "You can do as you choose, sir. If you reject this offer you will never get any thing; for the woman has friends who will convey her and her children out of the country."

Mr. Dodge concluded that "half a loaf was better than no bread," and he agreed to the proffered terms. By the next mail I received this brief letter from Mrs. Bruce: "I am rejoiced to tell you that the money for your freedom has been paid to Mr. Dodge. Come home to-morrow. I long to see you and my sweet babe."

My brain reeled as I read these lines. A gentleman near

me said, "It's true; I have seen the bill of sale." "The bill of sale!" Those words struck me like a blow. So I was *sold* at last! A human being *sold* in the free city of New York! The bill of sale is on record, and future generations will learn from it that women were articles of traffic in New York, late in the nineteenth century of the Christian religion. It may hereafter prove a useful document to antiquaries, who are seeking to measure the progress of civilization in the United States. I well know the value of that bit of paper; but much as I love freedom, I do not like to look upon it. I am deeply grateful to the generous friend who procured it, but I despise the miscreant who demanded payment for what never rightfully belonged to him or his.

I had objected to having my freedom bought, yet I must confess that when it was done I felt as if a heavy load had been lifted from my weary shoulders. When I rode home in the cars I was no longer afraid to unveil my face and look at people as they passed. I should have been glad to have met Daniel Dodge himself; to have had him see me and know me, that he might have mourned over the untoward circumstances which compelled him to sell me for three hundred dollars.

When I reached home, the arms of my benefactress were thrown round me, and our tears mingled. As soon as she could speak, she said, "O Linda, I'm so glad it's all over! You wrote to me as if you thought you were going to be transferred from one owner to another. But I did not buy you for your services. I should have done just the same, if you had been going to sail for California to-morrow. I should, at least, have the satisfaction of knowing that you left me a free woman."

My heart was exceedingly full. I remembered how my poor father had tried to buy me, when I was a small child, and how he had been disappointed. I hoped his spirit was rejoicing over me now. I remembered how my good old grandmother had laid up her earnings to purchase me in later years, and how often her plans had been frustrated. How that faithful, loving old heart would leap for joy, if she could look on me and my children now that we were free! My relatives had been foiled in all their efforts, but God had raised me up a friend among strangers, who had bestowed on me the precious, long-desired boon. Friend! It is a common word, often lightly used. Like other good and beautiful things, it may be tarnished by careless handling; but when I speak of Mrs. Bruce as my friend, the word is sacred.

My grandmother lived to rejoice in my freedom; but not long after, a letter came with a black seal. She had gone "where the wicked cease from troubling, and the weary are at rest."

Time passed on, and a paper came to me from the south, containing an obituary notice of my uncle Phillip. It was the only case I ever knew of such an honor conferred upon a colored person. It was written by one of his friends, and contained these words: "Now that death has laid him low, they call him a good man and a useful citizen; but what are eulogies to the black man, when the world has faded from his vision? It does not require man's praise to obtain rest in God's kingdom." So they called a colored man a *citizen*! Strange words to be uttered in that region!

Reader, my story ends with freedom; not in the usual way, with marriage. I and my children are now free! We are as free from the power of slaveholders as are the white people of the north; and though that, according to my ideas, is not saying a great deal, it is a vast improvement in *my* condition. The dream of my life is not yet realized. I do not sit with my children in a home of my own, I still long for a hearthstone of my own, however humble. I wish it for my children's sake far more than for my own. But God so orders circumstances as to keep me with my friend Mrs. Bruce. Love, duty, gratitude, also bind me to her side. It is a privilege to serve her who pities my oppressed people, and who has bestowed the inestimable boon of freedom on me and my children.

It has been painful to me, in many ways, to recall the dreary years I passed in bondage. I would gladly forget them if I could. Yet the retrospection is not altogether without solace; for with those gloomy recollections come tender memories of my good old grandmother, like light, fleecy clouds floating over a dark and troubled sea.

APPENDIX.

THE following statement is from Amy Post, a member of the Society of Friends in the State of New York, well known and highly respected by friends of the poor and the oppressed. As has been already stated, in the preceding pages, the author of this volume spent some time under her hospitable roof.

L. M. C.

The author of this book is my highly-esteemed friend. If its readers knew her as I know her, they could not fail to be deeply interested in her story. She was a beloved inmate of our family nearly the whole of the year 1849. She was introduced to us by her affectionate and conscientious brother, who had previously related to us some of the almost incredible events in his sister's life. I immediately became much interested in Linda; for her appearance was prepossessing, and her deportment indicated remarkable delicacy of feeling and purity of thought.

As we became acquainted, she related to me, from time to time, some of the incidents in her bitter experiences as a slave-woman. Though impelled by a natural craving for human sympathy, she passed through a baptism of suffering, even in recounting her trials to me, in private confidential conversations. The burden of these memories lay heavily upon her spirit—naturally virtuous and refined. I repeatedly urged her to consent to the publication of her narrative; for I felt that it would arouse people to a more earnest work for the disinthralment of millions still remaining in that soul-crushing condition, which was so unendurable to her. But her sensitive spirit shrank from publicity. She said, "You know a woman can whisper her cruel wrongs in the ear of a dear friend much easier than she can record them for the world to read." Even in talking with me, she wept so much, and seemed to suffer such mental agony, that I felt her story was too sacred to be drawn from her by inquisitive questions, and I left her free to tell as much, or as little, as she chose. Still, I urged upon her the duty of publishing her experience, for the sake of the good it might do; and, at last, she undertook the task.

Having been a slave so large a portion of her life, she is unlearned; she is obliged to earn her living by her own labor, and she has worked untiringly to procure education for her children; several times she has been obliged to leave her employments, in order to fly from the man-hunters and woman-hunters of our land; but she pressed through all these obstacles and overcame them. After the labors of the day were over, she traced secretly and wearily, by the midnight lamp, a truthful record of her eventful life.

This Empire State is a shabby place of refuge for the oppressed; but here, through anxiety, turmoil, and despair, the freedom of Linda and her children was finally secured, by the exertions of a generous friend. She was grateful for the boon; but the idea of having been *bought* was always galling to a spirit that could never acknowledge itself to be a chattel. She wrote to us thus, soon after the event: "I thank you for your kind expressions in regard to my freedom; but the freedom I had before the money was paid was dearer to me. God gave me that freedom; but man put God's image in the scales with the paltry sum of three hundred dollars. I served for my liberty as faithfully as Jacob served for Rachel. At the end, he had large possessions; but I was robbed of my victory; I was obliged to resign my crown, to rid myself of a tyrant."

Her story, as written by herself, cannot fail to interest the reader. It is a sad illustration of the condition of this country, which boasts of its civilization, while it sanctions laws and customs which make the experiences of the present more strange than any fictions of the past.

AMY POST.

ROCHESTER, N. Y., Oct. 30th, 1859.

The following testimonial is from a man who is now a highly respectable colored citizen of Boston.   L.M.C.

This narrative contains some incidents so extraordinary, that, doubtless, many persons, under whose eyes it may chance to fall, will be ready to believe that it is colored highly, to serve a special purpose. But, however it may be regarded by the incredulous, I know that it is full of living truths. I have been well acquainted with the author from my boyhood. The circumstances recounted in her history are perfectly familiar to me. I knew of her treatment from her master; of the imprisonment of her children; of their sale and redemption; of her seven years' concealment; and of her subsequent escape to the North. I am now a resident of Boston, and am a living witness to the truth of this interesting narrative.

GEORGE W. LOWTHER.

SELECTED BIBLIOGRAPHY

General

Andrews, William L. *African American Autobiography: A Collection of Critical Essays*. Englewood Cliffs, NJ: Prentice Hall, 1993.

——. *To Tell a Free Story: The First Century of Afro-American Autobiography, 1760–1865*. Urbana: University of Illinois Press, 1986.

Archer, Jermaine O. *Antebellum Slave Narratives: Cultural and Political Expressions of Africa*. New York: Routledge, 2009.

Baker, Houston A., Jr. *The Journey Back: Issues in Black Literature and Criticism*. Chicago: University of Chicago Press, 1980.

Beaulieu, Elizabeth Ann. *Black Women Writers and the American Neo-Slave Narrative: Femininity Unfettered*. Westport, CT: Greenwood Press, 1999.

Bland, Sterling L. *African American Slave Narratives: An Anthology*. Westport, CT: Greenwood Press, 2001.

——. *Voices of the Fugitives: Runaway Slave Stories and Their Fictions of Self-Creation*. Contributions to Afro-American and African Studies No. 199. Westport, CT: Greenwood Press, 2000.

Blassingame, John W. *The Slave Community: Plantation Life in the Antebellum South*. New York: Oxford University Press, 1972.

Blight, David W. *A Slave No More: Two Men Who Escaped to Freedom: Including Their Own Narratives of Emancipation*. Orlando, FL: Harcourt, 2007.

Bruce, Dickson D. *The Origins of African American Literature, 1680–1865*. Charlottesville: University Press of Virginia, 2001.

Connor, Kimberly Rae. *Imagining Grace: Liberating Theologies in the Slave Narrative Tradition*. Urbana: University of Illinois Press, 2000.

Costanzo, Angelo. *Surprising Narrative: Olaudah Equiano and the Beginnings of Black Autobiography. Contributions to Afro-American and African Studies* No. 104. New York: Greenwood Press, 1987.

Davis, Charles H. and Henry Louis Gates Jr., eds. *The Slave's Narrative.* New York: Oxford University Press, 1985.

Drexler, Michael J., and Ed White. *Beyond Douglass: New Perspectives on Early African-American Literature.* Lewisburg, PA: Bucknell University Press, 2008.

Escott, Paul D. *Slavery Remembered: A Record of Twentieth-Century Slave Narratives.* Chapel Hill: University of North Carolina Press, 1979.

Fisch, Audrey A. *The Cambridge Companion to the African American Slave Narrative.* Cambridge: Cambridge University Press, 2007.

Fisher, Dexter, and Robert B. Stepto, eds. *Afro-American Literature.* New York: Modern Language Association, 1979.

Fleischner, Jennifer. *Mastering Slavery: Memory, Family, and Identity in Women's Slave Narratives.* New York: New York University Press, 1996.

Foster, Frances Smith. *Witnessing Slavery: The Development of Ante-Bellum Slave Narratives.* Madison: University of Wisconsin Press, 1994.

Fulton, DoVeanna S. *Speaking Power: Black Feminist Orality in Women's Narratives of Slavery.* Albany: State University of New York Press, 2006.

Gates, Henry Louis, Jr. "The Trope of the Talking Book." In *The Signifying Monkey: A Theory of African-American Literary Criticism.* Oxford: Oxford University Press, 1988. 127–69.

Gray, James L. "Culture, Gender, and the Slave Narrative." *Proteus: A Journal of Ideas* 7.1 (Spring 1990): 37–42.

Hamilton, Cynthia S. "Revisions, Rememories and Exorcisms: Toni Morrison and the Slave Narrative." *Journal of American Studies* 30 (1996): 429–45.

Harris, Sharon M. "Early American Slave Narratives and the Reconfiguration of Place." *Journal of the American Studies Association of Texas* 21 (October 1990):15–23.

Heglar, Charles J. *Rethinking the Slave Narrative: Slave Marriage and the Narratives of Henry Bibb and William and*

Ellen Craft. Contributions to Afro-American and African Studies No. 204. Westport, CT: Greenwood Press, 2001.

Hopkins, Dwight N., and George C. L. Cummings. *Cut Loose Your Stammering Tongue: Black Theology in the Slave Narratives.* 2nd ed. Louisville, KY: Westminster John Knox Press, 2003.

James, Joy. *The New Abolitionists: (Neo)Slave Narratives and Contemporary Prison Writings.* Albany: State University of New York Press, 2005.

Jorif, Rolando Leodore. *How Slave Narratives Influenced American Literature: A Source for Herman Melville's Billy Budd.* Lewiston, NY: Edwin Mellen Press, 2009.

Lee, Julia Sun-Joo. *The American Slave Narrative and the Victorian Novel.* New York: Oxford University Press, 2010.

Li, Stephanie. *Something Akin to Freedom: The Choice of Bondage in Narratives by African American Women.* Albany: State University of New York Press, 2010.

McBride, Dwight A. *Impossible Witnesses: Truth, Abolitionism, and Slave Testimony.* New York: New York University Press, 2001.

Misrahi-Barak, Judith, ed. *Revisiting Slave Narratives.* Montpellier, France: Université Paul-Valéry-Montpellier III, 2005.

——, ed. *Revisiting Slave Narratives II. Les Avatars Contemporains des Récits d'Esclaves II.* Montpellier, France: Presses Universitaires de la Méditerranée, 2007.

Nichols, Charles H. *Many Thousand Gone: The Ex-Slaves' Account of Their Bondage and Freedom.* Bloomington: Indiana University Press, 1963.

Rice, Alan J. *Radical Narratives of the Black Atlantic.* New York: Continuum, 2003.

Rushdy, Ashraf H. A. *Neo-Slave Narratives: Studies in the Social Logic of a Literary Form.* New York: Oxford University Press, 1999.

Sekora, John, and Darwin T. Turner, eds. *The Art of the Slave Narrative.* Macomb: Western Illinois University Press, 1982.

Soto Garcia, Isabel. "Form as Ideology: The Antebellum Slave Narrative." In *Popular Texts in English: New Perspectives.* Mora, Lucía and Antonio Ballesteros, eds. Cuenca: Ediciones de la Universidad de Castilla-La Mancha, 2001. 103–11.

Spaulding, A. T. *Re-Forming the Past: History, the Fantastic, and the Postmodern Slave Narrative*. Columbus: Ohio State University Press, 2005.

Starling, Marion Wilson. *The Slave Narrative: Its Place in American History*. 2nd ed. Washington, D.C.: Howard University Press, 1988.

Stepto, Robert B. *From Behind the Veil: A Study of Afro-American Narrative*. Urbana: University of Illinois Press, 1979.

Taylor, Yuval. *I Was Born a Slave: An Anthology of Classic Slave Narratives*. 2 vols. Chicago: Lawrence Hill Books, 1999.

Thomas, Helen. *Romanticism and Slave Narratives: Transatlantic Testimonies*. Cambridge: Cambridge University Press, 2000.

Waters, Carver Wendell. *Voice in the Slave Narratives of Olaudah Equiano, Frederick Douglass, and Solomon Northrup*. Lewiston, NY: Edwin Mellen Press, 2002.

Williams, Roland Leander. *African American Autobiography and the Quest for Freedom. Contributions to Afro-American and African Studies* No. 191. Westport, CT: Greenwood Press, 2000.

Winter, Kari J. *Subjects of Slavery, Agents of Change: Women and Power in Gothic Novels and Slave Narratives, 1790–1865*. Athens: University of Georgia Press, 1992.

OLAUDAH EQUIANO

Editions

Allison, Robert J., ed. *The Interesting Narrative of the Life of Olaudah Equiano*. 2nd ed. New York: Palgrave Macmillan, 2006.

Brooks, Joanna, ed. *The Life of Olaudah Equiano: The Interesting Narrative of the Life of Olaudah Equiano, Or Gustavus Vassa, the African*. Chicago: Lakeside Press: R. R. Donnelley & Sons, 2004.

Eversley, Shelley, ed. *The Interesting Narrative of the Life of Olaudah Equiano, Or, Gustavus Vassa, the African*. Modern Library pbk. ed. New York: Modern Library, 2004.

Carretta, Vincent, ed. *The Interesting Narrative and Other Writings.* Rev. ed. New York: Penguin Books, 2003.

Costanzo, Angelo, ed. *The Interesting Narrative of the Life of Olaudah Equiano, Or, Gustavus Vassa, the African.* Peterborough, Ontario: Broadview Press, 2001.

Sollors, Werner, ed. *The Interesting Narrative of the Life of Olaudah Equiano, Or Gustavus Vassa, the African: An Authoritative Text.* 1st ed. New York: W. W. Norton & Co., 2001.

Gates, Henry Louis, Jr., and William L. Andrews, eds. *Pioneers of the Black Atlantic: Five Slave Narratives from the Enlightenment, 1772–1815.* Washington, D.C.: Civita Counterpoint 1998.

Edwards, Paul, ed. *Equiano's Travels. His Autobiography. The Interesting Narrative of Olaudah Equiano, or, Gustavus Vassa, the African.* Oxford: Heinemann, 1996.

Allison, Robert J. *The Interesting Narrative of the Life of Olaudah Equiano.* Boston: Bedford Books of St. Martin's Press, 1995.

Edwards, Paul, ed. *The Interesting Narrative of the Life of Olaudah Equiano, or Gustavus Vassa, the African. Written by Himself.* Harlow and White Plains, NY: Longman, 1989.

Samuels, Wilfred, ed. *The Interesting Narrative of the Life of Olaudah Equiano, or Gustavus Vassa, the African. Written by Himself.* Miami, FL: Mnemosyne Pub. Co., 1988.

Edwards, Paul, ed. *Equiano's Travels: The Interesting Narrative of the Life of Olaudah Equiano or Gustavus Vassa the African.* London: Heinemann, 1967.

Criticism

Acholonu, Catherine Obianuju. *The Igbo Roots of Olaudah Equiano: An Anthropological Research.* Owerri, Nigeria: AFA Publications, 1989.

Anderson, Douglas. "Division Below the Surface: Olaudah Equiano's Interesting Narrative." *Studies in Romanticism* 43.3 (2004): 439–60.

Aravamudan, Srinivas. "Equiano Lite." *Eighteenth-Century Studies* 34.4 (2001): 613–18.

Baker, Houston A., Jr. "Figurations for a New American

Literary History." In *Blues, Ideology, and Afro-American Literature: A Vernacular Theory.* Chicago, IL: University of Chicago Press, 1984.

Boulukos, George E. "Olaudah Equiano & the Eighteenth-Century Debate on Africa." *Eighteenth-Century Studies* 40.2 (2007): 241–55.

Bozeman, Terry S. "Interstices, Hybridity & Identity: Olaudah Equiano and the Discourse of the African Slave Trade." *Studies in the Literary Imagination* 36.2 (2003): 61–70.

Bugg, John. "The Other Interesting Narrative: Olaudah Equiano's Public Book Tour." *PMLA: Publications of the Modern Language Association of America* 121.5 (2006): 1424–42.

Byrd, Alexander X. "Eboe, Country, Nation & Gustavus Vassa's Interesting Narrative." *William & Mary Quarterly* 63.1 (2006): 123–48.

Cameron, Ann. *The Kidnapped Prince: The Life of Olaudah Equiano.* New York: Knopf: Distributed by Random House, 1995.

Carby, Hazel V. "Becoming Modern Racialized Subjects." *Cultural Studies* 23.4 (2009): 624–57.

Carey, Brycchain. "Olaudah Equiano." In Henry Louis Gates, Jr., and Eelyn Brooks Higginbotham, eds. *African American National Biography.* Vol. 3: 191–93. New York: Oxford University Press, 2008.

Carretta, Vincent. "Olaudah Equiano: African British Abolitionist and Founder of the African American Slave Narrative." In *The Cambridge Companion to the African American Slave Narrative.* Fisch, Audrey A., ed. Cambridge: Cambridge University Press, 2007.

——. *Equiano, the African: Biography of a Self-made Man.* Athens: University of Georgia Press, 2005.

——. "A New Letter by Gustavus Vassa, Olaudah Equiano?" *Early American Literature* 39.2 (2004): 355–61.

Collins, Janelle. "Passage to Slavery, Passage to Freedom: Olaudah Equiano & the Sea." *Midwest Quarterly* 47.3 (2006): 209–23.

Doherty, Thomas. "Olaudah Equiano's Journeys: The Geography of a Slave Narrative." *Partisan Review* 64.4 (1997): 572.

Earley, Samantha Manchester. "Writing from the Center or the Margins? Olaudah Equiano's Writing Life Reassessed." *African Studies Review* 46.3 (2003): 1–16.

Edwards, Paul. *Unreconciled Strivings and Ironic Strategies: Three Afro-British Authors of the Georgian Era: Ignatius Sancho, Olaudah Equiano, Robert Wedderburn* Edinburgh: Edinburgh University Press, 1992.

——. "Equiano's Lost Family: 'Master' and 'Father' in *The Interesting Narrative.*" *Slavery and Abolition* 11 (1990): 216–21.

——. "A Descriptive List of Manuscripts in the Cambridgeshire Record Office Relating to the Will of Gustavus Vassa (Olaudah Equiano)." *Research in African Literature* 20 (1989): 473–80.

Elrod, Eileen Razzari. "Moses and the Egyptian: Religious Authority in Olaudah Equiano's Interesting Narrative." *African American Review* 35.3 (2001): 409–25.

Field, Emily Donaldson. "'Excepting Himself': Olaudah Equiano, Native Americans, and the Civilizing Mission." *MELUS*, 2009. 15–38.

Filler, Louis. "Equiano." In *Dictionary of American Negro Biography.* Logan, Rayford W., and Michael R. Winston, eds. New York: W. W. Norton & Co., 1982. 212–13.

Ito, Akiyo. "Olaudah Equiano & the New York Artisans." *Early American Literature* 32.1 (1997): 82–101.

Jane, Wall Hinds. "The Spirit of Trade: Olaudah Equiano's Conversion, Legalism & the Merchant's Life." *African American Review* 32.4 (1998): 635–47.

Johnson, Sylvester A. "Colonialism, Biblical World-Making, and Temporalities in Olaudah Equiano's *Interesting Narrative.*" *Church History* 77.4 (2008): 1003–24.

Kaplan, Sidney. "Olaudah Equiano." In *The Black Presence in the Era of the American Revolution, 1770–1800.* Washington, D.C.: New York Graphic Society and the Smithsonian Institution Press, 1973. 193–207.

Kelleter, Frank. "Ethnic Self-Dramatization & Technologies of Travel in *The Interesting Narrative of the Life of Olaudah Equiano, Or Gustavus Vassa, the African, Written by Himself* (1789)." *Early American Literature* 39.1 (2004): 67–84.

Korieh, Chima J. (Chima Jacob). *Olaudah Equiano and the Igbo World : History, Society and Atlantic Diaspora Connections.* Trenton, NJ: Africa World Press, 2009.

Lovejoy, Paul E. "Autobiography and Memory: Gustavus Vassa, Alias Olaudah Equiano, the African." *Slavery & Abolition* 27.3 (2006): 317–47.

———. "'Freedom Narratives' of Transatlantic Slavery." *Slavery & Abolition* 32.1 (2011): 91–107.

Lowe, Lisa. "Autobiography Out of Empire." *Small Axe: A Caribbean Journal of Criticism* 28 (2009): 98–111.

Marren, Susan. "Between Slavery and Freedom: The Transgressive Self in Olaudah Equiano's Autobiography." *PMLA: Publications of the Modern Language Association*, 108 (Jan. 1993): 94–105.

McBride, Dwight. "Speaking as 'the African': Olaudah Equiano's Moral Argument Against Slavery." In McBride, Dwight A. *Impossible Witnesses: Truth, Abolitionism, and Slave Testimony.* New York: New York University Press, 2001.

Molesworth, Jesse M. "Equiano's Loud Voice: Witnessing the Performance of *The Interesting Narrative*." *Texas Studies in Language and Literature* 48.2 (2006). 123–44.

Murphy, Geraldine. "Olaudah Equino, Accidental Tourist." *Eighteenth-Century Studies* 27.4 (Summer 1994): 551–68.

Orban, Katalin. "Dominant and Submerged Discourses in 'The Life of Olaudah Equiano.'" *African American Review* 27.4 (Winter 1993): 655–64.

Osei-Nyame, Kwadwo. "The Politics of 'Translation' in African Postcolonial Literature: Olaudah Equiano, Ayi Kwei Armah, Toni Morrison, Ama Ata Aidoo, Tayeb Salih and Leila Aboulela." *Journal of African Cultural Studies* 21.1 (2009): 91–103.

Paul, Ronald. "'Whitened My Face, That They Might Not Know Me': Race and Identity in Olaudah Equiano's Slave Narrative." *Journal of Black Studies* 39.6 (2009): 848–64.

Pethers, Matthew J. "Talking Books, Selling Selves: Rereading the Politics of Olaudah Equiano's Interesting Narrative." *American Studies* 48.1 (2007): 101–34.

Potkay, Adam. "Olaudah Equiano and the Art of Spiritual

Autobiography." *Eighteenth-Century Studies* 27.4 (Summer 1994): 677–92.

Pudaloff, Ross J. "No Change Without Purchase: Olaudah Equiano and the Economies of Self and Market." *Early American Literature* 40.3 (2005): 499–527.

Rodgers, Nini. *Equiano and Anti-Slavery in Eighteenth-Century Belfast.* Northern Ireland: Belfast Society in association with the Ulster Historical Foundation, 2000.

Rust, Marion. "The Subaltern As Imperialist: Speaking of Olaudah Equiano." In *Passing and the Fictions of Identity.* Ginsberg, Elaine, ed. Durham, NC: Duke University Press, 1996. 21–36.

Sabino, Robin, and Jennifer Hall. "The Path Not Taken: Cultural Identity in the Interesting Life of Olaudah Equiano." *MELUS* 24.1 (1999): 5–20.

Samuels, Wilfred D. "Olaudah Equiano." In *Dictionary of Literary Biography,* Vol. 50. Harris, Trudier, and Thadious M. Davis, eds. Detroit, MI: Gale Research Company, 1986. 123–29.

Sandiford, Keith. *Measuring the Moment: Strategies of Protest in Eighteenth-Century Afro-English Writing.* London: Associated University Presses, 1988.

Tennenhouse, Leonard. "Is There an Early American Novel?" *Novel: A Forum on Fiction* 40.1 (2006): 5–17.

Thomas, Helen. "Olaudah Equiano's Interesting Narrative." In *Romanticism and Slave Narratives: Transatlantic Testimonies.* Cambridge: Cambridge University Press, 2000.

Waters, Carver Wendell. *Voice in the Slave Narratives of Olaudah Equiano, Frederick Douglass, and Solomon Northrup.* Lewiston, NY: Edwin Mellen Press, 2002.

Walvin, James. *An African's Life: The Life and Times of Olaudah Equiano, 1745–1797.* Washington, D.C.: Cassell, 1998.

Wheeler, Roxann. "Domesticating Equiano's Interesting Narrative." *Eighteenth-Century Studies* 34.4 (Summer 2001): 620–24.

Wiley, Michael. "Consuming Africa: Geography and Identity in Olaudah Equiano's *Interesting Narrative.*" *Studies in Romanticism* 44.2 (2005): 165–80.

MARY PRINCE

Editions

Salih, Sarah, ed. *The History of Mary Prince: A West Indian Slave.* London: Penguin Books, 2000.

Ferguson, Moira, ed. *The History of Mary Prince: A West Indian Slave.* Rev. ed. Ann Arbor: University of Michigan Press, 1997.

——. *The History of Mary Prince, a West Indian Slave.* Ann Arbor: University of Michigan Press, 1993.

Criticism

Aljoe, Nicole N. "Going to Law." *Early American Literature* 46.2 (2011): 351–81.

Andrews, William L. "Six Women's Slave Narratives, 1831–1909." In *Black Women's Slave Narratives.* New York: Oxford University Press, 1987.

Baumgartner, Barbara. "The Body as Evidence." *Callaloo: A Journal of African-American and African Arts and Letters* 24.1 (Winter 2001): 253–75.

Haynes, Rosetta R. "Voice, Body and Collaboration: Constructions of Authority in the History of Mary Prince." *Literary Griot: International Journal of Black Expressive Cultural Studies* 11.1 (1999): 18–32.

Larrabee, Mary Jeanne. "'I Know What a Slave Knows': Mary Prince's Epistemology of Resistance." *Women's Studies: An Interdisciplinary Journal* 35.5 (2006): 453–73.

McBride, Dwight. "'I Know What a Slave Knows': Mary Prince as Witness, or the Rhetorical Uses of Experience." In *Impossible Witnesses: Truth, Abolitionism, and Slave Testimony.* McBride, Dwight A., ed. New York: New York University Press, 2001.

Paquet, Sandra Pouchet. "The Heartbeat of a West Indian Slave: The History of Mary Prince." *African American Review* 26.1 (Spring 1992): 131–46.

Rauwerda, A. M. "Naming, Agency, and 'A Tissue of Falsehoods' in the History of Mary Prince." *Victorian Literature and Culture* 29.2 (2001): 397–411.

Saltus, Roiyah. "Mary Prince's Slave Narrative in the Context of Bermuda, Her 'Native Place' (1788–1815)." *MaComère: Journal of the Association of Caribbean Women Writers and Scholars* 7 (2005): 167–82.

Schroeder, Janice. "'Narrat[ing] Some Poor Little Fable': Evidence of Bodily Pain in the History of Mary Prince and 'Wife-Torture in England'." *Tulsa Studies in Women's Literature* 23.2 (2004): 261–81.

Sharpe, Jenny. "'Something Akin to Freedom': The Case of Mary Prince." *Differences: A Journal of Feminist Cultural Studies* 8.1 (1996): 31–56.

Shum, Matthew. "The Prehistory of the History of Mary Prince: Thomas Pringle's 'The Bechuana Boy'." *Nineteenth-Century Literature* 64.3 (2009): 291–322.

Simmons, K. M. "Beyond 'Authenticity': Migration and the Epistemology of 'Voice' in Mary Prince's *History of Mary Prince* and Maryse Conde's *I, Tituba*." *College Literature* 36.4 (2009): 75–99.

Thomas, Sue. "New Information on Mary Prince in London." *Notes & Queries* 58.1 (2011): 82–85.

——. "Pringle v. Cadell and Wood v. Pringle: The Libel Cases Over the History of Mary Prince." *Journal of Commonwealth Literature* 40.1 (2005): 113–35.

Todorova, Kremena. "'I Will Say the Truth to the English People': The History of Mary Prince and the Meaning of English History." *Texas Studies in Literature and Language* 43.3 (2001): 285–302.

Whitlock, Gillian. "Merry Christmas, Mary Prince." *Biography: An Interdisciplinary Quarterly* 26.3 (2003): 440–42.

FREDERICK DOUGLASS

Editions

Davis, Angela Y., ed. *Narrative of the Life of Frederick Douglass, an American Slave, Written by Himself: A New Critical Edition*. San Francisco: City Lights Books, 2010.

McDowell, Deborah, and John Charles, eds. *Narrative of the Life of Frederick Douglass: An American Slave*. Oxford: Oxford University Press, 2009.

Stepto, Robert, ed. *Narrative of the Life of Frederick Doug-*

lass, an American Slave. Cambridge: Belknap Press of Harvard University Press, 2009.

Gomes, Peter, and Gregory Stephens, eds. *Narrative of the Life of Frederick Douglass: An American Slave*. New York: Signet Classics, 2005.

Fulkerson, Gerald, John Blassingame and John McKivigan, eds. *Narrative of the Life of Frederick Douglass, an American Slave*. New Haven: Yale University Press, 2001.

Foner, Philip, and Yuvel Taylor, eds. *Frederick Douglass: Selected Speeches and Writings*. 1st ed. Chicago: Lawrence Hill Books, 1999.

Andrews, William L., and William McFeely, eds. *Narrative of the Life of Frederick Douglass: An American Slave Written by Himself; Authoritative Text, Contexts, Criticism*. New York: W. W. Norton & Co, 1997.

Andrews, William, L. ed. *The Oxford Frederick Douglass Reader*. New York: Oxford University Press, 1996.

Gates, Henry Louis, Jr. ed. *Douglass: Autobiographies*. New York: Library of America, 1994.

Criticism

Anderson, Douglas. "The Textual Reproductions of Frederick Douglass." *Clio* 27.1 (1997): 57–87.

Andrews, William L. *Critical Essays on Frederick Douglass*. Boston: G. K. Hall, 1991.

Archer, Jermaine O. "'Speaking Guinea and a Mixture of Everything Else': The Slave Narratives of Frederick Douglass Revisited." In Archer, Jermaine O. *Antebellum Slave Narratives: Cultural and Political Expressions of Africa*. New York: Routledge, 2009.

Awkward, Michael. "Negotiations of Power: White Critics, Black Texts, and the Self-Referential Impulse." *American Literary History* 2.4 (Winter 1990): 581–606.

Babb, Valerie. "'The Joyous Circle': The Vernacular Presence in Frederick Douglass's Narratives." *College English* 67.4 (2005): 365–77.

Bacon, Jacqueline. "Taking Liberty, Taking Literacy: Signifying in the Rhetoric of African-American Abolitionists." *Southern Communication Journal* 64.4 (1999): 271–87.

Bailey, Tyshawn, and Calil Yarbrough. "Frederick Douglass: A Light in Darkness." *Black History Bulletin* 69.2 (2006): 4–7.

Barnett, Timothy. "Politicizing the Personal: Frederick Douglass, Richard Wright, and Some Thoughts on the Limits of Critical Literacy." *College English* 68.4 (2006): 356–81.

Bernier, Celeste-Marie. "'Emblems of Barbarism': Black Masculinity and Representations of Toussaint L'Ouverture in Frederick Douglass's Unpublished Manuscripts." *American Nineteenth Century History* 4.3 (2003): 97–120.

Bland, Sterling L. "Authority, Power, and Determination of the Will: The Dilemma of Rhetorical Ownership in Frederick Douglass's *My Bondage and My Freedom* and Harriet Jacobs's *Incidents in the Life of a Slave Girl*." In *Voices of the Fugitives: Runaway Slave Stories and Their Fictions of Self-Creation. Contributions to Afro-American and African Studies* No. 199. Westport, CT: Greenwood Press, 2000.

——. "Behold a Man Transformed": Sacred Language and the Secular Self in Frederick Douglass's *Narrative*." In *Voices of the Fugitives: Runaway Slave Stories and Their Fictions of Self-Creation. Contributions to Afro-American and African Studies* No. 199. Westport, CT: Greenwood Press, 2000.

Blight, David W. *Frederick Douglass and Abraham Lincoln: A Relationship in Language, Politics, and Memory*. Milwaukee, WI: Marquette University Press, 2001.

——. "Up from 'Twoness': Frederick Douglass and the Meaning of W. E. B. Du Bois's Concept of Double Consciousness." *Canadian Review of American Studies* 21.3 (1990): 301–19.

Boxill, Bernard R. "Fear and Shame as Forms of Moral Suasion in the Thought of Frederick Douglass." *Transactions of the Charles S. Peirce Society* 31.4 (1995): 713–44.

——. "Frederick Douglass's Patriotism." *Journal of Ethics* 13.4 (2009): 301–17.

Brawley, Lisa. "Frederick Douglass's *My Bondage and My Freedom* and the Fugitive Tourist Industry." *Novel: A Forum on Fiction* 30.1 (1996): 98–128.

Brewton, Vince. "'Bold Defiance Took Its Place'—'Respect' and Self-Making in *Narrative of the Life of Frederick*

Douglass, an American Slave." *Mississippi Quarterly* 58.3 (2005): 703–17.

Bromell, Nick. "The Liberal Imagination of Frederick Douglass: Honoring the Emotions That Give Life to Liberal Principles." *American Scholar* 77.2 (2008): 34–45.

Buccola, Nicholas. "'Each for All and All for Each': The Liberal Statesmanship of Frederick Douglass." *The Review of Politics* 70.3 (2008): 400–19.

Burke, Ronald K. *Frederick Douglass: Crusading Orator for Human Rights.* New York: Garland Publishing, 1996.

Carter, J. Kameron. "Race, Religion, and the Contradictions of Identity: A Theological Engagement with Douglass's 1845 Narrative." *Modern Theology* 21.1 (2005): 37–65.

Cassuto, Leonard. "Frederick Douglass and the Work of Freedom: Hegel's Master-Slave Dialectic in the Fugitive Slave Narrative." *Prospects: An Annual Journal of American Cultural Studies* 21 (1996): 229–59.

Castronovo, Russ. "'As to Nation, I Belong to None': Ambivalence, Diaspora, and Frederick Douglass." *ATQ* 9.3 (1995): 245–60.

Cohen, Robert. "Was the Constitution Pro-Slavery? The Changing View of Frederick Douglass." *Social Education* 72.5 (2008): 246–50.

Colaiaco, James A. *Frederick Douglass and the Fourth of July.* 1st ed. New York: Palgrave Macmillan, 2006.

Davis, Reginald F. *Frederick Douglass: A Precursor of Liberation Theology.* 1st ed. Macon, GA: Mercer University Press, 2005.

DeLombard, Jeannine. "'Eye-Witness to the Cruelty': Southern Violence and Northern Testimony in Frederick Douglass." *American Literature* 73.2 (2001): 245–75.

Dorsey, Peter A. "Becoming the Other; the Mimesis of Metaphor." *PMLA: Publications of the Modern Language Association of America* 111.3 (1996): 435.

Drake, Kimberly. "Rewriting the American Self: Race, Gender, and Identity in the Autobiographies of Frederick Douglass and Harriet Jacobs." *MELUS* 22.4 (1997): 91–108.

Dunbar-Odom, Donna. "'Mastering' Representation: Rhetorical Constructions of the Life of Frederick Douglass." *Conference of College Teachers of English Studies (CCTEP)* 55 (1995): 26–32.

Dupuy, Edward J. "Linguistic Mastery and the Garden of the Chattel in Frederick Douglass' Narrative." *Mississippi Quarterly* 44.1 (Winter 1990–91): 23–33.

Dworkin, Ira. "Creative Conflict in African American Thought: Frederick Douglass, Alexander Crummell, Booker T. Washington, W. E. B. Du Bois, and Marcus Garvey." *American Literature* 77.2 (2005): 421–24.

Fanuzzi, Robert. "The Trouble with Douglass's Body." *ATQ* 13.1 (1999): 27.

Fichtelberg, Joseph. "The Writer Against Himself: Child and Man in the Autobiographies of Frederick Douglass." *Mid-Hudson Language Studies* 12.1 (1989): 72–80.

Ganter, Granville. "'He Made Us Laugh Some': Frederick Douglass's Humor." *African American Review* 37.4 (2003): 535–52.

Gates, Henry Louis, Jr. "From Wheatley to Douglass: The Politics of Displacement." In Sundquist, Eric J., ed. *Frederick Douglass: New Literary and Historical Essays.* Cambridge: Cambridge University Press, 1990.

——. "The Trope of a New Negro and the Reconstruction of the Image of the Black." *Representations* 24 (Autumn, 1988): 129–155.

——. "Frederick Douglass and the Language of the Self." In *Figures in Black: Words, Signs, and the 'Racial' Self.* Oxford: Oxford University Press, 1987. 98–124.

——. "Binary Oppositions in Chapter One of *Narrative of the Life of Frederick Douglass, an American Slave Written by Himself.*" In *Afro-American Literature: The Reconstruction of Instruction.* Fisher, Dexter and Robert Stepto, eds. New York: *MLA*, 1979. 212–32.

Gibson, Donald B. "Christianity and Individualism: (Re-) Creation and Reality in Frederick Douglass' Representation." *African American Review* 26.4 (1992): 591–603.

Gibson, Donald B. "Reconciling Public and Private in Frederick Douglass' Narrative." *American Literature* 57.4 (1985): 549–69.

Giles, Paul. "Narrative Reversals and Power Exchanges: Frederick Douglass and British Culture." *American Literature* 73.4 (2001): 779–810.

Goddu, Teresa A., and Craig V. Smith. "Scenes of Writing in Frederick Douglass's *Narrative*: Autobiography and the

Creation of Self." *The Southern Review* 25.4 (Autumn 1989): 822–40.

Jay, Gregory S. "American Literature and the New Historicism: The Example of Frederick Douglass." *Boundary 2: An International Journal of Literature and Culture* 17.1 (Spring 1990): 211–42.

Jenkins, Lee. "'The Black O'Connell': Frederick Douglass and Ireland." *Nineteenth Century Studies* 13 (1999): 22–46.

Jones, Paul Christian. "Copying What the Master Had Written: Frederick Douglass's 'The Heroic Slave' and the Southern Historical Romance." *Southern Quarterly* 38.4 (2000): 78–92.

Jorif, Rolando L. "Frederick Douglass's Providential Rediscovery of Africa: Agape." In *How Slave Narratives Influenced American Literature: A Source for Herman Melville's Billy Budd.* Lewiston, NY: Edwin Mellen Press, 2009.

Kibbey, Ann. "Language in Slavery: Frederick Douglass' Narrative." *Prospects: An Annual Journal of American Cultural Studies* 8 (1983): 163–82.

Kohn, Margaret. "Frederick Douglass's Master-Slave Dialectic." *Journal of Politics* 67.2 (2005): 497–514.

Lampe, Gregory P. *Frederick Douglass: Freedom's Voice, 1818–1845.* East Lansing: Michigan State University Press, 1998.

Lawson, Bill E., and Frank Kirkland. *Frederick Douglass: A Critical Reader.* Malden, MA: Blackwell Publishers, 1999.

Lee, Lisa Yun. "The Politics of Language in Frederick Douglass's Narrative." *MELUS* 17.2 (1991): 51–59.

Lee, Maurice S. *The Cambridge Companion to Frederick Douglass.* Cambridge: Cambridge University Press, 2009.

Leverenz, David Frederick. "Douglass's Self-Refashioning." *Criticism: A Quarterly for Literature and the Arts* 29.3 (Summer 1987) 41–70.

Levine, Robert S. "*Uncle Tom's Cabin* in *Frederick Douglass' Paper*: An Analysis of Reception." *American Literature* 64.1 (March 1992): 71–93.

Levine, Robert S., and Samuel Otter. *Frederick Douglass & Herman Melville: Essays in Relation.* Chapel Hill: University of North Carolina Press, 2008.

Lock, Helen. "The Paradox of Slave Mutiny in Herman

Melville, Charles Johnson, and Frederick Douglass." *College Literature* 30.4 (2003): 54–70.

Matterson, Stephen. "Shaped by Readers: The Slave Narratives of Frederick Douglass and Harriet Jacobs." In Kilcup, Karen L. ed. *Soft Canons: American Women Writers and Masculine Tradition.* Iowa City: University of Iowa Press, 1999. 82–96.

Matzke, Jason P. "The John Brown Way: Frederick Douglass and Henry David Thoreau on the Use of Violence." *Massachusetts Review* 46.1 (2005): 62–75.

McBride, Dwight A. "Consider the Audience: Witnessing to the Discursive Reader in Douglass's Narrative." In McBride, Dwight A. *Impossible Witnesses: Truth, Abolitionism, and Slave Testimony.* New York: New York University Press, 2001.

McClure, Kevin R. "Frederick Douglass' Use of Comparison in His Fourth of July Oration: A Textual Criticism." *Western Journal of Communication* 64.4 (2000): 425–44.

McDowell, Deborah. "In the First Place: Making Frederick Douglass and the Afro-American Narrative Tradition." In Andrews, William L. *African American Autobiography: A Collection of Critical Essays.* Englewood Cliffs, NJ: Prentice Hall, 1993.

McFeely, William S. *Frederick Douglass.* New York: W. W. Norton & Co., 1991.

Meer, Sarah. "Sentimentality and the Slave Narrative: Frederick Douglass' *My Bondage and My Freedom.*" In *The Uses of Autobiography.* Swindells, Julia, ed. London: Taylor & Francis, 1995. 89–97.

Mieder, Wolfgang. "'Do Unto Others as You Would Have Them Do Unto You': Frederick Douglass's Proverbial Struggle for Civil Rights." *Journal of American Folklore* 114.453 (2001): 331–57.

Miller, Keith D., and Kevin Quashie. "Slave Mutiny as Argument, Argument as Fiction, Fiction as America: The Case of Frederick Douglass's 'The Heroic Slave.'" *Southern Communication Journal* 63.3 (1998): 199–207.

Morgan, Winifred. "Gender-Related Difference in the Slave Narratives of Harriet Jacobs and Frederick Douglass." *American Studies* 35.2 (Fall 1994): 73–94.

Myers, Peter C. "'A Good Work for Our Race To-Day': Interests, Virtues, and the Achievement of Justice in Frederick Douglass's Freedmen's Monument Speech." *American Political Science Review* 104.2 (2010): 209–25.

——. *Frederick Douglass: Race and the Rebirth of American Liberalism.* Lawrence: University Press of Kansas, 2008.

Noble, Marianne. "Sympathetic Listening in Frederick Douglass's 'The Heroic Slave' and *My Bondage and My Freedom.*" *Studies in American Fiction* 34.1 (2006): 53–68.

Ochieng, Omedi. "A Ruthless Critique of Everything Existing: Frederick Douglass and the Architectonic of African American Radicalism." *Western Journal of Communication* 75.2 (2011): 168–84.

Pratt, Lloyd. "Human Beyond Understanding: Frederick Douglass's New Liberal Individual." *Novel: A Forum on Fiction* 43.1 (2010): 47–52.

Quarles, Benjamin, ed. *Frederick Douglass and the Woman's Rights Movement.* Baltimore: Morgan State Foundation, 1993.

——. *Frederick Douglass.* New York: Da Capo Press, 1997.

——. "Frederick Douglass." In *Dictionary of American Negro Biography.* Logan, Rayford W., and Michael R. Winston, eds. New York: W. W. Norton & Co., 1982. 181–186.

Quinn, John F. "'Safe in Old Ireland': Frederick Douglass's Tour, 1845–1846." *Historian* 64.3 (2002): 535–50.

Ramsey, William M. "Frederick Douglass, Southerner." *Southern Literary Journal* 40.1 (2007): 19–38.

Ray, Angela G. "Frederick Douglass on the Lyceum Circuit: Social Assimilation, Social Transformation?" *Rhetoric & Public Affairs* 5.4 (2002): 625–48.

Rice, Alan J., and Martin Crawford. *Liberating Sojourn: Frederick Douglass & Transatlantic Reform.* Athens: University of Georgia Press, 1999.

Ripley, C. Peter. "The Autobiographical Writings of Frederick Douglass." *Southern Studies* 24.1 (Spring 1985): 5–29.

Rowe, John Carlos. "Between Politics and Poetics: Frederick Douglass and Postmodernity." In *Reconstructing American Literary and Historical Studies.* Lenz, Gunter, H. Hartmut Keil, and Sabine Brock-Sallah, eds. Frankfurt: Campus, 1990. 192–210.

Royer, Daniel J. "The Process of Literacy as Communal Involvement in the Narratives of Frederick Douglass." *African American Review* 28.3 (1994): 363–74.

Sale, Maggie. "To Make the Past Useful: Frederick Douglass' Politics of Solidarity." *Arizona Quarterly* 51.3 (Autumn 1995): 25–60.

Schiller, Ben. "Learning Their Letters: Critical Literacy, Epistolary Culture, and Slavery in the Antebellum South." *Southern Quarterly* 45.3 (2008): 11–29.

Sekora, John. "Comprehending Slavery: Language and Personal History in Douglass' Narrative of 1845." *College Language Association Journal* 29.2 (December 1985): 157–70.

Selby, Gary S. "The Limits of Accommodation: Frederick Douglass and the Garrisonian Abolitionists." *Southern Communication Journal* 66.1 (2000): 52–66.

——. "Mocking the Sacred: Frederick Douglass's 'Slaveholder's Sermon' and the Antebellum Debate Over Religion and Slavery." *Quarterly Journal of Speech* 88.3 (2002): 326–41.

Sisco, Lisa. "'Writing in the Spaces Left': Literacy as a Process of Becoming in the Narratives of Frederick Douglass." *ATQ* 9.3 (1995): 195–232.

Slote, Ben. "Revising Freely: Frederick Douglass and the Politics of Disembodiment." *A/B: Auto/Biography Studies* 11.1 (Spring 1996): 19–37.

Smith, Sidonie. "Performativity, Autobiographical Practice, Resistance." *A/B: Auto/Biography Studies* 10.1 (Spring 1995): 17–33.

Stauffer, John. *Giants: The Parallel Lives of Frederick Douglass and Abraham Lincoln.* New York: Twelve, 2009.

——. "Frederick Douglass's Self-fashioning and the Making of a Representative American Man." In *The Cambridge Companion to the African American Slave Narrative.* Fisch, Audrey A., ed. Cambridge: Cambridge University Press, 2007.

——. "Frederick Douglass and the Aesthetics of Freedom." *Raritan* 25.1 (2005): 114–36.

Stepto, Robert. "Narration, Authentication, and Authorial Control in Frederick Douglass' Narrative of 1845." In Andrews, William L. *African American Autobiography:*

   A Collection of Critical Essays. Englewood Cliffs, NJ: Prentice Hall, 1993.

Stuckey, P. Sterling. "Afterword: Frederick Douglass and W. E. B. Du Bois on the Consciousness of the Enslaved." *Journal of African American History* 91.4 (2006): 451–58.

Sturdevant, Katherine Scott, and Stephen Collin. "Frederick Douglass and Abraham Lincoln on Black Equity in the Civil War: A Historical-Rhetorical Perspective." *Black History Bulletin* 73.2 (2010): 8–15.

Sundquist, Eric J. *Frederick Douglass: New Literary and Historical Essays*. Cambridge: Cambridge University Press, 1990.

——. "Slavery, Revolution, and the American Renaissance." In *The American Renaissance Reconsidered.* Michaels, W. B., and Donald E. Pease, eds. Baltimore: Johns Hopkins University Press, 1985. 1–33.

Sundstrom, Ronald. "Frederick Douglass's Longing for the End of Race." *Philosophia Africana* 8.2 (2005): 143–70.

Sweeney, Fionnghuala. *Frederick Douglass and the Atlantic World.* Liverpool: Liverpool University Press, 2007.

Tang, Edward. "Rebirth of a Nation: Frederick Douglass as Postwar Founder in *Life and Times*." *Journal of American Studies* 39.1 (2005): 19–39.

Terrill, Robert E. "Irony, Silence, and Time: Frederick Douglass on the Fifth of July." *Quarterly Journal of Speech* 89.3 (2003): 216–34.

Thompson, Julius Eric, James Conyers, and Nancy Dawson, eds. *The Frederick Douglass Encyclopedia.* Santa Barbara, CA: Greenwood Press, 2010.

Walter, Krista. "Trappings of Nationalism in Frederick Douglass's 'The Heroic Slave.'" *African American Review* 34.2 (2000): 233–47.

Wardrop, Daneen. "'While I Am Writing': Webster's 1825 Spelling Book, the Ell, and Frederick Douglass's Positioning of Language." *African American Review* 32.4 (1998): 649–60.

Waters, Carver Wendell. *Voice in the Slave Narratives of Olaudah Equiano, Frederick Douglass, and Solomon Northrup*. Lewiston, NY: Edwin Mellen Press, 2002.

Weinauer, Ellen. "Writing Revolt in the Wake of Nat Turner: Frederick Douglass and the Construction of Black Domesticity in 'The Heroic Slave.'" *Studies in American Fiction* 33.2 (2005): 193–202.

Wilson, Ivy G. "On Native Ground: Transnationalism, Frederick Douglass, and 'The Heroic Slave.'" *PMLA: Publications of the Modern Language Association of America* 121.2 (2006): 453–68.

Wohlport, A. J. "Privatized Sentiment and the Institution of Christianity: Douglass's Ethical Stance in the Narrative." *ATQ* 9.3 (1995): 181–95.

Wu, Jin-Ping. *Frederick Douglass and the Black Liberation Movement: The North Star of American Blacks.* New York: Garland, 2000.

Yancy, George. "The Existential Dimensions of Frederick Douglass's Autobiographical Narrative: A Beauvoirian Examination." *Philosophy & Social Criticism* 28.3 (2002): 297–320.

HARRIET JACOBS

Editions

Fleischner, Jennifer, ed. *Incidents in the Life of a Slave Girl: Written by Herself.* Boston: Bedford/St. Martin's, 2010.

Jacobs, John S., and Jean Fagan Yellin, eds. *True Tale of Slavery. Incidents in the Life of a Slave Girl: Written by Herself.* Enlarged ed. Cambridge: Belknap Press of Harvard University Press, 2009.

Child, Lydia Maria, ed. Introduction by Louise Meriwether. *Incidents in the Life of a Slave Girl.* New York: Washington Square Press, 2003.

McKay, Nellie, and Frances Smith Foster, eds. *Incidents in the Life of a Slave Girl: Contexts, Criticism.* New York: W. W. Norton & Co., 2001.

Yellin, Jean, and John S. Jacobs. *Incidents in the Life of a Slave Girl.* Cambridge: Harvard University Press, 2000.

Smith, Valerie, ed. *Incidents in the Life of a Slave Girl.* New York: Oxford University Press, 1988.

Yellin, Jean, ed. *Incidents in the Life of a Slave Girl.* Cambridge: Harvard University Press, 1987.

Criticism

Accomando, Christina." 'The Laws Were Laid Down to Me Anew': Harriet Jacobs and the Reframing of Legal Fictions." *African American Review* 32.2 (1998): 229–45.

Andrews, William L. "The Changing Moral Discourse of Nineteenth-Century African American Women's Autobiography: Harriet Jacobs and Elizabeth Keckley." In *De/Colonizing the Subject: The Politics of Gender in Women's Autobiography*. Smith, Sidonie and Julia Watson, eds. Minneapolis: University of Minnesota Press, 1992. 225–41.

Anonymous. "Linda: *Incidents in the Life of a Slave Girl. Written by Herself.*" *The Anti-Slavery Advocate* 53.2 (May 1, 1861): 1.

Bacon, Jacqueline. "Taking Liberty, Taking Literacy: Signifying in the Rhetoric of African-American Abolitionists." *Southern Communication Journal* 64.4 (1999): 271–88.

Barbeito, Patricia Felisa. " 'Making Generations' in Jacobs, Larsen and Hurston: A Genealogy of Black Women's Writing." *American Literature* 70.2 (1998): 365–95.

Bartholomaus, Craig. " 'What Would You Be?': Racial Myths and Cultural Sameness in *Incidents in the Life of a Slave Girl.*" *College Language Association Journal* 39.2 (Dec. 1995): 179–94.

Beardslee, Karen E. "Through Slave Culture's Lens Comes the Abundant Source: Harriet A. Jacobs's *Incidents in the Life of a Slave Girl.*" *MELUS* 24.1 (1999): 37–58.

Becker, Elizabeth C. "Harriet Jacobs's Search for Home." *College Language Association Journal* 35.4 (June 1992): 411–21.

Berlant, Lauren. "The Queen of America Goes to Washington City: Harriet Jacobs, Frances Harper, Anita Hill." *American Literature* 65.3 (1993): 549–74.

Blackford, Holly. "Figures of Orality: The Master, the Mistress, the Slave Mother in Harriet Jacobs's *Incidents in the Life of a Slave Girl: Written by Herself.*" *Papers on Language & Literature* 37.3 (2001): 314–36.

Braxton, Joanne M., and Sharon Zuber. "Silences in Harriet 'Linda Brent' Jacobs's *Incidents in the Life of a Slave*

Girl." In *Listening to Silences: New Essays in Feminist Criticism.* Hedges, Elaine and Shelley Fishkin, eds. New York: Oxford University Press, 1994. 146–55.

——. "Harriet Jacobs' *Incidents in the Life of a Slave Girl*: The Re-definition of the Slave Narrative Genre." *Massachusetts Review* 27.2 (Summer 1986): 379–87.

Burnham, Michelle. "Loopholes of Resistance: Harriet Jacobs' Slave Narrative and the Critique of Agency in Foucault." *Arizona Quarterly* 49.2 (Summer 1993): 53–73.

Cutter, Martha J. "Dismantling 'The Master's House': Critical Literacy in Harriet Jacobs' *Incidents in the Life of a Slave Girl*." *Callaloo: A Journal of African-American and African Arts and Letters* 19.1 (Winter 1996): 209–25.

Carson, Sharon. "Dismantling the House of the Lord: Theology as Political Philosophy in *Incidents in the Life of a Slave Girl*." *Journal of Religious Thought* 51.1 (1994): 53–66.

Cope, Virginia. "'I Verily Believed Myself to Be a Free Woman': Harriet Jacobs's Journey into Capitalism." *African American Review* 38.1 (2004): 5–20.

Dalton, Anne B. "The Devil and the Virgin: Writing Sexual Abuse in *Incidents in the Life of a Slave Girl*." In *Violence, Silence, and Anger: Women's Writing as Transgression.* Lashgari, Deirdre, ed. Charlottesville: University Press of Virginia, 1995. 38–61.

Daniel, Janice B. "A New Kind of Hero: Harriet Jacobs's *Incidents*." *The Southern Quarterly* 35.3 (Spring 1997): 7–12.

Davie, Sharon. "'Reader, My Story Ends with Freedom': Harriet Jacobs's *Incidents in the Life of a Slave Girl*." In *Famous Last Words: Changes in Gender and Narrative Closure.* Both, Alison and U. C. Knoepflmacher, eds. Charlottesville: University Press of Virginia, 1993. 86–109.

Dizard, Robin. "Native Daughters: My Place and *Incidents in the Life of a Slave Girl*." *MELUS* 22.4 (1997): 147–62.

Doriani, Beth Maclay. "Black Womanhood in Nineteenth-Century America: Subversion and Self-Construction in Two Women's Autobiographies." *American Quarterly* 43.2 (June 1991): 199–222.

Drake, Kimberly. "Rewriting the American Self: Race, Gender, and Identity in the Autobiographies of Frederick

Douglass and Harriet Jacobs." *MELUS* 22.4 (1997): 91–108.

Emsley, Sarah. "Harriet Jacobs and the Language of Auto-biography." *Canadian Review of American Studies* 28.2 (1998): 145–62.

Foreman, P. Gabrielle. "The Spoken and the Silenced in *Incidents in the Life of a Slave Girl* and *Our Nig*." *Callaloo: A Journal of African-American and African Arts and Letters* 13.2 (Spring 1990): 313–24.

Garfield, Deborah M., and Rafia Zafar. *Harriet Jacobs and Incidents in the Life of a Slave Girl: New Critical Essays.* Cambridge, New York: Cambridge University Press, 1996.

Gilmore, Leigh, and Elizabeth Marshall. "Girls in Crisis: Rescue and Transnational Feminist Autobiographical Resistance." *Feminist Studies* 36.3 (2010): 667–90.

Gomaa, Sally. "Writing to 'Virtuous' and 'Gentle' Readers: The Problem of Pain in Harriet Jacobs's *Incidents* and Harriet Wilson's *Sketches*." *African American Review* 43.2 (2009): 371–81.

Hanrahan, Heidi M. "Harriet Jacobs's *Incidents in the Life of a Slave Girl*: A Retelling of Lydia Maria Child's 'The Quadroons.'" *New England Quarterly* 78.4 (2005): 599–616.

Humphreys, Debra. "Power and Resistance in Harriet Jacobs' *Incidents in the Life of a Slave Girl*." In *Anxious Power: Reading, Writing, and Ambivalence in Narrative by Women*. Singley, Carol, and Susan Sweeney, eds. Albany: State University of New York Press, 1993. 143–55.

Kaplan, Carla. "Recuperating Agents: Narrative Contracts, Emancipatory Readers, and *Incidents in the Life of a Slave Girl*." In *Provoking Agents: Gender and Agency in Theory and Practice*. Gardiner, Judith, ed. Urbana: University of Illinois Press, 1995. 280–301.

Kaplan, Carla. "Narrative Contracts and Emancipatory Readers: *Incidents in the Life of a Slave Girl*." *The Yale Journal of Criticism* 6.1 (Spring 1993): 93–120.

Kreiger, Georgia. "Playing Dead: Harriet Jacobs's Survival Strategy in *Incidents in the Life of a Slave Girl*." *African American Review* 42.3 (2008): 607–21.

Larson, Jennifer. "Converting Passive Womanhood to Active Sisterhood: Agency, Power, and Subversion in Harriet Jacobs's *Incidents in the Life of a Slave Girl." Women's Studies* 35.8 (2006): 739–56.

——. "Renovating Domesticity in Ruth Hall, *Incidents in the Life of a Slave Girl*, and *Our Nig." Women's Studies* 39 (2009). 538–58.

Levy, Andrew. "Dialect and Convention: Harriet A. Jacobs's *Incidents in the Life of a Slave Girl." Nineteenth-Century Literature* 45.2 (1990): 206–19.

Logue, Cal M., and Eugene F. Miller. "Communicative Interaction and Rhetorical Status in Harriet Jacobs." *Southern Communication Journal* 63.3 (1998): 182.

Lovell, Thomas B. "By Dint of Labor and Economy: Harriet Jacobs, Harriet Wilson, and the Salutary View of Wage Labor." *Arizona Quarterly* 52.3 (Autumn 1996):1–32.

Lyons, Mary E. *Letters from a Slave Girl: The Story of Harriet Jacobs.* New York: Atheneum Books for Young Readers, 1992.

Marshall, Elaine. "Irruptions of the Grotesque in Harriet Jacobs' *Incidents in the Life of a Slave Girl." The Journal of the Association for the Interdisciplinary Study of the Arts* 2 .2 (Spring 1997): 17–34.

Matterson, Stephen. "Shaped by Readers: The Slave Narratives of Frederick Douglas and Harriet Jacobs." In Kilcup, Karen L., ed. *Soft Canons: American Women Writers and Masculine Tradition.* Iowa City: University of Iowa Press, 1999. 82–96.

McKay, Nellie Y. "The Girls Who Became the Women: Childhood Memories in the Autobiographies of Harriet Jacobs, Mary Church Terrell, and Anne Moody." In *Tradition and the Talents of Women.* Howe, Florence, ed. Urbana: University of Illinois Press, 1991. 105–24.

Miller, Jennie. "Harriet Jacobs and the 'Double Burden' of American Slavery." *International Social Science Review* 78.1 (2003): 31–41.

Mills, Bruce. "Lydia Maria Child and the Endings to Harriet Jacobs's *Incidents in the Life of a Slave Girl. American Literature* 64.2 (June 1982): 255–72.

Miskolcze, Robin. "The Middle Passages of Nancy Prince and Harriet Jacobs." *Nineteenth-Century Contexts* 29.2 (2007): 283–93.

Moody, Jocelyn K. "Ripping Away the Veil of Slavery: Literacy, Communal Love, and Self-Esteem in Three Slave Women's Narratives." *Black American Literature Forum* 24.4 (1990): 633–48.

Moore, Geneva Cobb. "A Freudian Reading of Harriet Jacobs' *Incidents in the Life of a Slave Girl.*" *Southern Literary Journal* 38.1 (2005): 3–20.

Morgan, Winifred. "Gender-Related Difference in the Slave Narratives of Harriet Jacobs and Frederick Douglass." *American Studies* 35.2 (Fall 1994): 73–94.

Naranjo-Huebl, Linda. "'Take, Eat': Food Imagery, the Nurturing Ethic, and Christian Identity in *The Wide, Wide World*, *Uncle Tom's Cabin*, and *Incidents in the Life of a Slave Girl.*" *Christianity & Literature* 56.4 (2007): 597–631.

Nudelman, Franny. "Harriet Jacobs and the Sentimental Politics of Female Suffering." *ELH* 59.4 (1992): 939–64.

Nussler, Ulrike. "'Across the Black Body': Herman Melville's 'Benito Cereno' and Harriet Jacobs's *Incidents in the Life of a Slave Girl.*" In *Boundaries: Critical Essays on American Literature*. Schmidt, Klaus and David Sawyer, eds. Frankfurt, Germany: Peter Lang, 1996. 55–79.

Perry, Lewis. "Harriet Jacobs and the 'Dear Old Flag.'" *African American Review* 42.3 (2008): 595–605.

Putzi, Jennifer. "'The Skin of an American Slave': African American Manhood and the Marked Body in Nineteenth-Century Abolitionist Literature." *Studies in American Fiction* 30.2 (2002): 181–206.

Randle, Gloria T. "Between the Rock and the Hard Place: Mediating Spaces in Harriet Jacobs's *Incidents in the Life of a Slave Girl.*" *African American Review* 33.1 (1999): 43–56.

Sherman, Sarah Way. "Moral Experience in Harriet Jacobs's *Incidents in the Life of a Slave Girl.*" *NWSA Journal* 2.2 (1990): 167–85.

Skinfill, Mauri. "Nation and Miscegenation: *Incidents in the Life of a Slave Girl.*" *Arizona Quarterly* 51.2 (Summer 1995): 63–79.

Smith, Stephanie A. "Harriet Jacobs: A Case History of Authentication." In Fisch, Audrey A. *The Cambridge Companion to the African American Slave Narrative.* Cambridge: Cambridge University Press, 2007.

Sorisio, Carolyn. "'There Is Might in Each': Conceptions of

Self in Harriet Jacobs's *Incidents in the Life of a Slave Girl, Written by Herself.*" *Legacy* 13.1 (1996): 1–18.

Stewart, Anna. "Revising 'Harriet Jacobs' for 1865." *American Literature* 82.4 (2010): 701–24.

Stone, Andrea. "Interracial Sexual Abuse and Legal Subjectivity in Antebellum Law and Literature." *American Literature* 81.1 (2009): 65–92.

Tricomi, Albert. "Dialect and Identity in Harriet Jacobs's Autobiography and Other Slave Narratives." *Callaloo: A Journal of African-American and African Arts and Letters* 29.2 (2006): 619–33.

Vermillion, Mary. "Reembodying the Self: Representations of Rape in *Incidents in the Life of a Slave Girl* and *I Know Why the Caged Bird Sings.*" *Biography: An Interdisciplinary Quarterly* 15.3 (Summer 1992): 243–60.

Walter, Krista. "Surviving in the Garret: Harriet Jacobs and the Critique of Sentiment." *ATQ* 8.3 (1994): 189–210.

Warhol, Robyn R. "'Reader, Can You Imagine? No, You Cannot': The Narratee as Other in Harriet Jacobs's Text." *Narrative* 3.1 (Jan. 1995): 57–72.

Warner, Anne Bradford. "Harriet Jacobs at Home in *Incidents in the Life of a Slave Girl.*" *Southern Quarterly* 45.3 (2008): 30–47.

Washington, Margaret. "'From Motives of Delicacy': Sexuality and Morality in the Narratives of Sojourner Truth and Harriet Jacobs." *Journal of African American History* 92.1 (2007): 57–73.

Whitsitt, Novian. "Reading Between the Lines." *Frontiers: A Journal of Women Studies* 31.1 (2010): 73–88.

Wolfe, Andrea Powell. "Double-Voicedness in *Incidents in the Life of a Slave Girl*: 'Loud Talking' to a Northern Black Readership." *ATQ* 22.3 (2008): 517–25.

Wong, Edlie. "'Freedom with a Vengeance': Choosing Kin in Antislavery Literature and Law." *American Literature* 81 (2009). 7–34.

Yellin, Jean Fagan. *Harriet Jacobs: A Life.* New York: Basic Civitas Books, 2004.

——. "Harriet Jacobs's Family History." *American Literature* 66.4 (1994): 765–67.

——. *Women & Sisters: The Anti-Slavery Feminists in American Culture.* New Haven: Yale University Press, 1989.

——. "Written by Herself: Harriet Jacobs' Slave Narrative." *American Literature* 53.3 (November 1981): 479–86.

Zafar, Rafia and Deborah Garfield, eds. *Harriet Jacobs and Incidents in the Life of a Slave Girl: New Critical Essays.* Cambridge: Cambridge University Press, 1996.

A NOTE ON THE TEXTS

The Interesting Narrative of the Life of Olaudah Equiano, or Gustavus Vassa is reprinted here from the 1794 edition published by the author in London; this was the ninth and last edition revised and published in his lifetime. *The Narrative of the Life of Frederick Douglass, An American Slave* is reprinted from the 1845 edition published by the Anti-Slavery Office in Boston. *The History of Mary Prince* is reprinted from the 1831 second edition, published by F. Westley and H. H. Davis in London. *Incidents in the Life of a Slave Girl* was reprinted from the 1861 edition, published for the author in Boston.

READ THE TOP 20
SIGNET CLASSICS

1984 by George Orwell

Animal Farm by George Orwell

Narrative of the Life of Frederick Douglass
   by Frederick Douglass

The Inferno by Dante

Romeo and Juliet by William Shakespeare

Why We Can't Wait by Dr. Martin Luther King, Jr.

Nectar in a Sieve by Kamala Markandaya

Frankenstein by Mary Shelley

Beowulf translated by Burton Raffel

Hamlet by William Shakespeare

The Federalist Papers by Alexander Hamilton

The Odyssey by Homer

Macbeth by William Shakespeare

Crime and Punishment by Fyodor Dostoyevsky

The Hound of the Baskervilles
   by Sir Arthur Conan Doyle

The Scarlet Letter by Nathaniel Hawthorne

Dr. Jekyll and Mr. Hyde by Robert L. Stevenson

A Midsummer Night's Dream by William Shakespeare

The Classic Slave Narratives by Henry L. Gates

A Tale of Two Cities by Charles Dickens

PENGUIN.COM
FACEBOOK.COM/SIGNETCLASSIC

S0154